Edge-Enabled 6G Networking

"This book discusses some interesting updates on edge-enabled 6G networking, covering a wide range of topics ranging from mmWave to THz communications and using technologies such as reconfigurable intelligent surfaces. Topics like VNF placement and NTN integration with terrestrial network have been also covered which are crucial for development of 6G—definitely worth a read."

—Prof. Aryan Kaushik, *Chief Innovation Officer (CIO), RakFort, UK and Adjunct Professor, IIIT Delhi, India*

"This book by Ojha et al. (eds.) covers how edge-based design of the 6G networks has the potential to overcome the challenges in delivering various newer services with strict QoS constraints. On the other hand, this book also discusses the AI-native design which is expected to be the backbone for enabling large-scale distributed services."

—Prof. Pascal Lorenz, *University of Haute Alsace, France*

Tamoghna Ojha · Md Muzakkir Hussain ·
Samaresh Bera · Nurzaman Ahmed · Sudip Misra
Editors

Edge-Enabled 6G Networking

Foundations, Technologies, and Applications

Springer

Editors
Tamoghna Ojha
Department of Mathematics and Computing
Indian Institute of Technology (ISM) Dhanbad
Dhanbad, Jharkhand, India

Md Muzakkir Hussain
Department of Computer Science and Engineering
SRM University-AP
Guntur, Andhra Pradesh, India

Samaresh Bera
Department of Computer Science and Engineering
Indian Institute of Technology Jammu
Nagrota, Jammu and Kashmir, India

Nurzaman Ahmed
Donald Danford Plant Science Center
Olivette, MO, USA

Sudip Misra
Department of Computer Science and Engineering
Indian Institute of Technology Kharagpur
Kharagpur, West Bengal, India

ISBN 978-3-032-19041-3 ISBN 978-3-032-19042-0 (eBook)
https://doi.org/10.1007/978-3-032-19042-0

This Springer imprint is published by the registered company Springer Nature Switzerland AG
The registered company address is: Gewerbestrasse 11, 6330 Cham, Switzerland

Foreword

The upcoming Sixth Generation (6G) of Communication Networks paradigm is expected to address the limitations of current network infrastructures. A defining characteristic of 6G will be its seamless integration of diverse network types, supported by intelligent decision-making capabilities embedded across every layer of the protocol stack. As a result, 6G will place unprecedented emphasis on the network "edge." The convergence of edge, fog, and cloud computing with 6G wireless systems will be essential for achieving ultra-fast, highly reliable communication and for enabling a wide range of emerging applications and use cases. A comprehensive overview of edge-enabled 6G networking, including its foundations, architectures, applications, and algorithms will serve to address the growing interest among the research community and demand for this technology.

Given the rapidly growing interest in this field, a comprehensive overview of edge-enabled 6G networking—covering its foundational concepts, architectures, applications, and underlying algorithms—will be invaluable to researchers and practitioners preparing for this next generation of wireless technology.

The book *Edge-Enabled 6G Networking: Foundations, Technologies, and Applications* distinguishes itself from existing literature through its unique and timely emphasis on the convergence of edge computing and 6G communication technologies. While several books address edge computing and a few of them focus specifically on 6G, there is a notable lack of resources that bridge these two rapidly evolving domains. This book fills that gap by examining the latest advancements, opportunities, and challenges associated with integrating edge intelligence into 6G networks.

It provides an in-depth exploration of how edge-enabled architectures, protocols, and algorithms can transform next-generation wireless systems, offering readers a holistic view of the emerging 6G ecosystem. By thoroughly covering the foundational principles, enabling technologies, and practical applications of edge-assisted 6G, this book serves as an essential and forward-looking reference for researchers, industry professionals, and students navigating the complexities of future communication networks.

Key strengths of this book include:

(a) *Foundational coverage of 6G technologies*, including detailed discussion and modeling of previously unused communication bands that will play a critical role in 6G.
(b) *A comprehensive treatment of AI-native network design*, which is central to supporting scalable, distributed services across future 6G infrastructures.
(c) *An in-depth exploration of edge-enabled architecture and their potential* to address major challenges associated with delivering diverse 6G services, ranging from healthcare, nano-networks, intelligent sensing, and cyber-physical systems, broadening the scope beyond conventional wireless networking.
(d) *Insightful coverage of satellite and non-terrestrial network integration*—a transformative feature of 6G—highlighting its role in enabling truly global, ubiquitous connectivity.

The concepts discussed in (a) will be of interest to beginner researchers such as UG/PG students for gaining introductory knowledge and overview of various aspects of the Edge-enabled 6G scenarios. On the other hand, (b), (c), and (d) will be suitable for Ph.D. scholars, researchers, and practitioners from academia and industry alike.

The editors of this book—Tamoghna Ojha, Md Muzakkir Hussain, Samaresh Bera, Nurzaman Ahmed, and Sudip Misra—are internationally recognized researchers with extensive contributions to the field. They have published widely in leading journals and conferences, including *IEEE Transactions on Mobile Computing*, *IEEE Transactions on Sustainable Computing*, *IEEE Journal on Selected Areas in Communications*, *IEEE Internet of Things Journal*, *IEEE Systems Journal*, and *IEEE Sensors Journal*, among others. Together the editors received multiple best paper awards in reputed international conferences, and held multiple prestigious international awards including Fellow of IEEE/ACM/INAE, IEEE Senior Membership, ERCIM Fellowship, and IEEE Richard E. Merwin Student Scholarship.

In closing, I would like to emphasize that this book is poised to be a valuable resource for students, researchers, and practitioners alike. Authored by respected experts in the field, it offers a well-balanced blend of theoretical foundations and practical applications, all presented in a clear and accessible manner.

I am confident that readers will find this book both insightful and enjoyable.

Prof. Vivek Ashok Bohara, Ph.D.
Senior Member, IEEE, CHANAKYA
Faculty Fellow, TiH-IIT Bombay
Indraprastha Institute of Information
Technology (IIIT), Delhi
New Delhi, India

Preface

Overview and Goals

With the advent of service-based architecture for cellular networking, starting with 5G, 6G networks support heterogeneous applications with diverse quality-of-service (QoS) requirements. The applications are broadly categorized as enhanced mobile broadband (eMBB), ultra-reliable and low-latency communication (uRLLC), and massive machine-type communication (mMTC). The eMBB applications are primarily concerned with high data rates. Whereas the uRLLC applications have high reliability and stringent latency requirements. On the other hand, the massive number of devices requires the underlying network to be supported for mMTC applications.

To achieve low latency for uRLLC applications, edge-enabled networking has emerged as a new paradigm in 6G networking. The edge-enabled networking involves the integration of edge computing, fog computing, and cloud computing with 6G wireless communication. Such integration enables faster and more reliable communication, supporting a variety of applications and use cases in 6G, unlike traditional cellular networking.

This book presents recent developments in 6G networking, specifically tailored to edge computing, on a unified platform to provide a concise overview of the concepts and technologies underlying 6G. It delves into the cutting-edge advancements and challenges of leveraging edge computing capabilities in the context of 6G networks, exploring how edge-enabled architectures, protocols, and algorithms can revolutionize the next generation of wireless communication systems. By providing a comprehensive understanding of the foundations, technologies, and applications in this emerging area, this book promises to offer a relevant and invaluable resource for researchers, professionals, and students seeking to navigate the complex landscape of edge-enabled 6G networking.

Organization

The book is divided into three parts. Part I primarily focuses on fundamental topics in wireless communications, specifically related to 6G mobile networks. Part II presents the enabling technologies for 6G radio access network, supporting various use cases with diverse quality-of-service requirements. Whereas Part III presents the enabling technologies for 6G core networks, primarily focusing on network function placement, network function virtualization, and 6G-enabled Internet of Things networking.

We believe readers will enjoy this book for its holistic overview of 6G communication and networking, covering fundamental concepts, enabling technologies, and use-case scenarios.

Dhanbad, India	Tamoghna Ojha
Guntur, India	Md Muzakkir Hussain
Nagrota, India	Samaresh Bera
Olivette, USA	Nurzaman Ahmed
Kharagpur, India	Sudip Misra

Contents

Foundation of 6G

mm-Wave Technology for 6G Communication 3
Anindya Ghosh and Tamoghna Ojha

Millimeter Wave and Terahertz Communication: An Overview 23
Poonam Maurya, Megha Sahu, Usha Kiran, Abhishek Hazra, and M. K. Askar

Intelligent Reflecting Surface for 6G Wireless Networks: Applications, Case Studies, Challenges and Future Directions 55
Debbarni Sarkar, Satyendra Singh Yadav, Vipin Pal, Yogita, and Sarat Kumar Patra

Cell-Free Massive MIMO for Future Generation Wireless Networks ... 81
Tasher Ali Sheikh, Shadab Haque, Mancharla Ravi, Anil Kumar Shaw, and Janmoni Borah

Enabling Technologies and Methods

Revolutionizing 6G Communication: Unleashing the Potential of Reconfigurable Intelligent Surfaces 105
Satish K. Tiwari, Shraddha Tripathi, Mahendra K. Shukla, and Om Jee Pandey

Synergistic Fusion of Terahertz and Molecular Communication for Futuristic 6G Networks 135
Chandrakant Shrivastava, Satish K. Tiwari, Nilay Pandey, and Gaurav Sharma

On Performance of UAV-Assisted RIS NOMA Network 169
Sayanti Ghosh, Abhijit Bhowmick, Sanjay Dhar Roy, and Sumit Kundu

D2D Communication in 6G Network 189
Srininvasarao Yarlagadda and Ajay Bhardwaj

Observability and Provenance for Distributed Microservices over Edge-Enabled 6G Networks 209
Subhankar Chakrabarti, Utkalika Satapathy, and Sandip Chakraborty

VNF Placement and Request Routing in 5G and Beyond Networks 235
Aqsa Sayeed and Samaresh Bera

Applications/Use-Cases/Case Studies

Edge-Enabled 6G Networking: Transforming IoT for a Hyperconnected Future 255
Nurzaman Ahmed, Tamoghna Ojha, Md. Muzakkir Hussain, and Samaresh Bera

OPUS: An Opportunistic Crowd-Sensing Framework for 5G Enabled Smart Campus 271
Ch Madhu Bhushan, Meka Naga Nandini Devi, A. Surayya, Firoj Gazi, and Md Muzakkir Hussain

LoRaWAN Based IoT to Satellite Communication for Integrated Terrestrial and Non-terrestrial Networks 301
Nikumani Choudhury, Jay Dave, and Tamoghna Ojha

Machine Learning Approach to Determine and Predict the Scattering Coefficients of Myocardium Tissue in the NIR Band for In-Vivo Communications—6G Networks 319
Raja Manjula, Adi Vishnu Avula, Abdul Jawad Khan, Chiranjeevi Thota, Venkata Kavyanjali Munipallle, and Sabita Langkam

Dielectric Characterization of Ovine Heart Tissues at Terahertz Frequencies via Machine Learning: A Use Case for In-Vivo Wireless Nano-Communication 347
Raja Manjula, Nalluri Sai Kusum Sarayu, Nelluri Sai Sruthi, Damavarapu Samaya, Kudeti Tarun Teja, and Langkam Sabita

Evolution of Intelligent Transportation Systems for the Next Generation: IRS Enabled 6G 371
Shaik Rajak, Vineela Chandra Dodda, Lakshmi, Koduru Hajarathaiah, Mohd Hamza Naim Shaikh Hamza, Inbarasan Muniraj, and Sunil Chinnadurai

Foundation of 6G

mm-Wave Technology for 6G Communication

Anindya Ghosh and Tamoghna Ojha

1 Introduction

The millimeter wave communication systems were first proposed and implemented by Sir Jagadish Chandra Bose in 1895. He proved his concept by successfully transmitting and receiving of 60 GHz electromagnetic signal. It was the first step towards today's mm-Wave technology. Prof. Bose introduced a spark transmitter, dielectric lens, horn antenna, coherer, polarizer, and cylindrical diffracting grating for his experiments [1]. In his experiments, he was successful in generating 2.5 cm to 5 mm wavelength electromagnetic signal [2, 3]. In his experiments, he used the spark gap as a mm-Wave source and point contact technology as a detector. In recent days technology, his invention is still useful and adopted in many systems.

Wireless communication techniques and the required system with trans-receiver systems have evolved in a parallel way. The improvement and the development of communication technology highly depend on the development of implementable systems and subsystems. These systems consist of trans-receiver channels including radio frequency subsystems. On the other hand, the communication techniques are frequency-division multiplexing access (FDMA), time-division multiplexing access (TDMA), code-division multiplexing access (CDMA), orthogonal frequency-division multiplexing (OFDM) and in recent days multiple-input multiple-output (MIMO).

The FDMA was first introduced with analog communication and implemented with first-generation (1G) mobile communication. The main limitation was it could only deal with voice signal and the spatial coverage was not stable [4]. The digital

A. Ghosh (✉)
Bosch Global Software Technology, Bangalore, India
e-mail: Anindya.Ghosh@in.bosch.com; anindyaghosh@ieee.org

T. Ojha
Mathematics and Computing, Indian Institute of Technology (ISM), Dhanbad, India
e-mail: tamoghnaojha@iitism.ac.in

T. Ojha et al. (eds.), *Edge-Enabled 6G Networking*,
https://doi.org/10.1007/978-3-032-19042-0_1

communication techniques resolved this issue and provided a comparatively stable communication link with a wider coverage area. The TDMA and CDMA communication techniques are the main backbone for 2nd generation wireless communication with the help of digitally evolved protocol [5, 6]. The next evolution in the wireless communication family was advanced CDMA which supported multimedia data transfer with the help of OFDM and MIMO technology. The required bandwidth, channel capacity, and data rate was improved by introducing 4th generation communication technique which was able to transfer data at megabytes per second speed [7, 8]. The advantages of 4th generation wireless communication technique are low-cost implementation and high efficiency as the operating frequency is below 4 GHz. Also, in this technology, the environmental effects and path loss are low as the frequency of operation is low. This is one of the major reasons that the 4th generation technology was rapidly adopted in the wireless ecosystem [9]. Increasing the demand on communication channel capacity and operational bandwidth, the 4th generation technology faced difficulties in meeting the data rate in present days [9], and was replaced by 5th generation technology in 2019. The 5th generation technology allows mm-Wave frequency band in wireless communication to improve data rate using available absolute wider bandwidth [10, 11].

The 5G can cover only the terrestrial area the 6G can extend it from terrestrial to space [12]. In other words, the coverage area is becoming three-dimensional using 6G technology. The 5G technology can be visualized as a quasi-two-dimensional network that covers terrestrial communication. On the other hand, a three-dimensional 6G network enables communication links between the Earth's surface to airborne satellite and water surface communication channels. Therefore, the 6G technology is targeted to access expanded global coverage with high-speed communication channels. The requirement of bandwidth for high-speed communication instigates to use mm-Wave frequency band due to the available absolute wider bandwidth. However the system-level implementation with mm-Wave technology for 6G is still progressing as the path loss, and fidelity become prominent for long-range communication links.

2 6G Technology and mm-Wave

Though the mm-Wave can provide wider bandwidth and high data rate communication the path loss at these frequencies is also very high. Therefore, efficient communication requires a beam-forming technique to direct the electromagnetic radiated wave toward the receiving unit. Another approach for increasing power efficiency and path loss is the asymmetrical communication system. Instead of using a reciprocal system where the receiving and transmitting antenna array are identical, the non-reciprocal transmitting and receiving antenna array can provide a system with low cost, low power consumption, and reduced signal processing requirements. The additional advantage of an asymmetric communication system is it can maintain wider instantaneous coverage with comparative less complex beam forming

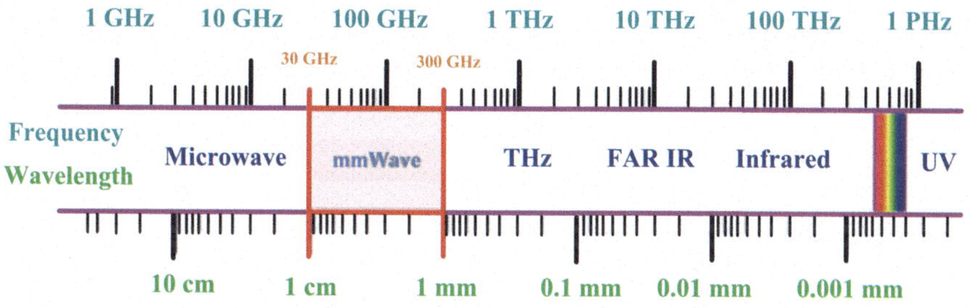

Fig. 1 The frequency bands and their corresponding wavelengths

strategies [13]. Another key factor in the 6G communication network is secure data transmission. The 3GPP ensures the use of a frequency band from 52.6 to 71 GHz which helps the communication link by increasing the physical layer [13]. This indicates the requirement to redesign the physical layer which was previously optimized for below 52.6 GHz.

Due to the smaller wavelength, as shown in Fig. 1, at mm-Wave frequency bands, the directive and a large number of antenna elements can be designed within the smaller physical dimension. The compactness of the overall system with a directive beam due to a large number of antenna elements provides a narrow beam and helps to provide immunity against the multi-path effect, jamming, and interruptions [13].

Interestingly, the spectrum sharing at mm-Wave frequency bands has the flexibility to avail uncoordinated spectrum sharing and also the high-end inter-cell coordination is not mandatory [16]. This is the key feature at 59–64 GHz and 64–71 GHz, unlicensed frequency bands which increases usability. Therefore, the key factor, spectrum sharing of unlicensed frequency bands features at mm-Wave 6G frequency bands demands the new licensing for spectrum allocation to improve usability. Further, the directional signal propagation and sensitivity blocking help to improve the interference in ultra-dense environments at mm-Wave frequency bands. It is necessary to investigate the communication channel modeling in a 6G ultra-dense network environment.

3 Challenges in Design of mm-Wave System Components

In this section, the challenges in mm-Wave technology for 6G communication are discussed. It is obvious that the channel capacity and data rate can be improved by using mm-Wave frequency bands but at the same time, the path loss, atmospheric absorption, and design complexity also increase. The path loss is a key factor for power efficient communication which is proportional to the frequency of operation, Therefore, the path loss would be high at mm-Wave frequency if we compare it with a communication channel at lower frequency bands. Another important factor is atmospheric absorption due to oxygen and moisture in the air, attenuation occurs due to rain.

3.1 Path Loss in Free Space

Path loss is a phenomenon that reduces the received signal power at the receiver when the transmitting signal frequency is increasing. Also, the signal power decreases when the distance between the transmitting and receiving antenna increases. Figure 2 explains a scenario when the signal is transmitted by the transmitting antenna towards the receiving antenna. More specifically the received power and transmitted power are maintained using the Eq. (1), where transmitting and receiving antenna gain are G_T, G_R, respectively. R denotes the distance between Tx and Rx antenna. The transmitted power is represented using P_T, λ denotes the wavelength of the operating frequency, and L is the system loss factor. The ratio $\frac{P_R}{P_T}$ defines the path loss of propagating electromagnetic signal. As mentioned, the received signal power reduces when R increases and lambda decreases. However, one can observe that even if R is small in value, the received power can be significantly low at higher frequencies.

$$\frac{P_R}{P_T} = \frac{G_T G_R \lambda^2}{16R^2 L\pi^2} \tag{1}$$

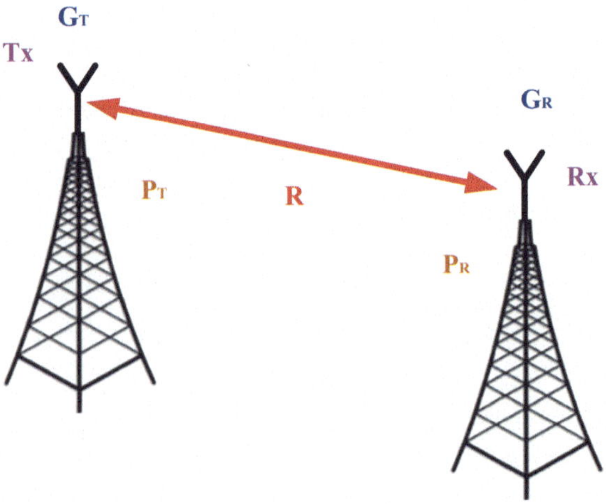

Fig. 2 Electromagnetic wave transmission

3.2 Atmospheric Absorption

The atmospheric absorption is more prominent for mm-Wave frequency as compared to the lower frequency of the signal. The losses are dominant at the troposphere layer when electromagnetic waves are traveling through the gas molecules. As the frequency goes higher, the possibilities of electron de-localization at resonance become higher. If the electromagnetic wave interacts with gas molecules such as O_2, N_2 moisture H_2O, the losses of energy occur due to the electric field which tries to align the electron along the direction of minimum potential with respect to the fields. This process introduces the absorption of energy when it is comparable to the quantum excitation energy of gas molecules. Therefore, the mechanical resonance frequency of gas molecules plays an important part in the atmospheric absorption phenomenon. For example, the oxygen O_2 and water vapour, this resonance is at 57–60 and 22 GHz.

The losses are 15 dB/km and 1.4 dB/km, observed at 60 GHz and 119 GHz respectively due to O_2 absorption. Similarly, the losses are 0.18 dB/km, 28.35 dB/km and 38.6 dB/km, at 23 GHz, 183 GHz and 323 GHz respectively due to H_2O absorption. The absorption at THz communication is more sensitive and the signal strength reduces to 10–20 dB for every hundred-meter distance. It is obvious that these values would be 100 to 200 dB/km at 600 GHz and 800 GHz respectively.

3.3 Precipitation

The scattering of electromagnetic waves is significant due to rain, as the size of a raindrop is comparable enough to interact with the wavelength of mm-Wave signals [14], This loss or attenuation due to the precipitation are function of rain rate and the size of raindrop. It is noticed that along with attenuation due to raindrops, an additional phenomenon which is depolarization takes place. The raindrop size distribution in [15] is useful to predict losses of electromagnetic signal for any frequency. It also confirms that the losses become more prominent at mm-Wave frequency bands as compared to the lower frequency bands such as L, S, C, and X. As an example, the lower mm-Wave frequency bands such as 28 and 3 GHz encounter less rain attenuation and atmospheric absorption as compared to 60 and 73 GHz frequency bands [16]. It is obvious as the size of raindrops is closer to the wave length of propagating electromagnetic waves and the absorption due to O_2 molecule is high at those frequency bands as suggested in Fig. 3.

The size of wavelengths in mm-Wave spectrum and the average size of a raindrop are comparable, within the order of a few millimeters. The propagating signals at mm-Wavegets obstructed up to 20 and 2.55 dB/km when the heavy rain (50 mm/hr) scenario and light rain (2 mm/hr) scenario in the communication path are established due to rainfall. It becomes more prominent at monsoon in the tropical regions in heavy rain scenarios (150 mm/hr) when signal strength reduces up to 42 dB/km from its actual power level at 60 GHz. These values are reduced to 7 dB/km at 28 GHz.

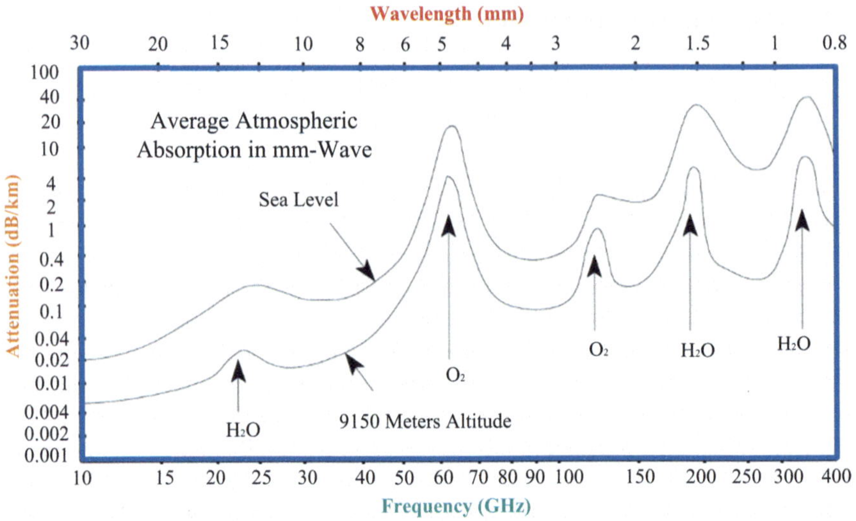

Fig. 3 Atmospheric attenuation at mm-Wave frequency

3.4 Dielectric Loss

The transmission line theory suggests that the complex propagation constant has a dependency on the frequency of wave propagation, conductivity of the conductor, permittivity, and the permeability of the dielectric constant. In Eqs. (2) and (3), the attenuation constant α and the phase constant β control the attenuation and phase velocity of the propagating wave. In the case of a perfectly matched transmission line (shown in Fig. 4), there is no reflection from the load which indicates the power flow $P(z)$ from a medium is in Eq. (4). The power loss per unit length can be expressed as Eq. (5).

Now, considering complex permittivity and permeability of dielectric substrate $\epsilon = \epsilon^{/} - j\epsilon^{//}$ and $\mu = \mu^{/} - j\mu^{//}$, the losses are mainly due to the bound charge and the free charge. This loss can be quantified by Eq. (7) using loss tangent $tan\delta$ for the electric field. Similarly, due to the magnetic field, the magnetic loss tangent $tan\delta_m$ can be expressed as Eq. (6).

$$\gamma = j\omega\sqrt{\mu\epsilon}\sqrt{1 - \frac{j\rho}{\omega\epsilon}} \tag{2}$$

$$P(z) = P_0 e^{-2\alpha z} \tag{3}$$

$$P_l = -\frac{\partial P(z)}{\partial z} \tag{4}$$

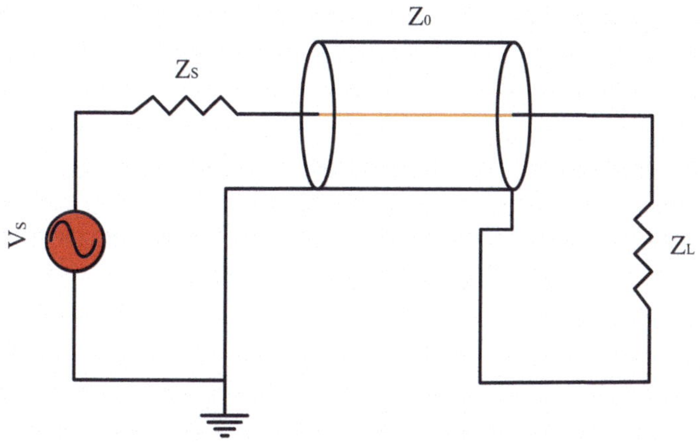

Fig. 4 Transmission line with characteristics impedance Z_0, source Z_S and load Z_L impedance

therefore,

$$P_l = 2\alpha P(z) \tag{5}$$

$$tan\delta \approx \frac{\epsilon^{//}}{\epsilon^{/}}, tan\delta_m \approx \frac{\mu^{//}}{\mu^{/}} \tag{6}$$

$$\alpha_d = 2.73\frac{tan\delta\epsilon(\epsilon_e - 1)}{\sqrt{\epsilon_e}(\epsilon - 1)\lambda_0}dB \tag{7}$$

The wave propagating medium such as waveguide, microstrip lines, H guide, and grove guide are formed with metal or metal-dielectric structure. Therefore, the geometry, electrical length, and most importantly losses due to dielectric and conductor decide the operating frequency of operations. The Table 1 presents different guiding structures with their frequency of operations.

Table 1 Guided medium for mm-Wave

Guided medium	Frequency range
Metallic waveguide	Up to 110 GHz
Planner transmission line	Up to 110 GHz
Substrate integrated waveguide	Up to 110 GHz
Quasi planner transmission line	30–120 GHz
Dielectric integrated waveguide	30–120 GHz
H guide	100–200 GHz
Groove guide	100–200 GHz

3.5 Conductor Loss

Assuming a smooth conductor surface, the conductor loss per unit length can be expressed as Eq. (8). It is easily understood that the conductor loss is proportional to the length of the transmission line and the surface resistance. Interestingly, the surface roughness is inversely proportional to the skin depth as a result, the conductor loss is also a function of frequency. Equation (9) suggests the dependency on material, and electrical parameters for conductor loss.

$$\alpha_c = \frac{R_S}{2Z_0\eta} \frac{Z_0}{dz} \tag{8}$$

In case of rough surfaces, the conductor loss formula can be found as presented in Eq. (9). Therefore, the surface roughness causes additional losses in the conductor,

$$\alpha_c^{/} = \alpha_c \left[1 + \frac{2}{\pi} tan^{-1} 1.4 \frac{\Delta}{\delta_s} \right] \tag{9}$$

As discussed above, the conductor, dielectric loss plays an important role for guided wave propagation, the Table 2 suggests different type of connectors for different frequency ranges. The operating frequency of different connectors is decided considering geometry, conductor, and dielectric losses.

3.6 Radiation Loss

The unwanted radiation loss is mainly introduced due to the higher order modes, surface wave in substrate, discontinuities, and leakages as shown in Fig. 5. The surface wave can be reduced by maintaining substrate height $h << \lambda$. The radiation losses increase with induced higher-order modes supported by the thicker dielectric

Table 2 Connectors for different frequency bands

Connector type	Frequency range
N	DC to 18 GHz
APC-7	DC to 18 GHz
SMA	DC to 18 GHz
Super SMA	DC to 27 GHz
3.5 mm	DC to 26.5 GHz
K	DC to 40 GHz
2.4 mm	DC to 50 GHz
V	DC to 65 GHz
1 mm	DC to 110 GHz

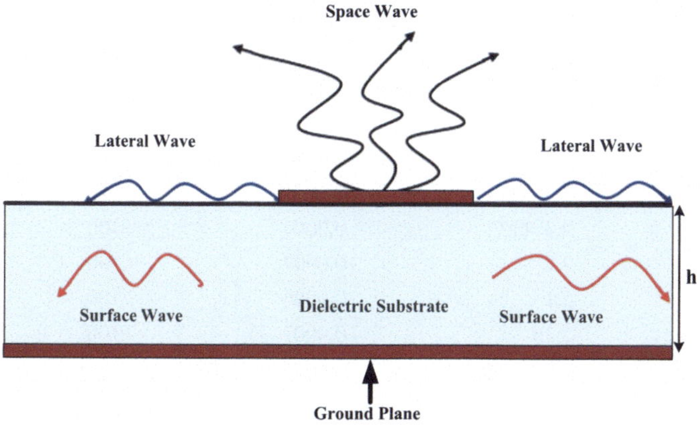

Fig. 5 Generation of surface wave in dielectric substrate

substrate. As the thickness of substrate becomes thicker, the radiation losses become more prominent. It is also recommended to use a high dielectric constant substrate as the radiation loss is high for lower values of dielectric constant. In case of mm-Wave frequency, the required height becomes very thin which causes bending and durability issues. The benching technique is required to resolve this issue which increases the profile of geometry.

The impedance transformers in mm-Wave are used to achieve reflection-less transmission, but in most cases, the impedance transformers create radiation loss due to discontinuity in geometry. Also, the stray reactance introduced by mode converters which are used to convert the TE to TM or TEM, causes radiation loss. The spurious frequency in the presence of resonating mode creates radiation losses which are more likely to happen in mm-Wave frequencies. In case of a CPW transmission line, the odd mode contributes to phase electric fields from the conductor to both grounding sides. As a result, the unwanted radiation mode creates interference with other components. Air bridges are useful to overcome these issues but shorter intervals of bridges are costly to implement from a manufacturing point of view. The same is true for making grounding vias in conductor-backed CPW to reduce surface waves. Hybrid technology with microstrip lines and grounded CPW lines combine to form a configuration called a co-planar launched microstrip line, which is useful to mitigate the radiation losses in mm-Wave frequencies.

Table 3 depicted the materials which are suitable for substrates at different frequency ranges considering conductor and dielectric loss.

Table 3 Dielectrics for different frequency bands

Material	Dielectric constant	Loss tangent	Frequency range (GHz)
Semi-insulating GaAs	16	0.016	10
Semi-insulating Si	12	0.001	10
Alumina	9.6–9.9	0.0001	10
Sapphire	9.3–11.7	0.0004	100
RT-Duroid	2.2	0.0009	100
Teflon	2.1	0.0006	100
Polypropylene	2.26	0.0007	100

4 Applications of mm-Wave 6G Technology

The typical applications in different operating frequency bands are presented in Table 4. The operational frequency and the applications are decided considering many factors, such as path loss, wave length, atmospheric absorption, and precipitation. Considering the advantages of the mm-Wave frequency band, available bandwidth, achievable bit rate and data rate. The 6G technology can be implementable for the following applications.

The available bandwidth at the 60 GHz band is capable enough to provide a high data rate for wireless personal area networks (WPAN) and wireless local area networks (WLAN). This leads to research and development on cutting-edge tech-

Table 4 Frequency bands

Bands	Range (GHz)	Typical applications
L	1–2	Telemetry, GPS, GSM and amateur radio
S	2–4	Radar, and satellites, Radio Astronomy, LAN, GPS and Bluetooth
C	4–8	Long distance telecommunication
X	8–12	Satellite communications, radar, space application
Ku	12–18	Satellite communications
K	18–26.5	Radar, satellite applications
Ka	26.5–40	Satellite applications
Q	33–50	Satellite, microwave communications and automotive radar
V	50–75	Millimetre wave radar
E	60–90	Ultra-high frequency communications
W	75–110	Satellite applications, millimeter-wave radar, tracking radar
F	90–140	Microwave devices, LAN and modern radars
D	110–170	Energy weapon, millimeter wave scanner

nologies with multi-dimensional applications in wireless communication, remote health care, energy harvesting and Simultaneous Wireless Information and Power Transfer.

These applications need advanced 6G technology to achieve high-speed gigabit transmission rates at least the same as IEEE 802.11ad and IEEE 802.11ay [17, 18]. It is expected that the IEEE 802.1ay network which is known as mm-Wave distribution networks (mDNs) could be a possible solution for point-to-point, point-to-multipoint networks for indoor and outdoor applications [17]. Though the above mDNs are capable of providing low-cost, high-speed communication links, the challenges are signal interference, path loss, and efficient beam training needs to be investigated for 6G technology [19].

4.1 Wireless Communication

The wireless technology for mobile communication has evolved significantly over the last four decades. The demands and as well as requirements are changed according to the specification of technology up gradation from 1st generation to 5th generation. These upgradations are depend on the bandwidth, channel capacity, data rate, and security requirements of wireless systems. The Fig. 6, illustrates the time span and evolving period for different wireless technologies from 1G to 6G. The 1G was mainly introduced with analog communication technology. Digital communications with improved integrated circuits have evolved from 1G according to system requirements using time division multiplexing technology.

These 1G and 2G technologies are limited to single input single output systems. Also, the gain of radiating elements is low to avail a wider angle of coverage. Though CDMA technology was one of the main elements for 3G wireless communication, the TDCDMA and WCDMA were also introduced at that time period. The 3G technology was suitable for providing high data rate but the main breakthrough was the multimedia technology.

The multiple input multiple output technology to avail the diversity gain and spacial multiplexing of system was introduced in 4G technology along with the high data rate capabilities. The next evolution was introduced as 5G technology which are mostly based on FR1 sub 6 GHz and FR2 mm-Wave frequency bands. It was first candidate who uses massive MIMO [20], mm-Wave [21], ultra-dense networking (UDN) technologies [22] to support higher data rate and lower latency. The mm-Wave frequency bands are adequately used for 5G technology. Now is the time for 6G technology where digital wireless technology with a massive MIMO concept is essential. The multi-beam massive MIMO mm-Wave wireless system can address the requirement of a number of transceiver channels greater than 64.

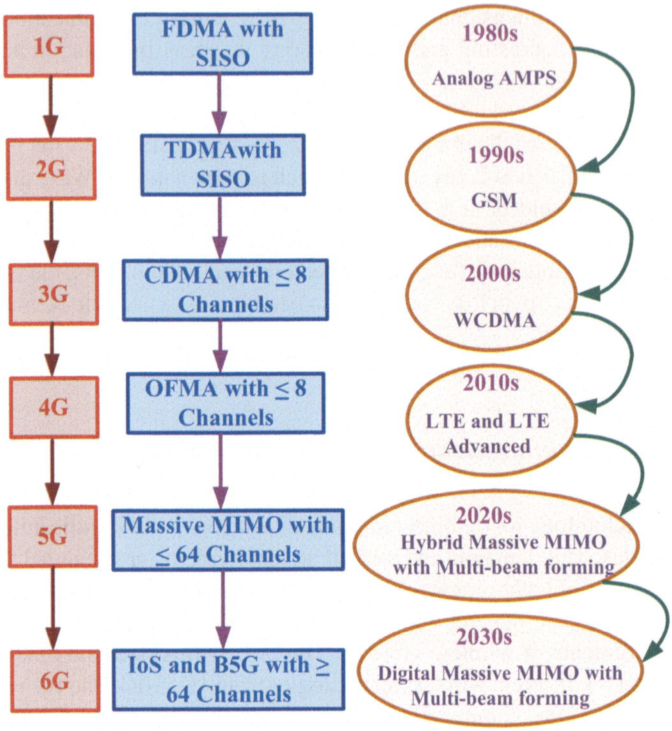

Fig. 6 Evolution of 6G technology

4.2 *Intelligent Health Care*

The limitation of 5G technology restricts the use of present technology in intelligent health care systems. The real time monitoring of a patient demands a high data rate with negligible latency. On the other hand the system requirements for intelligent health care such as data rate of ≥ 1 Tbps, time delay ≤ 1 ms, reliability of 10^{-9}, mobility of ≥ 1000 km/h, wavelength of $\leq 300\,\mu$m and operating frequency of ≥ 1 THz, [23] are only be achievable at 6G technology. This specification is decided to use the intelligence (AI) and entities (IE) [24] for the health care system. The wearable antenna along with 6G technology would be useful for remotely monitoring health care equipment such as telesurgery, holographic communications, and Hospital-to-Home (H2H) services [25]. The 6G technology in the present-day scenario is a key factor to allowing another evolution in the form of the Intelligent Internet of Medical Things (IIoMT) [26].

4.3 Energy Harvesting

One of the most promising applications of mm-Wave 6G technology is energy harvesting. The wireless power transform is basically, the generation of DC power from received RF power. The path loss and the atmospheric absorption problems can be mitigated using highly directive antennas.

The most reported work on 5G mm-Wave band is 24 GHz, using rectenna for conversion of electromagnetic signal into DC power. The 2.5 V DC power is converted from the 18 dBm received RF power at 24 GHz in [27]. The conversion efficiency is a key parameter for the energy harvesting technology which is defined by Eq. (10).

$$\eta = \frac{P_{out}}{P_{in}} \tag{10}$$

where P_{out} denotes converted DC output power and the P_{in} is input RF power.

The required circuit components for rectifying the RF power are rectifying diode, DC blocking capacitor, impedance matching network and output filter. The schematic of the circuit configuration is shown in Fig. 7a. The output DC voltage can be made double using voltage doubler circuit configuration in Fig. 7b. This concept can be useful at sixth generation (6G) frequency bands which will provide a wider bandwidth of operation. The maximum conversion efficiency in 6G is 67% reported in [28] at 35 GHz.

The 37.7% efficiency is reported in [29] at 94 GHz. In this work, the low-loss alumina substrate is used as the electric loss tangent value ($\tan \delta_e < 0.001$ at 60 GHz) is very low which leads to low dielectric loss.

Further, the multi-beam antenna in package approaches is reported at 57–66 GHz in [30], suggesting this can improve the efficiency as compared to on-chip antenna technology [31].

The main challenge is to maintain the performance of semiconductor devices from the aspect of semiconductor physics at mm-Wave frequencies. Table 5 suggests different devices and their applications in communication system blocks such as switches, rectifiers, oscillators and phase shifters.

4.4 Simultaneous Wireless Information and Power Transfer (SWIPT)

SWIPT technology empowers the devices to harness RF energy fully by enabling energy transfer along with information exchange.

In the futuristic 6G IoT networks, SWIPT will be a pivotal technology due to its ability to enhance energy efficiency and sustainability [32]. As 6G networks aim to support a massive number of low-power IoT devices with minimal environmental impact, SWIPT enables these devices to harvest energy from the same electromag-

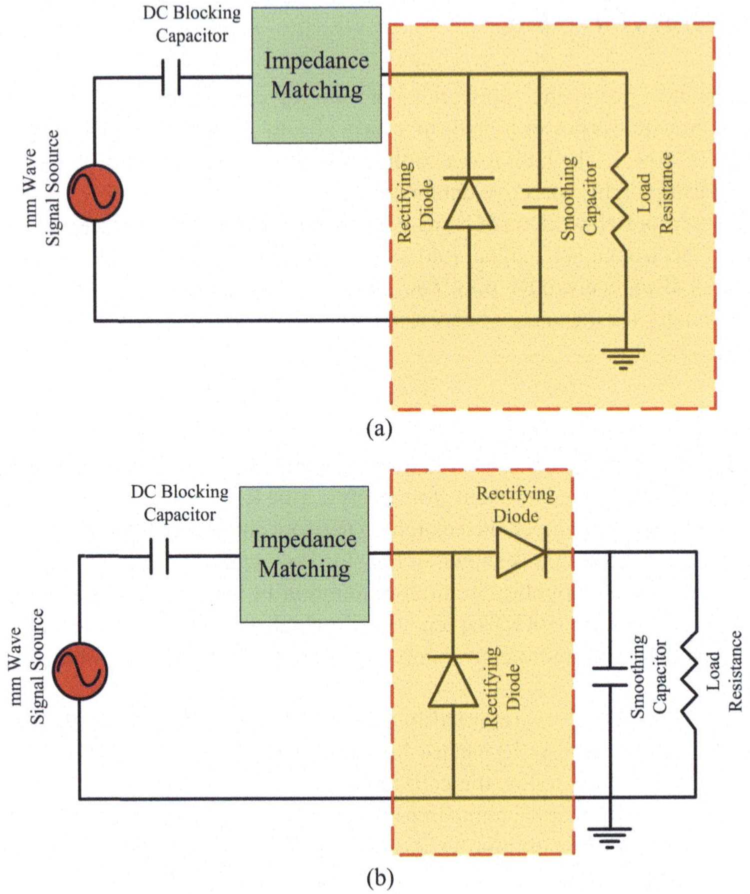

Fig. 7 Schematic for **a** Rectifier circuit **b** voltage doubler for energy harvesting

Table 5 Active devices for mm-Wave applications

Device	Frequency range	Material	Applications
PIN diode	Up to 100 GHz	Si, GaAs	Rectifier, switches and phase shifters
Gunn diode	Up to 140 GHz	GaAs, InP	Oscillators
Varactor diode	Up to 300 GHz	GaAs	Phase sifters and modulator
IMPATT diode	Up to 300 GHz	Si, GaAs, InP	Amplifiers
FET	Up to 100 GHz	GaAs, InP	Amplifiers, oscillators and mixer
HEMPT	Up to 100 GHz	GaAs, InP	Amplifiers, oscillators and mixer

netic waves used for data transmission, thereby reducing the need for frequent battery replacements and facilitating longer device lifetimes in remote or hard-to-access locations [42]. Additionally, SWIPT can contribute to the development of self-sustaining IoT ecosystems, promoting the deployment of dense IoT networks with improved reliability and reduced operational costs. Xue et al. [41] shows a mmWave-based SWIPT system.

Power-Splitting SWIPT: In power-splitting SWIPT, the receiver splits the received RF signal into two streams: one for information relaying (IR) and the other for energy harvesting (EH). This division allows devices with limited or no battery power, such as IoT sensors or mobile devices, to perform tasks while extending their operational lifetime by wirelessly receiving power.

A few important parameters of this system are—*Power-Splitting Ratio* (ρ_n): This ratio determines how much power is allocated to IR (ρ_n) and EH ($1 - \rho_n$), with an optimal value balancing power requirements for each. *Channel State Information (CSI)*: Knowledge of CSI helps adaptively adjust the power splitting ratio, improving efficiency in dynamic environments. Figure 8 depicts a power-splitting SWIPT system. Typically, in practical applications, the power splitting is done first for information processing and energy harvesting, and then, the information is relayed using the energy harvested by the system [33].

The power-splitting receiver is considered in both Unmanned Aerial Vehicles (UAVs) [33] and also in ground sensor nodes [34, 35]. Typically, the power-splitting profile is determined based on the energy requirements of the sensor node while maintaining the minimum data rate (when sensor node is the SWIPT receiver) or

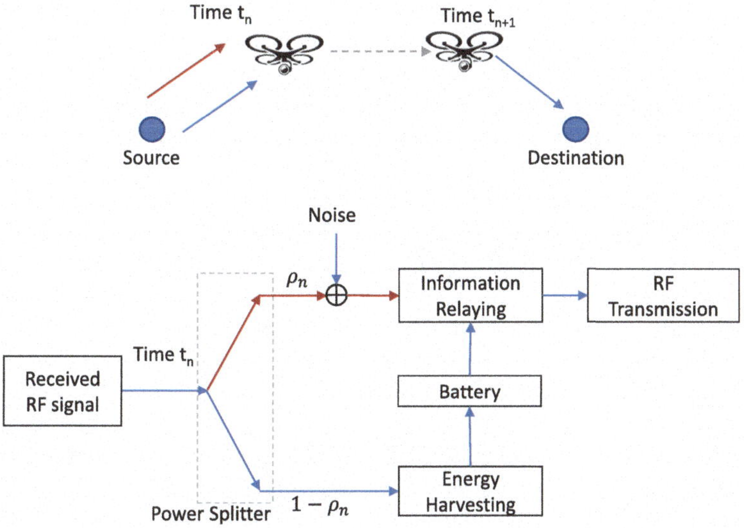

Fig. 8 Power-Splitting SWIPT architecture

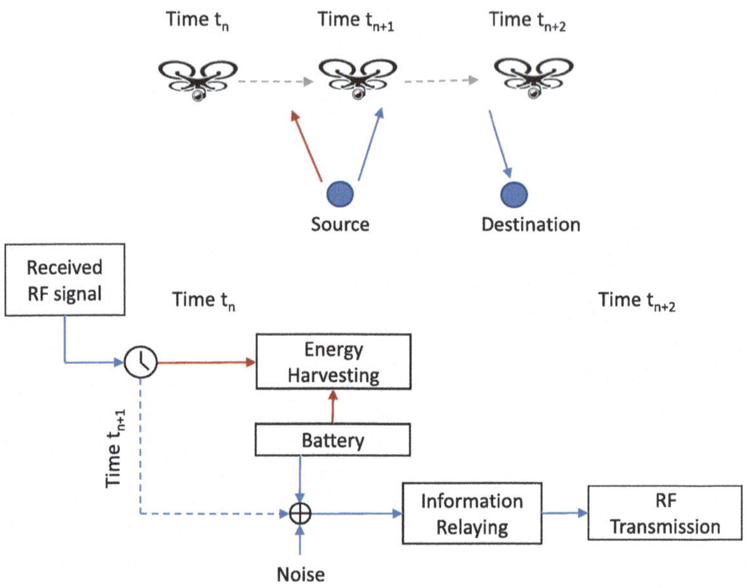

Fig. 9 Time-Sharing SWIPT architecture

both the trajectory and energy requirements of UAV (when UAV is the SWIPT receiver) [39]. Sun et al. [36] presented a mmWave-based secure communication system where UAV-based SWIPT is used.

Time-Sharing SWIPT: In time-sharing SWIPT, the receiver alternates between two modes, IR and EH, over different time intervals rather than simultaneously processing as used in power splitting SWIPT. In each time slot $(t_n | n = 1, 2, 3, \ldots, n, n+1, \ldots)$, the device either harvests energy from the RF signal or decodes information, with the time allocation optimized for the device's energy needs and data reception requirements. Figure 9 depicts a power-splitting SWIPT system.

A few important parameters in this regard are—*Time Allocation Ratio*: Denotes the fraction of time devoted to EH versus IR, balancing power needs with data throughput requirements. This parameter needs to be carefully chosen based on the system requirement. To be *adaptive to channel conditions*, time-sharing can be dynamically adjusted based on CSI, such that the efficiency can be maximized dynamically. *Synchronization*: This is a vital issue, as proper synchronization ensures the receiver switches seamlessly between IR and EH modes without loss of data or energy.

Although the power-splitting SWIPT is widely used, the time-sharing SWIPT system also finds in application in the existing literature such as [37, 38]. A system proposed in [40] uses both power-splitting and time-sharing types of SWIPT architectures.

5 Conclusion

This chapter discussed a possible approach and multiple applications of mm-Wave 6G technology considering environmental effects such as atmospheric loss, free space path loss, dielectric, and conductor loss. Also, the advantages of mm-Wave 6G technology are discussed in terms of data rate, wide bandwidth, secure data communication, and improved usability. A brief investigation on guided medium depending on dielectric loss at mm-Wave frequency, usable connector depending on dielectric and conductor loss, and active devices for different applications is presented. In recent days, the mm-Wave technology with 6G architecture has already become relevant in various applications such as wireless communication, intelligent health care, and energy harvesting. Effective and efficient communication channels can be implementable with suitable system specifications and appropriate typologies. It is predicted that the high data rate and channel capacity can be achievable and usable for communication links at mm-Wave frequency bands. The smaller wave length provides a large number of system components in smaller dimensions and therefore the upscaling of the communication channel would be an additional advantage.

References

1. D. T. Emerson, "The work of Jagadis Chandra Bose: 100 years of millimeter-wave research," in IEEE Transactions on Microwave Theory and Techniques, vol. 45, no. 12, pp. 2267-2273, Dec. 1997, https://doi.org/10.1109/22.643830.keywords: Semiconductor waveguides;Horn antennas;Dielectrics;Lenses;Polarization;Frequency;Receivers;Radio astronomy;Observatories;Telescopes,
2. Dod, G. L. Pearson and W. H. Brattain, "History of semiconductor research," Proc. IRE, vol. 43, pp. 1794–1806, 1955.
3. J. C. Bose, Collected Physical Papers. New York: Longmans, Green and Co., 1927.
4. T. Farley, "Mobile telephone history," Telektronikk, vol. 101, no. 3–4, pp. 22–34, 2005.
5. GSM Memorandum of Understanding, Copenhagen, Denmark, Eur. CEPT, Sep. 1987.
6. F. Hillebrand, "The creation of standards for global mobile communication: GSM and UMTS standardization from 1982 to 2000," IEEE Wireless Commun., vol. 20, no. 5, pp. 24–33, Oct. 2013.
7. S. Abeta, M. Tanno, and M. Iwamura, "Standardization trends in LTE enhancement," NTT DOCOMO Tech. J., vol. 12, no. 1, pp. 42–44, Jun. 2010.
8. C. Hoymann, D. Astely, M. Stattin, G. Wikstrom, J.-F. Cheng, A. Hoglund, "LTE release 14 outlook," IEEE Wireless Commun., vol. 54, no. 6, pp. 44–49, Jun. 2016.
9. A. Osseiran, F. Boccardi, V. Braun, K. Kusume, P. Marsch, M. Maternia, "Scenarios for 5G mobile and wireless communications: The vision of the METIS project," IEEE Commun. Mag., vol. 52, no. 5, pp. 26–35, May 2014.
10. T. S. Rappaport, S. Sun, R. Mayzus, H. Zhao, Y. Azar, K. Wang, "Millimeter wave mobile communications for 5G cellular: It will work!," IEEE Access, vol. 1, pp. 335–349, May 2013.
11. J. Qiao, X. Shen, J. Mark, Q. Shen, Y. He, and L. Lei, "Enabling deviceto-device communications in millimeter-wave 5G cellular networks," IEEE Commun. Mag., vol. 53, no. 1, pp. 209–215, Jan. 2015.
12. T. S. Rappaport, Y. Xing, O. Kanhere, S. Ju, A. Madanayake, S. Mandal, "Wireless communications and applications above 100 GHz: Opportunities and challenges for 6G and beyond," IEEE Access, vol. 7, pp. 78729–78757, Mar. 2019.

13. W. Hong, Z. H. Jiang, C. Yu, J. Zhou, P. Chen, Z. Yu,"Multibeam antenna technologies for 5G wireless communications," IEEE Trans. Antennas Propag., vol. 65, no. 12, pp. 6231–6249, Dec. 2017.
14. Z. Qingling, J. Li,"Rain attenuation in millimeter wave ranges". Inter. Symp. On Antennas, Propagation & EM Theory, Guilin, China, 2006, pp. 1–4.
15. J. S. Marshall, Palmer, W.Mc.K,"The distribution of rain drop with size", J. Meterol, 1948, 5, (4), pp. 165–166.
16. Niu, Y., Li, Y., Jin, D., et al.: "A survey of millimeter wave (mmWave)communications for 5G: opportunities and challenges", Wireless Netw., 2015,21, (8), pp. 2657–2676.
17. Y. Ghasempour, C. R. da Silva, C. Cordeiro, and E. W. Knightly, "IEEE 802.11 ay: Next-generation 60 GHz communication for 100 Gb/s Wi-Fi," IEEE Communications Magazine, vol. 55, no. 12, pp. 186–192, 2017.
18. T. Nitsche, C. Cordeiro, A. B. Flores, E. W. Knightly, E. Perahia, and J. C. Widmer, "IEEE 802.11 ad: Directional 60 GHz communication for multi-Gigabit-per-second Wi-Fi," IEEE Communications Magazine, vol. 52, no. 12, pp. 132–141, 2014.
19. P. Zhou, K. Cheng, X. Han, X. Fang, Y. Fang, R. He, Y. Long, and Y. Liu, "IEEE 802.11 ay-based mmWave WLANs: Design challenges and solutions," IEEE Communications Surveys and Tutorials, vol. 20, no. 3, pp. 1654–1681, 2018.
20. S. Tripathi, N. V Sabu, A.K Gupta, H.S Dhillon "Millimeter-wave and Terahertz Spectrum for 6G Wireless", arXiv:2102.10267
21. "The requirements, challenges, and technologies for 5G of terrestrial mobile telecommunication," IEEE Commun. Mag., vol. 52, no. 5, pp. 36–43, May 2014.
22. . Andrews et al., "Overview of millimeter wave communications for fifth-generation (5G) wireless networks—With a focus on propagation models," IEEE J. Sel. Areas Commun., vol. 32, no. 6, pp. 1065–1082, Jun. 2014.
23. W. Saad, M. Bennis, and M. Chen, "A vision of 6G wireless systems: Applications, trends, technologies, and open research problems," IEEE Netw., vol. 34, no. 3, pp. 134–142, May 2020.
24. M. Gezimati and G. Singh, "Terahertz Imaging and Sensing for Healthcare: Current Status and Future Perspectives," in IEEE Access, vol. 11, pp. 18590-18619, 2023, https://doi.org/10.1109/ACCESS.2023.3247196.
25. H. -S. Nguyen and M. Voznak, "A Bibliometric Analysis of Technology in Digital Health: Exploring Health Metaverse and Visualizing Emerging Healthcare Management Trends," in IEEE Access, vol. 12, pp. 23887-23913, 2024, https://doi.org/10.1109/ACCESS.2024.3363165.
26. Chamitha de Alwis; Quoc-Viet Pham; Madhusanka Liyanage, "6G for Healthcare," in 6G Frontiers: Towards Future Wireless Systems , IEEE, 2023, pp.189-196, https://doi.org/10.1002/9781119862321.ch14.
27. P. V. Matre, A. Kumbhare, R. Gedam, A. Sharma, N. K. Vaishnav and D. Naidu, "6G Enabled Smart IoT in Healthcare System: Prospect, Issues and Study Areas," 2023 International Conference on Artificial Intelligence for Innovations in Healthcare Industries (ICAIIHI), Raipur, India, 2023, pp. 1-6, https://doi.org/10.1109/ICAIIHI57871.2023.10489451.
28. S. Daskalakis, J. Kimionis, J. Hester, A. Collado, M. M. Tentzeris, and A. Georgiadis, "Inkjet printed 24 GHz rectenna on paper for millimeter wave identification and wireless power transfer applications," in IEEE MTT-S Int. Microw. Symp. Dig., Sep. 2017, pp. 1–3.
29. S. Hemour, C. H. P. Lorenz, and K. Wu, "Small-footprint wideband 94 GHz rectifier for swarm micro-robotics," in Proc. IEEE MTT-S Int. Microw. Symp., 2015, pp. 1–3.
30. H. Y. Kim, T. H. Jang, H. H. Bae, and C. S. Park, "A 60 GHz compact multidirectional-beam antenna-in-package for mobile devices," IEEE Antennas Wireless Propag. Lett., vol. 18 no. 11, pp. 2434–2438, Sep. 2019.
31. H. Gao et al., "A 71GHz RF energy harvesting tag with 8 for wireless temperature sensors in 65nm CMOS," in Proc. IEEE Radio Freq. Integr. Circuits Symp. (RFIC), 2013, pp. 403–406.
32. T. Ojha, T.P. Raptis, A. Passarella, M. Conti, "Wireless Power Transfer with Unmanned Aerial Vehicles: State of the Art and Open Challenges", Pervasive and Mobile Computing (Elsevier), vol. 93, pp. 101820, 2023.

33. S. Yin, Y. Zhao, L. Li and F.R. Yu, "UAV-assisted cooperative communications with power-splitting information and power transfer," in IEEE transactions on green communications and networking, vol. 3, issue 4, pp.1044-1057, 2019.
34. J. Wang, B. Li, G. Wang, Y. Hu and A. Schmeink, "Robust Design for UAV-Enabled Multiuser Relaying System With SWIPT," in IEEE Transactions on Green Communications and Networking, vol. 5, no. 3, pp. 1293-1305, Sept. 2021.
35. K. Heo, H.H. Choi and K. Lee, "Joint Trajectory and Resource Optimization for UAV-Assisted SWIPT Systems: A Comparative Study of Linear and Nonlinear Energy Harvesting Models," in IEEE Internet of Things Journal, 2024.
36. X. Sun, W. Yang and Y. Cai, "Secure Communication in NOMA-Assisted Millimeter-Wave SWIPT UAV Networks," in IEEE Internet of Things Journal, vol. 7, no. 3, pp. 1884-1897, March 2020.
37. S. Yin, Y. Zhao and L. Li, "UAV-Assisted Cooperative Communications with Time-Sharing SWIPT," 2018 IEEE International Conference on Communications (ICC), Kansas City, MO, USA, 2018, pp. 1-6,
38. S. Yin, Y. Zhao, L. Li and F. R. Yu, "UAV-Assisted Cooperative Communications With Time-Sharing Information and Power Transfer," in IEEE Transactions on Vehicular Technology, vol. 69, no. 2, pp. 1554-1567, Feb. 2020.
39. H. Yu, M. Ju and H. -C. Yang, "Aggregate Throughput Maximization for UAV-Enabled Relay Networks With Wireless Power Transfer: Joint Trajectory and Power Optimization," in IEEE Transactions on Vehicular Technology, vol. 73, no. 6, pp. 8253-8265, June 2024.
40. R. Jiang, K. Xiong, T. Liu, D. Wang and Z. Zhong, "Coverage Probability-Constrained Maximum Throughput in UAV-Aided SWIPT Networks," 2020 IEEE International Conference on Communications Workshops (ICC Workshops), Dublin, Ireland, 2020, pp. 1-6.
41. J. Xue, X. Zhou, C. Wang, D. Wang, Y. Zhao and Z. Li, "Hybrid precoding for IRS-assisted secure mmWave communication system with SWIPT", Proc. Int. Conf. Space-Air-Ground Comput. (SAGC), pp. 82-86, Dec. 2020.
42. C. Psomas, K. Ntougias, N. Shanin, D. Xu, K. Mayer and N.M. Tran , "Wireless Information and Energy Transfer in the Era of 6G Communications," in Proceedings of the IEEE, vol. 112, no. 7, pp. 764-804, July 2024.

Millimeter Wave and Terahertz Communication: An Overview

Poonam Maurya, Megha Sahu, Usha Kiran, Abhishek Hazra, and M. K. Askar

1 Introduction

With the evolution of 5G technology, 5G-driven use cases and applications are also increasingly demanding higher data rates and reliability with low latency requirements [1]. There are a few future potential use cases and novel applications such as Augmented Reality (AR)/Virtual Reality (VR), 4K and 8K UHD video streaming, 3D-gaming, vehicular communication, autonomous driving, and other applications and scenarios. However, the rapid increase in applications with high-bandwidth requirements has put huge pressure on wireless service providers due to the large volumes of data traffic contributing to overall network traffic and putting a significant load on the current network infrastructure. The most eminent difference between 5G technology and the prevalence of 4G (LTE) is that the 4G bandwidth of 6 GHz (sub-6 GHz cellular bands) is not sufficient to meet the requirements of newly emerging applications. 5G has made a significant leap with the introduction of millimetre (mmWave) technology from 4G to 5G in wireless communication capabilities [2].

P. Maurya (✉)
Aalborg University, Aalborg, Denmark
e-mail: poonamm@es.aau.dk

M. Sahu · U. Kiran · M. K. Askar
IIT Bhilai, Bhilai, India
e-mail: meghas@iitbhilai.ac.in

U. Kiran
e-mail: ushak@iitbhilai.ac.in

M. K. Askar
e-mail: askarmk@iitbhilai.ac.in

A. Hazra
IIIT Sri-city, Chittoor, India
e-mail: abhishek.hazra1@gmail.com

T. Ojha et al. (eds.), *Edge-Enabled 6G Networking*,
https://doi.org/10.1007/978-3-032-19042-0_2

The previous mmWaves were used for applications in higher bands (above 30 GHz), like satellite and radar communications. 5G mmWave extends the capabilities of existing mmWave for applications utilizing lower frequency bands, expanding into broader-user or market oriented applications, and leveraging advanced technologies. Also, modern devices and the antenna design in 5G have made previous mmWaves feasible for market-oriented applications such as AR/VR and autonomous driving.

As we are moving towards AR/VR, 3D Video streaming and gaming, which are putting more stricter constraints on the throughput, reliability, and latency requirements. The deployed 5G networks are struggling to fulfil these growing requirements of continuously emerging applications, and that pushes us towards the era of 6G [3]. Although 5G is still evolving and advancing, researchers have started working to better shape the next generation of 6G. The 6G wireless technology is making a significant difference from previous technologies by connecting the digital world with the physical world and revolutionizing the wireless evolution to provide intelligence, connectivity, and synchronization with emerging reality. 6G is redefining the spectrum to the terahertz (THz) band, which lies above the mmWave band. The previous THz waves were using the narrow frequency bands for applications like medical imaging, spectroscopy and security scannings. 6G THz is focusing more on the lower range of 0.1–1 THz for ultra high speed wireless communications such as immersive experiences and holographic communications.

1.1 Challenges in Traditional Communication Systems

Despite being well-established and widely utilized, conventional communication (like 1G–4G and beyond) systems face numerous challenges that are exacerbated by the constraints of modern technology and the need to adapt to the evolving wireless communication environment [4]. When examining these challenges in the context of mmWave and THz frequencies, several key distinctions and concerns come to the fore.

1. **Limited Bandwidth**: Broadband can be a challenge for older communication systems, especially those that operate below millimeter-wave frequencies as it has limited bandwidth and operates at lower frequency. This limitation restricts the amount of data that can be transmitted over a network simultaneously, which can cause issues during periods of high usage. Additionally, these systems often use old modulation methods and do not have the modern signal processing tools needed to handle high-bandwidth internet connections well. The problem is exacerbated by the growing demand for fast internet and data-intensive applications. As more individuals use video services, distant learning, and cloud computing, the available bandwidth becomes depleted, resulting in slower speeds and diminished service quality. Shifting to higher frequency bands, such as mmWave and THz, could be a solution, but it also presents some drawbacks.

2. **Interference and Signal Attenuation**: The main reason behind the impact of interference and signal attenuation on traditional wireless communication technologies is the dependence on lower frequency bands and less advanced modulation techniques. These frequency bands are more prone to interference from physical barriers like buildings and trees, and they experience greater signal attenuation over distance compared to higher frequency bands. Additionally, the modulation techniques employed in these technologies are less effective in combating these challenges, resulting in reduced performance in densely populated urban areas.
3. **Regulatory and Spectrum Management Issues**: Efficient operation of communication systems largely depends on the regulatory frameworks and spectrum management policies in place. Outdated regulations in traditional systems often hinder technological advancements, leading to suboptimal utilization of available spectrum. Furthermore, allocating spectrum for different purposes, including commercial, military, and scientific uses, may result in conflicts and inefficiencies. Effective spectrum management requires striking a balance between the needs of various stakeholders while guaranteeing access to resources for new technologies to function optimally.
4. **Latency sensitive Application**: The increasing demand for latency-sensitive applications, such as remote surgery, autonomous vehicles, and emergency system response, highlights the urgent need for low-latency communication systems. Traditional communication systems, particularly those based on outdated technologies, may not meet the rigorous demands of these applications, which may result in delays that could compromise performance and safety. Establishing ultra-low latency across extensive regions remains a formidable challenge, particularly in areas where infrastructure is scarce or geographical obstacles impede direct connectivity.

The Table 1 presents a comparison of traditional communication, mmWave, and THz communication, highlighting the key distinct feature among these technologies.

1.2 Need for Higher Data Rates and Emergence of mmWave and THz Communication

In recent years, the proliferation of smart mobile devices and the exponential growth in mobile data traffic have become evident. This trend is expected to persist and expand further in the future, driven by the incorporation of innovative technologies such as wireless Internet of Things (IoT) devices across various sectors, including supply chain management, biomedical research, and vehicular communication and transportation.

As the use of 5G technology has grown and data traffic continues to increase, it has become crucial for operators to use the available spectrum efficiently from both

Table 1 Comparison between traditional communication, mmWave, and THz communication

Feature	Traditional communication	mmWave	THz communication
Frequency range	Below 6 GHz	30–300 GHz	Above 100 GHz
Data rate	Moderate to high	Very high	Extremely high
Coverage	Wide coverage area	Limited coverage area	Very limited coverage area
Penetration through walls	Good	Poor	Very poor
Antenna size	Large	Small	Very small
Interference	Moderate	High	Very high
Line-of-sight required	No	Yes	Yes
Mobility	High	Moderate	Low
Deployment cost	Moderate	High	Very high
Applications	Mobile communication, broadcasting	5G networks, point-to-point links, backhaul	Wireless communication in environments with high data rate requirements

a technical and business standpoint. In order to meet the increasing digital demands of consumers and businesses, the mobile industry is constantly searching for ways to utilize the limited spectrum more effectively. Various techniques exist to enhance spectrum efficiency, particularly in FDD (Frequency Division Duplex) and TDD (Time Division Duplex) systems, such as carrier aggregation, which involves combining different spectrum channels, improving antenna capabilities, and upgrading radio resource management through Radio Access Network (RAN) software [5]. However, these methods are unlikely to provide significant improvements. An alternative solution to address the growing data demand is network densification [6], which involves increasing the number of base stations to improve coverage and spectral efficiency. However, this approach also leads to increased interference, limiting the performance gains that can be achieved. A more promising solution may be to expand the spectrum to mmWave and THz bands [7]. These frequencies offer a significantly larger amount of available spectrum—about 50–100 times more than sub-6 GHz frequencies.

2 Fundamentals of mmWave and THz Communication

This section serves to provide a foundational comprehension of mmWave and THz communication by exploring their spectrum utilization and distinctive characteristics.

2.1 Electromagnetic Spectrum

The electronic spectrum refers to the array of frequencies that can be utilized for transmitting and receiving signals. This spectrum is partitioned into multiple bands, with each band of the spectrum has different properties and uses. Radio waves are utilized in communication technologies, ranging from the initial 1G to the most recent 5G and beyond. Microwaves, on the other hand, are employed for heating food as well as communication, such as satellite communication. X-rays, meanwhile, are used primarily for medical imaging purposes. The importance of the electronic spectrum in wireless communication is manifold and encompasses the allocation of frequencies, the advancement of communication technologies, and the governance of spectrum usage.

As shown in Fig. 1, mmWave and THz communication utilize a segment of the electromagnetic spectrum that falls between microwave and infrared frequencies. The mmWave frequency range extends from 30 to 300 GHz, which corresponds to wavelengths ranging from 1 to 10 mm (named for their millimeter-order wavelength). The THz frequencies span from 0.1 to 10 THz (named for their terahertz-order frequencies), corresponding to wavelengths ranging from 3 mm to 30 μm [8]. These frequency bands provide expansive bandwidths and have the capacity for high data rates, making them well-suited for a range of applications, such as high-speed communication and sensing. Especially significant for the advancement of upcoming wireless communication technologies, such as 6G and beyond [9].

2.2 Characteristics and Properties of mmWave and THz Waves

The unique characteristics and properties of mmWave and THz waves distinguish them from lower-frequency communication technologies. These include their high frequency and large bandwidth, which enable the potential for ultra-high data rates, making them ideal for next-generation wireless applications. Despite the challenges

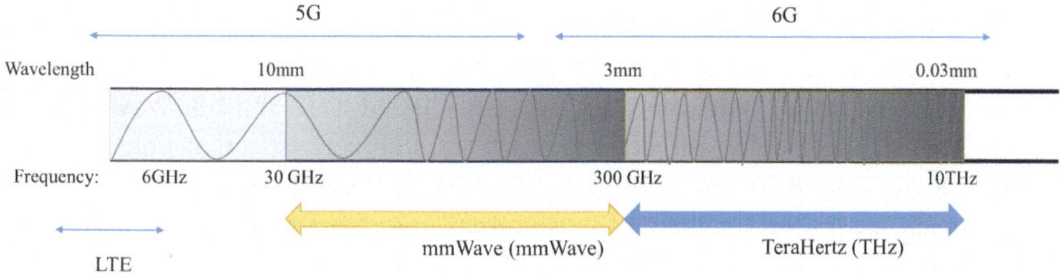

Fig. 1 Spectrum and wavelength of mmWave and THz communication

posed by their physical and propagation properties [10], these waves offer advantages over lower-frequency technologies.

1. **High Data Transmission Rates**: mmWave and THz frequencies can offer a broad frequency range that enables rapid data transmission, making them an ideal choice for the development of future wireless communication systems. As per Shannon's Capacity formula, the data rate (C) is directly proportional to the bandwidth (B), emphasizing the significance of these high-frequency bands for efficient communication.
$$C = B * \log_2(1 + SNR) \quad (1)$$
where SNR indicates signal-to-noise ratio. The mmWave and THz frequencies offer wider bandwidths that allow for significantly higher data rates compared to lower frequency bands [11]. For instance, mmWave systems that operate at frequencies around 60 GHz and possess a bandwidth of 2 GHz, which is a common feature in WiGig systems. These systems are capable of transmitting data at speeds exceeding 10 Gbps. The rationale behind this is that wider bandwidths provide more capacity for transferring data, leading to an increase in overall transmission throughput. Moreover, the utilization of mmWave and THz signals, characterized by their short wavelengths, facilitates highly targeted transmission. This feature may significantly enhance their compatibility with 6G that call for high-speed transmission and substantial data storage capabilities.
2. **Attenuation and Low Penetration**: The distinctive characteristics of mmWave and THz frequencies are mainly defined by their high absorption rates. The short wavelengths of these frequencies make them susceptible to interference from factors such as vegetation, walls, and atmospheric components like oxygen and water vapor. To overcome this, signals can be detuned through effective absorption, which occurs when waves interact with atmospheric molecules and common building materials. The limited penetrability of mmWave and THz frequencies renders them more adept for use cases necessitating communication over short distances. When it comes to indoor wireless networks and car radar systems, this feature is very useful. For these constrained applications in particular, the reduced signal-to-noise ratio improves security and decreases interference.
Additionally, mmWave and THz frequencies are resistant to outside interference and surveillance because of their low penetration and high absorption rates. This quality makes them ideal for uses that necessitate encrypted communication in confined spaces, where interference from outside sources is less likely to occur.
3. **Highly Directional Transmission**: The capacity of THz and mmWave signals to transmit in a specific direction is a critical characteristic that enhances the efficiency and security of communications due to their short wavelengths. This feature allows for the focusing of these signals into narrow beams, which significantly reduces interference and strengthens the security of the communication link. Using a narrow beam can decrease the likelihood of interference from external sources, which is especially beneficial in situations where several devices are operating simultaneously. By reducing interference, the quality of the com-

munication link can be maintained. The use of mmWave and THz signals in communication enhances security by making it difficult for unauthorized parties to intercept or eavesdrop on the signal. This helps to protect data privacy and security. Additionally, the directional characteristics of these signals play a role in reinforcing communication security. In addition, the ability to focus into narrow bands optimizes the use of the available spectrum in settings with a high density of devices or in concurrent transmission operation, where congestion in the spectrum can lead to reduced performance. The mmWave and THz frequencies are exceptionally advantageous for automotive and radar systems, as well as wireless communication systems (including 5G, 6G and beyond networks) that require secure and precise communication, on account of these characteristics.

The Fig. 2 illustrates the distinct properties of the mmWave and THz bands, highlighting their potential as next-generation wireless communication technologies and suitability for variety range of applications.

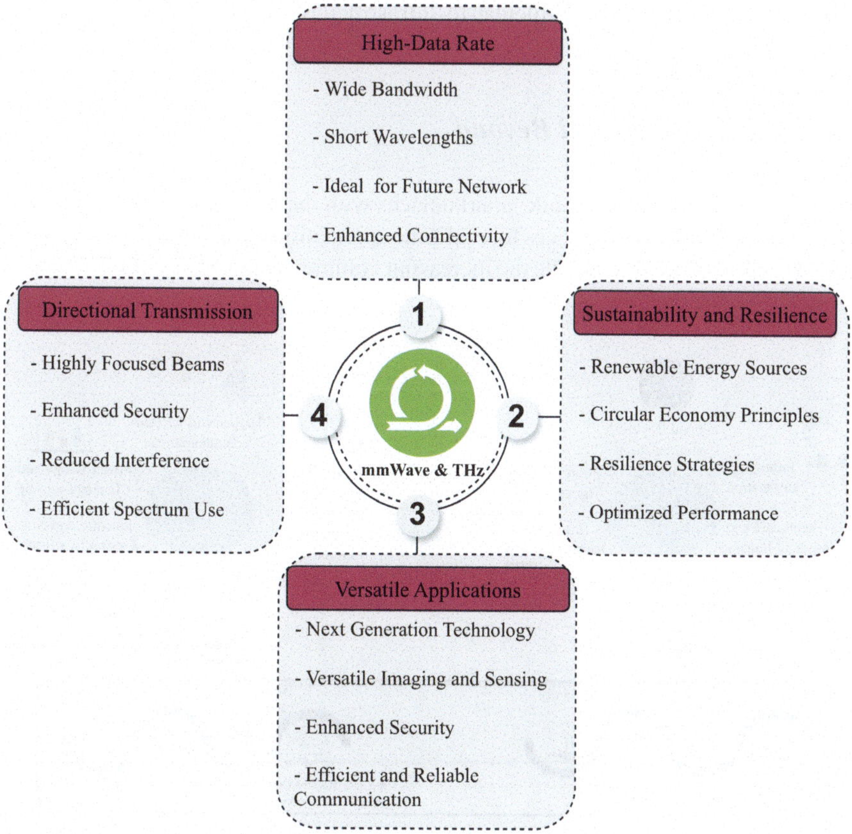

Fig. 2 Features of mmWave and THz communication

3 Applications and Use Cases

There is a wide range of applications of mmWave and THz in areas attracting a lot of attention in the domain of science and technology. A detailed view of mmWave and THz wave applications and use cases is given in Fig. 3 that also highlights their current potential use cases. The impact of mmWave and THz waves is influencing sectors such as telecommunications, healthcare, security, industrial automation, education, entertainment, and space exploration. The potential usecases of mmWave are in high-speed wireless communications like high-definition video streaming and video surveillance [12], AR/VR, connected vehicles [13], IoT networks for smart cities [14], and hospitals and emergency response [15]. THz communication is the next growing technology towards 6G and beyond. This aims to fulfil the demands for high data rates and ultra-large bandwidth requirements. The potential use cases of THz-band communication include: Extended Reality (XR) and Holographic Teleportation, Metaverse [16], Tactile Internet [17], Industry 4.0 [18] and Digital Twins [19], Connected Robotics and Autonomous Systems (CRAS) [20], Non-Terrestrial Networks (NTNs) [21], and Vehicular-to-Infrastructure (V2I) [22].

3.1 Role in 5G/6G and Beyond

There is a rapid growth in mobile smart devices with the capability to deliver highly intelligent and connected services for real-time applications demanding high capacity and reliability. In order to handle the increasing volume of data traffic, 4G (LTE) uses

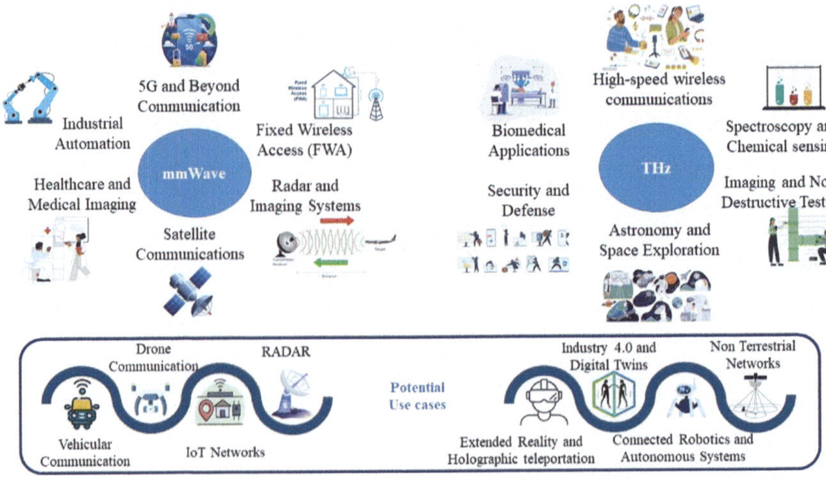

Fig. 3 Applications and use-cases of mmWave and THz across different domains and highlighting their current potential uses

sub-bands in conjunction with 5G and beyond, while the mmWave spectrum will be used to fulfil rising bandwidth requirements. The 5G mmWave wireless spectrum is ten times more prevalent than today's 4G (long-term evolution) bands. There will be more to 5G technology than just a new radio access standard. The primary innovation of 5G will instead be the amalgamation of several networks catering to a range of industries, fields, and uses. Beyond 5G networks, ultra-wideband transmission is used in the THz band.

To effectively utilize the high-bandwidth offered by (mmWave) 5G, [12] addresses the fundamental challenge of highly varying 5G throughput performance and its affect on QoE for ultra-HD (UHD) 4K/8K and volumetric video streaming applications. For high-speed wireless gaming and streaming applications, 5G accelerates FWA (Fixed Wireless Access), an alternative to wired connections. The use of mmWave in IEEE Standard 802.11ay for FWA is studied in [23]. A wide variety of use cases, diverse applications, and different verticals of 5G are discussed in [24] to understand specifically when, where, and how mmWave can be used in 5G and beyond applications. The mmwave 5G usecase for connected and automated driving is provided in [25], where real-time services in cross-border scenarios are discussed in context to challenges, 5G requirements, and technical features. Moving from 5G towards 6G eras, a B5G mobile system application: VR-based immersive service is presented in [26]. In 5G (B5G), remote applications are becoming extremely important, and [26] shows how a user remotely controls UAVs with 360°C cameras using hand mounted devices. The next-generation wireless technology, 6G, is predicted to provide ultra-large bandwidths in the THz range. The THz band is utilised for NTN communications. It supports high data rates for CRAS and V2I connectivity, as well as low latency and high dependability for XR services. The study [27], investigates dense THz networks for VR applications, and emphasises the inclusion of visual and haptic-based QoE requirements for VR users. It also offers a separate study for holographic and multi-media communications [28] due to their distinct QoE requirements. Another usecase of THz, Industry 4.0 is evolving towards automation involving machines and robots with minimal human input [18]. A digital twin technology can be incorporated into Industry 4.0 by creating its own model using real-world data to predict product or process performance. These two together can boost productivity. To bridge the physical and digital worlds, a framework based on THz wave communication is presented in [19] where the implementation of a digital twin prediction enables an extremely secure system for metamorphic objects. An NTN is a future wireless communication network that links terrestrial, satellite, ship, aerial, and underwater communications systems. Another cutting edge technology that has revolutionized the 6G and beyond systems is RIS. The use of RIS has improved the performance of THz systems [29]. In [29], a specific case is studied by integrating the RIS in non-orthogonal multiple access (NOMA)-based satellite networks and demonstrates the performance enhancement due to inclusion of RIS. Another work in [30] presents RIS equipped high altitude platform (HAP) are used to secure a communication link between Low Earth Orbit (LEO) satellite transmitter and UAV receivers.

mmWave communication is not only used for ultra-high-speed communication but is also well suited to provide efficient and flexible wireless backhauling. In recent years, a new RAN architecture has emerged, with different functions among the Centralized Unit (CU), a Distribution/BaseBand Unit (DU), and a Radio Unit (RU). Aggregated traffic at the CU, which links to many DUs, is still connected to the core network via the backhaul. These transport links must accommodate increasing traffic demands and low latency requirements for 5G and future mobile services. This huge data demand while providing high coverage, and high data-rates in 5G network can be fulfilled by using an ultra-dense network (UDN). The use of mmWave with massive-MIMO in wireless backhaul for 5G UDN is presented in [31]. Another, recent work deals with the mmWave backhaul scheduling problem that has proven to be an NPhard problem through simulations [32]. Wireless transport links in the THz band can support these higher capacity needs, achieving rates of up to 100 Gbps due to the large spectrum availability, which allows for channel spacing of up to 5 GHz, and the application of advanced multiplexing techniques [33].

The High-speed mobility applications primarily involves cooperation between communication nodes in a mobile scenario. Two common instances of utilizing mmWave and THz technology in situations include vehicle-to-everything (V2X) and train-to-train communications. This enhances V2X use cases like 4K/8K AR, extended sensors, autonomous platooning, remote driving, and advanced driving [13]. V2X applications demand the low response times and ultra-reliable communication that the THz spectrum can offer for communication and accurate sensing [22]. The Software Defined Networking (SDN)-controlled and Cognitive Radio (CR)-enabled V2X routing approach is presented in [34] where switching between ultrahigh- rate and minimized transmission delay for short-range (in THz bands) and middle-range (in mmWave) communications is supported.

3.2 Applications in Healthcare and Medical Imaging

The use of mmWaves in 5G healthcare has increased in recent years with the integration of potential technologies, IoT or the Internet of Medical Things (IoMT), artificial intelligence, and robotics to transform healthcare systems into an interconnected ecosystem. Remote surgery using robotic based tele-surgery relies broadly on the exchange of medical data, which includes high-quality images, audio, and video, digitized and transmitted over cable or wireless telecommunication networks. The surgeon present at the central healthcare station remotely controls the robot and instructs using voice controls from afar. In one such attempt in [35], a surgeon at the central healthcare centre controls the arms of the teleoperator (robot) at the remote site based on the multi-modal sensory (visual, auditory, and haptic data) feedback from the teleoperator. This expands into telemedicine and shares the vital parameters of the patient with the surgeon for real-time patient monitoring and treatment [36]. This work deals with challenges due to different types of information and different

QoS requirements. 5G healthcare is evolving more towards smart healthcare systems [37], particularly applications like remote patient monitoring and overall healthcare operations. The newer cutting-edge technology, edge computing, plays a crucial role in the field of telemedicine for real-time healthcare. Potential use cases in the healthcare sector include connected ambulances [38], remote expert collaborations, 5G-connected drones for e-health [39], and 5G private networks to ensure secure healthcare communications.

The demand for THz technology is increasing in healthcare due to emerging technologies, new diseases, growing health management techniques, awareness among customers, and many other advanced reasons. THz waves are used in biomedical applications, primarily in medical imaging, spectroscopy, and sensing [40]. These are further expanding in applications like non-invasive, non-destructive testing, and security and surveillance services. The THz radiations are used for medical diagnosis [41] and health monitoring for skin-related problems [42]. It is found that the use of THz technology for diagnostic applications should be performed in a controlled environment [43]. THz, in collaboration with other cutting-edge technologies like IoT, AI, and VR, enhances applications like telemedicine and telesurgery [44]. Tele-surgery or remote surgery utilizes potential THz by enabling surgeons to operate medical robots remotely at anytime from anywhere, where VR/AR technologies and haptic gloves could play a role in supporting these interventions. The role of THz communication is to provide human sensory capacities at the remote end through imaging and spectroscopy. Also, for the high-quality (4K/8K) video streaming of the patient for accuracy and good visuals, the THz provides the required bandwidth. Moreover, it enables high-definition video streaming with clarity. For the early detection and monitoring of diseases like cancer [45], dental issues [46], and skin problems [42], THz waves are used for non-invasive diagnostics by leveraging the unique property lies between microwave and infrared electromagnetic spectrum, without causing any damage to the biological tissue [47]. A detailed study of cancerous and healthy tissue is provided in [45] that finds cancerous tissue showing high absorption of THz waves.

3.3 New Services, Experiences and Security

The mmWave and THz bands are not just limited to healthcare, security and 5G/6G technological usecases, but also explored in the fields of entertainment, education, industrial automation, astronomy, and space, and many more.

In the field of entertainment, a specific use case of high-mobility bullet trains or airspace accessing video streaming, gaming, conferencing, and the internet is demanding. All such applications require high data rates and low latency in a highly crowded environment. The 5G mmWave based video streaming application for on road entertainment in vehicular networks is presented in [59].

THz technology is driven by applications in space where non terrestrial networks are used for deep space and inter-satellite communications. The light form of THz radio and antennas is attractive to NASA space applications to handle multiple space flight missions to avoid space Radio Frequency Interference (RFI) [54]. In space communication, latency remains an issue, but these services can be improved by combining THz/FSO links into space information networks [55]. An mmwave space application to deal with the data congestion in the nanosatellite mission is provided in [53]. The paper addresses the challenges of using mmWave for nano satellites and also state-of-the-art mmWave semiconductor technology in developing nano satellites.

Another growing application of THz and mmWaves is in the fields of industry and agriculture. The mmWave communications have regained popularity in industrial applications, expecting the next generation of manufacturing to deal with large amounts of data handling. Using wireless smart cameras and vision technologies enables remote visual monitoring, intelligent logistics tracking, automated assembly, and fault detection [56]. In the last few years, human capabilities have been automated, as has the development of mobile robots. Industrial automation helps with faster and more accurate inspections, where manual checks are time-consuming and prone to human error [57]. In industry, the THz potential application is THz sensors in industry [58]. THz sensors in a optical techniques that uses light in THz frequency range for measurement and analysis. It is used in industry for non destructive and condition monitoring.

Security is a major concern where these two: mmWave and THz technologies are adopted [49]. The use of mmWave and THz technologies in aviation security applications is increasing [50]. These waves are used for weapons detection by the smart security scanners at different security check-in points, say airports, hotels, malls, etc. The non-ionizing radiation of THz waves is proven to be absolutely harmless to people. THz waves are capable of detecting not only metals but also ceramics, plastics, and polymers that are transparent in THz waves and therefore can be easily detected. Also, there is the possibility of detecting hidden objects at a distance by THz. For the public safety applications, an mmWave-based solution [51] connects UAVs and remote control center, providing low latency and high throughput connectivity.

There are vast applications and use-cases that use the mmWave and THz bands. A summarized table for all the recent use cases in both bands is provided in Table 2.

4 Challenges in mmWave and THz

The challenges inherent in mmWave and THz communication must be addressed to fully realize their potential for future wireless communication systems. These high-frequency domains present unique obstacles that must be overcome in order to unlock their transformative capabilities.

Table 2 Recent use cases and applications of mmWave and THz technology in various fields of Science and Technology

Areas	Usecases and applications	mmWave	THz
Telecommunications	5G	[12] [24–26]	–
	5G FWA	[23]	–
	V2X	[13, 34]	[22, 34]
	6G and beyond	–	[17–19, 21, 27–29]
	Wireless backhaul	[31, 32]	[33]
	IoT networks	[14]	–
Healthcare	Tele-surgery	[35]	[44]
	Tele-medicine	[36–39, 48]	–
	Non invasive medical diagnostics	–	[41, 47]
Security	Airport security	[49]	[49, 50]
	Public safety	[51]	–
Scientific research	Spectroscopy	–	[40, 52]
Space exploration	Astronomy and space	[53]	[54, 55]
Industrial automation	Robotics and drone	[56, 57]	[58]

4.1 Technical Challenges

Technical obstacles in mmWave and THz communication span a broad range of challenges that must be overcome to fully exploit their potential. It is crucial to comprehend and tackle these intricate issues in order to unleash the revolutionary features of these advanced frequency bands in wireless communication systems.

- **High Power Requirements**
  In comparison to lower frequency bands, mmWave and THz communication systems typically necessitate significantly higher power levels for signal transmission. The shorter wavelengths of these signals are the primary cause of this, as they require the use of stronger signals to ensure that the link quality remains adequate over distances. The higher power requirements present several challenges [60, 61]. Achieving high data rates while minimizing energy consumption is essential for portable devices like smartphones and laptops. However, the significant energy demands of mmWave and THz technologies may exacerbate energy inefficiencies, making it necessary to develop innovative solutions to reduce power consumption. Moreover, effective thermal management techniques are vital to prevent heat buildup and ensure reliable device operation.
- **Complex Integration**
  Because of the unique features of mmWave and THz frequencies, integrating them into existing communication infrastructures is complicated. Specialized components, like as antennas and amplifiers, are required to efficiently transmit and

receive signals at mmWave and THz frequencies. However, developing these components to work successfully across a wide variety of frequencies and environmental conditions presents a substantial practical challenges. Additionally, to incorporate these components into compact, portable devices, novel packaging and assembly techniques must be used to accommodate the components' physical size and heat production characteristics.

- **Signal Propagation**
  The propagation of mmWave and THz signals is greatly affected by various elements such as scattering, absorption, and reflection from objects in their surroundings environment. One of the main obstacles is path loss, which gradually grows with frequency and decreases the effective range of the signal. To address this problem, techniques like beamforming and the use of highly directional antennas can be employed [60]. In urban areas, materials like buildings and vegetation commonly absorb and scatter mmWave and THz signals, which reduces their strength and reliability. To counteract these effects, advanced signal processing techniques are necessary. Additionally, signals at these frequencies have trouble penetrating certain materials like walls and leaves, which restricts their usefulness in both indoor and outdoor settings. As a result, ongoing research is aimed at discovering materials with lower absorption coefficients to overcome this limitation.
- **Signal Interference**
  Despite experiencing substantial signal attenuation, which limits their interference range compared to lower-frequency signals, mmWave and THz frequencies can still be susceptible to interference in crowded urban settings or when multiple systems operate in neighboring frequency bands. These high-frequency signals rapidly weaken due to obstacles such as buildings and atmospheric conditions, restricting long-range interference [62]. Nevertheless, in areas with high device density, the close proximity of various networks (including 5G, Wi-Fi, satellite, and radar systems) increases the likelihood of signal quality degradation caused by overlapping or adjacent frequency usage [63]. As an example, 5G technology, which functions in both sub-6 GHz and mmWave ranges (24–40 GHz), could potentially interfere with 6G systems that use higher mmWave and THz frequencies (exceeding 100 GHz), particularly in areas where there is a high concentration of base stations. Additionally, Wi-Fi networks, especially those operating in the 6 GHz and higher mmWave bands, may create interference issues as they share spectrum with 6G devices in densely populated areas. To address these issues, cutting-edge technologies like adaptive beamforming and massive MIMO are employed to spatially differentiate transmissions. Additionally, dynamic spectrum access (DSA) and interference cancellation methods are utilized to enhance spectrum efficiency and diminish interference. Crucial to minimizing the impact of interference from other wireless technologies on performance is the effective management and coordination of spectrum across various systems.

4.2 Regulatory Challenges

The use of mmWave and THz communication technologies is hindered by significant regulatory obstacles that must be overcome for their widespread adoption and utilization. Establishing appropriate regulatory frameworks, allocating sufficient spectrum, and ensuring compliance with relevant requirements are essential for seamlessly integrating these cutting-edge technologies into existing wireless networks and infrastructure

- **Spectrum Allocation and Licensing**
  A significant obstacle in implementing mmWave and THz technologies is the distribution of appropriate frequency bands. The lack of uniform regulations for these frequencies, especially those above 100 GHz, across different regions hinders the creation of worldwide 6G solutions. While certain bands have been designated for research and experimental purposes, there remains an absence of well-defined licensing structures for commercial applications. This inconsistency in spectrum allocation poses a major hurdle for the widespread adoption of these advanced communication technologies.
  Spectrum sharing also presents a significant challenge, especially in heavily populated regions where millimeter wave and terahertz frequencies coincide with existing services such as satellite communications, radar systems, and Wi-Fi networks. Further, as we have discussed in the previous section, interference is also a big challenge that must be considered. So, to effectively manage interference, it is essential to implement appropriate spectrum-sharing techniques and dynamic spectrum access (DSA) methods. Furthermore, the development of standards by organizations like 3GPP and IEEE plays a vital role in ensuring that various wireless systems and technologies can operate harmoniously alongside one another.
  Global entities like the International Telecommunication Union (ITU) are essential in coordinating spectrum usage worldwide [64, 65]. The ITU's World Radiocommunication Conference (WRC) is tasked with determining which spectrum bands can be allocated for emerging communications technologies. Nevertheless, various countries have their own spectrum management systems, implemented by national regulatory agencies. For instance, the United States has the Federal Communications Commission (FCC), Europe has the European Telecommunications Standards Institute (ETSI), and the Asia-Pacific region has the Asia-Pacific Telecommunity (APT). This diversity in regulatory frameworks can lead to a lack of uniformity across different regions. Addressing these issues requires joint action from governments, industry players, and regulatory agencies to harmonize spectrum policies and promote worldwide compatibility for 6G networks.
- **Safety and Health Concerns**
  Concerns regarding the potential health consequences of exposure to high-frequency radiation have been raised, with a specific focus on human contact with radio frequency electromagnetic (RFEM) fields [66]. As a result, power output limits have been established for radio transmitters. The mmWave frequencies, due to their ability to be absorbed by moisture in the human body, are incapable of

penetrating the outer layers of the skin. Thus, it is essential to ensure that the level of mmWave radiation does not exceed the maximum permissible exposure (MPE). To prevent any potential risks associated with exposure to high frequency radiation, extensive research is being carried out, and international safety standards are being followed.

4.3 Practical Challenges

The practical challenges and market acceptance of mmWave and THz communication are crucial factors affecting their implementation and commercial viability. Achieving cost-effectiveness, scalability, and user acceptance is essential for promoting the widespread adoption of these cutting-edge technologies in various applications and industries.

- **Deployment and Infrastructure**
  Utilizing mmWave and THz communication technologies presents various infrastructure challenges, such as the need to secure spectrum allocation and design networks capable of supporting their high data rates. The process of obtaining spectrum licenses can be costly and time-consuming, creating financial and logistical obstacles for operators. Regulatory agencies must balance the needs of new services with those of existing users while securing access to spectrum bands necessary for the deployment of these technologies. Complex network architecture and planning require many base stations and accurate beamforming to achieve high data speeds. The present infrastructure may not support mmWave and THz frequencies, requiring major renovations or new installations. Deploying these networks might be costly due to specialized equipment and new infrastructure [67]. Operators must weigh these expenses against the income and advantages of faster and more reliable connectivity.
- **Adoption and Market Acceptance**
  Market acceptance faces significant barriers, despite the technical benefits of mmWave and THz communications [68]. To facilitate adoption, it is crucial to educate consumers about the advantages of seamless streaming and faster downloads. However, high spectrum license costs and premium device pricing pose challenges. Moreover, device compatibility requires manufacturers to incorporate these technologies into new products, and consumers to upgrade their existing devices. The need for regulations that are aligned with technological advancements is emphasized by the potential for delayed market entry due to prolonged regulatory approval and review processes. It is essential to establish a comprehensive ecosystem that includes service providers, application developers, and content providers. Collaboration among stakeholders is crucial to create compelling value propositions that spark consumer interest. To overcome these obstacles, it is

necessary for industry actors, regulators, and standardization bodies to collaborate in addressing infrastructure concerns, promoting market acceptance, and navigating regulatory landscapes.

Additionally, Table 3 presents a thorough comparative analysis of the obstacles encountered by mmWave and THz communication, as well as potential solutions. This comparative examination provides valuable insights for addressing the unique challenges posed by these emerging technologies, enabling informed decision-making for their integration into future wireless networks.

5 Security Considerations Related to mmWave and THz Technologies

In this section, we discuss the security challenges associated with mmWave and THz technologies. A thorough examination of these challenges is imperative before deploying these technologies in any application to ensure their integration within a secure framework. Some of the major challenges include jamming attacks, authentication mechanisms, encryption mechanisms, and physical layer security etc.

5.1 Security Challenges

The mmWave technology is essential for applications that require high-speed communications like 5G, enabling high-speed data transfer and increased bandwidth [79]. However, they encounter a variety of cybersecurity and physical threats that demand detailed attention from the researchers [80]. Despite its short-range nature and directional signal transmission, mmWave technology is not immune to eavesdropping, which remains possible for determined attackers equipped with the right tools [81]. Jamming attacks, another significant risk, can disrupt mmWave signals by interfering with their narrow beams through various means, including physical obstruction or signal interference [82, 83].

As mentioned in the Table 4, the cybersecurity landscape surrounding mmWave technology is fraught with challenges, including signal interception vulnerabilities, susceptibility to jamming, and the potential for denial of Service (DoS) and Distributed Denia of Service (DDoS) attacks [84]. Inadequate encryption methods, limited authentication options, and shortcomings in key management practices may increase these risks, potentially exposing mmWave systems to vulnerabilities [85]. Moreover, threats like signal spoofing and side-channel attacks may pose additional challenges to the integrity and security of mmWave communications [83]. Physical threats to mmWave technology include the potential for eavesdropping via

Table 3 Comparative analysis of challenges and solutions in mmWave and THz communication

Challenge	mmWave	THz	Possible solutions
Propagation loss [69]	Significant free-space path loss	Extremely high free-space path loss	• Super-dense small cell networks • High-gain antennas • Sophisticated beamforming
Atmospheric absorption [70]	Moderate, especially affected by rain	Very high, strong absorption by water vapor and oxygen	• Frequency planning to avoid absorption peaks • Using short-range communication • Spectral windows with lower absorption
Penetration [69]	Poor, limited penetration through obstacles	Very poor, almost negligible penetration through obstacles	• Deployment of more base stations and relays • Use of reflective surfaces • Intelligent reconfigurable surfaces
Antenna design [71]	Requires advanced antenna technologies	Requires highly specialized and precise antenna design	• Development of compact, high-gain, phased array antennas • Research in nano-fabrication techniques
Signal attenuation [72]	High, due to atmospheric absorption and scattering	Very high, severe attenuation over short distances	• Use of repeaters and amplifiers • Development of low-loss waveguides • Advanced repeaters
Bandwidth availability [73]	Wide bandwidth, up to several GHz	Extremely wide bandwidth, up to several THz	• Efficient spectrum management • Exploiting the large available bandwidth while managing interference
Noise and interference [72]	Susceptible to thermal noise and interference	High susceptibility to noise due to high-frequency operations	• Advanced error correction • Noise mitigation techniques • Enhanced filtering • Robust error correction mechanisms

(continued)

Table 3 (continued)

Challenge	mmWave	THz	Possible solutions
Hardware cost [74]	High, but decreasing with technological advances	Very high, due to nascent technology and precision requirements	• Investment in scalable manufacturing techniques • Research and development to reduce costs through new manufacturing processes
Power consumption [75]	High power consumption	Extremely high power consumption	• Optimization of power-efficient circuit designs • Energy harvesting techniques • Innovations in low-power electronics • Efficient power management systems
Standardization [76]	Well underway (e.g., 5G standards)	In early stages, with ongoing research and development	• Continued efforts in global standardization bodies • Collaborative efforts to establish standards through international bodies
Heat dissipation [77]	Considerable heat generation	Severe heat generation, demanding efficient cooling mechanisms	• Advanced cooling solutions such as heat sinks • Development of new cooling technologies like advanced thermal materials • Microfluidic cooling systems
Beamforming and MIMO [78]	Essential for overcoming path loss and providing high data rates	Critical for efficient communication, highly complex implementation	• Implementation of advanced beamforming algorithms • Massive MIMO techniques • Research into advanced beamforming techniques and high-dimensional MIMO systems
Deployment complexity	High, requiring dense network of base stations	Extremely high, due to severe propagation and hardware challenges	• Strategic planning • Simulation-based deployment • Development of AI-based deployment strategies to optimize network layout

Table 4 Security challenges and solutions in mmWave and THz communication

Security challenge	Overview	Countermeasure techniques
Eavesdropping [87]	Signals that are transmitted can be intercepted and accessed by an unauthorized entity	• Lightweight Cryptographic Algorithms • Secure Communication Protocols • Intrusion Detection Systems (IDS) • Data Segmentation and Redundancy • Homomorphic Encryption
Jamming attacks [86]	It aims to flood the communication channel with excessive noise or deceptive signals, thereby preventing authorized users from accessing the network	• Spread Spectrum Techniques • IDS using Machine Learning solutions • Channel Hopping • Signal Processing Techniques
DoS or DDoS attack [84]	It can overwhelm communication channels by generating a high volume of traffic, rendering the network inaccessible to legitimate users.	• Network Infrastructure Protection • Traffic Filtering and Rate Limiting • Traffic Analysis and Anomaly Detection • Traffic Scrubbing • Web Application Firewalls (WAFs) • DNS Protection
Spoofing and side-channel attack [92]	The act of spoofing involves masquerading as a genuine device, while side-channel assaults target weaknesses in the execution of cryptographic algorithms to uncover secret keys.	• Uses of Secure Authentication Mechanisms • Constant-time algorithms • Physically unclonable functions • Use Randomization • Noise Injection • Side-Channel Resistant Hardware
Physical layer attacks [83]	This attack category target the hardware and transmission media of a network, aiming to disrupt communication, intercept data, or damage infrastructure.	• Tamper-Resistant Hardware • Network Redundancy and Robustness • Regular Audit, Monitoring and Response Mechanisms

strategic positioning within the signal path, jamming attacks using physical obstructions, signal spoofing, infrastructure sabotage, and disruptions caused by adverse weather conditions [86].

To address the above mentioned multifaceted security risks effectively, the deployment of mmWave technology requires the implementation of robust encryption protocols, stringent authentication mechanisms, and secure installation practices [87]. Additionally, advanced signal processing techniques, continuous monitoring, regular security audits, fine-grained access control, and network redundancy are vital components of a comprehensive security strategy aimed at enhancing the resilience of mmWave technology against both cybersecurity and physical threats [88].

THz frequencies are being explored for future high-speed wireless communication systems, promising significant data transfer speeds [89]. However, THz technology introduces nuanced security risks across various applications, requiring thorough examination and mitigation strategies. Privacy concerns arise due to THz's ability to penetrate materials, raising apprehensions about potential invasive surveillance, especially in sensitive areas like airport security [90]. There is also concern about unauthorized data gathering and potential misuse by THz imaging systems, highlighting the need for robust privacy protections and adherence to regulatory guidelines [91].

Cybersecurity risks in THz technology primarily affect communication systems, where interception, eavesdropping, and malicious attacks threaten data confidentiality and integrity. Effective cybersecurity strategies must include robust encryption algorithms, authentication mechanisms, and secure communication protocols. Ongoing research and development efforts are crucial to address emerging cyber threats and vulnerabilities in THz communication systems effectively [87].

Safety considerations regarding THz technology include potential health effects from THz radiation exposure, necessitating comprehensive research to establish safety standards and guidelines. While THz radiation is generally considered safe, understanding its long-term effects on biological tissues is essential for safe technology deployment. Addressing these complex security risks requires collaboration among researchers, regulatory bodies, and industry stakeholders to develop and implement appropriate safety measures and protocols [93].

Mitigating security risks in THz technology demands a comprehensive approach that addresses privacy, cybersecurity, and safety concerns. This approach should include robust privacy protections, secure communication protocols, ongoing safety research, and collaborative efforts across the board [93].

5.2 Protocol Support and Vulnerabilities

To support and to utilize mmWave and THz technology solutions effectively, IEEE has designed several protocols. One of the prominent protocol is IEEE 802.11ad, also known as WiGig. The 802.11ad standard is an extension of the IEEE 802.11 family of wireless networking standards. It operates in the 60 GHz frequency band, and the standard defines channels that are 2.16 GHz wide, enabling the transfer of large amounts of data. Moreover, it is designed to support multi-gigabit data rates over short distances and is commonly utilized in applications such as wireless docking stations, virtual reality (VR), and augmented reality (AR) devices [94]. Further, The IEEE 802.11ay standard, also known as Next-Generation WiGig, was developed to build upon the capabilities of the 802.11ad standard and address its limitations. IEEE 802.11ay extends the capabilities of IEEE 802.11 ad, operating in the 60 GHz frequency band with higher throughput and improved spectral efficiency, making it suitable for next-generation wireless communication systems [95].

As wireless technology continued to evolve, the demand for higher data rates and more efficient use of the spectrum grew. While standards like 802.11ad provided high-speed wireless communication, they were primarily designed for short-range applications in the 60 GHz frequency band. To address different requirements and applications, the IEEE developed the 802.15.3c standard. 802.15.3c specifies high-data-rate communication protocols for wireless personal area networks (WPANs) operating in the 60 GHz frequency band. This standard enables multimedia streaming, file sharing, and other high-bandwidth applications in close proximity. Additionally, the 5G NR (New Radio) standard includes specifications for mmWave frequencies above 24 GHz, supporting ultra-fast data rates and low latency for various use cases such as enhanced mobile broadband (eMBB), massive machine-type communications (mMTC), and ultra-reliable low-latency communications (URLLC) [96].

As the demand for higher data rates and better performance in wireless communication continued to increase, the IEEE introduced the 802.15.3d standard [97]. This new standard was developed to address specific needs that weren't fully met by previous standards like 802.15.3c. IEEE introduced to support data rates of up to 100 Gbps, significantly surpassing the capabilities of 802.15.3c. This makes it suitable for applications requiring extremely high bandwidth, such as ultra-high-definition video streaming and data-intensive wireless backhaul. Moreover, we have several other protocols like 3GPP NR (New Radio) for mmWave. It supports a wide range of frequencies, including millimeter-wave (mmWave) bands (24 GHz and above), which are crucial for achieving the high data rates and low latencies promised by 5G. mmWave frequencies enable enhanced mobile broadband (eMBB) and fixed wireless access (FWA) services due to their large available bandwidth [98]. Several other prominent protocols are IEEE 802.16 (WiMAX) [99] as mentioned in the Table 5

On the other hand, THz technology, being relatively new and still in its developmental stages, lacks standardized protocols specifically tailored for THz communication. However, potential protocols for THz communication are under exploration. These could include THz wireless communication protocols, designed to operate within the THz frequency range and facilitate high-speed data transmission over short distances [100]. Additionally, adaptations of existing wireless standards such as IEEE 802.11ad and 5G NR may be considered, with modifications to support THz frequencies while addressing the unique characteristics and challenges of THz communication. THz imaging protocols may also be developed, particularly for applications requiring THz imaging, to enable efficient capture, processing, and transmission of THz imaging data [101].

Furthermore, specialized security protocols may be devised for THz communication to mitigate potential security risks, ensuring the confidentiality, integrity, and authenticity of data transmitted over THz frequencies. Some of the security considerations related to protocol designed for these technologies are mentioned in the Table 5. Overall, while mmWave technology has established protocols for high-speed

Table 5 Specifications and security considerations of mmWave and THz Protocols

Protocol	Frequency	Use cases	Security considerations
802.11ad [94]	60 GHz	Wireless docking, VR/AR, high-speed data transfer	• DoS or DDoS Attack • Missing perfect forward secrecy
802.11ay [95]	60 GHz	Backhaul, dense deployments, high-throughput applications	• Interception and Eavesdropping • Side channel attack • DoS or DDoS attack
802.15.3c [96]	57–66 GHz	High-definition video streaming, wireless data transfer	• Interception and eavesdropping • Spoofing attack • Authentication mechanisms
3GPP NR [98]	24 GHz and above	Enhanced mobile broadband, fixed wireless access	• Jamming attack • Spoofing attack
802.15.3d [97]	6–10.6 GHz (UWB)	High-speed data transfer, multimedia streaming	• Jamming attack • Spoofing attack • Interception
802.16 (WiMAX) [99]	10–66 GHz	Broadband internet access, backhaul	• Jamming attack • Eavesdropping • Spoofing • DoS/DDoS attack

communication in the mmWave frequency range, the development of specific protocols for THz communication is ongoing and represents an area of active research and innovation in the field [102].

6 Future Trends and Outlook

Even though advancements in wireless communication technology, such as mmWave and THz communication, are significant and have several impacts on 5G or beyond wireless communications [103]. These technologies still suffer from several potential challenges, including hardware design, signal processing, propagation, penetration, and regulatory concerns. To effectively address these challenges, it is essential to revise existing methodologies with a new perspective by harnessing the power of data-driven techniques. Furthermore, incorporating cloud computing, edge computing, and cutting-edge quantum techniques can yield significant advantages.

Technologies such as artificial intelligence (AI) and machine learning (ML) can enhance signal pathways and adjust transmission settings dynamically. By deploying dense small-cell networks and relay stations, coverage can be improved and signal range extended [104]. Additionally, high-gain antennas and adaptive beamforming powered by AI algorithms can help reduce path loss. Other methods, such as energy harvesting and wireless power transfer, can also improve power economy and maintain signal strength over greater distances. Reflective and reconfigurable intelligent surfaces (RIS) offer the capability to divert the signal trajectory to bypass obstacles while simultaneously ensuring uninterrupted communication in challenging environments. Additionally, the implementation of edge computing and cloud computing technologies allows for data processing to be carried out locally, thereby reducing latency and improving performance in regions with limited internet connectivity.

Advanced antenna and beamforming techniques rely on cutting-edge materials to achieve higher efficiency. For instance, high-performance metamaterials can help create more efficient antennas that operate at higher frequencies. Furthermore, AI-powered beamforming techniques can optimize real-time performance by dynamically adjusting the direction and shape of the beam. Additionally, adaptive beamforming and large MIMO arrays can significantly enhance signal strength and reliability [105]. More efficient and precise beamforming techniques can be achieved by leveraging the power of quantum computing and distributed computing resources. These resources can provide innovative approaches to address intricate antenna design challenges, which is an ongoing research topic in the academic community.

Solving hardware and integration issues requires the use of cutting-edge technologies to improve component design and manufacturing processes. In this regard, advanced semiconductor materials, such as gallium nitride, can significantly enhance the functionality of RF components. Microfluidic cooling systems are a highly effective means of managing heat dissipation in high-power electronics. Furthermore, distributed processing, serverless computing, fog computing, and edge computing can aid in offloading and executing data on remote computing devices, thereby enhancing system efficiency. Adaptive modulation can employ ML techniques to continuously adjusting transmission parameters in accordance with the current state of the channel [106]. Advanced error correction codes can significantly improve data integrity by correcting errors caused by signal degradation. Quantum machine learning and cloud storage technology have numerous applications that cannot be overlooked, despite the fact that the research community has not yet fully explored them. Quantum machine learning has the potential to revolutionize complex signal processing by performing tasks at unprecedented speeds. In addition, cloud computing provides a scalable solution for storage and processing, capable of handling the massive amounts of data generated by these technologies. The extensive research is needed from the academic community to overcome the current obstacles in mmWave and THz communication and fully explore the potential applications of these technologies.

7 Conclusion

This chapter has offered an overview of mmWave and THz communication, delving into their emergence, fundamentals, applications, challenges, and future trends. The uses of mmWave and THz communication, emphasizing their essential role in 5G and 6G technology, influence on several industries and also present promising opportunities across various domains of Industry. The incorporation of mmWave and THz technologies with artificial intelligence and machine learning can significantly enhance their potential, resulting in more intelligent and efficient communication networks. This advancement places mmWave and THz communication as the forefront of revolutionizing digital connectivity, ushering in a new era of technological progress and societal advantages. Despite the current existing challenges, ongoing research and development efforts are poised to drive innovation and unlock the full potential of mmWave and THz communication in revolutionizing wireless communication for the future.

References

1. Mansoor Shafi, Andreas F. Molisch, Peter J. Smith, Thomas Haustein, Peiying Zhu, Prasan De Silva, Fredrik Tufvesson, Anass Benjebbour, and Gerhard Wunder. 5g: A tutorial overview of standards, trials, challenges, deployment, and practice. *IEEE Journal on Selected Areas in Communications*, 35(6):1201–1221, 2017.
2. Theodore S. Rappaport, Shu Sun, Rimma Mayzus, Hang Zhao, Yaniv Azar, Kevin Wang, George N. Wong, Jocelyn K. Schulz, Mathew Samimi, and Felix Gutierrez. Millimeter wave mobile communications for 5g cellular: It will work! *IEEE Access*, 1:335–349, 2013.
3. Khaled B. Letaief, Wei Chen, Yuanming Shi, Jun Zhang, and Ying-Jun Angela Zhang. The roadmap to 6g: Ai empowered wireless networks. *IEEE Communications Magazine*, 57(8):84–90, 2019.
4. Jyoti Goyal, Khushboo Singla, Akashdeep, and Sarbjeet Singh. A survey of wireless communication technologies from 1g to 5g. In *Second International Conference on Computer Networks and Communication Technologies: ICCNCT 2019*, pages 613–624, 2020.
5. Francesco Alessio Dicandia and Simone Genovesi. Spectral efficiency improvement of 5g massive mimo systems for high-altitude platform stations by using triangular lattice arrays. *Sensors*, 21(9), 2021.
6. Naga Bhushan, Junyi Li, Durga Malladi, Rob Gilmore, Dean Brenner, Aleksandar Damnjanovic, Ravi Teja Sukhavasi, Chirag Patel, and Stefan Geirhofer. Network densification: the dominant theme for wireless evolution into 5g. *IEEE Communications Magazine*, 52(2):82–89, 2014.
7. Jianhua Zhang, Kai Kang, Yongming Huang, Mansoor Shafi, and Andreas F. Molisch. Millimeter and thz wave for 5g and beyond. *China Communications*, 16(2):iii–vi, 2019.
8. Qing Xue, Chengwang Ji, Shaodan Ma, Jiajia Guo, Yongjun Xu, Qianbin Chen, and Wei Zhang. A survey of beam management for mmwave and thz communications towards 6g. *IEEE Communications Surveys & Tutorials*, pages 1–1, 2024.
9. Abhishek Hazra, Mainak Adhikari, Tarachand Amgoth, and Satish Narayana Srirama. Stackelberg game for service deployment of iot-enabled applications in 6g-aware fog networks. *IEEE Internet of Things Journal*, 8(7):5185–5193, 2021.

10. Ilias P. Misailidis and Konstantinos N. Voudouris. A review on propagation related issues for mm-wave and thz next generation cellular networks. In *Proceedings of the 24th Pan-Hellenic Conference on Informatics*, PCI '20, page 1–16, 2021.
11. Shuangfeng Han, Tian Xie, and Chih-Lin I. Greener physical layer technologies for 6g mobile communications. *IEEE Communications Magazine*, 59(4):68–74, 2021.
12. Eman Ramadan, Arvind Narayanan, Udhaya Kumar Dayalan, Rostand A. K. Fezeu, Feng Qian, and Zhi-Li Zhang. Case for 5g-aware video streaming applications. In *Proceedings of the 1st Workshop on 5G Measurements, Modeling, and Use Cases*, page 27–34, 2021.
13. Kei Sakaguchi, Ryuichi Fukatsu, Tao Yu, Eisuke Fukuda, Kim Mahler, Robert Heath, Takeo Fujii, Kazuaki Takahashi, Alexey Khoryaev, Satoshi Nagata, and Takayuki Shimizu. Towards mmwave v2x in 5g and beyond to support automated driving. *IEICE Transactions on Communications*, E104.B, 11 2020.
14. Daniel Minoli and Benedict Occhiogrosso. Practical aspects for the integration of 5g networks and iot applications in smart cities environments. *Wireless Communications and Mobile Computing*, 2019:1–30, 08 2019.
15. Chukwuka Elendu, Tochi Elendu, and Ijeoma Elendu. 5g-enabled smart hospitals: Innovations in patient care and facility management. *Medicine*, 103:38239, 05 2024.
16. Anjum Mohd Aslam, Rajat Chaudhary, Aditya Bhardwaj, Ishan Budhiraja, Neeraj Kumar, and Sherali Zeadally. Metaverse for 6g and beyond: The next revolution and deployment challenges. *IEEE Internet of Things Magazine*, 6(1):32–39, 2023.
17. Gerhard P. Fettweis. The tactile internet: Applications and challenges. *IEEE Vehicular Technology Magazine*, 9(1):64–70, 2014.
18. Tommaso Zugno, Lutfi Samara, Mate Boban, Per Hjalmar Lehne, and Thomas Kürner. Terahertz communications for industrial manufacturing: a use case analysis. In *2023 IEEE Conference on Standards for Communications and Networking (CSCN)*, pages 136–141, 2023.
19. Lin Zhang, Haochuan Wan, Xianhua Zheng, Meizi Tian, Yubao Liu, and Lingling Su. Digital-twin prediction of metamorphic object transportation by multi-robots with thz communication framework. *IEEE Transactions on Intelligent Transportation Systems*, 24(7):7757–7765, 2023.
20. From 5g to 6g vision - a connected and automated mobility (cam) perspective. *White Paper 6G SNS IA*, 2022.
21. Mehdi Harounabadi and Thomas Heyn. Toward integration of 6g-ntn to terrestrial mobile networks: Research and standardization aspects. *IEEE Wireless Communications*, 30:20–26, 12 2023.
22. Md. Noor-A-Rahim, Zilong Liu, Haeyoung Lee, Mohammad Omar Khyam, Jianhua He, Dirk Pesch, Klaus Moessner, Walid Saad, and H. Vincent Poor. 6g for vehicle-to-everything (v2x) communications: Enabling technologies, challenges, and opportunities. *Proceedings of the IEEE*, 110(6):712–734, 2022.
23. Khalid Aldubaikhy, Wen Wu, Ning Zhang, Nan Cheng, and Xuemin Shen. mmwave ieee 802.11ay for 5g fixed wireless access. *IEEE Wireless Communications*, 27(2):88–95, 2020.
24. Kei Sakaguchi, Thomas Haustein, S. Barbarossa, Emilio Strinati, Antonio Clemente, Giuseppe Destino, Aarno Pärssinen, Ilgyu Kim, Heesang Chung, Junhyeong Kim, Wilhelm Keusgen, Richard Weiler, Koji Takinami, Elena Ceci, Ali Sadri, Liang Xain, Alexander Maltsev, Gia Khanh Tran, Hiroaki Ogawa, and Robert Heath. Where, when, and how mmwave is used in 5g and beyond. *IEICE Transactions on Electronics*, E100.C, 04 2017.
25. Dirk Hetzer, Maciej Muehleisen, Apostolos Kousaridas, Sokratis Barmpounakis, Stefan Wendt, Kurt Eckert, Andreas Schimpe, Johan Löfhede, and Jesus Alonso-Zarate. 5g connected and automated driving: use cases, technologies and trials in cross-border environments. *EURASIP Journal on Wireless Communications and Networking*, 2021, 04 2021.
26. Tarik Taleb, Nassim Sehad, Zinelaabidine Nadir, and Jaeseung Song. Vr-based immersive service management in b5g mobile systems: A uav command and control use case. *IEEE Internet of Things Journal*, 10(6):5349–5363, 2023.
27. Christina Chaccour, Mehdi Naderi Soorki, Walid Saad, Mehdi Bennis, and Petar Popovski. Can terahertz provide high-rate reliable low-latency communications for wireless vr? *IEEE Internet of Things Journal*, 9(12):9712–9729, 2022.

28. Radostina Petkova, Ivaylo Bozhilov, Agata Manolova, Krasimir Tonchev, and Vladimir Poulkov. On the way to holographic-type communications: Perspectives and enabling technologies. *IEEE Access*, 12:59236–59259, 2024.
29. Parisa Ramezani, Bin Lyu, and Abbas Jamalipour. Toward ris-enhanced integrated terrestrial/non-terrestrial connectivity in 6g. *IEEE Network*, 37(3):178–185, 2023.
30. Jing Yuan, Gaojie Chen, Miaowen Wen, Rahim Tafazolli, and Erdal Panayirci. Secure transmission for thz-empowered ris-assisted non-terrestrial networks. *IEEE Transactions on Vehicular Technology*, 72(5):5989–6000, 2023.
31. Zhen Gao, Linglong Dai, De Mi, Zhaocheng Wang, Muhammad Ali Imran, and Muhammad Zeeshan Shakir. Mmwave massive-mimo-based wireless backhaul for the 5g ultra-dense network. *IEEE Wireless Communications*, 22(5):13–21, 2015.
32. Edgar Arribas, Antonio Fernández Anta, Dariusz R. Kowalski, Vincenzo Mancuso, Miguel A. Mosteiro, Joerg Widmer, and Prudence W. H. Wong. Optimizing mmwave wireless backhaul scheduling. *IEEE Transactions on Mobile Computing*, 19(10):2409–2428, 2020.
33. Vinay U. Pai, Pranay Bhardwaj, and S. M. Zafaruddin. Performance analysis of dual-hop thz wireless transmission for backhaul applications. In *2021 IEEE International Conference on Advanced Networks and Telecommunications Systems (ANTS)*, pages 438–443, 2021.
34. Angela Sara Cacciapuoti, Subramanian Ramanathan, Kaushik Roy Chowdhury, and Marcello Caleffi. Software-defined network controlled switching between millimeter wave and terahertz small cells. *ArXiv*, abs/1702.02775, 2017.
35. Qi Zhang, Jianhui Liu, and Guodong Zhao. Towards 5g enabled tactile robotic telesurgery. *ArXiv*, abs/1803.03586, 2018.
36. Abdullah K. Alhazmi, Mubarak A. Alanazi, Awwad H. Alshehry, Saleh M. Alshahry, Jennifer Jaszek, Cameron Djukic, Anna Brown, Kurt Jackson, and Vamsy P. Chodavarapu. Intelligent millimeter-wave system for human activity monitoring for telemedicine. *Sensors*, 24(1), 2024.
37. Abdul Ahad, Zahra Ali, Abdul Mateen, Mohammad Tahir, Abdul Hannan, Nuno M. Garcia, and Ivan Miguel Pires. A comprehensive review on 5g-based smart healthcare network security: Taxonomy, issues, solutions and future research directions. *Array*, 18:100290, 2023.
38. Yunkai Zhai, Xing Xu, Baozhan Chen, Huimin Lu, Yichuan Wang, Shuyang Li, Xiaobing Shi, Wenchao Wang, Lanlan Shang, and Jie Zhao. 5g-network-enabled smart ambulance: Architecture, application, and evaluation. *IEEE Network*, 35, 08 2020.
39. Naercio Magaia, Igor de L. Ribeiro, André W. O. de Aguiar, Ramon Fonseca, Khan Muhammad, and Victor Hugo C. de Albuquerque. An artificial intelligence application for drone-assisted 5g remote e-health. *IEEE Internet of Things Magazine*, 4(4):30–35, 2021.
40. Leili Afsah-Hejri, Elnaz Akbari, Arash Toudeshki, Taymaz Homayouni, Azar Alizadeh, and Reza Ehsani. Terahertz spectroscopy and imaging: A review on agricultural applications. *Computers and Electronics in Agriculture*, 177:105628, 2020.
41. Tahereh Amini, Fazel Jahangiri, Zoha Ameri, and Mohammad Amin Hemmatian. A review of feasible applications of thz waves in medical diagnostics and treatments. *Journal of Lasers in Medical Sciences*, 12, 2021.
42. Angelina I. Nikitkina, Polina Y. Bikmulina, Elvira R. Gafarova, Nastasia V. Kosheleva, Yuri M. Efremov, Evgeny A Bezrukov, Denis V Butnaru, Irina N. Dolganova, Nikita V. Chernomyrdin, Olga P. Cherkasova, Arsenii A. Gavdush, and Peter S. Timashev. Terahertz radiation and the skin: a review. *Journal of Biomedical Optics*, 26, 2021.
43. Mariia Borovkova, Maria Serebryakova, Viacheslav Fedorov, Egor Sedykh, Vladimir Vaks, Alexander Lichutin, Alina Salnikova, and M. Khodzitsky. Investigation of terahertz radiation influence on rat glial cells. *Biomedical Optics Express*, 8:273, 12 2016.
44. Amit Banerjee, Chinmay Chakraborty, and Megha Rathi. Chapter 8 - medical imaging, artificial intelligence, internet of things, wearable devices in terahertz healthcare technologies. In Amit Banerjee, Basabi Chakraborty, Hiroshi Inokawa, and Jitendra Nath Roy, editors, *Terahertz Biomedical and Healthcare Technologies*, pages 145–165. 2020.
45. Debamitra Chakraborty, Bradley N. Mills, Genyu Chen, Alaina Attanasio, Scott A. Gerber, and Roman Sobolewski. Pulsed terahertz time-domain spectroscopy of paraffin-embedded pancreatic ductal adenocarcinoma. In *2021 46th International Conference on Infrared, Millimeter and Terahertz Waves (IRMMW-THz)*, pages 1–2, 2021.

46. Nagendra Paradad Yadav, Guo-Zhen Hu, Zheng-Peng Yao, and Ashish Kumar. Diagnosis of dental problem by using terahertz technology. *Journal of Electronic Science and Technology*, 19(3):100082, 2021.
47. Liu Yu, Liu Hao, Meiqiong Tang, Huang Jiaoqi, Liu Wei, Dong Jinying, Chen Xueping, Fu Weiling, and Zhang Yang. The medical application of terahertz technology in non-invasive detection of cells and tissues: opportunities and challenges. *RSC Advances*, 9:9354–9363, 03 2019.
48. Abhishek Hazra, Alakesh Kalita, and Mohan Gurusamy. Meeting the requirements of internet of things: The promise of edge computing. *IEEE Internet of Things Journal*, 11(5):7474–7498, 2024.
49. Michael Kemp. Millimetre wave and terahertz technology for detection of concealed threats - a review. pages 1 – 2, 10 2008.
50. Frank Ellrich, Maris Bauer, N. Schreiner, Andreas Keil, T. Pfeiffer, J. Klier, Stefan Duran, Joachim Jonuscheit, Fabian Friederich, and Daniel Molter. Terahertz quality inspection for automotive and aviation industries. *Journal of Infrared, Millimeter, and Terahertz Waves*, 41, 04 2020.
51. William Xia, Michele Polese, Marco Mezzavilla, Giuseppe Loianno, Sundeep Rangan, and Michele Zorzi. Millimeter wave remote uav control and communications for public safety scenarios. In *2019 16th Annual IEEE International Conference on Sensing, Communication, and Networking (SECON)*, pages 1–7, 2019.
52. Tobias Kubiczek, Vladyslav Cherniak, Kevin Kolpatzeck, and Jan C. Balzer. 3d sar imaging enabled by terahertz time-domain spectroscopy. In *2023 24th International Radar Symposium (IRS)*, pages 1–8, 2023.
53. Ir. Visweswaran Karunanithi, C.J.M. Verhoeven, and E.W. McCune. Solutions to data congestion in space; mmwave communication for nano-satellites. In *2019 IEEE Aerospace Conference*, pages 1–12, 2019.
54. Shian U. Hwu, Kanishka B. deSilva, and Cindy T. Jih. Terahertz (thz) wireless systems for space applications. In *2013 IEEE Sensors Applications Symposium Proceedings*, pages 171–175, 2013.
55. Jingyuan Liang, Minghui Chen, and Xizheng Ke. Performance analysis of hybrid fso/rf-thz relay communication system. *IEEE Photonics Journal*, pages 1–10, 2024.
56. A. Soumya, C. Krishna Mohan, and Linga Reddy Cenkeramaddi. Recent advances in mmwave-radar-based sensing, its applications, and machine learning techniques: A review. *Sensors*, 23(21), 2023.
57. Jakub Mazguła, Jakub Sapis, Umair Hashmi, and Harish Viswanathan. Ultra reliable low latency communications in mmwave for factory floor automation. *Journal of the Indian Institute of Science*, 100, 04 2020.
58. Mira Naftaly, Nico Vieweg, and Anselm Deninger. Industrial applications of terahertz sensing: State of play. *Sensors*, 19(19), 2019.
59. Jian Qiao, Yejun He, and Xuemin Shen. Improving video streaming quality in 5g enabled vehicular networks. *IEEE Wireless Communications*, 25:133–139, 04 2018.
60. Ho-Jin Song and Namyoon Lee. Terahertz communications: Challenges in the next decade. *IEEE Transactions on Terahertz Science and Technology*, 12(2):105–117, 2022.
61. Ahmed Solyman and Ismail Elhaty. Potential key challenges for terahertz communication systems. *International Journal of Electrical and Computer Engineering (IJECE)*, 11:3403, 08 2021.
62. Vitaly Petrov, Mikhail Komarov, Dmitri Moltchanov, Josep Miquel Jornet, and Yevgeni Koucheryavy. Interference and sinr in millimeter wave and terahertz communication systems with blocking and directional antennas. *IEEE Transactions on Wireless Communications*, 16(3):1791–1808, 2017.
63. E. Udayakumar and V. Krishnaveni. Analysis of various interference in millimeter-wave communication systems: A survey. In *2019 10th International Conference on Computing, Communication and Networking Technologies (ICCCNT)*, pages 1–5, 2019.

64. Milos Tesanovic and Maziar M. Nekovee. mmwave-based mobile access for 5g: Key challenges and projected standards and regulatory roadmap. *2015 IEEE Global Communications Conference (GLOBECOM)*, pages 1–6, 2014.
65. Wijdan K. Alsaedi, Hamed Ahmadi, Zaheer Khan, and David Grace. Spectrum options and allocations for 6g: A regulatory and standardization review. *IEEE Open Journal of the Communications Society*, 4:1787–1812, 2023.
66. Phil Pietraski, David Britz, Arnab Roy, Ravi Pragada, and Gregg Charlton. Millimeter wave and terahertz communications: Feasibility and challenges. *ZTE communications*, 10(4):3, 2012.
67. Michele Polese, Francesco Restuccia, Abhimanyu Gosain, Josep Jornet, Shubhendu Bhardwaj, Viduneth Ariyarathna, Soumyajit Mandal, Kai Zheng, Aditya Dhananjay, Marco Mezzavilla, James Buckwalter, Mark Rodwell, Xin Wang, Michele Zorzi, Arjuna Madanayake, and Tommaso Melodia. Millimetera: Toward a large-scale open-source mmwave and terahertz experimental testbed. In *Proceedings of the 3rd ACM Workshop on Millimeter-Wave Networks and Sensing Systems*, page 27–32, 2019.
68. Barriers to terahertz-technology adoption. https://www.arrow.com/en/research-and-events/articles/terahertz-technology-adoption.
69. Yunchou Xing, Theodore S. Rappaport, and Amitava Ghosh. Millimeter wave and sub-thz indoor radio propagation channel measurements, models, and comparisons in an office environment. *IEEE Communications Letters*, 25(10):3151–3155, 2021.
70. Gustavo A. Siles, Jose Manuel Riera, and Padro Garcia-del Pino. Atmospheric attenuation in wireless communication systems at millimeter and thz frequencies [wireless corner]. *IEEE Antennas and Propagation Magazine*, 57(1):48–61, 2015.
71. Muhammad Ali Jamshed, Ali Nauman, Muhammad Ali Babar Abbasi, and Sung Won Kim. Antenna selection and designing for thz applications: Suitability and performance evaluation: A survey. *IEEE Access*, 8:113246–113261, 2020.
72. Vitaly Petrov, Joonas Kokkoniemi, Dmitri Moltchanov, Janne Lehtomäki, Markku Juntti, and Yevgeni Koucheryavy. The impact of interference from the side lanes on mmwave/thz band v2v communication systems with directional antennas. *IEEE Transactions on Vehicular Technology*, 67(6):5028–5041, 2018.
73. Preksha Jain, Akhil Gupta, Neeraj Kumar, and Mohsen Guizani. Dynamic and efficient spectrum utilization for 6g with thz, mmwave, and rf band. *IEEE Transactions on Vehicular Technology*, 72(3):3264–3273, 2023.
74. Donald Y.C. Lie, Jill C. Mayeda, and Jerry Lopez. Rf hardware design for 5g mm-wave and 6g revolutions: Challenges and opportunities. In *2021 IEEE International Conference on Consumer Electronics-Taiwan (ICCE-TW)*, pages 1–2, 2021.
75. Panagiotis Skrimponis, Sourjya Dutta, Marco Mezzavilla, Sundeep Rangan, Seyed Hadi Mirfarshbafan, Christoph Studer, James Buckwalter, and Mark Rodwell. Power consumption analysis for mobile mmwave and sub-thz receivers. In *2020 2nd 6G Wireless Summit (6G SUMMIT)*, pages 1–5, 2020.
76. Vitaly Petrov, Thomas Kurner, and Iwao Hosako. Ieee 802.15.3d: First standardization efforts for sub-terahertz band communications toward 6g. *IEEE Communications Magazine*, 58(11):28–33, 2020.
77. Li Zhou, Min Tang, Jiawei Qian, Yue-Ping Zhang, and Junfa Mao. Vivaldi antenna array with heat dissipation enhancement for millimeter-wave applications. *IEEE Transactions on Antennas and Propagation*, 70(1):288–295, 2021.
78. Shuai Nie and Ian F. Akyildiz. Beamforming in intelligent environments based on ultra-massive mimo platforms in millimeter wave and terahertz bands. In *ICASSP 2020 - 2020 IEEE International Conference on Acoustics, Speech and Signal Processing (ICASSP)*, pages 8683–8687, 2020.
79. Shazia Ashraf, Javaid A Sheikh, Ayash Ashraf, and Umhara Rasool. 5g millimeter wave technology: An overview. *Intelligent Signal Processing and RF Energy Harvesting for State of art 5G and B5G Networks*, pages 97–112, 2024.

80. Muhammad Adil, Houbing Song, Spyridon Mastorakis, Hussein Abulkasim, Ahmed Farouk, and Zhanpeng Jin. Uav-assisted iot applications, cybersecurity threats, ai-enabled solutions, open challenges with future research directions. *IEEE Transactions on Intelligent Vehicles*, 2023.
81. Yiwei Chen, Wenhao Li, XiuZhen Cheng, and Pengfei Hu. A survey of acoustic eavesdropping attacks: Principle, methods, and progress. *High-Confidence Computing*, page 100241, 2024.
82. Richa Priyadarshani, Ki-Hong Park, Yalcin Ata, and Mohamed-Slim Alouini. Jamming intrusions in extreme bandwidth communication: A comprehensive overview. *arXiv preprint* arXiv:2403.19868, 2024.
83. Jawhara Boodai, Aminah Alqahtani, and Mounir Frikha. Review of physical layer security in 5g wireless networks. *Applied Sciences*, 13(12):7277, 2023.
84. Umar Danjuma Maiwada, Shahbaz Ali Imran, Kamaluddeen Usman Danyaro, Aftab Alam Janisar, Anas Salameh, and Aliza Bt Sarlan. Security concerns of iot against ddos in 5g systems. *International Journal of Electrical Engineering and Computer Science*, 6:98–105, 2024.
85. Van-Linh Nguyen, Po-Ching Lin, Bo-Chao Cheng, Ren-Hung Hwang, and Ying-Dar Lin. Security and privacy for 6g: A survey on prospective technologies and challenges. *IEEE Communications Surveys & Tutorials*, 23(4):2384–2428, 2021.
86. Maya E Flores, Devon D Poisson, Colin J Stevens, Adriyel V Nieves, and Alexander M Wyglinski. Implementation and evaluation of a smart uplink jamming attack in a public 5g network. *IEEE Access*, 2023.
87. Fatima Salahdine, Tao Han, and Ning Zhang. Security in 5g and beyond recent advances and future challenges. *Security and Privacy*, 6(1):e271, 2023.
88. Prabhakar Krishnan, Kurunandan Jain, Ala-Saleh D Alluhaidan, and P Prabu. Highly secured authentication and fast handover scheme for mobility management in 5g vehicular networks. *Computers and Electrical Engineering*, 116:109152, 2024.
89. Rashmi Pant and Leeladhar Malviya. Thz antennas design, developments, challenges, and applications: A review. *International Journal of Communication Systems*, 36(8):e5474, 2023.
90. Vulugundam Anitha, Ankur Beohar, and Anveshkumar Nella. Thz imaging technology trends and wide variety of applications: a detailed survey. *Plasmonics*, 18(2):441–483, 2023.
91. Hussam N Fakhouri, Sadi Alawadi, Feras M Awaysheh, Imad Bani Hani, Mohannad Alkhalaileh, and Faten Hamad. A comprehensive study on the role of machine learning in 5g security: Challenges, technologies, and solutions. *Electronics*, 12(22):4604, 2023.
92. Faizan Shoaib, Yang-Wai Chow, Elena Vlahu-Gjorgievska, and Chau Nguyen. Mitigating timing side-channel attacks in software-defined networks: Detection and response. In *Telecom*, volume 4, pages 877–900, 2023.
93. Allanki Sanyasi Rao, Sreeja Mole SS, Sreeja Yelasani, and B Sandeep Kumar. Terahertz communications: Applications, challenges and open research issues for next generation 6g wireless networks. *Int. J. Innov. Eng. Manag. Res*, 12:295–315, 2023.
94. John Bellardo and Stefan Savage. 802.11 denial-of-service attacks: Real vulnerabilities and practical solutions. In *Proceedings of the 12th conference on USENIX Security Symposium*, volume 12, pages 2–2.
95. Khalid Aldubaikhy, Wen Wu, Ning Zhang, Nan Cheng, and Xuemin Shen. mmwave ieee 802.11 ay for 5g fixed wireless access. *IEEE Wireless Communications*, 27(2):88–95, 2020.
96. Yonggang Kim, Ryangsoo Kim, and Hyuk Lim. Hybrid weight link scheduling method for ieee 802.15. 3c-based millimeter-wave wireless networks. In *2019 IEEE International Conference on Consumer Electronics (ICCE)*, pages 1–6, 2019.
97. Hichem Guerboukha, Rabi Shrestha, Zhaoji Fang, Josep M Jornet, Edward Knightly, and Daniel M Mittleman. Jamming threats and countermeasures of the terahertz ook mode in ieee 802.15. 3d. In *2022 IEEE Future Networks World Forum (FNWF)*, pages 403–406, 2022.
98. Youness Arjoune and Saleh Faruque. Smart jamming attacks in 5g new radio: A review. In *2020 10th annual computing and communication workshop and conference (CCWC)*, pages 1010–1015. IEEE, 2020.

99. Ahmed Mohamed El-Amin, Alaa El-Din Rohiem, and Essam Abd-Elwanees. Wimax 802.16 networks: Threats, attacks, and solutions. In *The International Conference on Electrical Engineering*, volume 8, pages 1–15. Military Technical College, 2012.
100. Wei Jiang, Qiuheng Zhou, Jiguang He, Mohammad Asif Habibi, Sergiy Melnyk, Mohammed El-Absi, Bin Han, Marco Di Renzo, Hans Dieter Schotten, Fa-Long Luo, et al. Terahertz communications and sensing for 6g and beyond: A comprehensive review. *IEEE Communications Surveys & Tutorials*, 2024.
101. Rosario Giuseppe Garroppo and Maria Grazia Scutellà. Design model of an ieee 802.11 ad infrastructure for tsn-based industrial applications. *Computer Networks*, 230:109771, 2023.
102. Tanya Garg, Gurjinder Kaur, and Prashant Singh Rana. Protocol security in 6th generation (6g) networks. In *International Conference on Computation Intelligence and Network Systems*, pages 47–62, 2023.
103. Mainak Adhikari and Abhishek Hazra. 6g-enabled ultra-reliable low-latency communication in edge networks. *IEEE Communications Standards Magazine*, 6(1):67–74, 2022.
104. Mainak Adhikari, Abhishek Hazra, Varun G Menon, Brijesh K Chaurasia, and Shahid Mumtaz. A roadmap of next-generation wireless technology for 6g-enabled vehicular networks. *IEEE Internet of Things Magazine*, 4(4):79–85, 2021.
105. Dinh C. Nguyen, Ming Ding, Pubudu N. Pathirana, Aruna Seneviratne, Jun Li, Dusit Niyato, Octavia Dobre, and H. Vincent Poor. 6g internet of things: A comprehensive survey. *IEEE Internet of Things Journal*, 9(1):359–383, 2022.
106. Wei Jiang, Bin Han, Mohammad Asif Habibi, and Hans Dieter Schotten. The road towards 6g: A comprehensive survey. *IEEE Open Journal of the Communications Society*, 2:334–366, 2021.

Intelligent Reflecting Surface for 6G Wireless Networks: Applications, Case Studies, Challenges and Future Directions

Debbarni Sarkar, Satyendra Singh Yadav, Vipin Pal, Yogita, and Sarat Kumar Patra

1 Introduction

Fifth generation (5G) wireless communication networks can achieve 20 Gbit/s peak data rate, 0.1 Gbit/s user experience data rate, 1 ms end-to-end latency, and support 500 km/h mobility, 10^6 devices/km2 connection density and 10 Mbit/ (s·m2) area traffic capacity [1]. However, using massive multiple-input multiple-output (MIMO), millimeter wave, and ultra-dense network advanced technologies in these networks requires high costs, power, and energy. Moreover, first-generation (1G) to 5G wireless networks do not control dynamic wireless environments which is a significant barrier in wireless communication. Sixth-generation (6G) wireless communication networks can overcome these problems and meet high data rate requirements, high connectivity, global coverage, energy efficiency (EE), power efficiency, and low latency at low cost by intelligent reflecting surface (IRS) [2, 3]. The IRS is a novel concept and comprises many passive reflecting units (RUs). The amplitude and phase

D. Sarkar (✉) · S. S. Yadav
Department of ECE, National Institute of Technology Meghalaya, Shillong, India
e-mail: p21ec004@nitm.ac.in

S. S. Yadav
e-mail: satyendra@ieee.org

V. Pal
Department of CSE, Netaji Subhas University of Technology, Delhi, India
e-mail: vipin.pal@nsut.ac.in

Yogita
Department of CSE, National Institute of Technology Kurukshetra, Kurukshetra, India
e-mail: thakranyogita@gmail.com

S. K. Patra
Department of ECE, National Institute of Technology Agartala, Agartala, India
e-mail: skpatra@nitrkl.ac.in

T. Ojha et al. (eds.), *Edge-Enabled 6G Networking*,
https://doi.org/10.1007/978-3-032-19042-0_3

coefficients of the IRS's RUs are continuously adjusted according to channel circumstances to establish virtual line-of-sight (LoS) links between the base station (BS) and users [4, 5]. The IRS performs several attractive tasks, such as removing or reducing the co-channel interference of users, enhancing the channel condition by giving more signal links to the users, and reconstructing the fast-fading channel to low-fading channel for reliable communication [6, 7]. It enables more efficient energy usage and cost savings compared to traditional antenna and relay systems [8]. Further, in wireless communication, half and full duplex relays are affected by low spectral efficiency and interference, whereas the IRS operates in a full-duplex mode without experiencing interference and delivers high spectrum efficiency [9, 10]. In wireless communication, the IRS is easily installed or deployed in the environment with low cost since it is lightweight and portable dimensions [11]. In [12], the authors explore various applications of IRS in wireless communication and the associated challenges. The challenges of IRS hardware design and proposed solutions are briefly discussed in [13, 14]. Security and privacy issues of the IRS in wireless communication for different applications are in detail explained in [15, 16]. On the other hand, the prospects, implementations, and future trajectories of the IRS for sensing communication are illustrated in [17]. The contribution and limitations of the existing literature are outlined in Table 1. This chapter addresses the limitations of the existing study and presents the application, case examples, problems, and future directions of the IRS.

Table 1 Summary of the existing work

Reference	Contributions	Research gap
[12]	Discusses the different applications of the IRS and challenges	Few work on future directions
[13]	Highlights the challenges and offers solutions of the IRS hardware designing	Limited work on size and element, working principle, challenges on real-time application, and future directions
[15]	Provides a comprehensive survey on security and privacy of IRS	There is limited work on size and element, working principle, and different challenges such as channel estimation, beam-forming optimization, phase control, practical difficulty, etc.
[17]	Discuss the overview of integrated sensing and communication with IRS.	Few studies focus on challenges and future directions
[16]	Discusses IRS-aided physical layer security designs for 6G wireless networks.	Limited work on future directions
[14]	Addresses the challenges and presents solutions for IRS hardware design.	Few studies focus on working principle and application

The organization of the chapter is as follows: Sect. 2 discusses the structure and working principle of the IRS. Section 3 provides the applications of the IRS, and case studies of the IRS are illustrated in Sect. 4. Section 5 presents the challenges of the IRS. Section 6 discusses the future direction of the IRS for 6G wireless communication and Sect. 7 concludes this chapter.

2 Structure and Working Principle of Intelligent Reflecting Surface

A thorough overview of the IRS's structure is provided. The working principle of the IRS is also clearly illustrated.

2.1 *Structure of Intelligent Reflecting Surface*

The structure of the IRS depends on multiple components to manipulate electromagnetic waves in 6G wireless communications. The IRS design includes:

2.1.1 Number of Layers in Intelligent Reflecting Surface

An IRS comprises three layers: the outer, middle, and inner layers, as shown in Fig. 1. The outer layer is made of metallic or dielectric meta-atoms to control the direction of incident signals. The middle layer uses a copper plate to reduce signal energy leakage during reflection, and the inner layer contains a control circuit with a field-programmable gate array (FPGA) to adjust the amplitude and phase of the reflecting units (RUs).

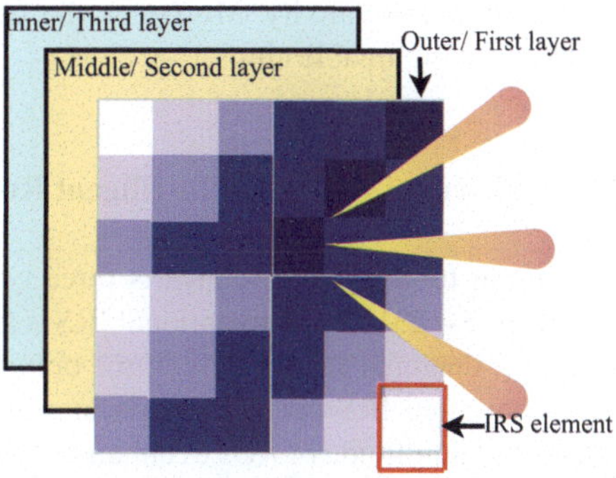

Fig. 1 Structure of IRS [18]

2.1.2 Size and Number of Intelligent Reflecting Surface Elements

The size and number of IRS elements are pivotal factors that impact the performance of an IRS-assisted communication system [19]. The large number of IRS elements precisely controls the phase shifts, amplifies the beam-forming gain, and augments signal strength, resulting in enhanced coverage and reliability, and constructive interference at the receiver. Further, larger element sizes possess a larger area for reflecting incoming signals, resulting in enhanced signal reflections and improved efficiency in power-limited systems. On the other hand, smaller components provide greater oversight of the phase and direction of the reflected signal, resulting in improved beam-forming accuracy, which is particularly crucial for multi-user and intricate situations that require accurate navigation. A large number of small elements delivers exceptional flexibility and precision in beam-forming, making it well-suited for environments that require meticulous signal control, such as densely populated urban areas or dynamic 6G networks. Conversely, a small number of large elements is appropriate for situations when signal strength takes precedence over exact beam control, such as in rural regions or basic communication configurations.

2.1.3 Elements and Phase Control Mechanisms of Intelligent Reflecting Surface

The IRS consists of varactors and diodes [20], and these elements can be modified by positive-intrinsic-negative (PIN) diodes, field-effect transistors, or micro-electromechanical system switches [21, 22]. The PIN diodes, field-effect transistors, or micro-electromechanical system switches are mainly used in the IRS as they have low hardware cost, low energy consumption, low reflection loss, and quick reflection response. In the IRS, amplitude and phase shift can be achieved by PIN diodes, varactor diodes, field-effect transistors, or micro-electromechanical systems. Activating or deactivating a PIN diode directly alters the reflective properties, which in turn, the phase shift of the reflected wave. Conversely, varactor diodes can continually alter their capacitance in response to an applied voltage, and micro-electromechanicals offer excellent sensitivity. Moreover, the IRS reduces the intercell communication interference by tunable chips.

2.1.4 Circuit Topology of Intelligent Reflecting Surface

The circuit topology of the IRS is three types: single, group, and fully-connected architectures [23]. The conventional IRS is a single-connected architecture and operates on a diagonal matrix to control only the signal's phase. The group IRS and fully-connected IRS operate on a scattering matrix that controls both the signal's phases and amplitude of RUs to enhance the performance over the conventional IRS. Moreover, according to the mathematical properties of the scattering matrix, the IRS can be split into beyond diagonal-IRS (BD-IRS). It has been introduced to overcome the conventional IRS's limitations and built based on the concept of block-diagonal IRS architecture. The block-diagonal IRS groups the RUs to enhance signal processing and flexibility [24, 25]. Simultaneous transmitting and reflecting IRS (STAR-IRS) is a part of the BD-IRS. It reflects and transmits the input signal to enhance the coverage. It belongs to the "cell-wise single-connected" branch, indicating no connections among different cells. Further, to overcome the limitation of cell-wise single-connected BD-IRS (STAR-IRS), "cell-wise group/fully-connected" BD-IRS has been considered, which indicates part of cells or all the cells are connected to each other [26].

2.2 *Working Principle of Intelligent Reflecting Surface*

The detailed overview of IRS-aided wireless networks function, and deployment considerations are illustrated.

2.2.1 Intelligent Reflecting Surface as a Signal Reflector in Wireless Networks

Figure 2 illustrates a structure of the IRS-aided network. The amplitude and phase coefficients of the RU of IRS can dynamically change its reflective properties in response to the incident signal and create virtual LoS links between BS to intended receivers to control the signals interact with obstacles, which improves the signal strength, mitigates the and reduces the non-line-of-sight (NLoS) regions effects [27]. The IRS creates beam-forming by integrating the reflection angles and phase shifts of

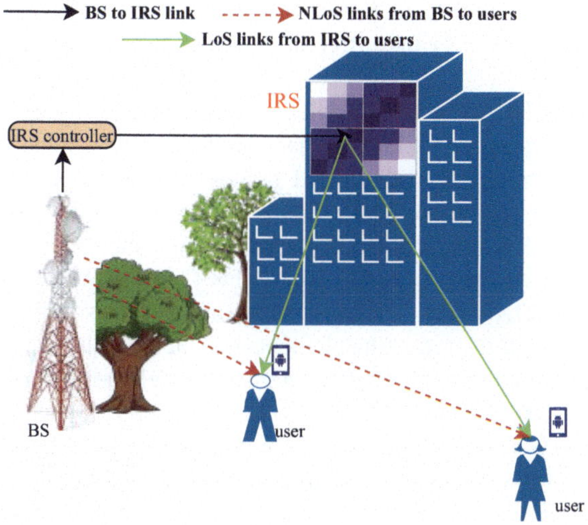

Fig. 2 System model of IRS-aided networks

its components to focus the reflected signal toward a certain user or direction, which is widely used in MIMO [28]. In densely populated urban regions, the IRS may utilize MIMO and beam-forming to deliver reliable connectivity in congested environments and to improve user experience in smart city applications. It can facilitate beam-forming in interior settings and enhance coverage in regions where conventional signals may be inadequate, such as expansive office spaces, shopping centers, or underground locations. Integrating IRS with MIMO and beam-forming can diminish the required power to get the necessary signal quality and making it a cost-effective solution for sustainable network designs. It also reflects the multiple data streams simultaneously without interference, thereby enhancing the network capacity and reliability. In IRS-assisted communication, the user transmits a pilot signal while both the BS and the IRS conduct channel estimation to acquire the channel information of the BS to the user and the IRS to the user, respectively. Then, the BS transmits a pilot signal while the IRS estimates the channel condition between the BS and the IRS. After that, the BS transmits the acquired channel status information (CSI). The IRS accesses the CSI for all links by using the aforementioned protocol and computing beam-forming and phase adjustments. Then the IRS controller sends the optimized beam-forming parameters to the BS for transmission [29]. The channel of the IRS-aided network is represented as

$$G = \overline{g}^H \Theta g \tag{1}$$

where g represents the channel from the BS to the IRS, $g \in \mathbb{C}^{N\times 1}$. Here, N represents the number of RUs of the IRS. $\overline{g}^H$ denotes channel from the IRS to the user, $\overline{g}^H \in \mathbb{C}^{1\times N}$. The coefficients of RU denoted by matrix, $\Theta = diag\left\{\beta_1 e^{j\varnothing_1}, \beta_2 e^{j\varnothing_2}, \ldots, \beta_N e^{j\varnothing_N}\right\}$, where, β_n and $\varnothing_n$ represent amplitude and phase reflecting coefficients of the nth RU, where $n \in \{1, \ldots, N\}$, $\beta_n \in (0, 1)$ and $\varnothing_n \in [0, 2\pi]$.

2.2.2 Intelligent Reflecting Surface as a Reflector as Well as a Transmitter in Wireless Networks

The IRS operates as a reflector and as well as a transmitter. The STAR-IRS reflects and transmits the input signal simultaneously to enhance the network's coverage. The system model of the STAR-IRS aided network is shown in Fig. 3. The front space of the area of the STAR-IRS is known as the reflection space, where the STAR-IRS operates in reflection mode, and behind the space of the area of the STAR-IRS is known as transmission space, where the STAR-IRS operates in transmission mode. The STAR-IRS consists of reflecting and transmitting elements. The amplitude and phase of the reflecting elements vary at the reflection mode operation. Similarly, the amplitude and phase of the transmitting elements vary during the transmission mode operation. The STAR-IRS operates based on the time switching, energy splitting, and mode switching protocols which improves the efficiency of the networks [30]. The energy splitting protocol uses input power variation, with the STAR-IRS operating in both transmission and reflection modes simultaneously. The STAR-IRS components

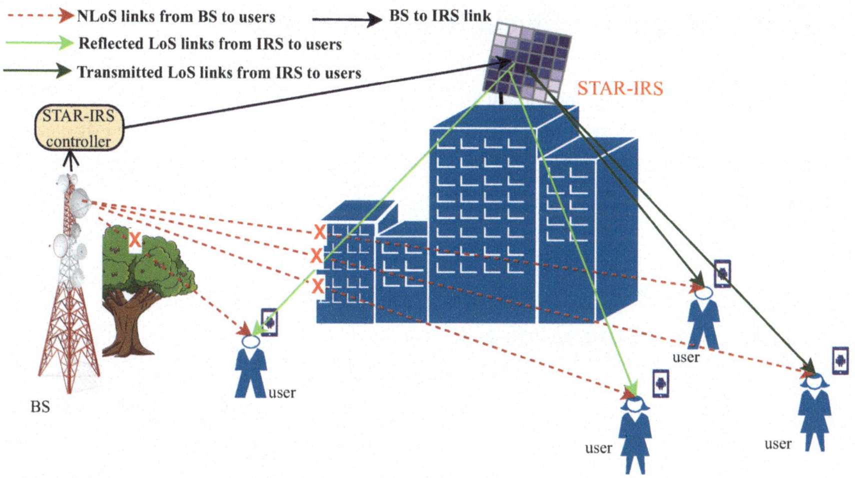

Fig. 3 System model of STAR-IRS-aided networks

are split between transmission and reflection modes in the mode-switching protocol. The STAR-IRS alternates between these modes in separate time slots in the time-switching protocol. Transmission and reflection are controlled by "ON/OFF" switches, typically using a PIN diode, which can be integrated during fabrication.

2.2.3 Security in Intelligent Reflecting Surface-Aided Networks

The IRS can accurately manipulate the direction and phase of reflected signals and keep them away from eavesdroppers. The optimized phase shifts of the IRS increase the confidentiality rate of the communication. The IRS can adjust its reflecting characteristics dynamically in response to current network circumstances and potential threats. It creates highly directional beams toward the intended receiver by dynamically adjusting the phase and amplitude of RUs that minimize signal leakage toward potential eavesdroppers [31]. It introduces multipath effects and creates artificial noise to confuse eavesdroppers to intercept or decode the signal [32]. It also can reflect the interference toward the eavesdroppers, which reduces the quality of the signals and makes it difficult to decode the information.

2.2.4 Deployment of Intelligent Reflecting Surface in Wireless Networks

In wireless networks, deployment of the IRS depends on the size of the IRS, locations, operating and maintaining costs, space availability, and the environment. The IRS must be placed close to the BS and users as its processing power is low and its power is decreased with distance [18].

3 Applications of Intelligent Reflecting Surface

IRS can be used in various applications of modern wireless communications. Here, some applications of the IRS in unmanned aerial vehicles (UAV), mobile edge computing (MEC), device-to-device (D2D), and Terahertz (THz) communications are illustrated.

3.1 Intelligent Reflecting Surface in Unmanned Aerial Vehicles Communication

UAV plays a key role in wireless communication. It provides great flexibility, mobility, and affordability in wireless communications. However, security, EE, and reliability are the main challenges in creating efficient UAV communication. To overcome the above problem, the IRS has been integrated into UAV networks. The IRS enhances physical layer security in IRS-aided UAV communication [33]. It also reduces the energy consumption of UAV communication by optimizing the propagation environment [34]. Further, it also maximizes the data rate of ground mobile users in IRS-aided UAV communication [35]. The IRS-aided UAV communication enhances the signal quality and coverage of the communication [36].

3.2 Intelligent Reflecting Surface in Mobile Edge Computing

In wireless communication, MEC is a prominent technology. It enhances privacy and saves mobile users energy. It also reduces the latency of the networks. However, latency is increased by the distance between edge servers and mobile devices. IRS can mitigate the problem of MEC. In IRS-aided MEC networks, the IRS is deployed to provide the LoS path and an optimized communication path between mobile devices and edge servers. Therefore, the IRS-aided MEC networks' propagation delay and overall latency are reduced [37]. IRS-aided MEC also enhances the network's security by dynamically adjusting signal reflections and creating secure signal paths [38]. Further, IRS-aided MEC minimizes energy consumption and increases the users' data rate of the networks [39, 40].

3.3 Intelligent Reflecting Surface in Device-to-Device Communication

D2D communication plays a crucial role in modern wireless communication. In D2D communication, devices communicate directly with each other without routing data through a BS, which improves efficiency and reduces the latency of the networks [41].

However, in dense environments, the overall performance of D2D communications is degraded due to interference. The D2D communication operates on short range and often relies on LoS connections. The IRS overcomes these problems. It intelligently reflects signals that minimize the interference of D2D communication and enhance the efficiency of the communication system [42]. D2D communication requires more power when obstacles are present, which is easily solved by the IRS. The IRS-aided D2D communication increases the sum rate and the EE of the networks [43, 44].

3.4 Intelligent Reflecting Surface in Terahertz Communication

THz communication meets the ever-growing demand for higher data rates, lower latency, and enhanced spectrum efficiency. However, THz communication is affected by the high free-space path loss and atmospheric attenuation. The performance of THz communication deteriorates when it passes through obstacles. Further, THz communication operates at high power and high energy. Therefore, device designing and EE are major challenges in THz communication. Further, THz communication is also affected by high-frequency signals and environmental noise. The IRS overcomes the limitation and extends the communication range of THz communication [45]. Moreover, the IRS provides multiple reflection paths and mitigates the high propagation losses. In IRS-aided THz communication, the networks' security and users' sum data rate are increased [46–48]. The detailed applications of the IRS have been presented in Table 2.

Table 2 Applications of IRS-assisted communication

Reference	IRS's applications	Key focus
[33–36]	IRS-assisted UAV communication	Enhance the physical layer security, spectrum efficiency, energy efficiency, efficient trajectories, coverage extension
[37–40]	IRS-assisted MEC	Latency minimization, secure computation task, energy minimization, achievable rate maximization
[41–44]	IRS-assisted D2D communication	Latency reduction, joint IRS selection and beam-forming optimization, sum rate optimization and enhance the energy efficiency
[45–48]	IRS-assisted THz communication	Enhance reliability, secure transmission and sum rate maximization

4 Case Studied

Here, two case studies on IRS-aided networks are discussed. The first case illustrates IRS-aided networks' performance over different fading channels. The second case presents the performance of IRS-aided orthogonal multiple access (OMA) and IRS-aided non-orthogonal multiple access (NOMA) networks.

4.1 Intelligent Reflecting Surface-Aided Network over Different Fading Channels

In wireless communication, fading decreases the strength of the signal. Multipath transmissions, the environment, and mobile objects generate fading. In 6G wireless communication, the users' performance is decreased because of fading. The IRS enhances the user's performance in fading environments. In [49], statistical CSI was designed for IRS-aided networks, where Rayleigh and Rician channels were considered based on LoS and NLoS paths. In [50], the average data rate and decoding error probability of IRS-aided networks were derived for different fading channels. This case study proposes an IRS-aided equal gain combine (EGC)-based MIMO wireless network over different fading channels.

4.1.1 System Model

The system model of IRS-aided MIMO wireless network over different fading channels is presented in Fig. 4. The system consists of one BS, one IRS, and user. The BS has N_t transmitting antennas and users have N_r receiving antennas. Here, Rayleigh,

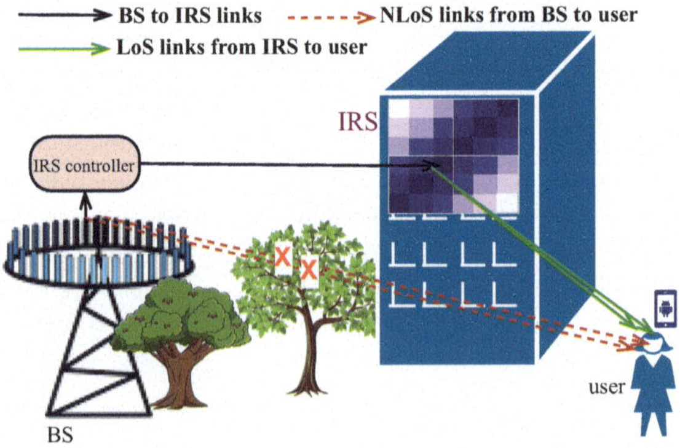

Fig. 4 System model of IRS-aided MIMO networks over different fading channels

Rician, and Nakagami fading channels are considered to examine the performance of the proposed network. The received signal by the user is represented as

$$\mathrm{Y} = \left(\overline{h}^{H}\Theta h\right)s + N_0 \tag{2}$$

where h indicates the BS to IRS channel with $d_{B,I}^{-\frac{\eta_{B,I}}{2}}$ and $\overline{h}^{H}$ indicate the IRS to user channel with $d_{I,U}^{-\frac{\eta_{I,U}}{2}}$. Here, $d_{B,I}$ and $d_{I,U}$ denote BS to IRS and IRS to user distance, respectively. $\eta_{B,I}$ and $\eta_{I,U}$ indicate the path loss component (PLC) of BS to IRS and IRS to the user, respectively. The coefficients of RUs represented by matrix, $\Theta = diag\left\{\beta_1 e^{j\varnothing_1}, \beta_2 e^{j\varnothing_2}, \ldots, \beta_N e^{j\varnothing_N}\right\}$, where, β_n and $\varnothing_n$ represent amplitude and phase reflecting coefficients of the nth RU, where $n \in \{1, \ldots, N\}$, $\beta_n \in (0, 1)$ and $\varnothing_n \in [0, 2\pi]$. s represents the transmitted signal and N_0 denotes the noise. To improve the user performance, $\varnothing_n$ needs to optimized which can be represented as

$$\varnothing_n^{*} = -arg[\overline{h}_n^{H}] - arg[h_n] \tag{3}$$

where h_n is the nth element of h, $\overline{h}_n^{H}$ is the nth element of $\overline{h}^{H}$ and $arg[.]$ indicates the phase of the complex term. The achievable data rate (ADR) of the user after EGC can be represented as

$$\mathrm{I} = \log_2\left(1 + \frac{\rho\sum_{j=1}^{k}\left|\overline{h}_j^{H}\Theta h_j e^{j\theta}\right|^2}{k}\right) \tag{4}$$

where θ indicates the phase of the incident signal, k denotes the number of receiving path of user and ρ indicates the signal-to-noise ratio (SNR).

4.1.2 Result and Discussion

Here, some simulation parameters are considered for simulation. $N = 4, 9$, the number of bits = 10^4, SNR $= 10:40$ dB are considered. $N_t = 2$ and $N_r = 2$, therefore, $k = 4$. Distance BS to user ($d_{B,U} = 50$ m), PLC of BS to user ($\eta_{B,U}$) = 2.4, $d_{B,I} = 20$ m, $\eta_{B,I} = 1.3$, $d_{I,U} = 50$ m and $\eta_{I,U} = 1.3$ are considered. The $\beta_n = 0.9$ and $\varnothing_n$ has been considered based on (3), where. $n \in \{1, \ldots, N\}$. Figure 5 presents the performance comparison between IRS-aided network and conventional network under the Rayleigh, Rician, and Nakagami fading channels, where $k = 2$ for the Rician fading channel and $m = 1.5$ and $s = 2.5$ for Nakagami fading channel. In Fig. 5a at 40 dB SNR for the Rician fading channel, the ADR of the conventional network is 1.281 bps/Hz, whereas, at $L = 4$ and $L = 9$, the ADR of the proposed network is 3.414 and 5.227 bps/Hz respectively, which is 1.67 times and 3.08 times better than the conventional network. Similarly, for the Nakagami fading channel,

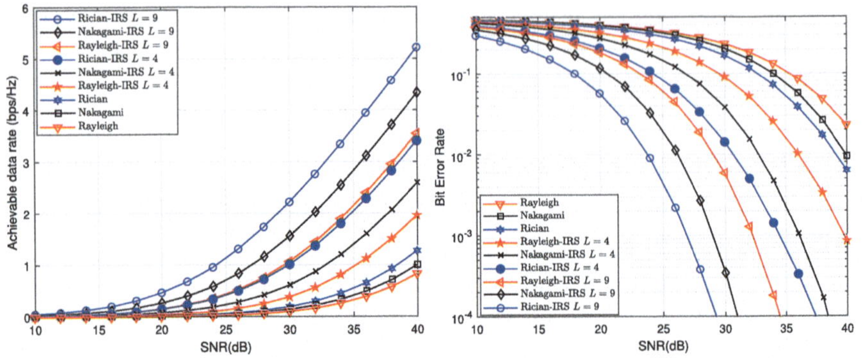

(a) (b)

Fig. 5 Performance comparison between IRS-aided network and conventional network under different fading channels, where, $k = 2$ for Rician fading channel and, $m = 1.5$ and $s = 2.5$ for Nakagami fading channel

the ADR of the conventional network is 1.003 bps/Hz, whereas, at $L = 4$ and $L = 9$, the ADR of the proposed network is 2.596 bps/Hz and 4.338 bps/Hz respectively, which is 1.59 times and 3.33 times superior to the conventional network. On the other hand, for the Rayleigh fading channel, the ADR of the conventional network is 0.842 bps/Hz, whereas, at $L = 4$ and $L = 9$, the ADR of the proposed network is 1.975 and 3.562 bps/Hz respectively, which is 1.35 times and 3.23 times outperform the conventional network. Similarly, in Fig. 5b, to achieve 10^{-4} BER at $L = 4$, the proposed network requires 29, 31 dB, and more than 40 dB SNR, respectively, and at $L = 9$ the proposed network needs 29, 31, and 34 dB SNR, respectively for the Rician, Nakagami, and Rayleigh fading channel, whereas the conventional network needs more than 40 dB SNR for all channels. The higher ADR and lower BER signify higher efficiency and, without error, how well a system can transmit data under various conditions. Therefore, it can be concluded that for all channels, the performance of the IRS-aided network is superior to the conventional network.

Figure 6 presents the performance comparison between the IRS-aided network and conventional network over Rician and Nakagami fading channels for different k and m, where $k = 2, 3$ for the Rician fading channel and $m = 1.5, 2.5$ and $s = 2.5$ for Nakagami fading channel. From Fig. 6, it has been seen that the performance of the IRS-aided network is increased with the increasing k and m. Figure 7 presents the performance comparison between IRS-aided network and conventional network over the Nakagami fading channels for different m and s, where. $m = 1.5, 2.5$ and $s = 2, 3$. From Fig. 7, it has been seen that the performance of the IRS-aided network is increased with the increasing m and s. Further, it has been observed that the proposed network' performance also increases with the value of s.

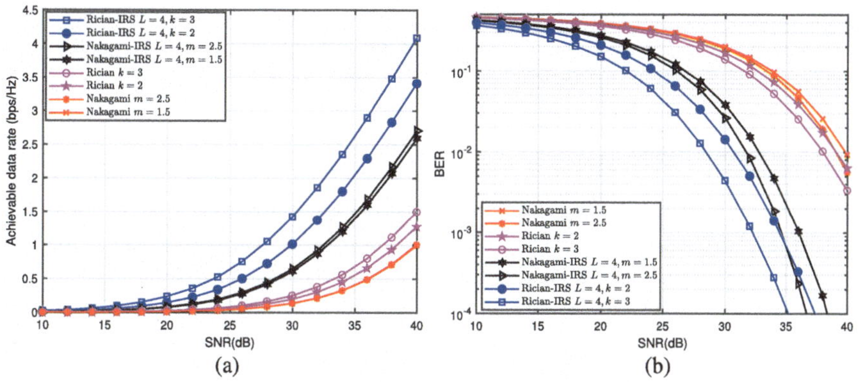

Fig. 6 Performances over Rician and Nakagami fading channels where $k = 2, 3$ for Rician fading channel and $m = 1.5, 2.5$ for the Nakagami fading channel

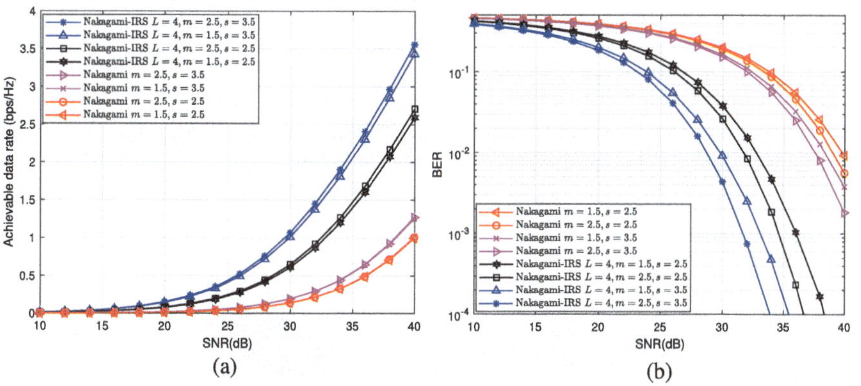

Fig. 7 Performances over Nakagami fading channels for $m = 1.3, 2.3$, and $s = 2, 3$

4.2 *Performance of Intelligent Reflecting Surface-Orthogonal Multiple Access and Intelligent Reflecting Surface-Non-Orthogonal Multiple Access*

In wireless communication, OMA and NOMA are two important key technologies. In OMA, users operate on different time bands, frequency bands, or codes to avoid collision or interference. On the other hand, in NOMA, users access the same time-frequency resources based on different power and code domains. However, in the NLoS regions, the performance of OMA and NOMA is degraded as users get the signal through the NLoS links. To improve the performance of users, OMA and NOMA are combined with the IRS-aided networks [51]. In [52, 53], the performances of IRS-aided NOMA networks for different wireless environments are illustrated. In [54], an overview and efficiency of IRS-NOMA has been discussed for both single input and single output and multiple input and single output communication scenarios. Here, the performance of IRS-NOMA and IRS-OMA are presented.

4.2.1 System Model

The system model of IRS-OMA and IRS-NOMA networks is presented in Fig. 8. The system model contains one BS, one IRS, and two users, where one user is located near the BS, and one user is located far from the BS. In IRS-OMA, the ADR of the user is represented as

$$\mathrm{I_{OMA}} = \frac{1}{N_u}\log_2\left(1 + \rho\left|\overline{h}^H\Theta h\right|^2\right) \tag{5}$$

where N_u represents the number of users, h indicates the BS to IRS channel with $d_{B,I}^{-\frac{\eta_{B,I}}{2}}$, it is a Rician channel with k Rician factor. $\overline{h}^H$ indicate the IRS to user channel with $d_{I,j}^{-\frac{\eta_{I,j}}{2}}$, it is a Rayleigh channel. Here, $d_{B,I}$ and $d_{I,j}$ denote BS to IRS and IRS to user distance, respectively. $\eta_{B,I}$ and $\eta_{I,j}$ indicate the PLC of BS to IRS and IRS to the user, respectively, where j indicates the near or far-user. The reflecting coefficients denoted by matrix, $\Theta = diag\left\{\beta_1 e^{j\varnothing_1}, \beta_2 e^{j\varnothing_2}, \ldots, \beta_N e^{j\varnothing_N}\right\}$, where, β_n and $\varnothing_n$ represent amplitude and phase reflecting coefficients of the nth RU, where

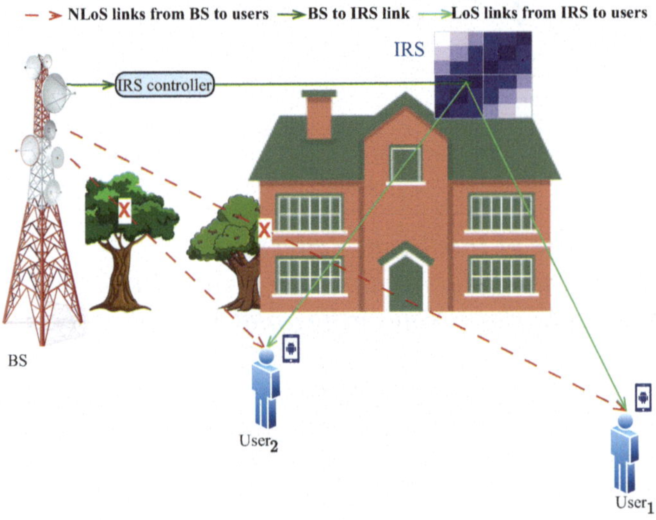

Fig. 8 System model of IRS-OMA and IRS-NOMA networks

$n \in \{1, \ldots, N\}$, $\beta_n \in (0, 1)$, $\varnothing_n \in [0, 2\pi]$ and ρ indicates SNR. In IRS-OMA, the outage probability (OP) of the user can be written as

$$\mathrm{P}_{\mathrm{OMA}} = \Pr\left(\mathrm{I}_{\mathrm{OMA}} < \gamma\right) \tag{6}$$

γ indicates the target data rate of the user.

In IRS-NOMA networks, the ADR of the far-user is represented as

$$\mathrm{I}_{\mathrm{NOMA,far}} = \log_2\left(1 + \frac{\alpha_{\mathrm{far}}\left|\overline{h}^H \Theta h_{\mathrm{far}}\right|^2}{\alpha_{\mathrm{near}}\left|\overline{h}^H \Theta h_{\mathrm{far}}\right|^2 + \frac{1}{\rho}}\right) \tag{7}$$

where α_{far} and α_{near} are the power allocation factors of far and near-users, respectively. h_{far} denotes the IRS to the far-user channel. In IRS-NOMA, the OP of the far-user can be written as

$$\mathrm{P}_{\mathrm{NOMA,far}} = \Pr\left(\mathrm{I}_{\mathrm{NOMA,far}} < \gamma_{\mathrm{far}}\right) \tag{8}$$

γ_{far} denotes the target data rate of the far-user.

The ADR of the near-user when it decodes the far-user signal is defined as

$$\mathrm{I}_{\mathrm{NOMA,near,far}} = \log_2\left(1 + \frac{\alpha_{\mathrm{near}}\left|\overline{h}^H \Theta h_{\mathrm{near}}\right|^2}{\alpha_{\mathrm{far}}\left|\overline{h}^H \Theta h_{\mathrm{near}}\right|^2 + \frac{1}{\rho}}\right) \tag{9}$$

The ADR of the near-user when it decodes its own signal is written as

$$\mathrm{I}_{\mathrm{NOMA,near}} = \log_2\left(1 + \rho\alpha_{\mathrm{near}}\left|\overline{h}^H \Theta h_{\mathrm{near}}\right|^2\right) \tag{10}$$

The OP of the near-user can be defined as

$$\mathrm{P}_{\mathrm{NOMA,near}} = \Pr\left(\mathrm{I}_{\mathrm{NOMA,near,far}} < \gamma_{\mathrm{far}} \bigcap \mathrm{I}_{\mathrm{NOMA,near}} < \gamma_{\mathrm{near}}\right) \tag{11}$$

h_{near} denotes the IRS to near-user channel and γ_{near} indicates the target data rate of the near-user.

4.2.2 Result and Discussion

The considered simulation parameters are $N_u = 2, N = 4, 9, k = 3, \rho = 10 : 40\,\mathrm{dB}$. Here, user$_1$ is the far-user and user$_2$ is the near-user. Distance of BS to user$_1$ ($d_{B,\mathrm{far}}$) = 60 m, PLC of BS to user$_1$ ($\eta_{B,\mathrm{far}}$) = 2, distance of BS to user$_2$ ($d_{B,\mathrm{near}}$) = 25 m, PLC of BS to user$_2$ ($\eta_{B,\mathrm{far}}$) = 2, $d_{B,I} = 20\,m$, $\eta_{B,I} = 1.1$, distance of IRS to user$_1$ ($d_{I,\mathrm{far}}$) = 55 m, PLC of IRS to user$_1$ ($\eta_{I,\mathrm{far}}$) = 1.1, distance of IRS to user$_2$ ($d_{I,\mathrm{near}}$) = 15 m

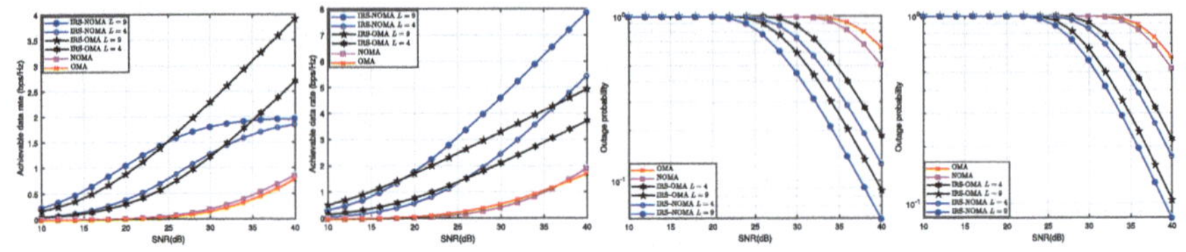

(a) $User_1$ (b) $User_2$ (c) $User_1$ (d) $User_2$

Fig. 9 The performance comparison among IRS-OMA, IRS-NOMA, OMA, and NOMA networks

and PLC of IRS to $user_1$ $(\eta_{I,\text{near}}) = 1.1$ are considered. $\alpha_{\text{far}} = 0.75$, $\alpha_{\text{near}} = 0.25$, $\gamma_{\text{near}} = 2$ bps/Hz and $\gamma_{\text{far}} = 1$ bps/Hz are considered. The $\beta_n = 0.9$ and $\varnothing_n$ has been considered based on (3), where $n \in \{1, \ldots, N\}$.

Figure 9 presents the performance comparison among IRS-OMA, IRS-NOMA, OMA, and NOMA networks of $user_1$ and $user_2$. In Fig. 9a, at 40 dB SNR, the ADR of $user_1$ for NOMA and OMA is 0.874 and 0.801 bps/Hz, respectively, whereas at $L = 4$ the ADR of $user_1$ for IRS-NOMA and IRS-OMA is 1.865 and 2.703 bps/Hz, respectively, which is 1.13 times and 2.37 times better than conventional NOMA and OMA respectively. On the other hand, at $L = 9$, the ADR of $user_1$ for IRS-NOMA and IRS-OMA is 1.978 and 3.917 bps/Hz, respectively, which is 1.47 times and 3.89 times superior to the conventional NOMA and OMA respectively where $user_1$ suffers from the interference of $user_2$ signal. Similarly, the ADR of $user_2$ for NOMA and OMA is 1.935 and 1.733 bps/Hz, respectively, whereas at $L = 4$ the ADR of $user_2$ for IRS-NOMA and IRS-OMA is 5.469 and 3.717 bps/Hz, respectively, which is 1.83 times and 1.44 times outperform to the conventional NOMA and OMA respectively. On the other hand, at $L = 9$, the ADR of $user_2$ for IRS-NOMA and IRS-OMA is 7.896 and 4.945 bps/Hz, respectively, which is 3.08 times and 1.85 times better than the conventional NOMA and OMA respectively. The higher ADR and lower OP indicate higher efficiency, system reliability, and performance. Further, from Fig. 9c and d, it has been observed that the OP of IRS-OMA and IRS-OMA networks outperform the OMA and NOMA networks and the performance of the IRS-aided networks is increased with the increasing N.

5 Challenges

In 6G wireless communications, IRS-aided networks overcome the limitations of the NLoS region effects, enhance signal coverage, and improve the reliability of communications. However, several challenges are associated with IRS-aided wireless networks based on their operations, design, and deployment. Here, some challenges of IRS-aided networks, such as channel estimation, beam-forming design, phase control, security enhancement, design and deployment, and practical difficulties, are illustrated.

5.1 *Channel Estimation of Intelligent Reflecting Surface*

In IRS-aided networks, based on CSI, the amplitude and phase shift coefficients of RUs are continuously updated to provide LoS links from the BS to users. Therefore, channel estimation plays an important role in IRS-aided networks [55]. In IRS-aided networks, each RU needs to be characterized, and large RUs create high dimensionality problems. Therefore, channel estimation is a critical and challenging aspect of IRS-aided networks. To solve this problem, compressed sensing techniques and dimensionality reduction techniques are required [56]. Further, channel estimation becomes difficult in IRS-aided networks with random variations of user positions and environmental factors [57].

5.2 *Beam-Forming Design of Intelligent Reflecting Surface*

In IRS-aided networks, beam-forming is an important technique as it effectively and efficiently manipulates signal propagation and improves the functionality of wireless communication systems. It focuses the transmission power in specific directions, which enhances signal strength and coverage, and reduces interferences [58]. However, the design of beam-forming is a challenging task as simultaneous optimization is required for beam-forming optimization. Therefore, alternating optimization techniques or semi-definite relaxation techniques are required. Further, accurate CSI is important for effective beam-forming design, which is very difficult. Moreover, the working capability of beam-forming is also affected by the rapid changes in the environments and user locations.

5.3 *Phase Control of Intelligent Reflecting Surface*

Phase control of an IRS is an essential part of IRS-aided networks. The IRS controls the phase of the reflected signals to enhance the overall network performance [29]. Each RU of an IRS is equipped with a phase shifter that adjusts the phase of the incoming signal to send the signal to the intended receiver. These phase shifters are electronically controlled and dynamically adjust the reflected beam to the desired directions [59]. However, controlling the phase shift of a large number of RUs leads to high optimization problems, which enhance the complexity of the networks. Frequently updating the phase shift is another challenging task due to rapid environmental changes. Accurate CSI is also important to control the phase effectively, which is also challenging. Further, in IRS-aided networks, more energy is required to control the IRS phase, which is another limitation in power-constrained environments.

5.4 Security Enhancement of Intelligent Reflecting Surface-Assisted Communication

Security has recently become an important and challenging task in wireless communication. In wireless communication, the IRS improves security and maximizes the data rate [60]. The IRS solves the information leakage problem in IRS-aided MEC networks by hiding physical layer details [61]. In IRS-aided networks, optimizing beamforming enhances the service quality for primary users while maximizing confidentiality for secondary users [62]. However, in IRS-aided 6G wireless communication, security becomes challenging because of the dynamic and adaptive characteristics of the IRS. Further, in IRS-aided communication, coordination, and synchronization are required among the BS, the IRS controller, and the users, so security needs to be maintained, which is also difficult. On the other hand, new risks may arise when attackers exploit gaps in the IRS controller, interrupt the connections between the BS and the IRS, or interfere with the methodology employed to modify the IRS's signal phase shifts. To solve this issue, the connection between the BS and the IRS controller must be secured with robust encryption and authentication protocols are essential. Along with this, an efficient ML/DL technique is also important to detect irregularities in IRS behavior, which can aid in identifying potential security. These algorithms can identify whether the IRS is being exploited or utilized in manners that differ from its intended purpose. Further, the intricacy of IRS systems and their integration with various technologies can generate multiple attack vectors that may be abused unexpectedly. To solve this problem, multi-layer security is essential.

5.5 Design and Deployment of Intelligent Reflecting Surface

In IRS-aided networks, an intricate hardware structure is essential for fabricating the IRS with many RUs, which is expensive [14]. Therefore, high energy and power are also required to design the IRS. Further, to control the IRS, an IRS controller is necessary, and to design this IRS controller, more controlling pins are essential. These increase the networks' complexity and expenditure. Moreover, to design the active IRS, a more complex hardware structure is required as active IRS consists of active components that enhance the energy and power consumption, which reduces the battery life and enhances the computational cost [63]. On the other hand, large elements necessitate more intricate optimization methods to determine the appropriate phase shifts for all elements, resulting in elevated computing and processing requirements at the IRS controller. A sophisticated design is also essential for the IRS to cover a large area. Further, the IRS's deployment is another difficult task, and to extend the coverage, more IRSs need to be deployed, which increases the deployment cost. In IRS-aided networks, the deployment also depends on the place where the IRS is located and the IRS's size. With the increasing size, the deployment complexity and cost also increase.

5.6 Practical Difficulties of Using Intelligent Reflecting Surface in Real-Life

Weather conditions influence the IRS's performance. The IRS panels suffer signal degradation and dispersion during heavy rain and snowfall. The reflected signal diminishes in strength and clarity, leading to a reduction in communication quality. The IRS may necessitate cleaning and repair after heavy rain and snowfall to maintain optimal functionality. Failure to fulfill these maintenance requirements the weather-related issues may result in ongoing problems with the quality and coverage of the signals. On the other hand, physical barriers such as buildings, trees, or other structures may block or modify signals unintendedly, thus impacting IRS performance [64]. This issue is more evident in urban regions, where numerous such impediments exist. Addressing these difficulties necessitates careful planning on the placing of IRS and implementing advanced signal processing techniques. Moreover, energy consumption in urban areas can fluctuate significantly, but it frequently rises due to the necessity for accurate signal management and frequent modifications to accommodate changing conditions.

6 Future Directions

The future directions of the IRS reveal the challenges of the IRS and elaborate the outstanding potential advantages. Here, the future direction of IRS-aided networks, such as covering large areas, machine (ML)/deep learning (DL) techniques, smart wireless sensing, BD-IRS, and standardization of IRS, are explained.

6.1 Intelligent Reflecting Surface for Large Area

Efficiently scaling IRS systems to encompass large areas while maintaining complexity and computing requirements is crucial in wide networks. The IRS systems can be segmented into smaller modular units, each of which functions autonomously and can be aggregated to encompass larger regions [65]. A multi-tiered control system may be established, wherein lower-level controllers can control smaller modules of the IRS while higher-level controllers can control the entire system. Adaptive beamforming algorithms can be developed to dynamically modify the focus of the IRS to include an extensive area.

6.2 Machine/Deep Learning Based Intelligent Reflecting Surface-Aided Networks

Accurate channel estimation is important for the IRS. The ML/DL-based techniques predict CSI by learning the complex patterns in the data [66, 67]. Further, the phase shift control of RUs is also important for effective beam-forming design, which ML/DL-based techniques can achieve. The ML-based algorithm alternately optimizes the beam-forming with low complexity [68]. The DL-based technique reduces the channel state overload for transmit beam-forming design [69]. It jointly designs the beam-forming in IRS-aided millimeter wave networks [70]. The ML/DL-based techniques enhance the overall performance of users [71, 72]. Still, these techniques have not been thoroughly investigated for 6G wireless communication, such as active IRS, which can be designed by ML or DL techniques. Further, other learning techniques, such as Q learning, transfer learning techniques, transformer-based learning, etc., can be used in IRS-aided networks.

6.3 Smart Wireless Sensing by Intelligent Reflecting Surface

In smart wireless networks, the IRS enhances the coverage and performance of wireless sensors. Moreover, in internet of things (IoT) networks, the IRS maximizes the data rate of IoT devices and provides smart city infrastructure through reliable connectivity and accurate sensing [40]. The IRS-aided IoT networks also enhance the flexibility and reliability of the users [73]. The IRS also monitors the industrial environment by communicating between sensors and control systems [50, 74]. Recently, it has been applied to health monitoring systems. In healthcare, it increases the capabilities of medical devices and sensors by improving signal reliability and reducing interference [75, 76]. However, it has not been fully explored in smart wireless communications. Therefore, there is a lot of opportunity to explore the IRS and enhance communication reliability.

6.4 Beyond Diagonal-Intelligent Reflecting Surface

The BD-IRS consists of active elements or hybrid elements. It reflects and transmits signals to provide more signal-processing capabilities. Along with the phase shift, the BD-IRS effectively controls the amplitude, frequency, and polarization of the reflected or transmitted signals [77]. The BD-IRS are applied in complex urban environments, MIMO networks, advanced beam-forming designing, and full space coverage [77]. However, more complex, high energy and high cost are required to design the BD-IRS, which are very challenging. Till now, there is no systematic method for designing the BD-IRS that achieves the best possible balance between circuit complexity and performance. Therefore, there are several chances to implement low-complexity the BD-IRS design in wireless communication.

6.5 The Standardization of Intelligent Reflecting Surface

6G system discussions are expected to start in 2026, as for 5G systems, the 3GPP took place in 2016. There are two main strategies for standardizing IRS in 3GPP: either integrating it into 5G-Advanced through a study item and work item or deferring its adoption to 6G. The International Telecommunication Union regarding the IRS is expected to become more defined after 2023. In 2021, the European Telecommunications Standards Institute approved the formation of an industry specification group on IRS technology for integration into future communication standards [78].

This chapter covers the structure and operational concepts of the IRS. Still, the various hardware designs have not been thoroughly analyzed. This chapter examines the IRS's implementation in UAV communication, MEC, D2D communication, and THz communication. However, the intricate working principle may not be comprehensively addressed, and other applications are not fully discussed. This chapter indicates that actual deployment has issues such as unanticipated interference, user mobility, and signal fading, which require further attention. Enhanced hardware presents opportunities for innovation to improve reflection and beam-forming while reducing power consumption. Additional research is required about the appropriate integration of the IRS with developing technologies such as artificial intelligence, sophisticated phase control and beam-forming methodologies.

7 Conclusion

In this chapter, IRS-aided 6G wireless communication has been discussed. First, the basic design and working principle of the IRS were briefly illustrated. Then, in 6G wireless communication, the IRS applications were discussed in detail. Moreover, the IRS's performance in different fading channels was studied. From this study, it has been observed that IRS-aided networks provide superior performance to conventional networks for all fading channels and the effectiveness of OMA and NOMA networks is enhanced with the IRS. This chapter briefly explained the challenges of the IRS in 6G wireless communications. Further, the future direction of the IRS illustrated to overcome the difficulties in 6G wireless communications.

References

1. Long, Wenxuan and Chen, Rui and Moretti, Marco and Zhang, Wei and Li, Jiandong. A Promising Technology for 6G Wireless Networks: Intelligent Reflecting Surface. *Journal of Communications and Information Networks*, 6(1):1–16, 2021.
2. Xingquan Li, Chiya Zhang, Chunlong He, Gaojie Chen, and Jonathon A Chambers. Sum-rate maximization in IRS-assisted wireless power communication networks. *IEEE internet of things journal*, 8(19):14959–14970, 2021.
3. Wenjing Wei, Xiaowei Pang, Jie Tang, Nan Zhao, Xianbin Wang, and Arumugam Nallanathan. Secure Transmission Design for Aerial IRS Assisted Wireless Networks. *IEEE Transactions on Communications*, 71(6):3528–3540, 2023.
4. Debbarni Sarkar, Yogita, Satyendra Singh Yadav, Vipin Pal, Neeraj Kumar, and Sarat Kumar Patra. A Comprehensive Survey on IRS-Assisted NOMA-Based 6G Wireless Network: Design Perspectives, Challenges and Future Directions. *IEEE Transactions on Network and Service Management*, 21(2):2539–2562, 2024.
5. Yaqi Mao, Xin Yang, Ling Wang, Dawei Wang, Osama Alfarraj, Keping Yu, Shahid Mumtaz, and F. Richard Yu. A High-Capacity MAC Protocol for UAV-Enhanced RIS-Assisted V2X Architecture in 3D IoT Traffic. *IEEE Internet of Things Journal*, pages 1–1, 2024.
6. Han Wen, Ahmad Massud Tota Khel, and Khairi Ashour Hamdi. Effects of Co-Channel Interference on the Performance of IRS-Assisted Communications. *IEEE Transactions on Vehicular Technology*, 2024.
7. Beixiong Zheng, Changsheng You, and Rui Zhang. Efficient channel estimation for double-IRS aided multi-user MIMO system. *IEEE Transactions on Communications*, 69(6):3818–3832, 2021.
8. Jian Chen, Yunhe Xie, Xidong Mu, Jie Jia, Yuanwei Liu, and Xingwei Wang. Energy efficient resource allocation for IRS assisted CoMP systems. *IEEE Transactions on Wireless Communications*, 21(7):5688–5702, 2022.
9. Gaofeng Pan, Jia Ye, Jianping An, and Mohamed-Slim Alouini. Full-duplex enabled intelligent reflecting surface systems: Opportunities and challenges. *IEEE Wireless Communications*, 28(3):122–129, 2021.
10. Yuhang Wu, Fuhui Zhou, Wei Wu, Qihui Wu, Rose Qingyang Hu, and Kai-Kit Wong. Multi-objective optimization for spectrum and energy efficiency tradeoff in IRS-assisted CRNs with NOMA. *IEEE Transactions on Wireless Communications*, 21(8):6627–6642, 2022.
11. Georgios C. Trichopoulos, Panagiotis Theofanopoulos, Bharath Kashyap, Aditya Shekhawat, Anuj Modi, Tawfik Osman, Sanjay Kumar, Anand Sengar, Arkajyoti Chang, and Ahmed Alkhateeb. Design and Evaluation of Reconfigurable Intelligent Surfaces in Real-World Environment. *IEEE Open Journal of the Communications Society*, 3:462–474, 2022.
12. Yishi Zhu, Bomin Mao, and Nei Kato. Intelligent reflecting surface in 6g vehicular communications: A survey. *IEEE Open Journal of Vehicular Technology*, 3:266–277, 2022.
13. Biswarup Rana, Sung-Sil Cho, and Ic-Pyo Hong. Review paper on hardware of reconfigurable intelligent surfaces. *IEEE Access*, 11:29614–29634, 2023.
14. Ertugrul Basar, George C. Alexandropoulos, Yuanwei Liu, Qingqing Wu, Shi Jin, Chau Yuen, Octavia A. Dobre, and Robert Schober. Reconfigurable intelligent surfaces for 6g: Emerging hardware architectures, applications, and open challenges. *IEEE Vehicular Technology Magazine*, pages 2–22, 2024.
15. Faisal Naeem, Mansoor Ali, Georges Kaddoum, Chongwen Huang, and Chau Yuen. Security and privacy for reconfigurable intelligent surface in 6g: A review of prospective applications and challenges. *IEEE Open Journal of the Communications Society*, 4:1196–1217, 2023.
16. Waqas Khalid, Muhammad Atif Ur Rehman, Trinh Van Chien, Zeeshan Kaleem, Howon Lee, and Heejung Yu. Reconfigurable intelligent surface for physical layer security in 6g-iot: Designs, issues, and advances. *IEEE Internet of Things Journal*, 11(2):3599–3613, 2024.
17. Rang Liu, Ming Li, Honghao Luo, Qian Liu, and A Lee Swindlehurst. Integrated sensing and communication with reconfigurable intelligent surfaces: Opportunities, applications, and future directions. *IEEE Wireless Communications*, 30(1):50–57, 2023.

18. Qingqing Wu, Shuowen Zhang, Beixiong Zheng, Changsheng You, and Rui Zhang. Intelligent reflecting surface-aided wireless communications: A tutorial. *IEEE transactions on communications*, 69(5):3313–3351, 2021.
19. Xilong Pei, Haifan Yin, Li Tan, Lin Cao, Zhanpeng Li, Kai Wang, Kun Zhang, and Emil Björnson. Ris-aided wireless communications: Prototyping, adaptive beamforming, and indoor/outdoor field trials. *IEEE Transactions on Communications*, 69(12):8627–8640, 2021.
20. Wankai Tang, Xiang Li, Jun Yan Dai, Shi Jin, Yong Zeng, Qiang Cheng, and Tie Jun Cui. Wireless communications with programmable metasurface: Transceiver design and experimental results. *China Communications*, 16(5):46–61, 2019.
21. Lei Zhang, Xiao Qing Chen, Shuo Liu, Qian Zhang, Jie Zhao, Jun Yan Dai, Guo Dong Bai, Xiang Wan, Qiang Cheng, Giuseppe Castaldi, et al. Space-time-coding digital metasurfaces. *Nature communications*, 9(1):4334, 2018.
22. Payam Nayeri, Fan Yang, and Atef Z Elsherbeni. Reflectarray antennas: theory, designs, and applications. 2018.
23. Shanpu Shen, Bruno Clerckx, and Ross Murch. Modeling and architecture design of reconfigurable intelligent surfaces using scattering parameter network analysis. *IEEE Transactions on Wireless Communications*, 21(2):1229–1243, 2021.
24. Hongyu Li, Shanpu Shen, and Bruno Clerckx. Synergizing Beyond Diagonal Reconfigurable Intelligent Surface and Rate-Splitting Multiple Access. *IEEE Transactions on Wireless Communications*, 23(8):8717–8729, 2024.
25. Hongyu Li, Shanpu Shen, Matteo Nerini, Marco Di Renzo, and Bruno Clerckx. Beyond Diagonal Reconfigurable Intelligent Surfaces With Mutual Coupling: Modeling and Optimization. *IEEE Communications Letters*, 28(4):937–941, 2024.
26. Hongyu Li, Shanpu Shen, and Bruno Clerckx. Beyond diagonal reconfigurable intelligent surfaces: From transmitting and reflecting modes to single-, group-, and fully-connected architectures. *IEEE Transactions on Wireless Communications*, 22(4):2311–2324, 2022.
27. Xin Tan, Zhi Sun, Dimitrios Koutsonikolas, and Josep M Jornet. Enabling indoor mobile millimeter-wave networks based on smart reflect-arrays. In *IEEE INFOCOM 2018-IEEE Conference on Computer Communications*, pages 270–278. IEEE, 2018.
28. Jinghe Wang, Hanqing Wang, Yu Han, Shi Jin, and Xiao Li. Joint transmit beamforming and phase shift design for reconfigurable intelligent surface assisted MIMO systems. *IEEE Transactions on Cognitive Communications and Networking*, 7(2):354–368, 2021.
29. Qingqing Wu and Rui Zhang. Intelligent reflecting surface enhanced wireless network via joint active and passive beamforming. *IEEE Transactions on Wireless Communications*, 18(11):5394–5409, 2019.
30. Yuanwei Liu, Xidong Mu, Jiaqi Xu, Robert Schober, Yang Hao, H Vincent Poor, and Lajos Hanzo. STAR: Simultaneous transmission and reflection for 360° coverage by intelligent surfaces. *IEEE Wireless Communications*, 28(6):102–109, 2021.
31. Jie Chen, Ying-Chang Liang, Yiyang Pei, and Huayan Guo. Intelligent reflecting surface: A programmable wireless environment for physical layer security. *IEEE Access*, 7:82599–82612, 2019.
32. Sheng Hong, Cunhua Pan, Hong Ren, Kezhi Wang, and Arumugam Nallanathan. Artificial-noise-aided secure mimo wireless communications via intelligent reflecting surface. *IEEE Transactions on Communications*, 68(12):7851–7866, 2020.
33. Wali Ullah Khan, Eva Lagunas, Zain Ali, Muhammad Awais Javed, Manzoor Ahmed, Symeon Chatzinotas, Björn Ottersten, and Petar Popovski. Opportunities for physical layer security in UAV communication enhanced with intelligent reflective surfaces. *IEEE Wireless Communications*, 29(6):22–28, 2022.
34. Yuhua Su, Xiaowei Pang, Shanzhi Chen, Xu Jiang, Nan Zhao, and F Richard Yu. Spectrum and energy efficiency optimization in IRS-assisted UAV networks. *IEEE Transactions on Communications*, 70(10):6489–6502, 2022.
35. Hazim Shakhatreh, Ahmad Sawalmeh, Ali H Alenezi, Sharief Abdel-Razeq, and Ala Al-Fuqaha. Mobile-IRS assisted next generation UAV communication networks. *Computer Communications*, 215:51–61, 2024.

36. Sota Yamamoto, Jin Nakazato, and Gia Khanh Tran. Multi-IRS-Assisted mmWave UAV-BS Network for Coverage Extension. *Sensors*, 24(6):2006, 2024.
37. Wei Zheng and Leibing Yan. Latency minimization for IRS-assisted mobile edge computing networks. *Physical Communication*, 53:101768, 2022.
38. Baogang Li, Jia Liao, Wenjing Wu, and Yonghui Li. Intelligent Reflecting Surface Assisted Secure Computation of Wireless Powered MEC System. *IEEE Transactions on Mobile Computing*, 23(4):3048–3059, 2024.
39. Chao Sun, Wei Ni, Zhiyong Bu, and Xin Wang. Energy minimization for intelligent reflecting surface-assisted mobile edge computing. *IEEE Transactions on Wireless Communications*, 21(8):6329–6344, 2022.
40. Baofeng Ji, Jingjing Zhang, Ying Wang, Jianghui Liu, and Weixing Wang. Achievable Rate Maximization for IRS Assisted System with Relay Cooperation of IoT Network. *IEEE Transactions on Consumer Electronics*, 2023.
41. Mengying Sun, Xiaodong Xu, Xiaofeng Tao, and Ping Zhang. Large-scale user-assisted multi-task online offloading for latency reduction in D2D-enabled heterogeneous networks. *IEEE Transactions on Network Science and Engineering*, 7(4):2456–2467, 2020.
42. Zhifeng Hou, Yuzhen Huang, Jin Chen, Guoxin Li, Xinrong Guan, Yifan Xu, Runfeng Chen, and Yuhua Xu. Joint IRS Selection and Passive Beamforming in Multiple IRS-UAV-Enhanced Anti-Jamming D2D Communication Networks. *IEEE Internet of Things Journal*, 10(22):19558–19569, 2023.
43. Fangmin Xu, Zhijian Ye, Haiyan Cao, and Zhirui Hu. Sum-rate optimization for irs-aided d2d communication underlaying cellular networks. *IEEE Access*, 10:48499–48509, 2022.
44. Qingsong Chen, Yinping Zhou, Weiyang Xu, and Yucheng Wu. Energy-Efficient Resource Allocation for IRS-Assisted SWIPT-enabled D2D Communications with Imperfect CSI. *IEEE Communications Letters*, 2024.
45. Hanwen Cao, Mate Boban, and Josef Eichinger. Terahertz communications enhanced by IRS. In *2021 IEEE 32nd Annual International Symposium on Personal, Indoor and Mobile Radio Communications (PIMRC)*, pages 1–5. IEEE, 2021.
46. Jingping Qiao and Mohamed-Slim Alouini. Secure transmission for intelligent reflecting surface-assisted mmWave and terahertz systems. *IEEE Wireless Communications Letters*, 9(10):1743–1747, 2020.
47. Jingping Qiao, Chuanting Zhang, Anming Dong, Ji Bian, and Mohamed-Slim Alouini. Securing intelligent reflecting surface assisted terahertz systems. *IEEE Transactions on Vehicular Technology*, 71(8):8519–8533, 2022.
48. Yijin Pan, Kezhi Wang, Cunhua Pan, Huiling Zhu, and Jiangzhou Wang. Sum-rate maximization for intelligent reflecting surface assisted terahertz communications. *IEEE Transactions on Vehicular Technology*, 71(3):3320–3325, 2022.
49. Xiaoling Hu, Junwei Wang, and Caijun Zhong. Statistical CSI based design for intelligent reflecting surface assisted MISO systems. *Science China Information Sciences*, 63:1–10, 2020.
50. Hong Ren, Kezhi Wang, and Cunhua Pan. Intelligent Reflecting Surface-Aided URLLC in a Factory Automation Scenario. *IEEE Transactions on Communications*, 70(1):707–723, 2022.
51. Debbarni Sarkar, Vipin Pal, Satyendra Singh Yadav, and Sarat Kumar Patra. IRS-Aided NOMA-based Communication Architecture for 6G Wireless Networks: An Enhanced Error-Control and Reliable Data Transmission. *Physical Communication*, 2024.
52. Arthur S. de Sena, Dick Carrillo, Fang Fang, Pedro H. J. Nardelli, Daniel B. da Costa, Ugo S. Dias, Zhiguo Ding, Constantinos B. Papadias, and Walid Saad. What Role Do Intelligent Reflecting Surfaces Play in Multi-Antenna Non-Orthogonal Multiple Access? *IEEE Wireless Communications*, 27(5):24–31, 2020.
53. Debbarni Sarkar, Satyendra Singh Yadav, Vipin Pal, Yogita, and Neeraj Kumar. Intelligent Reflecting Surface Aided NOMA-HARQ Based IoT Framework for Future Wireless Networks. *IEEE Transactions on Vehicular Technology*, 72(5):6268–6280, 2023.
54. Zhiguo Ding, Lu Lv, Fang Fang, Octavia A Dobre, George K Karagiannidis, Naofal Al-Dhahir, Robert Schober, and H Vincent Poor. A state-of-the-art survey on reconfigurable intelligent surface-assisted non-orthogonal multiple access networks. *Proceedings of the IEEE*, 110(9):1358–1379, 2022.

55. Beixiong Zheng, Changsheng You, Weidong Mei, and Rui Zhang. A survey on channel estimation and practical passive beamforming design for intelligent reflecting surface aided wireless communications. *IEEE Communications Surveys & Tutorials*, 24(2):1035–1071, 2022.
56. Tao Jiang, Hei Victor Cheng, and Wei Yu. Learning to reflect and to beamform for intelligent reflecting surface with implicit channel estimation. *IEEE Journal on Selected Areas in Communications*, 39(7):1931–1945, 2021.
57. Xiaoling Hu, Caijun Zhong, Mohamed-Slim Alouini, and Zhaoyang Zhang. Robust Design for IRS-Aided Communication Systems With User Location Uncertainty. *IEEE Wireless Communications Letters*, 10(1):63–67, 2021.
58. Boyu Ning, Zhi Chen, Wenjie Chen, and Jun Fang. Beamforming optimization for intelligent reflecting surface assisted mimo: A sum-path-gain maximization approach. *IEEE Wireless Communications Letters*, 9(7):1105–1109, 2020.
59. Samith Abeywickrama, Rui Zhang, Qingqing Wu, and Chau Yuen. Intelligent reflecting surface: Practical phase shift model and beamforming optimization. *IEEE Transactions on Communications*, 68(9):5849–5863, 2020.
60. Mevan Wijewardena, Tharaka Samarasinghe, Kasun T Hemachandra, Saman Atapattu, and Jamie S Evans. Physical layer security for intelligent reflecting surface assisted two–way communications. *IEEE Communications Letters*, 25(7):2156–2160, 2021.
61. Lianhong Zhang, Shiwei Lai, Junjuan Xia, Chongzhi Gao, Dahua Fan, and Jianghong Ou. Deep reinforcement learning based IRS-assisted mobile edge computing under physical-layer security. *Physical Communication*, 55:101896, 2022.
62. Zhangyu Liu, Ji Wang, Hao Jiang, Jun Wang, Xingwang Li, and Wenwu Xie. Physical Layer Security Performance Analysis of IRS-Aided Cognitive Radio Networks. *Electronics*, 12(12):2615, 2023.
63. Yiming Liu, Erwu Liu, and Rui Wang. Energy efficiency analysis of intelligent reflecting surface system with hardware impairments. In *GLOBECOM 2020-2020 IEEE Global Communications Conference*, pages 1–6. IEEE, 2020.
64. Qingqing Wu, Shuowen Zhang, Beixiong Zheng, Changsheng You, and Rui Zhang. Intelligent reflecting surface-aided wireless communications: A tutorial. *IEEE Transactions on Communications*, 69(5):3313–3351, 2021.
65. Marzieh Najafi, Vahid Jamali, Robert Schober, and H. Vincent Poor. Physics-based modeling and scalable optimization of large intelligent reflecting surfaces. *IEEE Transactions on Communications*, 69(4):2673–2691, 2021.
66. Yu Liu, Ibrahim Al-Nahhal, Octavia A. Dobre, and Fanggang Wang. Deep-Learning Channel Estimation for IRS-Assisted Integrated Sensing and Communication System. *IEEE Transactions on Vehicular Technology*, 72(5):6181–6193, 2023.
67. Yi Wei, Ming-Min Zhao, An Liu, and Min-Jian Zhao. Channel tracking and prediction for IRS-aided wireless communications. *IEEE Transactions on Wireless Communications*, 22(1):563–579, 2022.
68. Wencai Yan, Gangcan Sun, Wanming Hao, Zhengyu Zhu, Zheng Chu, and Pei Xiao. Machine learning-based beamforming design for millimeter wave IRS communications with discrete phase shifters. *IEEE wireless communications letters*, 11(12):2467–2471, 2022.
69. Chang Liu, Xuemeng Liu, Zhiqiang Wei, Shaokang Hu, Derrick Wing Kwan Ng, and Jinhong Yuan. Deep Learning-Empowered Predictive Beamforming for IRS-Assisted Multi-User Communications. In *2021 IEEE Global Communications Conference (GLOBECOM)*, pages 01–07, 2021.
70. Yongjun Ahn and Byonghyo Shim. Deep Learning-Based Beamforming for Intelligent Reflecting Surface-Assisted mmWave Systems. In *2021 International Conference on Information and Communication Technology Convergence (ICTC)*, pages 1731–1734, 2021.
71. Sohail Ahmad, Saud Khan, Komal S. Khan, Faisal Naeem, and Muhammad Tariq. Resource Allocation for IRS-Assisted Networks: A Deep Reinforcement Learning Approach. *IEEE Communications Standards Magazine*, 7(3):48–55, 2023.
72. Wei Wang and Wei Zhang. Intelligent reflecting surface configurations for smart radio using deep reinforcement learning. *IEEE Journal on Selected Areas in Communications*, 40(8):2335–2346, 2022.

73. Yuan Liu, Fengxia Han, and Shengjie Zhao. Flexible and reliable multiuser SWIPT IoT network enhanced by UAV-mounted intelligent reflecting surface. *IEEE Transactions on Reliability*, 71(2):1092–1103, 2022.
74. Shivani Dhok, Prasanna Raut, Prabhat Kumar Sharma, Keshav Singh, and Chih-Peng Li. Non-Linear Energy Harvesting in RIS-Assisted URLLC Networks for Industry Automation. *IEEE Transactions on Communications*, 69(11):7761–7774, 2021.
75. Umer Saeed, Syed Aziz Shah, Muhammad Zakir Khan, Abdullah Alhumaidi Alotaibi, Turke Althobaiti, Naeem Ramzan, and Qammer H Abbasi. Intelligent reflecting surface-based non-LOS human activity recognition for next-generation 6G-enabled healthcare system. *Sensors*, 22(19):7175, 2022.
76. Baofeng Ji, Yanan Wang, Ling Xing, Chunguo Li, Yi Wang, and Hong Wen. IRS-driven cyber-security of healthcare cyber physical systems. *IEEE Transactions on Network Science and Engineering*, 10(5):2564–2573, 2022.
77. Hongyu Li, Shanpu Shen, and Bruno Clerckx. Beyond Diagonal Reconfigurable Intelligent Surfaces: A Multi-Sector Mode Enabling Highly Directional Full-Space Wireless Coverage. *IEEE Journal on Selected Areas in Communications*, 41(8):2446–2460, 2023.
78. Yuanbin Chen, Ying Wang, Jiayi Zhang, Ping Zhang, and Lajos Hanzo. Reconfigurable intelligent surface (ris)-aided vehicular networks: Their protocols, resource allocation, and performance. *IEEE Vehicular Technology Magazine*, 17(2):26–36, 2022.

Cell-Free Massive MIMO for Future Generation Wireless Networks

Tasher Ali Sheikh, Shadab Haque, Mancharla Ravi, Anil Kumar Shaw, and Janmoni Borah

1 Introduction

In the upcoming days, future wireless networks will have to manage billions of devices all at once; where each terminal would demand high throughput to support many applications such as voice, real-time video, high-quality movies, etc. Cellular networks could not handle such large connections since user terminals at the cell boundary suffer from very high interference and therefore perform badly [1]. Furthermore, conventional cellular systems are designed mainly for human users. In future wireless networks, machine-type communications such as the Internet of Things, Internet of Everything, Smart X, massive device-to-device (D2D) and machine-to-machine (M2M) communications, etc. are expected to play an important role. The main challenge of machine-type communications is scalable and efficient connectivity for billions of devices. Centralized technology with cellular topologies does not seem to work in such scenarios, as each cell can cover a limited number of user terminals [1]. So why not cell-free (CF) structures with decentralized technology? Of course, to serve many user terminals and to simplify signal processing in a distributed manner, M-MIMO technology should be included. The overlay of the CF structure

T. A. Sheikh (✉) · A. K. Shaw
Assam down town University), Panikhaiti, Guwahati, Assam 781026, India
e-mail: tasher.ece@gmail.com

S. Haque
Department of Electrical and Computer Engineering, Virginia Tech, Virginia, USA

M. Ravi
Department of Electronics and Communication Engineering, KL University, Vaddeswaram, Vijayawada, Andhra Pradesh 522501, India

J. Borah
Madanapalle Institute of Technology and Science (Deemed to be University), Madanapalle, Andhra Pradesh, India

T. Ojha et al. (eds.), *Edge-Enabled 6G Networking*,
https://doi.org/10.1007/978-3-032-19042-0_4

and the M-MIMO technology yields the new concept, which is called CF M-MIMO. Recently, CF M-MIMO has been introduced as a practical and useful embodiment of the MIMO concept [28] of the network. In CF M-MIMO, a large number of Access Points (APs) are equipped with single or multiple antennas and distributed over a large area, coherently serving a large number of users in the same time-frequency resource.

In CF M-MIMO networks, all APs cooperate via a backhaul network, exchanging information with a central processing unit (CPU). As traditional M-MIMO [22], CF M-MIMO takes advantage of favorable propagation and channel hardening properties when the number of APs is large to multiplex many users in the same time-frequency resource with small interuser interference (IUI). Thus, it can offer a large SE with simple signal processing. More importantly, in a CF M-MIMO configuration, the service antennas are brought close to the users, which produces a high degree of macrodiversity and low path losses [28]; therefore, many users can be served simultaneously with a uniformly good quality of service (QoS). Furthermore, in [28], it was shown that CF M-MIMO has significantly better performance than conventional small cell systems, where each user is served by a single AP. For these reasons, CF M-MIMO is considered energy efficiency (EE), promising technology for next-generation wireless systems. However, despite its potential, in addition to [28], there is fairly little work on CF M-MIMO available in the literature. In [26], the performance of the CF M-MIMO with zero forcing (ZF) processing was analyzed, under the assumption that all pilot sequences assigned to users were mutually orthogonal. CF M-MIMO with beam-formed downlink training was investigated in [16]. The conclusion is that by beamforming the pilots, the performance of the CF M-MIMO downlink can be substantially improved. A compute and forward approach for CF M-MIMO was proposed and analyzed in [12] to reduce backhaul load. All the above-cited works assumed that the APs have only a single antenna. However, APs can be equipped with multiple antennas to increase diversity and array gains, as well as to reduce backhaul requirements. In addition, while it is well known that traditional M-MIMO is EE [7], it is not yet clear how good the EE of CF M-MIMO is. The argument is that in CF M-MIMO, more backhaul links are required, which potentially increase total power consumption to such a level that it can overwhelm SE gains.

In [18, 23], provide an overview of current research efforts on CF M-MIMO systems and their promising future application scenarios. In article [40], study the paradigm of massive MIMO communications mobile CF, including the main deployment architectures and associated application scenarios. Furthermore, exploit a novel predictor antenna, hierarchical cancelation, rate-splitting, and dynamic clustering system for mobile CF massive MIMO. In [29], we present a comprehensive survey of state-of-the-art research on CF M-MIMO and ultradense networks. Furthermore, discuss the key challenges of CF M-MIMO in ultradense scenarios such as low-complexity architecture and processing, low-complexity/scalable resource allocation, fronthaul limitation, massive access, synchronization, and channel acquisition. Inspired by the above points, the contribution of this paper is concise as follows.

- We provide an overview of the concept of CF M-MIMO in contemporary research on this topic.
- The substantial benefits of CF M-MIMO systems are quantified, and a range of open challenges issues are described.

The remainder of this paper is organized as follows. In Sect. 2, we have discussed the system model of the CF M-MIMO networks. In Sect. 3, we have explored the mechanism of CF M-MIMO networks. Section 4 discusses the signal processing techniques that are found to be suitable for CF M-MIMO technology in detail. The technological advancement of CF M-MIMO technology over traditional M-MIMO networks is discussed in Sect. 5. In Sect. 6 the advantages/benefits of CF M-MIMO networks are briefly explained. The transmission protocol, challenges, and possible research direction are described in Sects. 7 and 8, respectively. The feasibility of CF M-MIMO system design in a pre-existing environment is described in Sect. 9 and concluding remarks are given in Sect. 10.

2 CF M-MIMO System Model

Let us consider M single antenna APs, randomly distributed in a large area without boundaries, which simultaneously serve N single antenna users, $M > N$, by operating in the TDD mode shown in Fig. 1. All APs cooperate through a backhaul network and exchange information with a CPU. Only payload data and power control coefficients are exchanged. Each AP locally acquires channel state information (CSI) and precodes data signals without sharing CSI with the other APs. The time-frequency resources are divided into coherence intervals of length τ symbols. The channel is assumed to be static within a coherence interval, and it varies independently between each coherence interval.

Let g_{mn} denotes the channel coefficient between the nth user and the mth AP, defined as

$$g_{mn} = \sqrt{\beta_{mn}}\mathbf{h}_{mn}, \tag{1}$$

where β_{mn} is the large-scale fading (LSF) coefficient which accounts for path loss and shadowing effects. This coefficient changes slowly and hence can be learned and tracked. Unlike co-located systems, LSF is different for every pair of APs and users in the CF M-MIMO networks. The second factor $\mathbf{h}_{mn}$ $\mathbb{CN}(0, 1)$ is the small-scale fading (SSF) coefficient. We assume that these coefficients are independent and identically distributed (i.i.d.) random variables. We will use the block-fading model, that is, we assume that $\mathbf{h}_{mn}$ $(1 \leq m \leq M; 1 \leq n \leq N)$ stay constant during a coherent interval and are independent in different coherent intervals. We will assume channel reciprocity, that is, the channel coefficients for uplink and downlink transmissions are the same. The channel matrix between all antennas and users is denoted by $G \in \mathbb{C}^{(M \times N)}$.

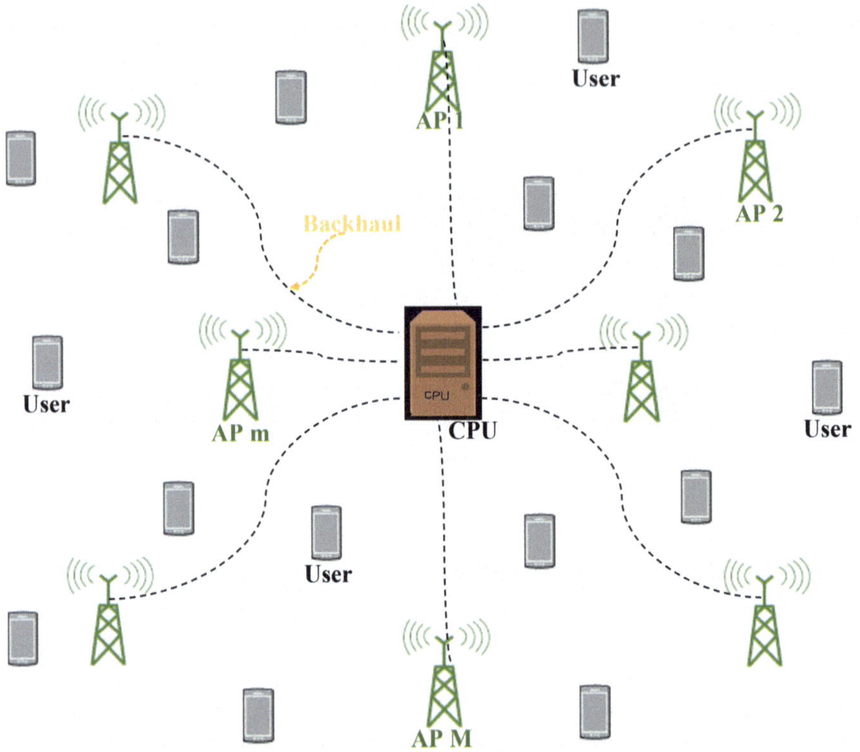

Fig. 1 CF M-MIMO network

The downlink system $SINR_n^{cellfree}$ of the CF M-MIMO network is calculated with the help of conjugal beamforming (CB) precoding from (1) under the assumption of estimating the minimum mean square error (MMSE) based on the orthogonal uplink pilot signal.

$$SINR_n^{cellfree} = \frac{\rho_d \left(\sum_{m=1}^{M} \sqrt{\alpha_{m,n}\eta_{m,n}}\right)^2}{1 + \rho_d \sum_{m=1}^{M} \beta_{m,n} \sum_{n'=1}^{N} \eta_{m,n'}}, \tag{2}$$

where,

$$\alpha_{m,n} = \frac{\rho_u \tau \beta_{m,n}^2}{1 + \rho_u \tau \beta_{m,n}} \tag{3}$$

where $\alpha_{m,n}$ is the mean square of the channel estimate, and ρ_u and ρ_d are the SNR uplink and downlink, respectively. The length of the pilot signal is τ sent by the user terminal which is used to estimate the channel. The $\beta_{m,n}$ represents the large-scale fading coefficient that accounts for path loss and shadowing effects. The downlink power control is represented with $\eta_{m,n}$ that is subjected to per AP power constraint which is express as below:

$$\sum_{n'=1}^{N} \eta_{m,n'} \leq 1, \forall m \in M \tag{4}$$

3 How Cell-Free Massive MIMO Works

In CF M-MIMO, the TDD operation is preferable and suitable. The TDD coherence interval is divided into four phases: uplink training, uplink payload data transmission, downlink training, and downlink payload data transmission, which are depicted in Fig. 2a–d.

In the uplink training phase, users synchronously send their pilot sequences to the APs and each AP estimates the channels to all users. The channel estimates are used by the APs to perform uplink signal detection and to beamform pilots and data during the downlink training phase and the downlink data transmission phase, respectively. The uplink training length corresponds to the pilot's length.

In uplink data transmission, each user sends its data symbol s_k to all APs, where $E\{|s_k|^2\} = 1$. s_k are mutually independent and independent of the noise and channel coefficients. The maximum transmit power is denoted by ρ_u. The user k transmits a fraction of $\triangleright_u$, determined by the power control coefficient $0 \leq \eta_k \leq 1$.

As the above state in CF M-MIMO TDD operation is preferred, therefore, by exploiting the perfect channel reciprocity, the estimates are then used in the downlink training to perform conjugate beamforming. The users decode the data relying only on the statistical CSI. For downlink data transmission, let q_k be the data symbol intended for user k and $E\{|q_k|^2\} = 1$. q_k are mutually independent and independent of the noise and channel coefficients. AP m serves k users by precoding the data symbol with the conjugate beamforming of the related channel estimate.

4 Signal Processing Technique in CF M-MIMO

In CF M-MIMO networks, choosing an appropriate signal processing technique is the most important issue. This signal processing must be very simple and different from conventional M-MIMO systems in terms of practical constraints, channel fading model, and configurations.

Fig. 2 **a** Uplink training. **b** Uplink payload data transmission. **c** Downlink training. **d** Downlink payload data transmission

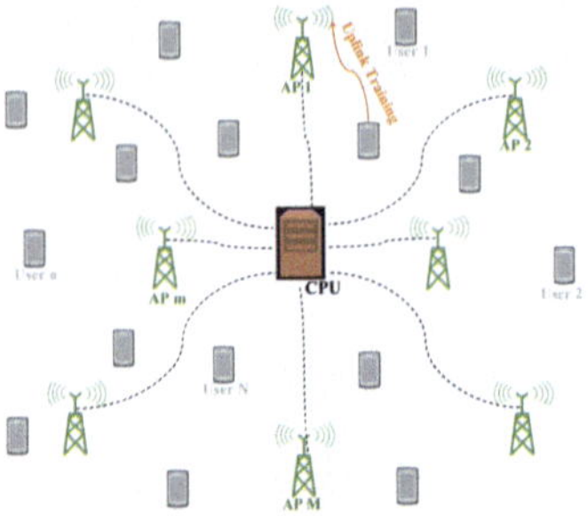

(a) Uplink training

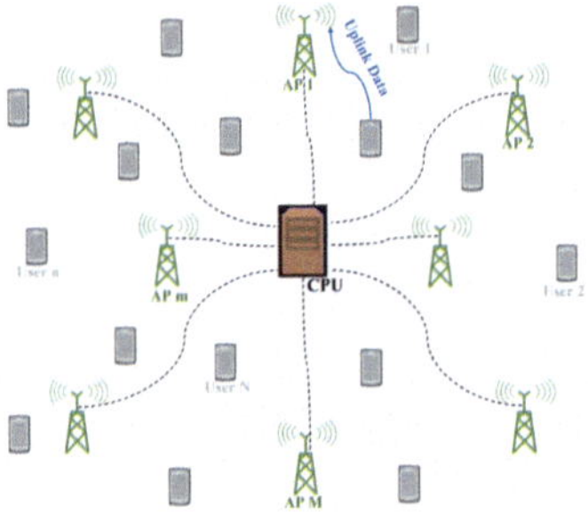

(b) Uplink Payload Data Transmission

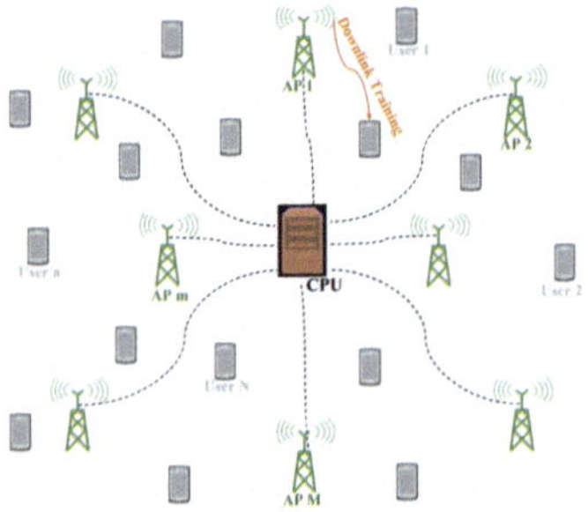

(c) Downlink Training

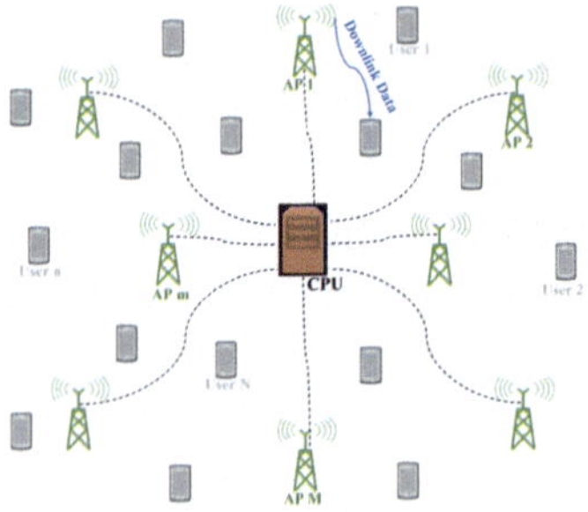

(d) Downlink Payload Data Transmission

4.1 Channel Estimation

For supporting efficient signal detection and precoding schemes to decrease IUI, accurate channel estimation is the most important concern in CF M-MIMO networks. To estimate the channel in the uplink, all users send pilot sequences to all distributed APs. In [9], it has advocated that channel hardening does not always offer benefits. Upon simply using $E\mathbf{h}_{mn}$, performance has degraded, therefore instantaneous channel gains are h_{mn} fluctuating. In [16], a downlink training method with a power control scheme based on a max-min fairnes has been proposed that significantly increases achievable throughput. The study of a non-orthogonal downlink pilot with efficient pilot assignments algorithm needs to be studied in the future to improve the number of users served. In [15], it has been shown that, from the primary study and analysis, downlink-based training can significantly improve SE with low pilot overhead. In [30], it was also noticed that the blind algorithm with downlink pilot and channel estimation may perform better in the CF M-MIMO network.

4.2 Signal Detection in Uplink

The users sent their uplink data signals to the APs during the uplink signal detection phase. Fully or partially centralizing uplink processing on the CPU could magnificently enhance the SE advocated in [26]. In this context for uplink signal detection, four different levels of cooperation have been introduced [6]. With uplink receiver weighted coefficient vector optimization, the CPU can maximize the SE with the aid of channel statics. In a cellular M-MIMO system, this strategy is called LSF decoding (LSFD) [2]. In this study, it is also shown that the SE with LSFD is much better than the maximum ratio (MR) receiver in CF M-MIMO systems. In [5], it is explored that the rate of uplink users is significantly enhanced by optimizing the receiver filter coefficient on the CPU. However, the problem with this technique is non-convex and the computational complexity is very high. Therefore, it is impractical to implement it in the CF M-MIMO network. Therefore, it is an open challenge for researchers to design optimal and low-complexity distributed uplink signal detection schemes in CF M-MIMO networks.

5 What Difference in CF M-MIMO from Conventional M-MIMO?

CF M-MIMO is different from distributed M-MIMO [16]. Both systems use many service antennas in a distributed way to serve many user terminals, but they are not entirely the same. The distinction between CF M-MIMO and conventional distributed M-MIMO [12] is the number of antennas involved in coherently serving a given user. In canonical CF M-MIMO, every antenna serves every user. The conventional M-MIMO system has a cell boundary, but in CF M-MIMO systems there is no concept of cell or cell boundaries. Compared to traditional M-MIMO, CF M-MIMO has the potential to improve coverage and EE due to increased macro-diversity gain [16]. Moreover, CF M-MIMO reaps all benefits obtained from M-MIMO and network MIMO, and hence is expected to offer many advantages compared with conventional wireless systems such as huge data throughput, EE, and high coverage probability. Cellular M-MIMO benefits from spatial interference suppression and channel hardening, but cell edge users can have poor channel conditions. However, CF M-MIMO benefits from strong macro-diversity but its interference suppression ability highly depends on how it is operated. Thus, CF M-MIMO is a disruptive technology for next-generation densified wireless systems. Figure 3a, b compare the structures of CF M-MIMO and distributed M-MIMO.

6 Benefits of Cell-Free Massive MIMO

The significant features of CF M-MIMO over traditional cellular M-MIMO networks are strong multi-user interference suppression and macro-diversity capabilities. In this technology, usually, there are a huge number of serving APs around the users, and hence there is a high probability that it may have very good channel conditions. Therefore, the throughput and capacity of a system are significantly enhanced. The main benefits of the CF M-MIMO technology are presented in Table 1 and some of them are discussed in detail below.

Figure 4 compares cellular M-MIMO and CF M-MIMO with $L = 400$ and $N = 1$. The figure shows the cumulative distribution function (CDF) of the SE of a randomly located UE, when combining MMSE or L-MMSE in the cell-free cases. At the 90% or 95% likely SE points i.e., where the vertical axis is 0.1 or 0.05), the cell-free cases perform according to their level: Level 4 provides by far the highest SEs, while Level 1 gives the lowest SEs but is anyway preferable as compared to Cellular M-MIMO. Looking at the complete CDF curves, the situation is more complicated since the Level 1 and Cellular M-MIMO curves are crossing the Level 2 and Level 3 curves. Hence, UEs with good channel conditions get better performance with these methods. However, Level 4 performs better than Cellular M-MIMO for every UE [6].

Figure 5 considers the case $L = 400$, $N = 1$ and MR combining, which is the receiver processing on CF M-MIMO. More precisely, Level 2 was considered in [28], and Level 3 in [24]. Poor processing leads to a large SE loss, compared to Fig. 4, for all levels of CF M-MIMO receiver cooperation, except level 1. In fact, Level 2 is outperformed by both small cells (Level 1) and Cellular M-MIMO for every UE.

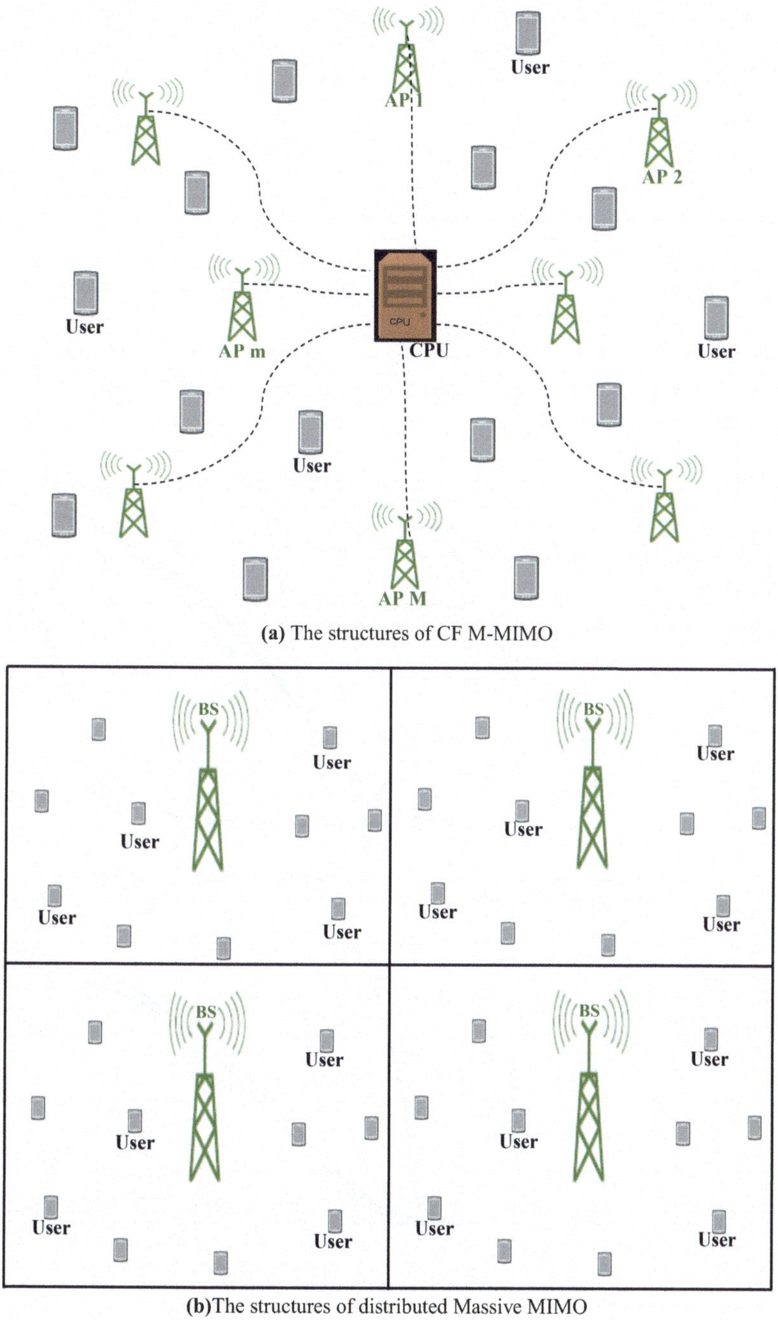

Fig. 3 **a** The structures of CF M-MIMO. **b** The structures of distributed massive MIMO

Table 1 Comparison between Network MIMO, Centralized M-MIMO, and CF M-MIMO

Architecture	Network	Centralized	Cell-free
Number of antennas	Moderate	Large	Large
Macro diversity	Moderate	Small	Large
Interference suppression capacity	Moderate	Weak	Very strong
Coverage area	Moderate	Bad	Good
Favorable propagation	Weak	Strong	Moderate
Channel estimation	Global	Global	Local
Channel hardening	Weak	Strong	Moderate
Front-haul resource	Large	Small	Moderate
Energy efficiency	Small	Large	Very large
Implementation cost	High	High	Low

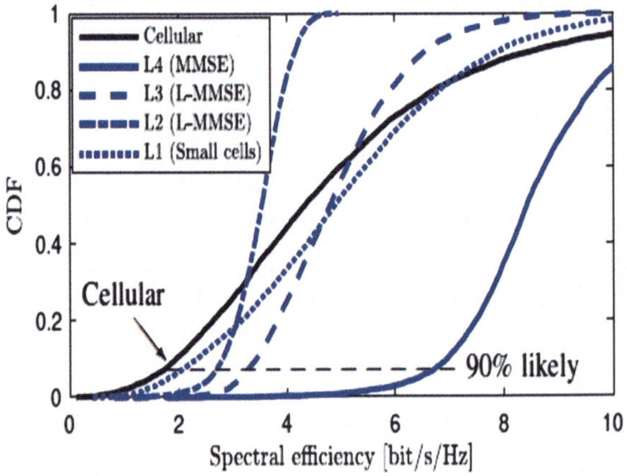

Fig. 4 Comparison of cellular M-MIMO and CF M-MIMO (L = 400, N = 1) when using MMSE or L-MMSE combining

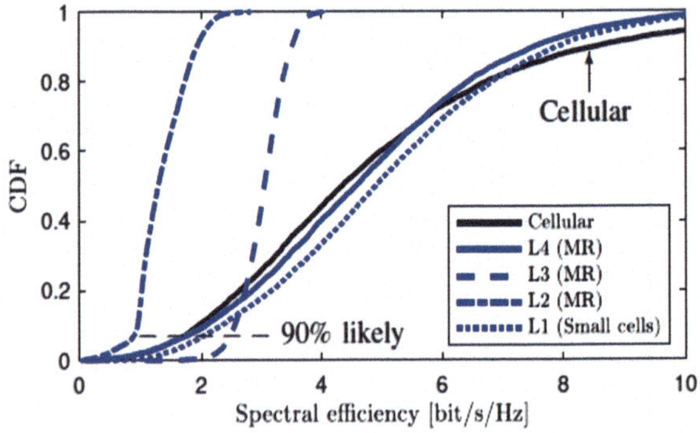

Fig. 5 Comparison of cellular M-MIMO with CF M-MIMO (L = 400, N = 1) when using MR combining

6.1 Takes Advantages of Favorable Propagation and Channel Hardening

To some extent, M-MIMO technology based on favorable propagation and channel hardening properties is used in the CF M-MIMO network [36]. This technology offers favorable propagation channels, and hence, all users can share the same time-frequency resource with a not very high IUI. In this technology, synchronization can be done locally.

In CF M-MIMO, the channel still hardens but is not as good as the channel in collocated M-MIMO in terms of hardening property. In fact, in [28], the signal processing in users is done relying on the channel hardening property. The performance of the system is still very good. Furthermore, a downlink pilot can be sent via a beamforming training scheme to improve system performance. Note that the corresponding channel overhead for this downlink pilot scheme does not depend on the number of APs. Furthermore, in CF M-MIMO, the large number of APs is distributed over a wide area, and many APs are very far from a given user; therefore, each user is effectively served by a smaller number of APs [11, 20]. As a result, channel hardening is less pronounced than in M-MIMO, and the potential gain from using downlink pilots is larger. So channel hardening is not a problem for CF M-MIMO [9].

6.2 Flexible and Low Implementation Cost

In CF M-MIMO the APs have very few antennas. Therefore, it can be easily accommodated in space constraint environment. This environment like traffic lights mounted on lampposts, offices, smart factories, train stations, shopping malls, stadiums, subways, hospitals, community centers, and college campuses, etc. This means that CF M-MIMO gives a substantial improvement in EE. In [17], a cost analysis of cell-free massive MIMO and building a unified model with varying numbers of antennas per AP. Their objective was to explore whether employing multi-antenna APs could reduce system costs while maintaining performance. In addition, they analyze and evaluate the result in the identification of a cost-effective design for a cell-free massive MIMO, providing valuable insight for practical implementation. These characteristics of this network could be implemented and operated at a very low cost. Therefore, this technology is considered the EE solution for next-generation wireless technology.

6.3 It Is Energy Efficiency Technology

The CF M-MIMO is much more EE than the traditional M-MIMO system if employed with some adequate power control strategy. In this technology a great increase in radiated EE might be due to two causes. The first cause is that it is well-known fact that in the CF M-MIMO configuration the service antennas are brought close to the users, which yields a high degree of macro-diversity and low path losses leading to the cellular M-MIMO configuration. The second cause is that it is a surprising fact that in CF M-MIMO a large number of AP's do not transmit with max-min power control with full power. In [34] the EE of cellular M-MIMO and CF M-MIMO with lab demo. It is also seen that in suburban and rural areas the radiated EE is double and the per-user throughput is also increasing to 95% in CF M-MIMO with the same time-frequency resource [31, 32]. In an urban scenario, the radiate EE gain is moderate. It is also shown that CF M-MIMO with max-min power control is naturally EE without losing any SE. However, searching for max-min power control for the CF M-MIMO network is a time-consuming process. In this technology, a faster algorithm is immediately needed. To maximize global downlink EE in the paper [3], the authors have proposed an optimal power allocation algorithm for CF M-MIMO mmWave networks. The radiated EE of the CF M-MIMO system $EE^{cell-free}$ is express as:

$$EE^{cell-free} = \frac{B \sum_{n=1}^{N} \log(1 + SINR_n^{cell-free})}{P_d \sum_{m=1}^{M} \sum_{n'=1}^{K} \eta_{m,n'}}, \tag{5}$$

where the per AP downlink radiated power is P_d, carrier spectral bandwidth is B, signal to interference plus noise ration of the CF M-MIMO is $SINR_n^{cell-free}$ for n user and $\eta_{m,n'}$ is denote the sum of the power control coefficients from antenna m to user n', which is the optimization parameter in power allocation and adjusts each antenna's transmit power.

6.4 Increases the Coverage Range

It is already discussed that in the CF M-MIMO network there is a huge number of APs installed in the large geographic area. Using a larger number of CPUs and APs can extend the service area with this technology [13]. However, for a highly large dimension of CF M-MIMO networks, it is infeasible to connect all APs with single CPUs to serve a single user jointly and simultaneously. In [14], the authors proposed a distributed and scalable CF M-MIMO framework in which it is considered that the disjoint cluster of APs can serve by multiple CPUs. This scalable nature of CF M-MIMO can reduce the data payload in the fronthaul and enhance each user's SE. Therefore, this technology can enhance the coverage range.

6.5 *It Uniformly Maintains the Quality of Services (QoS)*

A huge number of APs are deployed in the CF M-MIMO network; therefore, the average distances between the closest APs and arbitrary users are substantially reduced. As in this technology only one and the closest APs are served to the users, hence this technology performs better. In this technology, when shadow fading is uncorrelated, user-per-user throughput is enhanced up to 95% compared to a small cell network [35]. Moreover, under the condition of correlated shadow fading, the performance improvement is achieved up to tenfold with this technology. Hence, this technology can be used to provide enhanced service to all users across the entire network. Moreover, with the aid of the max-min power control algorithm in CF M-MIMO networks regardless of the geographic area of the user, the same good quality of services is provided to all users.

7 Transmission Protocol in CF M-MIMO

7.1 *Transmit Precoding*

For exchanging the payload data in CF M-MIMO networks connected all APs to the CPU via the fronthaul network. In this network, by exploiting a large number of APs in large-scale systems, the performance of EE is neglected in maximum cases in terms of bit/Joule is a major figure of merit. Therefore, it is important to design precoding techniques to improve system performance and EE. This technology can be designed with simple linear processing such as ZF and CB. It is examined that very low complexity CB [4] or maximum ratio transmit (MRT) pre-processing [28] is highly suitable for CF M-MIMO networks for enhancing the SE. As in this technology, transmit precoding is done locally by APs rather than at the CPU [28]. ZF processing has higher deployment complexity with higher backhaul requirements, but can handle the IUI. In contrast, the CB scheme is very simple and has low backhaul requirements. But it suffers from high IUI. Hence, it is of high importance to find and design optimal precoding schemes to provide higher system performance with low fronthaul requirements.

7.2 *Transmit Decoding*

The same as in cellular M-MIMO, either implemented centrally for the entire system or on a per-AP basis. In this technology, the non linear successive interference cancelation (SIC) method is used in CF M-MIMO, which means that the CPU decodes one user signal at a time, and then sequentially suppresses interference that the decoded signal caused to the remaining signals. The interference cannot be fully canceled since the CPU has an imperfect CSI, but it can still improve the SE of the users compared to the linear combination [6].

7.3 Pilot Contamination Effect

In CF M-MIMO systems, the length of the coherence interval (τ) is limited. Therefore, the non-orthogonal pilot sequences must be used by the different users. Moreover, in CF M-MIMO networks, the same pilot signals are assigned to multiple users. Hence, the performance of channel estimation is degraded due to the pilot signal transmitted from other users. This leads to pilot contamination effects between users served by a particular AP. This causes called the pilot contamination effect. To resolve this effect, one usually uses random and greedy pilot assignment schemes which may effectively mitigate this problem in this network. Additionally, using a max-min power control scheme and pairwise orthogonal pilot sequences can also be used in this network to avoid pilot contamination effects significantly.

7.4 Power Control

Power control is usually performed on the LSF time scale and is performed on the CPU of the CF M-MIMO networks. To improve each user's performance and QoS in downlink CF M-MIMO networks, the CPU may use a classical max-min power control algorithm. In [35], it has been explored that the SE achieved per user with accurate power control is much better than the system without power control. It is also explored that all users have almost the same SE under an accurate max-min power control algorithm. However, the bisection algorithm may also be used for the same purpose, but it has a huge implementation complexity. Therefore, an optimal power control algorithm is urgently essential in CF M-MIMO networks that are the hot topic for future research.

7.5 Selection of Access Point

It is found in the literature that all exiting contributions considered that all APs combinedly sent their signals to all users on the CF M-MIMO networks. This is an impractical and power-inefficient consideration. As in this technology, a fraction of APs sent signals to a particular user to their benefit [35]. These networks dynamically allocate a group of APs that has the best channel gain with each user. In [8], has explored that even a very simple channel estimation algorithm, i.e., the selected-APs-based schemes outperform the all-APs-based method in terms of the 95% likely per-user rate. Moreover, in the CF M-MIMO network, a large number of APs are deployed, and hence backhaul power consumption is significantly struck on EE. Additionally, the largest proportion of the total energy utilized is exploit in the APs for data transmission. Transfer of data from the APs and CPU required more backhaul connections. In addition, CSI is acquired in APs through TDD operation and reception of pilot signals sent by the users. In APs multiplexing and de-multiplexing operation is performed on downlink with CB and uplink with match filter. Closed-from expression for individual user's uplink and downlink throughput need power control algorithm for efficient power consumption in APs. Moreover, in this technology network, each user is served by one signle AP. Hence, to reduce this issue, AP selection algorithms are urgently needed. In those cases, the largest LSF selection schemes and the average power-based selection schemes are mostly workable in this technology. The AP selection process is usually done by the users in random order.

7.6 Address the Proper Issue of Handovers

For a sufficiently small time scale, handovers between APs do not occur in CF M-MIMO networks, but for large-scale networks, the concept of time handover is required. For performance analysis in CF M-MIMO networks, a good handover model is necessary. In the future, work may address the issue of handovers in this technology.

8 Challenges and Possible Research Direction of CF M-MIMO

CF M-MIMO can offer enhanced broadband services in future wireless networks. 5G networks are expected to support a wide variety of wireless services in areas ranging from information technology to healthcare, smart homes and cities, manufacturing, military equipment, automotive companies, and many others. This technology can be tailored to support a massive number of Massive Machine Type Communication (MTC) devices. Also, it is an excellent candidate to realize Ultra-Reliable Communication as it can establish very robust physical links. Since CF M-MIMO is a very new research topic, several issues and questions still need to be addressed before rolling it out into practice. Some of the issues include simple signal processing architecture is needed, channel estimation should be very low complexity, the pilot assignment should not be contaminated, efficient power controls architecture, and suitable AP selection schemes, NOMA, shadow fading correlation, mobile scenario analysis, low backhaul constraint, mmWave communication compatible, secure security issue and hardware impairments, etc.

8.1 Non-Orthogonal Multiple Access (NOMA)

Recently, NOMA is considered the most favorable multiple access technology to enhance the SE of a wireless communication system. In CF M-MIMO networks, the distance between APs and users is very minimal. Therefore, when combining the CF M-MIMO concept with NOMA becomes more beneficial. The performance of the CF M-MIMO-NOMA concept has been first addressed in [19]. But so far has not addressed any uplink issues of CF M-MIMO networks. Therefore, in future research, the protocol stack design and performance analysis of such a system should be considered in future research.

8.2 Effect of Shadow Fading Correlation

The spatial correlation and cross-correlation are the two most common exiting correlation models for the shadow fading model, often effects from the user's perspective. The spatial correlation effects signify the correlation due to the relative location between the users. The cross-correlation signifies the correlation between the shadowing coefficients of various BSs with the users [27]. In CF M-MIMO both the users and APs are distributed randomly in the network, and typically they are near each other. Moreover, the elevation of the APs antenna is not very high. Therefore, the correlation of shadow fading on the APs and the users' side must be taken into account for better system performance.

8.3 Mobile Environment Scenarios

In CF M-MIMO networks, most of the previous works are conducted for very low mobility users whose mobility rate is less than 10 Km/h. In a high-mobility environment, the users communicating at a higher rate with a short symbol duration may exceed the coherence interval due to the multipath dispersion. This technology usually has a limited number of pilot signals. Hence, users in each other are unable to reuse the pilot signals in each other's immediate vicinity. This results in the production of the pilot contamination effect that generates excessive interference which may corrupt the channel estimation. Moreover, in high-mobility environments, there may occur significant phase shift of multipath signals. To cope with high vehicular speed, efficient power allocation and a sophisticated transmit precoding algorithm should be designed. One optimal solution for such scenarios is to separate the users into some sub-group based on their different mobility. If the same is done, a few of the APs may choose to serve users associated with high mobility, and the remaining APs serve the rest of the users. On the other hand, the orthogonal pilot signals are allocated for the high mobility users and a long-term statistical CSI is used for low mobility users. Hence, for performance evaluation of CF M-MIMO networks, it is essential to study the effect of phase shift.

8.4 Design Significant Backhaul Constraint

In CF M-MIMO networks, all APs are connected to the CPU through backhaul for data transmission. In it, all APs are connected via perfect backhaul which offers the error-free and infinite capacity to the CPU. In practice, backhaul will be subject to significant practical constraints and costly [21]. Therefore, future work is needed to quantify the impact of backhaul constraints on system performance.

8.5 mmWave Communication

Recently, mmWave communication gains significant attention in research institutions around the world. The frequency range of the mmWave band is 10GHz to 300GHz. For indoor short-range communications as both CF M-MIMO and mmWave communication, techniques are very suitable; hence the implementation is very easy. In CF M-MIMO networks, the users are very close to the APs hence it reduces the path loss. Additionally, this providing macro-diversity gain so decreases the shadow fading effect. It is very beneficial to implement a large number of APs with small antenna arrays to use mmWave with low complexity and hardware cost algorithm. However, due to distributed APs in CF M-MIMO networks, multipath diversity signals are blocked by the obstacle effect of mmWave [3]. Therefore, design of a mmWave CF M-MIMO network should be taken into account for future research. Due to the high bandwidth of the CF M-MIMO network, could possibly deliver a high data rate for which it needs a high backhaul rate. The optimal solution to such a problem is to use wireless cables in lieu of fiber optic cables that also decrease the implementation cost.

8.6 Security in Physical Layer

The security issues in the physical layer play a vital role in next-generation wireless communication networks. It is an extension of the traditional cryptographic security method deployed in the upper layers. The density of users and APs is very high in CF M-MIMO networks, hence the probability to attack confidential information is very high. In the existing literature in very few papers jointly deal with the CF M-MIMO and security in physical layers. As pilot signals and transmission protocol are public, there is a high chance of attacking the network and exploiting the data by smart eavesdroppers. In [38], it has been noticed that in CF M-MIMO networks secrecy performance is degraded due to the eavesdropper pilot spoofing attack. For detecting the pilot spoofing attacks in the paper, [39] has proposed a very efficient and simple minimum description length scheme based on the sub-space dimension of the received signal correlation matrix. The suspicion of eavesdroppers in the CF M-MIMO networks could be suppressed by resolving the power optimization problem [10]. In this concept, the pilot signals assigned to each user must be mutually orthogonal. This concept is not possible to implement practically, as when pilot signals are reused, then the pilot contamination effect arises that reduces the performance of the network. Moreover, exploiting the high correlation of CF M-MIMO networks and separate the networks into groups based on user-centric could be able to suppress the required leaving pilot signals. Therefore, active attack detection schemes are needed for better system performance and error-free data connection.

8.7 Hardware Impairment

Based on the ideal hardware concept in [28] study the basic principle of CF M-MIMO networks. However, with the increase of the number of APs the hardware cost and system power consumption increase drastically. In a practical situation, these are assumed to be bottlenecks in CF M-MIMO networks. Additionally, the limited fronthaul restricts the data traffic coming from APs. Evaluating the effects of realistic imperfect hardware components also requires further research. In [37], it has been shown that when the number of APs increases, the impact of hardware impairments on the APs becomes less severe. Furthermore, [35] also designed hardware impairments by additive white Gaussian noise. Here, we explore that the impact of hardware impairments in APs is more pronounced than in users.

8.8 Prototypes

As the advantages and idea of CF M-MIMO networks have already been confirmed, therefore, the design of a comprehensive hardware prototype of a complex system is a challenging and emerging topic of research for next-generation wireless networks. Initially, it would be very beneficial if conduct the link-level simulation of the networks to pre-checked the design and implementation before going for the final construction of the prototype. As CF M-MIMO works under the philosophy of distributed networks, therefore, the synchronization with the various APs in a precise time and frequency makes the design more challenging. This effect could be handled by deploying trigger and clock signals on the distributed network. When partitioning the whole CF M-MIMO network into some sub-systems then each connects with the most suitable number of APs results in reducing the processing burden of the networks.

9 Will CF M-MIMO Possible to Design Practically?

CF M-MIMO does work in practice? pCell technology [33] is an example of a centralized CF system, demonstrating that it is practically feasible. It has started to be demonstrated to achieve a record average SE of approximately 59.3 bps/Hz in a real-life testbed experiment with 32 APs and 16 users [33]. This demonstration shows an improvement of SE 34.88 times more than cellular 4G systems, yet was achieved in a controlled laboratory environment. In [25] shows that the CF M-MIMO systems give a more than 10-fold significant gain over small-cell systems. Adding more APs and deploying more dedicated hardware could support more simultaneous users and provide higher SE compared to conventional exiting technology [33]. The efficient operation has been validated in a wide range of propagation conditions, including indoor and outdoor situations. The solutions to compensate for the non-reciprocity of front-ends in TDD-based channel estimation have been confirmed to be robust. Recently, the proof was extended to true mobile access: communication with pedestrians and cures can be maintained. These experiments show that channels can be tracked sufficiently fast to spatially multiplex moving users, which is also demonstrated in [33].

In parallel, hardware implementations have progressed very favorably [33]. Mostly, it has been technically proven that CF M-MIMO systems can be built with very low-complexity hardware, both for the digital baseband and the analog RF chains. In addition, innovative architectures and circuits that take advantage of the specific nature of CF M-MIMO systems are being designed. These will further reduce power, cost, and promote an attractive deployment of CF M-MIMO systems for future-generation wireless networks.

10 Conclusion

In this chapter, we have highlighted the state of the art in CF M-MIMO networks and explored their performance characteristics. The most important benefits of CF M-MIMO are that it offers uniform performance to a large coverage area with low power consumption. Furthermore, it offers a higher data rate, EE, and SE. However, further research is required for proper implementation of CF M-MIMO networks, such as perfect signal processing architecture, good APs selection, and a sophisticated power control algorithm are desirable for enhancement of system performance. In our chapter, in the end, we have enlightened some key research issues and directions for the CF M-MIMO network. Those solutions will lead to next-generation wireless networks for quick practical implementation. This chapter may serve as an enlightening guide for future research work in CF M-MIMO networks.

References

1. Cell-Free Massive MIMO: New Concept I Wireless Future Blog, November 2016.
2. Ansuman Adhikary, Alexei Ashikhmin, and Thomas L. Marzetta. Uplink Interference Reduction in Large-Scale Antenna Systems. *IEEE Transactions on Communications*, 65(5):2194–2206, May 2017.
3. Mario Alonzo, Stefano Buzzi, Alessio Zappone, and Ciro D'Elia. Energy-Efficient Power Control in Cell-Free and User-Centric Massive MIMO at Millimeter Wave. *IEEE Transactions on Green Communications and Networking*, 3(3):651–663, September 2019.
4. Masoud Attarifar, Aliazam Abbasfar, and Angel Lozano. Modified Conjugate Beamforming for Cell-Free Massive MIMO. *IEEE Wireless Communications Letters*, 8(2):616–619, April 2019.
5. Manijeh Bashar, Kanapathippillai Cumanan, Alister G. Burr, Mérouane Debbah, and Hien Quoc Ngo. On the Uplink Max–Min SINR of Cell-Free Massive MIMO Systems. *IEEE Transactions on Wireless Communications*, 18(4):2021–2036, April 2019.
6. Emil Björnson and Luca Sanguinetti. Making Cell-Free Massive MIMO Competitive With MMSE Processing and Centralized Implementation. *IEEE Transactions on Wireless Communications*, 19(1):77–90, January 2020.
7. Emil Björnson, Luca Sanguinetti, Jakob Hoydis, and Mérouane Debbah. Optimal Design of Energy-Efficient Multi-User MIMO Systems: Is Massive MIMO the Answer? *IEEE Transactions on Wireless Communications*, 14(6):3059–3075, June 2015.
8. Stefano Buzzi and Carmen D'Andrea. Cell-Free Massive MIMO: User-Centric Approach. *IEEE Wireless Communications Letters*, 6(6):706–709, December 2017.
9. Zheng Chen and Emil Björnson. Channel Hardening and Favorable Propagation in Cell-Free Massive MIMO With Stochastic Geometry. *IEEE Transactions on Communications*, 66(11):5205–5219, November 2018.
10. Tiep M. Hoang, Hien Quoc Ngo, Trung Q. Duong, Hoang Duong Tuan, and Alan Marshall. Cell-Free Massive MIMO Networks: Optimal Power Control Against Active Eavesdropping. *IEEE Transactions on Communications*, 66(10):4724–4737, October 2018.
11. Jakob Hoydis, Stephan ten Brink, and Merouane Debbah. Massive MIMO in the UL/DL of Cellular Networks: How Many Antennas Do We Need? *IEEE Journal on Selected Areas in Communications*, 31(2):160–171, February 2013.
12. Qinhui Huang and Alister Burr. Compute-and-forward in cell-free massive MIMO: Great performance with low backhaul load. In *2017 IEEE International Conference on Communications Workshops (ICC Workshops)*, pages 601–606, May 2017.
13. Giovanni Interdonato. Cell-Free Massive MIMO : Scalability, Signal Processing and Power Control. 2020.
14. Giovanni Interdonato, Pal Frenger, and Erik G. Larsson. Scalability Aspects of Cell-Free Massive MIMO. In *ICC 2019 - 2019 IEEE International Conference on Communications (ICC)*, pages 1–6, May 2019.
15. Giovanni Interdonato, Hien Quoc Ngo, Pål Frenger, and Erik G. Larsson. Downlink Training in Cell-Free Massive MIMO: A Blessing in Disguise. *IEEE Transactions on Wireless Communications*, 18(11):5153–5169, November 2019.
16. Giovanni Interdonato, Hien Quoc Ngo, Erik G. Larsson, and Pal Frenger. How Much Do Downlink Pilots Improve Cell-Free Massive MIMO? In *2016 IEEE Global Communications Conference (GLOBECOM)*, pages 1–7, December 2016.
17. Wei Jiang and Hans D. Schotten. Cost-Effectiveness Analysis and Design of Cost-Efficient Cell-Free Massive MIMO Systems. In *2024 IEEE 35th International Symposium on Personal, Indoor and Mobile Radio Communications (PIMRC)*, pages 1–6, September 2024.
18. Joumana Kassam, Daniel Castanheira, Adão Silva, Rui Dinis, and Atílio Gameiro. A Review on Cell-Free Massive MIMO Systems. *Electronics*, 12(4):1001, January 2023.
19. Yikai Li and Gayan Amarasuriya Aruma Baduge. NOMA-Aided Cell-Free Massive MIMO Systems. *IEEE Wireless Communications Letters*, 7(6):950–953, December 2018.

20. David López-Pérez, Ming Ding, Holger Claussen, and Amir H. Jafari. Towards 1 Gbps/UE in Cellular Systems: Understanding Ultra-Dense Small Cell Deployments. *IEEE Communications Surveys & Tutorials*, 17(4):2078–2101, 2015.
21. Patrick Marsch and Gerhard Fettweis. Uplink CoMP under a Constrained Backhaul and Imperfect Channel Knowledge. *IEEE Transactions on Wireless Communications*, 10(6):1730–1742, June 2011.
22. Thomas L. Marzetta, Erik G. Larsson, Hong Yang, and Hien Quoc Ngo. *Fundamentals of Massive MIMO*. Cambridge University Press, Cambridge, 2016.
23. Mohammadali Mohammadi, Zahra Mobini, Hien Quoc Ngo, and Michail Matthaiou. Next-Generation Multiple Access With Cell-Free Massive MIMO. *Proceedings of the IEEE*, 112(9):1372–1420, September 2024.
24. Elina Nayebi, Alexei Ashikhmin, Thomas L. Marzetta, and Bhaskar D. Rao. Performance of cell-free massive MIMO systems with MMSE and LSFD receivers. In *2016 50th Asilomar Conference on Signals, Systems and Computers*, pages 203–207, November 2016.
25. Elina Nayebi, Alexei Ashikhmin, Thomas L. Marzetta, and Hong Yang. Cell-Free Massive MIMO systems. In *2015 49th Asilomar Conference on Signals, Systems and Computers*, pages 695–699, November 2015.
26. Elina Nayebi, Alexei Ashikhmin, Thomas L. Marzetta, Hong Yang, and Bhaskar D. Rao. Precoding and Power Optimization in Cell-Free Massive MIMO Systems. *IEEE Transactions on Wireless Communications*, 16(7):4445–4459, July 2017.
27. Hien Quoc Ngo, Alexei Ashikhmin, Hong Yang, Erik G. Larsson, and Thomas L. Marzetta. Cell-Free Massive MIMO: Uniformly great service for everyone. In *2015 IEEE 16th International Workshop on Signal Processing Advances in Wireless Communications (SPAWC)*, pages 201–205, June 2015.
28. Hien Quoc Ngo, Alexei Ashikhmin, Hong Yang, Erik G. Larsson, and Thomas L. Marzetta. Cell-Free Massive MIMO Versus Small Cells. *IEEE Transactions on Wireless Communications*, 16(3):1834–1850, March 2017.
29. Hien Quoc Ngo, Giovanni Interdonato, Erik G. Larsson, Giuseppe Caire, and Jeffrey G. Andrews. Ultradense Cell-Free Massive MIMO for 6G: Technical Overview and Open Questions. *Proceedings of the IEEE*, 112(7):805–831, July 2024.
30. Hien Quoc Ngo and Erik G. Larsson. No Downlink Pilots Are Needed in TDD Massive MIMO. *IEEE Transactions on Wireless Communications*, 16(5):2921–2935, May 2017.
31. Hien Quoc Ngo, Le-Nam Tran, Trung Q. Duong, Michail Matthaiou, and Erik G. Larsson. On the Total Energy Efficiency of Cell-Free Massive MIMO. *IEEE Transactions on Green Communications and Networking*, 2(1):25–39, March 2018.
32. Long D. Nguyen, Trung Q. Duong, Hien Quoc Ngo, and Kamel Tourki. Energy Efficiency in Cell-Free Massive MIMO with Zero-Forcing Precoding Design. *IEEE Communications Letters*, 21(8):1871–1874, August 2017.
33. Stephen Perlman and A. Forenza. An Introduction to pCell - White Paper. 2015.
34. Hong Yang and Thomas L. Marzetta. Energy Efficiency of Massive MIMO: Cell-Free vs. Cellular. In *2018 IEEE 87th Vehicular Technology Conference (VTC Spring)*, pages 1–5, June 2018.
35. Jiayi Zhang, Shuaifei Chen, Yan Lin, Jiakang Zheng, Bo Ai, and Lajos Hanzo. Cell-Free Massive MIMO: A New Next-Generation Paradigm. *IEEE Access*, 7:99878–99888, 2019.
36. Jiayi Zhang, Linglong Dai, Ziyan He, Shi Jin, and Xu Li. Performance Analysis of Mixed-ADC Massive MIMO Systems Over Rician Fading Channels. *IEEE Journal on Selected Areas in Communications*, 35(6):1327–1338, June 2017.
37. Jiayi Zhang, Yinghua Wei, Emil Björnson, Yu Han, and Shi Jin. Performance Analysis and Power Control of Cell-Free Massive MIMO Systems With Hardware Impairments. *IEEE Access*, 6:55302–55314, 2018.
38. Xianyu Zhang, Daoxing Guo, and Kang An. Secure communication in multigroup multicasting cell-free massive MIMO networks with active spoofing attack. *Electronics Letters*, 55(2):96–98, January 2019.

39. Xianyu Zhang, Daoxing Guo, Kang An, Zhiguo Ding, and Bangning Zhang. Secrecy Analysis and Active Pilot Spoofing Attack Detection for Multigroup Multicasting Cell-Free Massive MIMO Systems. *IEEE Access*, 7:57332–57340, 2019.
40. Jiakang Zheng, Jiayi Zhang, Hongyang Du, Dusit Niyato, Bo Ai, Mérouane Debbah, and Khaled B. Letaief. Mobile Cell-Free Massive MIMO: Challenges, Solutions, and Future Directions. *Wireless Commun.*, 31(3):140–147, June 2024.

Enabling Technologies and Methods

Revolutionizing 6G Communication: Unleashing the Potential of Reconfigurable Intelligent Surfaces

Satish K. Tiwari, Shraddha Tripathi, Mahendra K. Shukla, and Om Jee Pandey

1 Introduction

In the rapidly evolving field of wireless communication, the pursuit of more efficient, reliable, and adaptive communication systems has led to the exploration of novel technologies. Among these, Reconfigurable Intelligent Surfaces (RIS) have emerged as a groundbreaking solution poised to revolutionize the landscape of 6G communication networks [1]. This chapter delves into the concept of RIS, its significance in 6G networks, and the transformative impact it is expected to have on wireless communication.

S. K. Tiwari (✉)
Department of Electronics and Communication Engineering, PDPM IIITDM Jabalpur, Jabalpur, India
e-mail: sktiwari@iiitdmj.ac.in

S. Tripathi
Department of Network and Systems Engineering (NSE), School of EECS, KTH Royal Institute of Technology, Stockholm, Sweden
e-mail: shrtri@kth.se

M. K. Shukla
Department of Information Technology, ABV-Indian Institute of Information Technology and Management (ABV-IIITM) Gwalior, Gwalior, India
e-mail: mahendra@iiitm.ac.in

O. J. Pandey
Department of Electronics Engineering, Indian Institute of Technology (BHU) Varanasi, Varanasi, India
e-mail: omjee.ece@iitbhu.ac.in

T. Ojha et al. (eds.), *Edge-Enabled 6G Networking*,
https://doi.org/10.1007/978-3-032-19042-0_5

1.1 Introduction to RIS

The quest for more efficient and robust communication systems has driven researchers and engineers to explore the potential of RIS. RIS, also known as intelligent reflecting surfaces or metasurfaces, are innovative technologies designed to manipulate electromagnetic waves in a controlled manner to enhance signal strength, coverage, and overall network performance [2]. These surfaces consist of numerous small, passive or active elements that can dynamically adjust their electromagnetic properties, such as phase, amplitude, and polarization, in response to environmental conditions and user requirements.

RIS operates on the principle of reconfigurability and intelligence. By strategically altering the properties of incident waves, RIS can steer signals towards desired destinations, effectively shaping the propagation environment. This capability enables RIS to enhance communication links by improving signal quality, reducing interference, and optimizing the performance of wireless networks. The emergence of RIS represents a paradigm shift from traditional communication technologies, which rely primarily on active transmitters and receivers, towards a more flexible and adaptive approach to wireless communication.

Figure 1 illustrates the concept and application of RIS in various scenarios within a 6G network, demonstrating how RIS enhances signal propagation and overcomes obstacles like buildings and trees. The diagram shows clustering of IoT devices for different applications such as defence, social, healthcare, and commercial sectors, where RIS ensures secure, reliable, and seamless connectivity. Buildings and trees that obstruct signal paths can be bypassed using strategically placed RIS panels, maintaining strong signal strength and coverage. The base station (BS) acts as the primary signal source/recipient, with RIS panels controlled by an RIS controller to manip-

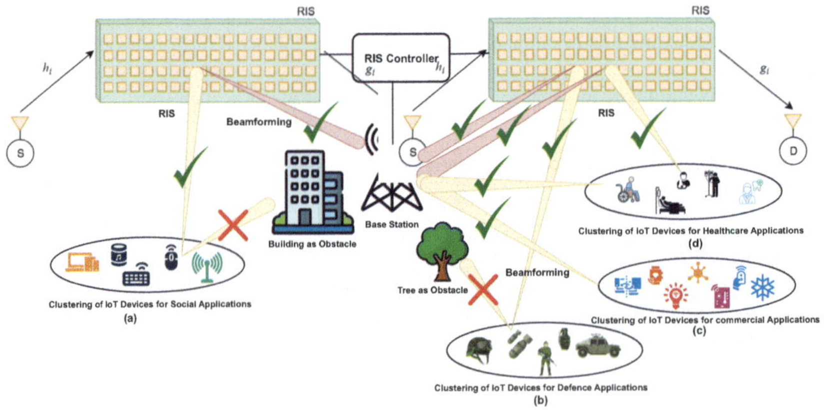

Fig. 1 Illustration of RIS-assisted 6G communication network across various applications–' demonstrating how RIS addresses signal blockages and enhances device localization in Non-Line-of-Sight (NLoS) scenarios

ulate electromagnetic waves and achieve beamforming. This process focuses and directs signals from specific IoT clusters, optimizing signal strength and minimizing interference. Overall, Fig. 1 underscores the pivotal role of RIS in transforming the 6G network landscape by facilitating advanced beamforming techniques to ensure optimal connectivity and overcoming environmental challenges, which is essential for the next-generation IoT ecosystem.

1.2 Importance of RIS in Revolutionizing 6G Communication

As the demand for higher data rates, lower latency, and ubiquitous connectivity continues to escalate, the role of RIS in shaping the future of 6G communication cannot be overstated. The integration of RIS into 6G networks offers a multitude of benefits that address the limitations of traditional communication infrastructures and pave the way for a new era of ultra-efficient and adaptive wireless networks [3].

One of the primary advantages of RIS is its ability to enhance coverage and capacity in challenging environments, such as urban areas with high attenuation or indoor spaces with significant multipath propagation. By intelligently redirecting and focusing electromagnetic waves, RIS enables more reliable communication links, increasing the overall capacity of 6G networks. This capability is particularly crucial in densely populated areas where maintaining high-quality connectivity is challenging.

Furthermore, RIS significantly improves energy efficiency by reducing the transmit power required to establish communication links. By exploiting passive signal manipulation techniques, RIS minimizes energy consumption while maintaining high-quality connectivity. This makes RIS an attractive solution for sustainable and eco-friendly communication systems, aligning with the growing emphasis on energy-efficient technologies in modern communication networks.

In addition to enhancing coverage and energy efficiency, RIS facilitates dynamic and adaptive communication environments. Through real-time control and optimization, RIS can adapt its configuration to optimize signal propagation, mitigate interference, and accommodate diverse applications and services [4]. This adaptability enables more flexible and responsive 6G networks capable of meeting the evolving demands of modern communication scenarios.

The integration of RIS into 6G networks also holds the potential to mitigate common challenges in wireless communication, such as multipath fading and interference. By manipulating the propagation environment to create constructive interference patterns and suppress unwanted signals, RIS improves link reliability and spectral efficiency. This capability is particularly valuable in environments with high user density or reflective surfaces, where maintaining high-quality communication links is often challenging.

Hence, after reviewing the brief introduction of RIS and their importance in revolutionizing 6G communication, in this chapter, first in Sect. 2, the fundamentals of RIS is discussed which covers the basic principles of RIS, their architecture, functionalities, and a comparison with conventional communication technologies. Thereafter, various advantages of RIS such as improving energy efficiency, SINR, data latency, complexity, cost, and interference are highlighted in Sect. 3. Subsequently, in Sect. 4, the hardware design consideration of RIS is presented along with beamforming techniques and channel estimation methods. Section 5, describes the various applications of RIS in 6G communication networks such as indoor/outdoor communication, mmWave communication, smart city communication, and satellite communication. The challenges and operation of RIS deployment, interference management, and security and privacy concerns are elaborated in Sect. 7. Section 8 provides future directions and emerging research areas with respect to RIS-assisted wireless communication. Finally, conclusions are given in Sect. 9.

2 Fundamentals of RIS

To fully understand the transformative potential of RIS in 6G communication networks, it is essential to delve into their fundamental principles, architecture, operating mechanisms, and how they compare with conventional communication technologies. This section provides a comprehensive overview of these aspects, laying the groundwork for understanding the advantages and applications of RIS.

2.1 Definition and Basic Principles of RIS

RIS operates on the principle of reconfigurability and intelligence, leveraging a multitude of passive reflecting elements (REs) to dynamically adjust their electromagnetic properties [5]. These elements, often referred to as meta-atoms or metamaterial structures, can manipulate incident electromagnetic waves by altering their phase, amplitude, and polarization. By strategically controlling these properties, RIS can steer signals towards desired destinations, effectively shaping the propagation environment and enhancing communication performance.

The basic principle of RIS involves the constructive and destructive interference of electromagnetic waves. By adjusting the phase of reflected waves at each element, RIS can create constructive interference patterns that enhance signal strength at specific locations, or destructive interference patterns that suppress unwanted signals. This capability allows RIS to optimize signal propagation, mitigate interference, and improve overall network performance.

2.2 Architecture and Components of RIS

The architecture of RIS typically comprises a grid of passive and active elements integrated with control units, sensing mechanisms, and communication mechanisms [6]. These elements collectively form a flexible platform for controlling and manipulating electromagnetic waves in real-time. The key components of RIS include:

- **Passive Elements**: These are the fundamental building blocks of RIS, responsible for manipulating the properties of incident waves. They can be made from various materials, such as metamaterials or meta-atoms, and are designed to operate at specific frequencies.
- **Active Elements**: Unlike passive elements, active elements can amplify or generate signals. They provide additional functionalities, such as signal regeneration and enhancement, thereby increasing the overall capability and flexibility of RIS in managing electromagnetic waves.
- **Control Units**: These units manage the configuration of both passive and active elements, adjusting their electromagnetic properties in response to environmental conditions and user requirements. Control units can be implemented using various technologies, such as microelectromechanical systems (MEMS) or integrated circuits (ICs).
- **Sensing Mechanisms**: These mechanisms detect changes in the environment and provide feedback to the control units, enabling real-time adaptation of RIS configuration. Sensing mechanisms can include antennas, sensors, and other devices that monitor signal quality and propagation characteristics.
- **Communication Mechanisms**: These mechanisms facilitate the exchange of information between the RIS and external devices, such as BSs or user equipment. They ensure that the RIS can receive control commands and transmit status updates or performance metrics. Communication mechanisms may include wireless transceivers, wired interfaces, and communication protocols tailored for real-time control and coordination.

The integration of these components allows RIS to dynamically optimize signal propagation, enhancing communication performance in a wide range of scenarios. The combination of passive and active elements, sophisticated control and sensing, and robust communication mechanisms makes RIS a powerful tool in modern communication systems.

2.3 Operating Principles and Functionalities of RIS

RIS fundamentally operate through the manipulation of electromagnetic waves using passive signal control [7]. The core mechanisms enabling RIS to enhance wireless communication include phase shifting, beamforming, and polarization control. These functionalities allow RIS to shape the wireless environment by dynamically adjusting signal propagation and enabling real-time adaptation to changing conditions. Below, we explore these mechanisms in greater depth.

- **Phase Shifting and Interference Management**: Phase shifting is a critical operating principle of RIS that enables precise control over the propagation of electromagnetic waves. Each RE of an RIS can adjust the phase of incident waves, either to create constructive interference (enhancing signal strength) or destructive interference (cancelling unwanted signals). This ability allows RIS to fine-tune the signal reaching the receiver, optimizing coverage and communication quality.
  Mathematically, the phase shift θ_i applied at the i-th element alters the total phase of the reflected wave as:

$$\phi_r = \phi_i + \theta_i, \tag{1}$$

  where ϕ_i is the phase of the incident wave and ϕ_r is the resulting phase of the reflected wave. This adjustment ensures that signals can be steered and focused toward desired locations, improving signal reliability and minimizing interference.

  Beamforming for Targeted Communication: Beamforming is one of the most powerful functionalities enabled by RIS. By intelligently controlling the phase and amplitude of reflected waves, RIS can steer beams toward specific directions or users, significantly improving signal strength and coverage in challenging environments, such as urban areas with high obstacles.
  By dynamically adjusting the phase shift of each element, RIS can create narrow, directed beams of electromagnetic waves that are focused on specific receivers, thus optimizing communication links. The directional steering of beams not only reduces interference from unwanted directions but also enables multi-user communication by forming multiple beams simultaneously.
  The phase shift required for beamforming toward a user at angle ψ can be expressed as:

$$\theta_i = -\frac{2\pi d_i \sin(\psi)}{\lambda}, \tag{2}$$

  where d_i is the distance between the i-th element and a reference point, λ is the wavelength, and ψ is the desired beam angle. This allows RIS to focus energy where it is most needed, improving both signal-to-noise ratio (SNR) and capacity.

  Polarization Control for Enhanced Propagation: Polarization control offers additional flexibility in manipulating electromagnetic waves. Polarization refers to the orientation of the wave's electric field, and by controlling this aspect, RIS can further optimize signal transmission.
  In environments where certain polarization orientations may lead to higher levels of multipath interference or signal degradation, RIS can adaptively rotate or adjust the polarization of reflected waves to improve signal strength and quality. This technique can be particularly valuable in environments with high interference

or complex reflective surfaces, such as indoor urban environments or crowded networks.
Polarization control is described by manipulating the Jones vector representation of an electromagnetic wave:

$$\mathbf{E} = \begin{pmatrix} E_x \\ E_y \end{pmatrix}, \quad (3)$$

where E_x and E_y represent the horizontal and vertical components of the electric field. By adjusting these components, RIS can dynamically shift the polarization to reduce interference and optimize link reliability.

- **Real-Time Adaptation and Environmental Sensing**: A distinguishing feature of RIS is its ability to adapt in real-time to changes in the environment or network conditions. Equipped with sensing mechanisms and feedback systems, RIS can monitor signal quality, interference levels, and user locations, allowing it to adjust the configuration of its reflective elements on-the-fly.
For instance, in a scenario where a user moves behind a physical obstruction (e.g., a building), causing a loss of line-of-sight (LoS), the RIS can automatically reconfigure the phase shifts to redirect the signal around the obstacle. This real-time adaptability ensures that communication links remain reliable, even in dynamic environments.

These techniques collectively enable RIS to optimize signal propagation, improve link reliability, and enhance overall network performance, making it a powerful tool for modern wireless communication systems.

2.4 Comparison with Conventional Communication Technologies

RIS represent a significant departure from traditional communication technologies, which rely primarily on active transmitters and receivers [8]. In conventional systems, signal propagation is controlled by adjusting the power and directionality of transmitted signals, often leading to high energy consumption and limited flexibility in adapting to changing environmental conditions.

In contrast, RIS introduces a paradigm shift by leveraging passive elements to reshape the wireless propagation environment. This approach offers several advantages:

- **Reduced Power Consumption**: RIS relies on passive elements to manipulate electromagnetic waves, significantly reducing the power required to establish and maintain communication links. This results in more energy-efficient systems, which is particularly important in the context of sustainable communication networks.

- **Improved Spectral Efficiency**: By dynamically controlling the phase, amplitude, and polarization of incident waves, RIS can optimize signal propagation and mitigate interference, leading to higher spectral efficiency. This enables more efficient use of available spectrum, supporting higher data rates and improved network capacity.
- **Enhanced Flexibility**: RIS provides greater flexibility in network deployment and optimization. Unlike traditional systems, which require extensive infrastructure and active components, RIS can be easily deployed in various environments and adapted to different communication scenarios, making it a versatile solution for a wide range of applications.
- **Cost-Effectiveness**: The use of passive elements in RIS reduces the need for complex and expensive active components, potentially lowering the overall cost of network deployment and maintenance. This makes RIS an attractive option for expanding network coverage and capacity in cost-sensitive applications.
- **Robustness**: The architecture of RIS, with its ability to adapt to changing environmental conditions and mitigate interference, contributes to the robustness of communication systems. This adaptability ensures reliable performance even in challenging conditions, such as urban environments with high signal attenuation.
- **Scalability**: RIS technology offers excellent scalability, allowing for easy integration into existing networks and the ability to support a large number of users and devices. The modular nature of RIS elements facilitates seamless scaling of network infrastructure to meet growing demand.
- **Security**: RIS can enhance the security of wireless communication systems by creating controlled and configurable propagation environments. This capability enables the implementation of advanced security measures, such as secure beamforming and signal obfuscation, to protect against eavesdropping and unauthorized access.

The combination of reduced power consumption, improved spectral efficiency, enhanced flexibility, cost-effectiveness, robustness, scalability, and security makes RIS a revolutionary technology for modern communication systems, offering significant improvements over conventional approaches. These advantages make RIS a highly flexible and energy-efficient technology compared to conventional systems. However, to fully appreciate its role in the evolving landscape of 6G networks, it is essential to compare RIS with other emerging technologies like Massive Multiple-Input Multiple-Output (Massive MIMO), which also play a significant role in enhancing network performance.

2.4.1 Comparison Between RIS and Massive MIMO

Massive MIMO is one of the cornerstone technologies of 5G and is expected to evolve further in 6G networks. Massive MIMO utilizes large arrays of antennas at the base station to simultaneously serve multiple users by spatial multiplexing, significantly increasing spectral efficiency.

Key Advantages of Massive MIMO:

- *Spectral Efficiency*: Massive MIMO can increase spectral efficiency by serving multiple users simultaneously with the same time-frequency resources, making it suitable for high-density environments like urban areas.
- *Beamforming*: Massive MIMO's beamforming capabilities allow for precise signal targeting, which reduces interference and improves signal quality.
- *Active Technology*: Unlike RIS, Massive MIMO actively transmits and receives signals, offering higher control over signal power and coverage area.

Key Differences with RIS:

- *Passive versus Active*: RIS is a passive technology that reflects and manipulates signals without generating new ones, whereas Massive MIMO requires active transmission of signals. As a result, RIS is inherently more energy-efficient but may have limitations in terms of coverage and signal strength compared to the power output of Massive MIMO.
- *Deployment Complexity*: Massive MIMO systems require complex hardware and significant power consumption for their operation, whereas RIS systems are composed of passive, low-power reflective elements that can be easily deployed in diverse environments, such as on walls or building facades.
- *Interference Management*: Massive MIMO excels in environments where high interference exists due to its advanced beamforming and interference suppression capabilities. In contrast, RIS can help mitigate interference in a more passive manner by dynamically controlling how signals are reflected or directed, but it relies on external sources for signal transmission.

Synergy: The two technologies are not mutually exclusive. In fact, RIS can complement Massive MIMO by enhancing the propagation environment in challenging locations such as NLoS areas. For instance, while Massive MIMO provides the active beamforming, RIS can improve the channel by reflecting signals to optimize their path, making hybrid solutions a strong possibility for 6G (Table 1).

Table 1 Comparative summary

Feature	RIS	Massive MIMO
Control	Passive control of signal reflection	Active control with large antenna arrays
Energy efficiency	High, due to passive nature	Moderate, high power consumption
Deployment complexity	Low, flexible and scalable	High, requires significant infrastructure
Interference management	Passive interference mitigation	Advanced interference suppression
Suitability for NLoS scenarios	High	High

Both technologies contributes uniquely to 6G networks. RIS stands out for its energy efficiency, low-cost deployment, and its ability to complement other technologies by enhancing the propagation environment without the need for active transmission. On the other hand, Massive MIMO excel in specific high-performance applications but require more complex infrastructure and higher energy consumption.

3 Advantages and Benefits of RIS in 6G Networks

RIS into 6G networks offers numerous advantages that address the limitations of existing communication systems and unlock new opportunities for enhancing network performance [4, 9–12]. This section explores the key benefits of RIS, including its ability to enhance coverage and capacity, improve energy efficiency, enable dynamic and adaptive communication environments, and mitigate multipath fading and interference.

3.1 Enhancing Coverage and Capacity

One of the primary benefits of RIS is its ability to significantly extend the coverage area of wireless networks and enhance signal strength in challenging environments. In urban areas with high user density or indoor spaces with significant attenuation, traditional communication systems often struggle to maintain reliable connectivity. RIS addresses this challenge by intelligently redirecting and focusing electromagnetic waves, thereby enhancing signal coverage and strength.

By strategically positioning RIS elements in areas with poor coverage, it becomes possible to create more reliable communication links, reducing dead zones and improving overall network performance. For instance, as illustrated in Fig. 2, RIS

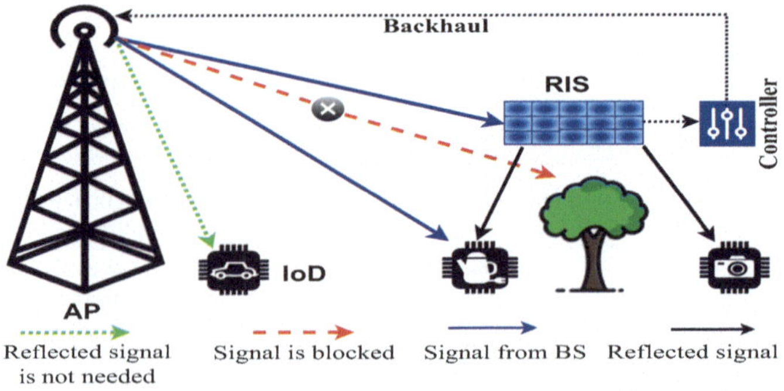

Fig. 2 RIS-assisted IoT network where RE are grouped together for the beam power management

can group REs to optimize beam power management by selectively directing signals toward IoT devices, while blocking or redirecting non-essential signals. This capability ensures efficient signal propagation, making it particularly valuable in densely populated areas, where maintaining high-quality connectivity is essential for supporting the growing demand for data-intensive applications and services.

3.2 Improving Energy Efficiency

Energy efficiency is a critical consideration in modern communication networks, especially as the demand for data continues to grow. RIS offers significant improvements in energy efficiency by reducing the transmit power required to establish communication links. By leveraging passive signal manipulation techniques, RIS minimizes energy consumption while maintaining high-quality connectivity.

This reduction in power consumption is achieved through the intelligent control of electromagnetic waves, enabling RIS to optimize signal propagation without the need for additional power-hungry active components. As a result, RIS presents an attractive solution for sustainable and eco-friendly communication systems, aligning with the growing emphasis on energy-efficient technologies in modern communication networks.

Figure 3 illustrates the impact of varying transmit power levels on the achieved Signal-to-Interference-plus-Noise Ratio (SINR) levels. The proposed method in [4] consistently achieves higher SINR values at each transmit power level compared to the benchmark methods. This performance improvement is attributed to power control in both the direct and reflected paths. If the signal strength in the direct path is low, the proposed method allocates more power to the reflected link.

Fig. 3 An illustration of variation in SINR with varying transmit power in RIS-assisted wireless network [4]

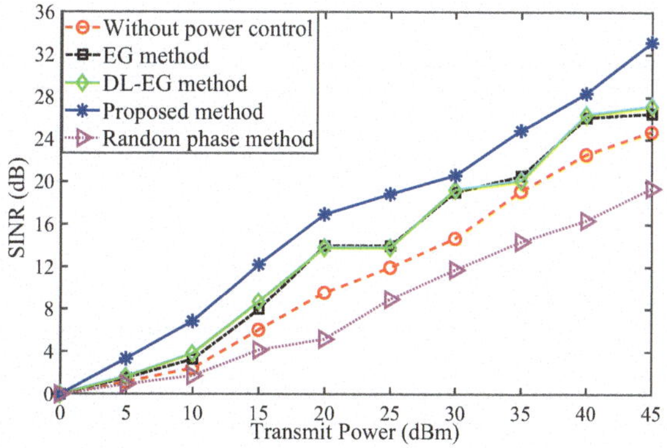

3.3 Improving SINR at BS

SINR is a critical metric for evaluating the quality and reliability of wireless communication links. Enhancing SINR at BS is essential for improving overall network performance, particularly in environments with high interference and signal degradation. As can be seen from Fig. 3, RIS play a vital role in enhancing SINR at BS by dynamically manipulating the propagation environment to optimize signal quality.

RIS can intelligently control the phase, amplitude, and polarization of incident waves to create constructive interference patterns and suppress unwanted signals. This ability to fine-tune the propagation environment helps in reducing interference and enhancing the desired signal strength at the BS. By optimizing the reflection and scattering of electromagnetic waves, RIS can effectively improve the SINR, leading to more reliable and high-quality communication links.

The deployment of RIS in strategic locations within the network can significantly boost SINR, particularly in areas with challenging propagation conditions. This enhancement in SINR translates to better data rates, improved network capacity, and more robust communication links, making RIS a valuable component in the evolution of 6G networks.

3.4 Improving Data Latency

RIS significantly reduce data latency in wireless networks. Data latency, the delay between sending and receiving information, is critical for applications requiring real-time communication, such as autonomous driving, telemedicine, and industrial automation. RIS can optimize the signal paths dynamically, ensuring that data travels the shortest and most efficient route possible. As illustrated in Fig. 4, incorporating more RIS element groups into the network consistently decreases data latency [4]. This reduction is attributed to the intelligent manipulation of electromagnetic waves, which minimizes delays caused by signal reflection and scattering. By optimizing the

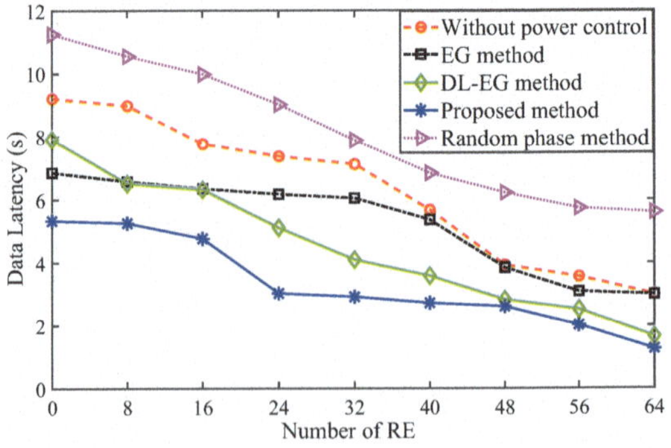

Fig. 4 Data transmission latency versus varying number of RIS element groups using various methods [4]

configuration of RIS elements, the proposed method in [4] achieves lower latency compared to traditional communication systems, making it a vital component for latency-sensitive applications in 6G networks.

3.5 Improving Time Complexity

The integration of RIS in communication networks can also lead to improvements in computational efficiency, particularly in terms of time complexity associated with network operations. Figure 5 demonstrates a comparative analysis of time complexity across various algorithms, where the proposed method [4], despite its higher complexity, shows optimized performance due to the intelligent control of both direct and reflected signal paths. This method assigns optimal power levels and adjusts the RIS reflection matrix in real-time, ensuring efficient use of computational resources. By reducing the computational burden on network nodes and optimizing signal processing tasks, RIS contributes to more efficient network management and faster response times, crucial for maintaining high performance in 6G networks.

3.6 Improving Cost

Implementing RIS in wireless communication networks also brings significant cost efficiency benefits. As shown in Fig. 6, the proposed method [4] enhances the average reward across different network sizes by optimizing the use of RIS elements. The efficient use of RIS can reduce the need for additional infrastructure investments, such as deploying more base stations or relay nodes, thus lowering the overall network deployment and maintenance costs. Furthermore, RIS can operate with minimal energy consumption, reducing operational expenses associated with power usage.

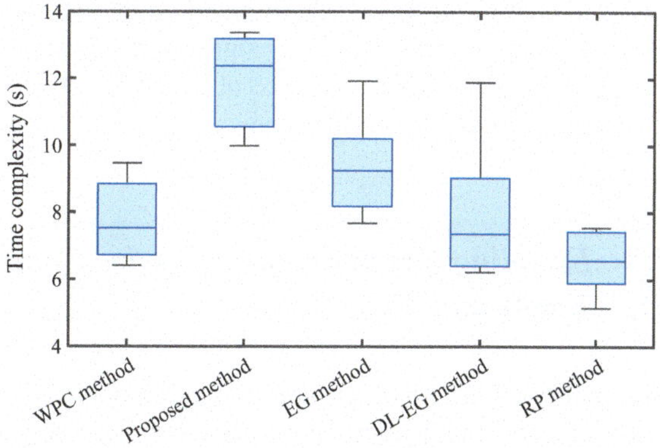

Fig. 5 Time complexity analysis of methods [4]

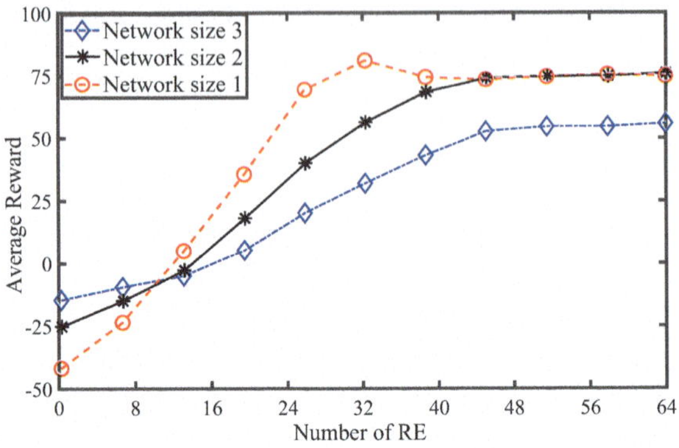

Fig. 6 Variation of the average reward achieved at different network sizes [4]

This cost efficiency, coupled with the improved network performance and reliability provided by RIS, makes it a compelling solution for future 6G networks, enabling more cost-effective and scalable communication systems.

3.7 Mitigating Multipath Fading and Interference

Multipath fading and interference are common challenges in wireless communication, particularly in densely populated areas or environments with reflective surfaces. These issues can degrade signal quality, reduce link reliability, and limit overall network performance.

RIS effectively addresses these challenges by manipulating the propagation environment to create constructive interference patterns and suppress unwanted signals. By intelligently controlling the phase, amplitude, and polarization of incident waves, RIS can mitigate the effects of multipath fading and interference, resulting in improved link reliability and spectral efficiency.

This capability is particularly valuable in environments with high user density or reflective surfaces, where maintaining high-quality communication links is often challenging. By optimizing signal propagation and reducing interference, RIS enhances the overall performance of wireless networks, making it a powerful tool for modern communication systems.

3.8 Enabling Dynamic and Adaptive Communication Environments

The ability of RIS to facilitate dynamic adaptation to changing communication environments and user requirements is a key advantage in the context of 6G networks. Through real-time control and optimization, RIS can adapt its configuration to optimize signal propagation, mitigate interference, and accommodate diverse applications and services.

This adaptability enables more flexible and responsive networks capable of meeting the evolving demands of modern communication scenarios. For example, RIS can dynamically adjust its configuration to enhance signal quality in areas with high user density, improve coverage in challenging environments, and support a wide range of applications, from high-speed data transmission to low-latency communication for critical applications.

3.9 Addressing Issue of Time Varying IoT Networks

IoT networks are characterized by their dynamic nature, with devices frequently joining and leaving the network, varying communication patterns, and changing environmental conditions. Addressing the issue of time-varying IoT networks is crucial for maintaining reliable and efficient communication.

RIS offers a promising solution to this challenge by providing a flexible and adaptive platform for optimizing signal propagation in real-time. The ability of RIS to dynamically adjust its configuration in response to changes in the network and environment allows it to maintain high-quality communication links even in time-varying conditions.

By leveraging advanced sensing mechanisms and control units, RIS can continuously monitor the network status and environmental factors, such as signal strength, interference levels, and the presence of obstacles. This real-time feedback enables RIS to adapt its reflection and scattering properties to optimize signal paths and enhance communication performance.

In time-varying IoT networks, RIS can effectively mitigate issues such as signal degradation, interference, and connectivity loss by dynamically reconfiguring the propagation environment. This adaptability ensures that IoT devices maintain reliable and efficient communication, supporting a wide range of applications, from smart homes and industrial automation to healthcare and transportation.

Incorporating RIS into time-varying IoT networks enhances their resilience, scalability, and overall performance, making it a crucial technology for the future of IoT and 6G networks.

4 Technologies and Techniques for Implementing RIS

The successful implementation of RIS in communication networks requires the development of advanced technologies and techniques. This section explores the key considerations for RIS hardware design, beamforming and beam steering techniques, channel estimation and optimization methods, and the integration of RIS with existing communication systems [13–17].

4.1 RIS Hardware Design Considerations

The design of RIS hardware involves careful consideration of factors such as element geometry, material properties, and integration with control and sensing modules. Advanced fabrication techniques, such as metamaterial engineering and nanoscale manufacturing, play a crucial role in realizing compact and efficient RIS architectures capable of achieving desired communication objectives.

- **Element Geometry**: The shape and size of RIS elements, or meta-atoms, are critical factors in determining their electromagnetic properties and overall performance. Optimizing the geometry of these elements enables precise control over the phase, amplitude, and polarization of incident waves, enhancing the ability of RIS to manipulate signal propagation.
- **Material Properties**: The choice of materials used in RIS elements is essential for achieving desired electromagnetic properties. Advanced materials, such as metamaterials and nanomaterials, offer unique advantages in terms of flexibility, durability, and performance, making them ideal for RIS applications.
- **Integration with Control and Sensing Modules**: Integrating RIS elements with control units and sensing mechanisms enables real-time adaptation to changing environmental conditions and user requirements. This integration involves the development of sophisticated control algorithms and sensing technologies capable of optimizing RIS configurations in response to dynamic communication scenarios.

4.2 Beamforming and Beam Steering Techniques

Beamforming and beam steering are essential techniques for maximizing the effectiveness of RIS in directing electromagnetic waves towards desired receivers or destinations. By dynamically adjusting the phase and amplitude of reflected waves, RIS can steer beams with high precision, enabling targeted communication links and efficient spectrum utilization in 6G networks.

- **Phase Shifting**: Each element of RIS can adjust the phase of the reflected wave, allowing for precise control over the direction and strength of the reflected signal. This capability enables RIS to steer beams towards specific directions, enhancing signal coverage and capacity.

- **Amplitude Control**: In addition to phase shifting, RIS can control the amplitude of reflected waves, further optimizing the beamforming process. By adjusting the amplitude of each element, RIS can create more focused beams, improving signal strength and quality at the desired destination.
- **Adaptive Beamforming**: Adaptive beamforming techniques leverage real-time feedback from sensing mechanisms to dynamically adjust the phase and amplitude of reflected waves. This enables RIS to continuously optimize beam direction and strength in response to changing communication environments and user requirements.

4.3 Channel Estimation and Optimization Methods

Accurate channel estimation and optimization are critical for the effective deployment and operation of RIS in real-world communication scenarios. Advanced signal processing algorithms and machine learning techniques can be employed to estimate channel characteristics, optimize RIS configurations, and adaptively control signal propagation, thereby enhancing the overall performance of 6G networks.

- **Signal Processing Algorithms**: Advanced signal processing algorithms are used to estimate channel characteristics, such as path loss, multipath propagation, and interference. These algorithms provide the necessary information for optimizing RIS configurations and ensuring reliable communication links.
- **Machine Learning Techniques**: Machine learning techniques can be employed to predict channel conditions and optimize RIS configurations based on historical data and real-time feedback. By leveraging data-driven approaches, RIS can achieve higher levels of intelligence and self-optimization, leading to more efficient and adaptive communication systems.
- **Optimization Methods**: Various optimization methods, such as convex optimization and evolutionary algorithms, can be used to find the optimal configuration of RIS elements. These methods ensure that RIS can adaptively control signal propagation to achieve desired communication objectives, such as maximizing signal strength, minimizing interference, and improving spectral efficiency.

4.4 Integration with Existing Communication Systems

Integration of RIS with existing communication systems poses both technical and practical challenges, including compatibility issues, interoperability considerations, and deployment complexity. However, by leveraging standardized interfaces and protocols, seamless integration of RIS into 6G networks can be achieved, unlocking new opportunities for enhancing communication performance and scalability.

- **Compatibility Issues**: Ensuring compatibility between RIS and existing communication systems requires careful consideration of factors such as frequency bands, modulation schemes, and communication protocols. Developing standardized interfaces and protocols can facilitate seamless integration and interoperability.
- **Interoperability Considerations**: Interoperability between RIS and different communication technologies, such as Massive MIMO and mmWave communication, is essential for realizing the full potential of RIS-enabled systems. This requires the development of flexible and adaptive RIS architectures capable of supporting diverse communication scenarios.
- **Deployment Complexity**: Deploying RIS in large-scale communication networks involves significant complexity in terms of installation, configuration, and maintenance. Developing efficient deployment strategies, optimization algorithms, and scalable hardware architectures is essential for addressing these challenges and ensuring the successful implementation of RIS.

5 Applications of RIS in 6G Communication Networks

The integration of RIS into 6G communication networks opens up numerous application possibilities. This section explores the potential applications of RIS in indoor and outdoor wireless communication, massive MIMO and mmWave communication, Internet of Things (IoT) and smart city applications, and satellite communication and backhaul optimization [18–25].

5.1 Indoor and Outdoor Wireless Communication

RIS can significantly improve indoor and outdoor wireless communication by extending coverage, enhancing signal quality, and enabling seamless connectivity in challenging environments. In indoor scenarios, RIS can mitigate multipath propagation and shadowing effects, while in outdoor settings, it can enhance coverage and capacity, particularly in urban areas with high user density.

- **Indoor Wireless Communication**: In indoor environments, RIS can be strategically deployed to enhance signal strength and coverage in areas with high attenuation, such as office buildings, shopping malls, and residential complexes. By mitigating multipath propagation and shadowing effects, RIS enables more reliable and high-quality indoor communication links.

- **Outdoor Wireless Communication**: In outdoor settings, RIS can be used to extend coverage and enhance signal quality in urban areas with high user density and complex propagation environments. By intelligently redirecting and focusing electromagnetic waves, RIS can overcome obstacles and interference, ensuring seamless and high-performance outdoor communication.

5.2 Massive MIMO and MmWave Communication

RIS holds great potential for enhancing Massive Multiple Input Multiple Output (MIMO) and millimeter-wave (mmWave) communication systems, which are key enablers of 6G networks. By providing additional degrees of freedom for signal manipulation and propagation control, RIS can overcome the limitations of conventional antenna technologies and unlock new possibilities for high-capacity, high-frequency communication.

- **Massive MIMO**: In Massive MIMO systems, RIS can enhance the performance of communication links by optimizing the propagation environment and mitigating interference. By intelligently controlling the phase and amplitude of reflected waves, RIS can improve signal strength, increase spectral efficiency, and enhance overall network capacity.
- **mmWave Communication**: In mmWave communication systems, RIS can address the challenges of high path loss and limited coverage by providing precise control over signal propagation. By dynamically steering beams and focusing electromagnetic waves, RIS can extend coverage, enhance signal quality, and enable reliable high-frequency communication links.

5.3 Internet of Things (IoT) and Smart City Applications

In the context of IoT and smart city applications, RIS can play a crucial role in optimizing communication networks, improving connectivity, and enabling diverse IoT devices and sensors to exchange data efficiently. By enhancing coverage, reducing latency, and conserving energy, RIS can support a wide range of smart city initiatives, from traffic management to environmental monitoring.

- **IoT Applications**: In IoT applications, RIS can optimize communication networks to ensure reliable and low-latency connectivity for a vast array of IoT devices and sensors. By enhancing coverage and signal quality, RIS enables efficient data exchange and supports the diverse communication requirements of IoT ecosystems.

- **Smart City Initiatives**: In smart city initiatives, RIS can enhance communication networks to support a wide range of applications, such as traffic management, environmental monitoring, and public safety. By improving coverage, reducing latency, and conserving energy, RIS enables the seamless integration of smart technologies and enhances the overall efficiency and sustainability of urban environments.

5.4 Satellite Communication and Backhaul Optimization

RIS can also be deployed in satellite communication systems to improve link reliability, enhance spectral efficiency, and optimize backhaul connectivity. By strategically positioning RIS elements on satellite payloads or ground stations, it becomes possible to overcome signal attenuation and interference challenges, thereby enabling more robust and resilient satellite communication networks.

- **Satellite Communication**: In satellite communication systems, RIS can enhance link reliability and spectral efficiency by optimizing signal propagation and mitigating interference. By dynamically controlling the phase and amplitude of reflected waves, RIS can improve signal strength and quality, ensuring reliable and high-performance satellite communication links.
- **Backhaul Optimization**: In backhaul networks, RIS can optimize connectivity between different network nodes by enhancing signal propagation and reducing interference. By strategically deploying RIS elements, it becomes possible to improve the efficiency and reliability of backhaul links, supporting the overall performance of communication networks.

6 Recent Advancements in RIS Technology

The evolution of RIS continues to shape the future of wireless communication, especially in the context of 6G and the IoT. Recent research has introduced novel techniques and applications, enhancing the performance, energy efficiency, and scalability of RIS-enabled systems. This section highlights three key advancements: channel estimation techniques, unmanned aerial vehicles (UAV)-assisted IoT data harvesting, and energy-efficient multiuser localization.

6.1 Parallel Channel Estimation Techniques in RIS-Assisted IoT Networks

Accurate channel estimation is a critical challenge in RIS-assisted systems, as direct and reflected signals can overlap, making traditional methods insufficient. Recent advancements introduce parallel channel estimation techniques, which utilize separate processes for direct and reflected channels. Methods proposed in [26] significantly improve the accuracy of channel state information (CSI). These techniques not only enhance the performance of RIS-assisted massive MIMO systems but also reduce hardware complexity and power consumption, making them ideal for large-scale IoT networks.

6.2 RIS-Assisted UAVs for IoT Data Harvesting

UAVs integrated with RIS have demonstrated significant improvements in IoT data harvesting. By leveraging the mobility of UAVs and the signal-reflecting capabilities of RIS, the framework proposed in [27] enables dynamic optimization of UAV trajectories and RIS phase shifts. Reinforcement learning algorithms are used to maximize data collection efficiency, ensuring better coverage and reduced energy consumption. This approach has been shown to improve data collection by up to 50%, offering a scalable solution for IoT networks that face energy and connectivity challenges.

6.3 Energy-Efficient Multiuser Localization in RIS-Assisted IoT Networks

Localization in IoT networks, particularly for energy-constrained devices, is another area where RIS technology has made significant advancements. The introduction of energy-efficient multiuser localization leverages the difference in signal propagation delays between direct and reflected paths to achieve high-precision positioning [28]. By optimizing RIS phase shifts and employing semidefinite relaxation (SDR) techniques, decimeter-level accuracy is achieved with minimal power consumption. This advancement is crucial for large-scale IoT networks, where energy efficiency is a top priority.

7 Challenges and Solutions

While RIS offer significant advantages for 6G communication networks, their deployment and operation present several challenges. This section explores the key challenges associated with RIS deployment and scalability, hardware complexity and cost considerations, interference management and coordination issues, and security and privacy concerns. It also discusses potential solutions to address these challenges.

7.1 Deployment and Scalability Challenges

One of the primary challenges in deploying RIS is ensuring scalability and cost-effectiveness, particularly in large-scale communication networks. Addressing this challenge requires the development of efficient deployment strategies, optimization algorithms, and scalable hardware architectures capable of supporting diverse deployment scenarios and network configurations.

- **Efficient Deployment Strategies**: Developing efficient deployment strategies involves optimizing the placement and configuration of RIS elements to maximize coverage and performance. This requires careful planning and analysis of the propagation environment, user density, and communication requirements.
- **Optimization Algorithms**: Advanced optimization algorithms are essential for managing the complexity of large-scale RIS deployments. These algorithms can optimize the configuration of RIS elements in real-time, ensuring that the network adapts to changing conditions and user demands.
- **Scalable Hardware Architectures**: Scalable hardware architectures are crucial for supporting the widespread deployment of RIS in large-scale networks. This involves designing RIS elements and control units that can be easily integrated and scaled to meet the needs of different communication scenarios.

7.2 Hardware Complexity and Cost Considerations

The hardware complexity and cost of RIS pose significant barriers to widespread adoption, especially in resource-constrained environments or cost-sensitive applications. To overcome this challenge, ongoing research efforts focus on developing low-cost, energy-efficient RIS designs, leveraging advances in materials science, fabrication techniques, and system integration.

- **Low-Cost RIS Designs**: Developing low-cost RIS designs involves optimizing the materials and fabrication processes used to create RIS elements. Advances in materials science, such as the use of metamaterials and nanomaterials, can reduce costs while maintaining high performance.
- **Energy-Efficient Designs**: Energy-efficient RIS designs are essential for minimizing power consumption and ensuring sustainable operation. This requires the development of innovative control algorithms and energy-efficient hardware components that can operate effectively in low-power environments.
- **System Integration**: Effective system integration involves developing RIS elements and control units that can be seamlessly integrated with existing communication systems. This requires careful consideration of compatibility, interoperability, and deployment complexity to ensure that RIS can be easily adopted and scaled in diverse communication scenarios.

7.3 Interference Management and Coordination Issues

Interference management and coordination among multiple RIS elements represent another critical challenge in realizing the full potential of RIS in 6G networks. Effective interference mitigation techniques, such as coordinated beamforming and interference alignment, are essential for maximizing spectral efficiency and minimizing performance degradation in dense RIS deployments.

- **Coordinated Beamforming**: Coordinated beamforming techniques involve the simultaneous control of multiple RIS elements to optimize signal propagation and minimize interference. By coordinating the phase and amplitude of reflected waves, RIS can create constructive interference patterns and suppress unwanted signals.
- **Interference Alignment**: Interference alignment techniques can be used to align interfering signals in such a way that they cancel each other out, reducing the overall level of interference in the network. This requires advanced signal processing algorithms and real-time coordination among multiple RIS elements.
- **Spectral Efficiency**: Maximizing spectral efficiency involves optimizing the use of available spectrum by minimizing interference and enhancing signal quality. This requires the development of sophisticated control algorithms and optimization techniques capable of managing the complex interactions between multiple RIS elements and communication devices.

7.4 Security and Privacy Concerns

The integration of RIS into communication networks introduces new security and privacy considerations, including potential vulnerabilities, unauthorized access, and data interception. Robust encryption, authentication, and access control mechanisms are essential for safeguarding RIS-enabled systems against malicious attacks and ensuring the integrity and confidentiality of sensitive information.

- **Encryption**: Robust encryption techniques are essential for protecting data transmitted over RIS-enabled communication links. This involves developing advanced cryptographic algorithms that can secure data against eavesdropping and unauthorized access.
- **Authentication**: Strong authentication mechanisms are necessary to verify the identity of users and devices accessing the network. This ensures that only authorized entities can interact with RIS-enabled systems, preventing unauthorized access and potential security breaches.

- **Access Control**: Effective access control mechanisms are essential for managing the permissions and privileges of users and devices in the network. This involves developing policies and protocols that define who can access and control RIS elements, ensuring that the system remains secure and resilient against malicious attacks.

8 Future Directions and Emerging Research Areas

The future of RIS in 6G networks holds exciting possibilities for advanced research and development. This section explores emerging research areas and future directions for RIS, including advanced RIS architectures and designs, machine learning and AI-driven optimization techniques, integration with other emerging technologies, and standardization efforts and regulatory considerations.

8.1 Advanced RIS Architectures and Designs

Future research in RIS will focus on developing advanced architectures and designs capable of supporting higher frequencies, wider bandwidths, and more complex signal processing capabilities. Novel materials, such as graphene and metamaterials, hold promise for enabling next-generation RIS with enhanced performance and functionality.

- **High-Frequency Support**: Developing RIS architectures that can support higher frequencies, such as mmWave and terahertz frequencies, is essential for meeting the demands of 6G networks. This requires advances in materials and fabrication techniques capable of operating effectively at high frequencies.
- **Wider Bandwidths**: Future RIS designs will need to support wider bandwidths to accommodate the increasing data rates and communication requirements of modern networks. This involves optimizing the design and configuration of RIS elements to ensure efficient operation across a broad range of frequencies.
- **Complex Signal Processing**: Advanced signal processing capabilities are essential for enabling sophisticated RIS functionalities, such as adaptive beamforming, interference mitigation, and dynamic optimization. This requires the development of powerful control algorithms and hardware architectures capable of handling complex signal processing tasks.

8.2 *Machine Learning and AI-Driven Optimization Techniques*

Machine learning and artificial intelligence (AI) will play an increasingly important role in optimizing RIS configurations, predicting channel conditions, and autonomously adapting to changing communication environments. AI-driven techniques can enhance the intelligence and adaptability of RIS, enabling more efficient and resilient communication systems.

- **Predictive Optimization**: Machine learning algorithms can be used to predict channel conditions and optimize RIS configurations based on historical data and real-time feedback. This enables RIS to anticipate changes in the environment and proactively adjust its settings to maintain optimal performance.
- **Autonomous Adaptation**: AI-driven optimization techniques can enable RIS to autonomously adapt to changing communication scenarios, such as varying user density, mobility patterns, and interference levels. This enhances the flexibility and responsiveness of RIS-enabled systems, ensuring reliable and high-performance communication links.
- **Intelligent Control**: AI and machine learning can be used to develop intelligent control algorithms that optimize the configuration of RIS elements in real-time. These algorithms can learn from the environment and user behavior, continuously improving their performance and adapting to new challenges.

8.3 *Integration with Other Emerging Technologies*

The integration of RIS with other emerging technologies, such as edge computing, blockchain, and quantum communication, offers new opportunities for enhancing the performance, security, and scalability of 6G networks. These synergies can unlock novel applications and services, driving the evolution of next-generation communication systems.

- **Edge Computing**: Integrating RIS with edge computing can enhance the performance and efficiency of communication networks by enabling local processing and optimization of data. This reduces latency and improves the responsiveness of RIS-enabled systems, supporting real-time applications and services.
- **Blockchain**: Blockchain technology can enhance the security and trustworthiness of RIS-enabled communication systems by providing decentralized and tamper-proof mechanisms for data management and access control. This ensures the integrity and confidentiality of data transmitted over RIS-enabled networks.
- **Quantum Communication**: The integration of RIS with quantum communication technologies holds promise for enabling ultra-secure and high-capacity communication links. By leveraging the unique properties of quantum mechanics, such as

entanglement and superposition, RIS can enhance the security and performance of next-generation communication systems.

8.4 Standardization Efforts and Regulatory Considerations

Standardization efforts and regulatory considerations are crucial for ensuring the successful deployment and operation of RIS in 6G networks. Developing standardized interfaces, protocols, and guidelines can facilitate interoperability, compatibility, and widespread adoption of RIS, driving the evolution of communication networks.

- **Standardized Interfaces**: Developing standardized interfaces and protocols for RIS is essential for ensuring compatibility and interoperability with existing communication systems. This involves defining common frameworks and specifications that enable seamless integration and operation of RIS in diverse communication scenarios.
- **Regulatory Considerations**: Regulatory considerations play a critical role in shaping the deployment and operation of RIS-enabled systems. This involves developing guidelines and policies that address issues such as frequency allocation, spectrum management, and compliance with safety and performance standards.
- **Industry Collaboration**: Collaboration between industry stakeholders, researchers, and regulatory bodies is essential for driving the standardization and adoption of RIS. By working together, these stakeholders can develop common frameworks and guidelines that support the widespread deployment of RIS in 6G networks.

9 Conclusions and Future Research Directions

RIS represent a transformative technology poised to revolutionize 6G communication networks. By leveraging the principles of reconfigurability and intelligence, RIS offers numerous advantages, including enhanced coverage and capacity, improved energy efficiency, dynamic and adaptive communication environments, and mitigation of multipath fading and interference.

After reviewing the brief introduction of RIS and their importance in revolutionizing 6G communication, this chapter discussed the fundamentals of RIS, covering their basic principles, architecture, functionalities, and a comparison with conventional communication technologies. Various advantages, hardware design considerations, beamforming techniques, and channel estimation methods were presented. The chapter also described state-of-the-art applications of RIS in 6G communication networks, as well as challenges related to deployment, interference management, and security concerns. Future directions and emerging research areas concerning RIS-assisted wireless communication were provided.

This comprehensive exploration of RIS has highlighted its fundamental principles, advantages, challenges, and future directions, providing a deep understanding of the potential and opportunities that RIS brings to the field of wireless communication. As research and development in RIS continue to advance, it is poised to play a pivotal role in shaping the future of 6G networks, unlocking new possibilities for high-performance, efficient, and resilient communication systems.

Future Research Directions

Despite its promising potential, RIS is still an emerging technology, and several key areas warrant further research to unlock its full capabilities in 6G networks. One critical direction is the integration of AI and machine learning with RIS, which can enable real-time optimization and intelligent adaptation to dynamic environments. By leveraging AI, RIS systems could autonomously adjust their configurations to optimize beamforming, interference management, and energy efficiency, making them more responsive to fluctuating network conditions. Another vital area is the development of RIS for mmWave and terahertz communication, where higher frequencies suffer from significant signal attenuation and limited range. Researchers must explore new architectures and materials that allow RIS to operate effectively in these high-frequency bands, thereby expanding their applicability in future wireless networks.

Energy efficiency remains a critical challenge, especially for large-scale RIS deployments. Future studies should focus on designing low-power RIS hardware and energy-efficient communication protocols, ensuring sustainable operation in 6G systems. Additionally, research into the joint design of RIS with other technologies, such as massive MIMO, can reveal new hybrid systems that capitalize on the strengths of both. Combining RIS's passive, energy-efficient capabilities with massive MIMO's active control could lead to enhanced performance, particularly in complex urban environments where NLoS communication is common.

Security and privacy are also emerging concerns, as RIS introduces new vulnerabilities, including the potential for signal manipulation and eavesdropping. Future work should explore novel security frameworks, such as secure beamforming and blockchain-based solutions, to safeguard RIS-enabled networks. Moreover, research is needed to optimize RIS for ultra-low-latency applications, such as autonomous driving, virtual reality, and telemedicine, where real-time communication is crucial. Lastly, RIS's integration with UAVs and satellite communication presents exciting possibilities for extending coverage to remote and hard-to-reach areas. Investigating how RIS can be utilized in aerial platforms or satellite systems will open new avenues for global connectivity and enhance communication reliability in underserved regions.

By addressing these future research directions, RIS can evolve into a key enabler of next-generation wireless communication, driving forward the development of 6G networks and beyond.

References

1. Rihan M., Zappone A., Buzzi S., Fodor G. and Debbah M. (2024): Passive Versus Active Reconfigurable Intelligent Surfaces for Integrated Sensing and Communication: Challenges and Opportunities, IEEE Network 38, 218–226
2. Li H., Shen S., Nerini M. and Clerckx B. (2024): Reconfigurable Intelligent Surfaces 2.0: Beyond Diagonal Phase Shift Matrices, IEEE Communications Magazine 62, 102–108
3. Sang J., et al. (2024): Coverage Enhancement by Deploying RIS in 5G Commercial Mobile Networks: Field Trials, IEEE Wireless Communications 31, 172–180
4. Tripathi S., Pandey O. J. and Hegde R. M. (2023): An optimal reflective elements grouping model for RIS-assisted IoT networks using Q-learning. IEEE Transactions on Circuits and Systems II: Express Briefs 70, 3214–3218
5. Shrivastava A. K., Agrawal U. K., Shukla M. K. and Pandey O. J. (2023): Neural Networks-Based Phase Estimation and Symbol Detection for RIS-Assisted Wireless Communications, IEEE Communications Letters 27, 3245–3249
6. Chepuri S. P., Shlezinger N., Liu F., Alexandropoulos G. C., Buzzi S. and Eldar Y. C. (2023): Integrated Sensing and Communications With Reconfigurable Intelligent Surfaces: From signal modeling to processing, IEEE Signal Processing Magazine 40, 41–62
7. Liu R., Li M., Luo H., Liu Q. and Swindlehurst A. L. (2023): Integrated Sensing and Communication with Reconfigurable Intelligent Surfaces: Opportunities, Applications, and Future Directions, IEEE Wireless Communications 30, 50–57
8. Chen Z., et al. (2023): Reconfigurable-Intelligent-Surface-Assisted B5G/6G Wireless Communications: Challenges, Solution, and Future Opportunities, IEEE Communications Magazine 61, 16–22
9. Tripathi S., Pandey O. J. and Hegde R. M. (2023): Optimal Data Transfer Over RIS-Assisted Edge Networks Using Coordinated 3D Beamforming, 2023 National Conference on Communications (NCC), Guwahati, India, 1–6
10. Almekhlafi M., Arfaoui M. A., Assi C. and Ghrayeb A. (2022): Enabling URLLC Applications Through Reconfigurable Intelligent Surfaces: Challenges and Potential, IEEE Internet of Things Magazine 5, 130–135
11. Tripathi S., Pandey O. J. and Hegde R. M. (2022): Low-latency Data Transfer over SNR Constrained IoT Networks Using Optimal Active RIS Elements: A Q-learning Framework, IEEE 8th World Forum on Internet of Things (WF-IoT), Yokohama, 1–6
12. Tripathi S., Pandey O. J., Cenkeramaddi L. R. and Hegde R. M. (2022): Optimal Active Elements Selection in RIS-Assisted Edge Networks for Improved QoS, 2022 IEEE 12th Sensor Array and Multichannel Signal Processing Workshop (SAM), Trondheim, Norway, 21–25
13. Dai Y., Guan Y. L., Leung K. K. and Zhang Y. (2021): Reconfigurable Intelligent Surface for Low-Latency Edge Computing in 6G, IEEE Wireless Communications 28, 72–79
14. Basharat S., Hassan S. A., Pervaiz H., Mahmood A., Ding Z. and Gidlund M. (2021): Reconfigurable Intelligent Surfaces: Potentials, Applications, and Challenges for 6G Wireless Networks, IEEE Wireless Communications 28, 184–191
15. Yang B., et al. (2021): Spectrum-Learning-Aided Reconfigurable Intelligent Surfaces for Green 6G Networks, IEEE Network 35, 20–26
16. Pan C., et al. (2021): Reconfigurable Intelligent Surfaces for 6G Systems: Principles, Applications, and Research Directions, IEEE Communications Magazine 59, 14–20
17. Basar E. and Yildirim I. (2021): Reconfigurable Intelligent Surfaces for Future Wireless Networks: A Channel Modeling Perspective, IEEE Wireless Communications 28, 108–114
18. Alexandropoulos G. C., Shlezinger N. and del Hougne P. (2021): Reconfigurable Intelligent Surfaces for Rich Scattering Wireless Communications: Recent Experiments, Challenges, and Opportunities, IEEE Communications Magazine 59, 28–34
19. Wu Q., Zhang S., Zheng B., You C., and Zhang R. (2021): Intelligent reflecting surface aided wireless communications: a tutorial, IEEE Transactions on Communications 69, 3313–3351

20. Gong S., Lu X., Hoang D. T., Niyato D., Shu L., Kim D. I., and Liang Y.-C. (2020): Towards smart radio environment for wireless communications via intelligent reflecting surfaces: a comprehensive survey, IEEE Communications Surveys and Tutorials 22, 2283–2314
21. Dai L., Wang B., Wang M., Yang X., Tan J., Bi S., Xu S., Yang F., Chen Z., Renzo M. D., Chae C. B., and Hanzo L. (2020): Reconfigurable intelligent surface-based wireless communications: antenna design, prototyping, and experimental results, IEEE Access 8, 45913–45923
22. Wu Q. and Zhang R. (2020): Towards smart and reconfigurable environment: intelligent reflecting surface aided wireless network, IEEE Communications Magazine 58, 106–112
23. Renzo M. D., et al. (2019): Smart radio environments empowered by AI reconfigurable meta-surfaces: an idea whose time has come, EURASIP Journal on Wireless Communications and Networking
24. Basar E., Renzo M. D., Rosny J. D., Debbah M., Alouini M.-S., and Zhang R. (2019): Wireless communications through reconfigurable intelligent surfaces, IEEE Access 7, 116753–116773
25. Huang C., Zappone A., Alexandropoulos G. C., Debbah M., and Yuen C. (2019): Reconfigurable intelligent surfaces for energy efficiency in wireless communication, IEEE Transactions on Wireless Communications 18, 4157–4170
26. Chen Z., Huang L., Xia S., Tang B., Haardt M. and Zhang X. Y. (2024): Parallel channel estimation for RIS-assisted Internet of Things, IEEE Transactions on Intelligent Transportation Systems 25, 9762–9773
27. Abualhayjaa M. et al. (2024): RIS-assisted UAV for IoT data harvesting, IEEE International Conference on Communications Workshops (ICC Workshops), Denver, CO, USA, 816–821
28. Zhang J., Zheng Z., Fei Z. and Han Z. (2022): Energy-efficient multiuser localization in the RIS-assisted IoT networks, IEEE Internet of Things 9, 20651–20665

Synergistic Fusion of Terahertz and Molecular Communication for Futuristic 6G Networks

Chandrakant Shrivastava, Satish K. Tiwari, Nilay Pandey, and Gaurav Sharma

1 Introduction

1.1 Importance of THz and MC in 6G

As the demand for higher data rates, lower latency, and ubiquitous connectivity continues to grow, the exploration of new communication paradigms becomes imperative. Two promising technologies, Terahertz (THz) communication and Molecular Communication (MC), have emerged as potential game-changers for 6G networks. THz communication offers ultra-wide bandwidths and high data rates, while MC leverages biochemical signaling for nanoscale communication. The convergence of these technologies holds the key to addressing the diverse requirements of future wireless networks.

C. Shrivastava · S. K. Tiwari (✉)
Department of Electronics and Communication Engineering, PDPM IIITDM Jabalpur, Jabalpur, India
e-mail: sktiwari@iiitdmj.ac.in

C. Shrivastava
e-mail: 24pecv01@iiitdmj.ac.in

N. Pandey
Department of Electronics and Communication Engineering, Birla Institute of Technology, Mesra (Patna Campus), Patna, India
e-mail: nilaypandey@bitmesra.ac.in

G. Sharma
Department of Electrical and Electronics Engineering, Atal Bihari Vajpayee-Indian Institute of Information Technology and Management Gwalior, Gwalior, India

T. Ojha et al. (eds.), *Edge-Enabled 6G Networking*,
https://doi.org/10.1007/978-3-032-19042-0_6

1.2 Objective of the Chapter

This chapter aims to explore the synergistic fusion of Terahertz and Molecular Communication and its implications for futuristic 6G communication networks. By examining the fundamentals, challenges, and potential applications of both technologies, this chapter seeks to elucidate the transformative potential of their integration in shaping the future of wireless communication.

2 Fundamentals of THz Communication

2.1 Introduction to THz Frequency Band

By 2030, data rates exceeding 1 Tera-bit per second (Tbps) would be required for ubiquitous and seamless connectivity in the next-generation communication systems. According to a report published by the International Telecommunication Union (ITU), by the year 2030, the performance of wireless systems will be at par with wired networks, thereby supporting reliable communication in resource-constrained environments, as demonstrated in Fig. 1. Additionally, with global mobile data traffic reaching 226 ExaBytes per month by 2026, there is an immediate requirement for higher capacity spectrums. Very high data rates for wireless systems are essential in indoor locations where the requirement of low-cost high bandwidth equipment is

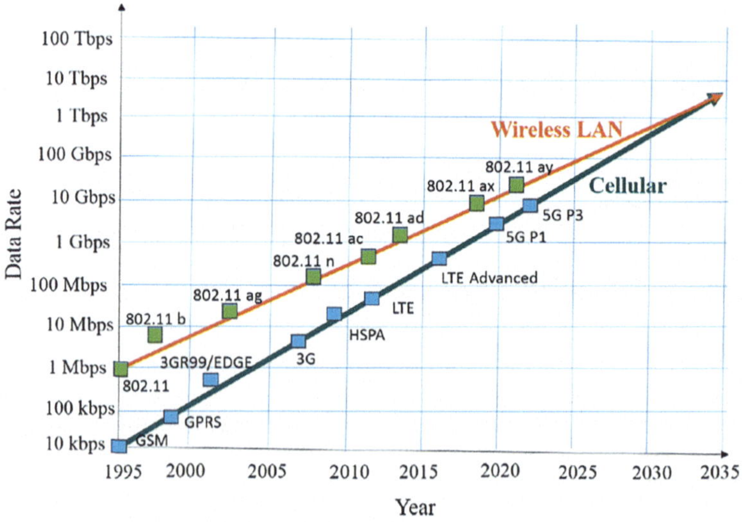

Fig. 1 Wireless roadmap up to the year 2035 [5]

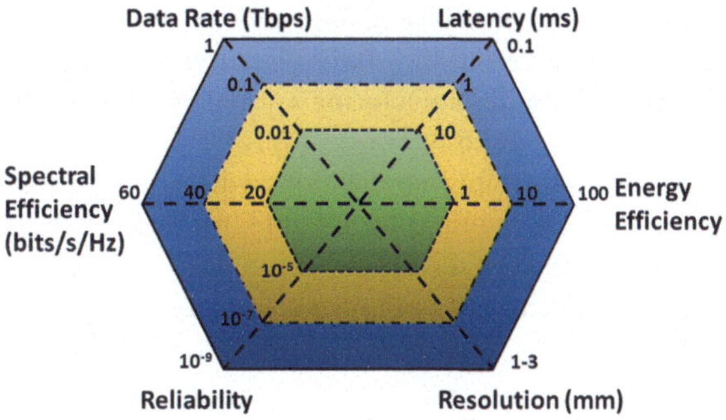

Fig. 2 6G key performance indicators

significant to address the communication needs in applications such as intra-wagon communication, point-to-point scenarios such as kiosk downloads, intra-device communications, power grid stations, and wireless links in data centres.

In 6G wireless communication systems, to quench the increasing demand for higher data rates and better coverage, the terahertz spectrum (0.1–10 THz), is viewed as a promising candidate [1–3]. Devices that would be employed in 6G-based wireless systems are expected to deliver one terabit per second (Tbps), with a peak spectral efficiency of 60 bps/Hz and 100 times improved energy efficiency [4, 5]. Figure 2, highlights the performance indicators for 6G systems. In addition to the aforementioned key performance indicators (KPIs), the 6G-based communication devices are evaluated based on extended KPIs such as reliability, positioning accuracy, connection density, etc. The enhanced KPIs of the 6G-based communication systems lead to the realization of numerous applications such as Industry 4.0, virtual reality, intra-device communication, high-speed wireless data centers, and high-speed backhaul links [6]. In current 5G-based cellular systems, millimetre-wave (mm-wave) communication is the primary technology. However, because of the stringent quality of service (QoS) requirements, mm-wave under 100 GHz has been implemented in current 5G-based wireless communication systems [7]. Conversely, because of the multi-GHz bandwidth, the picosecond-level symbol duration, and the coexistence with the standardized spectrum, the THz frequency band is considered one of the critical technologies which would fulfil the requirements and subsequently lead towards the realization of 6G-based cellular devices [8–10]. However, compared to mm-wave and optical-based communication systems, the THz-based communication systems exhibit resilience towards atmospheric effects. This characteristic facilitates simplified beamforming and beam-tracking tasks, enabling the subsequent deployment of the THz-based communication systems in environments with high QoS requirements.

Traditionally, the THz band in the electromagnetic (EM) wave spectrum has been the least explored band due to the unavailability of practical transceivers and antennas. However, with the advancements in photonics and microwave solid-state devices, the availability of highly directive antennas has paved the path for the practical deployment of THz-based systems. Currently, THz-spectrum finds its applications in spectroscopy for sensing applications such as material characterization, weather characterization, and the study of astronomical objects. However, with the advent of sophisticated manufacturing equipment nowadays, the THz band is utilized in Wireless Local Area Networks (WLANs), High-Speed Train communications, and Vehicle-to-everything applications where appropriate beam-steering and tracking capabilities are required for reliable information transmission. Furthermore, due to the compatibility of the THz spectrum with cellular biology nowadays, the THz spectrum has applications in the medical industry, particularly in invivo nanonetworks.

2.1.1 Terahertz Device Technologies

In this subsection, we will highlight the hardware building blocks, namely, the front-ends, the antenna systems, and digital back-ends, in a THz-based system.

THz Front-End Technologies: Although the THz-based communication systems are envisioned as the fundamental building blocks in the 6G-based applications, the advancements in the development of practical and commercial systems are still ongoing [11]. Currently, three main technological pathways, i.e., the electronic, the plasmonics, and the photonics approach, are essential for realising practical systems. In the electronic approach, the frequency multiplying chains are employed for up-converting a lower-frequency signal [12]. In general, Silicon (Si) CMOS and Silicon-Germanium (SiGe) BiCMOS-based electronic devices offering higher integration with the existing electronic systems are utilized [13]. In the plasmonics approach, by leveraging the properties of the plasma waves, the devices are created that intrinsically operate at THz frequencies [14]. Metamaterials such as graphene are utilised nowadays to create THz-based systems that can operate at room temperature [15]. In addition to the electronics and plasmonics approach, the photonics approach [16] utilizes optical signal generators such as quantum cascade lasers (QCLs) [17, 18], photoconductive antennas [19], and photomixer-like frequency-difference generators (DFG) [20]. Further, depending on the use case scenarios, particular types of antenna architecture are utilized to realise the THz-based practical signal generators. Particularly, open-ended waveguides, horn antennas, and parabolic antennas provide numerous options for directivity; advanced antenna and array techniques like electronically steerable antennas, beamforming, and beam switching are employed for seamless and dynamic services [21]. Other non-conventional devices currently explored for the design of THz-based communication systems include phase-change materials, such as vanadium dioxide (VO_2) and liquid crystals [22].

Antenna Systems for Transmission, Reception, and Reflection: Antennas are required for the conversion of the on-chip voltage/current signals into wireless signals. The antenna systems are much more flexible than the THz transceiver systems [23]. Generally, conventional antennas are employed in conjunction with electronic and photonic front-end, whereas plasmonic antennas are used with the plasmonic systems. Concurrently, to obtain a collimated beam towards the receivers, the optical lens is used in conjunction with antennas and front-end systems [24]. The high-frequency THz spectrum results in very small wavelength signals, enabling the development of very small conventional THz antennas. For instance, to exhibit a quasi-omnidirectional radiation pattern and tunable resonant frequency of 1 THz, a 150 μm long printed dipole or patch antenna is utilized. Moreover, utilizing graphene and other plasmonic materials leads to even smaller THz antennas. For example, a graphene-based nano-patch antenna of 1 μm $\times$ 10 nm generates a signal with the resonant frequency of 1 THz [25]. Miniaturized antenna size contributes towards the realization of next-generation applications of networks on chips and wearable and implantable devices. There are primarily two types of directional antenna systems:

- **Fixed directional antennas** which include horn antenna (directivity of 20–25 dBi), Cassegrain dish reflector antennas (directivity around 40–45 dBi) [26], or multi-reflector antennas (30–35 dBi) [27]. Furthermore, leaky wave antennas with radiation direction dependent on excitation frequency are used for spatial and frequency multiplexing.
- **Beamforming Antenna Arrays** include fixed or dynamic antenna arrays built with either traditional metals or nanomaterials. Metallic antenna arrays with 16 controllable in association with electronic front-ends are used in applications under 300 GHz [28].

Table 1 represents the properties of different antenna systems currently utilized in THz-based systems.

Digital Bottleneck: Attaining 1 Tbps links requires not only reliable front-ends or antennas that operate at high frequencies but also require a robust digital signal processing back-end that can generate information signals at a very high rate at the transmitting and receiving side [29]. The major difficulty in the realization of ultra-broadband digital THz communications is posed by the performance of the digital-to-analogue converters (DACs) and analogue-to-digital converters (ADCs) [30]. Currently, the state-of-the-art DACs at the transmitters are able to sample at a rate of 128 Giga samples per second (GSaps); however, this sampling rate comes with major

Table 1 Properties of different antenna systems

Structures	Use case			Element size	Mode of operation			
	Tx.	Rx.	Ref.		Beamform.	Spatial Mod.	Absorp.	Polar.
Antenna and antenna arrays	Yes	Yes	Yes	$\simeq\lambda/2$	Yes	Yes	No	No
Dielectric lenses and lens arrays	Yes	Yes	Yes	$\geq\lambda$	Yes	Yes	No	Yes
Metasurfaces	Yes	Yes	Yes	$\ll\lambda/2$	Yes	Yes	Yes	Yes

challenges such as low resolution and high power requirements [31]. Simultaneously, high sampling frequency and higher resolution ADCs have been developed at the receiver, but these devices also suffer from higher costs and higher thermal and spatial requirements.

2.1.2 THz Standardization

First standardization at 300 GHz by IEEE 802.15 THz interest group is known as IEEE 802.15.3d-2017 [32]. This is an amendment to the previous standard IEEE 802.15.3-2016 [33] working at 60 GHz and achieving operation data rate of up to 100 Gbps. As illustrated in Fig. 3, the 300 GHz standard utilizes 8 different channel bandwidths between 252 and 321 GHz at multiples of 2.16 GHz [34]. Currently, for active services, such as earth exploration satellite services and radio astronomy, up to 275 GHz is allocated. Furthermore, at the World Radiocommunication Conference (WRC) 2019 [35], four contiguous bands (275–296 GHz, 306–313 GHz, 318–333 GHz, 356–450 GHz) were identified for mobile and fixed services. In addition, the ThoR project [36] identified three bands (296–306 GHz, 313–318 GHz, 33–356 GHz) for interference mitigation while considering the operational characteristics of passive and active services.

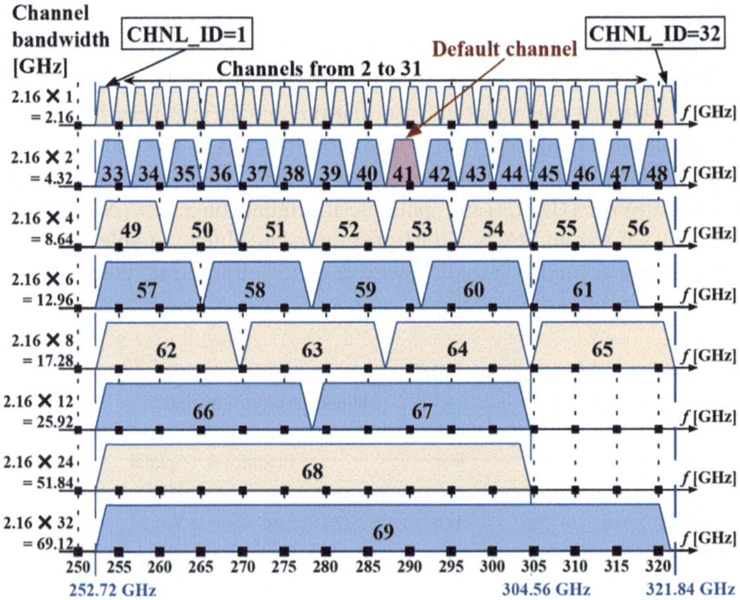

Fig. 3 IEEE 802.15.3d-2017 standard for 0.252–0.321 THz spectrum allocation [34]

2.2 *Properties and Characteristics of THz Waves*

THz waves exhibit unique properties, including low absorption by biological tissues, non-ionizing radiation, and strong interactions with molecular vibrations. These characteristics make THz communication suitable for a wide range of applications, from high-speed data transmission to biomedical sensing and imaging. Due to the numerous opportunities, the THz spectrum will empower the 6G-based systems by providing solutions to real-world challenges in conjunction with the existing 5G technologies. The physical characteristic traits of the wireless channel medium, where the information propagation from the transmitting source to the receiving destination occurs, determines the overall performance of the communication system. Figure 4 highlights the THz-channel modeling. The THz-channel modeling comprises outdoor channel modeling, indoor channel modeling and nanoscale channel modeling.

Outdoor channel models are scarce and focus primarily on point-to-point links. For outdoor environment measurement, the interference from unintentional non-line-of-sight (NLoS) paths impacts the bit error rate (BER) performance. The THz links suffer from significant attenuation due to atmospheric conditions, especially for long-distance wireless communication. Figure 5 illustrates the impact of environmental and weather conditions in terms of attenuation on various frequency bands. Unlike outdoor models, several indoor channel models are available, which can be categorized into deterministic, stochastic, and hybrid models. Ray tracing (RT), finite difference time domain (FDTD), and measurement-based models collectively represent the deterministic channel modeling category. The ray tracing technique utilizes the

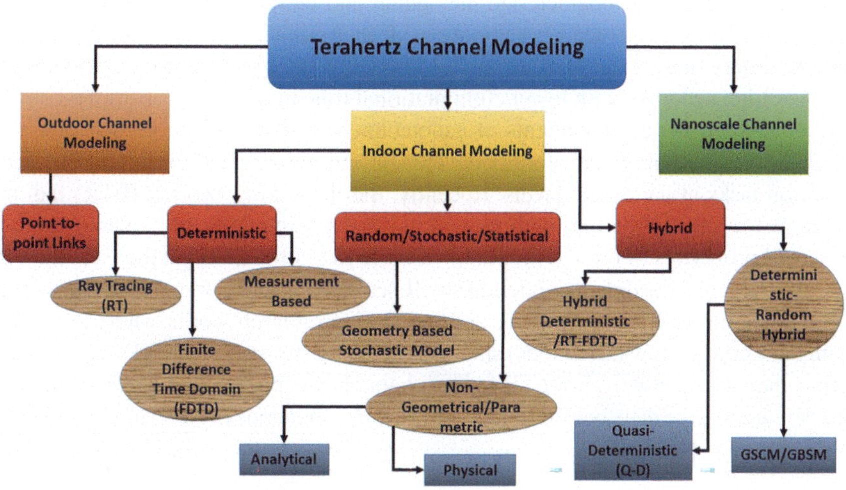

Fig. 4 THz channel modeling

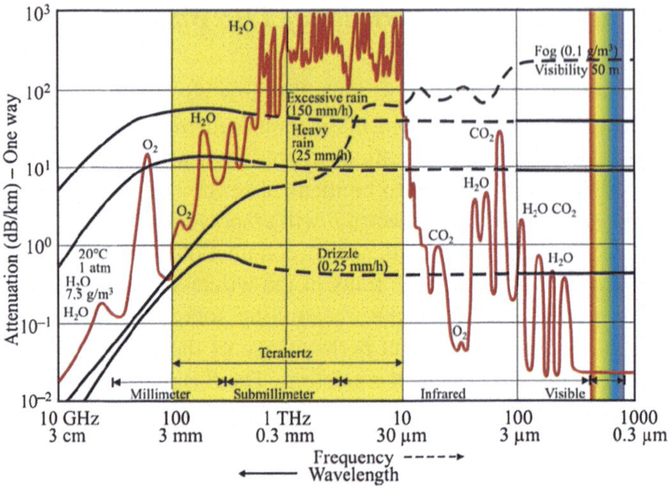

Fig. 5 Attenuation impact due to environmental effects over different frequencies [43]

fundamentals of wave transmission and is employed in line-of-sight (LoS) and NLoS environments. The Yee's or FDTD method numerically derives the channel model from Maxwell's equations, wherein the channel is divided into grids to accelerate the computations; finally, the electric and magnetic fields are analyzed. On the contrary, stochastic channel modeling (SCM) enables the utilization of large datasets obtained from empirical channel measurements. Using probabilistic approaches (cumulative distribution function, moment generating function, and probability density function), the SCM models characterize the spatial and temporal characteristics of the THz channel. Furthermore, a combination of deterministic and stochastic channel models results in a newer channel model known as the hybrid channel model that achieves high accuracy with lower computational time in resource-constrained environments. With the advancements in nanotechnology, the realization of nanoscale sensing, computational, and storage devices has allowed data storing, sensing, and actuation tasks at nanoscale levels. Recently, the fluctuating two-ray (FTR) fading has drawn a lot of attention, with numerous works being dedicated to analyze the statistical properties of the FTR random variable [37–39]. Although the FTR fading distribution is used widely in modeling small-scale fading environments in mm-wave communication technologies, there are only a few research works where the FTR fading distribution is used to model small-scale fading statistics of the THz communication channel accurately. For FTR fading channels, the probability density function and the cumulative distribution function of the instantaneous SNR γ_r are expressed, respectively, as [40]

$$f_\Gamma(\gamma) = \frac{m^m}{\Gamma(m)} \sum_{i=0}^{\infty} \frac{K^i \, d_i}{i! \, i!} \frac{\gamma_r^i}{(2\sigma^2)^{i+1}} \, \mathrm{e}^{\left(-\frac{\gamma}{2\sigma^2}\right)}, \tag{1}$$

$$F_\Gamma(\gamma) = \frac{m^m}{\Gamma(m)} \sum_{i=0}^{\infty} \frac{K^i \, d_i}{i! \, i!} \, \gamma\left(i+1, \frac{\gamma}{2\sigma^2}\right), \tag{2}$$

where $\Gamma(\cdot)$ is the gamma function and the lower incomplete gamma function $\gamma(i+1, \gamma/2\sigma^2)$ is given by

$$\gamma\left(i+1, \frac{\gamma}{2\sigma^2}\right) = 1 - \mathrm{e}^{-\frac{\gamma}{2\sigma^2}} \sum_{j=0}^{i} \frac{(\gamma)^j}{(2\sigma^2)^j \, j!}. \tag{3}$$

The multiplicative factor d_i in (1) and (2) is given by [41].

$$\begin{aligned} d_i \triangleq & \sum_{q=0}^{i} \binom{i}{q} \sum_{s=0}^{q} \binom{q}{s} \frac{\Gamma(i+m+2s-q) \, K^{2s-q}}{(m+K)^{(i+m+2s-q)}} \\ & \times \left(\frac{\Delta}{2}\right)^{2s} \times (-1)^{2s-q} \times R_{i+m}^{q-2s}\left(\left\{\frac{K\Delta}{m+K}\right\}^2\right), \end{aligned} \tag{4}$$

where m, K, and $\Delta \in [0, 1]$ are the parameters representing the fading severity, the average power ratio of the dominant component to the remaining diffuse multipath, and the dominant waves similarity index. The factor $R_\omega^\epsilon(y)$, in (4) is defined as [41, Eq. (20)]

$$R_\omega^\epsilon(y) \triangleq \begin{cases} \left(\frac{\omega-\epsilon}{2}\right)_\epsilon \left(\frac{\omega-\epsilon+1}{2}\right)_\epsilon \frac{y^\epsilon}{\epsilon!} \\ \times \; {}_2F_1\left(\frac{\omega+\epsilon}{2}; \frac{\omega+\epsilon+1}{2}; 1+\epsilon; y\right) & \text{for } \epsilon \in \mathbb{N}^+, \\ \frac{{}_2F_1\left(\frac{\omega-\epsilon}{2}; \frac{\omega-\epsilon+1}{2}; 1-\epsilon; y\right)}{\Gamma(1-\epsilon)} & \text{otherwise}, \end{cases} \tag{5}$$

where $\omega = i + m, \epsilon = q - 2s, {}_2F_1(a; b; c; x)$ is the Gauss hypergeometric function, and $(\cdot)_b$ represents the Pochhammer symbol, written as $(a)_b = \Gamma(a+b)/\Gamma(a) = a(a+1)...(a+b-1)$. Substituting (3) in (2), the c.d.f. expression of (2) is simplified to

$$F_\Gamma(\gamma) = 1 - \frac{m^m}{\Gamma(m)} \sum_{i=0}^{\infty} \frac{K^i \, d_i \, \mathrm{e}^{-\frac{\gamma_r}{2\sigma^2}}}{i!} \sum_{j=0}^{i} \frac{(\gamma)^j}{(2\sigma^2)^j \, j!}, \tag{6}$$

where $2\sigma^2$ represents the average power of the diffuse component over FTR fading. In addition to small-scale fading, THz-based systems also experience free space path loss (FSPL), attenuation due to atmospheric gasses, and molecular absorption caused by rain and fog. The FSPL is expressed through Friis' transmission expression given as

$$P_{Rx}(l) = \frac{P_{Tx} A_{eTx} A_{eRx}}{l^2 \lambda^2}, \tag{7}$$

where P_{rx}, P_{Tx}, A_{eTx}, A_{eTx}, l, and λ represents the received power, transmit power, effective transmitter and receiver antenna area, propagation distance, and wavelength respectively. Based on Friis' transmission expression, the mathematical expression of FSPL can be written as

$$FSPL = \left(\frac{4\pi l}{\lambda}\right)^2. \tag{8}$$

Moreover, according to the ITU recommendations, attenuation due to rain follows a power-law distribution, given by

$$\gamma_R = kR^a, \tag{9}$$

where γ_R and R denotes rain attenuation in dB/km and rain rate in mm/hr, respectively, while k and a are frequency-dependent coefficients derived from scattering calculations. Figure 5 illustrates the impact of various environmental factors on signal attenuation across different frequency ranges.

The impact of small and large-scale path loss models in THz-based networks is crucial to accurately characterize and model the line-of-sight (LOS) communication in THz-based systems. Particularly, in small-scale fading, the signal arriving at the receiver results from numerous multipath components, causing both constructive and destructive interferences. Therefore, it is critical to account for both FSPL and small-scale fading simultaneously to create a reliable and efficient THz communication system for 6G networks.

In THz-based networks, FSPL leads to significant attenuation, especially at higher frequencies, necessitating novel antenna designs and short-range communication models to address this high signal loss. At the same time, small-scale fading caused by multipath propagation can be mitigated using adaptive beamforming and diversity techniques to minimize interference, thereby ensuring more reliable and efficient communication, which is essential for the success of 6G networks (Table 2).

2.3 Current Applications and Challenges in THz Communication

The THz frequency band is envisioned as a promising candidate for various applications, ranging from the nano-to-macro scale. The ability to provide terabits per second (Tbps) data rates with reliable and efficient information transmission,

Table 2 THz channel measurement techniques

	Vector network analyzer based	Sliding correlation based	Direct pulse based
Domain	Frequency	Time	Time
Signal	Single carrier	Auto-correlated sequence	THz pulse
Distance	Limited by physical link	Support long distance	Limited by pulse power
Physical link	Required	Not required	Required
Synchronization	Implicit	Required	Required
Bandwidth	Large (dozens of GHz)	Small ($\leq$10 GHz)	Very Large $(THz - level)$
Measuring speed	Low	High	High
Use cases/applications	Indoor conference hall	University and train station environment	Network on chip and Internet of nano things

alongside minimal latency, makes the THz spectrum a key enabler for 6G networks and beyond. Despite its immense potential, THz communication faces several technical and regulatory challenges.

One major challenge is propagation loss, which becomes significant at high frequencies due to atmospheric absorption and molecular absorption. Environmental factors such as rain, fog, and even oxygen in the air can severely attenuate THz signals. Regulatory constraints also pose a challenge, as spectrum allocation for THz frequencies is still in its infancy.

Another key challenge in THz communication is interference, particularly due to the narrow and highly directional nature of pencil beams used in THz systems [42]. These beams are produced by small-sized antenna arrays with multiple antenna elements, making them highly sensitive to alignment errors. If the receiver's beam is accidentally directed toward a dominant multipath interference link, significant interference can occur. Additionally, in scenarios involving mobile users, where the transceiver system must continuously update the beam direction to maintain communication, frequent adjustments can result in increased interference and degraded performance.

To mitigate interference, various techniques are being explored. Adaptive beamforming is a crucial strategy, where the system dynamically adjusts the direction and shape of the beam to focus on the intended receiver while minimizing interference from unwanted sources. Additionally, placing nulls in the antenna gain pattern towards interfering signals can reduce the impact of interference. Cognitive radio techniques also offer a potential solution by allowing THz systems to intelligently sense the environment and dynamically adjust their frequency usage and beam direction based on real-time conditions, thus avoiding interference with other systems.

THz communication has several applications, including short-range wireless links, imaging systems, intra-device communications, wireless backhaul/fronthaul networks, and high-speed train communication networks. It also supports nano-networks, vehicle-to-everything (V2X) networks, and spectroscopy. Ongoing research aims to overcome technical barriers to extend these systems' capabilities for long-range and high-capacity communication.

Despite the significant advancements in THz communication, several challenges still need to be addressed before large-scale commercial deployment can be achieved. These include complexities in channel measurement and modeling, such as dealing with multipath propagation, diffuse particle scattering, and capturing the time-varying characteristics of THz channels. Additionally, concerns regarding RF-EMF (Radio Frequency Electromagnetic Fields) exposure at THz frequencies remain unresolved. The development of enhanced channel simulators and the integration of Reconfigurable Intelligent Surfaces (RIS) or hybrid channel models are also critical for improving the overall performance of THz communication systems.

In conclusion, while the THz band holds tremendous promise for future communication systems, several challenges–especially those related to interference management and channel modeling–must be addressed. Innovative solutions such as adaptive beamforming, cognitive radio, and advanced antenna designs will be crucial in ensuring the successful deployment of THz communication systems.

2.4 Potential Benefits of THz Communication in 6G Networks

Integrating THz communication into 6G networks offers numerous benefits, including increased data rates, enhanced spectrum efficiency, and support for emerging applications such as virtual reality, augmented reality, and ultra-high-definition video streaming. By leveraging the bandwidth available in the THz band, 6G networks can achieve unprecedented performance and connectivity. The availability of very large bandwidth, particularly at THz frequencies, alleviates the spectrum scarcity problem of current wireless networks and opens the door to the practical realization of wireless terabit-per-second (Tbps) links. Furthermore, the availability of miniaturized-sized THz transceivers and antennas has contributed towards the realization of extremely small radios that are non-intrusively installed, thereby creating a possibility of realization of numerous applications such as the Internet of Nano-Things and wireless networks on chip. Moreover, the utilization of the THz-band paved the path for next-generation wireless sensing and localization.

3 Fundamentals of MC

3.1 Introduction to MC

The traditional communication engineering paradigm has mostly been focused on electromagnetic (EM) communication where the information is transferred through the EM waves propagating either through a wired channel or a wireless one. However, the recent advancements in the fields of biology and nanotechnology have enabled scientists and engineers to create biologically inspired bio-nanomachines that are capable of interacting with biological systems at the nano and micro scale environments [44, 45]. Some of the envisioned applications of such bio-nanomachines include the development and deployment of bio-hybrid systems [46], nanoscale sensors [47], targeted drug delivery [44], internet of nano things (IoNT) [45], and body area networks (BAN) [48]. These nanomachines have simple architecture, leading to limited computational and networking capabilities. To overcome these limitations, many nanomachines can be interconnected, where they cooperate and communicate with each other forming a nanonetwork [47, 48]. Using EM communication in such nanoscale environments is very difficult and inefficient, and other communication paradigms need to be explored [49].

Molecular Communication (MC) is a bio-inspired communication paradigm that utilizes chemical signals to exchange information between nanoscale devices. In MC, information is encoded in the concentration, type, and timing of signaling molecules, enabling communication at the molecular level. Even though there are other communication paradigms for such nanoscale environments like nano-mechanical, acoustic, and terahertz [48], MC has emerged as the most promising one [50–58]. MC, a nature-inspired communication method, is inherently energy-efficient, bio-compatible, and employable in physiological systems, making it suited for applications such as nanonetworks and IoNT.

3.2 Basic Principles and Components of MC Systems

MC is the most common form of communication in nature and is ubiquitous in biological systems, as it is the primary mode of communication in biological systems for both macroscopic and microscopic scales [44, 50]. At the microscopic scale, MC is employed for inter-cellular and intra-cellular communications, while MC using pheromones is used for long range communications [48]. A simple MC system consists of a message source, a transmitter, a propagation channel, and a receiver as shown in Fig. 6. The transmitter encodes the information and releases information molecules in to a fluid or a gaseous medium that forms the communication channel. These information molecules are sensed at the receiver, and the receiver makes a

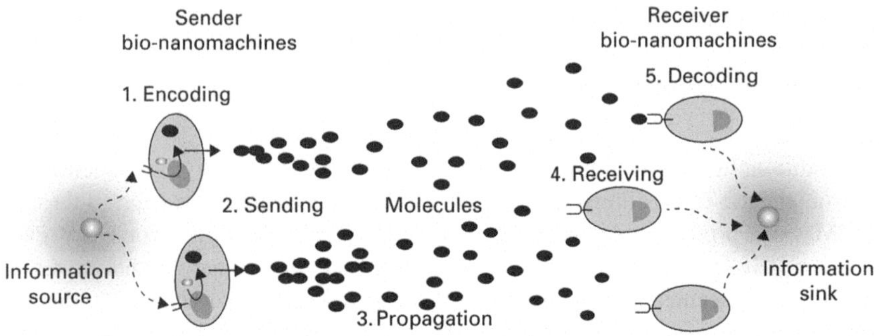

Fig. 6 A representation of a MC system [44]

decision about the transmitted symbol based on this information. Various properties associated with information molecules can be modulated to convey the information including:

- Number: Here, the information is modulated on the number of information molecules being released into the fluid medium. Different symbols are represented using different concentrations of molecules. This type of modulation is also known as amplitude modulation (AM) in the context of MC [48].
- Concentration: Here, the information is modulated on the concentration of information molecules being released into the fluid medium. Different symbols are represented using different numbers of molecules. This type of modulation is also known as concentration shift keying (CSK) in context of MC [59].
- Timing: In this scheme, the release time of the information molecules is modulated to convey the information. The receiver measures the time of arrival, and makes a decision regarding the symbol transmitted based on this information [60, 61].
- Position: Here, the release position of the information molecules is modulated to convey the information. The receiver measures the arrival position, and makes a decision regarding the symbol transmitted based on this information [62].

It has been known for long that MC is the prominent mode of communication in nature, including microorganisms and body cells that exchange information through the exchange of chemicals [46, 63]. However, the pioneering work in the field of MC from the perspective of an engineered communication system was started by Suda and colleagues in 2005 [50], and since then the research in this area has made considerable progress with increased focus on nanonetworks.

In the next section, we discuss the model of a typical MC system and the design considerations.

3.3 MC Model: Overview and Considerations

In this section, we discuss MC from a communication engineering perspective, identifying primary processes and components required for designing and analyzing such systems.

3.3.1 MC Model

Shannon's model of communication can easily be extended to describe an MC system. As with any communication system, an MC system has three basic components: the transmitter, the receiver, and the propagation channel. The physical components necessary to implement an MC system are shown in Fig. 7. These components are responsible for carrying out the primary processes that are involved in MC including:

- Encoding: Encoding is the process of modulating the pattern of information molecules at the transmitter to convey the message in a way that the receiver can detect. Properties such as number, time of release, concentration, etc., of information molecules can be modulated.
- Releasing: This is the process of releasing information molecules into the propagation medium. This can be done in two ways: the information molecules unbind from the transmit nanomachine, or the information molecules diffuse away through a molecular gate.
- Propagation: During propagation, the information molecules move from the transmitter to the receiver. The propagation paradigm can be broadly classified into two modes: active and passive. We will dive a bit deeper into the channel and propagation mechanisms in the next Section.

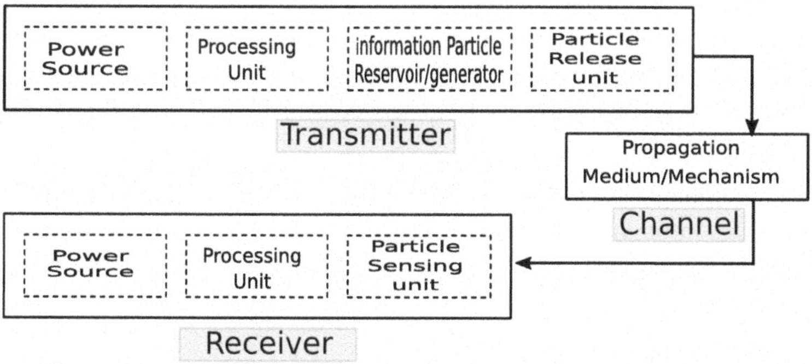

Fig. 7 Key physical components for MC

- Receiving: During this phase, the receiver captures the information molecules from the fluid environment. The receiver can also be modeled as either being active or passive.
- Decoding: Decoding is the process of estimating the transmitted message based on the received information molecules.

3.3.2 Channel and Propagation

For communicating at smaller scales, two approaches are feasible: miniaturizing the traditional electronic or electromagnetic communication systems and utilizing/mimicking the existing MC systems in nature. However, for communication at nano and micro scales, MC is the obvious choice for communication scientists. There are many options: diffusion based propagation, flow assisted propagation, active transport using molecular motors and cytoskeletal filaments, and bacteria assisted propagation [48].

- Free diffusion: Diffusion, or Brownian motion, is the random motion of a particle suspended in a fluid and arises from the collisions with other molecules in its neighborhood. As free diffusion utilizes the thermal energy of the fluid environment itself, diffusive propagation does not require any external source of energy.
- Flow assisted propagation: Though diffusion has the advantage of requiring no external source of energy for transmission, information particles can take very long to reach the receiver. Introducing a flow in the fluid medium from transmitter towards receiver is one way to significantly increase the propagation speed as compared to free diffusion.
- Motor protein moving over microtubule tracks: Using microtubules and motor proteins is an efficient way to actively transport the information particles from the transmitter to the receiver.
- Bacteria assisted propagation: In this scheme, bacteria are used as packets inside which information molecules are placed and are released into the channel. The bacteria travels through channel and releases the information molecules upon reaching the receiver. This propagation can be enhanced by using self propelling flagellated bacteria.

As with any communication channel, the channel introduces some noise in the signal as it propagates through it. Noise in the context of communication is some form of distortion that degrades the received signal quality. In case of MC, the sources of the noise can be many:

- diffusion noise due to random propagation
- transmitter noise
- receiver noise (reception/counting)
- environmental degradation of information molecules
- stray molecules present in the environment, acting as noise
- left over molecules from previous transmissions, resulting in ISI.

3.4 Applications and Challenges of MC

MC allows using nanomachines to form nanonetworks that are capable of sensing, transporting, and modifying information carrying molecules. Most promising application areas include biomedical and environmental applications [44]. In this section, we briefly discuss these applications:

3.4.1 Biomedical Applications

- Lab-on-a-chip: In such applications, a biological sample can be chemically analyzed on a small chip. Such a chip will have certain modules that perform specific functions, and MC can be employed to carry specific molecules to specific modules on the chip.
- Health monitoring: Monitoring of specific molecules within the body of an animal or a plant can be carried out using MC. These specific molecules can be used to biomark a disease or some medical condition. Bio-nanomachines can be implanted in the body and MC can be used to collect information about these marker molecules, interpret the information, and transfer it to some external unit.
- Drug delivery: Drug supply systems make it easier to manage and distribute drugs in an organism. Implanted bio-nanomachines or nano-robots can use MC for targeted drug delivery and help reduce the side-effects, while increasing the efficacy.

3.4.2 Environmental Applications

- Environment monitoring: MC can be employed to identify certain agents present in the environment that may be toxic or radioactive. This information can be used to detect problems and provide an environment-cleaning map. Nanomachines that are integrated into such environments can map the locations of such molecules and used MC to process this molecular information and communicate the result to other some central monitoring device.
- Pollution management: Nanomachines could be used to not only detect the kind of pollutants present in an environment by detecting specific molecules and their sources, but can also be used to manage the pollutants by limiting such molecules by activating counter reactions as specific locations.

3.4.3 Security and Privacy Challenges

MC offers tremendous potential for bio-medical applications like in-body nanonetworks for disease diagnostics and targeted drug delivery. However, given its nature, it also raises some significant security and privacy concerns, like the privacy, security, and ownership of a person's sensitive health information. Other concerns include reliability and the biological compatibility of the data.

One way to address these concerns is by deploying encryption in the MC setting. Given that MC vastly differs from conventional communication paradigms, novel encryption techniques must be deployed. Some of the most suited encryption techniques include chemical-based cryptography, where specific chemical reactions are used to encode and decode the data. Another promising encryption technique quite suited for MC is molecular stenography, where the communication is hidden by embedding the information in the naturally occurring biological and molecular processes within the body. Bio-molecular encryption can also be used to secure sensitive data. Here, biological components like DNA, RNA, and protein are used to encode the data.

3.5 Definitions and Mathematical Preliminaries

In this section, we give some of the basic terms and definitions used in the MC literature.

3.5.1 Diffusion, Brownian Motion, and Weiner Process

A molecule suspended freely in a fluid medium propagates through the underlying process of Brownian motion, which results from the random collisions with the fluid's molecules. A mathematical description of diffusion was first provided by Adolf Fick. This description, known as Fick's second law, is based on the diffusion coefficient D and gives a deterministic solution for the concentration of diffusing molecules, governed by the partial differential equation

$$\frac{\partial c'}{\partial t} = D\nabla^2 c', \tag{10}$$

where c' is the local concentration of the diffusing quantity (the concentration field) at a given position and time, and D is the diffusion coefficient that depends on the temperature T, the fluid viscosity η, and the molecule's Stokes radius R and is given as

$$D = \frac{k_B T}{6\pi \eta R} \tag{11}$$

where k_B is the Boltzmann constant.

While the bulk transport of the diffusing molecules is a deterministic process, the movement of individual molecules undergoing Brownian motion (discrete Brownian motion) is not. A Wiener process is a simple physical model for a discrete Brownian motion [44]. If $B(t)$ represents the position of a molecule undergoing Brownian motion at time $t \geq 0$, where $B(0)$ represents the initial position, then $B(t)$ is a one-dimensional Wiener process if the following two criteria are satisfied:

1. For time instances t_1 and t_2, where $t_2 > t_1 \geq 0$, and some constant σ^2

$$B(t_2) - B(t_1) \sim \mathcal{N}(0, \sigma^2(t_2 - t_1)), \tag{12}$$

   where $\mathcal{N}\left(m, \sigma^2\right)$ represents a Gaussian distribution with mean m and variance σ^2;

2. For two non-overlapping intervals $[t_1, t_2]$ and $[t_3, t_4]$, the increments $B(t_4) - B(t_3)$ and $B(t_2) - B(t_1)$ are statistically independent.

In physical Brownian motion, the variance parameter σ^2 is given as $\sigma^2 = \alpha D$, with $\alpha = 2, 4, 6$ for one, two, three dimensional diffusion, respectively. The independent increments are a key property of the Wiener process and allow the use of the Markov chain.

Using this Markovian property, diffusion can be simulated in a precise way using the Monte-Carlo method. In a 2-dimensional environment, given an initial position (x_0, y_0, z_0) at time $t = 0$, and any integer $k > 0$, the motion of the particles can be described by the sequence of coordinates (x_i, y_i, z_i) for $i = 1, 2, \cdots, k$, where coordinate (x_i, y_i, z_i) is the particle's location at time instance $t = it$, and can be given as

$$(x_i, y_i, z_i) = (x_{i-1}, y_{i-1}, z_{i-1}) + (\Delta x_i, \Delta y_i, \Delta z_i), \tag{13}$$

where, $\Delta x_i \sim N(0, 2D\Delta t)$, $\Delta y_i \sim N(0, 2D\Delta t)$, and $\Delta z_i \sim N(0, 2D\Delta t)$ in case there is no drift present in the fluid medium. In the case of a constant drift in the fluid medium, $\Delta x_i = v_x \Delta t + N(0, 2D\Delta t)$, $\Delta y_i = v_y \Delta t + N(0, 2D\Delta t)$, and $\Delta z_i = v_z \Delta t + N(0, 2D\Delta t)$, where v_x, v_y, v_z, represent the velocity components in the x, y, z-directions, respectively.

3.5.2 First Passage Time

In any MC system, an information molecule Once released into the fluid medium, takes a random path to the receiver. The time taken for the information molecule to travel to the receiver surface for the first time, also called the first passage time, is also random. This random arrival time plays an important role in the design and analysis of an MC system. Note that the notion of first passage time is important as given the random path taken by a Brownian particle, the information molecule may cross the receiver surface many times. Usually, the receiver is modeled as a perfectly absorbing surface, where the information molecules are pulled out of the system as soon as they arrive at the receiver (Dirichlet boundary condition), or as a transparent passive observer that does not affect the movement of information molecules.

In case of molecular timing channels, this random first passage time of the information molecules acts as an additive noise, i.e., if T_x is the release time of the molecule and T_y is the time when this molecule arrives at the receiver, then we can express T_y as

$$T_y = T_x + T_n, \tag{14}$$

where T_n is the random first passage time of the information particle and is highly dependent on the presence or the absence of any drift in the fluid medium. In the presence of a positive drift from the transmitter to the receiver, the additive noise term has an inverse Gaussian (IG) distribution, while in case of a drift free fluid medium, the additive noise term follows a Lévy distribution [48].

3.6 Integration of MC in 6G Networks

Many models of the smart 6G networks of the future will be inspired from biological organisms, which are known for their efficiency. In fact, the idea to incorporate a biological layer as part of future 6G's (Sixth-Generation) networks is one of the most fascinating ones. Integrating MC into 6G networks offers unique opportunities for communication at scales and in environments never before imaginable. Ushering in new applications such as intra-body communication, targeted drug delivery, and environmental sensing. The concept of a biological layer has evolved in tandem with the emergence of two new nanoscale communication paradigms: MC and THz. Using MC and THz nanonetworks as its primary enabling technologies. This biological layer will give the future 6G networks unprecedented levels of connectivity and functionality.

4 Synergistic Fusion of THz and MC

THz communication and MC offer unique synergies that can mitigate the limitations inherent in each technology when used independently [64]. By combining their strengths, we can develop innovative communication systems with enhanced capabilities, paving the way for groundbreaking applications in diverse fields.

Figure 8 illustrates a conceptual model of synergetic fusion in medical technology, emphasizing the role of MC for sensing and communication within the body. Biomedical sensors are strategically placed to monitor physiological parameters and use MC to relay this information within the circulatory system. The collected data is then conveyed externally through THz communication to healthcare provider, enabling real-time health monitoring and personalized medical interventions. This integration

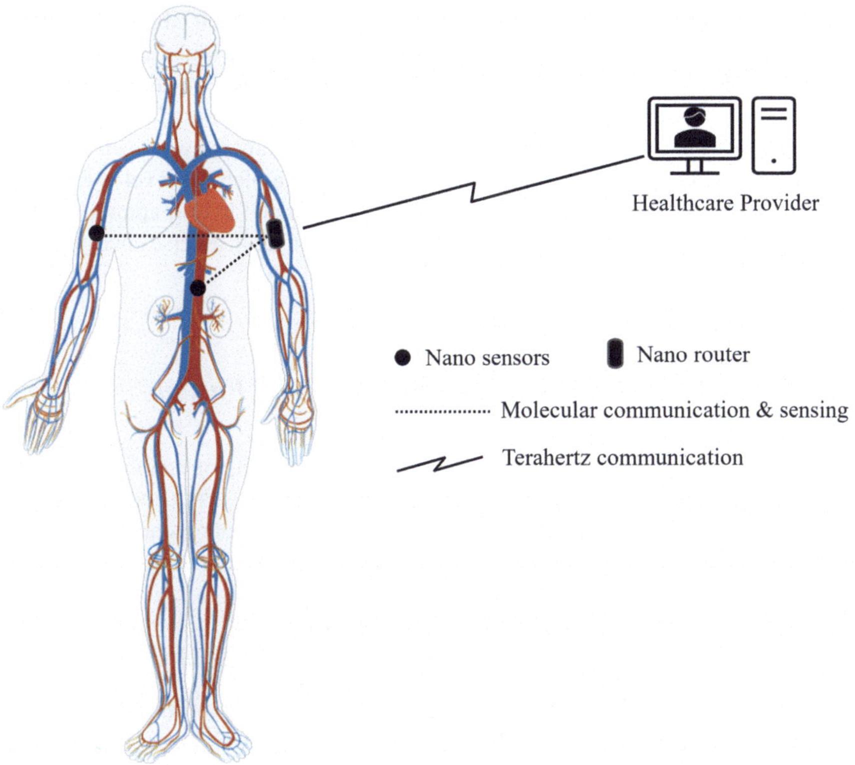

Fig. 8 Synergistic fusion of THz and MC for the state-of-the-art healthcare applications

leverages the body's natural pathways for efficient data transmission, highlighting the potential of advanced biomedical engineering to revolutionize healthcare by ensuring continuous, accurate, and responsive medical care.

4.1 Rationale for Combining THz and MC

The fusion of THz communication and MC is driven by the need to leverage the complementary strengths of each technology. THz communication excels in providing high-speed, long-range connectivity with large bandwidth, making it ideal for macroscopic communication networks. On the other hand, MC enables effective communication at the nanoscale, with minimal energy consumption and low interference, making it suitable for applications within biological environments and other complex mediums where traditional electromagnetic communication methods fall short.

The rationale for combining these technologies lies in their ability to address each other's limitations. THz communication, while offering high data rates, faces challenges such as high path loss and atmospheric absorption, which limit its range and reliability in certain environments. MC, with its diffusion-based propagation, is inherently slow and limited in range but excels in environments where electromagnetic waves cannot penetrate or where precision at the molecular level is required. By integrating THz and MC, it becomes possible to create hybrid communication systems that are both high-speed and capable of functioning in diverse environments, from the macro to the nanoscale.

4.2 *Potential Synergies and Advantages of the Fusion*

Combining THz and MC technologies opens up the possibility of establishing seamless communication links that span multiple length scales, from macroscopic to nanoscopic. This hybrid approach enables the creation of heterogeneous networks capable of supporting a wide range of applications, from macrocellular communication to intra-body sensing and targeted drug delivery.

The potential synergies and advantages of this fusion are manifold:

- **Enhanced Connectivity:** By leveraging the high-speed capabilities of THz communication and the precise, localized communication of MC, it becomes possible to establish robust communication networks that can operate efficiently across different scales and environments.
- **Energy Efficiency:** The fusion of THz and MC technologies significantly enhances energy efficiency, especially in resource-constrained environments like implantable medical devices. MC inherently mimics biological processes, using chemical signals for communication, which results in low power consumption ideal for long-term operation in devices such as bio-nanosensors and targeted drug delivery systems. This bio-compatible, energy-efficient nature of MC complements THz communication, which, while requiring more power, offers high-speed data transmission. By leveraging MC for nanoscale, intra-body communication and selectively utilizing THz for high-data tasks, the hybrid system optimizes overall energy consumption. Moreover, integrating energy harvesting techniques, such as utilizing kinetic or thermal energy from the human body, enhances the sustainability of these devices, allowing them to function autonomously for extended periods without the need for frequent battery replacements.
- **Reduced Interference:** MC's minimal interference characteristics can help mitigate the interference challenges faced by THz communication, particularly in densely populated or complex environments.

- **Seamless Integration:** The fusion of THz and MC can enable the development of integrated systems that can seamlessly transition between macroscopic and nanoscopic communication, supporting applications that require both broad coverage and high precision.

4.3 Challenges and Solutions in Integrating the Two Communication Paradigms

Integrating THz and MC presents several technical challenges that need to be addressed to realize their full potential. These challenges include synchronization, channel modeling, and signal processing across disparate timescales and length scales.

- **Synchronization:** Achieving synchronization between THz and MC systems is challenging due to the vastly different propagation speeds and timescales involved. Innovative synchronization techniques that can align the timing of these systems are required to ensure seamless communication.
- **Channel Modeling:** Accurate channel models that capture the unique characteristics of both THz and MC propagation are essential for predicting performance and optimizing system design. This includes modeling path loss, multipath propagation, and molecular diffusion, and developing hybrid models that can integrate these different phenomena.
- **Signal Processing:** Signal processing techniques need to be adapted to handle the distinct challenges of both THz and MC systems. This includes developing algorithms for error correction, interference mitigation, and adaptive modulation that can operate effectively across different scales and environments.

Addressing these challenges requires innovative solutions in hardware design, signal processing algorithms, and system integration techniques. Advanced materials, novel device architectures, and hybrid signal processing frameworks are key to overcoming these obstacles and realizing the full potential of THz and MC fusion.

4.4 Technologies and Techniques for Synergistic Fusion

4.4.1 Hardware and Device Considerations

Designing hardware for the synergistic fusion of THz and MC requires careful consideration of device architectures, fabrication techniques, and integration challenges. Advanced materials, such as graphene and nanomaterials, hold promise for realizing compact and energy-efficient devices capable of operating across multiple frequency bands.

- **Device Architectures:** The design of hybrid devices that can support both THz and MC communication is critical. This includes developing transceivers that can switch between electromagnetic and molecular communication modes, and integrating these devices into compact, multifunctional units.
- **Fabrication Techniques:** Advanced fabrication techniques are required to create the nanoscale components necessary for MC, as well as the high-frequency components needed for THz communication. Techniques such as nanoimprint lithography and atomic layer deposition can be leveraged to achieve the precision and scalability needed for these devices.
- **Integration Challenges:** Integrating THz and MC components into a single system presents significant challenges, including ensuring compatibility between different materials and technologies, and managing the thermal and power requirements of the system. Innovative integration techniques, such as 3D integration and system-on-chip designs, are essential for overcoming these challenges.

4.4.2 Signal Processing and Modulation Techniques

Signal processing and modulation techniques play a crucial role in optimizing communication performance and reliability in THz and MC systems. Adaptive modulation schemes, error correction codes, and interference mitigation algorithms are essential for mitigating channel impairments and maximizing spectral efficiency.

- **Adaptive Modulation:** Developing modulation schemes that can dynamically adapt to the varying conditions of THz and MC channels is crucial for maintaining reliable communication. Techniques such as adaptive coding and modulation (ACM) can be used to optimize data rates and reliability based on channel conditions.
- **Error Correction Codes:** Robust error correction codes are necessary to compensate for the high error rates and signal degradation in THz and MC channels. Techniques such as low-density parity-check (LDPC) codes and polar codes can be adapted to the unique characteristics of these channels.
- **Interference Mitigation:** Effective interference mitigation algorithms are essential for ensuring reliable communication in environments with high interference levels. Techniques such as interference alignment and coordinated multipoint (CoMP) transmission can be used to manage interference in THz and MC systems.
- **AI and Machine Learning:** The real-time integration of Artificial Intelligence (AI) and Machine Learning in THz-MC systems presents an enhancement for the future. AI-driven techniques can improve channel estimation, resource management, and adaptive modulation in dynamic environments. Machine learning algorithms can be employed for optimizing resource allocation, predicting channel conditions, and reducing system latency, making the fusion more efficient and robust for advanced 6G applications.

4.4.3 Channel Modeling and Optimization

Accurate channel modeling and optimization are essential for predicting communication performance and designing efficient transmission schemes in THz and MC systems. Channel characteristics such as path loss, multipath propagation, and molecular diffusion must be carefully modeled and optimized to ensure reliable and robust communication links.

- **Path Loss Models:** Developing accurate path loss models for both THz and MC channels is crucial for predicting signal attenuation and designing effective transmission schemes. This includes modeling the impact of different materials and environments on signal propagation.
- **Multipath Propagation:** Understanding and modeling multipath propagation in THz and MC channels is essential for optimizing signal processing and modulation techniques. This includes developing models that can capture the complex interactions between signals and the environment.
- **Molecular Diffusion:** Accurate modeling of molecular diffusion is critical for predicting the behavior of MC channels and designing effective communication schemes. This includes understanding the impact of factors such as temperature, pressure, and chemical reactions on molecular propagation.

4.4.4 Security and Privacy Concerns

Security and privacy considerations are paramount in designing and deploying THz and MC-enabled systems. The information transfer, from source to destination becomes challenging due to the intrusion of an unauthorized receiver in the communication channel [65]. Particularly, in a targeted drug delivery scenario, the critical aspect is to ensure the delivery of the drug at the desired tumor node without interference from the adjacent healthy node to prevent drug overdose and drug wastage. Here, the adjacent healthy node behaves as a malicious node, and would unnecessarily try to destroy the drug molecule by considering it a foreign entity. Another classic example of the presence of a malicious entity at the macroscale level is the case of bioterrorism [65]. Here, the malicious entity present inside the water bodies transmits chemoattractant, preventing the authorized node from analyzing the chemical and physical composition of water inside the water bodies. On the contrary, in the event of oil spillage, the breakdown process of the hydrocarbons on the oceanic surfaces is inhibited by releasing chemorepellents from the malicious node. Recently, various physical layer security (PLS) techniques are utilized, with the PLS exploiting various characteristic features of the wireless channel medium in order to provide information-theoretic security. Further, the PLS approach has certain advantages, namely, (1) the PLS techniques do not require a shared private key, (2) the PLS approach can be employed in those environments where constraints on resources are experienced, and (3) the PLS techniques are independent of the limited computational power assumption of the eavesdropper. Apart from PLS techniques, numerous encryption, authentication, and access control mechanisms are employed to protect sensitive information and prevent unauthorized access or tampering.

- **Encryption:** Developing robust encryption techniques that can secure THz and MC communication channels is critical for ensuring data privacy. This includes adapting traditional encryption methods to the unique characteristics of these channels and developing new techniques that can provide high levels of security with minimal overhead.
- **Authentication:** Effective authentication mechanisms are necessary to ensure that only authorized devices can access the communication system. This includes developing techniques that can authenticate devices based on their unique physical and chemical properties.
- **Access Control:** Implementing robust access control mechanisms is essential for preventing unauthorized access to the communication system. This includes developing techniques that can dynamically manage access based on the current state of the system and the identities of the devices involved.

4.5 Use Cases and Scenarios for Synergistic Fusion in 6G Networks

The fusion of THz and MC in 6G networks opens up numerous application possibilities:

- **Intra-body Communication for Healthcare:** Enabling precise communication between nanoscale devices within the body for health monitoring and medical interventions. This includes applications such as real-time monitoring of vital signs, targeted drug delivery, and early detection of diseases.
- **Environmental Monitoring:** Using nanoscale sensors for detailed and accurate monitoring of environmental conditions. This includes applications such as monitoring air and water quality, detecting hazardous substances, and tracking changes in environmental parameters over time.
- **Targeted Drug Delivery Systems:** Leveraging MC for precise drug delivery at the cellular level, coordinated by THz communication for control and monitoring. This includes applications such as delivering drugs to specific cells or tissues, controlling the release of drugs over time, and monitoring the effects of drug delivery in real-time.

These use cases demonstrate how the unique strengths of THz and MC can be harnessed to address specific challenges in wireless communication and sensing.

4.6 Future Directions

The synergistic fusion of THz and MC opens up new possibilities for a wide range of applications in 6G communication networks, including healthcare, environmental monitoring, industrial automation, and smart cities. These applications leverage the unique capabilities of THz and MC to address diverse communication and sensing requirements.

4.6.1 Emerging Research Directions and Opportunities

Emerging research directions in THz and MC focus on overcoming technical challenges and exploring new applications and use cases. Key research areas include advanced modulation schemes, efficient channel coding techniques, and novel device architectures for THz and MC-enabled systems.

- **Advanced Modulation Schemes:** Developing new modulation schemes that can take advantage of the unique characteristics of THz and MC channels is a key area of research. This includes techniques such as pulse-based modulation for THz communication and molecular concentration modulation for MC.
- **Efficient Channel Coding Techniques:** Designing channel coding techniques that can provide high levels of error correction with minimal overhead is essential for ensuring reliable communication in THz and MC systems. This includes techniques such as fountain codes and rateless codes.
- **Novel Device Architectures:** Developing new device architectures that can support both THz and MC communication is a key area of research. This includes techniques such as hybrid transceivers that can switch between electromagnetic and molecular communication modes.
- **Simulation and Analytical Tools:** The use of simulation to evaluate the various performance indices like data rates, communication range, latency, energy consumption, bit error rate (BER), and channel capacity has an essential role in understanding MC-THz hybrid systems for various biomedical applications. Since these systems are still in the nuance stage, these simulations are primarily based on various analytical models. Various simulation studies in both MC and THz literature try to quantify the metrics mentioned above. For example, MC systems typically have a low data range ranging from 10 to 100 bits per second (Bps) when simulating an MC channel between two nano-machines 1 cm apart in an aqueous medium like blood. On the contrary, THz systems generally have very high deter rates, typically 100 Mbps to 100 Gbps, when simulating in-body communication over a distance of 1 cm. Considering these contrasting characteristics of MC and THz systems, a communication paradigm integrating these two will have to carefully balance the low data rates originating from the MC-based short-range but highly precise and localized information and the high data rates originating from the THz-based longer-range information exchange.

4.6.2 Challenges and Open Research Issues

Despite the promise of synergistic fusion, several challenges and open research issues remain to be addressed, including synchronization, interference management, and scalability in heterogeneous networks.

- **Regulatory and standardization challenges:** Given that the fields of MC and THz are relatively new and highly specialized in their own right, it is crucial to address the various regulatory and standardization challenges to ensure the interoperability, security, and scalability of the MC-THz hybrid systems. This involves establishing common protocols, frameworks, and standards compatible with existing and future communication and networking systems. Some current standards being developed include the "IEEEP1096.1" standard for MC and the "IEEE 802.15.3d" standard for THz. "ISO/TC 229" is the International Organization for Standardization (ISO) technical committee working on nanotechnology standards. The International Telecommunication Union (ITU) is already working on identifying suitable frequency ranges for THz spectrum allocation. The integration of MC and THz requires new combined standards addressing aspects like the MC-THz interface, energy efficiency, safety, and quality of service (QoS).
- **Synchronization:** Achieving synchronization between THz and MC systems is a significant challenge due to the different propagation speeds and timescales involved. Research efforts are focused on developing new synchronization techniques that can align the timing of these systems.
- **Interference Management:** Managing interference in environments with high levels of interference is a critical challenge for THz and MC systems. Research efforts are focused on developing new interference mitigation techniques that can ensure reliable communication in these environments.
- **Scalability:** Ensuring that THz and MC systems can scale to support large numbers of devices and communication links is a key challenge. Research efforts are focused on developing new techniques for managing scalability in heterogeneous networks.

4.6.3 Future Prospects and Implications

The integration of THz and MC technologies holds the promise of revolutionizing wireless communication and sensing in 6G networks and beyond. By harnessing the complementary strengths of both technologies, it becomes possible to create adaptive, resilient, and efficient communication systems capable of supporting the diverse needs of modern society.

- **Revolutionizing Healthcare:** The integration of THz and MC technologies has the potential to revolutionize healthcare by enabling new applications such as real-time monitoring of vital signs, targeted drug delivery, and early detection of diseases.

- **Enhancing Environmental Monitoring:** The fusion of THz and MC technologies can enhance environmental monitoring by enabling detailed and accurate monitoring of environmental conditions, detecting hazardous substances, and tracking changes in environmental parameters over time.
- **Transforming Industrial Automation:** The integration of THz and MC technologies can transform industrial automation by enabling new applications such as real-time monitoring of manufacturing processes, precise control of industrial equipment, and early detection of equipment failures.
- **Enabling Smart Cities:** The fusion of THz and MC technologies can enable smart cities by supporting applications such as real-time monitoring of urban infrastructure, intelligent traffic management, and efficient energy management.

By addressing these challenges and leveraging the unique strengths of THz and MC, it becomes possible to create communication systems that are more versatile, efficient, and capable of supporting a wide range of applications in the upcoming 6G era and beyond.

5 Conclusion

5.1 Summary of Key Points

The THz and MC represents a transformative and forward-thinking approach to wireless communication and sensing within future 6G networks. By combining the high-speed, long-range capabilities of THz communication with the nanoscale precision of MC, heterogeneous networks can be designed to support a wide variety of advanced applications. These include real-time healthcare monitoring, environmental sensing, and communication on biological scales, paving the way for innovations that are not feasible with current technologies alone. The amalgamation of these two technologies enhances network performance, efficiency, and adaptability, catering to an expanding range of use cases in the future.

5.2 Importance of Synergistic Fusion for Future 6G Networks

The integration of THz and MC technologies into 6G networks offers immense potential in addressing the evolving demands of wireless communication, healthcare, environmental monitoring, and other domains. By leveraging the complementary strengths of both technologies, 6G networks can achieve unprecedented levels of connectivity, efficiency, and functionality. This convergence opens doors to an entirely new realm of communication possibilities, including nanoscale biomedical applications like targeted drug delivery, biosensing, and intra-body communication.

Furthermore, the ability to overcome existing technological limitations such as high atmospheric absorption in THz communication or the need for precise coordination in MC systems highlights the strength of this synergy.

Looking ahead, the fusion of THz and MC technologies promises to significantly reshape the technological landscape, impacting sectors ranging from smart cities and environmental monitoring to healthcare and industrial automation. By addressing the core challenges associated with both technologies such as synchronization, interference management, and scalability, research and development efforts are set to produce communication systems that are more adaptive, resilient, and efficient. The vision of 6G is not just about faster networks but also about expanding the scope of communication to cover previously inaccessible domains, such as the human body at a molecular level, or extreme environments where conventional electromagnetic waves struggle.

5.3 Future Directions

As we move towards realizing the full potential of this integration, future research should focus on further optimizing the fusion of these technologies to overcome existing challenges, such as improving the synchronization between THz and MC systems, minimizing interference, and scaling the system to handle a larger number of devices. These areas require innovative solutions, particularly in hardware development, system design, and signal processing techniques. Addressing these challenges will not only enhance the technical viability of 6G networks but will also unlock a new era of interdisciplinary applications that merge biology, nanotechnology, and wireless communication.

The integration of diverse technologies like THz and MC will be pivotal for advancing 6G networks, and it calls for collaborative efforts across various domains to bring this vision to fruition. Further research and development are necessary to fully realize the transformative potential of this technology, paving the way for the next generation of communication systems.

References

1. Akyildiz, I. F., et al. (2014): Terahertz band: Next frontier for wireless communications. Physical communication 12, 16–32
2. Akyildiz, I. F., et al. (2014): TeraNets: Ultra-broadband communication networks in the terahertz band. IEEE Wireless Communications 21, 130–135
3. Kürner, T., & Priebe, S, (2014): Towards THz communications-status in research, standardization and regulation. Journal of Infrared, Millimeter, and Terahertz Waves 35, 53–62
4. Akyildiz, I. F., et al. (2020): 6G and beyond: The future of wireless communications systems. IEEE Access 8, 133995–134030
5. Elayan, H., et al. (2019): Terahertz band: The last piece of RF spectrum puzzle for communication systems. IEEE Open Journal of the Communications Society 1, 1–32

6. Chowdhury, M. Z., et al. (2020): 6G Wireless Communication Systems: Applications, Requirements, Technologies, Challenges, and Research Directions. IEEE Open Journal of the Communications Society, 1, 957–975.
7. Rappaport, T. S., et al. (2019): Wireless communications and applications above 100 GHz: Opportunities and challenges for 6G and beyond. IEEE Access 7, 78729–78757
8. Boulogeorgos, A. A. A., et al. (2018): Terahertz technologies to deliver optical network quality of experience in wireless systems beyond 5G. IEEE Communications Magazine 56, 144–151
9. Akyildiz, I. F., et al. (2022): Terahertz band communication: An old problem revisited and research directions for the next decade. IEEE Transactions on Communications 70, 4250–4285
10. Petrov, V., et al. (2018): Last meter indoor terahertz wireless access: Performance insights and implementation roadmap. IEEE Communications Magazine 56, 158–165
11. Han, C., et al. (2021): Terahertz Wireless Channels: A Holistic Survey on Measurement, Modeling, and Analysis. IEEE Communications Surveys & Tutorials 24, 1670–1707
12. Leong, K. M. K. H., et al. (2017): 850 GHz Receiver and Transmitter Front-Ends Using InP HEMT. IEEE Transactions on Terahertz Science and Technology 7, 466–475
13. Kenneth, K. O., et al., (2019): Opening Terahertz for Everyday Applications. IEEE Communications Magazine 57, 70–76, August 2019
14. Knap, W., et al. (2004): Plasma wave detection of sub-terahertz and terahertz radiation by silicon field-effect transistors. Applied Physics Letter (85), 675—677
15. Novoselov, K., et al. (2012): A roadmap for graphene. Nature 490, 192—200.
16. Yao J., (2009): Microwave photonics. Journal of Lightwave Technology 27, 314—335
17. Williams, B. S., (2007): Terahertz quantum-cascade lasers. Nature Photonics 1, 517—525.
18. Wang, X. et al. (2016): High-power terahertz quantum cascade lasers with 0.23 W in continuous wave mode. AIP Advances 6, Art. no. 075210
19. Yardimci, N. T. and Jarrahi, M. (2018): Nanostructure-enhanced photoconductive terahertz emission and detection. Small 14, Art. no. 1802437
20. Nagatsuma, T., et al. (2016): Advances in terahertz communications accelerated by photonics. Nature Photonics 10, 371—379
21. Chaloun, T., et al. (2022): Electronically Steerable Antennas for Future Heterogeneous Communication Networks: Review and Perspectives. IEEE Journal of Microwaves 2, 545–581
22. Wang, J., et al. (2022): Liquid crystal terahertz modulator with plasmon-induced transparency metamaterial. Optics Express 26, 5769–5776
23. Kissinger, D., et al. (2021): Millimeter-Wave and Terahertz Transceivers in SiGe BiCMOS Technologies. IEEE Transactions on Microwave Theory and Techniques 69, 4541–4560
24. Popovic, Z. and Mortazawi, A. (1998): Quasi-optical transmit/receive front ends. IEEE Transactions on Microwave Theory and Techniques 46, 1964–1975
25. Jornet, J. M. and Akyildiz, I. F. (2013): Graphene-based Plasmonic Nano-Antenna for Terahertz Band Communication in Nanonetworks. IEEE Journal on Selected Areas in Communications 31, 685–694
26. Fan, K., et al. (2017): Development of a High Gain 325–500 GHz Antenna Using Quasi-Planar Reflectors. IEEE Transactions on Antennas and Propagation 65, 3384–3391
27. Mi-Wave Antennas, (2019), [online] Available: https://www.miwv.com/millimeter-wave-products/antenna-products/
28. Sengupta, K., and Hajimiri, A. (2012): A 0.28 THz Power-Generation and Beam-Steering Array in CMOS Based on Distributed Active Radiators. IEEE Journal of Solid-State Circuits 47, 3013–3031
29. Xie, Y., et al. (2017): Programmable optical processor chips: Toward photonic RF filters with DSP-level flexibility and MHz-band selectivity. Nanophotonics 7, 421–454
30. Tang, R., et al. (2021): Ten-port unitary optical processor on a silicon photonic chip. ACS Photonics 8, 2074–2080
31. Nagatani, M., et al. (2018): A 256-Gbps PAM-4 Signal Generator IC in $0.25 - \mu$m InP DHBT Technology. In 2018 IEEE BiCMOS and Compound Semiconductor Integrated Circuits and Technology Symposium (BCICTS) 28–31

32. Serghiou, D., et al. (2022): Terahertz channel propagation phenomena, measurement techniques and modeling for 6G wireless communication applications: A survey, open challenges and future research directions. IEEE Communications Surveys & Tutorials 24, 1957–1996
33. Rappaport, T. S., et al. (2015): Wideband millimeter-wave propagation measurements and channel models for future wireless communication system design. IEEE Transactions on Communications 63, 3029–3056
34. Petrov, V., et al. (2020): IEEE 802.15. 3d: First standardization efforts for sub-terahertz band communications toward 6G. IEEE Communications Magazine 58, 28–33
35. Kürner, T., & Hirata, A. (2020): On the impact of the results of WRC 2019 on THz communications. In 2020 Third International Workshop on Mobile Terahertz Systems (IWMTS) 1–3
36. Rey, S., (2021). Initial results on sharing studies, Thor Deliverable D5. 1. Available: https://thorproject.eu/results
37. Al-Hmood, H. and Al-Raweshidy, H. S. (2021): Performance analysis of mmwave communications with selection combining over fluctuating-two ray fading model. IEEE Communication Letters 25, 2531–2535
38. Badarneh, O. S., and Da Costa, D. B., (2019): Cascaded fluctuating two-ray fading channels, IEEE Communication Letters 23, 1497–1500
39. Badarneh, O. S., et al. (2019): Ratio of products of fluctuating two-ray variates. IEEE Communication Letters 23, 1944–1948
40. Sharma, G., and Mallik, R. K. (2023): Secrecy Performance of Terahertz Based Systems Over Fluctuating Two-Ray Fading. IEEE Transactions on Wireless Communications 23, 5600–5615
41. López-Benítez, M., and Zhang, J., (2021): Comments and Corrections to "New Results on the Fluctuating Two-Ray Model With Arbitrary Fading Parameters and Its Applications". IEEE Transactions on Vehicular Technology 70, 1938–1940
42. Petrov, V., et al. (2017): Interference and SINR in Millimeter Wave and Terahertz Communication Systems With Blocking and Directional Antennas, IEEE Transactions on Wireless Communications 16, 1791–1808
43. Rogalski, A., & Sizov, F. (2011): Terahertz detectors and focal plane arrays. Opto-electronics review 19, 346–404
44. Nakano, T., Eckford, A. W., Haraguchi, T. (2013): Molecular communication. Cambridge University Press, Cambridge
45. Akyildiz, I. F.,Pierobon, M., Balasubramaniam, S., Koucheryavy, Y. (2015): The internet of bio-nano things. IEEE Communications Magazine 53, 32–40
46. Hiyama, S., Moritani, Y. (2010): Molecular communication: Harnessing biochemical materials to engineer biomimetic communication systems. Nano Communication Networks 1, 20–30
47. Akyildiz, I. F., Brunetti, F., Blázquez, C. (2008): Nanonetworks: A new communication paradigm. Computer Networks 52, 2260–2279
48. Farsad, N., Yilmaz, H. B., Eckford, A., Chae, C., Guo, W. (2016): A comprehensive survey of recent advancements in molecular communication. IEEE Communications Surveys Tutorials 18, 1887–1919
49. Guo, W., Mias, C., Farsad, N., Wu, J. L. (2015): Molecular versus electromagnetic wave propagation loss in macro-scale environments. IEEE Transactions on Molecular, Biological and Multi-Scale Communications 1, 18–25
50. Suda, T., Moore, M., Nakano, T., Egashira, R., Enomoto, A., Hiyama, S., Moritani, Y. (2005): Exploratory research on molecular communication between nanomachines. Genetic and Evolutionary Computation Conference (GECCO), Late Breaking Papers Washington, D.C, USA
51. Tiwari, S. K., and Upadhyay, P. K. (2017): Estimate-and-forward relaying in diffusion- based molecular communication networks: Performance evaluation and threshold optimization. IEEE Transactions on Molecular, Biological and Multi- Scale Communications 3, 183–193
52. Tiwari, S. K., and Upadhyay, P. K. (2016): Maximum likelihood estimation of SNR for diffusion-based molecular communication. IEEE Wireless Communications Letters 5, 320–323

53. Tiwari, S. K., Reddy, T. R. T., and Upadhyay, P. K. (2017): Error performance optimization using logarithmic barrier function in molecular nanonetworks. IEEE Communications Letters 21, 2408–2411
54. Tiwari, S. K., Reddy, T. R. T., Upadhyay, P. K., and Da Costa, D. B. (2018): Joint optimization of molecular resource allocation and relay positioning in diffusive nanonetworks. IEEE Access 6, 67681–67687
55. Ayaluru, S. R. K., Shrivastava, C., Tiwari, S. K., Pandey, N., Sharma, G., and Pandey, O. J. (2024): A two-way synchronization method for molecular bio-nanosensor networks using truncated L'evy distribution. International Conference on Informa- tion Communication Technology (CICT), IIIT Allahabad, India
56. Tiwari, S. K., and Upadhyay, P. K. (2018): Estimate-and-forward relaying in molecular communication using brownian motion with drift. International Conference on Signal Processing and Communications (SPCOM), IISc Bangalore, In- dia
57. Pandey, N., Mallik, R. K., and Lall, B. (2017): Truncated Lévy statistics for diffusion based molecular communication. IEEE Global Communications Conference (GLOBECOM), Singapore
58. Pandey, N., Joshi, S., and Mallik, R. K. (2021): Characterizing the probability of collision between information particles in molecular communications. IEEE Wireless Communications Letters 10, 1252-1255
59. Mahfuz, M. U., Makrakis, D., Mouftah, H. T. (2010): On the characterization of binary concentration-encoded molecular communication in nanonetworks. Nano Communication Networks 1, 289—300
60. Srinivas, K. V., Eckford, A., Adve, R. S. (2012): Molecular communication in fluid media: The additive inverse gaussian noise channel. IEEE Transactions on Information Theory 58, 4678–4692
61. Pandey, N., Mallik, R. K., Lall, B. (2019): Performance analysis of diffusive molecular timing channels. IET Communications 13, 3059—3067
62. Pandey, N., Mallik, R. K., Lall, B. (2019): Molecular communication: The first arrival position channel. IEEE Wireless Communications Letters 8, 508—511
63. Hancock, J.T. (2017): Cell signalling. Oxford University Press
64. Yang K., et al. (2020): A comprehensive survey on hybrid communication in context of molecular communication and terahertz communication for body-centric nanonetworks. IEEE Transactions on Molecular, Biological, and Multi-Scale Communications 6, 107–133
65. Sharma, G., Mallik, R. K., Pandey, N., Singh, A. (2024): Effect of interfering transmitter on the secrecy of diffusive molecular timing channels. IEEE Transactions on Communications 72(6), 3323–3337. https://doi.org/10.1109/TCOMM.2024.3365629

On Performance of UAV-Assisted RIS NOMA Network

Sayanti Ghosh, Abhijit Bhowmick, Sanjay Dhar Roy, and Sumit Kundu

1 Introduction

Reliable communication is still a significant difficulty in today's highly populated areas [1]. Device-to-device (D2D) communication plays an important role in disaster management. In this context, D2D refers to direct communication between users without the need to route through the base station (BS) [1]. When the traditional communication infrastructure breaks down during a crisis. Unmanned aerial vehicles (UAVs) possess the ability to operate as aerial base stations, providing an efficient way to increase coverage. It facilitates the transport of wireless information and fulfils a number of functions, including package delivery, disaster management, search and rescue, and surveillance [2]. In the event that a UAV manages to provide communication between users within the disaster area, conventional multiple access technologies, such as frequency division and time division, may have limitations that prohibit numerous users from concurrently utilizing the spectrum band. However, a promising option for 5G networks is non-orthogonal multiple access (NOMA) technology, which improves spectral efficiency by allowing users share resource blocks and employing a successive interference cancellation (SIC)

S. Ghosh (✉)
Institute of Engineering and Management Kolkata, Kolkata, India
e-mail: sayantighosh.1991@gmail.com

University of Engineering and Management Kolkata, Kolkata, India

A. Bhowmick
Vellore Institute of Technology, Vellore, India

S. D. Roy · S. Kundu
National Institute of Technology, Durgapur, India
e-mail: sdroy.ece@nitdgp.ac.in

S. Kundu
e-mail: skundu.ece@nitdgp.ac.in

T. Ojha et al. (eds.), *Edge-Enabled 6G Networking*,
https://doi.org/10.1007/978-3-032-19042-0_7

scheme for effective signal extraction [3]. Reconfigurable intelligent surfaces (RIS), NOMA, and simultaneous wireless information and power transfer have emerged as enabling technologies in 5G and beyond wireless networks to improve communication reliability, energy issues with power-constrained nodes, and increase spectral efficiency [4–10]. According to [5], RIS recently unveiled a ground-breaking technique for wireless communication that can passively modify wave fronts to improve spectrum and energy efficiency at a low cost. RIS integration onto mobile UAVs, as opposed to stationary structures like walls or buildings, enables flexible deployment and a wide range of signal reflection, which eventually results in better coverage. As discussed in [5], this integration can help UAV systems operate with far less channel complexity, interference, access delay, and energy usage. The authors have focused on imperfect SIC-based decoding over Nakagami-m fading channels in [6]. For the ergodic capacity and outage probability, they have obtained closed-form formulas using selection combining (SC). In [7], closed-form expressions for the outage probability and ergodic capacity have been derived. Following this, UAV-assisted communications with energy harvesting are studied. Additionally, the influence of element splitting in a UAV-RIS-assisted NOMA network on the outage probability has been examined, as discussed in [8]. In [13], the authors have explored RIS-assisted UAVs, addressing a number of concerns like optimization and communication strategies while outlining potential obstacles and future directions. The use of RIS for improving UAV communication to increase coverage and reliability has been suggested in [14]. In [15], the authors have investigated the use of UAVs and RISs to improve 6G mobile networks (0.3–3 THz). While RISs maximize signal reflection and energy efficiency, UAVs offer mobility but come with security concerns. In [16], the authors have examined an air-to-ground network that uses RIS and UAVs to facilitate energy-efficient communication. A 145% increase in energy efficiency over a standard relay is demonstrated by an optimized deployment method. Wireless control is improved by RIS, and connectivity is improved by UAVs. The use of RIS and UAVs in a multiuser NOMA system has been investigated in [17]. While RIS emphasizes energy economy and improves signal quality, UAVs optimize signal strength. Simulations show substantial power savings and improved user satisfaction with the integrated UAV and RIS. In [18], the authors have worked on a UAV-RIS-assisted communication network where they have estimated the channel. For disaster areas or non-functional areas (NFAs), where traditional base stations are out of order, a UAV-enabled downlink multi-hop NOMA network to extend coverage effectively is proposed in [19]. To improve wireless communication during disasters, in [20], the authors have proposed a communication network where RIS-assisted UAVs played a major role. It optimizes user equipment transmit power, RIS phase shifts, and trajectories to maximize communication capacity. Numerical results highlight that the significant improvement can be achieved with the NOMA scheme, despite some limitations in RIS gain. An energy-efficient beam training method for UAV-RIS communication in emergency situations has been proposed in [21]. It takes into account RIS-induced phase shifts under communication rate limits and minimizes transmission power while satisfying communication requirements. Simulation is used to demonstrate power consumption reduction. In [22], the authors have presented a network that combines RIS with a full-duplex UAV to improve communication. For both uplink and downlink users, the RIS increases signal strength and lowers interference. When compared to benchmark schemes, simulation results demonstrate a significant rate gain. A mean score opinion-based quality of experience model for web browsing has been introduced in [23], wherein the authors have examined indoor NOMA systems with RIS in κ–μ fading channels in order to address quality of service. Nevertheless, instead of evaluating the traditional quality of experience, they have argued in favor of the mean opinion score component, which converts the objective technical criterion into a subjective quality acknowledged by the users. In [24], the authors have used a 1-bit coding approach to study RIS-assisted NOMA networks with imperfect and perfect SIC. They have examined the ergodic rate and outage probability asymptotic formulations. They have also covered throughput, energy efficiency, and diversity order in delay-tolerant and delay-limited transmission modes. In [25], the authors investigated a D2D network assisted by a UAV and a RIS, employing NOMA with the assumption of perfect SIC.

1.1 Research Gaps and Contributions

Previous studies on UAV-RIS-assisted communication have predominantly concentrated on non-disaster scenarios, neglecting the specific challenges and applications of UAV-RIS communication in disaster-stricken areas [6, 7, 12, 22]. Additionally, while various diversity strategies, such as MRC and energy harvesting systems have been explored, their network performance has not been extensively evaluated [6–8]. This chapter provides a more comprehensive analysis by focusing on UAV-RIS communication in disaster scenarios, incorporating energy harvesting at the UAV. It evaluates the system outage probability and ergodic capacity, considering both SC and MRC for signals received via UAV and RIS mounted on the UAV. We specifically focus on both SC and MRC to provide a detailed analysis of system performance, considering energy harvesting at the UAV under the Nakagami-m fading model in both uplink (i.e., temporary base station (T-BS) to UAV-RIS) and downlink (i.e., UAV-RIS to ground users). Additionally, we investigate the impact of element splitting in the UAV-RIS-assisted NOMA network, offering further insights into the optimal number of RIS elements. This aspect of splitting RIS elements has not been considered in [6, 7, 10, 20].

2 UAV-RIS Assisted NOMA Network

Section 2 discusses the challenges of establishing reliable communication in disaster-affected regions, which presents several significant challenges. Physical obstacles, such as collapsed buildings and infrastructure, can obstruct signal paths, creating NFAs where traditional ground-based communication system is disrupted. Moreover, environmental factors like dense urban layouts, or mountainous terrain exacerbate signal attenuation and loss, making it difficult to maintain stable connections between the BS and ground users. Additionally, network congestion due to emergency situations and power outages can further degrade communication reliability. To overcome these challenges, we propose using UAVs as mobile aerial relays to extend network coverage and provide communication services to NFAs. UAVs can dynamically adjust their position to avoid obstacles and maintain a line-of-sight connection with ground users. The system can further improve the quality and efficiency of communication links by equipping UAVs with RIS and utilizing NOMA. The UAV is outfitted with an RIS to manipulate the wireless environment, reflecting and focusing signals to ensure better coverage and signal strength, even in environments with complex physical obstructions. NOMA Access allows the transmission of signals to multiple users simultaneously, assigning different power levels based on their channel conditions. This enables efficient spectrum utilization, crucial for disaster scenarios where communication demand is high. Ground users in this network are considered D2D users, who can benefit from enhanced communication channels provided by the UAV and RIS. This setup ensures that even when traditional networks fail due to disasters, users can still communicate effectively. In this Sect. 2, we investigate the performance of a network involving a single UAV equipped with an RIS, utilizing NOMA-based transmission between a T-BS and two destination (ground) users. Specifically, we evaluate the end-to-end outage probability and ergodic capacity of such a network under Nakagami-m fading channels. Furthermore, diversity combining techniques such as SC and MRC are applied to the signals received via the UAV and RIS at the end users. The impact of diversity combining and imperfect SIC-based decoding on outage probability and ergodic capacity is also analysed. We derive analytical expressions for the outage probability and ergodic capacity based on SC and MRC and compare NOMA-based transmission with conventional OMA. Additionally, we assess the effect of splitting the RIS elements between the two users and identify an optimal split factor in the following section.

3 Network Model

In the proposed UAV-RIS-assisted network, as depicted in Fig. 1, a significant challenge arises due to the blocked and heavily faded direct communication path between the T-BS and the ground users. In this system model, the RIS is mounted on the UAV, which is positioned at a height H from the ground users. To establish communication, the T-BS employs NOMA by transmitting a superimposed signal through the UAV and the RIS to reach the ground users. Specifically, we have two ground users as U_i, denoted by $i = 1, 2$ as the user index. The communication process involves the T-BS transmitting the NOMA signal through the UAV, which acts as a DF relay. The UAV then retransmits the signal in the downlink using NOMA to the ground users. Simultaneously, a NOMA signal is transmitted from the T-BS to a RIS with N reflecting elements. The RIS then reflects the signal to nearby D2D users. This

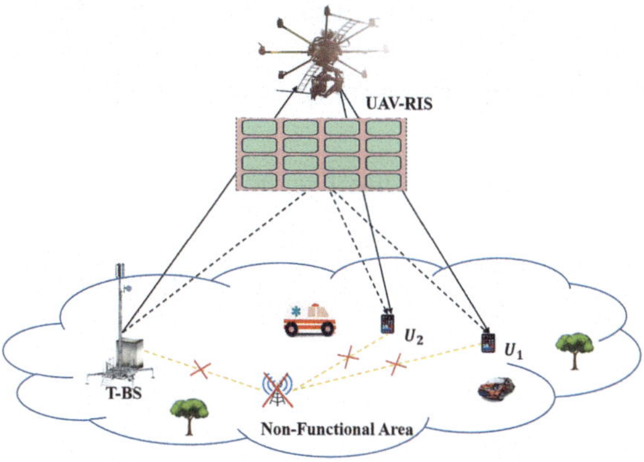

Fig. 1 System model for NOMA network assisted by UAV and RIS

NOMA transmission in addition to the NOMA signal relayed by UAV, helps ground users to decode the combined NOMA signal from both the UAV and the T-BS. Consequently, each ground user receives two copies of the signal. To enhance the reliability and diversity of the communication, the ground users perform either SC or MRC to obtain estimates of the signal using diversity combining techniques. The link between the T-BS and the kth reflecting element of the RIS is represented as $\widehat{h}_k$, while the link between the kth element of the RIS and the D2D users are denoted as $\widehat{g}_k$. These first and second-hop links are assumed to be Nakagami-m faded, independent, and identically distributed (i.i.d). To decode their respective information, the destination users employ the perfect and imperfect SIC process under two different situations. The power allocation from the UAV to the ground users is dependent on the corresponding link conditions. A power allocation scheme is implemented such that transmissions associated with good links (stronger and less faded) are assigned lower power compared to transmissions associated with bad links (weaker and more faded), following the principle of downlink NOMA. The coordinates of the T-BS, UAV, and ground users are represented as $(a_0, b_0, 0)$, (x, y, H), $(a_1, b_1, 0)$, and $(a_2, b_2, 0)$, respectively. The distances between the links (T-BS-UAV, UAV-U_1, UAV-U_2) are denoted as d_{sr}, d_{ru_1}, and d_{ru_2}, respectively. The corresponding distances are expressed as:

$$d_{ur} = \sqrt{(x - a_0)^2 + (y - b_0)^2 + H^2} \tag{1}$$

$$d_{ru_1} = \sqrt{(x - a_1)^2 + (y - b_1)^2 + H^2} \tag{2}$$

$$d_{ru_2} = \sqrt{(x - a_2)^2 + (y - b_2)^2 + H^2} \tag{3}$$

3.1 Signal Transmission Through UAV

3.2 Energy Harvesting at the UAV

For the first-hop transmission, the received signal at the UAV is expressed as:

$$y_{u,i} = h_{xx}\left(\sum_{i=1}^{2}\sqrt{l_{u,i}}u_i\right) + \acute{n}_{u,i} \tag{4}$$

A general expression of the links mentioned below:

$$h_{xx} = \sqrt{\frac{P_x}{d_x^c}}h_x \tag{5}$$

where $h_{xx} \in \{h_{ur}, h_{r\acute{u}_i}, \widehat{h}_k, \widehat{g}_{k,i}\}$, $P_x \in \{P_u, P_R\}$, $d_x^c \in \{d_{ur}^c, d_{ru_1}^c, d_{ru_2}^c\}$, u_i represents the information signal meant for the ith user, P_u denotes the allocated power of source node, $l_{u,i}$ denotes the power allocation factor for ith user from (T-BS-UAV), and $\sum_{i=1}^{2} l_{u,i} = 1$. Here, $l_{u,1} > l_{u,2}$, h_x is the contribution from small scale fading which follow Nakagami-m distribution. U_1 is considered as a far user while U_2 is considered as a near user, c represents the path-loss exponent and $\acute{n}_{u,i}$ denotes noise. The received SINR ($\gamma_{s,1}$) at UAV to decode U_1 can be expressed as:

$$\gamma_{u,1} = \frac{l_{u,1}|h_{ur}|^2}{l_{u,2}\rho'|h_{ur}|^2 + \sigma_{d,1}^2} \tag{6}$$

where $\sigma_{d,1}^2$ denotes the noise power for U_1. The SNR ($\gamma_{u,2}'$) to decode U_2 after performing perfect SIC at the UAV can be expressed as [7]:

$$\gamma_{u,2}' = \frac{l_{u,2}|h_{ur}|^2}{\sigma_{d,2}^2} \tag{7}$$

where $\sigma_{d,2}^2$ denotes the noise power for U_2. Assuming, $\sigma_{d,1}^2 = \sigma_{d,2}^2 = \sigma_d^2$. The UAV relay employs an RF signal from the BS for energy harvesting, utilizing a time-switching relay (TSR) scheme [7]. The SINR ($\gamma_{u,2}$), for decoding U_2 after imperfect SIC at the UAV, can be expressed as [6]:

$$\gamma_{u,2} = \frac{l_{u,2}|h_{ur}|^2}{\Upsilon l_{u,1}|h_{ur}|^2 + \sigma_{d,2}^2} \tag{8}$$

where Υ denotes an error due to imperfection in SIC while $\Upsilon = 0$ represents perfect SIC. The UAV relay utilizes RF signals from the BS for energy harvesting, the energy level achieved at the UAV relay can be represented as:

$$E_{UAV} = \alpha\eta|h_{ur}|^2 T \tag{9}$$

where α denotes the fraction of the EH time, T is the total time period and η represents the EH efficiency. The transmit power of the relay is a function of harvested energy during the first phase. It is expressed as:

$$P_R = \frac{E_{UAV}}{(1-\alpha)\frac{T}{2}} = \frac{2\alpha\eta|h_{ur}|^2}{(1-\alpha)} \tag{10}$$

In the second hop transmission, the UAV relay utilizes the harvested energy to transfer information to ground users with a power level denoted as P_R. The received signal at user U_i from the UAV can be expressed as:

$$y_{d,i} = h_{r\acute{u}_i}\left(\sum_{i=1}^{2}\sqrt{l_{d,i}}u_i\right) + \acute{n}_{d,i} \tag{11}$$

where $l_{d,i}$ denotes the power allocation factor for ith user from (UAV-U_i), and $\sum_{i=1}^{2} l_{d,i} = 1$. Here, $l_{d,1} > l_{d,2}$ as $h_{r\acute{u}_1} < h_{r\acute{u}_2}$. At U_1, the received SINR ($\gamma_{d,1}$) from UAV, to detect U_1, is expressed as:

$$\begin{aligned}\gamma_{d,1} &= \frac{l_{d,1}|h_{r\acute{u}_1}|^2}{l_{d,2}|h_{r\acute{u}_1}|^2 + \sigma_{d,1}^2}\\ &= \frac{Vl_{d,1}|h_{ur}|^2|h_{r\acute{u}_1}|^2}{Vl_{d,2}|h_{ur}|^2|h_{r\acute{u}_1}|^2 + \sigma_{d,1}^2}\end{aligned} \tag{12}$$

where $V = \frac{2\alpha\eta}{1-\eta}$. The SNR ($\gamma_{d,2}^{'}$) after successfully information decoding of U_1 can be expressed as:

$$\gamma_{d,2}^{'} = \frac{Vl_{d,2}|h_{ur}|^2|h_{r\acute{u}_2}|^2}{\sigma_{d,2}^2} \tag{13}$$

The SINR ($\gamma_{d,2}$) at the U_2 incorporating imperfect SIC can be expressed as:

$$\gamma_{d,2} = \frac{Vl_{d,2}|h_{ur}|^2|h_{r\acute{u}_2}|^2}{\Upsilon Vl_{d,1}|h_{ur}|^2|h_{r\acute{u}_2}|^2 + \sigma_{d,2}^2} \tag{14}$$

3.3 Signal Transmission Through RIS

The end-to-end link (T-BS to D2D users) is denoted as $\widehat{H}$, $\widehat{H} = \sum_{k=1}^{N}\widehat{H}_k$ where $\widehat{H}_k = \widehat{h}_k\widehat{g}_k$. To determine the PDF of the equivalent channel coefficient $\widehat{H}_k$, we can start with the PDFs of the individual fading components, $\widehat{h}_k$ and $\widehat{g}_k$ [9]. In this case,

$\widehat{H}_k$ becomes the product of two Nakagami-m faded, independent, and identically distributed random variables, which is given as [9].

$$f_{\widehat{H}_k}(x) = \frac{4x^{m_1+m_2-1}}{\Gamma(m_1)\Gamma(m_2)}\left(\frac{m_1 m_2}{\bar{\Omega}_1\bar{\Omega}_2}\right)^{\frac{m_1+m_2}{2}} K_{m_1-m_2}\left(2x\sqrt{\frac{m_1 m_2}{\bar{\Omega}_1\bar{\Omega}_2}}\right) \tag{15}$$

where $\Gamma(.)$ is a gamma function, m_1, and m_2 are the fading parameters. Now, the PDF of $\widehat{H}$ can be expressed as:

$$f_{\widehat{H}}(x) = \sum_{k_1=0}^{m_1-1}\cdots\sum_{k_N=0}^{m_1-1}\Pi_{j=1}^{N}\frac{(m_2)_{m_1-1-k_j}(1-m_2)_{k_j}}{(m_1-1-k)!k_j!}$$
$$\times\frac{4\left(\frac{m_1 m_2}{\bar{\Omega}_1\bar{\Omega}_2}\right)^{\frac{u+1}{2}}}{(u-1)!}x^u K_{u-1}\left(2\sqrt{\frac{m_1 m_2}{\bar{\Omega}_1\bar{\Omega}_2}}x\right) \tag{16}$$

where $u = N(m_1+m_2-1) - \sum_{j=1}^{N} k_j$, $K_\upsilon(.)$ is the υth order modified bessel function of the 2nd kind [9]. The composite received signal $(y_{d,i})$ at U_i from the RIS can be expressed as:

$$y_{d,i} = \sum_{k=1}^{N}\widehat{h}_k\beta e^{j\theta_k}\left(\sum_{i=1}^{2}\sqrt{l_{u,i}}u_i\right)\widehat{g}_{k,i} + \acute{n}_{d,i} \tag{17}$$

where β represents the reflection loss parameter ($\beta = 1$, when there is no loss), and θ_k denotes the phase error of the kth reflection element of RIS, $\theta_k = -arg(\widehat{h}_k\widehat{g}_{k,i})$ [10]. The received SINR $(\bar{\gamma}_{d,1})$ at the U_1 via RIS can be expressed as:

$$\bar{\gamma}_{d,1} = \frac{l_{u,1}|\widehat{H_1}|^2}{l_{u,2}|\widehat{H_1}|^2 + \sigma\prime^2_{d,1}} \tag{18}$$

where $\widehat{H_1} = \sum_{k=1}^{N}\widehat{h}_k\widehat{g}_{k,1}$, and $\sigma\prime^2_{d,1}$ denotes the noise power for U_1. The SNR $(\bar{\gamma}\prime_{d,2})$ at the U_2 after successfully decoding of U_1 can be expressed as:

$$\bar{\gamma}\prime_{d,2} = \frac{l_{u,2}|\widehat{H_2}|^2}{\sigma\prime^2_{d,2}} \tag{19}$$

The SINR $(\bar{\gamma}_{d,2})$ at the U_2 after imperfect SIC can be expressed as:

$$\bar{\gamma}_{d,2} = \frac{l_{u,2}|\widehat{H_2}|^2}{\Upsilon l_{u,1}|\widehat{H_2}|^2 + \sigma\prime^2_{d,2}} \tag{20}$$

where $\widehat{H_2} = \sum_{k=1}^{N} \widehat{h}_k \widehat{g}_{k,2}$, and $\sigma{\prime}_{d,2}^2$ denotes the noise power for U_2. Assuming, $\sigma{\prime}_{d,1}^2 = \sigma{\prime}_{d,2}^2 = \sigma{\prime}_{d}^2$.

$Perfect\ SIC$: In a perfect SIC scheme, the receiver is assumed to have perfect knowledge of the interfering signals and can perfectly cancel them out. This means that the receiver can successfully decode the strongest desired signal first, remove its contribution from the received signal, and then decode the next strongest signal, and so on.

$Imperfect\ SIC$: In an imperfect SIC scheme, the receiver's capability to eliminate interference is somewhat compromised. These imperfections result in residual interference persisting even after the cancellation process, thereby reducing the overall effectiveness of interference mitigation which degrades the performance.

3.3.1 Elements Splitting on RIS for U_1 and U_2

The distribution of elements within the RIS involves splitting them between two ground users. To elaborate, the total count of elements is N, out of which N_1 elements are designated for creating beamforming signals aimed at U_1. In this context, the value of N in (34) should be substituted with N_1. The remaining set of elements, amounting to $N_2 = N - N_1$, is then configured to serve U_2. This allocation of elements is employed in the formulation of the expression of (35) or (36), where the original variable N is replaced by N_2, thus reflecting the resources assigned to U_2, as detailed in [8].

4 Outage Analysis of UAV-RIS Network

In this section, a detailed analytical framework for outage probability and achievable ergodic capacity is given under perfect and imperfect SIC. The outage probability (Pr_{out}) is defined as the probability that the received SINR falls below a target threshold (γ_{th}).

For transmission through UAV, we need to calculate the minimum SINR between the first hop and the second hop to evaluate the system outage probability.

Effective SINR of the ith *user for two-hop communication via UAV*

$$W = min(\gamma_{u,i}, \gamma_{d,i}) \tag{21}$$

where $\gamma_{s,i}$ is the SINR at the UAV for ith user, and $\gamma_{d,i}$ is the SINR at the ith user for the signal coming through UAV. Now, the outage probability ($Pr^U_{out_{s,i}}$) is given as

$$\begin{aligned} Pr^U_{out_{u,i}} &= P(W \leq \gamma_{th}) \\ &= 1 - (1 - F_{\gamma_{u,i}}(\gamma_{th}))(1 - F_{\gamma_{d,i}}(\gamma_{th})) \end{aligned} \tag{22}$$

4.1 Diversity Combining

Let Q_i be the SINR applying SC on the received signals via UAV and RIS. Thus,

$$Q_i = max(W, \bar{\gamma}_{d,i}) \tag{23}$$

where $\bar{\gamma}_{d,i}$ is the end-to-end SINR of ith user via the RIS. The outage probabilities for the end-to-end link when applying SC and MRC with information coming from UAV and RIS at U_1 can be evaluated as:

$$\begin{aligned} Pr_{out,sc,1} &= P(max(W, \bar{\gamma}_{d,i}) \leq \gamma_{th}) \\ &= [1 - (1 - F_{\gamma_{u,1}}(\gamma_{th}))(1 - F_{\gamma_{d,1}}(\gamma_{th}))F_{\bar{\gamma}_{d,1}}(\gamma_{th})] \end{aligned} \tag{24}$$

The PDF and CDF of a single Nakagami-m faded channel are expressed as:

$$f_{\gamma_{s,i}}(x) = \frac{2{m_1}^{m_1}}{\Gamma(m_1)\bar{\Omega}_1^{m_1}} x^{2m_1-1} exp\left(-\frac{m_1 x^2}{\bar{\Omega}_1}\right) \tag{25}$$

$$F_{\gamma_{u,i}}(x) = \gamma\left(m_1, \frac{m_1}{\bar{\Omega}_1} x^2\right) \tag{26}$$

where γ is the incomplete gamma function. The CDF of $F_{\gamma_{u,1}}(\gamma_{th})$ and $F_{\gamma_{u,2}}(\gamma_{th})$ based on single Nakagami-m faded channel are expressed as:

$$F_{\gamma_{u,1}}(\gamma_{th}) = \gamma\left(m_1, \frac{m_1}{\bar{\Omega}_1}\left(\gamma_{th}\frac{\mathbb{E}1}{\mathbb{E}2}\right)^2\right) \tag{27}$$

For perfect SIC, the $F_{\gamma'_{u,2}}(\gamma_{th})$ is

$$F_{\gamma'_{u,2}}(\gamma_{th}) = \gamma\left(m_2, \frac{m_2}{\bar{\Omega}_2}\left(\frac{\gamma_{th}}{\mathbb{E}2}\right)^2\right) \tag{28}$$

where $\mathbb{E}1 = \frac{l_{u,1}P_u}{d^c_{ur}\sigma^2_{d,1}}$, and $\mathbb{E}2 = \frac{l_{u,2}P_u}{d^c_{ur}\sigma^2_{d,2}}$. For imperfect SIC, the $F_{\gamma_{u,2}}(\gamma_{th})$ is

$$F_{\gamma_{u,2}}(\gamma_{th}) = \gamma\left(m_2, \frac{m_2}{\bar{\Omega}_2}\left(\gamma_{th}\frac{\mathbb{E}1}{\mathbb{E}2}\right)^2\right) \tag{29}$$

where $\mathbb{E}1 = \frac{l_{u,2}P_u}{d_{ur}^c \sigma_{d,2}^2}$, and $\mathbb{E}2 = \frac{\Upsilon l_{u,1}P_u}{d_{ur}^c \sigma_{d,1}^2}$. The CDF of $F_{\gamma_{d,1}}(\gamma_{th})$ and $F_{\gamma_{d,2}}(\gamma_{th})$ are expressed as:

$$\begin{aligned} F_{\gamma_{d,1}}(\gamma_{th}) &= P(\gamma_{d,1} \le \gamma_{th}) \\ &= P\left(\frac{\frac{Vl_{d,1}\rho'|h_{ur}|^2|h_{r\acute{u}_1}|^2}{d_{ur}^c d_{r\acute{u}_1}^c}}{1+\frac{Vl_{d,2}\rho'|h_{ur}|^2|h_{r\acute{u}_1}|^2}{d_{ur}^c d_{r\acute{u}_1}^c}} \le \gamma_{th}\right) \\ &= \int_0^{\gamma_{th}^\star} \frac{4x^{m_1+m_2-1}}{\Gamma(m_1)\Gamma(m_2)}\left(\frac{m_1m_2}{\bar{\Omega}_1\bar{\Omega}_2}\right)^{\frac{m_1+m_2}{2}} K_{m_1-m_2}\left(2x\sqrt{\frac{m_1m_2}{\bar{\Omega}_1\bar{\Omega}_2}}\right)dx \end{aligned} \tag{30}$$

where $\bar{\mathbb{E}}1 = \frac{Vl_{d,1}P_u}{d_{ur}^c d_{r\acute{u}_1}^c \sigma_{d,1}^2}$, $\bar{\mathbb{E}}2 = \frac{Vl_{d,2}P_u}{d_{ur}^c d_{r\acute{u}_2}^c \sigma_{d,2}^2}$, and $\gamma_{th}^\star = \sqrt{\frac{\gamma_{th}}{\bar{\mathbb{E}}1-\bar{\mathbb{E}}2\gamma_{th}}}$.

For a perfect SIC, the CDF of $F_{\gamma'_{d,2}}(\gamma_{th})$ is found out in a similar manner,

$$F_{\gamma'_{d,2}}(\gamma_{th}) = P(\gamma'_{d,2} \le \gamma_{th}) \tag{31}$$

For an imperfect SIC, the CDF of $F_{\gamma_{d,2}}(\gamma_{th})$ is

$$F_{\gamma_{d,2}}(\gamma_{th}) = P(\gamma_{d,2} \le \gamma_{th}) \tag{32}$$

where $\bar{\mathbb{E}}1 = \frac{Vl_{d,2}P_u}{d_{ur}^c d_{r\acute{u}_2}^c \sigma_{d,2}^2}$, $\bar{\mathbb{E}}2 = \frac{\Upsilon Vl_{d,1}P_u}{d_{ur}^c d_{r\acute{u}_1}^c \sigma_{d,1}^2}$.

The CDF of $F_{\bar{\gamma}_{d,1}}(\gamma_{th})$ and $F_{\bar{\gamma}_{d,2}}(\gamma_{th})$ are expressed as:

$$\begin{aligned} F_{\bar{\gamma}_{d,1}}(\gamma_{th}) &= P(\bar{\gamma}_{d,1} \le \gamma_{th}) \\ &= \int_0^{\gamma_{th}^\star} \sum_{k_1=0}^{m_1-1} \cdots \sum_{k_N=0}^{m_1-1} \Pi_{j=1}^N \frac{(m_2)_{m_1-1-k_j}(1-m_2)_{k_j}}{(m_1-1-k)!k_j!} \\ &\times \frac{4\left(\frac{m_1m_2}{\bar{\Omega}_1\bar{\Omega}_2}\right)^{\frac{u+1}{2}}}{(u-1)!} x^u K_{u-1}\left(2\sqrt{\frac{m_1m_2}{\bar{\Omega}_1\bar{\Omega}_2}x}\right)dx \end{aligned} \tag{33}$$

where $\bar{\mathbb{E}}'1 = \frac{l_{u,1}P_u}{d_{ur}^c d_{r\acute{u}_1}^c \sigma'^2_{d,1}}$, and $\bar{\mathbb{E}}'2 = \frac{l_{u,2}P_u}{d_{ur}^c d_{r\acute{u}_2}^c \sigma'^2_{d,2}}$, and $\gamma_{th}^\star = \sqrt{\frac{\gamma_{th}}{\bar{\mathbb{E}}'1-\bar{\mathbb{E}}'2\gamma_{th}}}$.

For perfect SIC, the CDF of $F_{\bar{\gamma}'_{d,2}}(\gamma_{th})$ is

$$\begin{aligned} F_{\bar{\gamma}'_{d,2}}(\gamma_{th}) &= P(\bar{\gamma}'_{d,2} \le \gamma_{th}) \\ &= P\left(\frac{l_{u,2}P_u|\widehat{H_2}|^2}{\sigma'^2_{d,2}} \le \gamma_{th}\right) \end{aligned} \tag{34}$$

For imperfect SIC, the CDF of $F_{\bar{\gamma}_{d,2}}(\gamma_{th})$ is

$$F_{\bar{\gamma}_{d,2}}(\gamma_{th}) = P(\bar{\gamma}_{d,2} \leq \gamma_{th}) \tag{35}$$

where $\bar{\mathbb{E}}'1 = \frac{l_{u,2} P_u}{d_{ur}^c d_{r\acute{u}_2}^c \sigma r_{d,2}^2}$, and $\bar{\mathbb{E}}'2 = \frac{\Upsilon l_{u,1} P_u}{d_{ur}^c d_{r\acute{u}_1}^c \sigma r_{d,1}^2}$.

4.2 Outage for MRC Case

The overall SINR at U_1 after MRC is $Z = X + Y$, where $X = W$, and $Y = \bar{\gamma}_{d,1}$. Now, outage for U_1

$$\begin{aligned} Pr_{out,mrc,1} &= P(Z \leq \gamma_{th}) \\ &= \int_{y=0}^{\gamma_{th}} F_X(\gamma_{th} - y) f_Y(y)\, dy \end{aligned} \tag{36}$$

Here, X is +ve, then we can consider $\gamma_{th} > y$. After some algebraic manipulation and utilizing the above (15), (27), and (30), we can write

$$\begin{aligned} Pr_{out,mrc,1} = & \int_{y=0}^{\gamma_{th}} \Bigg[1 - (1 - F_{\gamma_{u,1}}(\gamma_{th} - y))(1 - F_{\gamma_{d,1}}(\gamma_{th} - y)) \Bigg] \\ & \times \Bigg[\sum_{k_1=0}^{m_1-1} \cdots \sum_{k_N=0}^{m_1-1} \Pi_{j=1}^{N} \frac{(m_2)_{m_1-1-k_j}(1 - m_2)_{k_j}}{(m_1 - 1 - k)!k_j!} \\ & \times \frac{4\left(\frac{m_1 m_2}{\bar{\Omega}_1 \bar{\Omega}_2}\right)^{\frac{u+1}{2}}}{(u-1)!} y^u K_{u-1}\left(2\sqrt{\frac{m_1 m_2}{\bar{\Omega}_1 \bar{\Omega}_2} y}\right)\Bigg] dy \end{aligned} \tag{37}$$

Similarly, in the above (24) and (37) we can find out for the $Pr_{out,sc,2}$ and $Pr_{out,mrc,2}$.

4.3 System Outage Probability

We consider the system goes into an outage whenever any one of the two users is in an outage. Considering the individual outage probabilities $Pr_{out,sc,1}$ and $Pr_{out,sc,2}$, the system outage for SC is [25]:

$$Pr_{sys_{out,sc}} = Pr_{out,sc,1} + Pr_{out,sc,2} - Pr_{out,sc,1} Pr_{out,sc,2} \tag{38}$$

Similarly, the system outage for MRC is:

$$Pr_{sys_{out,mrc}} = Pr_{out,mrc,1} + Pr_{out,mrc,2} - Pr_{out,mrc,1}Pr_{out,mrc,2} \tag{39}$$

5 Ergodic Capacity Analysis

The ergodic capacity (C^U_{d,u_i}) of the ith user for transmission through UAV can be expressed as:

$$C^U_{d,u_i} = \frac{1}{2}\int_0^\infty log_2(1+w)f_W(w) \quad dw \tag{40}$$

$$F_W(w) = P(W \leq w) = P(min(\gamma_{s,i}, \gamma_{d,i}) \leq w) \tag{41}$$

$F_W(w)$ is already evaluated in (36). The ergodic capacities of U_1 and U_2 for UAV through transmission are represented as:

$$\begin{aligned}
C^U_{d,u_1} &= \frac{1}{ln2}\int_0^\infty \frac{1}{1+w}\left[1-\gamma\left(m_1, \frac{m_1}{\bar{\Omega}_1}\left(w\frac{\mathbb{E}1}{\mathbb{E}2}\right)^2\right)\right] \\
&\left[1 - B\left[2^{-\upsilon-2}\pi\left(\sqrt{\frac{w}{\bar{\mathbb{E}}1-\bar{\mathbb{E}}2w}}\right)^{\acute{a}}\left(c\left(\sqrt{\frac{w}{\bar{\mathbb{E}}1-\bar{\mathbb{E}}2w}}\right)\right)^{-\upsilon}\right.\right. \\
&csc(\pi\upsilon)\left[4^{\upsilon}\Gamma\left(\frac{\acute{a}-\upsilon}{2}\right){}_1\bar{F}_2\left[\frac{\acute{a}-\upsilon}{2}; 1-\upsilon, \frac{1}{2}(\acute{a}-\upsilon+2); \frac{c^2\left(\sqrt{\frac{w}{\bar{\mathbb{E}}1-\bar{\mathbb{E}}2w}}\right)^2}{4}\right]\right. \\
&-\left(c\left(\sqrt{\frac{w}{\bar{\mathbb{E}}1-\bar{\mathbb{E}}2w}}\right)\right)^{2\upsilon}\Gamma\left(\frac{\acute{a}+\upsilon}{2}\right) \\
&\left.\left.\left.{}_1\bar{F}_2\left[\frac{\acute{a}+\upsilon}{2}; \upsilon+1, \frac{1}{2}(\acute{a}+\upsilon+2); \frac{c^2\left(\sqrt{\frac{w}{\bar{\mathbb{E}}1-\bar{\mathbb{E}}2w}}\right)^2}{4}\right]\right]\right]\right]dw
\end{aligned} \tag{42}$$

where $B = \frac{4}{\Gamma(m_1)\Gamma(m_2)}\left(\frac{m_1m_2}{\bar{\Omega}_1\bar{\Omega}_2}\right)^{\frac{m_1+m_2}{2}}$, $\acute{a} = m_1+m_2, \upsilon = m_1 - m_2$, and $c = 2\sqrt{\frac{m_1m_2}{\bar{\Omega}_1\bar{\Omega}_2}}$.

For a perfect SIC, the C^U_{d,u_2} is

$$\begin{aligned}
C^U_{d,u_2} &= \frac{1}{ln2}\int_0^\infty \frac{1}{1+w}\left[1-\gamma\left(m_2, \frac{m_2}{\bar{\Omega}_2}\left(\frac{w}{\mathbb{E}2}\right)^2\right)\right]\left[1 - A\left[2^{-\upsilon-2}\pi\left(\frac{w}{\bar{\mathbb{E}}'2}\right)^{\acute{a}}\right.\right. \\
&\left(c\left(\frac{w}{\bar{\mathbb{E}}'2}\right)\right)^{-\upsilon}csc(\pi\upsilon)\left[4^{\upsilon}\Gamma\left(\frac{\acute{a}-\upsilon}{2}\right){}_1\bar{F}_2\left[\frac{\acute{a}-\upsilon}{2}; 1-\upsilon, \frac{1}{2}(\acute{a}-\upsilon+2); \frac{c^2\left(\frac{w}{\bar{\mathbb{E}}'2}\right)^2}{4}\right]\right. \\
&\left.\left.\left.-\left(c\left(\frac{w}{\bar{\mathbb{E}}'2}\right)\right)^{2\upsilon}\Gamma\left(\frac{\acute{a}+\upsilon}{2}\right){}_1\bar{F}_2\left[\frac{\acute{a}+\upsilon}{2}; \upsilon+1, \frac{1}{2}(\acute{a}+\upsilon+2); \frac{c^2\left(\frac{w}{\bar{\mathbb{E}}'2}\right)^2}{4}\right]\right]\right]\right]dw
\end{aligned} \tag{43}$$

Now, we find the ergodic capacity (C^R_{d,u_i}) through RIS

$$C^R_{d,u_i} = \int_0^\infty log_2(1 + w')f_{\widehat{W}}(w') \quad dw' \tag{44}$$

where $\widehat{W}$ represents the SINR of the end-to-end link from the (T-BS - U_i) through RIS, $\widehat{W}$ is expressed in (18) for U_1 and (19) for U_2. The ergodic capacities of U_1 and U_2 through RIS are represented as:

$$C^R_{d,u_1} = \frac{1}{ln2}\int_0^\infty \frac{1}{1+w'}\Bigg[1 - \Bigg\{\sum_{k_1=0}^{m_1-1}\cdots\sum_{k_N=0}^{m_1-1}\Pi_{j=1}^N \frac{(m_2)_{m_1-1-k_j}(1-m_2)_{k_j}}{(m_1-1-k)!k_j!} \times\left(1-\frac{2}{(u-1)!}\right)\left(\sqrt{\frac{m_1m_2}{\bar{\Omega}_1\bar{\Omega}_2}}\sqrt{\frac{w'}{\bar{\mathbb{E}}'1-\bar{\mathbb{E}}'2w'}}\right)^u K_u\left(2\sqrt{\frac{m_1m_2}{\bar{\Omega}_1\bar{\Omega}_2}}\sqrt{\frac{w'}{\bar{\mathbb{E}}'1-\bar{\mathbb{E}}'2w'}}\right)\Bigg\}\Bigg]dw' \tag{45}$$

For a perfect SIC, the C^R_{d,u_2} is

$$C^R_{d,u_2} = \frac{1}{ln2}\int_0^\infty \frac{1}{1+w'}\Bigg[1 - \Bigg\{\sum_{k_1=0}^{m_1-1}\cdots\sum_{k_N=0}^{m_1-1}\Pi_{j=1}^N \frac{(m_2)_{m_1-1-k_j}(1-m_2)_{k_j}}{(m_1-1-k)!k_j!} \times\left(1-\frac{2}{(u-1)!}\right)\left(\sqrt{\frac{m_1m_2}{\bar{\Omega}_1\bar{\Omega}_2}}\left(\frac{w'}{\bar{\mathbb{E}}'2}\right)\right)^u K_u\left(2\sqrt{\frac{m_1m_2}{\bar{\Omega}_1\bar{\Omega}_2}}\left(\frac{w'}{\bar{\mathbb{E}}'2}\right)\right)\Bigg\}\Bigg]dw' \tag{46}$$

Similarly, following the above (43) and (46), we can find C^U_{d,u_2} and C^R_{d,u_2} for imperfect SIC.

The achievable ergodic capacity of the end-to-end link at U_1 and U_2 using signals from UAV and RIS, after applying SC, can be expressed as [6, 25]:

$$C_1 = max(C^U_{d,u_1}, C^R_{d,u_1}) \tag{47}$$

$$C_2 = max(C^U_{d,u_2}, C^R_{d,u_2}) \tag{48}$$

Similarly, the achievable ergodic capacity can be found by considering imperfect SIC, incorporating the above procedures, and following the same steps. In this case, the imperfections in the SIC scheme, represented by $\Upsilon > 0$, will introduce residual interference even after the cancellation process and are likely to degrade the performance.

6 Results on Outage and Ergodic Capacity

We now present numerical results following our analytical formulation and validate the same with MATLAB-based simulation. Specifically, we will analyze the outage probability and achievable ergodic capacity, considering both SC and MRC diversity combining techniques under the Nakagami-m fading channel. The simulation outcomes will be presented for different scenarios, including variations in the number of reflecting elements in the RIS, the SNR in dB, and the distance between users. Nakagami-m fading channel with $m_1 = 4$, $m_2 = 2$ is considered. The following parameters are summarized in Table 1.

The outage probability performance for U_2 in the context of both OMA and NOMA cases is compared in Fig. 2. The outcomes of the simulation show that NOMA has a lower outage probability than OMA. For example, it is found that the outage probability for NOMA relative to OMA decreases by 66% at an SNR of 7 dB. The SIC technique used at U_2 is responsible for the enhanced outage performance of NOMA. By utilizing this approach, U_2 may effectively decode and subtract interference from the signal of the other user, improving its capacity to decode and retrieve the transmitted data with greater reliability.

Figure 3 presents the relationship between the system outage probability and SNR (in dB). With the increase in SNR, outage reduces. The system outage probability decreases as the number of reflecting elements increases. For the same number of N, and under the same SNR, imperfect SIC increases the outage probability compared to perfect SIC case. As the number of reflecting elements increases, outage reduces.

Figure 4 illustrates the impact of splitting RIS elements on system outage. Here, N_1 represents the number of reflecting elements dedicated to U_1's signal in the downlink. When N_1 is low, the received SINR at U_1 is also low, leading to an increased outage

Table 1 Simulation parameters and values

Parameters	Values
η	0.8
α	0.7
c	2
H	30 meter (m)
d_{ur}	20 m
$d_{r\acute{u}_1}$	30 m
$d_{r\acute{u}_2}$	15 m
$\bar{\Omega}_1 = \bar{\Omega}_2$	1
$a_{u,1} = a_{d,1}$	0.6
$a_{u,2} = a_{d,2}$	0.4
N	10, 20, 30
SNR	18 dB
γ_{th}	10 dB

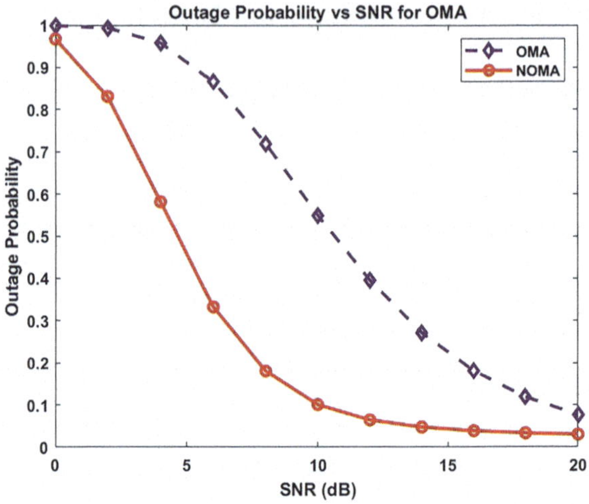

Fig. 2 Outage performance comparison between OMA and NOMA

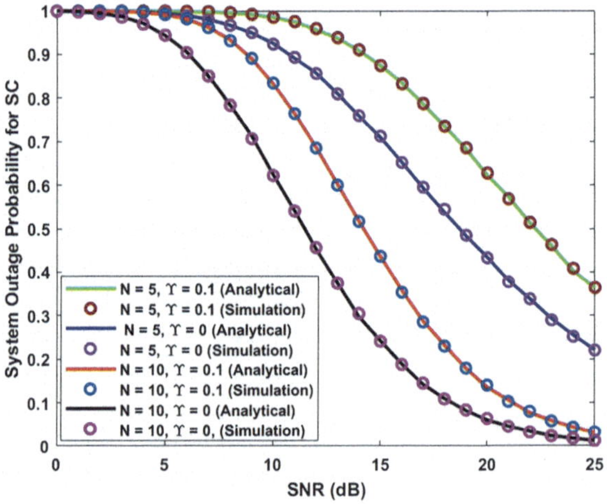

Fig. 3 System outage comparison for perfect SIC and imperfect SIC

probability for U_1 and, consequently, a higher overall system outage. Conversely, when N_1 is very high, the remaining RIS elements ($N_2 = N - N_1$) available for reflecting U_2's signal are insufficient, resulting in a low received SINR at U_2 and an increased outage for both U_2 and the entire system outage. Therefore, there exists an optimal intermediate value of N_1 that minimizes the system outage. In this scenario, the optimal N_1 is 6 for an SNR of 25 dB, and 7 for an SNR of 18 dB. Since U_1 is the farther user, it has a more significant influence on the overall system outage. At higher SNR levels, fewer reflecting elements N_1 are needed to achieve the same outage level at U_1, resulting in a lower optimal N_1. Additionally, as the SNR increases, the system outage consistently decreases. Moreover, for the same SNR levels, MRC shows a lower system outage compared to SC.

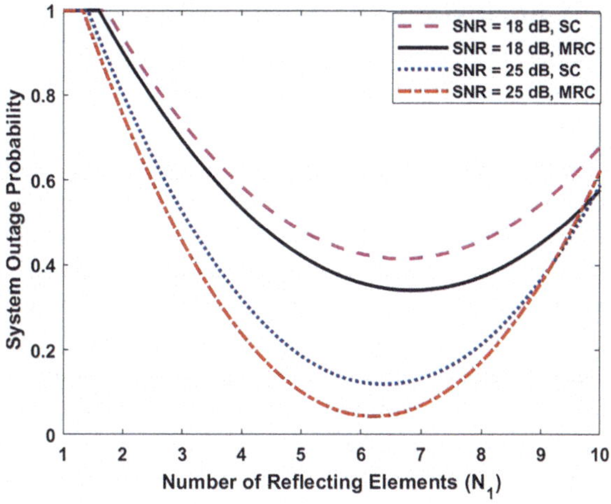

Fig. 4 Performance of system outage probability on SNR (in dB), $\Upsilon = 0$

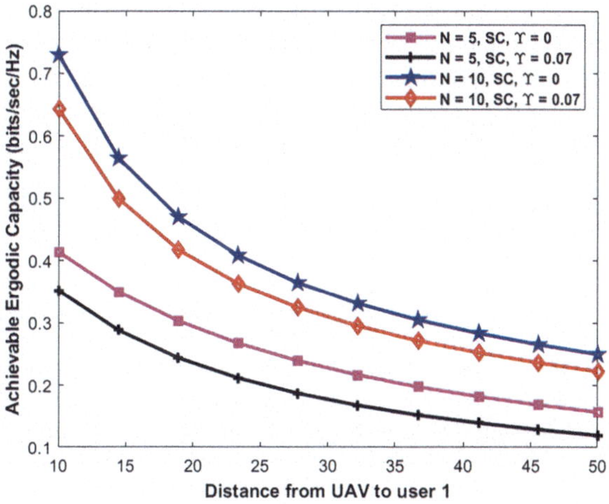

Fig. 5 Achievable ergodic capacity versus distance from UAV to user 1

In Fig. 5, the achievable ergodic capacity is depicted for two scenarios: $N = 5$ and $N = 10$. Figure 5 highlights several key insights regarding the effects of distance and the number of reflecting elements on system performance. Firstly, it is evident that as the distance between the UAV and U_1 increases, the achievable ergodic capacity decreases. This observation suggests that greater user distance from the UAV diminishes the capacity for reliable data transmission, leading to a reduction in overall system performance. However, an increase in the value of N results in an increase in the achievable ergodic capacity. This finding implies that the loss in ergodic capacity due to increased distance can be mitigated by augmenting the number of reflecting elements. Additionally, imperfect SIC leads to a reduction in ergodic capacity compared to perfect SIC.

7 Conclusions and Future Work

An integrated UAV-RIS scheme-based NOMA network has been investigated. To realistically capture the wireless channel conditions, we account for the presence of Nakagami-m fading in both the uplink and downlink scenarios. Specifically, we consider Nakagami-m fading channels from the T-BS to the UAV-RIS and from the UAV-RIS to the D2D users. Further, we have considered diversity combining techniques and observed that MRC outperforms SC. Our analysis has focused on assessing the outage and ergodic capacity performance of the network through the development of analytical expressions. The RIS plays a vital role in enhancing the signal by intelligently reflecting it, and the number of reflecting elements in the RIS affects its capability to improve the signal quality. Moreover, we have observed that the proposed UAV-RIS-based NOMA outperforms the OMA scheme. Imperfection in SIC degrades the performance compared to perfect SIC. Allocation of more reflecting elements improves outage and ergodic capacity. The optimal value of N_1 has been evaluated with respect to the SNR. Our framework can be used to analyse for Rician fading channel and this study can be extended to accommodate multiple users encompassing imperfection in phase error.

References

1. A. Alnoman, and A. Anpalagan. "On D2D communications for public safety applications". IEEE Canada international humanitarian technology conference (IHTC), pp. 124-127, Jul. 2017.
2. M. Z. Khan, M. Rahim, M. A. Javed, F. Ghabban, O. Ameerbakhsh, and I. Alfadli. "A D2D-assisted multi-hop data dissemination protocol for inter-UAV communication". International Journal of Communication Systems, vol. 34, no. 11, pp. e4857, Jul. 2021.
3. Z. Ding, P. Fan, and H. V. Poor. "Impact of user pairing on 5G nonorthogonal multiple-access downlink transmissions". IEEE Transactions on Vehicular Technology, vol. 65, no. 8, pp. 6010-6023, Sep. 2015.
4. J. Ren, X. Lei, Z. Peng, X. Tang, and O. A. Dobre. "Ris-assisted cooperative NOMA with SWIPT". IEEE Wireless Communications Letters, vol. 12, no. 3, pp. 446-450, Dec. 2022.
5. S. A. H. Mohsan, M. A. Khan, M. H. Alsharif, P. Uthansakul, and A. A. Solyman. "Intelligent reflecting surfaces assisted UAV communications for massive networks: current trends, challenges, and research directions". Sensors, vol. 22, no. 14, pp. 5278, Jul. 2022.
6. S. K. Singh, K. Agrawal, K. Singh, C. P. Li, and Z. Ding. "NOMA enhanced hybrid RIS-UAV-assisted full-duplex communication system with imperfect SIC and CSI". IEEE Transactions on Communications, 70(11), Oct. 2022, pp. 7609-7627.
7. D. T. Do, A. T. Le, Y. Liu, and A. Jamalipour. "User grouping and energy harvesting in UAV-NOMA system with AF/DF relaying". IEEE Transactions on Vehicular Technology, vol. 70, no. 11, pp. 11855-11868, Sep. 2021.
8. B. Tahir, S. Schwarz, and M. Rupp. "Outage analysis of uplink IRS-assisted NOMA under elements splitting". IEEE 93rd Vehicular Technology Conference (VTC2021-Spring), pp. 1-5, Apr. 2021.

9. S. A. Tegos, D. Tyrovolas, P. D. Diamantoulakis, C. K. Liaskos, and G. K. Karagiannidis. "On the distribution of the sum of double-Nakagami-m random vectors and application in randomly reconfigurable surfaces". IEEE Transactions on Vehicular Technology, vol. 71, no. 7, pp. 7297-7307, Apr. 2022.
10. B. C. Nguyen, N. T. Phuong, X. N. Tran, and P. T. Hiep. On performance of RIS-aided ground-to-air and air-to-ground communications in multi-user NOMA systems. Computer Networks, 228, 109754, Jun. 2023.
11. The Wolfram Functions Site [Online]. Available: http://functions.wolfram.com
12. M. A. Badiu, and J. P. Coon. Communication through a large reflecting surface with phase errors. IEEE Wireless Communications Letters, vol. 9, no. 2, pp. 184-188, Oct. 2019.
13. A. C. Pogaku, D. T. Do, B. M. Lee, and N. D. Nguyen. UAV-assisted RIS for future wireless communications: A survey on optimization and performance analysis. IEEE Access, 10, pp. 16320-16336, Feb. 2022.
14. L. Yang, F. Meng, J. Zhang, M. O. Hasna, and M. Di Renzo. On the performance of RIS-assisted dual-hop UAV communication systems. IEEE Transactions on Vehicular Technology, 69(9), pp. 10385-10390, Jun. 2020.
15. N. Rahmatov, and H. Baek. RIS-carried UAV communication: Current research, challenges, and future trends. ICT Express, Mar. 2023.
16. Y. Yao, K. Lv, S. Huang, X. Li, and W. Xiang. UAV trajectory and energy efficiency optimization in RIS-assisted multi-user air-to-ground communications networks. Drones, vol. 7, no. 4, p. 272, Apr. 2023.
17. M. Diamanti, M. Tsampazi, E. E. Tsiropoulou, and S. Papavassiliou. Energy efficient multi-user communications aided by reconfigurable intelligent surfaces and UAVs. In IEEE International Conference on Smart Computing (SMARTCOMP), pp. 371-376, Aug. 2021.
18. Y. Byun, H. Kim, S. Kim, and B. Shim. Channel Estimation and Phase Shift Control for UAV-carried RIS Communication Systems. IEEE Transactions on Vehicular Technology, May 2023.
19. N. Zhao, X. Pang, Z. Li, Y. Chen, F. Li, Z. Ding, and M. S. Alouini. "Joint trajectory and precoding optimization for UAV-assisted NOMA networks". IEEE Transactions on Communications, vol. 67, no. 5, pp. 3723-3735, Jan. 2019.
20. S. Shang, and D. Xu. Beamforming Design for Double-RIS Assisted UAV Communication with Limited Feedback in Disaster Scenarios. In IEEE 97th Vehicular Technology Conference (VTC2023-Spring), pp. 1-5, Jun. 2023.
21. Y. Zhang, Z. Gao, M. Jiang, Y. Zhang, X. Lu, and L. Zhang. UAV-Mounted RIS Assisted UAV Communications Incorporating NOMA: Performance Evaluation and Optimization. In 2023 IEEE 6th International Conference on Electronic Information and Communication Technology (ICEICT), pp. 712-716, Jul. 2023.
22. K. Tian, B. Duo, S. Li, Y. Zuo, and X. Yuan. Hybrid uplink and downlink transmissions for full-duplex UAV communication with RIS. IEEE Wireless Communications Letters, vol. 11, no. 4, pp. 866-870, Feb. 2022.
23. A. Alqahtani, and E. Alsusa. On the Quality of Service and Experience in IRS-NOMA Over $\kappa-\mu$ Generalized Fading Channels. IEEE Open Journal of the Communications Society, vol. 3, pp.2272-2283, Nov. 2022.
24. X. Yue, and Y. Liu. Performance analysis of intelligent reflecting surface assisted NOMA networks. IEEE Transactions on Wireless Communications, vol. 21, no. 4, pp.2623-2636, Oct. 2021.
25. S. Ghosh, A. Bhowmick, S.D. Roy, and S. Kundu. Outage and Ergodic Capacity Analysis in UAV-RIS Assisted NOMA-D2D Network. In IEEE International Conference on Advanced Networks and Telecommunications Systems (ANTS), pp. 762-767, Dec. 2023.

D2D Communication in 6G Network

Srininvasarao Yarlagadda and Ajay Bhardwaj

1 Introduction

The forthcoming six-generation (6G) wireless network eventually will replace the ongoing 5G networks. The 6G network seems to have the potential of providing an ultra-high-speed data rate, highly reliable and low latency end-to-end communication, better privacy and security compared to the 5G networks [1]. According to the CISCO VNI report [2], mobile users have been experiencing significant and rapid growth with different types of applications that require a lot of data, such as streaming videos or downloading large files. This increased demand for data puts a heavy load on the base stations. D2D communication emerge as one of the significant solution to this problem and is critical to the upcoming 6G network. It allows the devices to communicate directly with each other without the help of base stations. Hence, it reduces the burden on the base station and improves spectral efficiency, reducing the latency and improves the throughput. In D2D communication, D2D users (DUs) may share the spectrum of cellular users which inherently leads to several challenges that may need to be addressed, such as resource allocation, interference management, and security [3, 4].

Resource management is critical to enable the D2D communication in the 6G network. The efficient allocation of power, time, and spectrum ensures optimal performance in improving energy efficiency and maintaining high service quality, which is crucial for battery-powered mobile devices. Additionally, it supports network scalability [5], allowing smooth communication among many devices. Another significant challenge is interference management, which must be addressed cautiously to implement the 6G network successfully. As previously mentioned, DUs share the

S. Yarlagadda · A. Bhardwaj (✉)
SRM University, Amaravati, AP, India
e-mail: ajay.b@srmap.edu.in

S. Yarlagadda
e-mail: srinivasarao_y@srmap.edu.in

T. Ojha et al. (eds.), *Edge-Enabled 6G Networking*,
https://doi.org/10.1007/978-3-032-19042-0_8

uplink or downlink spectrum allocated to the cellular users (CUs) to make the system spectral efficient. DUs interfere with CUs when they use downlink resources, while interference is generated at the base station when DUs share the uplink resource. However, interference handling at the base station is more manageable than CUs because of more computational power at the base station.

Another significant challenge is secure communication via D2D-enabled networks. The absence of central authorities in D2D-enabled networks poses security challenges. As more devices connect and sensitive data is exchanged, robust security measures are needed. This has led to interest in developing techniques to enhance secrecy and protect against eavesdropping and other malicious activities. Integrating reconfigurable intelligent surfaces (RIS) into D2D communication networks offers a promising approach to supporting secrecy [6]. RIS can manipulate the wireless environment to improve signal quality and steer signals away from potential eavesdroppers, thereby enhancing the security of D2D communication. By intelligently reconfiguring the propagation environment, RIS can create more secure communication channels that are resilient to interception and jamming attempts. Some scenarios in 6G networks need to be considered, as discussed below.

D2D communication in upcoming 6G networks aims to achieve ultra-low latency, massive connectivity, and enhanced energy efficiency. Additionally, it also ensures the advanced security and privacy while leveraging AI and machine learning to optimize network performance. Furthermore, it aims to supports the emerging use cases, such as, augmented reality, vehicle-to-everything (V2X) communication, and public safety. However, to support these key applications, we need to address the proximity-based communication and dynamic spectrum sharing problems. One promising solution seems is network slicing and virtualization which ensures ultra-reliable, low-latency, and energy-efficient connectivity for a wide range of applications.

This book chapter highlights the importance of D2D communication in 6G networks, focusing on resource management, interference management, and security. Further, it will explore challenges and opportunities related to these topics and highlight present research. The overall structure of the book chapter is as follows.

Organization Section 2 provides applications of D2D Communication in 6G Networks. Section 3 offers various challenges and prospective solutions proposed in the literature. Section 4 provides security and privacy in D2D-enabled 6G networks, while Sect. 5 concludes the chapter.

2 Applications of D2D Communication in 6G Networks

The prominent feature of D2D communication in 6G networks is to leverage the shared data from nearby mobile devices which eventually extends the user equipment's view scope. This uprising demands of local data exchanges will become the

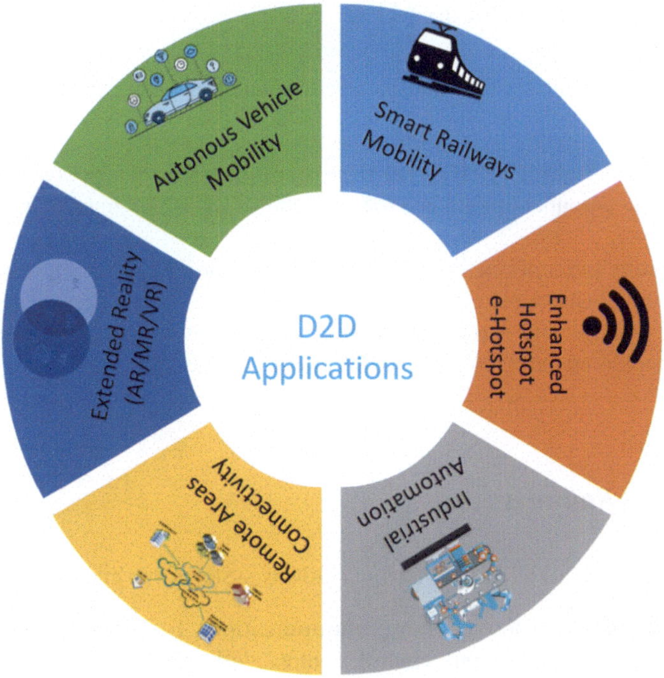

Fig. 1 Exploring D2D applications within the next-generation 6G network landscape

basis for designing new applications of D2D communication. The various applications of D2D communication in 6G networks, showcasing its pivotal role across multiple domains are illustrated in Fig. 1.

From enabling seamless communication among Autonomous Vehicles (AVs) to enhancing efficiency in Smart Railways, facilitating Enhanced Hotspot connectivity, powering immersive experiences in Extended Reality (AR/MR/VR), to bridging connectivity gaps in Remote Areas, D2D communication emerges as a fundamental enabler of connectivity and innovation in the next-generation wireless landscape.

D2D communication is vital across various applications by enhancing efficiency and connectivity. Autonomous vehicles allow them to share real-time information, have low latency, and improve safety. By directly interacting with each other, vehicles can choose the best routes, avoid collisions, and better understand their surroundings. Smart railways enable real-time data exchange between trains and control systems, improving safety and coordination. For enhanced hotspots (e-Hotspots), D2D communication boosts network performance by allowing devices to share access directly, reducing congestion in high-density areas. Extended reality (AR/MR/VR) applications ensure low-latency, high-bandwidth connections for seamless, immersive experiences. Additionally, D2D communication bridges connectivity gaps in remote areas by forming ad-hoc networks, providing essential connectivity without relying on traditional infrastructure.

2.1 Autonomous Vehicles (AVs)

6G will be instrumental in the widespread adoption of safe and efficient autonomous vehicles:

- **Ultra-high-definition (UHD) real-time mapping:** 6G will support the transmission of vast amounts of data needed for detailed, real-time maps crucial for AV navigation.
- **Cooperative perception:** Vehicles can share sensor data in real-time, creating a more comprehensive picture of the environment.
- **Remote control and intervention:** 6G's high bandwidth and low latency will enable human operators to control AVs in emergencies remotely.

2.2 Smart Railways

6G will play a crucial role in transforming railway systems into intelligent networks:

- **Ultra-reliable and low-latency communication:** Real-time communication between trains, tracks, and control centres will enable tighter control over operations and improved safety.
- **Advanced sensor networks:** Denser sensor networks will provide real-time data for predictive maintenance and to prevent breakdowns.
- **Immersive training for personnel:** Virtual reality (VR) simulations powered by 6G can provide highly realistic training experiences.

2.3 Enhanced Hotspot (e-Hotspot)

e-Hotspots will be significantly enhanced with the capabilities of 6G:

- **Holographic communication:** 6G's high bandwidth could enable holographic communication for more immersive collaboration.
- **Multi-gigabit internet access:** e-Hotspots could provide significantly faster Internet speeds for bandwidth-intensive applications.
- **Dynamic network slicing:** 6G will allow e-Hotspots to simultaneously cater to different user needs, prioritizing bandwidth for critical applications.

2.4 *Extended Reality (AR/MR/VR)*

6G will revolutionize extended reality experiences:

- **Haptic feedback and sensory experiences:** Ultra-low latency will enable the integration of haptic feedback for a more realistic VR experience.
- **Scalable cloud-based rendering:** Complex VR experiences can be streamed to less powerful devices by offloading processing to the cloud.
- **Multi-user AR experiences:** Seamless interaction between multiple users in shared AR environments will foster collaboration and innovation.

2.5 *Remote Areas Connectivity*

6G will bridge the digital divide by providing internet access to remote areas:

- **Satellite-based 6G networks:** Constellations of 6G satellites could provide high-speed internet access to even the most remote areas.
- **Integration with terrestrial networks:** Seamless integration with terrestrial networks will ensure constant connectivity regardless of location.

3 Challenges and Prospective Solutions

In 6G D2D communication, numerous challenges arise concerning resource and interference management, as DUs share the cellular spectrum with CUs. There are two types of D2D communication: inband and outband. Inband D2D communication occurs within the same spectrum as the CUs. There are two further subdivisions: underlay and overlay D2D communication. In underlay mode, DUs operate in the same frequency band as CUs however are treated as secondary users, allowing them to access the spectrum opportunistically. This enhances spectral efficiency by increasing the reuse of frequency bands. However, it introduces interference management challenges as DUs must avoid causing significant interference to CUs. Techniques like power control, resource allocation, and interference cancellation are necessary to mitigate interference [7, 8]. Underlay communication offers significant spectral efficiency improvements but requires sophisticated algorithms to balance D2D performance with minimal interference to cellular users. In overlay communication, a portion of the cellular spectrum is dedicated exclusively to D2D communication, meaning that DUs do not interfere with CUs. This can simplify interference management, however, may lead to inefficient spectrum utilization if the allocated resources are not fully used by DUs. Overlay D2D provides a balance between minimizing interference and maintaining the performance of cellular networks [9]. In outband

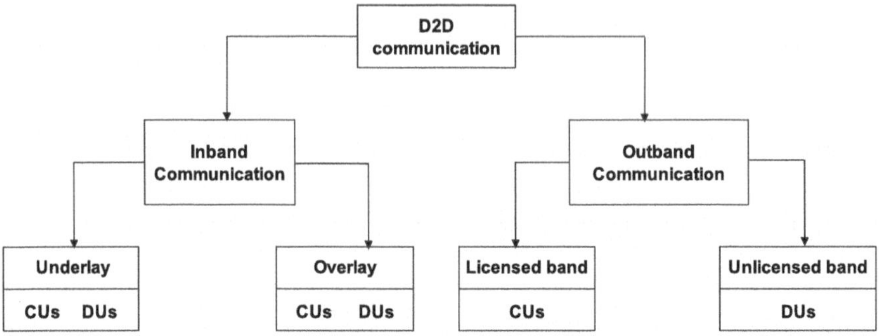

Fig. 2 Categories of D2D communication based on the spectrum use

D2D communication involves the use of spectrum outside the licensed cellular band. This approach leverages unlicensed frequency bands (e.g., ISM bands) for D2D communication while leaving licensed spectrum for CUs. The main advantage of outband communication is that it completely avoids interference with cellular users. However, the use of unlicensed bands comes with its own set of challenges, such as congestion, spectrum sharing, and regulatory limitations since many other devices also utilize the unlicensed spectrum [10]. Moreover, outband communication often requires additional coordination mechanisms to manage interference from other D2D and non-D2D devices operating in the same band. Figure 2 shows the categories of D2D communication based on the spectrum use.

3.1 Resource Management

Resource management for D2D communication focuses on addressing key issues such as spectrum sharing, power control, and interference mitigation. Since D2D links reuse cellular network resources, careful coordination is required to avoid conflicts between cellular and D2D transmissions. This ensures that network capacity is maximized, while maintaining the required quality of service (QoS) for both cellular and D2D users. Effective resource management not only optimizes the performance of D2D communications but also enhances the overall network's scalability, energy efficiency, and spectral utilization, making it a fundamental aspect of future wireless systems.

The authors in [11] propose an EHA-CRD model to maximize energy efficiency in D2D communication networks through joint time allocation and relay selection. They divide the problem into two sub-problems: relay selection and time optimization. They introduce the weighted sum maximum algorithm for relay selection and an iterative optimization algorithm for time optimization. Simulation results demonstrate improvement compared to existing algorithms, showcasing the potential of the novel network model design to enhance energy efficiency. Additionally, the model transforms non-convex optimization problems into convex ones using fractional programming theory. The proposed model combines D2D communication and energy harvesting technology, investigating maximizing energy efficiency through joint time allocation and relay selection. It attains higher energy efficiency compared to other schemes in simulation and offers advantages over exhaustive relay selection schemes using the PSO algorithm. The future work includes studying resource allocation based on 5G communication networks.

The authors in [12] propose a joint optimization approach for transmission rate selection and power control (TRSPC) to minimize total transmission energy consumption for relay-assisted D2D and CC links. The study also investigates interference control for relay-assisted D2D and cellular-cellular links, considering different transmission rates based on channel conditions. The proposed TRSPC approach aims to minimize energy consumption while meeting transmission delay and data volume requirements, and simulation results demonstrate its effectiveness in reducing total transmission energy consumption. This contrasts with existing approaches in typical cellular network scenarios.

The authors in [13] propose optimization of power allocation for NOMA-enabled D2D communication using dual theory and the sub-gradient method. The proposed scheme aims to enhance cellular networks' spectral efficiency and connection density. This specific scheme brings about a notable enhancement in the data rate of D2D communication and possesses a lower level of complexity, ultimately converging after a few iterations. The integration of Non-Orthogonal Multiple Access (NOMA) and D2D communication demonstrates an improvement in both spectral efficiency and connection density, emphasizing the efficacy of the suggested power optimization approach for NOMA-enabled D2D communication, even with imperfect successive interference cancellation (SIC) decoding. Table 1 summarizes the resource management for D2D-enabled wireless communication in the literature to delineate the contributions, highlighting the objectives they addressed and the methodologies used. This table offers an overview of the various research works and their approaches within the field.

The authors in [14] propose an efficient relay selection strategy for D2D communication, considering link stability, social connections, and users' willingness. They address the resource allocation problem using a nested algorithm based on Dinkelbach theory and Lagrange dual decomposition to maximize energy efficiency while meeting data rate and power constraints. The iterative algorithm improves solution efficiency, and simulations confirm its effectiveness in relay selection and overall energy efficiency. The research underscores the importance of considering social attributes for efficient resource allocation and emphasizes social-aware relay selection for enhanced system energy efficiency. The proposed scheme demonstrates better average energy efficiency than other methods, suggesting its potential for enhancing D2D communication in 5G networks.

The authors in [15] investigate resource allocation algorithms in D2D communication, focusing on improving resource utilization, throughput, energy efficiency, and latency. It categorizes the surveyed algorithms into four groups: conventional, NOMA, game theory, and machine learning techniques, and evaluates them based

Table 1 Works on resource management in D2D communication

Ref.	Objective	Methodology
[11]	To maximize energy efficiency in D2D communication networks through joint time allocation and relay selection	Energy harvesting aided D2D communication network under the cognitive radio (EHA-CRD)
[12]	To minimize total transmission energy consumption for relay-assisted D2D and CC links	Joint optimization approach for transmission rate selection and power control (TRSPC)
[13]	Optimizing power allocation for NOMA-enabled D2D communication	Dual theory and the sub-gradient
[14]	Develop an efficient relay selection strategy for D2D communication aiming to maximize energy efficiency	Dinkelbach theory and Lagrange
[15]	Improvement of resource utilization, throughput, energy efficiency, and latency	Conventional, NOMA, game theory, and machine learning techniques
[16]	It focuses on optimizing relay deployment, channel allocation, and relay assignment in UAVs to maximize network capacity	Reinforcement learning algorithms like stochastic
[17]	Spectrum and power allocation in high-rate D2D networks	Coloring Algorithm (CA)
[18]	Minimize total transmit power for all cellular and D2D network users	It uses a three-step mixed integer linear program to optimize subchannel assignment, user pairing, and power control to minimize total transmit power
[19]	Maximize the sum rate of D2D pairs in a NOMA cellular network, subject to minimum rate requirements for cellular users	Uses a dual-based iterative algorithm to optimize resource allocation for D2D communication in a NOMA cellular network, maximizing the D2D sum rate while meeting cellular user minimum rates

on various metrics. The study highlights the challenges of high interference levels introduced by frequency reuse in D2D communication and emphasizes enabling concurrent communication sessions through channel and power allocation. Additionally, it discusses enhancing cellular framework performance, the viability of D2D communication within LTE networks, architectural requirements for integration, and standardization in 3GPP. The paper also identifies the limitations of conventional and NOMA-based resource allocation algorithms and presents open challenges for future research.

The authors in [16] emphasize optimizing relay deployment, channel allocation, and relay assignment in UAVs to maximize network capacity. They propose an alternating optimization approach, dividing the problem into sub-problems and effectively addressing the interconnectedness between variables through decentralized methods. This approach is extended to UAV-aided D2D networks, demonstrating improved performance. Introducing reinforcement learning algorithms like stochastic learning automata and online learning algorithms based on real-time capacity measures further enhances relay network performance compared to conventional methods. The proposed approach has been validated through simulation results, demonstrating its effectiveness and highlighting increased relay network capacity. However, achieving convergence to the optimum requires specific learning step sizes due to potential selfish behaviour among nodes. Overall, the study showcases the significance of alternating optimization methods and reinforcement learning algorithms in improving relay network capacity within D2D-enabled UAV environments.

The authors in [17] emphasize spectrum and power allocation in D2D networks. It proposes energy-efficient resource allocation methods, utilizing the colouring algorithm (CA) technology for aggregating multiple Control Channels (CCs) for D2D pairs. They develop iterative algorithms, such as independent-power greedy-based outer approximation (IPGOA) and uniform-power greedy-based outer approximation (UPGOA). Simulation results demonstrate superior performance in energy-efficient spectrum allocation compared to existing methods. The research studies spectrum and power allocation in high-rate D2D networks and offers energy-efficient solutions to enhance performance.

The authors in [18] focuses on a NOMA-based D2D communication system in a cellular network. The focus is on resource allocation optimization to reduce the total transmit power for coexisting users. The paper investigates various aspects of power optimization, including sub-channel assignments, user pairings, and power control. It utilizes Rayleigh fading channels to find optimal solutions. The paper also explores centralized models for the coexistence of NOMA-D2D downlink and uplink cellular systems. It provides a framework for joint subchannel allocation, user pairing, and power control. The achievable rates for D2D and cellular users are calculated.

The work in [19] address the problem of control overhead and resource allocation in D2D communications under a NOMA cellular network. It aims to maximize the D2D sum rate while ensuring the requirements of cellular users. The study proposes a dual-based iterative algorithm for resource allocation and shows its superiority over existing orthogonal multiple access schemes through simulation results. It also derives optimal conditions for power control of cellular users and evaluates the performance of the proposed algorithm through simulations.

Resource management for D2D communication has seen significant advancements through various approaches such as energy harvesting, transmission rate optimization, relay selection, power control, and the incorporation of NOMA, each contributing to improved energy efficiency, spectral utilization, and interference mitigation. However, several challenges remain under-explored. The integration of machine learning for dynamic, real-time resource optimization is still in its early stages, and interference management in dense, multi-cell networks continues to be a significant hurdle. Additionally, achieving scalability and low-latency communication in ultra-dense networks while maintaining QoS is an ongoing challenge. Future research should explore innovative strategies combining optimization algorithms with real-time adaptability, potentially integrating emerging technologies like RIS and AI, to make D2D communication more efficient and scalable for next-generation wireless networks.

3.2 Interference Management

The significant challenges faced by researchers while designing architecture of D2D-enabled 6G network is interference management. To reduce the interference between D2D and cellular users, the authors [20] introduce efficient power allocation schemes such as power control scheme-1 (PCS1) and power control scheme-2 (PCS2). These power control schemes enhance data rates in downlink and uplink communication modes. Additionally, D2D communication has broader applications, including power control mechanisms in smart grids and power management optimization in IoT networks. Overall, D2D communication in 6G cellular networks presents opportunities and challenges, with power control schemes essential in alleviating interference and optimizing network performance.

The authors in [21] investigate cooperative D2D communication with relay techniques to reduce interference, presenting two approaches to interference management and cancellation using the Amplify and forward (AF) strategy. It also identifies the optimal relay location and evaluates the impact of varying the number of D2D pairs. In the context of inband D2D communication, the authors [21] introduce two protocols for interference management and cancellation, resulting in reduced BER at lower SNR values and a 20% increase in D2D link throughput. Additionally, a comparison with another method demonstrates a 9 dB reduction in BER, and the study analyzes the outcome of changing the number of D2D pairs on the outage ratio. Overall, the proposed cooperative D2D communication minimizes interference, enhances BER, boosts D2D link throughput, and optimizes relay location, highlighting its potential to improve network performance and reliability.

The authors in [22] focus on the coverage probability analysis of D2D networks, employing a Poisson cluster process (PCP) approach to capture spatial configurations of devices. It considers Nakagami-m fading for more realistic performance analysis and utilizes stochastic geometry for interference and coverage probability analysis. The authors derive a closed-form approximate expression and bound for coverage probability, including analysis for interference-limited D2D networks. Numerical results support the analysis, evaluating the impact of the Nakagami-m fading environment on the coverage probability, the relationship between coverage probability and the average number of active D2D transmitters, and the relationship between coverage probability, interference, link quality, and threshold. The paper's analytical framework provides valuable insights into the coverage probability in D2D networks, offering a comprehensive understanding of the impact of various factors on network performance.

The authors in [23] propose a novel greedy-based channel assignment algorithm for D2D communication. It aims to mitigate interference and improve network capacity and fairness among devices. The proposed method constructs a novel interference graph to describe interferences between communication links and converts the channel assignment problem into a robust graph coloring problem. This approach has been tested with numerical methods, which has dramatically increased the efficiency of the network, and devices get a fair share of resources compared to robust graph colouring and higher values of Jain's fairness index, highlighting its usefulness in real-world applications.

The authors in [24] propose a D2D communication network interference coordination scheme based on an improved Stackelberg-model based on a deep-Q-network (DQN), which suggests a dynamic interference coordination approach, which involves optimizing resource allocation and power control. The model establishes a master-slave game between cellular and multiplexing resource users to improve transmission power and resource allocation schemes. This algorithm, through simulations, achieved higher throughput and improved interference management compared to similar approaches.

The authors in [25] propose the integration of D2D communication with radio frequency energy harvesting (RFEH) and interference management in a cellular network. They introduce a technique based on time division duplexing (TDD) that enables devices to capture energy from the downlink transmissions of the base station. While managing interference between devices in the uplink. This method has adaptive transmission probability (ATP) and fixed transmission probability (FTP) for transmission coordination.

The authors in [26] propose a resource allocation strategy for managing interference. The base station allocates sub-channels to D2D User Equipments to maximizing the network data rate. To understand how interference affects the network, the author calculated the receiver coverage probability by modeling the spatial distribution of user equipment using a Poisson Point Process. They then developed a resource allocation problem to address this interference. They introduced a matching algorithm to maximize network throughput and proposed three new protocols: time division duplexing, fixed transmission probability, and adaptive transmission probability.

The following Table 2 provides an overview of various interference management schemes' objectives and methodologies authors put forth.

The authors in [27] introduce an innovative approach to managing interference in heterogeneous cellular networks (HetCNets) that enables direct device communication. This scheme uses power control to adjust the area affected by interference in real-time, allowing users to choose different communication modes based on this dynamic adjustment. They introduced a method called Power Control with Interference Limited Area (PC-ILA). Their approach achieves exceptional performance in mode selection and effectively suppresses interference in D2D networks while demonstrating superior spectrum resource utilization.

The authors in [28] propose integrating D2D communication within cellular networks to support high data rates. They introduce two novel schemes: Enhanced Dynamic Activation of Heterogeneous Networks (EDAH) and Enhanced Dynamic Activation of Small Cells (EDAS). These schemes aim to suppress interference and facilitate the activation of D2D communication, which improves spectrum allocation. Based on the activation scheme, users are classified into CUs and edge users (EUs). Using stochastic geometry, the authors analyzed the success probabilities for CUs, DUs, and EUs. Additionally, they evaluate area spectral efficiency (ASE) to assess network performance. Their findings indicate that both EDAH and EDAS effectively suppress interference in D2D networks, thereby significantly enhancing the success

Table 2 Summary of works on interference management in D2D communication

Ref.	Objective	Methodology
[20]	Enhances data rates in downlink and uplink communication approaches	PCS1 and PCS2
[21]	Reduced BER at lower SNR values and increase in D2D link throughput	AF strategy
[22]	Improve coverage using Poisson cluster process	Poisson cluster process
[23]	Improve network capacity and enhance fairness among devices	Greedy-based channel assignment algorithm
[24]	A dynamic interference coordination approach to enhance spectrum resource utilization and user communication quality	Stackelberg model based on a deep Q network (DQN)
[25]	TDD-based protocol for D2D communication with RFEH and interference management to improve efficiency in next-generation networks	TDD-based protocol with two transmission coordination schemes, FTP and ATP
[26]	Aims to optimize resource allocation in D2D networks for throughput and fairness by proposing a matching algorithm	A two-sided exchange stable matching where devices and base station iteratively find optimal sub-channel assignments
[27]	Joint mode selection and power control to maximize data rate by managing interference in D2D cellular networks	Jointly selects communication modes and adjusts power control dynamically to optimize D2D performance in cellular networks
[28]	Exclusion-based D2D activation schemes (EDAH and EDAS) to reduce interference and improve reliability in D2D/cellular networks, especially for edge users	EDAH and EDAS schemes (exclusion-based D2D activation) for interference suppression in D2D/cellular networks, analyzed using stochastic geometry
[29]	The distance-based dynamic algorithm to minimize interference and ensure QoS for cellular and D2D links in HetCNets	AIR, which enforces a minimum distance between devices to guarantee QoS in D2D-enabled cellular networks
[30]	Analyzes femtocell, D2D, and macrocell coexistence in HetNets, proposing an FFR scheme for interference management and energy-efficient resource allocation	Dinkelbach iterative algorithm that transforms optimization problems into concave forms for energy-efficient resource allocation
[31]	Analyze coverage probability in a D2D network considering interference, comparing Laplace transform and interference functional approaches for efficiency	Uses stochastic geometry and both interference functional and Laplace transform approaches to analyze coverage probability in a D2D network considering Nakagami-m fading and interference from cellular links

probabilities of CUs and DUs. Specifically, EDAH improves transmission reliability for users, while EDAS increases ASE. Interestingly, EDAH offers a more substantial improvement in the ASE of the cellular tier compared to EDAS.

The authors in [29] propose a dynamic algorithm for interference management in D2D-enabled HetCNets through a combined approach of mode selection and power control. They introduce the concept of power control with an interference-limited area (PC-ILA) to dynamically adjust the ILA using power control, aiming to optimize the utilization of spectrum resources. By segmenting the system into distinct regions based on the signal-to-interference-plus-noise ratio (SINR) thresholds, the proposed scheme effectively addresses interference issues from D2D and femto-cellular users towards the macro base station (MBS). Emphasis is placed on the significance of mode selection based on ILA to prevent wastage of spectrum resources and ensure a minimum quality of service (QoS) for all users. The research demonstrates the benefits of the proposed method in adapting to varying levels of interference and enhancing network performance, particularly in high-SINR scenarios. Simulation results showcase substantial improvements in coverage probability and sum data rate compared to existing approaches, highlighting the efficacy of the PC-ILA strategy. This research advances efficiency and performance in D2D-enabled HetCNets by integrating power control, interference management, and mode selection strategies, providing valuable insights for developing next-generation cellular networks.

The authors in [30] analyze HetNets with femtocells, D2D, and macrocells to achieve high data rates. They propose a fractional frequency reuse (FFR)-based spectrum partitioning method to mitigate cross-tier interference. Distinct optimization techniques are used for resource allocation in various tiers, and these problems are modeled as non-cooperative games to reduce complexity. The study also includes a mathematical analysis of spectral efficiency and proposes optimization problems based on energy efficiency and spectral efficiency for power allocation. The proposed FFR structure enhances system performance with different optimizations, and it is found that energy efficiency-based D2D optimization and spectral efficiency-based femtocell and macrocell optimizations are effective. The fast convergence of iterative algorithms is demonstrated through computer simulations.

The authors in [31] shed lights on various aspects of interference analysis and coverage probability in D2D communication networks. The analysis utilizes stochastic geometry and the Nakagami-m fading model to study the performance of D2D links. The Laplace transform and interference functional approach derive the coverage probability expressions. The research focuses on the impact of fading parameter values on coverage computations and presents numerical results to support the coverage analysis. Additionally, the papers explore resource optimization, dedicated and shared D2D communication, and the use of the Poisson cluster process to analyze coverage and interference in D2D networks. The Nakagami-m fading model is applied to D2D communication links, and a bound on coverage probability simplifies computations at higher fading values.

Interference management in D2D communication for 6G networks has introduced various approaches, such as power control schemes (PCS1 and PCS2), cooperative communication with relay techniques, dynamic interference coordination using game theory and machine learning, and TDD-based protocols for energy harvesting. These methods have improved network capacity, fairness, and resource allocation, while reducing interference and enhancing D2D link throughput. However, challenges remain under explored, including real-time interference management in ultra-dense networks, integrating AI-driven resource management for dynamic environments, and achieving scalable, low-latency communication while ensuring QoS for both D2D and cellular users. Addressing these challenges is essential for maximizing the potential of D2D communication in 6G networks, calling for further advancements in interference mitigation, power control, and resource optimization strategies.

4 Security and Privacy in D2D-Enabled 6G Network

The authors in [32] emphasize the need to manage the increasing traffic generated by humans and machines while ensuring data security. They highlight the crucial role played by D2D and Multicasting technologies in optimizing network resource utilization and catering to emerging scenarios where disseminating identical content to numerous devices is necessary. Their proposed protocol that is Secure and Trust D2D (SeT-D2D) uses trustworthiness gauged from direct interactions and social-awareness metrics to choose relay nodes, enhancing both the performance and security of data transmission within 5G-oriented networks. The research introduces a framework for evaluating the trustworthiness of network nodes and integrates security measures to safeguard data exchanged through D2D communications and the privacy of users involved. The proposed SeT-D2D protocol effectively selects trustworthy D2D transmitters, improves network performance, and ensures efficient data delivery, as demonstrated in a simulation campaign using the Matlab tool. The study also suggests future research directions, including mode selection schemes, adaptive resource allocation based on user distribution, and the utilization of D2D clustering to enhance network performance.

The authors in [33] investigate the impact of channel estimation errors on physical layer security (PLS) in wireless networks, focusing on optimal power allocation to maximize achievable secrecy rate and studying scenarios with and without friendly jamming. It derives a closed-form definition for ergodic secrecy rate (ESR) in Rayleigh fading channels and calculates a high SNR slope and power offset of optimized scenarios. They proposed that power allocation techniques enhance secrecy rate performance compared to others while demonstrating a reduction in secrecy rate performance with increasing channel estimation error. Additionally, the study emphasizes the effect of imperfect channel state information (ICSI) on ESR performance, showcasing that optimizing power allocation can enhance ESR performance in the presence of a jammer, with specific insights into the performance of scenarios with and without jamming.

The authors in [34] explore secure communications in a D2D-underlaid cellular network, where D2D communication operates using both millimeter-wave (mmWave) and microwave frequency bands. It employs covert communication techniques to conceal legitimate D2D transmissions from vigilant adversaries. The study utilizes stochastic geometry modeling to delineate the spatial arrangement of the network and uses a two-stage Stackelberg game framework to simulate the interaction between D2D users and adversaries. The objective of the adversaries is to minimize detection errors, while D2D users seek to maximize their utilities while ensuring covert communication. The paper also explores the advantages of hybrid D2D communication regarding security and throughput, substantiating these advantages through numerical simulations. Furthermore, it incorporates covert communication techniques to bolster the security of hybrid D2D communication within a large-scale D2D-underlaid cellular network against adversaries and confirms the optimality of the resultant Stackelberg equilibrium.

The authors in [35] address the growing demand for wireless traffic management by proposing underlying cellular networks with D2D communication. It suggests leveraging covert communication techniques to secure D2D transmissions against detection by adversaries. A two-stage Stackelberg game is formulated to model the conflict between adversaries seeking to detect D2D communications and the legitimate entity, which aims to maximize its utility while ensuring communication covertness and cellular users QoS. Utilizing stochastic geometry allows for a comprehensive understanding of network dynamics. A bi-level algorithm, coupled with the successive convex approximation (SCA) method, determines optimal strategies for both adversaries and legitimate entities to achieve Stackelberg equilibrium. The study underscores the importance of covert communication in enhancing security and privacy within D2D-underlaid cellular networks. It provides insights into optimizing network performance amidst strategic interactions between adversaries and legitimate entities. Key findings include the delicate balance required when utilizing interference from cellular networks for covert communication, the positive impact of decreased communication distances on both link reliability and communication covertness, and the similar influence of cellular QoS constraints on legitimate utility and D2D communication covertness. Table 3 summarizes security and privacy in the literature to delineate the contributions, highlighting the objectives they addressed and the methodologies used. This table offers a comprehensive overview of the various research works and their approaches within the field.

The authors in [36] propose integrating relay-assisted D2D communication into a cellular network as an underlay, with a selection of consecutive best relay nodes based on different criteria. Innovative analytical formulations are introduced to assess the probability of nonzero secrecy capacity (PNSC) and the secrecy outage probability (SOP) for evaluating secrecy performance. They derive a straightforward approximation of SOP under high SNR conditions to reveal the impact of system parameters. Analytical expressions for SOP are provided in scenarios without D2D interference and with cooperation between cellular and D2D networks, along with an analytical expression for the mutual outage probability (MOP) and an asymptotic analysis of MOP under high SNR conditions. The proposed mathematical framework is validated through Monte Carlo simulations. Contributions include considering two relay selection criteria in a relay-assisted D2D underlaying cellular network, deriving a

Table 3 Works on secrecy and privacy in D2D communication

Ref.	Objective	Methodology
[32]	To improve 5G network performance and security through better relay node selection and addressing D2D communication challenges	Secure and Trust D2D (SeT-D2D) protocol
[33]	Focusing on optimal power allocation to enhance accomplishable secrecy rate with and without friendly jamming	AF strategy
[34]	Improve coverage using the Poisson cluster process	Poisson cluster process
[35]	Analyze the coexistence of femtocells, D2D communication, and macrocells in HetNets, focusing on interference management and energy-efficient resource allocation	A bi-level approach using gradient descent and local approximation to minimize D2D interference on cellular users in a D2D-underlaid network
[36]	Improve network capacity and enhance device fairness	Greedy-based channel assignment algorithm
[37]	To leverage RIS to improve secrecy and outage probability for D2D communication while maximizing cellular network capacity	Utilizes SOP formulation and analysis to optimize D2D communication with RIS in cellular networks
[38]	To improve cellular network security with D2D communication by combining ESN and LSTM for antenna selection and D2D establishment	LSTM and ESN for secure D2D communication in cellular networks
[39]	Proposes a D2D user access scheme to improve cellular user privacy by leveraging interference for jamming against eavesdroppers	A D2D user access scheme with an iterative algorithm to optimize a threshold, maximizing cellular user secrecy throughput against eavesdropping
[40]	To improve the PLS and data transmission in cellular networks through full-duplex jamming relay-aided D2D communications	A cooperative scheme involving FD transmission, dual antenna selection, and practical combining techniques at the D2D relay node

novel expression for SOP over-generalized η–μ fading channels, and analyzing cooperative benefits between D2D and cellular networks. Additionally, the study explores the effects of increasing the number of base station antennas on cooperative benefits and the advantageous impacts of a densely populated D2D network on both D2D transmission and the cellular network.

The authors in [37] focus on investigating the application of RIS in an inband underlay D2D communication system where the direct link between D2D users is unavailable. The RIS is employed to dynamically adjust its reflecting elements, thereby enhancing the transmission of D2D communication data while concurrently bolstering the secrecy performance of the cellular network. Analytical formulas for various performance metrics, including SOP, PNSC, and D2D outage probability, are derived for cellular networks. The critical contributions of the study lie in leveraging RIS to fortify the resilience and dependability of D2D communication, augmenting the PLS of the cellular network, and acting as a cooperative jammer to ensure heightened security for the cellular network. Furthermore, the study furnishes closed-form expressions for the probability of non-zero secrecy capacity and SOP for the cellular network, along with asymptotic analysis, to elucidate the effect of critical parameters on system performance. The validity of analyses is substantiated through comprehensive Monte-Carlo simulations, affirming the efficacy of the proposed framework.

The authors in [38] propose a collaborative scheme for enhancing the physical layer security of the D2D-enabled cellular network through deep learning-based transmit antenna selection and optimal D2D pair establishment. The echo state network (ESN) is utilized for transmit antenna selection, while the long short-term memory (LSTM) is employed for D2D pair establishment. The collaborative scheme effectively improves the security capacity of the cellular network with D2D, prolongs the life of the base station, and reduces energy consumption. The main contributions include the development of an ESN-based antenna selection framework that considers physical layer security and maximizes jamming to D2D eavesdroppers. An LSTM-based D2D pair establishment framework is proposed based on prediction results to improve system security. The collaborative scheme demonstrates a higher positive secrecy capacity and a lower secret outage probability than individual LSTM-based and ESN-based schemes while requiring less energy. The analysis results confirm the practical improvement of the cellular network's security capacity with D2D and the increased life of the temporary base station due to the collaborative scheme.

The authors in [39] discuss various aspects of physical layer security for D2D communications in cellular networks. It includes a proposed access selection scheme to protect cellular users from eavesdropping, secrecy throughput to quantify security performance, and an optimization method to determine the optimal threshold for security enhancement. The research focuses on PLS for D2D communications, considering factors such as secrecy throughput, optimal threshold, and access selection scheme. Stochastic geometry and optimization methods are utilized to evaluate security performance. The studies also involve deriving closed-form expressions for secrecy throughput, proof of an optimal threshold, and the design of iterative algorithms.

The authors in [40] enhance PLS and data transmission within cellular networks, mainly focusing on full-duplex (FD) transmission and dual antenna selection at D2D relays. They propose a scheme involving friendly jamming relays to aid secrecy performance and evaluate the secrecy performance of the cellular network and D2D communications, analyzing outage probability and reliability. Through analytical expressions and simulation, they verify the efficacy of the proposed methods, emphasizing improvements in secrecy and reliability. Additionally, it highlights the benefits of dual antenna selection at relays and increasing jamming antennas to enhance transmission performance and secrecy within the network.

Security and privacy in D2D communication are key to improving network performance and PLS. Techniques like trust-based protocols, optimal power allocation, covert communication, and resource optimization using game theory and deep learning help enhance security. Technologies such as RIS and full-duplex transmission also improve secrecy and reduce eavesdropping risks. However, challenges remain, such as adapting security measures in real-time for dense networks, balancing security with energy efficiency, and developing advanced PLS techniques for future threats. More research is needed to address these issues and optimize security, performance, and scalability in D2D communication for 6G networks.

5 Conclusion

The evolution of 6G networks has brought significant advancements in D2D communication, presenting challenges in resource management, interference, security, and privacy. Effective resource allocation and advanced interference management strategies are crucial for optimizing D2D communication in 6G networks, especially in densely populated areas. Equally important is the progress of privacy-preserving protocols and robust security mechanisms to safeguard sensitive data and ensure user privacy. Moving forward, industry, researchers, policymakers, and stakeholder's collaborative efforts are imperative to address these challenges and unlock the full potential of D2D communication within 6G networks, ushering in a new era of connectivity and efficiency.

References

1. Jiadai Wang, Jiajia Liu, Jingyi Li, and Nei Kato. Artificial intelligence-assisted network slicing: Network assurance and service provisioning in 6G. *IEEE Vehicular Technology Magazine*, 18(1):49–58, 2023.
2. CISCO. Visual network index report, Annual Internet Report— cisco.com, 2024. [Accessed 19-01-2024].
3. Bomin Mao, Jiajia Liu, Yingying Wu, and Nei Kato. Security and privacy on 6G network edge: A survey. *IEEE communications surveys & tutorials*, 2023.
4. Ajay Bhardwaj and Samar Agnihotri. Multiple D2D multicasts in underlay cellular networks. *arXiv preprint* arXiv:1908.08866, 2019.
5. Safwan Alwan, Ilhem Fajjari, and Nadjib Aitsaadi. A scalable joint routing and OFDMA resource allocation in LTE-D2D networks. In *Proc. WCNC*, pages 1–8. IEEE, 2019.
6. Liang Yang, Jinxia Yang, Wenwu Xie, Mazen O Hasna, Theodoros Tsiftsis, and Marco Di Renzo. Secrecy performance analysis of RIS-aided wireless communication systems. *IEEE Transactions on Vehicular Technology*, 69(10):12296–12300, 2020.
7. Lina Yang, Qiang Wang, Wei Wei, and Xin Hu. Resource allocation and power control for D2D underlay communication. In *Proc. WPMC*, pages 513–517. IEEE, 2016.
8. Hongyuan Yu, Ying Peng, and Jianjun Wu. Interference mitigation in d2d underlay networks. *IEEE Communications Letters*, 20(6):1175–1178, 2016.
9. Klaus Doppler, Mika Rinne, Carl Wijting, Cássio B Ribeiro, and Klaus Hugl. Device-to-device communication as an underlay to LTE-advanced networks. *IEEE communications magazine*, 47(12):42–49, 2009.

10. Dongfeng Wu, Xiaodong Liu, and Jian Zhang. Outband D2D communication: Mode selection and spectrum sharing. *IEEE Transactions on Vehicular Technology*, 66(9):8573–8584, 2017.
11. Gang Feng, Xizhong Qin, Zhenhong Jia, and Shaohua Li. Energy efficiency resource allocation for D2D communication network based on relay selection. *Wireless networks*, 27:3689–3699, 2021.
12. Zitian Zhang, Yue Wu, Xiaoli Chu, and Jie Zhang. Energy-efficient transmission rate selection and power control for relay-assisted device-to-device communications underlaying cellular networks. *IEEE Wireless Comm.Letters*, 9(8):1133–1136, 2020.
13. Shanshan Yu, Wali Ullah Khan, Xiaoqing Zhang, and Ju Liu. Optimal power allocation for NOMA-enabled D2D communication with imperfect SIC decoding. *Physical Communication*, 46:101296, 2021.
14. Jing Cao, Xin Song, Zhigang Xie, Suyuan Li, and Fangyuan Si. Social-aware relay selection and energy-efficient resource allocation for relay-aided D2D communication. *Physical Communication*, 52:101665, 2022.
15. Pimmy Gandotra and Rakesh Kumar Jha. Energy-efficient device-to-device communication using adaptive resource-block allocation. *International Journal of Communication Systems*, 32(8):e3922, 2019.
16. Xijian Zhong, Yan Guo, Ning Li, and Yancheng Chen. Joint optimization of relay deployment, channel allocation, and relay assignment for UAVs-aided D2D networks. *IEEE/ACM Transactions on Networking*, 28(2):804–817, 2020.
17. Runzhou Li, Peilin Hong, Kaiping Xue, Ming Zhang, and Te Yang. Energy-efficient resource allocation for high-rate underlay D2D communications with statistical csi: A one-to-many strategy. *IEEE Transactions on Vehicular Technology*, 69(4):4006–4018, 2020.
18. Taehyun Yoon, Tien Hoa Nguyen, Xuan Tung Nguyen, Daeseung Yoo, Byungtae Jang, et al. Resource allocation for NOMA-based D2D systems coexisting with cellular networks. *IEEE Access*, 6:66293–66304, 2018.
19. Yijin Pan, Cunhua Pan, Zhaohui Yang, and Ming Chen. Resource allocation for D2D communications underlaying a noma-based cellular network. *IEEE Wireless Communications Letters*, 7(1):130–133, 2017.
20. R Zeeshan Ahamad, A Rehman Javed, Shakir Mehmood, M Zubair Khan, Abdulfattah Noorwali, and Muhammad Rizwan. Interference mitigation in D2D communication underlying cellular networks: Towards green energy. *CMC-COMPUTERS MATERIALS & CONTINUA*, 68(1):45–58, 2021.
21. Rna Ghallab and Mona Shokair. Proposed protocols for interference managements and interference cancellation with AAF relay in D2D communication. In *Proc. NRSC*, pages 113–120. IEEE, 2018.
22. Sandeep Joshi and Ranjan K Mallik. Coverage and interference in D2D networks with poisson cluster process. *IEEE Communications Letters*, 22(5):1098–1101, 2018.
23. Liqun Zhao, Hongpeng Wang, and Xiaoxiong Zhong. Interference graph based channel assignment algorithm for D2D cellular networks. *IEEE Access*, 6:3270–3279, 2018.
24. Xinzhou Li, Guifen Chen, Guowei Wu, Zhiyao Sun, and Guangjiao Chen. D2D communication network interference coordination scheme based on improved stackelberg. *Sustainability*, 15(2):961, 2023.
25. Nasrin Razmi, Mehdi Mahdavi, Mohammadali Mohammadi, and Petar Popovski. Analysis of D2D communication with RF energy harvesting and interference management. *arXiv preprint* arXiv:2002.01686, 2020.
26. Shiva Shamaei, Siavash Bayat, and Ali Mohammad Afshin Hemmatyar. Interference-aware resource allocation algorithm for D2D-enabled cellular networks using matching theory. *IEEE Transactions on Network and Service Management*, 2023.
27. Xiaolan Liu, Hailin Xiao, and Anthony Theodore Chronopoulos. Joint mode selection and power control for interference management in D2D-enabled heterogeneous cellular networks. *IEEE Transactions on Vehicular Technology*, 69(9):9707–9719, 2020.
28. Libo Chen, Na Deng, and Haichao Wei. Performance analysis of D2D and cellular coexisting networks with interference management. *IEEE Access*, 8:82747–82759, 2020.

29. Md Kamruzzaman, Nurul I Sarkar, and Jairo Gutierrez. A dynamic algorithm for interference management in D2D-enabled heterogeneous cellular networks: Modeling and analysis. *Sensors*, 22(3):1063, 2022.
30. Azadeh Khazali, Sima Sobhi-Givi, Hashem Kalbkhani, and Mahrokh G Shayesteh. Energy-spectral efficient resource allocation and power control in heterogeneous networks with D2D communication. *Wireless Networks*, 26(1):253–267, 2020.
31. Sandeep Joshi and Ranjan K Mallik. Coverage probability analysis in a device-to-device network: Interference functional and laplace transform based approach. *IEEE Communications Letters*, 23(3):466–469, 2019.
32. Chiara Suraci, Sara Pizzi, David Garompolo, Giuseppe Araniti, Antonella Molinaro, and Antonio Iera. Trusted and secured D2D-aided communications in 5G networks. *Ad Hoc Networks*, 114:102403, 2021.
33. Marzieh Izanlou, Abbas Mohammadi, and Mohamad Dosaranian-Moghadam. Impact of imperfect channel state information on the physical layer security in D2D wireless networks using untrusted relays. *Wireless Personal Communications*, 116:341–368, 2021.
34. Shaohan Feng, Xiao Lu, Dusit Niyato, Yuan Wu, and Wenbo Wang. System-level security solution for heterogeneous D2D-underlaid cellular network. In *Proc. WCSP*, pages 797–802. IEEE, 2023.
35. Shaohan Feng, Xiao Lu, Kun Zhu, Dusit Niyato, and Ping Wang. Covert D2D communication underlaying cellular network: A system-level security perspective. *IEEE Transactions on Wireless Communications*, 2024.
36. Jules M Moualeu and Telex MN Ngatched. Physical-layer security enhancement via relay-aided D2D communications underlaying cellular networks. *IEEE Open Journal of the Communications Society*, 1:413–427, 2020.
37. Majid H Khoshafa, Telex MN Ngatched, and Mohamed Hossam Ahmed. Reconfigurable intelligent surfaces-aided physical layer security enhancement in D2D underlay communications. *IEEE Communications Letters*, 25(5):1443–1447, 2020.
38. Lixin Li, Youbing Hu, Huisheng Zhang, Wei Liang, and Ang Gao. Deep learning based physical layer security of D2D underlay cellular network. *China Communications*, 17(2):93–106, 2020.
39. Lei Wang, Jiaming Liu, Mingkai Chen, Guan Gui, and Hikmet Sari. Optimization-based access assignment scheme for physical-layer security in D2D communications underlaying a cellular network. *IEEE Transactions on Vehicular Technology*, 67(7):5766–5777, 2018.
40. Majid H Khoshafa, Telex MN Ngatched, Mohamed H Ahmed, and Ahmed Ibrahim. Improving physical layer security of cellular networks using full-duplex jamming relay-aided D2D communications. *IEEE Access*, 8:53575–53586, 2020.

Observability and Provenance for Distributed Microservices over Edge-Enabled 6G Networks

Subhankar Chakrabarti, Utkalika Satapathy, and Sandip Chakraborty

1 Introduction

The convergence of distributed microservices, edge computing, and 6G networks promises to transform the landscape of modern communication systems in the form of *Communication Platform as a Service* (CPaaS) [19]. As a software architectural style, microservices provide flexibility and scalability by breaking down applications into smaller, self-contained services. On the other hand, edge computing brings computational resources closer to the end-user, reducing latency, and improving real-time data processing. The future 6G networks promise ultra-high-speed connectivity and low-latency communication, essential for applications like autonomous systems, the Internet of Things (IoT), and smart cities. However, these advances introduce unique challenges for ensuring observability and provenance in distributed systems [29]. Observability refers to the ability to understand and monitor the behavior of microservices, while provenance focuses on tracing the origins and transformations of data as it flows through distributed systems. In an edge-enabled 6G environment, these challenges are amplified due to the decentralized nature of edge nodes, dynamic service interactions, and high data volume [21].

5G deployments have reached critical markets and are fast evolving towards 6G, promising higher performance and near sub-millisecond latency. Higher automation in use cases fueled by artificial intelligence techniques is expected to be the core of future applications and services. The service providers have started re-focusing on use cases that can leverage the new and improved capabilities for better *average*

S. Chakrabarti (✉) · U. Satapathy · S. Chakraborty
Indian Institute of Technology Kharagpur, Kharagpur, India
e-mail: subhankarchakrabarti.t24@kgpian.iitkgp.ac.in

U. Satapathy
e-mail: utkalika.satapathy01@kgpian.iitkgp.ac.in

S. Chakraborty
e-mail: sandipc@cse.iitkgp.ac.in

T. Ojha et al. (eds.), *Edge-Enabled 6G Networking*,
https://doi.org/10.1007/978-3-032-19042-0_9

revenue per unit (ARPU) for both consumers and enterprises. Subsequently, the information industry has been evolving from physical infrastructure-centric, predefined, and preconfigured services to increasingly virtual infrastructure-centric, on-demand, and dynamically configured services, which poses new challenges for provenance and observability for large-scale systems. In addition, centralized data center (DC)-anchored cloud services are rapidly embracing hybrid cloud and distributed edge services at the usage proximities targeting near real-time latency. The future vision is shaped by the compelling need for agility, virtualization, customization, and programmability in infrastructure and networking (network slicing, etc.) and approaching optimum scalability. Artificial intelligence (AI), decentralization, adaptive and cognitive security, multi-access edge computing, and serverless paradigm with cluster/container orchestration (e.g., Kubernetes, Docker Swarm, Redhat Openshift) are some of the essential ingredients presently nurtured to build the road to these destinations and beyond, which brings up new challenges for developing observability and provenance frameworks for edge-enabled 6G networks.

Notably, 6G builds on the foundation of 5G: enhanced mobile broadband (eMBB), massive machine-type communications (mMTC), and ultra-reliable low-latency communications (URLLC) by introducing new paradigms such as integrated sensing and communication (ISAC), terahertz (THz) bands, and ubiquitous AI integration. 6G aims to achieve global coverage, enhanced spectral efficiency, and intelligent network management, necessitating a shift from centralized cloud architectures to distributed edge systems. Edge computing in 6G decentralizes processing, reduces end-to-end latency and increases spectral efficiency while supporting applications like holographic communications and autonomous networked systems [34]. Considering such architectural factors and the requirements for dynamic observability and provenance over decentralized infrastructure, it will be essential to focus on new research and developments on such a paradigm.

However, distributed edge computing introduces complexity. Networks must manage heterogeneous devices, dynamic workloads, and densified topologies. This evolution demands robust mechanisms to monitor and optimize real-time performance, making runtime observability indispensable. Unlike 5G, where observability was often reactive, 6G requires proactive and predictive approaches to handle scale and diversity. The transition to Beyond 5G (B5G) and 6G networks marks a significant evolution in mobile communications, driven by the need for ultra-low latency, high reliability, and massive connectivity to support emerging applications like autonomous vehicles, augmented reality (AR), and massive Internet of Things (IoTs) deployments. An on-demand computing (ODC) platform for distributed microservices in edge-enabled networks is pivotal to meeting these stringent requirements by dynamically provisioning computing resources at the network edge. Modern applications demand computational capabilities closer to the data source to minimize latency and enhance efficiency. Traditional centralized cloud paradigms fall short due to their distance from end-users, introducing delays beyond the minimum threshold for latency-sensitive use cases in B5G and 6G networks. Edge computing bridges this gap by placing resources at the network periphery, but static resource allocation struggles with the dynamic workloads and mobility inherent in advanced networks.

An ODC platform addresses this by enabling on-demand allocation of computational resources to support distributed microservices, i.e., modular, independently deployable services that form a complete application. Leveraging intent-based orchestration, serverless computing, and AI-driven resource allocation, the platform addresses ultra-low latency (<1 ms), scalability, and energy efficiency.

In edge-enabled B5G and 6G networks, such a platform must seamlessly integrate with 3GPP-defined architectures, leveraging advancements like Multi-Access Edge Computing (MEC) and anticipating a decentralized, AI-driven paradigm of 6G. Some potential components of the ODC platform are: (1) *AI-driven dynamic resource allocation*: A method using reinforcement learning to predictively allocate edge resources based on UE mobility and traffic patterns, (2) *Seamless microservice scheduling*: A framework for microservice scheduling across edge nodes without service disruption, (3) *Secure computation offloading*: A security protocol for offloading tasks to edge nodes with AI-based anomaly detection, and (4) *In-Network compute orchestration*: A protocol for orchestrating computations within the network using programmable data planes. The 3GPP has standardized edge computing in 5G (e.g., TR 23.758 [6]) and continues to evolve its framework for B5G and 6G. The ODC platform builds on this foundation, adapting to distributed control and intelligent resource management. Considering such factors, in this book chapter, we discuss the requirements for observability and provenance for edge-enabled 6G ecosystem, propose a potential framework to support the same, and deliberate on the research gaps and possible areas for further investigation.

The remainder of this book chapter is organized as follows. Section 2 presents the related works as a brief literature review and explains how this work differs from previous works. Section 3 presents the definition of observability from the scope of 3GPP. Section 4 presents the importance of runtime observability for distributed microservices over an edge-enabled 6G network. Section 5 presents a generic observability framework for 3GPP-complied edge networks. Section 6 presents dynamic provenance as a use case of observability. Section 7 presents the future research challenges following the concluding remarks in Sect. 8.

List of Abbreviations and Definition

ML-Machine Learning, AI-Artificial Intelligence, EC-Edge Computing, CN-Core Network, 5G-Fifth-generation technology for wireless communications, 6G-Sixth-generation technology for wireless communications, B5G-Beyond 5G, NC-Network Core, 5GC-5G network Core, RAN-Radio Access Network, KPIs-Key Performance Indicators, 3GPP-Third Generation Partnership Project, SBI-Service-based Interfaces, EES-Edge Enabler Server, AF -Application Function, EAS -Edge Application Server, ECS -Edge Configuration Server, UPF-User Plane Function, AMF-Access and Mobility Management Function, SMF-Session Management Function, RAN-Radio Access Network, NFV-Network Function Virtualization, 3D -Three-dimensional, DevOps-Development Operations, CDN-Content Delivery Network.

2 Related Work

In this section, we present a review of the existing research on observability and provenance tracking in distributed microservice architecture and also the work done around 5G and 6G networks.

Researchers have used data provenance techniques to investigate attacks in large-scale systems. [3, 10, 16, 54] have explored audit logs that capture the detailed history of how the system has been used. The provenance tracking and observability of monolithic architecture have been extensively studied in previous work. The components of observability in distributed systems are metrics[4, 9, 46], logs[35], and traces[8, 15, 28, 43]. However, these works face challenges such as scaling the data collection and adding meaningful information or context to the collected data, which can be used further for analysis and performing some actionable events.

3 Defining Observability from the Scope of 3GPP

In the context of 5G and beyond (i.e., upcoming 6G technology), as standardized by the 3GPP, the network architecture has evolved significantly, shifting toward more modular, flexible, and scalable systems with the adoption of microservices and virtualization of network functions. Combining cloud services through microservice architecture with the telecommunication infrastructure creates a new paradigm of edge computing-based integrated networks, where both are interdependent. The concept of microservices has emerged as the core architectural paradigm, especially in dynamic deployments. Dynamic microservices deployment, where services are instantiated, scaled, or terminated on demand, introduces unparalleled flexibility and complexity in mobile networks. These microservices are components within the network that offer specific functionalities, often running in containers, and can be dynamically orchestrated and scaled. As these architectures gain prominence, observability becomes an essential aspect of understanding system states from the operational parameters (e.g., metrics, logs, traces), maintaining system health, ensuring network reliability, and managing performance. So, in a nutshell, observability refers to the ability to monitor, measure, and analyze various operational parameters across the network, including the Radio Access Network (RAN), Core Network (CN), and the host platform where the microservices are deployed. In dynamic microservices environments, observability becomes more complex for the following reasons. First, microservices are lightweight, independent components that dynamically scale. Second, they operate in containers that may move between hosts and nodes, adding a layer of complexity in terms of network visibility. Third, traditional monitoring tools or methods may be insufficient to understand the health or status of a system where individual services are constantly deployed, decommissioned, or updated. From a 3GPP perspective, observability must address the unique challenges of multi-domain monitoring (spanning RAN, Core, Edge), real-time telemetry (for latency-sensitive services (e.g., URLLC)), telecom-grade reliability, standardized interfaces (leveraging 3GPP-defined APIs (e.g., Nnrf, Nsmf)), real-time performance analysis, security (compliance with 3GPP TS 33.501 (security assurance) [23]), and multi-vendor interoperability while aligning with dynamic nature of microservices.

3.1 Observability for Network Management from 3GPP Perspective: Transition from Monolithic to Microservice Architecture

In traditional 3GPP frameworks, observability is implicitly embedded in network management practices (e.g., TS 32.101, TS 28.532) [33]. It focuses on collecting Key Performance Indicators (KPIs) such as latency, handover success, and throughput through Operations, Administration, and Maintenance (OAM) interfaces. Techniques like Minimization of Drive Tests (MDT, TS 37.320) provide visibility into radio conditions, while fault management systems detect and resolve issues [17]. However, these mechanisms were designed for monolithic or semi-distributed architectures, not the containerized microservice architecture of modern 5G Core (5GC).

The 5GC, introduced in Release 15 (TS 23.501) [38] adopts a Service-Based Architecture (SBA) where Network Functions (NFs) like the Access and Mobility Management Function (AMF) or Session Management Function (SMF) are deployed as microservices. These NFs communicate through Service-Based Interfaces (SBIs) using Hypertext Transfer Protocol/2 (HTTP/2) and Representational State Transfer (REST) compliant application programming interfaces (REST APIs), enabling dynamic scaling and orchestration, often in Kubernetes clusters. Traditional observability tools fall short here, lacking the granularity and adaptability required for rapidly changing deployments [44]. Research insights from recent literature highlight the growing complexity of microservices deployment in edge-enabled networks along with the core network function management [53]. In that aspect, designing an efficient and comprehensive observability framework will be pivotal in managing inter-service dependencies to reduce the failure rate, and meeting service-level agreements (SLAs) and service-level objectives (SLOs) [50]. The 3GPP's work on Management and Orchestration (MANO, TS 28.533) integrates with ETSI NFV to orchestrate microservices, but observability lags. The introduction of the Network Data Analytics Function (NWDAF) in Release 16 offers a breakthrough, providing real-time analytics for traffic patterns and anomalies–akin to an observability hub for microservices [12]. So, there is a need to redefine the observability comprehensively for distributed microservices over the next-generation edge-enabled network from a 3GPP perspective.

Table 1 presents the contrast between the static and network-centric focus of traditional observability and the dynamic and service-centric needs of microservices, highlighting the shift in scope.

Table 1 Comparison of traditional network-oriented observability framework versus microservices deployment oriented observability framework in 3GPP

Feature	Traditional 3GPP observability focusing on network functioning	Microservices-based observability
Data sources	Key performance indicators (KPIs)	Metrics/Events/Logs/Traces
Granularity	Node-level	Service-level
Scalability	Static	Dynamic
Latency focus	Network-wide	Per-service

3.2 *Redefining Observability for Distributed Microservices over Edge-Enabled Network: 3GPP Perspective*

3GPP has played an essential role in defining the technical specifications for the Mobile-Edge-Cloud continuum, including the next-generation wireless network (i.e., 5G architecture and beyond), where microservices are increasingly being integrated. 3GPP's 5G core network adopts a Service-Based Architecture (SBA), where Network Functions (NFs) like AMF (Access and Mobility Management Function) and SMF (Session Management Function) are deployed as microservices. Observability in this context must support dynamic scaling and orchestration (e.g., Kubernetes) and integrate with 3GPP Management and Orchestration (MANO) frameworks (NFV-MANO). The complete communication platform as a service (CPaaS), which is central to the edge-enabled network, has two inter-connected segments: (1) the core of the network where network functions are deployed in the form of microservices, (2) services in the host edge-server are deployed in the form of distributed microservices. From a 3GPP perspective, observability for dynamic microservices deployment can be defined as follows.

Comprehensive observability framework. *The multi-layered capability to monitor, infer, and predict the operational state, performance, and interdependencies of microservices-based Network Functions in real-time, using standardized telemetry, distributed and slice-aware tracing, and AI-driven intelligent analytics, while ensuring telecom-grade QoS and fault resilience in a multi-domain, dynamically orchestrated environment.*

This definition merges telecom-specific requirements such as standardization, reliability, and low latency with the requirement for agility and scalability from microservices deployment perspective. It not only aligns with current standards but also anticipates future needs, positioning observability as a cornerstone of next-generation networks. Observability in 3GPP's dynamic microservices deployment and orchestration context is a fusion of standardized telecom practices and modern software paradigms. By leveraging SBI tracing, slice-aware metrics, and NWDAF analytics, 3GPP can meet the demands of beyond 5G (B5G) and 6G (Table 2).

Table 2 3GPP standardization related to edge-enabled network, technical reports, and corresponding summary

Technical reports	Objectives	Summary
3GPP TS 28.533 (Release 17, 2022) [5]	Management and orchestration; Architecture framework	Defines performance management requirements for cloud-native network functions (NFs)
3GPP TR 28.805 (Release 18, 2023) [30]	Study on enhancement of management & Orchestration for network automation	Discusses AI/ML-driven observability for dynamic microservices in 5G core networks
3GPP TR 23.700-91 (Release 18, 2023) [41]	Study on enablers for network automation for 5G	Observability as a key enabler for autonomous 5G networks
3GPP TS 23.548 (Release 19, 2024) [48]	Enhancements for edge computing in 5G systems	Highlights observability needs for edge-deployed microservices

The broader definition of dynamic observability in the context of 3GPP edge-enabled networked systems includes following key building components.

1. **Performance monitoring and metrics**. 3GPP focuses on key performance indicators (KPIs) such as latency, throughput, availability of resources, and quality of service (QoS). These are essential for assessing the health of microservices running in dynamic environments.
2. **Configuration and network slice management**. In a microservices-based 5G architecture, the concept of network slicing which stands for virtualized, isolated network segments tailored to specific use cases, is crucial. Observability framework needs to track the state of slices and ensures the components of a slice (often composed of several microservices) are operating optimally.
3. **Dynamic instrumentation and unified data model**. Automatically instruments microservices for observability and uses a standardized data model for telemetry, logs, and traces.
4. **Standardized telemetry**. Leveraging 3GPP's Network Resource Model (NRM, TS 28.541) [39] and performance measurements (TS 28.552) [52] to collect metrics like resource utilization and SBI latency.
5. **Distributed Tracing**: Adapting tracing concepts to track requests across NF microservices, akin to software observability but enriched with radio-layer context.
6. **Intelligent analytics**. Incorporating AI/ML (TR 28.809) to predict failures, anomaly detection, and root cause analysis. Based on that, it optimizes microservices deployments dynamically.
7. **Fault management and recovery mechanism**. Fault detection, isolation, and recovery mechanisms are the core components of 3GPP's observability approach. For dynamic deployments, microservices require real-time monitoring to detect failures, service unavailability, or misconfigurations.

Table 3 Architectural components of observability framework in terms of functional properties and corresponding 3GPP alignments

Layer	Functional properties	3GPP alignment
Data collection	Collects metrics, logs, and traces from microservices (including network core functions)	3GPP TS 28.532 (performance- management) [1, 20, 47]
Data aggregation and processing	Correlates data across domains (RAN, core, edge)	3GPP TS 28.545 (fault -supervision) [7, 49]
Analytics and AI/ML	Applies ML models for anomaly detection and root cause analysis	3GPP TR 28.805 (AI-driven network automation) [37]
Visualization	Provides dashboards and graphical interfaces for operators via 3GPP-compliant interfaces	3GPP TS 28.533 (reporting services) [13]

8. **Security monitoring**. With the increasing attack surface in microservices environments, 3GPP observability frameworks must also include tools for detecting security threats in real-time, including distributed denial-of-service (DDoS) attacks, unauthorized access attempts, and data breaches.
9. **Telecom-Grade assurance**. Ensuring observability supports ultra-reliable low-latency communication (URLLC) and network slicing.

As 6G takes shape from the 3GPP standardization perspective, observability will evolve further. Research from 3GPP TR 22.874 [27] on AI-native networks suggests embedding observability into the protocol stack, with self-observing NFs reporting their state autonomously. This could significantly reduce latency in detecting failures.

4 Importance of Runtime Observability for Distributed Edge-Enabled 6G

Runtime observability encompasses three pillars: monitoring (collecting metrics), logging (recording events), and tracing (tracking request flows across distributed microservices which are deployed in the host edge nodes). In 6G, it provides visibility into the network's operational state, enabling fault detection, performance optimization, and adaptive resource allocation.

The emergence of microservices architectures, together with the Development and Operations (DevOps) design philosophy, has made considerable changes to the way user applications are developed, deployed, and managed. Compared to a typical monolithic application, where the entire application is built as a single unified system, a microservices architecture decomposes the application into several independent executable pieces that coherently interoperate to provide specific application functionalities. Techniques like lightweight RESTful Application Programming Interfaces (APIs) are extensively adopted to facilitate runtime communication among microservices. As IT infrastructures continue to grow and become more distributed, enticed by a prospect of faster innovation, cost reduction, and boost agility, many businesses are migrating their traditional monolithic applications to microservices.

For smooth execution, the requirement to monitor these infrastructures at different levels of the software stack appears to be seamlessly crucial with the introduction of distributed environments and the transition to microservices. Monitoring is by no means a new problem or new requirement. Traditional monitoring tools, however, do fall short of meeting the challenges posed by operation monitoring demands of containerized microservices deployed over distributed IT infrastructures. The emergence of the Industrial Internet of Things (IIoT), along with edge and cloud, where mission-critical IIoT applications are hosted, introduces significant complexity for operators. In these setups, multi-site resource islands are connected via heterogeneous networks requiring several operation monitoring tools to manage aspects such as users, application data, tenants, nodes, or networks. Naive monitoring of bare-metal servers, virtual machine (VM) instances, or application container metrics without understanding the topological relationships between these various entities is incomplete for diverse operations (Ops) teams when troubleshooting performance issues.

Even though monitoring has served as a core function of IT for the last few decades, it started to prove itself limited due to various factors, including agile development methodologies, cloud-native deployments, and new DevOps practices. These factors have altered how the entire IT ecosystem (e.g., infrastructures, systems, and applications) should be monitored to respond promptly to incidents. For example, most edge infrastructures are orchestrated through Kubernetes, which is intended to abstract a lot of the underlying complexity. However, the platform itself consists of multiple independent projects as well as interconnected components. As such, simply choosing and applying traditional monitoring tools does not work out of the box for several reasons, e.g., several influencing components are hosted outside the containerized application, the underlying environment is more dynamic, and applications have more rapid deployment cycles. To this end, observability is an emerging set of practices combined with tools that go beyond monitoring to provide insight into the internal state of a system by analyzing its external outputs. The core of observability is to quickly learn what is happening within the IT infrastructure to avoid extended outages and during an outage, quickly enable so-called root cause analysis of the problem. For example, the Mean Time to Resolution (MTTR) metric measures outages, and the objective of observability is to drive the MTTR value as close to zero as possible.

5 A Generic Observability Framework for 3GPP-Complied Edge Networks

As 5G and beyond (i.e., 6G) networks increasingly adopt microservices for their deployment at the network edge, efficient management and observability of these microservices become critical. Microservices enable flexibility, scalability, and resilience, but they also create challenges in terms of monitoring, troubleshooting, and ensuring optimal performance. With edge computing environments being deployed in compliance with 3GPP standards, effective observability of microservices becomes a necessity to ensure that edge network services meet Quality of Service (QoS) requirements, operate securely, and remain reliable. This section introduces a generic observability framework for microservices deployed within 3GPP-compliant edge networks, highlighting the fundamental role of observability in enhancing network reliability, security, and performance. A *generic observability framework* for microservices deployed in 3GPP-compliant edge networks aims to provide comprehensive monitoring, tracing, and analysis capabilities to ensure the successful operation of edge applications. The comparative analysis of existing observability frameworks and tools are provided in Table 4.

Table 4 Comparative analysis of existing observability frameworks and tools which may be applicable to edge-enabled networks. However, when it comes to 3GPP-compliant edge networks, not all solutions are suitable

Framework	Supported network/service	Features	Strengths	Limitations
Prometheus [26]	General networking	Metrics collection, alerting	Open-source, real-time data	Lack of built-in tracing, Limited integration with 3GPP
Kubernetes [22]	Edge computing	Orchestration, scalability	Highly flexible, widely used	Complex for edge use cases
OpenStack [11]	Cloud & Edge computing	Virtualization, orchestration	Mature, scalable	Not optimized for low-latency
Grafana [42]	General networking	Data visualization, monitoring	Visualization	Requires integration with Prometheus for full observability
OpenTelemetry [36]	General networking	Distributed tracing, metrics	Open-source, flexible	Complex setup for edge nodes

5.1 A Generic Observability Framework: Key Architectural Components

The generic observability framework consists of several key architectural components (refer Table 3) that work in synergy to provide a holistic view of the operational health and performance of the networked systems. In Fig. 1, the workflow for the 3GPP-aligned observability pipeline for an end-to-end observability framework is presented in the form of a layered architecture. We explain these key components in detail as follows.

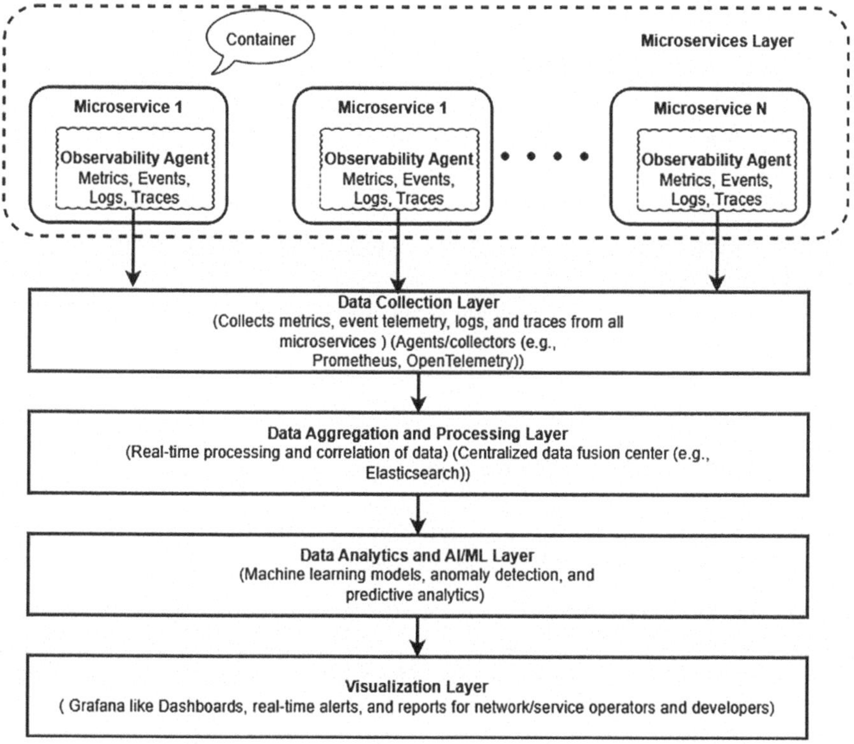

Fig. 1 Schematic diagram of the 3GPP-aligned data pipeline for observability framework consists of various inter-connected layers considering N numbers of containerized microservices deployed in the host edge server

5.1.1 Data Collection Layer

The first component of the observability framework is the data collection layer, which is responsible for gathering key metrics, logs, and traces from the microservices deployed at the edge. This layer must be able to capture the following:

1. **Metrics**. Performance indicators like CPU utilization, memory consumption, throughput, and latency. These metrics provide insights into the operational health of the microservices and corresponding host edge server.
2. **Logs**. Event logs generated by microservices, which provide a detailed record of service interactions, errors, and system behaviors.
3. **Traces**. Distributed traces that track the flow of requests as they traverse multiple microservices. Tracing helps in visualizing the interaction between different components and identifying bottlenecks.

Popular tools for data collection in microservices environments include Prometheus for metrics collection, ELK stack (*Elasticsearch, Logstash, Kibana*) for log aggregation, and Jaeger for distributed tracing.

The data collection layer must consist of the following components.

1. **3GPP-Specific Exporters**. Collect metrics from UPF, AMF, and SMF via 3GPP's Northbound APIs.[1]
2. **Observability Agents**. Lightweight agents for application-level telemetry from the application space and the kernel space.
3. **IoT Gateway Integration**. MQTT/CoAP[2] support for sensor data [24].

5.1.2 Data Aggregation and Processing Layer

The data aggregation and processing layer consists of the following major components along with the specifications for data storage.

1. **Data Stream Processing**. Apache Kafka for ingestion; Apache Flink for real-time aggregation.
2. **Context Enrichment**. Augment raw metrics with network slice IDs and geolocations.
3. **Data Sampling**. Strategically select a representative subset of data from a large volume of system telemetry, like logs, metrics, and traces, to analyze and monitor system behavior without being overwhelmed by the sheer amount of data, allowing for efficient troubleshooting and performance insights while still capturing critical events.
4. **Time-Series Databases**. InfluxDB for performance metrics.

[1] Application programming interfaces (APIs) that allow third-party applications to use a mobile network's core functions.

[2] MQTT stands for Message Queuing Telemetry Transport and CoAP stands for Constrained Application Protocol.

5. **Graph Databases**. Neo4j for topology and dependency mapping.
6. **Long-term Storage**. Amazon S3 for compliance logs.

5.1.3 Data Analytics and AI/ML Layer

This layer consists of the following components.

1. **Anomaly Detection**. Isolation Forest for latency spikes [25].
2. **Predictive Maintenance**. Long short-term memory (LSTM) networks, which is a type of recurrent neural network (RNN), can be utilized for UPF congestion forecasting through effectively learning long-term dependencies in sequential data flow [2].

5.1.4 Visualization Layer

The visualization layer provides an integrated interface that presents the collected data, analysis results, and predictive insights to networks/systems administrators and application developers. This layer typically involves interactive dashboards and visualization tools like Grafana or Kibana [45], which allow developers to monitor the functional health and performance of microservices and corresponding systems in real-time. This layer enables up/down side scaling of the deployed microservices based on the volume of incoming traffic. The Key functionalities of the visualization layer is as follows.

1. **Real-time performance monitoring**. Displaying KPIs and performance metrics for each microservice.
2. **Service interaction mapping**. Visualizing the interactions between different microservices to detect issues related to inter-service communication.
3. **Alerting and notifications**. Configuring thresholds for metrics and logs to trigger alerts when performance drops below acceptable levels.
4. **Dashboards**. Grafana for operators; custom command line interface (CLI) for DevOps [40].

5.1.5 Compliance with 3GPP Standards

For the observability framework to be effective in 3GPP-compliant edge networks, it must be integrated seamlessly with existing 3GPP network functions and protocols. The framework must adhere to:

1. **QoS specifications**. Ensuring that the observability tools do not violate the stringent latency and throughput requirements for 5G and beyond networks.
2. **Security protocols**. Ensuring that data collection and processing do not compromise the security of the network. Encryption, access controls, and secure log management must be enforced.

3. **Network slicing**. The observability framework should support the monitoring and analysis of different network slices (i.e., isolated network segments) in compliance with 3GPP standards.

5.2 eMELT: A Conceptual Self-Learning Observability and Orchestration Framework

In this section, we propose a conceptual observability and orchestration framework, eMELT (Edge MELT, *MELT* corresponds to "*Metrics, Events, Logs and Traces*"), and discuss its technical aspects for real-time implementation. One of the major aspects of this framework is the ability to collect MELT data from the deployed containerized (e.g., Docker) microservices across the distributed host edge servers without snooping into the application. After collecting observability data, it will have the ability to analyze data patterns through automated data analysis and convert those data into decisions/actions through machine learning models for the orchestration of microservices containers in the distributed edge nodes. Optimum resource management and service placement are two major objectives behind this. So, this self-learning observability framework will have four components (refer Fig. 2), (1) eMELT agent, (2) eMELT collector, (3) mlMELT, and (4) esOrchestrator. eMELT agent will be deployed in each microservice container to extract MELT data from the host worker node. Collected data from the deployed microservices over distributed edge server nodes will be collated and sampled by the eMELT collector deployed in the manager node. So, the manager node and the worker nodes create the overall edge server mesh for an edge-enabled network. The mlMELT (i.e., machine learning-enabled MELT data analyzer) module will create patterns from observability data. The esOrchestrator (i.e., edge services orchestrator) will translate those data analysis patterns into decisions/actions for service deployment (i.e., scaling and maintenance) considering demand in terms of the incoming traffic from users in the edge server service region. We also discuss the positioning of this observability framework in the edge-enabled network stack in compliance with 3GPP.

1. **eMELT agent**. This observability agent is proposed considering two aspects: (1) MELT (i.e., metrics, events, logs, and traces) data extracting tools are required to be installed/configured independently in the host and inside each Docker container, and (2) combining the logs generated from the running microservices with the logs from the host OS kernel. The eMELT agent will have two broad components, (1) user space component and (2) kernel space component. The Userspace component will create the interface between the MELT data extractor and the host OS kernel. Throughput, CPU usage, memory usage, network latency, and cache hit ratio are some important system parameters along with the event logs and traces. There are open-source tools to measure these parameters, like New Relic, iostat, and traceroute, to assess system state at the run time. For collecting event-based logging information, we propose to use eBPF (extended Berkeley Packet

Filter) to inject customized byte-codes to specific kernel hook points. The Kernelspace component will have modules like tracepoints, eBPF probes, and eBPF maps to extract and order the log messages from both applications and the host kernel. Then through implementing atomic system event logging, causally consistent and event execution order preserving logs are generated for the microservices running over a single host. All the system state measuring tools, along with the eBPF-based tools, are interconnected through API gateways such that at run time, all these tools are triggered at the same time.

2. **eMELT collector**. This observability component is placed on the manager node to collect all the MELT data from microservices running in the distributed edge servers. However, there are two challenges. First, how to synchronize the collection of data from various distributed edge servers at runtime while the physical clocks of all the servers are not synchronized in real-time. The event triggers are random in nature. To solve this, the concept of a vector clock can be implemented to combine system tracing with application event logs while preserving causality. The second challenge is the huge volume of observability data which are generated from multiple distributed edge servers. Creating a data fusion center at the collector by accumulating and storing this huge volume of data is memory inefficient. Designing an efficient data sampling algorithm for this will solve this problem. eBPF maps are used at the collector to store and retrieve data in a wide set of data structures: Hash tables, Arrays, LRU (Least Recently Used), Ring Buffer, LPM (Longest Prefix match), and Stack Trace.
3. **mlMELT**. This component of our proposed observability framework namely machine learning-enabled MELT data analyzer (mlMELT) aims to create data patterns from the MELT data stored at the data fusion center. There are several machine learning models based on federated and reinforcement-based learning. Output from this module can be utilized in two ways. First, the output can be

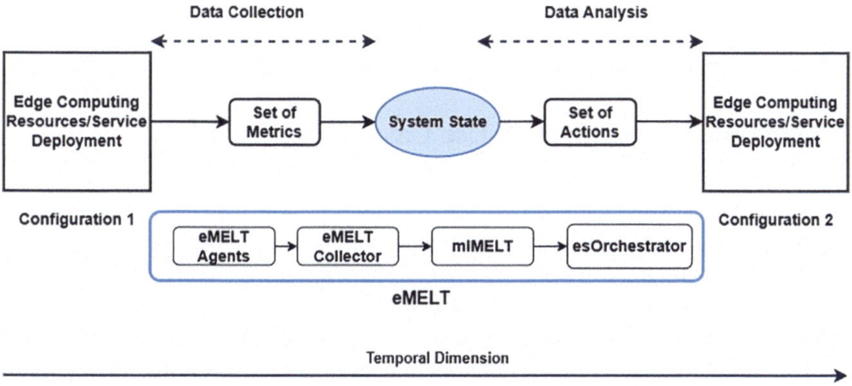

Fig. 2 Schematic diagram of the workflow of the proposed self-learning observability and orchestration framework where system configuration evolves based on observability data analysis

interfaced with visualization tools like Grafana Dashboards. Secondly, the output can be fed to a microservice orchestrator tool for automated decision-making.

4. **esOrchestrator**. This component namely edge services orchestrator (esOrchestrator) is the integration of machine learning-based decision-making module and Kubernetes/Docker Composer-based orchestration module. According to demand or incoming traffic for a specific edge server service region, esOrchestrator enables auto-scaling of deployed microservices and automated resource management (i.e., data storage, application processing memory, computing and network resources, etc.). This AI-integrated module not only makes this observability framework intelligent and robust, it also increases system efficiency.

Remark 1 Training a machine learning model, corresponding inference, and computing load at the edge server related to deployed services affects the power consumption of the bare metal directly. So, analyzing the effect of various observed system and network parameters on power consumption is important for sustainable network functioning. Power consumption measurement is an important aspect of an observability framework.

5.3 Methodology for Effectiveness and Viability Analysis of an Observability Framework

Analysis of the effectiveness and viability of an observability framework is important for real-time deployment. Some major parameters are as follows: (1) Computation overhead: minimizing computation overhead is necessary for edge servers as it has fewer computational capabilities in comparison with cloud servers, (2) Network overhead: it should be minimized to reduce end-to-end latency and spectrum inefficiency, (3) Central processing units (CPU) and memory usage are two parameters to characterize the efficacy of an observability framework.

6 Dynamic Provenance: A Use Case of Observability

Observability in next-generation networked systems is more than just data collection. It involves understanding the flow and transformations of data, operations, and activities that occur within the system. As systems grow more complex, particularly with the advent of edge computing, cloud-native architectures, and large-scale distributed systems, traditional methods of monitoring and logging fall short of providing full visibility into data flows and operations. Provenances in computing refer to the origin, creation, modification, and usage history of data, providing a record that establishes authenticity, reliability, and context. In comparison with observability, provenance enables tracking not just the outputs but the entire journey of data across different components, giving system operators/developers insight into how and why a result was produced. *Dynamic provenance* extends this concept to systems that change over time, such as distributed applications and networks that continuously adapt based on usage patterns, incoming traffic, faults, or performance requirements with low latency (e.g., latency<100ms). This section focuses on dynamic provenance as a powerful tool for improving observability in modern networks and systems, exploring its use cases and benefits in the context of real-time decision-making, fault detection, and system optimization.

6.1 A Methodology to Create Provenance from Observability Data for Distributed Edge Enabled Network and Corresponding Analysis

Creating provenance from observability data involves systematically collecting, correlating, and contextualizing to reconstruct a verifiable record of events, actions, and dependencies in the distributed edge computing environment. The goal is to establish a comprehensive and contextually enriched view of the data flow and transformations across the entire system, linking observability data such as logs, metrics, traces, and events. We provide a step-wise methodology to create provenance from observability data as follows.

1. **Correlation of Observability Data**. In a distributed microservices architecture, the first step is to correlate observability data across the various services and edge components. This is typically done using a correlation ID or a trace ID, which is passed along as metadata in each request. These identifiers ensure that logs, traces, and metrics from different microservices are linked to the same request or transaction. For example *Correlation IDs* are attached to requests when they enter the system and are propagated through headers, metadata, or tags as the request traverses multiple services. This makes it possible to correlate logs, metrics, and traces from different sources.
2. **Enriching Observability Data with Metadata**. Once data is correlated, the next step is to enrich the observability data with metadata that provides additional context. This metadata may contain the attributes namely *service information, timestamps, device/user information, network data* and *network slice information* which are described as follows.
   Service Information. Names of the services that processed the request, including RAN, core network, and edge server services.
   Timestamps. Exact times of when each service processed the data, which helps in identifying latencies and pinpointing performance bottlenecks.
   Device or User Information. Context on which device or user initiated the request, geographic location, and other contextual details.
   Network Data. Collecting network-related data (e.g., routing paths, network delays) with the same trace ID, enabled by coordination between application and network layers are useful to create provenance graph. This approach lever-

ages 3GPP's edge computing framework, where the network functions, such as the SMF and EES play a central role in managing interactions between applications and the network, as outlined in 3GPP technical reports like TR 23.700-48 [14].

Network Slice Information. In the case of *B5G slicing*, identifying which slice handled the request (e.g., eMBB, URLLC).

Enriching observability data with the above informations helps to build a *comprehensive timeline* of the request as it flows through different network functions and microservices.

3. **Building the Provenance Graph**. Once the data is enriched, a provenance graph can be constructed. The provenance graph is typically a Directed Acyclic Graph (DAG) that represents the flow of data through the system. The two major components of the provenance graph namely *nodes* and *edges* are described as follows.
   Nodes. Each node in the graph represents a specific event or state of the system (e.g., a service call, data transformation, or service state change).
   Edges. Edges represent relationships or dependencies between nodes, indicating how data flows or how events in one service trigger actions in another.
4. **Distributed Tracing across Edge Nodes for Provenance**. In B5G networks, *distributed tracing* is particularly useful for visualizing the journey of a request across multiple microservices and network functions. Tools like Jaeger and OpenTelemetry are used to instrument the system with trace IDs, enabling operators to track the performance and identify bottlenecks. Distributed tracing enables precise *latency measurements* between each hop in the graph. For example, developer/system operator can measure how long it took to retrieve a video from the CDN versus the core network or identify where the video transcoding service caused any delays.
5. **Storage and Verification**. One prominent mechanism is to store the provenance graph in a distributed ledger (e.g., Hyperledger Fabric) hosted across edge servers for tamper-proof auditability. Alternatively, a lightweight database like SQLite can be utilized for real-time access. Integrating with 3GPP's Network Data Analytics Function (NWDAF) to validate provenance across network performance data is useful for ensuring consistency.

6.2 Analyzing Provenance Data and Visualization in the Form of Graphical Representation

Once the provenance graph is created, it can be analyzed for various purposes which are discussed as follows.

1. **Performance Optimization**. By analyzing the provenance graph, operators can identify areas where latency occurs and optimize the performance of microservices and network paths.

2. **Fault Detection, Debugging, and Root Cause Analysis**. Provenance data helps in tracing the root cause of failures. For example, if video playback is delayed, the graph will highlight whether the delay occurred during the transcoding process or in fetching content from the core network. By considering both the service sequence and network path simultaneously, operators/developers can identify whether delays are due to application processing or network routing, thus enhancing fault isolation.
3. **Security and Auditing**. Provenance provides a detailed audit trail, which is useful for tracking suspicious activities and ensuring data integrity. Security teams can analyze how data was handled and identify potential security risks.
4. **Graph Visualization and Analysis**. The visualization in the form of graph maps the end-to-end request flow, from the user device initiating the request, through various edge servers and network components, and back to the device. Each stage of the flow is recorded with relevant metadata, which can later be used for performance analysis, troubleshooting, or security auditing.

Remark 2 In the context of B5G networks, provenance extends beyond application-level tracking to include network-level information, such as the routing path through the network, network delays, and interactions with network functions like the Session Management Function (SMF) and Policy Control Function (PCF). This comprehensive provenance is essential for debugging, optimizing performance, and ensuring security and ultra-low latency, especially in critical applications like autonomous driving, real-time gaming, and automated healthcare in hospitals etc.

7 Research Challenges

6G requirements and system design will be driven by (i) the persistent pursuit of spectral (bits/Hz/area), energy (bits/Joule), and cost (bits/dollar) efficiencies, and (ii) three new service enhancements: sensing/localization/awareness, compute, and global broadband/emergency connectivity [18]. Throughout the protocol stack (i.e., from the physical layer to the application layer), there will be more complexity in terms of network function virtualization and network slicing (Table 5). In that aspect, microservice architecture is the potential approach for developing scalable and flexible applications and deploying containerized network functions. So, designing a dynamic observability framework will be crucial for understanding system behavior, diagnosing issues, and ensuring performance and reliability. Provenance, on the other hand, refers to the ability to track the origin and history of data. Provenance is critical for security, compliance, and debugging, particularly in distributed environments where data may traverse multiple services and nodes. Both are important for ensuring the reliability, security, and performance of distributed microservices over edge-enabled 6G networks. In this section, we discuss some of the important research challenges (refer Table 6) along with potential research directions as follows.

Table 5 Research challenges across different layers considering different functionalities and corresponding 3GPP Mapping. EES -Edge enabler server, AF -Application function, EAS -Edge application server, ECS -Edge configuration server, AMF -Access and mobility management function, SMF -Session management function, RAN -Radio access network, NFV -Network function virtualization

Layer	Functionality	3GPP components	Key challenges
Application	Microservice hosting, QoS enforcement	EAS, AF	Service discovery latency
Service enabler	Resource allocation, orchestration	EES, ECS	Dynamic resource management
Network	Ultra-low latency, traffic steering	UPF, SMF, RAN	Network slicing overhead
Infrastructure	Compute and storage provisioning	NFV, Edge Nodes	Energy efficiency

Table 6 Comparison between several research challenges for developing a dynamic observability framework across key aspects: complexity, current solutions, and research gaps

Challenge	Complexity	Current solutions	Research challenges
Real-time monitoring	High	AI-based anomaly detection	Handling 3D topology dynamics
Scalability	Medium	Distributed tracing (e.g., Jaeger)	Edge-specific scalability frameworks
Provenance tracking	High	Blockchain, metadata tagging	Heterogeneous node integration
Security/Privacy	High	Encryption, federated learning	Lightweight security framework for edge
Resource constraints	Medium	Lightweight agents (e.g., eBPF)	Balancing granularity versus overhead
Interoperability	Medium	OpenTelemetry, gRPC[a]	6G-specific standards
Latency-sensitive logging	High	In-memory logging, sampling	Real-time provenance optimization

[a] gRPC is a cross-platform high-performance remote procedure call framework. gRPC was initially created by Google, but is open source and is used in many organizations. Use cases range from microservices to the "last mile" of computing [51]

1. **Scalability and Complexity**. One of the primary challenges in observability and provenance for distributed microservices over edge-enabled 6G networks is the scalability and complexity of the environment. The distributed nature of microservices means that data may traverse multiple services and nodes, making it difficult to track and monitor. Additionally, the dynamic and heterogeneous nature of edge environments introduces further complexity, as resources may be added or removed dynamically, and the network topology may change frequently. Current tools like Prometheus or Jaeger [31] are designed for small-scale systems.

Scaling them to 6G requires distributed tracing paradigms, which face bottlenecks in aggregating telemetry data across edge clusters.

2. **Data Aggregation and Creating Data Fusion Center**.: Observability relies on collecting and aggregating data from distributed nodes. Edge nodes might not have centralized logging facilities, leading to fragmented data. Edge nodes (e.g., mobile devices, robots, automated vehicles, etc.) are resource-constrained, and aggregating metrics from all of them without overwhelming the network becomes a key challenge.
3. **Real-Time Monitoring in Dynamic and Heterogeneous Environments**. The dynamic and heterogeneous nature of edge environments introduces significant challenges in observability and provenance. In edge-enabled 6G networks, resources may be added or removed dynamically, and the network topology may change frequently. This makes it difficult to maintain a consistent view of the system and track the origin and history of data. The high mobility of user equipment (UE) and edge nodes in 6G networks, combined with frequent microservice orchestration, demands real-time monitoring. Traditional centralized monitoring fails due to latency and bandwidth constraints. AI-driven monitoring can be a potential solution but introduces computational overhead. Along with that, high-frequency logging strains edge resources, necessitating efficient *compression* or *sampling* techniques without losing critical data.
4. **Security, Privacy, and Provenance Tracking**. Security and privacy are critical concerns in observability and provenance for distributed microservices over edge-enabled 6G networks. The distributed nature of microservices means that data may traverse multiple services and nodes, increasing the risk of security breaches and privacy violations. Ensuring consistent provenance metadata in a multi-vendor, multi-protocol environment is complex. Blockchain-based solutions are suggested but face latency and energy trade-offs in edge contexts [32]. Federated learning for observability offers privacy-preserving solutions but increases complexity.
5. **Latency, Maintaining Service-Level Objectives, Dynamic Orchestration, and Mobility**. Latency, maintaining service-level objectives, dynamic orchestration, and high mobility are critical concerns in observability and provenance for distributed microservices over edge-enabled 6G networks. Handoffs between edge nodes cause trace fragmentation.
6. **Interoperability, Cross-Domain Provenance, and Standardization**. Interoperability, cross-domain provenance, and standardization are critical concerns in observability and provenance for distributed microservices over edge-enabled 6G networks. In a 6G network, services might span multiple administrative domains (e.g., different telecom providers and cloud infrastructures). This makes it difficult to maintain a consistent view of the system and track the origin and history of data. Ensuring provenance tracking across different trust boundaries and governance models is complex.
7. **Resource Constraints at the Edge**. Edge devices have limited CPU, memory, and energy, challenging the deployment of observability and provenance mech-

anisms. Lightweight solutions are needed, but reducing overhead often compromises granularity, impacting fault diagnosis, and data trustworthiness.

8. **Temporal Granularity for Dynamic Topologies**. Provenance information must be accurate and reflect the precise transformations and actions that occur over time. Maintaining this level of granularity for distributed microservices deployment is complex. Ensuring accurate time synchronization across geographically distributed edge nodes is essential for precise provenance tracking. Blockchain can be a potential solution for immutable and verifiable data provenance. Its decentralized nature aligns with the distributed nature of microservices. Blockchain provides a trusted, tamper-proof ledger for tracking data across microservices, ensuring transparent provenance.

Observability and provenance in distributed microservices over edge-enabled 6G networks face multifaceted challenges rooted in the technology's scale, heterogeneity, and real-time demands. Challenges like real-time monitoring and provenance tracking exhibit high complexity due to 6G's dynamic and distributed nature. Security remains a critical gap, with existing solutions insufficient for edge constraints. Scalability and interoperability show progress but lack 6G-tailored approaches. Recent research underscores the need for innovative, edge-centric solutions to ensure system reliability and trustworthiness. Future work should prioritize adaptive, scalable, and secure frameworks to unlock 6G's full potential. Comparison between several research challenges for developing a dynamic observability framework across key aspects (i.e., complexity, current solutions, and research gaps) are presented in Table 6.

8 Conclusion

As 6G networks evolve to support ultra-low latency, dynamic scalability, and pervasive edge computing, robust observability and provenance frameworks become increasingly critical. This chapter presented a comprehensive observability analysis from the 3GPP perspective, redefining it to align with distributed microservices deployed over edge-enabled infrastructures. We introduced a generic observability framework tailored for 3GPP-compliant networks and proposed eMELT, a self-learning architecture capable of collecting, analyzing, and acting on runtime telemetry. Through the use case of dynamic provenance, we emphasized how observability is a foundation for trustworthy, adaptive, and secure systems. Furthermore, we outlined various research challenges in the directions, ranging from scalability to resource constraints, from the deployment perspective to interoperability and real-time monitoring, which must be addressed to realize the full potential of edge-native observability in 6G. Future research in this direction must focus on lightweight, AI-enabled, and standard-compliant solutions that can operate under the constraints of edge environments while ensuring end-to-end visibility, reliability, and resilience across heterogeneous and decentralized networks.

References

1. ADS, A.L., Atxutegi, E., Giust, G.U.F., Munaretto, D., IHP, J.G.T., IHP, E.G., IT, A.J.M., KAU, A.B., Marie, A., LMI, C.B., et al.: Standardization and regulation report (release a) (2019)
2. Ali, A., Ullah, I., Shabaz, M., Sharafian, A., Khan, M.A., Bai, X., Qiu, L.: A resource-aware multi-graph neural network for urban traffic flow prediction in multi-access edge computing systems. IEEE Transactions on Consumer Electronics (2024)
3. Bates, A., Tian, D.J., Butler, K.R., Moyer, T.: Trustworthy {Whole-System} provenance for the linux kernel. In: 24th USENIX Security Symposium (USENIX Security 15). pp. 319–334 (2015)
4. Chen, S., Delimitrou, C., Martínez, J.F.: Parties: Qos-aware resource partitioning for multiple interactive services. In: Proceedings of the Twenty-Fourth International Conference on Architectural Support for Programming Languages and Operating Systems. pp. 107–120 (2019)
5. Chen, W., Lin, X., Lee, J., Toskala, A., Sun, S., Chiasserini, C.F., Liu, L.: 5g-advanced toward 6g: Past, present, and future. IEEE Journal on Selected Areas in Communications **41**(6), 1592–1619 (2023)
6. Collin, J., Pellikka, J., Penttinen, J.: New capabilities of 5g sa. 5G Innovations for Industry Transformation: Data-driven Use Cases p. 51 (2023)
7. Ferrús, R., Sallent, O., Pérez-Romero, J., Agusti, R.: On the automation of ran slicing provisioning and cell planning in ng-ran. In: 2018 European Conference on Networks and Communications (EuCNC). pp. 37–42. IEEE (2018)
8. Fonseca, R., Porter, G., Katz, R.H., Shenker, S.: {X-Trace}: A pervasive network tracing framework. In: 4th USENIX Symposium on Networked Systems Design & Implementation (NSDI 07) (2007)
9. Gan, Y., Zhang, Y., Hu, K., Cheng, D., He, Y., Pancholi, M., Delimitrou, C.: Seer: Leveraging big data to navigate the complexity of performance debugging in cloud microservices. In: Proceedings of the twenty-fourth international conference on architectural support for programming languages and operating systems. pp. 19–33 (2019)
10. Gehani, A., Tariq, D.: Spade: Support for provenance auditing in distributed environments. In: ACM/IFIP/USENIX International Conference on Distributed Systems Platforms and Open Distributed Processing. pp. 101–120. Springer (2012)
11. Giorgi, L., Puliafito, C., Virdis, A., Mingozzi, E.: Service continuity in edge computing through edge proxies and http alternative services. IEEE Open Journal of the Communications Society (2024)
12. Giuliano, R.: From 5g-advanced to 6g in 2030: New services, 3gpp advances and enabling technologies. IEEE Access (2024)
13. Groenendijk, J., Lan, Z.: 5g management and orchestration architecture framework. Journal of ICT Standardization **7**(2), 81–92 (2019)
14. Gür, G., Kalla, A., De Alwis, C., Pham, Q.V., Ngo, K.H., Liyanage, M., Porambage, P.: Integration of icn and mec in 5g and beyond networks: Mutual benefits, use cases, challenges, standardization, and future research. IEEE Open Journal of the Communications Society **3**, 1382–1412 (2022)
15. Hassan, W.U., Bates, A., Marino, D.: Tactical provenance analysis for endpoint detection and response systems. In: 2020 IEEE symposium on security and privacy (SP). pp. 1172–1189. IEEE (2020)
16. Ji, Y., Lee, S., Downing, E., Wang, W., Fazzini, M., Kim, T., Orso, A., Lee, W.: Rain: Refinable attack investigation with on-demand inter-process information flow tracking. In: Proceedings of the 2017 ACM SIGSAC conference on computer and communications security. pp. 377–390 (2017)
17. Johansson, J., Hapsari, W.A., Kelley, S., Bodog, G.: Minimization of drive tests in 3gpp release 11. IEEE Communications Magazine **50**(11), 36–43 (2012)
18. Kaushik, A., Singh, R., Dayarathna, S., Senanayake, R., Di Renzo, M., Dajer, M., Ji, H., Kim, Y., Sciancalepore, V., Zappone, A., et al.: Toward integrated sensing and communications for 6g:

Key enabling technologies, standardization, and challenges. IEEE Communications Standards Magazine **8**(2), 52–59 (2024)
19. Keller, E., Rexford, J.: The "platform as a service" model for networking. INM/WREN **10**, 95–108 (2010)
20. Keysight, M.M.B.f.: 5g transport network survey-huawei sponsored. ai-artificial intelligence, whitepaper on its footfalls. (2018)
21. Kosińska, J., Baliś, B., Konieczny, M., Malawski, M., Zieliński, S.: Toward the observability of cloud-native applications: The overview of the state-of-the-art. IEEE Access **11**, 73036–73052 (2023)
22. Koukis, G., Skaperas, S., Kapetanidou, I.A., Mamatas, L., Tsaoussidis, V.: Performance evaluation of kubernetes networking approaches across constraint edge environments. In: 2024 IEEE Symposium on Computers and Communications (ISCC). pp. 1–6. IEEE (2024)
23. Kumar, A., Thing, V.L.: A public key infrastructure for 5g service-based architecture. In: 2023 IEEE 22nd International Conference on Trust, Security and Privacy in Computing and Communications (TrustCom). pp. 1532–1539. IEEE (2023)
24. Lalhriatpuii, Ruchi, Wasson, V.: Comprehensive exploration of iot communication protocol: Coap, mqtt, http, lorawan and amqp. In: International Conference on Machine Learning Algorithms. pp. 261–274. Springer (2024)
25. Larian, H., Safi-Esfahani, F.: Intec: integrated things-edge computing: a framework for distributing machine learning pipelines in edge ai systems. Computing **107**(1), 41 (2025)
26. Liu, H.X.: Instrumenting Observability in a Decentralized Microservice Architecture. Ph.D. thesis, Massachusetts Institute of Technology (2024)
27. Lyu, X., Li, Y., He, Y., Ren, C., Ni, W., Liu, R.P., Zhu, P., Cui, Q.: Objective-driven differentiable optimization of traffic prediction and resource allocation for split ai inference edge networks. IEEE Transactions on Machine Learning in Communications and Networking (2024)
28. Mace, J., Roelke, R., Fonseca, R.: Pivot tracing: Dynamic causal monitoring for distributed systems. ACM Transactions on Computer Systems (TOCS) **35**(4), 1–28 (2018)
29. Mahmoud, H.H.H., Amer, A.A., Ismail, T.: 6G: A comprehensive survey on technologies, applications, challenges, and research problems. Transactions on Emerging Telecommunications Technologies **32**(4), e4233 (2021)
30. Majumdar, S., Trivisonno, R., Poe, W.Y., Carle, G.: Distributing intelligence for 6g network automation: Performance and architectural impact. In: ICC 2023-IEEE International Conference on Communications. pp. 6224–6229. IEEE (2023)
31. Marangozova, V., Soares, J., Koagne, Y.N.: D 1.2-1 Tools for Microservice Characterization. Ph.D. thesis, Université Grenoble-Alpes (2024)
32. Mertens, D., Kim, J., Xu, J., Kim, E., Lee, C.: Smart flow: a provenance-supported smart contract workflow architecture. Cluster Computing **27**(6), 8173–8187 (2024)
33. Moltsen, L., Jacobsen, R.H., Inceoglu, F., Antoci, V., Marcano, N.J.H., Alminde, L.K., Michaelsen, P.H., Sorensen, C.I., Jensen, M.: Positioning 5g management interfaces for mega-constellations management (megaman). Journal of ICT Standardization **7**(2), 109–126 (2019)
34. Nguyen, D.C., Ding, M., Pathirana, P.N., Seneviratne, A., Li, J., Niyato, D., Dobre, O., Poor, H.V.: 6G internet of things: A comprehensive survey. IEEE Internet of Things Journal **9**(1), 359–383 (2021)
35. Oliner, A., Ganapathi, A., Xu, W.: Advances and challenges in log analysis. Communications of the ACM **55**(2), 55–61 (2012)
36. Otero, M., Garcia, J.M., Fernandez, P.: Towards a lightweight distributed telemetry for microservices. In: 2024 IEEE 44th International Conference on Distributed Computing Systems Workshops (ICDCSW). pp. 75–82. IEEE (2024)
37. Ouyang, Y., Wang, L., Yang, A., Shah, M., Belanger, D., Gao, T., Wei, L., Zhang, Y.: The next decade of telecommunications artificial intelligence. arXiv preprint arXiv:2101.09163 (2021)
38. Perdigão, A., Quevedo, J., Aguiar, R.L.: Is release 15 ready for the industry? IEEE Access **12**, 17651–17668 (2024)
39. Ping, J.: Network resource model for 5g network and network slice. Journal of ICT Standardization **7**(2), 127–140 (2019)

40. Puolitaival, V.: Enhancing development efficiency with devsecops template: a design science approach for iac and ci/cd implementation for aws (2024)
41. Qu, M., Tang, X., Zhang, Y., Chen, Z., Zhang, T., Zhao, Y., Li, Y.: An overview of enabling artificial intelligence in 3gpp 5g-advanced networks. In: 2023 IEEE International Conferences on Internet of Things (iThings) and IEEE Green Computing & Communications (GreenCom) and IEEE Cyber, Physical & Social Computing (CPSCom) and IEEE Smart Data (SmartData) and IEEE Congress on Cybermatics (Cybermatics). pp. 65–70. IEEE (2023)
42. Rayhana, R., Yun, H., Wang, T., Chen, J., Fan, Y., Liu, Z., Gao, W.: Distributed predictive maintenance through edge computing. In: 2024 IEEE 22nd International Conference on Industrial Informatics (INDIN). pp. 1–13. IEEE (2024)
43. Sigelman, B.H., Barroso, L.A., Burrows, M., Stephenson, P., Plakal, M., Beaver, D., Jaspan, S., Shanbhag, C.: Dapper, a large-scale distributed systems tracing infrastructure (2010)
44. Song, P., Peng, H., Zhang, X.: A micro-service approach to cloud native ran for 5g and beyond. IEEE Access **11**, 130257–130271 (2023)
45. Team, F.B.U.: Service observability. In: Cloud-Native Application Architecture: Microservice Development Best Practice, pp. 213–281. Springer (2024)
46. Thalheim, J., Rodrigues, A., Akkus, I.E., Bhatotia, P., Chen, R., Viswanath, B., Jiao, L., Fetzer, C.: Sieve: Actionable insights from monitored metrics in distributed systems. In: Proceedings of the 18th ACM/IFIP/USENIX middleware conference. pp. 14–27 (2017)
47. Tovinger, T., Cornily, J.M., Gardella, M., Shan, C., Ai, C., Andrianov, A., Chou, J., Groenendijk, J., Kai, Z., Lan, Z., et al.: Management, orchestration and charging in the new era. Journal of ICT Standardization **6**(1-2), 159–178 (2018)
48. Tran, M.N., Kim, Y.: Design of 5g architecture enhancements for supporting serverless computing. IEEE Access (2024)
49. Wang, Y., Qin, S., Feng, G., Zhou, J., Wei, F.: Gan-based pareto optimization for self-healing of radio access network slices. IEEE Transactions on Network and Service Management **19**(1), 146–157 (2021)
50. Wu, X., Farooq, J., Chen, J.: Adaptive risk-aware resource orchestration for 5g microservices over multi-tier edge-cloud systems. In: 2024 IEEE International Conference on Communications Workshops (ICC Workshops). pp. 359–364. IEEE (2024)
51. Yan, X.: Web API Development with ASP. NET Core 8: Learn techniques, patterns, and tools for building high-performance, robust, and scalable web APIs. Packt Publishing Ltd (2024)
52. Yao, Y., Sun, X.: Performance assurance for 5g networks including network slicing. Journal of ICT Standardization **7**(2), 93–108 (2019)
53. Zeb, S., Rathore, M.A., Hassan, S.A., Raza, S., Dev, K., Fortino, G.: Toward ai-enabled nextg networks with edge intelligence-assisted microservice orchestration. IEEE Wireless Communications **30**(3), 148–156 (2023)
54. Zengy, J., Wang, X., Liu, J., Chen, Y., Liang, Z., Chua, T.S., Chua, Z.L.: Shadewatcher: Recommendation-guided cyber threat analysis using system audit records. In: 2022 IEEE symposium on security and privacy (SP). pp. 489–506. IEEE (2022)

VNF Placement and Request Routing in 5G and Beyond Networks

Aqsa Sayeed and Samaresh Bera

1 Introduction

Rapid growth in digitization opens up the door for multiple applications across multiple industries. Hence, support for multi-dimensional requirements necessitates that the network be flexible and scalable. However, traditional network architectures depend on hardware-based infrastructure; thus, they face challenges in implementing the heterogeneous demands of modern technology and applications. Due to heterogeneity in device logic, centralized control may not be feasible in a traditional network, making it difficult to scale. The network devices such as middleboxes are required to be configured according to the vendor-specific configuration in traditional networks. However, the network applications of upper-layer and business requisites are always subject to change due to rapid technological changes as mentioned earlier. This necessitates that the hardware infrastructure should be dynamic to support newer technologies [8]. However, traditional architecture limits the dynamic configuration and makes it hard to meet the needs of modern applications and business [11]. Various vendors produce network devices, generally with self-configurable proprietary protocols and hardware. This causes a significant challenge for complex debugging and configuration management of heterogeneous hardware devices. The devices from multiple vendors may not work seamlessly together, causing interoperability issues and communication problems between devices. Hence, the vendor-specific networking creates issues with traffic congestion, data analysis, and inefficient resource utilization [2].

A. Sayeed (✉) · S. Bera
Department of Computer Science and Engineering, Indian Institute of Technology Jammu, Jammu, India
e-mail: 2023rcs1015@iitjammu.ac.in

S. Bera
e-mail: s.bera.1989@ieee.org

T. Ojha et al. (eds.), *Edge-Enabled 6G Networking*,
https://doi.org/10.1007/978-3-032-19042-0_10

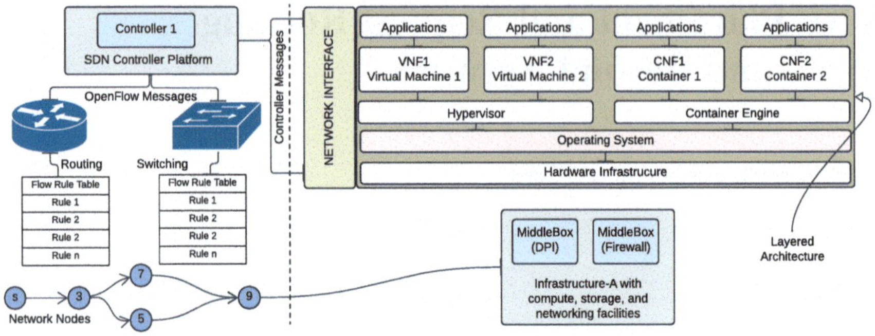

Fig. 1 A comprehensive architecture of SDN and NFV architecture

To overcome these challenges, there is a requirement of a flexible, scalable, and interoperable network system. As a result, researchers have introduced the concepts of software-defined networking (SDN) and network function virtualization (NFV) [14]. SDN creates a programmable network by keeping centralized control over all networking devices, and NFV virtualizes the network system's physical resources and network functions. In practical, SDN takes care of traffic forwarding in the network. Whereas NFV enables virtualized network function (VNF) placement on commodity hardware instead of using closed-box hardware platform. The VNFs are placed using hypervisors or container engines, as discussed below [17].

Figure 1 illustrates the SDN-NFV architecture. This diagram depicts a network with numerous nodes, including routers and switches. The network is connected to an infrastructure, which consists of several middleboxes responsible for operations and network traffic processing [5]. An SDN controller centrally manages the network devices in the architecture via southbound protocol, such as OpenFlow. The devices include hardware components, an operating system, and flow tables in the data plane [6]. A network interface connects the SDN segment and the virtualized network segment. Figure 2 provides an illustration of dedicated hardware devices to virtualized network functions. The diagram of the SDN-NFV architecture depicts the interconnection and layers of VNFs and cloud-native network functions (CNFs) on the host machine using either hypervisors or container engines [10].

2 Prerequisites of VNF Placement

The VNF placement architecture should be vendor-independent. Figure 3 illustrates the deployment of end-to-end virtual network services using the NFV-MANO architecture [7]. The diagram considers a service from point A to point B within an NFV-enabled infrastructure. Let us assume that a network service S requires the following network functionalities [9]:

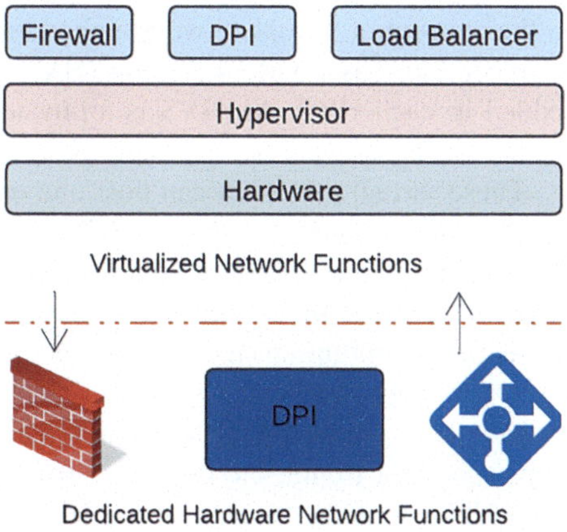

Fig. 2 An illustration of dedicated hardware devices to virtualized network functions

$$S = \{firewall \rightarrow load\ balancing \rightarrow encryption \rightarrow DPI \rightarrow decryption\}$$

Several VNFs make up this service, working together to complete a task. In Fig. 3, there is a virtualization layer that abstracts the physical resources, connecting the VNFs to the physical infrastructure. This architecture integrates virtual elements

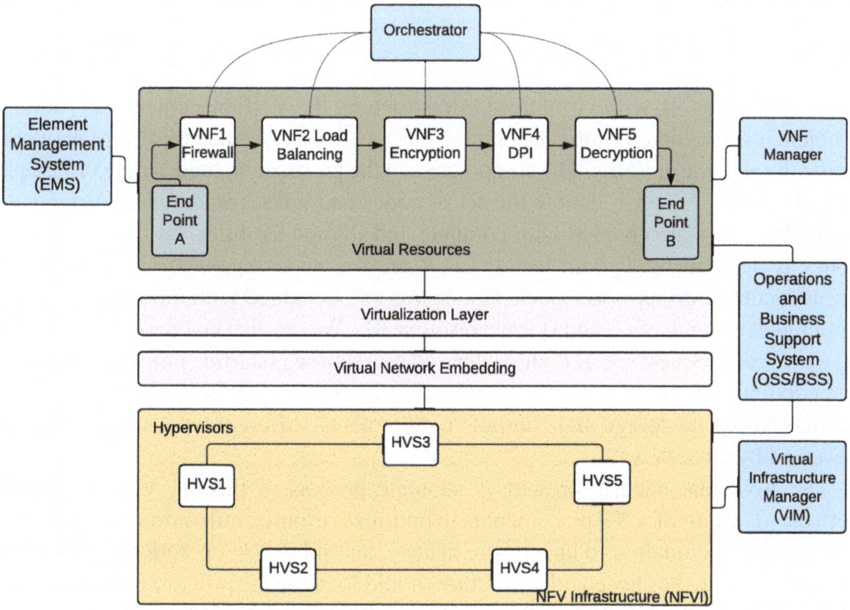

Fig. 3 The ETSI's MANO architecture for vitualization

with physical ones via the concept of virtual network embedding (VNE) [7]. In the example, we have four hypervisor-based virtual systems (HVSs) for the four VNFs, with each VNF embedded in each HVS. An HVS is a physical network node in an NFV-based architecture, using a hypervisor to manage virtual machines based on available resources. These virtual machines can host one or more VNFs of the same type. The network function virtual infrastructure (NFVI) includes computing, storage, software, and networking hardware. It provides resources for VNFs to process data traffic. A VNF is managed by an element management system (EMS), which is in charge of creating, configuring, monitoring, and guaranteeing its performance and security. Operations and business support systems help infrastructure providers deploy and manage end-to-end telecommunications services such as ordering, billing, renewals, and troubleshooting. A virtual infrastructure manager (VIM) manages the NFVI in accordance with the NFV-MANO architecture. The NFV orchestrator dynamically allocates and manages virtualized infrastructure resources. It handles the entire lifecycle of network services, including setup, configuration, monitoring, and termination. The orchestrator arranges and links VNFs to establish comprehensive network services, automated workflows, and collaborates with various components of the NFV environment, including VNFs, VM managers, NFVI, and VIM. This centralized management improves flexibility, efficiency, and service quality [11, 13].

3 Overview of VNF Placement and Request Routing Problem

For a given network with virtualized infrastructure, the VNF placement and routing problem involves determining the optimal placement of VNFs and routing of network traffic through these VNFs. The components of the problem include: a network graph G(N, L) where N and L denote the set of nodes and links, respectively. Among all the nodes, a few are enabled with compute and storage facilities, let the set of such nodes is denoted by P, and let $(P') \in P$ are the nodes enables with virtualized infrastructure. Furthermore, let each node $k \in (P')$, enabled with infrastructure, has a compute resource of C_k and storage resource D_k. We are also given a set of requests R, where each request $r \in R$ is characterized by a source s (starting point), destination d (endpoint). We are also given a nominal bandwidth b_r requirement of a link, and set of VNFs with storage and compute requirements, different types of VNFs to be traversed by edge flows.

The VNF placement represents a strategic process of placing VNFs within a network. The aim of VNF placement is to optimize resource utilization in a network, improve service quality, reduce traffic latency, and minimize operational costs. For VNF placement, the chosen infrastructure should focus on the primary factors such as CPU resource availability, storage, network topology, bandwidth, and traffic patterns. The request routing process entails addressing incoming service requests to the most appropriate VNF instance. The routing certifies that the network can handle the load efficiently by applying load balancing across VNF instances and eliminating infrastructure overloading. Also, routing certifies that it meets performance demands by minimizing request-routing response time to the appropriate VNF instance, for example, the nearest VNF instance. Therefore, the concept of VNF placement and request routing is indispensable to modern NFV environments. Furthermore, it entails a holistic approach for managing network resources and traffic delivery. Also, it benefits the network system by providing improved performance due to reduced traffic latency.

The dynamic adaptability of network operators in response to changing service requirements and traffic patterns achieves a flexible network system. Similarly, integrating VNF and request routing improves scalability and cost efficiency. However, the combination of VNF placement and request routing can present significant challenges. Since this task is complex, it requires sophisticated algorithms and real-time data analysis to find a location to place a VNF. Next, we need to ensure that the placement and routing strategies remain optimal. The adjustment of VNF placement and request routing strategies is very resilient, as it requires continuous monitoring. Also, resource balancing among VNFs can be challenging while meeting performance and policy requirements. In this chapter, the objective of the VNF placement and routing problem is to find the optimal placement of NF nodes and to serve the maximum number of service requests. For optimal system operation, the proposed concept of VNF pacement and routing must adhere to several constraints. The considered constraints are VNF resources capacity, VNF forwarding bandwidth, and VNF node sharing rules [2, 10, 12].

4 Key Questions

The network infrastructure, encompassing resources and requests, necessitates the resolution of the following queries:

1. What are the various VNFs required to fulfill the requests?
2. What are the resources, such as compute, storage, and bandwidth, required to serve the requests based on the VNF requirements?
3. Which infrastructures should we place the VNFs in?
4. How do we route the service requests to the desired VNFs, considering the bandwidth resources in the network?

To answer these questions, we present the problem by creating six scenarios in an incremental way of considering the network infrastructure. We consider six scenarios with different assumptions. And, as we discuss the scenarios from 1 to 6, will keep removing the assumptions to make the model more realistic and practical. We believe this discussion provides an incremental and clear understanding to the readers.

5 Scenario 1

Assumptions:

- One infrastructure considered with certain compute and storage
- VNFs are dedicated to individual service requests
- Each requiring specific compute and storage resources

Figure 4 illustrates Scenario 1 with the service requests $request1$, $request2$, and $request3$, fulfilled by VNFs of single infrastructure A. It has a total capacity of computation and storage resources as 6 and 35, respectively. Therefore, considering the available compute and storage resources, requests $request1$, $request2$, and $request3$, are served by placing the VNFs with required compute and storage resources. In this optimization problem, we consider the computation and storage constraints, with the decision variables x_r, $\forall r \in R$ for VNF placement. Mathematically,

$$\text{Maximize} \quad \sum_{r \in R} x_r \qquad \rightarrow \text{objective} \tag{1}$$

$$\text{Subject to} \quad \sum_{r \in R} x_r \, c_r \leq C, \qquad \rightarrow \text{computation constraint} \tag{2}$$

$$\sum_{r \in R} x_r \, d_r \leq D, \qquad \rightarrow \text{storage constraint} \tag{3}$$

$$x_r \in \{0, 1\}. \qquad \rightarrow \text{binary decision variable} \tag{4}$$

We are given an infrastructure with compute and storage resources denoted by C and D respectively, to place VNFs. We are also given a set of requests denoted as R, each request $r \in R$ with a VNF requirement. Our objective is to maximize the number of served requests while considering the associated constraints. Equation (1) defines the objective which is the maximization of served requests. Equations (2) and (3) define that the utilized compute and storage resources must be within the capacity, respectively. Equation (4) denotes that a request is either fully admitted, i.e., $x_r = 1$, or rejected, i.e., $x_r = 0$.

This concept of VNF placement is very simple to implement and manage because each request uses only one VNF. VNFs dedicate specific compute and storage resources to individual service requests, considering only one infrastructure. However, this strategy may face various challenges, including the possibility of a single-point infrastructure failure. Furthermore, the scenario does not consider the possibility of distributing VNFs across multiple infrastructures, due to which it can lead to suboptimal placement decisions and underutilization of resources. This makes VNF placement less scalable by limiting its applicability to more sophisticated real-world use cases [2, 10].

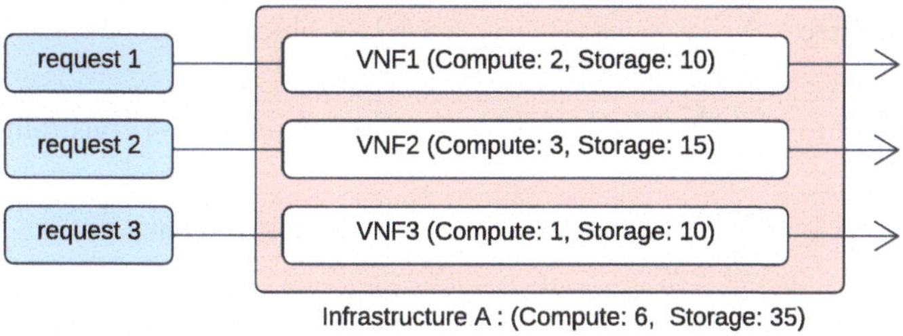

Fig. 4 An example of VNF placement with different requests as per Scenario 1

6 Scenario 2

Assumptions:

- One infrastructure considered with certain compute and storage
- VNFs are dedicated to individual service requests
- Multiple VNFs associated per request

Figure 5 illustrates Scenario 2 with the service requests $request1$, $request2$, and $request3$, fulfilled by VNFs of types VNF1, VNF2, and VNF3 of single infrastructure A. It has a total capacity of computation and storage resources as 14 and 65, respectively. Considering the requirements of requests with one or more VNFs with compute and storage requirements, the requests are admitted. In this optimization problem, we consider the computation and storage constraints, with the decision variable $x_r, \forall r \in R$ for VNF placement. Mathematically,

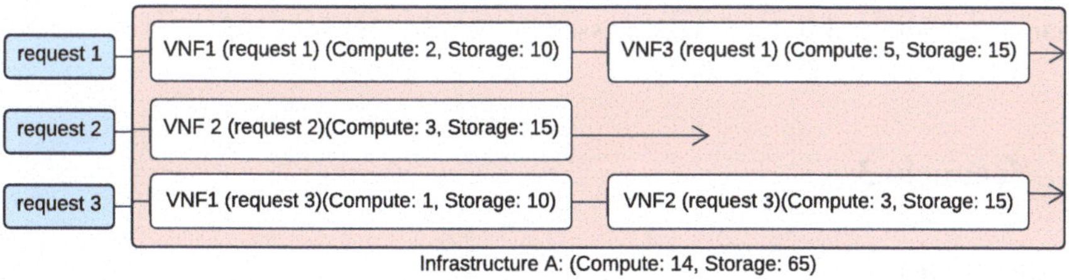

Fig. 5 An example of VNF placement with different requests as per Scenario 2

$$\text{Maximize} \quad \sum_{r \in R} x_r \qquad \rightarrow \text{objective} \tag{5}$$

$$\text{Subject to} \quad \sum_{r \in R} \sum_{v \in V} c_{rv}\, x_r \leq C, \qquad \rightarrow \text{computation constraint} \tag{6}$$

$$\sum_{r \in R} \sum_{v \in V} d_{rv}\, x_r \leq D, \qquad \rightarrow \text{storage constraint} \tag{7}$$

$$x_r \in \{0, 1\}. \qquad \rightarrow \text{binary decision variable} \tag{8}$$

We are given an infrastructure with compute and storage resources denoted by C and D, respectively, to place VNFs. We are also given a set of requests denoted as R, and multiple VNFs are associated per request, $r \in R$. Our objective is to maximize the number of served requests while considering the associated constraints. Equation (5) defines the objective which is the maximization of number of requests. Equation (6) represents the compute constraint, where c_{rv} represents the compute resource required by VNF type v of request r. Similarly, (7) represents the storage constraint, where d_{rv} represents the storage resource required by VNF type v of request r. Equation (8) denotes that a request is either fully admitted, i.e., $x_r = 1$, or rejected, i.e., $x_r = 0$.

This VNF placement scenario can handle more complex service requests that require multiple VNFs. Despite that, the VNF placement scenario encounters certain limitations, such as increased complexity due to multiple VNFs per request. This leads to a longer computation time and challenges in finding optimal solutions as the number of VNFs and requests increases. The presence of multiple VNFs per request can lead to higher competition for limited resources within a single infrastructure, potentially leading to the denial of some requests despite the availability of overall capacity [10]. Similar to Scenario 1 (refer to Sect. 5), the static nature of the resource requirements does not account for dynamic changes in demand, leading to potential inefficiencies. In order to overcome this, we can utilize multiple infrastructures with shared compute and storage, as discussed in the next scenarios [9].

7 Scenario 3

Assumptions:

- Multiple infrastructures with specific computation and storage capabilities
- Multiple VNFs associated per request
- All VNFs associated with a request must be placed at one place
- VNFs are not shared among different service requests

Figure 6 illustrates Scenario 3 with the service requests $request1$, $request3$, and $request5$, fulfilled by VNFs of types VNF1, VNF2, and VNF3 of infrastructure A and infrastructure B. Infrastructure A has a total capacity of computation and storage resources as 6 and 35, respectively, and infrastructure B has a total capacity

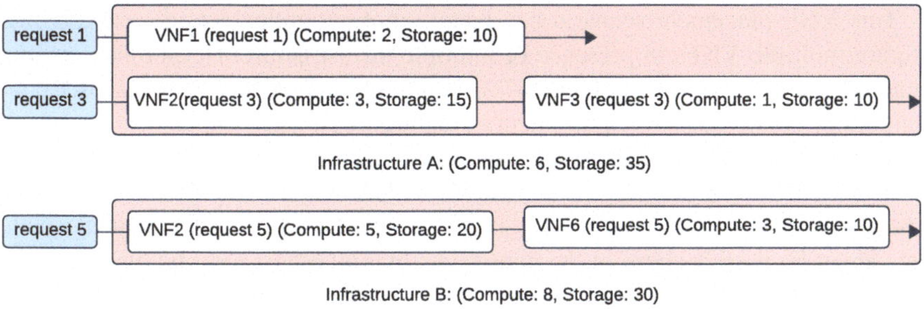

Fig. 6 An example of VNF placement with different requests as per Scenario 3

of computation and storage resources as 8 and 30, respectively. We are also given a set of requests denoted as R, each with multiple VNF requirement. As, shown in Fig. 6, we have three requests with different VNFs requirements. The VNFs associated with request $request_1$ and $request_3$ are placed in Infrastructure A. The VNFs associated with request $request_5$ is placed in infrastructure B. Thus, multiple infrastructure helps in accommodating more number of requests. In this optimization problem, we consider the computation and storage constraints, with the decision variable $x_r^{[k]}, \forall r \in R$ for VNF placement and resources. We also consider the k infrastructure for resource utilization. Mathematically,

$$\text{Maximize} \quad \sum_{r \in R} \sum_{k \in P'} x_r^{[k]} \qquad \rightarrow \text{objective} \tag{9}$$

$$\text{Subject to} \quad \sum_{r \in R} \sum_{v \in V} c_{rv}\, x_r^{[k]} \leq C^{[k]}, \quad \forall k \in P', \qquad \rightarrow \text{computation constraint} \tag{10}$$

$$\sum_{r \in R} \sum_{v \in V} d_{rv}\, x_r^{[k]} \leq D^{[k]}, \quad \forall k \in P', \qquad \rightarrow \text{storage constraint} \tag{11}$$

$$x_r^{[k]} \in \{0, 1\}. \qquad \rightarrow \text{binary decision variable} \tag{12}$$

Our objective is to maximize the number of served requests while considering the associated constraints. Equation (9) defines the objective which is the maximization of served requests. Equation (10) represents the computation constraint, where c_{rv} represents the compute resource required by VNF type v of request r, and $C^{[k]}$ represents the computation limit of an infrastructure k. Similarly, (11) represents the storage constraint, where d_{rv} represents the storage resource required by VNF type v of request r, and $D^{[k]}$ represents the computation limit of an infrastructure k. Equation (12) denotes that a request is either fully admitted, i.e., $x_r = 1$, or rejected, i.e., $x_r = 0$.

This VNF placement scenario can handle more complex service requests that require multiple VNFs in presence of multiple infrastructure. Despite its potential benefits, this optimization problem faces certain limitations, including resource concentration. This is due to the placement of required VNFs at a single location, which could potentially overload a specific infrastructure. Hence, by that time, other infrastructures will have an underutilization problem. This scenario might lead to situations where resources with compute and storage constraints at each location are available but cannot be used because of the constraints that all VNFs must be placed in one place, resulting in suboptimal resource utilization. For this scenario, the solution is to use load balancers across infrastructures over the same network area. We can also use advanced scheduling algorithms to enhance scalability and ensure efficient resource utilization [1, 9].

8 Scenario 4

Assumptions:

- Multiple infrastructure with compute capacity and storage
- Multiple VNFs associated per request
- All VNFs associated with a request must be placed at one place
- Requests need to be routed to the selected infrastructure
- VNFs are not shared among different service requests

Figure 7 represents a network model of VNF placement and routing. In this network, we consist of multiple nodes N_1, N_2, N_3, and N_4. The substrate nodes N_3 and N_4 connect infrastructure A and infrastructure B, respectively to the network. A source s generates requests, which can either flow via path A or path B to reach the

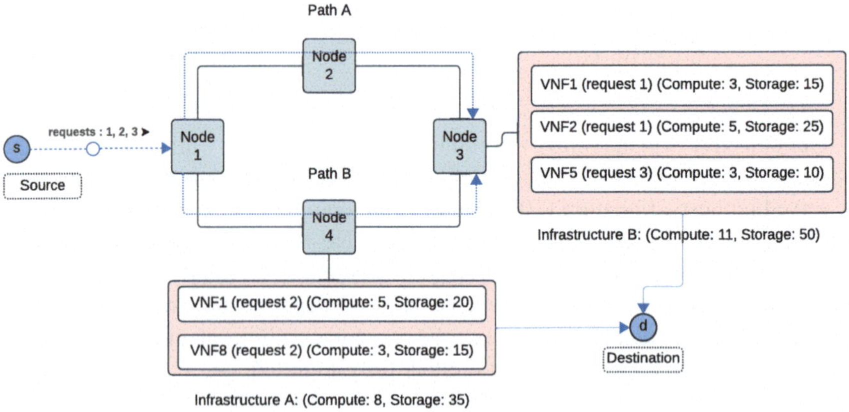

Fig. 7 An example of VNF placement with different requests as per Scenario 4

destination d. We consider infrastructure A has a total capacity of computation and storage resources as 8 and 35, respectively. Infrastructure B has a total capacity of computation and storage resources as 11 and 50, respectively. We are also given a set of requests denoted as R, each with multiple VNF requirement. In this optimization problem, we consider the computation, storage, bandwidth, and routing constraints, with the decision variables $x_r^{[k]}$ and $y_r^{[j,i]}$ for VNF placement resources and for edge routing, respectively. Mathematically,

$$\text{Maximize} \quad \sum_{r\in R}\sum_{k\in P'} x_r^{[k]} \qquad \rightarrow \text{objective} \tag{13}$$

$$\text{Subject to} \quad \sum_{r\in R}\sum_{v\in V} c_{rv}\, x_r^{[k]} \le C^{[k]}, \forall k \in P', \qquad \rightarrow \text{computation constraint} \tag{14}$$

$$\sum_{r\in R}\sum_{v\in V} d_{rv}\, x_r^{[k]} \le D^{[k]}, \forall k \in P', \qquad \rightarrow \text{storage constraint} \tag{15}$$

$$\sum_{k\in P'} x_r^{[k]} \le 1, \forall r \in R, \qquad \rightarrow \text{at most one admission} \tag{16}$$

$$x_r^{[k]} \in \{0,1\}, \forall r \in R, \forall k \in P', \qquad \rightarrow \text{binary decision variable} \tag{17}$$

$$\sum_{r\in R} b_r\, y_r^{[i,j]} \le B_{[i,j]}, \forall [i,j] \in A, \forall b_r \in B, \qquad \rightarrow \text{link bandwidth (B) constraint} \tag{18}$$

$$y_r^{[i,j]} \in \{0,1\}, \forall r \in R, \forall [i,j] \in A. \qquad \rightarrow \text{binary decision variable} \tag{19}$$

$$\sum_{j\in P} y_r^{[i,j]} - \sum_{j\in P} y_r^{[j,i]} = \begin{cases} \sum_{k\in P'} x_r^{[k]} & \text{if } i = s_r \in P, \\ -x_r^{[k]} & \text{if } i \in P' \setminus \{s_r\}, \\ 0 & \text{otherwise} \end{cases} \qquad \rightarrow \text{routing constraint} \tag{20}$$

Our objective is to maximize the number of served requests and maintain optimal traffic route while considering the associated constraints. We are also considering the k infrastructure for resource utilization. Equation (13) defines the objective which is the maximization of served requests. Equation (14) represents the computation constraint, where c_{rv} represents the compute resource required by VNF type v of request r, and $C^{[k]}$ represents the computation limit of an infrastructure k. Similarly, (15) represents the storage constraint, where d_{rv} represents the storage resource required by VNF type v of request r, and $D^{[k]}$ represents the storage limit of an infrastructure k. Equation (16) ensures that each resource r is allocated to at most one of the possible configurations k in the set $P\prime$. This can be interpreted as a constraint that enforces exclusive selection, meaning that each resource can only be assigned to one configuration at a time. This helps in avoiding over-commitment of resources across multiple configurations, maintaining a clear and efficient allocation.

Equation (17) denotes that a request is either fully admitted, i.e., $x_r^{[k]} = 1$, or rejected, i.e., $x_r^{[k]} = 0$. Equation (18) represents the bandwidth constraint, where b_r represents the bandwidth resource and $B_{[i,j]}$ represents the bandwidth capacity of link (i, j), where $(i, j) \in A$. Equation (19) denotes that a request is either fully routed, i.e., $y_r^{[i,j]} = 1$, or rejected, i.e., $y_r^{[i,j]} = 0$. Equation (20) represents the network's routing constraint (the flow conservation principle of flow requests). $\sum_{j \in P} y_r^{[i,j]}$ represents the total outgoing flow of request r from node i to all other nodes j in the set of infrastructure P. Similarly, $\sum_{j \in P} y_r^{[j,i]}$ represents the total incoming flow of requests r to node i from all other nodes j in set P. Source node $i = s_r$ represents if node i is the source node s_r of request r, then the net flow out of the source node should be equal to the total number of requests originating from this node, i.e., $\sum_{k \in P'} x_r^{[k]}$. For the intermediate node i, the net flow should be equal to the negative of the requests at that node, implying that these nodes do not generate new requests but only forward them, i.e., $-x_r^{[k]}$. For other nodes, the net flow should be zero, indicating that these nodes neither generate nor consume the flow of requests, i.e., 0.

This method yields the optimized routing. However, there can still be some challenges, such as network and bandwidth congestion, as multiple requests routed via the same network path to a particular infrastructure can violate assumed bandwidth, resulting in network congestion. Furthermore, the interaction between VNF placement and routing decisions necessitates sophisticated coordination for effective management. This extra coordination required effort, resulting in reduced system efficiency. Placing all the VNFs for a request at a single location can result in suboptimal resource utilization. Additionally, the need to route requests to these locations might result in non-optimal paths, further reducing efficiency. In order to improve network optimization, we can share the network infrastructure [8, 12, 15].

9 Scenario 5

Assumptions:

- Multiple infrastructure with compute capacity and storage
- Multiple VNFs associated per request
- All the VNFs associated with each request must be placed at multiple places, and requests need to be routed through these VNFs one by one to the selected infrastructure, creating a chain of VNFs called service function chains (SFCs)
- VNFs are not shared among different service requests.

Figure 8 represents a network consisting of multiple nodes N_1, N_2, N_3, and N_4. The nodes N_3 and N_4 serve as substrate nodes, linking infrastructure A and infrastructure B to the network. A source s generates requests, which can either flow via path A or path B to reach the destination d. We consider infrastructure A has a total capacity of computation and storage resources as 8 and 35, respectively, and infrastructure B has a total capacity of computation and storage resources as 11 and 50, respectively.

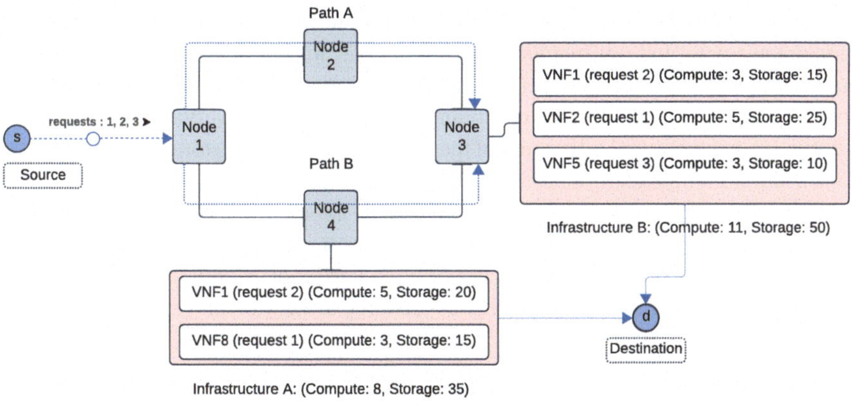

Fig. 8 An example of VNF placement with different requests as per Scenario 5

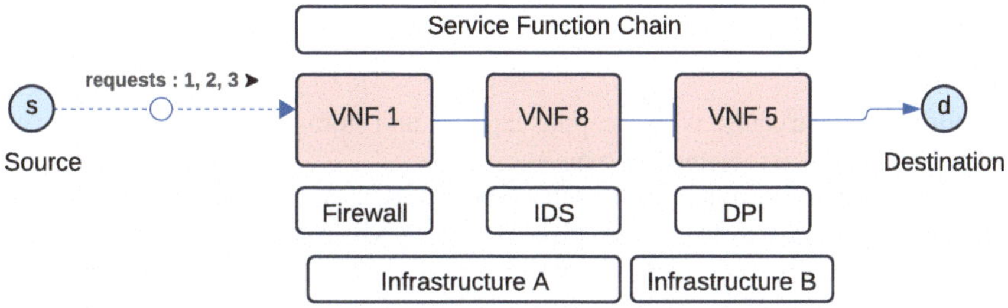

Fig. 9 An example of SFCs with different requests as per Scenario 5

We are also given a set of requests denoted as R, each with a VNF requirement. Our objective is to maximize the number of served requests and maintain optimal traffic path while considering the associated constraints. Figure 9 illustrates a chain of VNFs followed to fulfill a service request. This diagram considers the routing of data requests from source s to destination d through various VNFs, including firewalls, IDS, and DPI. These VNFs share the same infrastructure, including firewalls and IDS.

This concept demonstrates the possibility of achieving improved resource utilization, and optimized performance. This logic favors partially and fully ordered SFCs for more strategic placement and routing decisions. Placing VNFs at multiple locations can enhance scalability, allowing for dynamic allocation and adjustment of resources based on demand and availability. Some limitations may arise from managing multiple infrastructures, routing through VNFs, and ensuring the correct sequence of VNFs in an SFC, all of which significantly increase the complexity of the problem. The network becomes more challenging due to the need to manage additional constraints related to ordering, placement, and routing. Maintaining the order of SFCs and ensuring seamless interaction between VNFs across different infrastructures can introduce coordination complexity. Routing through multiple VNFs can lead to network congestion. To overcome these problems, we can develop and implement integrated optimization algorithms that jointly address VNF placement and routing, balance the load across multiple infrastructures, and minimize latency and congestion. Dynamic resource management can handle varying demands efficiently, ensuring optimal utilization of the following resources: storage, compute, and bandwidth. Machine learning models, through their predictive analytics, can forecast traffic patterns and proactively manage resource allocation and routing. Predictive analysis will prevent congestion and improve overall system performance. Allowing for flexible SFC strategies, such as the full and partial distribution of VNFs within an SFC, where it is feasible, will enhance resource utilization and reduce latency [3, 8, 10].

10 Scenario 6

Assumptions:

- Multiple infrastructure with compute capacity and storage
- Multiple VNFs associated per request
- All the VNFs associated with each request must be placed at multiple places, and requests need to be routed through these VNFs one by one to the selected infrastructure, creating a chain of VNFs called service function chains (SFCs)
- VNFs are shared among different service requests.

The diagrammatic model of routing and VNF placement that depicts the data path to be followed and directs data via chain of VNFs of multiple infrastructures to reach its destination is mentioned in Fig. 10.

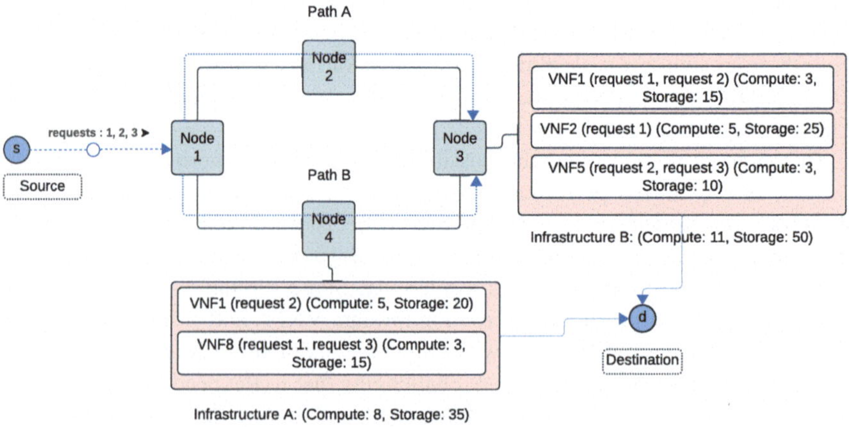

Fig. 10 An example of VNF placement with different requests as per Scenario 6

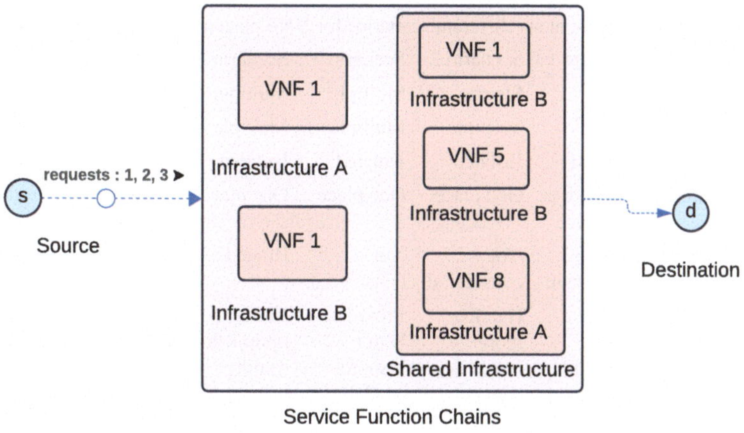

Fig. 11 SFC including shared resources

The network consists of multiple nodes N_1, N_2, N_3, and N_4. The nodes N_3 and N_4 serve as substrate nodes, linking infrastructure A and infrastructure B to the network. A source s generates requests, which can either flow via path A or path B to reach the destination d. We consider infrastructure A has a total capacity of computation and storage resources as 8 and 35, respectively, and infrastructure B has a total capacity of computation and storage resources as 11 and 50, respectively. We are also given a set of requests denoted as R, each with a VNF requirement. Our objective is to maximize the number of served requests and maintain optimal traffic path while considering the associated constraints. Figure 11 depicts the SFC of multiple infrastructures to be followed, and a shared chain can also be used for serving a demand or request. In this diagrammatic model of SFCs, VNF_1 and VNF_5 of Infrastructure A are shared and VNF_8 of Infrastructure A is also shared among the requests $request1$, $request2$, and $request3$ as illustrated clearly in Fig. 10.

This scenario can improve resource efficiency, cost-effectiveness, scalability, and load balancing, i.e., properly managed shared VNFs can facilitate better load balancing across requests, improving overall system performance and reliability. Still, there can be some limitations, such as shared resource contention and performance degradation, i.e., without proper management, shared VNFs can experience performance degradation, especially during peak times when multiple requests demand high resource utilization. Also, implementing priority handling mechanisms can introduce complexity to the system. It is crucial to develop and manage the priority methods carefully. We must serve high-priority requests to avoid conflicts and delays. For example, consider a VNF with specific compute and storage capacities, denoted as $VNF_X = (4, 20)$. Let these values represent the peak traffic capacities. If two routers, R_1 and R_2, both use VNF_X, the utilization of R_1 can affect R_2, and vice versa. To address this issue, a Linux tool such as the TC command can be used to set the priority of routers for resource utilization. Also, we can overcome network issues

Table 1 Comparison table of six different scenarios for VNF placement and request routing

Parameter	Scenario 1	Scenario 2	Scenario 3	Scenario 4	Scenario 5	Scenario 6
Infrastructure	Single	Single	Multiple	Multiple	Multiple	Multiple
VNF	Single	Multiple	Multiple	Multiple	Multiple	Multiple
VNF shared	Isolated	Isolated	Isolated	Isolated	Isolated	Shared
VNF placement strategy	All VNF at one place	One place	One place	One place	Multiple places	Multiple places
Request routing	Not considered	Not considered	Not considered	Routed	Routed	Routed
Advantages	Simple implementation	Handles more complex service requests	Provides better resource availability	Yields optimized routing	Improved resource utilization, optimized latency, and optimized performance	Scalable and reliable network system
Limitations	Suboptimal placement due to single VNF	Longer computation time and more complexities	Suboptimal resource utilization	Same network path leads to congestion	Increases complexity in network	Shared resource contention
Solution	Multiple VNFs and shared resources	Multiple infrastructures with shared compute and storage	Load balancers across infrastructures	Shared network infrastructure	Use of flexible SFC strategies	Use of Linux tools and network slicing

by the concept of network slicing [3, 4, 16]. Comparison of all different scenarios for VNF placement and request routing is given in Table 1.

11 Summary

In the chapter, we discussed the limitations of traditional hardware-based network architectures in handling modern technology's heterogeneous demands, as well as the solutions offered by SDN and NFV. The chapter introduces the SDN-NFV architecture, highlighting the interaction between physical and virtual resources. A significant focus is on VNF placement and routing within NFV-enabled networks. VNF placement involves strategically placing VNFs to optimize resource utilization, service quality, and operational costs. To balance load and minimize latency, request routing directs service requests to appropriate VNF instances. The chapter provides six different scenarios that gradually look at different VNF placement and routing strategies. The scenarios range from simple single-infrastructure setups to complex multi-infrastructure environments, and each has its own optimization goals and constraints. The optimization problems involve constraints related to computation, storage, and bandwidth, aiming to maximize the number of service requests handled. Each scenario addresses different levels of complexity and resource management, with specific mathematical models and constraints tailored to the setup. The study finds that combining VNF placement and routing makes the network more flexible, efficient, and scalable. However, combining VNF placement and routing complicates real-time traffic analysis, constant resource monitoring, and resource balancing. As a result, the use of advanced algorithms and flexible strategies for optimal performance, such as shared resources and network slicing, are required to address issues effectively.

References

1. Sherif Abdelwahab, Bechir Hamdaoui, Mohsen Guizani, and Taieb Znati. Network function virtualization in 5G. *IEEE Communications Magazine*, 54:84–91, 2016.
2. Bernardetta Addis, Dallal Belabed, Mathieu Bouet, and Stefano Secci. Virtual network functions placement and routing optimization. In *IEEE International Conference on Cloud Networking (CloudNet)*, pages 171–177, 2015.
3. Samuel M. A. Araújo, Fernanda S. H. de Souza, and Geraldo R. Mateus. A composition selection mechanism for chaining and placement of virtual network functions. In *International Conference on Network and Service Management (CNSM)*, pages 1–5, 2019.
4. Wissal Attaoui, Essaid Sabir, Halima Elbiaze, and Mohsen Guizani. VNF and CNF placement in 5G: Recent advances and future trends. *IEEE Transactions on Network and Service Management*, 20:4698–4733, 2023.
5. Samaresh Bera, Sudip Misra, and Athanasios Vasilakos. Software-defined networking for internet of things: A survey. *IEEE Internet of Things Journal*, 2017.
6. Christos Bouras, Anastasia Kollia, and Andreas Papazois. SDN & NFV in 5G: Advancements and challenges. In *IEEE Conference on Innovations in Clouds, Internet and Networks (ICIN)*, pages 107–111, 2017.
7. ETSI. Network functions virtualisation (NFV); management and or- chestration. Technical report, ETSI, 2014.
8. Ivan Farris, Tarik Taleb, Yacine Khettab, and Jaeseung Song. A survey on emerging SDN and NFV security mechanisms for IoT systems. *IEEE Communications Surveys and Tutorials*, 21:812–837, 2019.
9. Juliver Gil Herrera and Juan Felipe Botero. Resource allocation in NFV: A comprehensive survey. *IEEE Transactions on Network and Service Management*, 13:518–532, 2016.
10. Morteza Golkarifard, Carla Fabiana Chiasserini, Francesco Malandrino, and Ali Movaghar. Dynamic VNF placement, resource allocation and traffic routing in 5G. *Computer Networks*, 188:107–830, 2021.
11. Fei Hu, Qi Hao, and Ke Bao. A survey on software-defined network and OpenFlow: From concept to implementation. *IEEE Communications Surveys & Tutorials*, 16:2181–2206, 2014.
12. Iqbal Jovan, Kashif Sharif, Fan Li, Zohaib Latif, Md Monjurul Karim, Sujit Biswas, Yu Wang, and Boubakr Nour. A survey of network virtualization techniques for internet of things using SDN and NFV. *ACM Computing Surveys*, 53:1–40, 2020.

13. Ola Salman, Imad H. Elhajj, Ayman Kayssi, and Ali Chehab. SDN controllers: A comparative study. In *2016 18th Mediterranean Electrotechnical Conference (MELECON)*, pages 1–6, 2016.
14. Liran Sidki, Yehuda Ben-Shimol, and Akiva Sadovski. Fault tolerant mechanisms for SDN controllers. In *IEEE Conference on Network Function Virtualization and Software Defined Networks (NFV-SDN)*, pages 173–178, 2016.
15. Shaoyang Wang, Chau Yuen, Wei Ni, Yong Liang Guan, and Tiejun Lv. Multiagent deep reinforcement learning for cost- and delay-sensitive virtual network function placement and routing. *IEEE Transactions on Communications*, 70:5208–5224, 2022.
16. Xue Yu, Ran Wang, Jie Hao, Qiang Wu, Changyan Yi, Ping Wang, and Dusit Niyato. Priority-aware deployment of autoscaling service function chains based on deep reinforcement learning. *IEEE Transactions on Cognitive Communications and Networking*, pages 1–1, 2024.
17. Manare Zerifi, Abdellatif Ezzouhairi, and Abdelhak Boulaalam. Overview on SDN and NFV based architectures for IoT environments: Challenges and solutions. In *International Conference on Intelligent Computing in Data Sciences (ICDS)*, pages 1–5, 2020.

Applications/Use-Cases/Case Studies

Edge-Enabled 6G Networking: Transforming IoT for a Hyperconnected Future

Nurzaman Ahmed, Tamoghna Ojha, Md. Muzakkir Hussain, and Samaresh Bera

1 Introduction

The rapid digital transformation of society is giving rise to an unprecedented level of hyperconnectivity, driven by advancements in wireless communication technologies and the expanding reach of the Internet of Things (IoT) [1, 2]. As we transition from 5G to 6G, the focus is shifting from human-centric communication to machine-centric networks capable of supporting billions of interconnected devices. Hyperconnectivity, defined by the seamless, real-time integration of IoT devices and systems across diverse domains such as ground, air, space, and underwater, underpins the vision of 6G [3]. This interconnected framework enables a unified IoT ecosystem, where autonomous vehicles on the ground can communicate with drones in the air, satellites in space, and underwater sensors in marine environments. Such a network fosters innovations across applications ranging from smart agriculture and industrial automation to Earth observation and marine exploration. However,

N. Ahmed (✉)
Donald Danforth Plant Science Center, Saint Louis, MO, USA
e-mail: nahmed@danforthcenter.org

T. Ojha
Department of Mathematics and Computing, Indian Institute of Technology (ISM) Dhanbad, Dhanbad, India
e-mail: tamoghnaojha@iitism.ac.in

Md. M. Hussain
Department of Computer Science and Engineering, SRM University AP, Kuragallu, India
e-mail: muzakkirhussain.m@srmap.edu.in

S. Bera
Department of Computer Science and Engineering, Indian Institute of Technology Jammu, Jammu, India
e-mail: samaresh.bera@iitjammu.ac.in

T. Ojha et al. (eds.), *Edge-Enabled 6G Networking*,
https://doi.org/10.1007/978-3-032-19042-0_11

achieving this vision is fraught with challenges. Massive data generation, ultra-low latency requirements, and the need for energy-efficient, sustainable systems push the boundaries of existing wireless technologies.

The IoT is poised to redefine connectivity across these diverse domains, leveraging 6G's transformative capabilities. Ground-based IoT applications, including smart agriculture, healthcare, industrial IoT (IIoT), and environmental monitoring, enhance efficiency and sustainability in critical sectors. In the air, drones, aviation systems, and airborne Internet services revolutionize logistics, surveillance, and connectivity. IoT applications extend even further, reaching space and underwater environments. As shown in Fig. 1, space-based IoT supports Earth observation, space exploration, and IoT-enabled space stations, driving advancements in global navigation and space-based weather monitoring. Underwater IoT facilitates marine research, aquaculture, deep-sea exploration, and subsea defense operations. These applications demonstrate how 6G's hyperconnectivity ensures seamless IoT integration across these domains, enabling a unified and intelligent network while addressing challenges unique to each environment.

The advent of 6G aims to address these gaps through novel architectures and the integration of edge computing, paving the way for IoT ecosystems that are more intelligent, responsive, and scalable. It envisions a paradigm shift in connectivity, introducing transformative technologies such as terahertz communication, intelligent reflective surfaces, and AI-driven network management [4]. These advancements address the unique requirements of IoT, including massive machine-type communication (mMTC), ultra-low latency, and high reliability, enabling robust support for applications like immersive extended reality, high-fidelity mobile holograms, and digital twins. IoT devices are evolving from passive network entities to active participants in a decentralized, intelligent ecosystem. In this new paradigm, the integration of edge computing enables localized data processing, reducing dependency on cen-

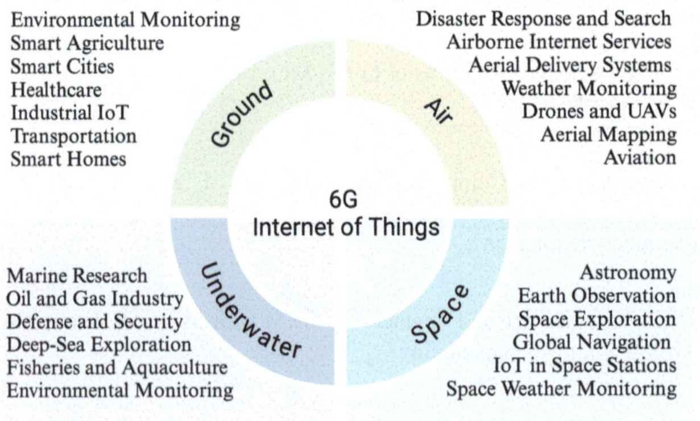

Fig. 1 Future 6G-IoT applications across ground, air, space, and underwater domains

tralized cloud servers and ensuring real-time responsiveness for latency-sensitive applications [5]. AI-driven optimization at every layer of the network stack further enhances scalability, sustainability, and performance, making 6G networks the backbone of a hyperconnected IoT world.

While most recent 6G-related surveys have primarily focused on foundational technologies such as terahertz communication, reconfigurable intelligent surfaces, and AI for network management, this chapter takes a distinct approach. Specifically, the key contributions of this chapter are:

- We emphasize the key challenges associated with 6G architectures, particularly in the context of hyperconnectivity IoT applications, addressing device heterogeneity, interoperability, privacy, security, and energy consumption.
- We analyze the existing state of 6G architectures, bridging the gap between conceptual frameworks and real-world implementation for IoT-driven hyperconnectivity across ground, air, space, and underwater domains.

This comprehensive focus highlights both the current capabilities and the future potential of edge-enabled 6G networking to meet the hyperconnectivity demands of IoT.

2 Feasible Network Architecture for 6G and Edge-Enabled IoT

To realize seamless IoT integration across ground, air, space, and underwater domains, 6G requires a robust network architecture supported by cutting-edge technologies and innovative frameworks.

2.1 Key Enabling Technologies for 6G IoT

To meet the demands of hyperconnectivity and massive IoT applications, 6G networks are underpinned by transformative enabling technologies. Figure 2 shows the key enabling technologies for 6G IoT. The Terahertz (THz) communication offers ultra-high bandwidth and low latency, enabling unprecedented data transfer speeds critical for real-time applications like autonomous vehicles, immersive extended reality, and augmented reality [6]. Intelligent Reflective Surfaces (IRS) are another pivotal technology, allowing dynamic manipulation of electromagnetic waves to optimize signal strength and coverage, especially in dense urban environments and remote regions. Massive URLLC ensures reliable and low-latency connectivity, addressing mission-critical IoT use cases like autonomous driving and telemedicine [7]. The integration of space-air-ground-underwater communication systems facilitates global coverage, supporting seamless connectivity across diverse

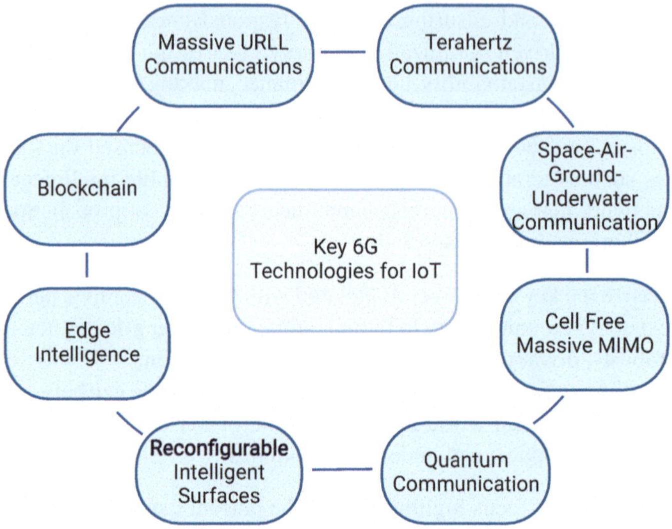

Fig. 2 The key enabling technologies of 6G Internet of Things

terrains and environments. Edge intelligence extends AI capabilities to the network edge, enabling distributed data processing and decision-making, which are essential for latency-sensitive IoT applications. Blockchain technology ensures secure, decentralized data management, providing robust solutions for privacy and trust in 6G IoT ecosystems [8]. Together, these technologies create a unified framework capable of addressing the stringent requirements of hyperconnectivity in future IoT systems. The key features and use cases of these technologies are summarized in Table 1.

Moreover, AI-driven network optimization enhances resource allocation and network management by leveraging predictive analytics and autonomous decision-making. This capability ensures seamless operation in dynamic IoT environments. Quantum communication introduces unparalleled security through quantum key distribution, addressing privacy challenges in hyperconnected ecosystems. Reconfigurable optical networks provide flexible and adaptive high-capacity optical links, critical for handling the massive data backhaul required by 6G applications. Meanwhile, cell-free massive MIMO architectures leverage distributed antenna systems to eliminate inter-cell interference, ensuring high spatial resolution and seamless connectivity. Energy harvesting networks promote sustainability by powering IoT devices through ambient energy sources, reducing dependency on conventional batteries. Lastly, Integrated Sensing and Communication (ISAC) combines data sensing and communication into a unified infrastructure, optimizing resource utilization and reducing costs [16].

Table 1 Key enabling technologies for 6G IoT

Technology	Key features	Use cases in 6G IoT
Terahertz communication [6]	Ultra-high bandwidth, low latency	Real-time applications, high-speed data transfer, autonomous vehicles, augmented reality
Intelligent Reflective Surfaces (IRS) [9]	Wave manipulation, enhanced signal coverage	Smart urban environments, signal optimization, coverage in remote regions
Massive URLLC [10]	Ultra-reliable, low-latency communications	Telemedicine, autonomous driving, industrial automation
Space-air-ground-underwater communications [11, 12]	Global coverage, seamless integration	Disaster recovery, global IoT connectivity, maritime and aerospace communications
Edge intelligence [13]	AI at the edge, reduced latency, localized decision-making	Smart factories, healthcare IoT, real-time analytics
Blockchain [8]	Decentralized, secure, immutable	Data security, IoT trust management, decentralized device authentication
Quantum communication [14]	High-security, quantum key distribution	Secure communications, defense IoT, financial data protection
Cell-free massive MIMO [15]	Distributed antenna arrays, seamless connectivity	Dense urban IoT, industrial IoT, high spatial resolution applications

2.2 *Enabling Network Architectures for 6G IoT*

The integration of these enabling technologies necessitates transformative changes in network architectures, which can be categorized into communication-based and computing-based paradigms.

2.2.1 Communication-Based Architectures

Communication-based network architectures are central to enabling hyperconnectivity in 6G IoT systems across diverse domains. These architectures include Cell-Free Massive MIMO, which utilizes distributed antenna systems to eliminate inter-cell interference, providing seamless connectivity in dense urban areas and industrial IoT deployments. Space-Air-Ground-Underwater Integration bridges communication gaps between terrestrial, aerial, space, and underwater networks, ensuring global IoT coverage and supporting critical applications like disaster recovery and environmental monitoring. Intelligent Reflective Surfaces (IRS) dynamically optimize signal propagation, enhancing coverage and capacity in challenging environments

Table 2 Suitability of communication-based architectures for hyperconnectivity across domains

Architecture	Ground	Air	Space	Underwater
Cell-free massive MIMO	High-density urban IoT, industrial IoT	UAV and aerial IoT integration	Limited	Limited
Space-air-ground-underwater integration	Urban-rural IoT bridging	UAV and aerial IoT integration	Global satellite IoT	Maritime IoT, disaster recovery
Intelligent Reflective Surfaces (IRS)	Urban smart cities, indoor environments	UAV communication optimization	Limited	Limited
Quantum communication networks	Secure IoT data transmission in smart cities	Secure UAV-to-ground communication	Satellite communication security	Subsea IoT security
Reconfigurable optical networks	Scalable backhaul for dense IoT deployments	High-throughput UAV backhaul	Optical links for satellites	Limited
Integrated Sensing and Communication (ISAC)	Autonomous vehicles, environmental monitoring	Real-time sensing for UAV applications	Earth observation, satellite sensing	Oceanographic sensing

such as urban landscapes and indoor spaces. To address the growing need for secure communication, Quantum Communication Networks leverage quantum cryptography to ensure ultra-secure data transmission, particularly in sensitive applications like defense and finance. Additionally, Reconfigurable Optical Networks offer high-capacity backhaul solutions that adapt dynamically to data demands, making them vital for urban and rural IoT scalability. Lastly, Integrated Sensing and Communication (ISAC) reduces redundancy by combining sensing and communication functions, supporting resource-efficient applications like autonomous vehicles and large-scale environmental monitoring. The suitability of these architectures for hyperconnectivity across ground, air, space, and underwater domains is summarized in Table 2.

2.2.2 Computing-Based Architectures

Computing-based architectures are critical for enabling hyperconnectivity in 6G IoT by addressing the computational demands of diverse applications across ground, air, space, and underwater domains. Edge Computing processes data closer to the source, reducing latency and bandwidth usage, making it indispensable for real-time applications such as industrial automation and telemedicine. Complementing this, Split Computing distributes tasks between IoT devices and edge/cloud servers to optimize resource utilization and energy efficiency, particularly for resource-intensive AI inference tasks. Federated Learning enhances privacy and accelerates AI model training by enabling collaborative learning across distributed IoT devices without sharing raw data, ensuring compliance with privacy regulations in sectors like healthcare and finance.

For secure and transparent data management, Blockchain-Based Computing establishes decentralized infrastructures that foster trust and authentication in IoT ecosystems, essential for supply chain management and decentralized device interactions. Additionally, AI-Driven Network Optimization leverages predictive analytics to dynamically allocate network resources, enhancing operational efficiency in hyperconnected environments. Finally, Energy Harvesting Systems provide sustainable solutions by powering IoT devices through energy harvesting techniques, reducing reliance on traditional power sources and enabling deployments in remote or off-grid locations. Table 3 highlights the suitability of these architectures for hyperconnectivity across various domains.

Table 3 Suitability of computing-based architectures for hyperconnectivity across domains

Architecture	Ground	Air	Space	Underwater
Edge computing	Industrial IoT, healthcare IoT	Onboard UAV processing for real-time analytics	Spacecraft data pre-processing	Real-time underwater sensor analytics
Split computing	AI inference for smart cities	UAV and aerial IoT optimization	Task distribution between satellites and ground stations	Data compression and transmission in underwater IoT
Federated learning	Privacy-preserving healthcare AI	UAV swarm coordination	Collaborative satellite AI models	Distributed learning in oceanographic research
Blockchain-based computing	Supply chain management, IoT authentication	UAV flight log security	Satellite-to-ground transaction integrity	Decentralized subsea IoT security
AI-driven network optimization	Smart city traffic management	UAV network resource optimization	Satellite resource allocation	Subsea communication optimization
Energy harvesting systems	Renewable-powered IoT for rural areas	Solar-powered UAV systems	Space-based solar energy collection	Ocean wave energy for subsea IoT

3 Hyperconnectivity Challenges and Requirements in IoT

The proliferation of the IoT has ushered in an era of hyperconnectivity, presenting multifaceted challenges that must be addressed to fully harness its potential (Table 4).

3.1 Scalability and Device Density

The exponential increase in IoT devices intensifies the complexity of network resource management. Traditional networks are often ill-equipped to handle the concurrent data transmissions from billions of devices. To mitigate this, 6G networks are anticipated to implement innovations such as massive machine-type communication (mMTC) and resource-efficient protocols. Techniques like network slicing and dynamic spectrum allocation are pivotal for the dynamic distribution of resources based on real-time demand [17]. Moreover, channel access mechanisms like Non-Orthogonal Multiple Access (NOMA) have demonstrated suitability for massive IoT access. Enhanced techniques such as LoCoNOMA [18] further improve its efficiency by enabling grant-free resource allocation, effectively addressing the growing scalability demands in massive machine-type communication (MTC). The integration of space-air-ground-underwater networks, augmented by edge computing, has been proposed to facilitate massive IoT, offering a holistic solution to scalability challenges. However, scalability remains a significant challenge in different domains:

Ground IoT: Dense urban environments and smart cities face high device density and interference, making resource allocation and real-time data management challenging. Advancements in machine learning algorithms for predictive resource allocation are essential to enhance scalability and efficiency. Additionally, the development of adaptive network slicing techniques that can respond dynamically to IoT traffic is crucial for managing urban IoT infrastructures effectively.

Air IoT: UAV networks require efficient spectrum sharing and collision-free communication, especially as the number of drones increases for logistics, surveillance, and monitoring. Future research should focus on designing real-time interference mitigation algorithms and decentralized spectrum management techniques to support scalable UAV operations.

Space IoT: Satellite constellations handling massive IoT devices must address limited spectrum availability and efficient routing between satellites and ground stations. Techniques such as AI-driven satellite routing and dynamic frequency allocation are critical to optimizing resource usage and managing scalability in space-based IoT networks.

Table 4 Domain-specific challenges for scalability, energy, interoperability, security, and edge computing in 6G IoT

Challenge	Ground	Air	Space	Underwater
Scalability and device density	High device density in urban areas causes congestion, requiring advanced resource allocation and real-time data management	UAVs need dynamic spectrum allocation to prevent interference in growing aerial networks	Satellite constellations face challenges in spectrum allocation and inter-satellite routing	Limited communication channels and high attenuation make scaling underwater networks challenging
Energy efficiency and sustainability	Frequent battery replacements in IoT devices highlight the need for energy harvesting and sustainable power sources	UAV operations are limited by battery life, requiring lightweight solar panels and energy-efficient communication protocols	Satellites rely on solar power, but advancements in energy storage and efficiency are needed for prolonged missions	Underwater IoT depends on innovative energy harvesting methods, such as current and thermal gradient utilization
Interoperability across heterogeneous networks	Diverse communication standards in urban IoT environments hinder seamless integration and require adaptive middleware	UAV networks need standardized protocols for integration with ground and satellite networks	Satellite-based IoT demands advanced interoperability frameworks to ensure seamless data exchange	Underwater acoustic communications face significant challenges when interfacing with terrestrial and aerial networks
Security and privacy concerns	Ground IoT systems, especially in smart cities, are vulnerable to cyberattacks, necessitating decentralized and resilient security frameworks	UAV communications are prone to eavesdropping and spoofing attacks, requiring secure communication protocols	Space-based IoT systems face risks from interception and spoofing, necessitating quantum cryptography and secure routing	Underwater IoT networks must address challenges such as jamming and secure acoustic communication
Edge computing challenges	Ground-based edge nodes have limited computational power and energy resources, impacting real-time analytics.	UAVs require lightweight onboard edge computing for latency-sensitive applications	Space-based edge nodes operate under harsh conditions and limited hardware capabilities, demanding adaptive solutions	Underwater edge nodes face severe constraints in energy availability and computational power due to aquatic environments

Underwater IoT: The deployment of numerous underwater sensors is constrained by limited communication channels and high signal attenuation. Future efforts should explore innovative underwater communication techniques, such as adaptive acoustic modulation and multi-hop networking, to improve scalability and maintain network performance in challenging underwater environments.

3.2 Energy Efficiency and Sustainability

The simultaneous operation of billions of IoT devices significantly elevates concerns regarding energy efficiency. The concept of zero-energy IoT devices, powered by energy harvesting technologies, represents a transformative step forward [19, 20]. These devices, when coupled with efficient communication protocols and hardware advancements, can achieve continuous operation, significantly reducing the environmental footprint of IoT deployments. Studies have highlighted the potential of zero-energy devices in 6G networks, underscoring their role in driving sustainable IoT solutions. We highlight the energy efficiency and sustainability challenges in different domains as below:

Ground IoT: Ground-based IoT systems, including smart cities and industrial IoT, often rely on battery-powered devices, leading to frequent replacements and increased waste. Enhancing energy harvesting technologies, such as solar and piezoelectric systems, can provide sustainable energy alternatives. Future work should explore adaptive energy management techniques to balance device energy consumption and network efficiency.

Air IoT: UAVs and other aerial IoT devices face critical energy constraints due to limited battery life, affecting prolonged operations. Integrating lightweight solar panels and advanced energy-efficient flight algorithms can extend UAV endurance. Research should also focus on optimizing communication protocols to minimize energy usage during data transmission.

Space IoT: Satellites and space-based IoT devices rely heavily on solar power, making energy storage and efficiency crucial. Future efforts should investigate advanced energy storage systems and radiation-resistant energy harvesting technologies to sustain operations in harsh space environments.

Underwater IoT: Energy efficiency is a significant challenge for underwater sensors due to the absence of solar energy and reliance on battery power. Innovative approaches, such as harvesting energy from underwater currents or thermoelectric gradients, can support long-term underwater IoT operations. Developing ultra-low-power acoustic communication protocols will further enhance sustainability in underwater networks.

3.3 *Interoperability Across Heterogeneous Networks*

Achieving seamless integration of diverse networks, encompassing various protocols, frequencies, and technologies, is imperative for hyperconnectivity. This necessitates standardized communication frameworks and intelligent gateways capable of adapting to varying network conditions [21, 22]. The convergence of blockchain, IoT, and 6G has been identified as a potential solution to interoperability challenges, offering a decentralized approach to managing heterogeneous networks. For example, Multi Glass-Wafer Stacked Technology for 3D Heterogeneously-Integrated Scalable 6G Arrays [23]. However, interoperability presents unique challenges across different domains:

Ground IoT: Ground-based IoT systems encounter significant interoperability issues due to the diversity of devices and communication protocols in smart cities and industrial IoT environments. Developing universal communication standards and adaptive middleware solutions is critical to ensure seamless integration among these heterogeneous devices.

Air IoT: UAV networks face challenges in integrating with terrestrial and satellite networks due to differing communication standards. Future work should focus on designing flexible protocols that enable seamless communication between UAVs, ground stations, and satellites.

Space IoT: Space-based IoT systems must achieve interoperability between satellites and ground networks to enable efficient data exchange. Advanced AI-based protocol adaptation mechanisms can help address the dynamic network conditions in space.

Underwater IoT: The use of acoustic communication in underwater networks poses challenges when interfacing with terrestrial and aerial networks. Future efforts should explore adaptive gateways and cross-domain protocol translation techniques to bridge these systems effectively.

3.4 *Security and Privacy Concerns*

As data becomes a central asset in IoT ecosystems, ensuring its security and privacy is paramount. 6G networks must embed trust at all levels, from the physical layer to application protocols. Techniques such as physical-layer security, decentralized identity management, and privacy-preserving data-sharing frameworks are critical in building resilient networks. For example, Field-Programmable Gate Array-Based Implementation of Zero-Trust Stream Data Encryption [24]. Security challenges, however, vary significantly across domains:

Ground IoT: Ground-based IoT systems, such as smart cities, are vulnerable to cyberattacks due to their extensive exposure to public networks. Developing robust encryption methods and implementing decentralized security frameworks, such as blockchain, can significantly enhance trust and data integrity.

Air IoT: UAV networks are susceptible to eavesdropping and spoofing attacks during communication with ground and satellite systems. Future research should prioritize lightweight cryptographic protocols and secure UAV communication frameworks to mitigate these risks.

Space IoT: Satellite-based IoT networks face unique security challenges due to their reliance on long-distance communication links. Techniques like quantum cryptography and physical-layer encryption can address the critical need for secure data transmission in space.

Underwater IoT: Underwater IoT systems are prone to jamming and interception due to the limited security options in acoustic communication. Research should focus on developing secure acoustic communication protocols and anomaly detection mechanisms to enhance privacy and data integrity.

3.5 Security and Privacy Concerns

As data becomes a central asset in IoT ecosystems, ensuring its security and privacy is paramount. 6G networks must embed trust at all levels, from the physical layer to application protocols. Techniques such as physical-layer security [25], decentralized identity management [26], privacy-preserving data-sharing [27] and zero-trust stream data encryption [24] frameworks are critical in building resilient networks. Security challenges, however, vary significantly across domains:

Ground IoT: Ground-based IoT systems, such as smart cities, are vulnerable to cyberattacks due to their extensive exposure to public networks. Developing robust encryption methods and implementing decentralized security frameworks, such as blockchain, can significantly enhance trust and data integrity.

Air IoT: UAV networks are susceptible to eavesdropping and spoofing attacks during communication with ground and satellite systems. Future research should prioritize lightweight cryptographic protocols and secure UAV communication frameworks to mitigate these risks.

Space IoT: Satellite-based IoT networks face unique security challenges due to their reliance on long-distance communication links. Techniques like quantum cryptography and physical-layer encryption can address the critical need for secure data transmission in space.

Underwater IoT: Underwater IoT systems are prone to jamming and interception due to the limited security options in acoustic communication. Research should focus on developing secure acoustic communication protocols and anomaly detection mechanisms to enhance privacy and data integrity.

3.6 Edge Computing Challenges with IoT

The integration of edge computing into IoT ecosystems introduces unique challenges that must be addressed to achieve hyperconnectivity and scalability in 6G networks. A substantial body of literature proposes various edge computing frameworks and edge intelligence techniques aimed at enhancing IoT performance and scalability [28–30]. While edge computing enables low-latency data processing and reduced bandwidth usage, its deployment across diverse domains presents a range of domain-specific challenges:

Ground IoT: Ground-based edge nodes face constraints in computational power and energy resources, limiting their ability to handle real-time data processing. Future work should explore energy-efficient edge devices and scalable frameworks to accommodate dense urban IoT environments.

Air IoT: UAVs equipped with edge computing capabilities must address limitations in onboard power and processing capacity. Research should focus on optimizing flight energy consumption and implementing lightweight edge computing algorithms to support real-time aerial data processing.

Space IoT: Space-based edge computing systems, such as those on satellites, must operate under harsh environmental conditions and limited hardware capabilities. Developing radiation-resistant hardware and adaptive computing frameworks can enhance the scalability of edge computing in space.

Underwater IoT: Underwater edge nodes face severe constraints in energy availability and communication efficiency due to the aquatic environment. Innovative energy harvesting techniques and ultra-low-power edge computing frameworks are necessary to sustain underwater IoT operations.

4 Conclusion

The advent of 6G networks promises a transformative era of hyperconnectivity, seamlessly integrating IoT systems across ground, air, space, and underwater domains. This chapter has reviewed the enabling technologies, such as terahertz communication, edge intelligence, and blockchain, alongside communication and computing-based network architectures, highlighting their role in addressing critical challenges like scalability, energy efficiency, interoperability, and security. While each domain presents unique constraints—ranging from dense urban IoT deployments to energy limitations in underwater systems—the integration of innovative solutions offers a unified framework for sustainable, scalable, and secure IoT ecosystems. By addressing these challenges, 6G IoT stands poised to revolutionize global connectivity, unlocking new possibilities across diverse applications and driving the evolution of a truly hyperconnected world.

References

1. O. Vermesan and J. Bacquet, *Cognitive Hyperconnected Digital Transformation: Internet of Things Intelligence Evolution*. River Publishers, 2017.
2. R. Prasad, D. S. Mantri, S. K. Pandey, and A. D. Mihovska, *6G Connectivity-Systems, Technologies, and Applications: Digitalization of New Technologies, 6G and Evolutio*. CRC Press, 2024.
3. R. Chataut, M. Nankya, and R. Akl, “6g networks and the ai revolution—exploring technologies, applications, and emerging challenges,” *Sensors*, vol. 24, no. 6, p. 1888, 2024.
4. N. H. Mahmood, H. Alves, O. A. López, M. Shehab, D. P. M. Osorio, and M. Latva-Aho, “Six key features of machine type communication in 6g,” in *2020 2nd 6G Wireless Summit (6G SUMMIT)*. IEEE, 2020, pp. 1–5.
5. Y. Xiao, G. Shi, Y. Li, W. Saad, and H. V. Poor, “Toward self-learning edge intelligence in 6g,” *IEEE Communications Magazine*, vol. 58, no. 12, pp. 34–40, 2020.
6. H. Chen, H. Sarieddeen, T. Ballal, H. Wymeersch, M.-S. Alouini, and T. Y. Al-Naffouri, “A tutorial on terahertz-band localization for 6g communication systems,” *IEEE Communications Surveys & Tutorials*, vol. 24, no. 3, pp. 1780–1815, 2022.
7. W. Jiang, B. Han, M. A. Habibi, and H. D. Schotten, “The road towards 6g: A comprehensive survey,” *IEEE Open Journal of the Communications Society*, vol. 2, pp. 334–366, 2021.
8. T. Hewa, G. Gür, A. Kalla, M. Ylianttila, A. Bracken, and M. Liyanage, “The role of blockchain in 6g: Challenges, opportunities and research directions,” *2020 2nd 6G Wireless Summit (6G SUMMIT)*, pp. 1–5, 2020.
9. J. Zhao, “A survey of intelligent reflecting surfaces (irss): Towards 6g wireless communication networks,” *arXiv preprint* arXiv:1907.04789, 2019.
10. M. E. Haque, F. Tariq, M. R. Khandaker, K.-K. Wong, and Y. Zhang, “A survey of scheduling in 5g urllc and outlook for emerging 6g systems,” *IEEE access*, vol. 11, pp. 34 372–34 396, 2023.
11. H. Luo, J. Wang, F. Bu, R. Ruby, K. Wu, and Z. Guo, “Recent progress of air/water cross-boundary communications for underwater sensor networks: A review,” *IEEE Sensors Journal*, vol. 22, no. 9, pp. 8360–8382, 2022.

12. A. Higuchi, E. Takeshita, D. Hisano, Y. Inoue, K. Maruta, T. Nishio, Y. Hara-Azumi, and Y. Nakayama, "Aquatic fronthaul for underwater-ground communication in 6g mobile communications," in *2022 IEEE 95th Vehicular Technology Conference:(VTC2022-Spring)*. IEEE, 2022, pp. 1–6.
13. Q. Liu, S. Wang, Z. Qi, K. Zhang, and Q. Liu, "Edge intelligence for iot services in 6g integrated terrestrial and non-terrestrial networks," *IEEE Network*, vol. 38, no. 4, pp. 80–87, 2024.
14. M. Z. Ali, A. Abohmra, M. Usman, A. Zahid, H. Heidari, M. A. Imran, and Q. H. Abbasi, "Quantum for 6g communication: A perspective," *IET Quantum Communication*, vol. 4, no. 3, pp. 112–124, 2023.
15. H. He, X. Yu, J. Zhang, S. Song, and K. B. Letaief, "Cell-free massive mimo for 6g wireless communication networks," *Journal of Communications and Information Networks*, vol. 6, no. 4, pp. 321–335, 2021.
16. F. Liu, Y. Cui, C. Masouros, J. Xu, T. X. Han, Y. C. Eldar, and S. Buzzi, "Integrated sensing and communications: Toward dual-functional wireless networks for 6g and beyond," *IEEE journal on selected areas in communications*, vol. 40, no. 6, pp. 1728–1767, 2022.
17. B. Ramesh, R. Changala, P. K. Kalangi, M. Bhavsingh *et al.*, "Optimizing 6g network slicing with the evonetslice model for dynamic resource allocation and real-time qos management," *International Research Journal of Multidisciplinary Technovation*, vol. 6, no. 3, pp. 325–340, 2024.
18. I. Oueslati, O. Habachi, J.-P. Cances, and V. Meghdadi, "Loconoma: A grant-free resource allocation for massive mtc," *Computer Networks*, p. 110859, 2024.
19. M. T. Abbas, K.-J. Grinnemo, G. Ferré, P. Laurent, S. Alfredsson, M. Rajiullah, and J. Eklund, "Towards zero-energy: Navigating the future with 6g in cellular internet of things," *Journal of Network and Computer Applications*, p. 103945, 2024.
20. O. López, R. K. Singh, D.-T. Phan-Huy, E. Katranaras, N. Mazloum, R. Jäntti, H. Khan, O. Rosabal, P. Alexias, P. Raghuwanshi *et al.*, "Zero-energy devices for 6g: Technical enablers at a glance," *arXiv preprint* arXiv:2402.09244, 2024.
21. Q. Wang, L. Liu, S. Zhang, B. Di, and F. C. M. Lau, "A heterogeneous 6g networked sensing architecture with active and passive anchors," *IEEE Transactions on Wireless Communications*, vol. 23, no. 8, pp. 9502–9517, 2024.
22. D. A. George and G. R. Murthy, *Towards Wireless Heterogeneity in 6G Networks*. CRC Press, 2024.
23. S. Z. Aslam, O. Boomhower, J. Popp, and N. Ebrahimi, "Multi glass-wafer stacked technology for 3d heterogeneously-integrated scalable 6g arrays," in *2024 IEEE Wireless and Microwave Technology Conference (WAMICON)*. IEEE, 2024, pp. 1–4.
24. W.-C. Tsai, "Field-programmable gate array-based implementation of zero-trust stream data encryption for enabling 6g-narrowband internet of things massive device access," *Sensors*, vol. 24, no. 3, p. 853, 2024.
25. S. Zhang, D. Zhu, and Y. Liu, "Artificial intelligence empowered physical layer security for 6g: State-of-the-art, challenges, and opportunities," *Computer Networks*, p. 110255, 2024.
26. E. Zeydan, L. Blanco, J. Mangues-Bafalluy, A. Aydeger, S. Arslan, and Y. Turk, "Integrating quantum-secured blockchain identity management in open ran for 6g networks," in *2024 IEEE 49th Conference on Local Computer Networks (LCN)*. IEEE, 2024, pp. 1–7.
27. M. F. Ahammed and M. R. Labu, "Privacy-preserving data sharing in healthcare: Advances in secure multiparty computation," *Journal of Medical and Health Studies*, vol. 5, no. 2, pp. 37–47, 2024.
28. X. Wang, A. Shankar, K. Li, B. D. Parameshachari, and J. Lv, "Blockchain-enabled decentralized edge intelligence for trustworthy 6g consumer electronics," *IEEE Transactions on Consumer Electronics*, vol. 70, no. 1, pp. 1214–1225, 2024.

29. A. Kaushik, R. Singh, M. Li, H. Luo, S. Dayarathna, R. Senanayake, X. An, R. A. Stirling-Gallacher, W. Shin, and M. Di Renzo, "Integrated sensing and communications for iot: Synergies with key 6g technology enablers," *IEEE Internet of Things Magazine*, vol. 7, no. 5, pp. 136–143, 2024.
30. S. I. Loutfi, I. Shayea, U. Tureli, A. A. El-Saleh, and W. Tashan, "An overview of mobility awareness with mobile edge computing over 6g network: Challenges and future research directions," *Results in Engineering*, p. 102601, 2024.

OPUS: An Opportunistic Crowd-Sensing Framework for 5G Enabled Smart Campus

Ch Madhu Bhushan, Meka Naga Nandini Devi, A. Surayya, Firoj Gazi, and Md Muzakkir Hussain

1 Introduction

The efficient management of urban areas and communities heavily depends on monitoring dynamic urban phenomena to support decision-making. Traditional sensing methods, such as wireless sensor networks (WSNs) [1], use distributed sensors to capture real-world conditions. Despite significant research, the implementation of commercial sensor network techniques in practical scenarios encounters obstacles like limited node coverage, high costs for installation and maintenance, and scalability concerns (Table 1).

Mobile Crowd Sensing (MCS) [2] offers an innovative sensing model that leverages the extensive use of mobile devices. The proliferation of user-associated devices, such as mobile phones, wearables, and smart vehicles [3], along with their mobility, fosters a rapidly expanding sensing paradigm [4]. MCS allows the collection of local data via sensor-enhanced mobile devices, capturing information like location, environmental context, noise levels, traffic conditions, and specific data such as pollution. This data can be shared with social networks, healthcare services, and utility providers. By merging ground-collected information with cloud-based data fusion,

C. M. Bhushan · M. N. N. Devi · A. Surayya · F. Gazi · M. M. Hussain (✉)
SRMAP University, Guntur, India
e-mail: muzakkirhussain.m@srmap.edu.in

C. M. Bhushan
e-mail: madhubhushan_chakka@srmap.edu.in

M. N. N. Devi
e-mail: naganandinidevi_meka@srmap.edu.in

A. Surayya
e-mail: surayya.a@srmap.edu.in

F. Gazi
e-mail: firoj.g@srmap.edu.in

T. Ojha et al. (eds.), *Edge-Enabled 6G Networking*,
https://doi.org/10.1007/978-3-032-19042-0_12

Table 1 Acronyms

Abbreviation	Description
AQI	Air Quality Index
IoT	Internet of Things
MCS	Mobile Crowd Sensing
WSN	Wireless Sensor Network
POI	Points of Interest
LBSN	Location-Based Social Network
MQ135	Air Quality Sensor
HEPA	High Efficiency Particulate Air
ESP8266	Wi-Fi Module
NodeMCU	Open Source IoT Platform

MCS offers a versatile platform that can often replace static sensing infrastructures, aiding in applications like urban dynamics analysis [5], public safety, traffic management [6], and environmental monitoring [7].

Mobile Crowd Sensing (MCS) is defined as a system where everyday users gather data through their mobile devices. This data is then collected and analyzed in the cloud to derive insights and provide services centered around people [8]. MCS differs from participatory sensing in several key aspects [9]. MCS also reutilizes user-contributed data from mobile Internet services, often termed as participatory media, for secondary purposes. Additionally, MCS integrates and fuses data from heterogeneous, cross-space sources.

Figure 1 depicts a smart campus enabled by 5G technology. The illustration shows various interconnected devices and systems utilizing 5G for efficient communication

Fig. 1 5G enabled smart campus

and data exchange. Key elements include edge computing, solar-powered buildings, and extensive wireless connectivity. The visual representation highlights how 5G supports real-time data processing and integration across different campus facilities, enhancing overall operational efficiency and user experience.

The Urban Sensing Scenario exemplifies the features of MCS. Route planning is a common MCS application. Participatory sensing can utilize GPS trajectory data [10] from vehicles to determine the optimal route for a given query. However, more intricate queries, such as creating an itinerary for a visitor with time constraints, require additional data like points of interest (POIs) [11], their categories, optimal visiting times, and user preferences. This information can be obtained by reusing user-contributed data from mobile social networks like FourSquare. Another example is noise mapping, where mobile audio sensing generates noise maps. Understanding the causes of noise in specific areas often involves correlating the location with its category (e.g., market, school, street), which can be derived from location-based social network (LBSN) check-in datasets [12]. Thus, MCS leverages both online and offline participant data, exploring cross-space data fusion for innovative applications.

MCS presents unique research challenges, including data collection methods, incentive mechanisms, quality of user-contributed data, and cross-space data fusion [13]. Moreover, MCS represents a hybrid of human and machine intelligence [14], a relatively unexplored area. The key contributions of this paper are as follows:

- Conduct a thorough review of existing literature on Mobile Crowd Sensing (MCS), detailing its progression from the concept of participatory sensing.
- Describe the technical principles underpinning MCS, highlighting the best practices for combining human input and machine intelligence, and pinpoint major research obstacles.
- Develop a conceptual framework for MCS and explore potential avenues for future research in this domain.

2 Related Works

Many research works are carried out on air pollution monitoring systems [15], focusing on fixed sensor deployments and mobile sensing [4]. Systems like U-Air [16] analyze data from fixed stations to understand spatial correlations of air quality across urban areas. These systems employ artificial neural networks [17] to process data from various sources, including meteorological conditions and traffic flow, to infer air quality (Table 2).

Recent advancements have seen the deployment of portable sensors attached to public and private vehicles, allowing for data collection on the move. For instance, the MESSAGE project developed low-cost portable devices for high-density deployment [28] in urban environments [29]. These efforts demonstrate the potential of mobile crowd-sensing for environmental monitoring, providing a more granular view of air

Table 2 Existing methodology

Citation	Year	Use case	Hardware	Methodology
[18]	2022	MCS in smart cities to improve public services	Smartphones, UAVs, Robots	Utilizes an ontology-based framework for managing heterogeneous MCS systems. Comprehensive functional and performance testing. Classification of human, machine, and object subclasses
[19]	2024	Traffic congestion, Mobile Crowd Sensing, Urban Traffic Management	Smartphones, GPS, IoT devices	Utilizes Mobile Crowd Sensing (MCS) for real-time data collection. Proposes a dynamic traffic efficiency model. Leverages IoT and smartphones for low-cost traffic monitoring
[20]	2018	Tracking activities within social networks, lifestyle habits, healthcare, environmental applications, and smart transportation systems.	Smart mobile devices (Android, iOS)	Utilizes mobile phones for data collection. Explores monitoring applications in various fields. Discusses capabilities of sensing and wireless communication
[21]	2019	Real-time mobile applications like tracking missing persons or capturing event highlights	Mobile devices (smartphones)	Proposes ContextAiDe, an end-to-end architecture for data-driven distributed applications. Utilizes Edge computing to support real-time applications. Optimizes quality and cost of acquiring contextual data
[22]	2024	Crowd density estimation in heterogeneous environments	Mobile devices	Proposes an architecture for estimating crowd density. Uses opportunistic data collection methods. Integrates heterogeneous data sources
[23]	2020	Environmental monitoring using mobile crowdsensing	Smart devices (smartphones)	Establishes opportunistic crowdsensing for reliable monitoring. Advocates cost-effective data collection. Utilizes edge computing for inference

(continued)

Table 2 (continued)

Citation	Year	Use case	Hardware	Methodology
[24]	2020	Hybrid crowdsensing architectures supporting 5G	Mobile edges, IoT devices	Proposes optimization strategies for selecting mobile edges. Enhances communication infrastructures for lower latency and higher reliability. Uses hybrid crowdsensing architecture
[25]	2021	Tracking and managing crowd movements during pandemics	Smart devices (smartphones), Edge nodes	Proposes ParticipAct, an edge-enabled mobile crowdsensing platform. Utilizes edge nodes for crowd management. Implements a federated blockchain network for rewards. Uses smart push notifications
[26]	2020	Reducing data collection costs while maintaining high delivery probability in MCS	Mobile devices, Cellular networks, Opportunistic networks	Proposes optimal data collection scheme using integrated cellular and opportunistic networks. Uses data collecting paths. Minimizes crowdsensing cost under data delivery constraints. Implements a greedy heuristic algorithm
[27]	2018	IoT solution for data sensing in a smart campus using smartphone sensors	Smartphones	Proposes an IoT solution for data sensing in a smart campus. Uses smartphone sensors for data collection. Integrates data for smart ambient environments and services
Our work	–	crowd-sensing frameworks to monitor and manage various environmental parameters using smartphone sensors	IOT devices, Smart devices	Proposes an multi-tier system architecture that incorporates edge computing. This section outlines the key components and processes involved in our e-Sense framework

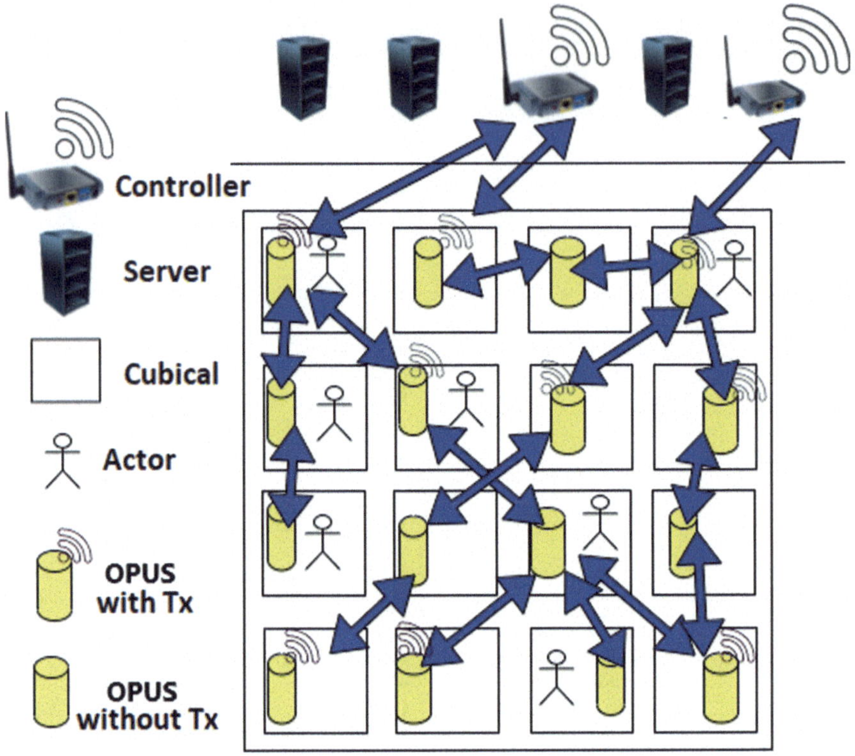

Fig. 2 Architecture of the system

quality. However, integrating such systems with the high-speed connectivity offered by 5G can significantly enhance data collection and real-time analysis capabilities.

Figure 2 illustrates a network architecture where controllers manage servers and communication devices (OPUS) within a grid of cubicles. Each cubicle houses actors (people) and OPUS devices, some with transmission capabilities (Tx) and some without. The blue arrows depict data flow between OPUS devices and controllers. Controllers facilitate communication and data exchange across the network, ensuring connectivity and coordination within the system. This setup is designed to enable efficient data management and communication in an office environment.

2.1 Fixed Sensor Deployments

Fixed sensor deployments provide continuous monitoring of air quality at specific locations. These systems use a network of sensors placed at strategic points to measure pollutants like CO, NO_2, and $PM_{2.5}$. Examples include government-operated air quality monitoring stations and research-based sensor networks.

Fixed sensor deployments, such as the ones used by government agencies and environmental organizations, provide valuable long-term data on air quality. These sensors are often highly accurate and capable of measuring a wide range of pollutants. However, their high cost and maintenance requirements limit their deployment to a few strategic locations. This results in a lack of spatial resolution, making it difficult to capture localized variations in air quality.

2.2 *Mobile Sensing*

Mobile sensing involves using portable devices to collect air quality data while in motion. This approach increases the spatial resolution of air quality measurements. Projects like Citi-Sense [30] and Air Quality Egg [29] have shown the feasibility of using low-cost sensors to gather air quality data through mobile sensing.

Mobile sensing offers a promising alternative to fixed sensor deployments. By attaching portable sensors to vehicles or carrying them on person, it is possible to collect air quality data across a wide area. This approach provides a more detailed and dynamic picture of air quality, capturing variations that fixed sensors might miss. However, mobile sensing faces challenges related to sensor calibration, data integration, and ensuring consistent data quality.

Figure 3 categorizes various sensing techniques into two main groups: fixed sensor deployments and mobile sensing. Fixed sensor deployments include traditional meth-

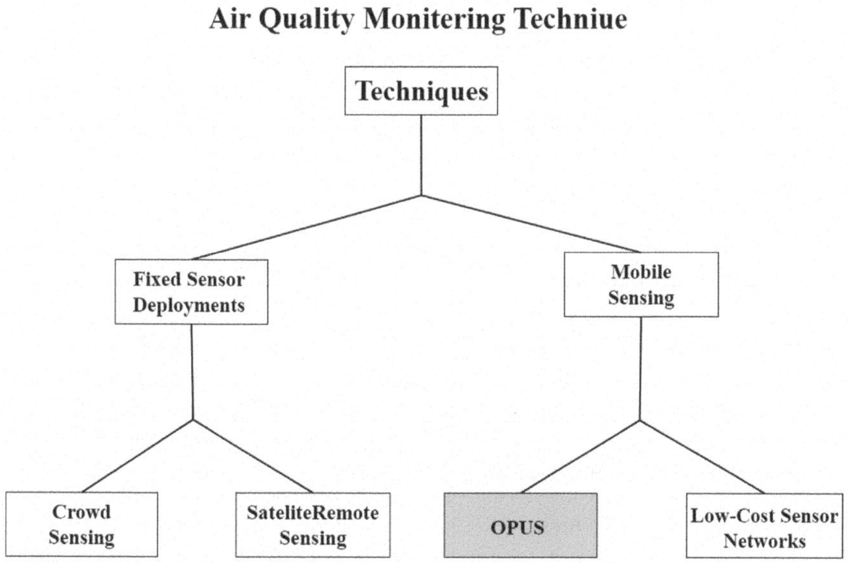

Fig. 3 Classification of state of the art techniques of air quality monitoring

ods such as crowd sensing and satellite remote sensing. Mobile sensing is divided into OPUS (a specific sensing method) and low-cost sensor networks. These techniques collectively contribute to data collection and monitoring across different environments, enhancing the overall efficiency and effectiveness of sensing applications.

3 Methodology

The methodology of our opportunistic crowd-sensing framework for a 5G-enabled smart campus involves the design, development, and deployment of a multi-tier system architecture that incorporates edge computing. This section outlines the key components and processes involved in our e-Sense framework, including data collection, edge processing, transmission, and user interaction.

3.1 System Architecture

The system architecture is segmented into four layers: data acquisition, edge processing, data communication, and user interface. Each layer is optimized to utilize the advantages of 5G technology and edge computing, thereby improving the efficiency and functionality of the e-Sense framework.

Figure 4 illustrates a multi-layered architecture for urban planning, smart campus monitoring, and smart power management applications. The end-user layer involves users interacting with IoT devices. Data from these devices is processed at the edge layer, which includes local servers and wireless communication. The processed data is then transmitted to the cloud layer for further analysis and storage. Finally, the application layer utilizes this data to provide services such as urban planning, campus monitoring, and power management, enabling efficient and intelligent management of urban and campus environments.

3.1.1 Data Collection Layer

This layer is responsible for gathering environmental data from various sensors embedded in smartphones and IoT devices. The sensors include air quality sensors, temperature sensors, humidity sensors, and noise level sensors. Data collection is performed opportunistically, meaning that data is gathered whenever a significant change is detected or when devices are in predefined areas of interest.

- **Smartphones and IoT Devices**: Serve as the primary data collection points in the e-Sense framework. They are equipped with sensors to measure various environmental parameters.

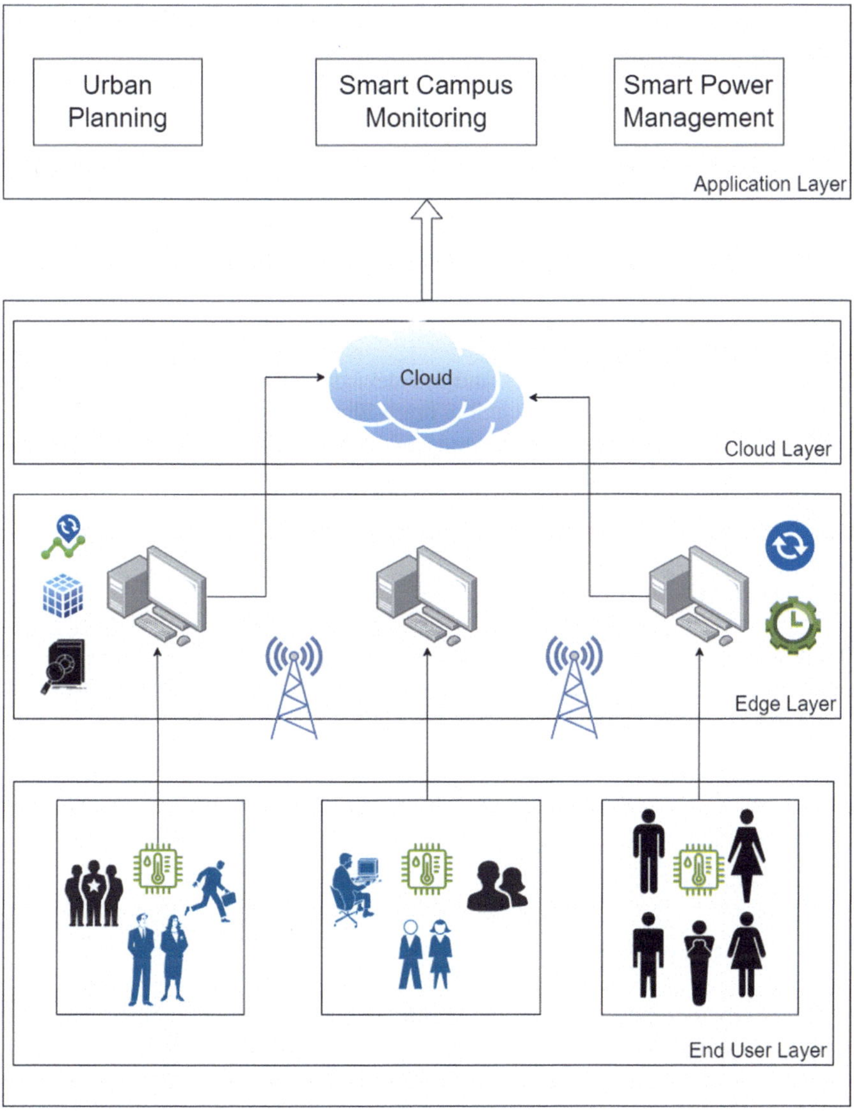

Fig. 4 Architecture of the system

- **Trigger Mechanism**: Data collection is triggered by significant changes in sensor readings or by the presence of the device in specific locations.

3.1.2 Edge Processing Layer

The collected data is processed locally at the edge using the computational power of smartphones and IoT devices before being transmitted to the cloud. This reduces latency and bandwidth usage, ensuring that only relevant and processed data is sent to the cloud for further analysis.

- **Local Processing**: Smartphones and IoT devices in the e-Sense framework perform initial data processing, including noise filtering and preliminary analysis.
- **Edge Analytics**: Basic machine learning algorithms run on edge devices to provide quick insights and reduce the volume of data transmitted to the cloud.

3.1.3 Data Transmission Layer

The processed data is transmitted to the cloud using the high-speed, low-latency capabilities of 5G networks. This ensures that data is sent in real-time, which is crucial for timely processing and feedback.

- **5G Connectivity**: Enables rapid and reliable data transmission to the cloud.
- **Data Security**: Ensures that data is transmitted securely to prevent unauthorized access and tampering.

3.1.4 User Interaction Layer

This layer provides users with real-time feedback and visualization of environmental conditions through a mobile application. The application allows users to view current data, historical trends, and receive notifications about significant changes in the environment.

- **Mobile Application**: Available for Android and iOS platforms, providing an intuitive interface for users to interact with the e-Sense system.
- **Real-Time Updates**: Delivers real-time information about environmental conditions on the smart campus.
- **User Contributions**: Allows users to manually report anomalies or additional data, enhancing the system's accuracy and reliability.

4 Implementation

The implementation of the e-Sense framework involves the integration of various hardware and software components to achieve the desired functionality.

4.1 Hardware Components

- **Sensors**: Include air quality sensors (e.g., MQ135), temperature sensors, humidity sensors, and noise sensors embedded in smartphones and IoT devices.
- **5G-Enabled Devices**: Smartphones and IoT devices equipped with 5G connectivity for real-time data transmission.
- **Edge Devices**: Devices with local processing capabilities to perform edge analytics.
- **Cloud Infrastructure**: Provides the necessary computational and storage resources for data processing.

4.2 Software Components

- **Mobile Application**: Developed using cross-platform frameworks to ensure compatibility with both Android and iOS devices. The app collects data from sensors and displays real-time environmental conditions.
- **Edge Processing Software**: Implements local data processing and preliminary analysis on edge devices.
- **Cloud Platform**: Utilizes cloud services for data storage, aggregation, and processing. The platform is designed to scale based on the volume of data collected.
- **Analytics Engine**: Implements machine learning models to analyze the collected data and generate insights. The engine is capable of real-time processing to provide immediate feedback.

4.3 Data Collection Process

The data collection process in the e-Sense framework begins with the detection of significant changes in environmental parameters or the presence of devices in predefined areas. Sensors embedded in smartphones and IoT devices capture the data, which is then pre-processed locally to reduce noise and irrelevant information. The pre-processed data is then transmitted to the cloud via 5G networks.

4.4 Edge Processing

Once data is collected, it is processed locally on the edge devices. This includes initial filtering, aggregation, and basic analytics to reduce the volume of data sent to the cloud and ensure timely insights. Edge processing in e-Sense helps in minimizing latency and reducing bandwidth usage.

4.5 Data Transmission Process

The data transmission process leverages the high-speed capabilities of 5G networks to ensure that the collected data reaches the cloud servers in real-time. Data security measures, such as encryption and secure transmission protocols, are implemented to protect the data during transit.

4.6 Data Processing and Analysis

Once the data reaches the cloud, it undergoes a series of processing steps. Initially, the data is cleaned to remove any noise or irrelevant information. It is then aggregated with data from other sources to create a comprehensive dataset. Machine learning algorithms analyze this dataset to identify patterns, detect anomalies, and generate actionable insights.

4.7 User Interaction and Feedback

The processed data and insights are made available to users through a mobile application. Users can view real-time environmental conditions, historical trends, and receive notifications about significant changes. The application also allows users to manually report anomalies or provide additional data, which enhances the system's accuracy and reliability.

5 Proposed Model

The main aim of our proposed model is to create a robust and efficient framework for environmental monitoring in a 5G-enabled smart campus using opportunistic crowdsensing and edge computing. This section details the components and operation of the proposed e-Sense model, including the hardware setup, software architecture, and the interaction between different system components. The overall working of OPUS framework is depicted through Algorithm 1.

Algorithm 1: OPUS Framework for 5G-Enabled Smart Campus

Inputs: Set of mobile devices M, Set of IoT devices I, Set of edge nodes E, Cloud server C, Sensors data D, Threshold for significant change θ

Output: Processed and transmitted data to cloud, Real-time feedback to users

```
InitializeSystem()
Algorithm OpportunisticCrowdSensing
    foreach device m ∈ M do
        if significantChangeDetected(m, θ) then
            D_m ← collectData(m)
            e ← selectNearestEdgeNode(m, E)
            transmitDataToEdge(D_m, e)
        end
    end
    foreach edge node e ∈ E do
        D_e ← receiveData(e)
        D_processed ← edgeProcessing(D_e)
        transmitDataToCloud(D_processed, C)
    end
    D_cloud ← receiveDataFromEdgeNodes(C)
    D_aggregated ← cloudAggregation(D_cloud)
    insights ← analyzeData(D_aggregated)
    updateMobileApplication(insights)
```

5.1 Implementation Setup

The implementation setup for MCS involves deploying sensor-enhanced mobile devices across the target area to collect various data types. These devices, including smartphones and wearables, capture data such as location, environmental conditions, and user activity. Data is then transmitted to a cloud-based platform where it is aggregated and analyzed using machine learning algorithms to extract actionable insights. The setup also integrates edge computing for real-time data processing and utilizes 5G technology to ensure seamless communication and data transfer between devices and the cloud.

5.1.1 Essential Components

- **MQ135 Air Quality Sensor**: This sensor is instrumental in detecting various airborne contaminants such as ammonia, smoke, carbon dioxide, and other noxious gases. It functions within a voltage range of 2.5–5.0 V and offers both digital and analog outputs for versatility.
- **HEPA Filter**: High Efficiency Particulate Air (HEPA) filters are designed to capture at least 99.97% of particles that are 0.3 microns in size, effectively removing allergens, dust, pollen, and other minute particles from the air.

- **Ultraviolet (UV) Lamps**: UV lamps are utilized to sanitize the air by eliminating biological contaminants such as bacteria and viruses. UV light is a potent method for disinfecting air and water systems.
- **ESP8266 E-12 based NodeMCU**: NodeMCU, built on the ESP8266 Wi-Fi module, serves as an open-source platform for IoT applications, providing essential processing power and network connectivity for the air quality monitoring setup.
- **Arduino IDE**: The Arduino Integrated Development Environment (IDE) facilitates coding and uploading programs to the NodeMCU, supporting languages like C and C++ for seamless development and deployment.

Figure 5 illustrates the real-time OPUS environment. Figure 6a shows the deployment of sensor nodes in a real-world office setting. Figure 6b presents the actual

(a) Real-world node deployment

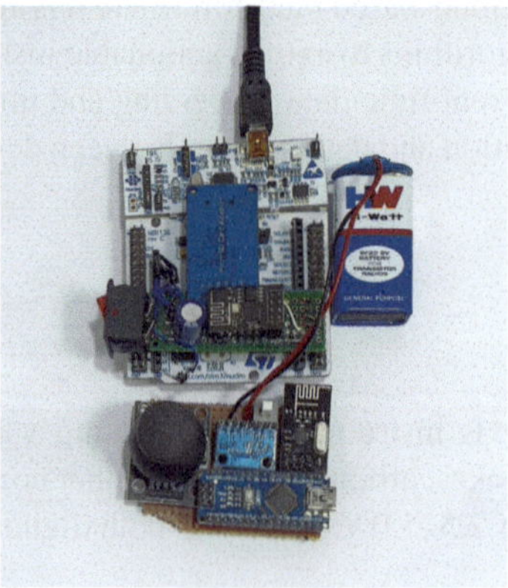

(b) Realtime tespbed

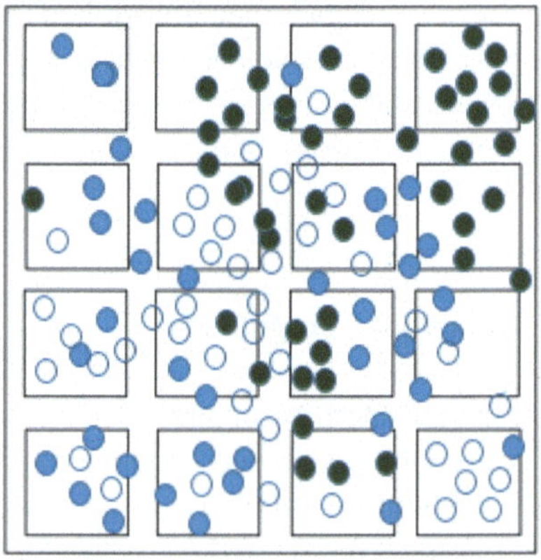

(c) Cubical air pollution map

Fig. 5 Realtime OPUS environment

Fig. 6 Wave generated by OPUS node in various conditions

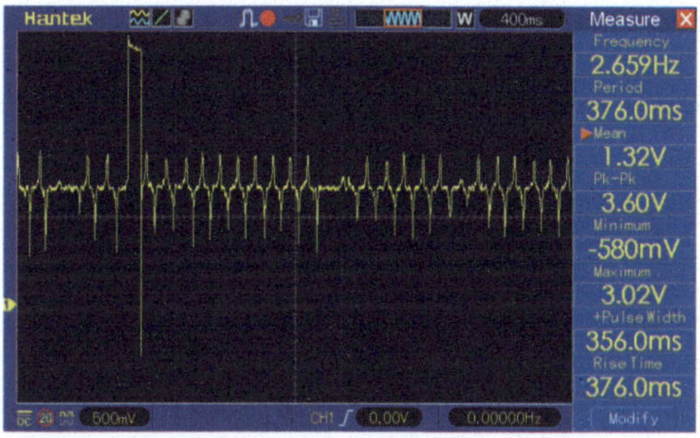

(a) Idle condition

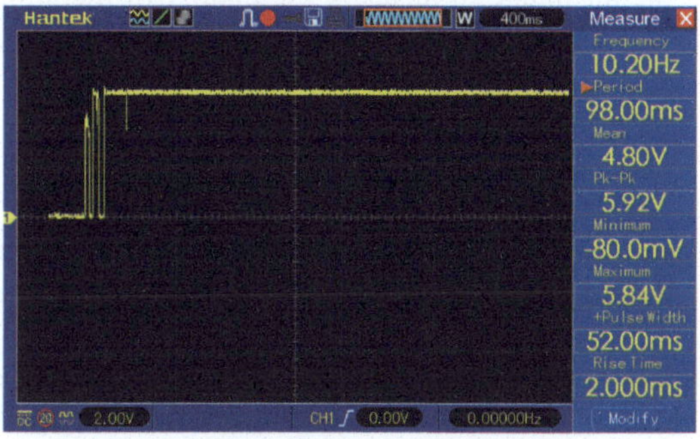

(b) While sensing and actuating

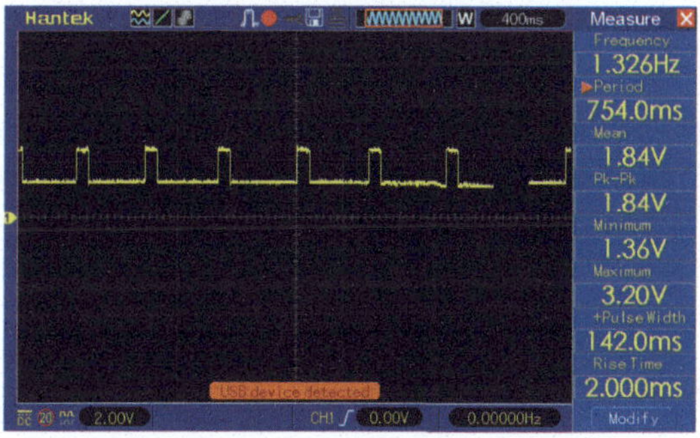

(c) Communication phase

testbed used for real-time data collection, consisting of interconnected hardware components. Figure 6c displays a cubical air pollution map, highlighting the distribution of air quality measurements within the office cubicles. Together, these images demonstrate the setup and functionality of the OPUS system in monitoring and mapping environmental conditions in an office environment.

5.1.2 Proposed Model

The proposed e-Sense model consists of several stages that work together to ensure efficient air quality monitoring and purification. These stages include data collection, air filtration, data transmission, and user interaction.

5.1.3 Data Collection

The data collection process in the e-Sense model starts with the MQ135 air quality sensors, which detect the presence of pollutants in the air. The first sensor is placed at the air intake to measure the quality of incoming air. The data collected by this sensor is sent to the NodeMCU for processing.

5.1.4 Air Filtration

Air is drawn into the system through an intake vent and directed through a HEPA filter, which efficiently captures 99.97% of particles exceeding 0.3 microns in size. Post-filtration, the air undergoes sterilization via UV lamps, which effectively neutralize bacteria and viruses. The cleaned air is subsequently released back into the environment.

5.1.5 Edge Processing and Data Transmission

The NodeMCU processes the sensor data locally and transmits it to the cloud via a 5G network. This high-speed transmission ensures real-time updates and accurate monitoring. Data security measures, such as encryption and secure transmission protocols, are implemented to protect the data during transit.

5.1.6 User Interaction

Users can interact with the e-Sense system through a mobile application. The app provides real-time updates on air quality, historical data, and notifications about significant changes in environmental conditions. Users can also manually input additional data or report anomalies to enhance system accuracy.

5.2 Filtering Process

The filtering process involves several steps to ensure that the air is thoroughly cleaned and safe for indoor environments.

- **Air Intake**: Air is drawn into the system through an inlet.
- **HEPA Filtration**: The air passes through the HEPA filter, which captures 99.97% of airborne particles larger than 0.3 microns.
- **UV Sterilization**: The filtered air is exposed to UV lamps, which destroy any remaining biological pollutants.
- **Air Output**: The purified air is expelled back into the environment through an exhaust fan.

5.3 Data Processing

The data collected by the sensors in the e-Sense framework is transmitted to the cloud, where it undergoes several processing steps:

- **Data Cleaning**: Noise and irrelevant information are removed from the data.
- **Data Aggregation**: Data from multiple sensors is combined to create a comprehensive dataset.
- **Data Analysis**: Machine learning algorithms analyze the data to identify patterns, detect anomalies, and generate insights.
- **Visualization**: The processed data is visualized on the mobile application, providing users with real-time information about air quality.

5.4 User Interaction

The mobile application serves as the primary interface between the e-Sense system and the users. It offers several features:

- **Real-Time Updates**: Users receive real-time updates about air quality.
- **Historical Data**: Users can view historical trends in air quality data.
- **Notifications**: Users are notified about significant changes in environmental conditions.
- **Manual Input**: Users can manually report anomalies or provide additional data.

The proposed e-Sense model leverages the capabilities of 5G technology, IoT devices, and advanced data processing techniques to create a comprehensive and efficient air quality monitoring and purification system for smart campuses.

6 System Description

The proposed opportunistic crowd-sensing framework for a 5G-enabled smart campus is designed to monitor and enhance environmental conditions through real-time data collection, edge processing, transmission, and user interaction. This section provides a detailed description of the system components and their interactions.

6.1 System Architecture

The system is built on a multi-tier architecture that includes the following layers: data collection, edge processing, data transmission, and user interaction. Each layer is designed to optimize the use of 5G technology and edge computing to ensure efficient and effective operation.

6.1.1 Data Collection Layer

The data collection layer is responsible for gathering environmental data from various sensors embedded in smartphones and IoT devices distributed across the smart campus. These sensors measure air quality, temperature, humidity, and noise levels.

- **Sensors**: The primary data collection points in the e-Sense framework, including air quality sensors (e.g., MQ135), temperature sensors, humidity sensors, and noise level sensors.
- **Trigger Mechanism**: Data is collected opportunistically, triggered by significant changes in sensor readings or the presence of devices in predefined areas of interest.

6.1.2 Edge Processing Layer

The collected data is processed locally at the edge using the computational power of smartphones and IoT devices before being transmitted to the cloud. This reduces latency and bandwidth usage, ensuring that only relevant and processed data is sent to the cloud for further analysis.

- **Local Processing**: Smartphones and IoT devices in the e-Sense framework perform initial data processing, including noise filtering and preliminary analysis.
- **Edge Analytics**: Basic machine learning algorithms run on edge devices to provide quick insights and reduce the volume of data transmitted to the cloud.

6.1.3 Data Transmission Layer

This layer ensures the real-time transmission of collected data to the cloud using the high-speed, low-latency capabilities of 5G networks.

- **5G Connectivity**: Facilitates rapid and reliable data transmission to the cloud infrastructure.
- **Data Security**: Implements encryption and secure transmission protocols to protect data during transit.

6.1.4 Data Processing Layer

Once the data reaches the cloud, it undergoes several processing steps to generate meaningful insights.

- **Cloud Computing**: Provides computational power and storage for processing large volumes of data.
- **Data Aggregation**: Combines data from various sensors to create a comprehensive view of the smart campus environment.
- **Analytics Engine**: Uses machine learning algorithms to analyze data, identify patterns, detect anomalies, and generate insights.

6.1.5 User Interaction Layer

The user interaction layer offers an interface for users to access real-time updates, historical data, and notifications through a mobile application.

- **Mobile Application**: Available on Android and iOS platforms, providing an intuitive user interface.
- **Real-Time Updates**: Displays current environmental conditions and historical trends.
- **Notifications**: Alerts users about significant changes in environmental conditions.
- **User Contributions**: Allows users to manually report anomalies and provide additional data.

6.2 Data Collection Process

The data collection process in the e-Sense framework starts with sensors detecting changes in environmental parameters. The data is pre-processed locally on the device to filter out noise and irrelevant information before being transmitted to the cloud via 5G networks.

6.3 Edge Processing

Once data is collected, it is processed locally on the edge devices. This includes initial filtering, aggregation, and basic analytics to reduce the volume of data sent to the cloud and ensure timely insights. Edge processing in e-Sense helps in minimizing latency and reducing bandwidth usage.

6.4 Data Transmission Process

Leveraging 5G technology, the system ensures that the collected data is transmitted to the cloud servers in real-time. Data security measures, such as encryption and secure transmission protocols, are employed to safeguard the data during transmission.

6.5 Data Processing and Analysis

Upon reaching the cloud, the data undergoes several processing stages:

- **Data Cleaning**: Removes noise and irrelevant information from the raw data.
- **Data Aggregation**: Integrates data from multiple sensors to create a unified dataset.
- **Data Analysis**: Machine learning algorithms analyze the aggregated data to identify patterns, detect anomalies, and generate actionable insights.
- **Visualization**: The processed data is visualized on the mobile application, providing users with clear and comprehensive information about the environmental conditions.

6.6 User Interaction and Feedback

The mobile application serves as the primary interface for user interaction, offering features such as:

- **Real-Time Updates**: Users receive immediate information about the current environmental conditions on the smart campus.
- **Historical Data**: Users can access historical trends and analyze changes over time.
- **Notifications**: Users are alerted to significant changes in the environment, enabling them to take timely action.
- **Manual Input**: Users can manually report any anomalies or additional data, which helps improve the accuracy and reliability of the e-Sense system.

This comprehensive system description outlines the key components and processes involved in our opportunistic crowd-sensing framework for a 5G-enabled smart campus. The integration of advanced technologies and user-centric design ensures that the e-Sense system effectively monitors and enhances the campus environment.

7 Experimental Results

The proposed opportunistic crowd-sensing framework was deployed in a university campus for a pilot study. The primary objective was to evaluate the effectiveness of the e-Sense system in collecting, transmitting, and analyzing environmental data in real-time. This section presents the results of our deployment, including data collection efficiency, data accuracy, and overall system performance.

In Fig. 6, we observe the waveforms generated by an OPUS node under three distinct conditions: idle, while sensing and actuating, and during the communication phase.

(a) Idle Condition:

In the idle condition, the waveform (Fig. 6a) shows periodic small fluctuations with low amplitude. This indicates that the OPUS node is in a low-power standby mode. The minimal background processes are reflected by the relatively stable signal with slight variations, suggesting energy conservation while remaining ready to activate as needed.

(b) While Sensing and Actuating:

When the OPUS node is actively sensing and actuating, the waveform (Fig. 6b) changes significantly. There is a noticeable increase in both the frequency and amplitude of the signal. This reflects higher power consumption and increased activity levels as the node engages its sensors and actuators to perform its tasks. The waveform demonstrates a consistent high level of activity, indicative of continuous operation during this phase.

(c) Communication Phase:

During the communication phase, the waveform (Fig. 6c) displays periodic pulses. These pulses represent data transmission between OPUS nodes. The amplitude is moderate, reflecting balanced power consumption during communication activities. The regular intervals of the pulses suggest a structured and consistent communication protocol, where the node periodically sends and receives data to and from other nodes. This phase is crucial for maintaining synchronization and effective data exchange within the network of OPUS devices.

These detailed observations illustrate how the OPUS device operates under different conditions. In the idle state, it conserves energy with minimal activity. During sensing and actuating, it ramps up power usage to perform necessary tasks. In the communication phase, it maintains a regular pattern of data transmission, ensuring effective communication with other devices. The oscilloscope waveforms provide a clear picture of the device's operational characteristics in each of these states.

7.1 *Data Collection Efficiency*

Over a period of three months, data was collected from various sensors embedded in smartphones and IoT devices distributed across the smart campus. The e-Sense system successfully captured and transmitted environmental data with minimal latency, leveraging the high-speed capabilities of 5G networks.

7.2 *Data Accuracy*

The accuracy of the data collected was validated through continuous monitoring and cross-verification with standard measurement tools placed strategically across various zones on the campus. The sensors exhibited high precision in capturing environmental parameters such as air quality, temperature, humidity, and noise levels. This high degree of accuracy ensures the reliability of the e-Sense system in providing real-time environmental insights.

7.3 *System Performance*

The performance of the e-Sense system was comprehensively evaluated based on multiple criteria including data processing time and overall system reliability.

7.3.1 Data Processing Time

The e-Sense system demonstrated an impressive data processing time, averaging less than 5 s from data collection to insight generation. This rapid processing capability is critical for providing real-time feedback and supports dynamic decision-making in a smart campus environment.

7.3.2 System Reliability

The reliability of the e-Sense system was evaluated by monitoring the uptime and recording any system failures during the deployment period. The system achieved an impressive uptime of 99.5.

7.4 *Data Visualization and Analysis*

The collected data was visualized using a variety of graphical representations to facilitate analysis and decision-making. Below are some key visualizations:

The arc diagram in Fig. 7 visualizes the communication between different zones based on SSID interactions. Nodes represent SSIDs, while edges indicate connections, weighted by the average RSSI values. Higher weights (thicker edges) denote stronger signals, suggesting closer proximity or fewer obstacles between SSIDs. The diagram helps in understanding the network topology and the relative strength of connections across zones. For example, SSIDs with thicker connections are likely key nodes in the network, facilitating robust communication. This visualization is crucial for identifying central SSIDs, optimizing network performance, and troubleshooting connectivity issues within the zones.

Figure 8 presents a violin plot illustrating the distribution of RSSI values for different SSIDs. Each violin represents the spread and density of RSSI values, with wider sections indicating higher density. The central black bar shows the interquartile range, while the white dot represents the median RSSI value. This plot highlights the variability in signal strength for each SSID, aiding in the identification of consistently strong or weak signals. For instance, SSIDs with wider violins and lower median values indicate more variability and generally weaker signals, crucial for network optimization and ensuring consistent connectivity across different areas.

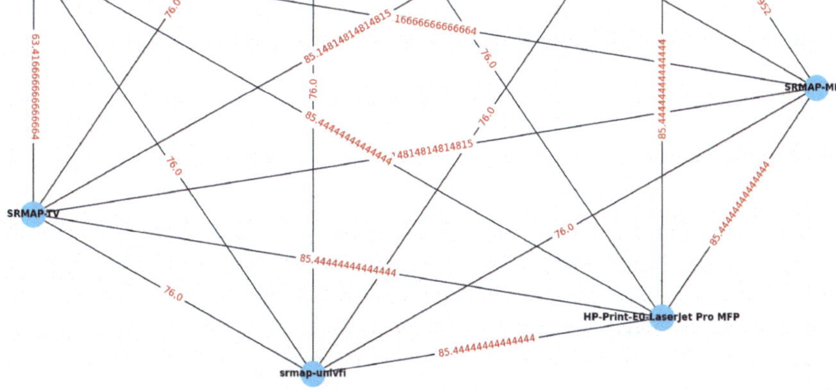

Fig. 7 Arc diagram showing communication between zones

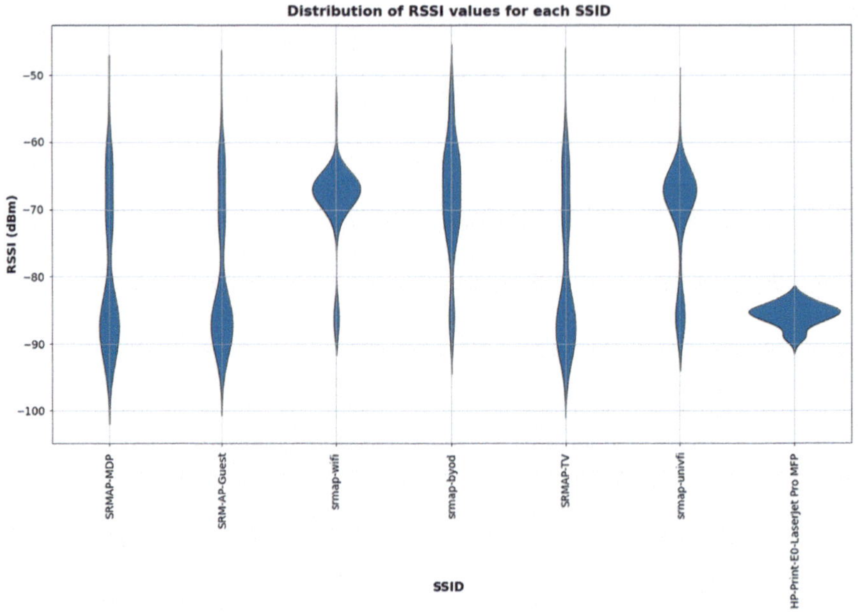

Fig. 8 Violin plot of RSSI values by SSID

Figure 9 illustrates the signal strength variations for various SSIDs over time across different zones. Each subplot corresponds to a specific zone, with the X-axis representing the timestamp (in seconds) and the Y-axis indicating RSSI values (in dBm). Zones 1 to 8 display significant RSSI fluctuations, suggesting dynamic environments with potential interference or varying distances from the signal source. In contrast, Zones 9 to 16 show more consistent RSSI patterns, indicating stable conditions or controlled environments. This analysis aids in identifying zones with high variability that may require additional network optimization, such as deploying more access points or adjusting configurations to enhance connectivity.

7.5 Discussion

The deployment of the e-Sense system demonstrated significant advantages in real-time environmental monitoring on a 5G-enabled smart campus. The arc diagram (Fig. 7) illustrates the communication between different zones, highlighting the robust connectivity and data sharing facilitated by the system. The violin plot (Fig. 8) provides a detailed view of the RSSI values by SSID, emphasizing the system's capability to monitor signal strength variations across different zones.

The zone-specific graphs (Fig. 9) show the dynamic changes in RSSI values over time, providing a comprehensive overview of network performance and environmental conditions across the campus. These visualizations underscore the effectiveness of the e-Sense framework in leveraging crowd-sensing and edge computing for enhanced environmental monitoring.

The successful deployment and high user satisfaction validate the e-Sense framework's potential for broader implementation. Future work will focus on incorporating additional environmental parameters and enhancing data analytics capabilities to provide more detailed insights. The integration of more sophisticated machine learning algorithms and the expansion of sensor networks will further improve the system's accuracy and reliability.

7.6 Conclusion

The e-Sense framework has proven to be a robust and efficient solution for real-time environmental monitoring in a 5G-enabled smart campus. The system's ability to collect, transmit, and process data quickly and accurately provides valuable insights that can enhance campus safety and resource management. Ongoing improvements and expansions to the e-Sense system will continue to drive advancements in smart campus initiatives, making significant contributions to environmental monitoring and management.

8 Discussion

The deployment of our opportunistic crowd-sensing framework on a 5G-enabled smart campus has yielded promising results, showcasing the e-Sense system's potential to significantly enhance environmental monitoring and management. This section discusses the implications of the results, the advantages of the proposed framework, and potential areas for future research and development.

8.1 Implications of the Results

The experimental results indicate that the e-Sense system is highly efficient in collecting, transmitting, and processing environmental data in real-time. The high data collection efficiency and accuracy demonstrate the effectiveness of using opportunistic crowd-sensing and 5G technology for environmental monitoring. The ability to provide real-time updates and accurate information allows campus authorities to make informed decisions promptly, improving the overall smart campus environment and safety.

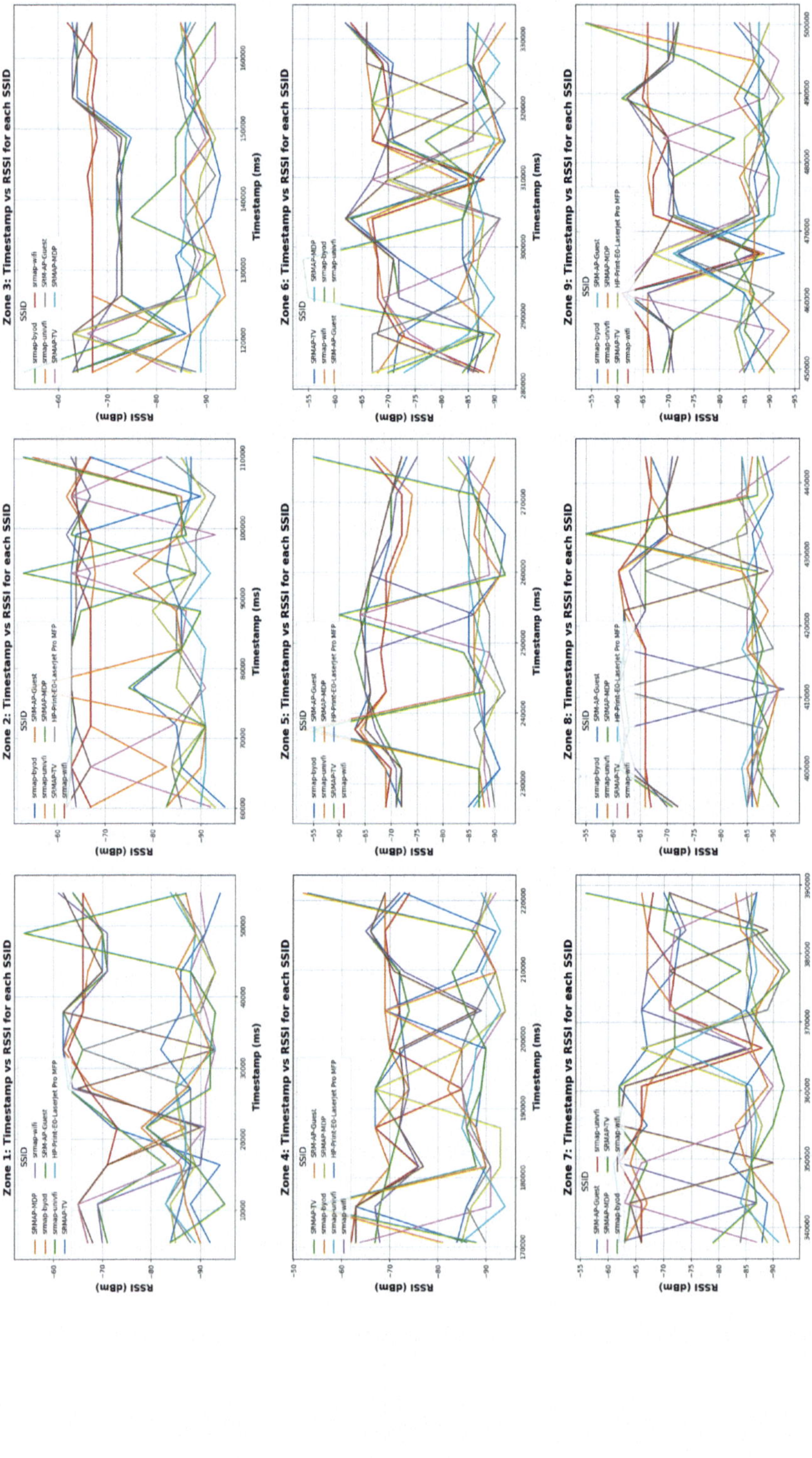

Fig. 9 RSSI values by SSID across different zones

8.2 Advantages of the Proposed Framework

The proposed e-Sense framework offers several advantages over traditional environmental monitoring systems:

- **Cost-Effectiveness**: By leveraging existing smartphones and IoT devices, the framework reduces the need for expensive fixed sensor networks.
- **Scalability**: The system can easily scale with the addition of more sensors and devices, providing comprehensive coverage of large campus areas.
- **Real-Time Monitoring**: The use of 5G technology enables real-time data transmission and processing, ensuring timely updates and alerts.
- **User Engagement**: The mobile application enhances user engagement by allowing users to access real-time data, historical trends, and provide manual inputs.
- **Flexibility**: The opportunistic sensing approach allows for flexible data collection, adapting to changes in environmental conditions and user behavior.

8.3 Challenges and Limitations

Despite the promising results, the deployment also highlighted several challenges and limitations:

- **Data Privacy and Security**: Ensuring the privacy and security of the collected data is crucial, especially when dealing with sensitive environmental information.
- **Network Coverage**: Although 5G provides high-speed connectivity, network coverage can be inconsistent in certain areas, affecting data transmission reliability.
- **Battery Consumption**: Continuous data collection and transmission can lead to increased battery consumption in smartphones and IoT devices.
- **Sensor Calibration**: Ensuring the accuracy and calibration of sensors over time is essential to maintain data reliability.

8.4 Future Work

Future research and development efforts will focus on addressing the identified challenges and expanding the capabilities of the e-Sense framework:

- **Enhanced Data Analytics**: Developing more sophisticated machine learning algorithms to analyze the collected data and provide deeper insights into environmental patterns and trends.
- **Extended Sensor Integration**: Integrating additional sensors to monitor a broader range of environmental parameters, such as particulate matter (PM2.5, PM10), CO_2 levels, and more.

- **Improved User Interface**: Enhancing the mobile application interface to provide more intuitive and interactive data visualizations and user feedback mechanisms.
- **Energy Optimization**: Implementing strategies to optimize battery usage in smartphones and IoT devices during data collection and transmission.
- **Data Privacy Measures**: Strengthening data privacy and security measures to protect the collected information and ensure compliance with relevant regulations.
- **Wider Deployment**: Conducting larger-scale deployments in diverse smart campus environments to validate the e-Sense system's scalability and adaptability.

9 Conclusion

The deployment of our opportunistic crowd-sensing framework on a 5G-enabled smart campus demonstrates its potential to enhance environmental monitoring and management. The e-Sense system's ability to collect, transmit, and process data in real-time provides valuable insights that can improve campus safety and resource management. While challenges remain, ongoing research and development efforts will continue to refine and expand the e-Sense framework, further contributing to the advancement of smart campus initiatives.

Acknowledgements The authors would like to acknowledge the support of the Future Ubiquitous Networking (FUN) LAB and the research facilities at SRM University for providing the seed grant SRMAP/URG/SEED/2023-24/036 that made this research possible.

References

1. Ian F Akyildiz and Mehmet Can Vuran. *Wireless sensor networks*. John Wiley & Sons, 2010.
2. Andrea Capponi, Claudio Fiandrino, Burak Kantarci, Luca Foschini, Dzmitry Kliazovich, and Pascal Bouvry. A survey on mobile crowdsensing systems: Challenges, solutions, and opportunities. *IEEE communications surveys & tutorials*, 21(3):2419–2465, 2019.
3. Abdalla Abdelrahman, Amr S El-Wakeel, Aboelmagd Noureldin, and Hossam S Hassanein. Crowdsensing-based personalized dynamic route planning for smart vehicles. *Ieee Network*, 34(3):216–223, 2020.
4. Bin Guo, Zhu Wang, Zhiwen Yu, Yu Wang, Neil Y Yen, Runhe Huang, and Xingshe Zhou. Mobile crowd sensing and computing: The review of an emerging human-powered sensing paradigm. *ACM computing surveys (CSUR)*, 48(1):1–31, 2015.
5. Cristina Martinez-Fernandez, Chung-Tong Wu, Laura K Schatz, Nobuhisa Taira, and José G Vargas-Hernández. The shrinking mining city: Urban dynamics and contested territory. *International Journal of Urban and Regional Research*, 36(2):245–260, 2012.
6. Wilfried Steiner, Silviu S Craciunas, and Ramon Serna Oliver. Traffic planning for time-sensitive communication. *IEEE Communications Standards Magazine*, 2(2):42–47, 2018.
7. Silvia Liberata Ullo and Ganesh Ram Sinha. Advances in smart environment monitoring systems using iot and sensors. *Sensors*, 20(11):3113, 2020.

8. Ke Mao, Mark Harman, and Yue Jia. Crowd intelligence enhances automated mobile testing. In *2017 32nd IEEE/ACM International Conference on Automated Software Engineering (ASE)*, pages 16–26. IEEE, 2017.
9. Bin Guo, Zhiwen Yu, Xingshe Zhou, and Daqing Zhang. From participatory sensing to mobile crowd sensing. In *2014 IEEE international conference on pervasive computing and communication workshops (PERCOM WORKSHOPS)*, pages 593–598. IEEE, 2014.
10. Shuming Sun, Juan Chen, and Jian Sun. Traffic congestion prediction based on gps trajectory data. *International Journal of Distributed Sensor Networks*, 15(5):1550147719847440, 2019.
11. Lih Wei Yeow, Raymond Low, Yu Xiang Tan, and Lynette Cheah. Point-of-interest (poi) data validation methods: An urban case study. *ISPRS International Journal of Geo-Information*, 10(11):735, 2021.
12. Yu Zheng. Location-based social networks: Users. In *Computing with spatial trajectories*, pages 243–276. Springer, 2011.
13. Wenqian Nan, Bin Guo, Shenlong Huangfu, Zhiwen Yu, Huihui Chen, and Xingshe Zhou. A cross-space, multi-interaction-based dynamic incentive mechanism for mobile crowd sensing. In *2014 IEEE 11th Intl Conf on Ubiquitous Intelligence and Computing and 2014 IEEE 11th Intl Conf on Autonomic and Trusted Computing and 2014 IEEE 14th Intl Conf on Scalable Computing and Communications and Its Associated Workshops*, pages 179–186. IEEE, 2014.
14. Sandip Garai and Ranjit Kumar Paul. Development of mcs based-ensemble models using ceemdan decomposition and machine intelligence. *Intelligent Systems with Applications*, 18:200202, 2023.
15. Zeba Idrees and Lirong Zheng. Low cost air pollution monitoring systems: A review of protocols and enabling technologies. *Journal of Industrial Information Integration*, 17:100123, 2020.
16. Yu Zheng, Furui Liu, and Hsun-Ping Hsieh. U-air: When urban air quality inference meets big data. In *Proceedings of the 19th ACM SIGKDD international conference on Knowledge discovery and data mining*, pages 1436–1444, 2013.
17. Guangyu Robert Yang and Xiao-Jing Wang. Artificial neural networks for neuroscientists: a primer. *Neuron*, 107(6):1048–1070, 2020.
18. Yimeng Liu, Zhiwen Yu, Jiangtao Wang, Bin Guo, Jiangbin Su, and Jiahao Liao. Crowdmanager: An ontology-based interaction and management middleware for heterogeneous mobile crowd sensing. *IEEE Transactions on Mobile Computing*, 22(11):6358–6376, 2022.
19. Akbar Ali, Nasir Ayub, Muhammad Shiraz, Niamat Ullah, Abdullah Gani, and Muhammad Ahsan Qureshi. Traffic efficiency models for urban traffic management using mobile crowd sensing: A survey. *Sustainability*, 13(23):13068, 2021.
20. Khalid Abualsaud, Tarek M Elfouly, Tamer Khattab, Elias Yaacoub, Loay Sabry Ismail, Mohamed Hossam Ahmed, and Mohsen Guizani. A survey on mobile crowd-sensing and its applications in the iot era. *Ieee access*, 7:3855–3881, 2018.
21. Madhurima Pore. *Mobile Crowd Sensing in Edge Computing Environment*. Arizona State University, 2019.
22. Lavanya Addepalli. *An Architecture for Crowd Density Estimation in Heterogenous Opportunistic Environment*. PhD thesis, Universitat Politècnica de València, 2024.
23. Yifan Du. *Collaborative crowdsensing at the edge*. PhD thesis, Sorbonne Université, 2020.
24. Dimitri Belli, Stefano Chessa, Antonio Corradi, Luca Foschini, and Michele Girolami. Optimization strategies for the selection of mobile edges in hybrid crowdsensing architectures. *Computer Communications*, 157:132–142, 2020.
25. Luca Foschini, Giuseppe Martuscelli, Rebecca Montanari, and Michele Solimando. Edge-enabled mobile crowdsensing to support effective rewarding for data collection in pandemic events. *Journal of Grid Computing*, 19(3):28, 2021.
26. Doaa Mohsin Majeed, Lin Zhang, and Ke Shi. Optimal data collection for mobile crowdsensing over integrated cellular and opportunistic networks. *IEEE Access*, 8:157270–157283, 2020.
27. Jaime Alonso, Carlos Bayona, Omar Rojas, Marco Terán, Juan Aranda, Henry Carrillo, and Carlos Parra. Iot solution for data sensing in a smart campus using smartphone sensors. In *2018 IEEE Colombian conference on communications and computing (COLCOM)*, pages 1–6. IEEE, 2018.

28. Alexander Pyattaev, Kerstin Johnsson, Sergey Andreev, and Yevgeni Koucheryavy. Communication challenges in high-density deployments of wearable wireless devices. *IEEE Wireless Communications*, 22(1):12–18, 2015.
29. MI Mead, OAM Popoola, GB Stewart, Peter Landshoff, M Calleja, M Hayes, JJ Baldovi, MW McLeod, TF Hodgson, J Dicks, et al. The use of electrochemical sensors for monitoring urban air quality in low-cost, high-density networks. *Atmospheric Environment*, 70:186–203, 2013.
30. Nuria Castell, Mike Kobernus, Hai-Ying Liu, Philipp Schneider, William Lahoz, Arne J Berre, and Josef Noll. Mobile technologies and services for environmental monitoring: The citi-sense-mob approach. *Urban climate*, 14:370–382, 2015.

LoRaWAN Based IoT to Satellite Communication for Integrated Terrestrial and Non-terrestrial Networks

Nikumani Choudhury, Jay Dave, and Tamoghna Ojha

1 Introduction

The Internet of Things (IoT) has revolutionized the way we collect, process, and utilize data across various industries, including environmental monitoring, disaster management, precision agriculture, and defence. However, traditional IoT deployments, with inherent geographical limitations, rely on terrestrial communication networks, such as cellular, Wi-Fi, and Long Range Wide Area Networks (LoRaWAN) [7, 8, 16, 17]. Remote and inaccessible regions such as oceans, dense forests, deserts, and polar areas remain largely unconnected due to the lack of infrastructure, making it difficult to deploy IoT solutions effectively.

To overcome these limitations, integrating LoRaWAN with satellite communication has emerged as a promising solution [2, 6, 12]. LoRaWAN is a low-power, long-range communication protocol widely used for IoT applications due to its energy efficiency and ability to support large-scale sensor networks. However, conventional LoRaWAN networks depend on terrestrial gateways to relay data to the internet, restricting their reach to areas with existing network infrastructure [10]. IoT devices can achieve global coverage by extending LoRaWAN connectivity through Low Earth Orbit (LEO) satellite constellations and other satellite architectures, enabling seamless data transmission even in the most remote locations [1, 4, 19, 25].

N. Choudhury (✉) · J. Dave
Department of CSIS, BITS Pilani Hyderabad, Hyderabad, India
e-mail: nikumani@hyderabad.bits-pilani.ac.in

J. Dave
e-mail: Jay.dave@hyderabad.bits-pilani.ac.in

T. Ojha
Department of Mathematics and Computing, IIT (ISM) Dhanbad, Dhanbad, India
e-mail: tamoghnaojha@iitism.ac.in

T. Ojha et al. (eds.), *Edge-Enabled 6G Networking*,
https://doi.org/10.1007/978-3-032-19042-0_13

Despite its potential, IoT-to-satellite communication faces several technical challenges, including high latency, intermittent connectivity, spectral efficiency constraints, interference management, and power limitations of IoT devices [18, 23, 26]. Unlike traditional terrestrial networks, satellite links introduce delays due to longer transmission distances and the movement of satellites. Additionally, since many IoT sensors operate on battery power in remote locations, energy-efficient communication strategies are essential to prolong network lifespan.

As we move toward the sixth-generation (6G) wireless networks, the integration of Terrestrial and Non-Terrestrial Networks (ITNTN) with LoRaWAN will be a game-changer in ensuring ubiquitous, ultra-reliable, and low-latency connectivity [9, 13, 14, 21, 22]. 6G envisions a fully connected world where satellite, aerial, and terrestrial networks seamlessly interoperate to provide global coverage, supporting applications such as autonomous systems, real-time environmental monitoring, and smart cities. By integrating LoRaWAN with ITNTN, IoT devices can dynamically switch between terrestrial and satellite links, ensuring uninterrupted connectivity even in challenging environments. In Fig. 1, we discuss the key features and aspects of 6G network vision. Additionally, 6G-enabled AI-driven network management can optimize spectrum allocation, enhance data prioritization, and improve energy efficiency, making LoRaWAN-based IoT-to-satellite communication more scalable and resilient. This fusion of technologies will be critical in enabling next-generation IoT applications, bridging the digital divide, and supporting a wide range of mission-critical operations.

This chapter explores the integration of LoRaWAN and satellite communication, detailing its system architecture, key challenges, and potential solutions. It also highlights real-world applications across various industries and discusses future research directions to improve resource allocation, security, and efficiency in satellite-enabled

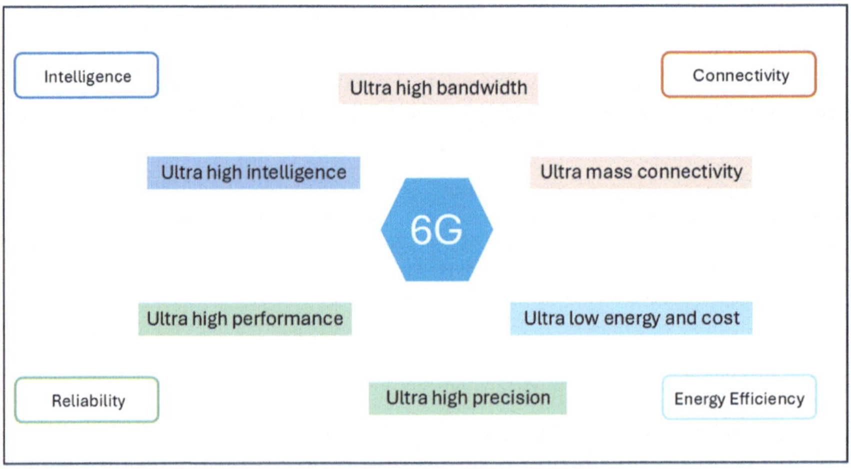

Fig. 1 Key features and aspects of the 6G network vision

IoT networks. By addressing these issues, LoRaWAN-based IoT-to-satellite communication can play a pivotal role in expanding the reach of IoT applications, ensuring connectivity in remote and harsh environments, and supporting a wide range of sectors, from environmental conservation to global security.

1.1 Motivation

The rapid growth of the Internet of Things (IoT) has revolutionized industries such as environmental monitoring, agriculture, disaster management, and defense by enabling real-time data collection and automation. However, a significant challenge remains in the form of the limited reach of traditional IoT networks, which rely on terrestrial infrastructures such as cellular, Wi-Fi, and conventional LoRaWAN gateways. These networks fail to provide coverage in remote and inaccessible regions, such as oceans, deserts, mountains, and polar areas, where IoT applications are most needed [15, 24]. This gap in connectivity hinders the deployment of critical services, including wildlife conservation, early disaster warnings, military surveillance, and global logistics tracking.

To overcome these limitations, the integration of LoRaWAN with satellite communication offers a promising solution (as shown in Fig. 2). LoRaWAN is known for its low power consumption and long-range communication, making it ideal for IoT applications. However, conventional LoRaWAN networks require terrestrial gateways to relay data, restricting their deployment to areas with existing infrastructure. By leveraging Low Earth Orbit (LEO) satellite constellations and other non-terrestrial networks , LoRaWAN can achieve global coverage, enabling seamless IoT connectivity even in remote environments [3, 5]. This integration aligns with the vision

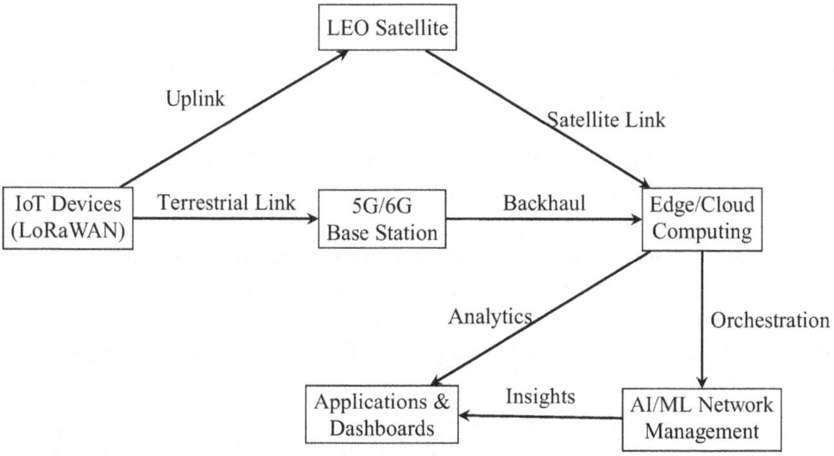

Fig. 2 Conceptual architecture of integrated terrestrial and satellite networks in 6G

of 6G networks, where Terrestrial and Non-Terrestrial Networks will work together to ensure uninterrupted connectivity for IoT applications. This work is motivated by the urgent need to develop scalable, reliable, and energy-efficient IoT-to-satellite communication solutions. By addressing the key challenges, this integration can unlock new opportunities for global IoT applications, supporting industries ranging from environmental conservation and precision agriculture to defense and emergency response.

1.2 Contribution

This chapter explores the integration of LoRaWAN with satellite communication, addressing the key challenges and opportunities in extending IoT connectivity to remote and underserved regions. The major contributions of this chapter are as follows:

1. Provides an in-depth overview of LoRaWAN technology and its limitations in terrestrial networks. It further explains how satellite communication, particularly Low Earth Orbit (LEO) satellite constellations, can extend LoRaWAN's coverage globally.
2. It proposes a three-layer architecture consisting of IoT end devices, satellite-enabled gateways, and ground stations.
3. The chapter discusses critical issues such as high latency, spectrum efficiency, interference management, and power constraints in IoT-to-satellite communication.

2 Overview of LoRaWAN and Satellite Communication

Long Range Wide Area Network (LoRaWAN) is a low-power, long-range wireless communication protocol designed for IoT applications. It operates on license-free sub-GHz frequency bands, such as 868 MHz in Europe and 915 MHz in the US, making it cost-effective and widely accessible. LoRaWAN utilizes chirp spread spectrum (CSS) modulation, allowing data transmission over long distances while maintaining low power consumption. Key advantages of LoRaWAN include its long-range communication capability, with coverage of up to 10–15 km in rural areas and 2–5 km in urban settings, as well as its low power requirements, enabling IoT devices to operate for years on battery power. The network follows a star-of-stars topology, where end devices transmit data to gateways, which then forward it to network servers. However, LoRaWAN also has limitations, primarily due to its dependence on terrestrial gateways, restricting deployment to areas with existing network infrastructure. Additionally, it faces coverage limitations in remote regions such as oceans, mountains,

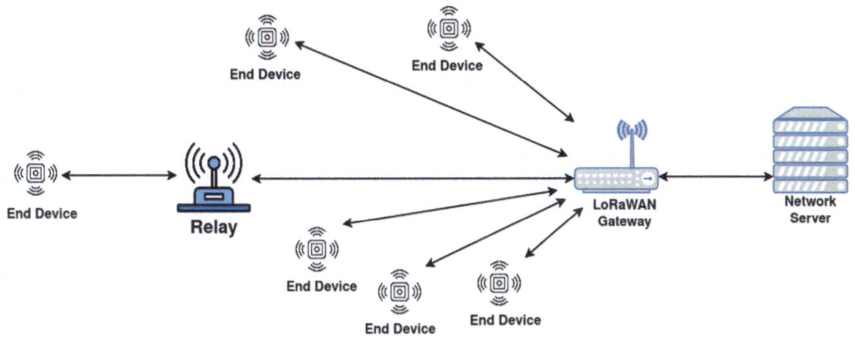

Fig. 3 LoRaWAN architecture

and polar zones, and is vulnerable to interference from other devices operating in unlicensed frequency bands. A typical LoRaWAN architecture is shown in Fig. 3.

To address these challenges, satellite communication presents a viable solution for extending IoT connectivity beyond terrestrial constraints. By integrating LoRaWAN with satellite networks, IoT applications can operate in remote and inaccessible locations, enabling critical services such as environmental monitoring, disaster response, and military surveillance. Different types of satellites serve IoT communication needs, categorized based on their orbital altitude. Low Earth Orbit (LEO) satellites, positioned between 500–1,500 km, offer low latency (50–100 ms) and frequent data transmission, making them ideal for IoT applications requiring real-time updates. Examples include Starlink, Swarm, Kepler, and Lacuna Space. Medium Earth Orbit (MEO) satellites, at altitudes between 5,000–20,000 km, balance latency and coverage and are commonly used for applications like GPS tracking. Meanwhile, Geostationary Orbit (GEO) satellites, positioned at 35,786 km, provide extensive coverage but suffer from high latency (250–600 ms), making them less suitable for real-time IoT applications. Notable GEO satellite providers include Inmarsat, HughesNet, and Viasat.

The integration of LoRaWAN with satellite networks provides numerous benefits, including global coverage, scalability, and resilience. Unlike terrestrial networks, satellite communication can connect IoT devices without requiring dense gateway deployments, making it more cost-effective for large-scale applications. Additionally, satellite networks remain operational during disasters and infrastructure failures, ensuring reliable connectivity in emergency situations. The LoRaWAN-to-satellite communication architecture typically consists of three layers: IoT end devices, which collect and transmit data using LoRa modulation; satellite-enabled gateways, which receive and relay data to ground stations; and ground stations and cloud platforms, which process the data and distribute it for analysis and decision-making. However, integrating LoRaWAN with satellites introduces challenges such as high latency, intermittent connectivity, spectrum efficiency, and power constraints of IoT devices.

To overcome these limitations, advanced techniques such as Delay-Tolerant Networking (DTN), adaptive modulation, AI-driven data prioritization, and energy-efficient transmission strategies are being explored. DTN ensures reliable data delivery despite connectivity disruptions, while adaptive modulation and coding optimize transmission rates under varying link conditions. Additionally, AI-driven network optimization can enhance resource allocation and reduce redundant transmissions, improving efficiency and extending device battery life. By leveraging LEO satellite constellations, LoRaWAN-based IoT-to-satellite networks can achieve ubiquitous, energy-efficient, and cost-effective connectivity, supporting next-generation IoT applications in remote and challenging environments.

3 System Model

The proposed LoRaWAN-to-Satellite communication system consists of three primary layers: IoT end devices, satellite-enabled gateways, and ground stations with cloud processing. This is presented in Fig. 4. At the IoT end devices layer, sensors and other low-power IoT devices are deployed in remote and inaccessible locations, such as forests, mountains, oceans, and deserts. These devices utilize LoRa modulation to transmit data over long distances with minimal power consumption. Since traditional LoRaWAN networks depend on terrestrial gateways, integrating satellite communication eliminates coverage limitations, enabling seamless global connectivity.

The satellite-enabled gateway layer consists of Low Earth Orbit (LEO), Medium Earth Orbit (MEO), and Geostationary Earth Orbit (GEO) satellites equipped with LoRa receivers. These satellites act as relays, collecting data from IoT devices and forwarding it to ground stations. Due to the intermittent nature of satellite links, a store-and-forward mechanism using Delay-Tolerant Networking (DTN) is employed to ensure reliable data transmission. Satellites also communicate with each other to optimize data routing and reduce latency before relaying information to Earth.

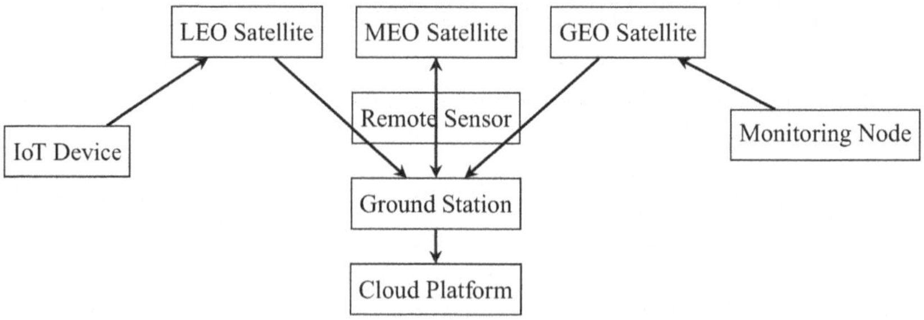

Fig. 4 Three-tier satellite architecture with IoT devices, satellite relay, and cloud integration

At the ground station and cloud processing layer, ground stations receive data from satellites and forward it to cloud platforms for further processing and analysis. Cloud-based systems enable real-time monitoring, analytics, and decision-making, making the network suitable for applications such as environmental monitoring, disaster response, precision agriculture, and military surveillance. Additionally, AI-driven data prioritization and adaptive resource allocation help optimize bandwidth usage and minimize redundant transmissions. The integration of multipath routing across LEO, MEO, and GEO satellites further enhances network resilience and Quality of Service (QoS). Overall, this system model leverages satellite-enabled LoRaWAN networks to provide scalable, energy-efficient, and globally accessible IoT connectivity, overcoming the limitations of traditional terrestrial infrastructures.

3.1 LoRaWAN Relay Support in NS-3: Overview and Functionality

This NS-3 module [20] implements a comprehensive framework to simulate LoRaWAN relay-assisted communication. It consists of three main modules: the end device application (`lorawan-test-app`), the relay node application (`lorawan-relay`), and the simulation configuration (`lorawan-realworld-simulation.cc`). Each component plays a distinct role in modeling the interactions within a LoRaWAN system involving uplink and downlink traffic with relay support.

The end device functionality is implemented through the `LoRaWanTestApp` class, derived from `ns3::Application`. Each end device sets up UDP sockets to send uplink frames to the relay and to listen for downlink messages on port 10001. The application schedules three key types of messages: uplink frames, MAC command frames, and timing update frames. The `SendUplinkFrame()` method sends a standard uplink packet. The `SendMacCommandFrame()` sends a relay configuration request using command ID `0x40`, allowing remote tuning of the relay's forward delay. The `SendTimingUpdateFrame()` method configures timing-related parameters on the relay (e.g., CAD periodicity, CAD-to-RX symbol delay, and time offset) using command ID `0x41`. The application also includes a downlink receiver via `HandleDownlink()`, which enables end devices to process packets forwarded by the relay.

The relay node functionality is encapsulated in the `LoRaWanRelay` class. This component sets up two sockets: one to receive uplink packets on port 10000 and another to receive downlink traffic on port 30000. The `HandleRead()` method parses received packets, verifies their structure and content, and processes MAC commands. The relay filters out Join Requests and uses placeholder MIC verification to simulate security checks. MAC commands received from end devices are handled by `ProcessMacCommand()`, which interprets and applies the appropriate configuration changes. Command `0x40` modifies the forwarding delay, while `0x41` adjusts internal timing parameters. Valid frames are scheduled for forwarding to the network server via the `ForwardPacket()` method, introducing a controlled delay as configured. The relay also handles downlink packets from the network server, broadcasting them to all end devices on UDP port 10001 using the `HandleDownlink()` method.

The complete simulation is orchestrated in `lorawan-realworld-simulation.cc`, which sets up a network consisting of 16 end devices, one relay node, one gateway, and one network server. All nodes are connected using a CSMA channel, and IP addresses are assigned accordingly. The gateway runs the `LoRaWanGatewayApp`, which listens on port 40000 for uplink packets from the relay and on port 40001 for downlink packets from the network server. It forwards uplink traffic to the server and routes downlink traffic to the relay. The network server is configured as a UDP server, and a scheduled event sends a downlink packet at 70 s.

This modular architecture provides a robust simulation environment for evaluating the performance and behavior of relay-assisted LoRaWAN networks. It supports dynamic MAC command configuration, timing updates, and bi-directional traffic flow between end devices and the network server. The framework is ideal for analyzing protocol performance, relay behavior, and timing-critical applications in IoT scenarios. A UML diagram depicting the interdependencies of the various functions are shown in Fig. 5.

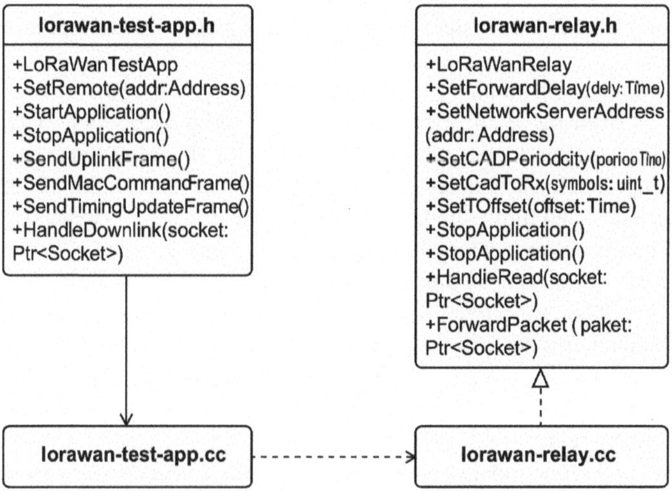

Fig. 5 UML diagram for LoRaWAN relay

3.2 Testbed with LoRaWAN

The testbed employed an ESP-32 microcontroller paired with an RFM95W radio transmitter, operating at 868MHz, to function as the end device. The gateway component was realized using a Dragino PG 1302 Concentrator connected to a Raspberry Pi 4. This concentrator efficiently aggregates the LoRa signals, while the Raspberry Pi facilitates data transmission to the network server. This is shown in Fig. 6.

3.3 Space-Aerial-Ground Integrated Network (SAGIN) Simulation with NS-3

The SAGIN NS-3 module [11] implements a simulation framework that enables the modeling and performance evaluation of hybrid communication infrastructures spanning satellite, aerial, and terrestrial layers. The module is designed to support experimentation with integrated routing, mobility, MAC/PHY behaviors, and node coordination strategies that are foundational to next-generation non-terrestrial networks (NTNs) and 6G research.

At its core, the module defines an extensible node hierarchy through the `SaginNode` class, which serves as the base abstraction for all types of SAGIN entities. Specialized node classes—`AerialNode`, `GroundNode`, and `SpaceNode`—inherit from `SaginNode`, each extending the base functionality with behaviors suited to their respective domains. This object-oriented structure allows users to instantiate and interconnect heterogeneous nodes while maintaining a unified network abstraction.

The MAC and PHY layers are implemented via `SaginMac` and `SaginPhy`, respectively. The `SaginMac` class handles medium access control and encapsulates logic for data transmission coordination and frame handling. It is responsible for scheduling access and resolving contentions among nodes. The `SaginPhy` class

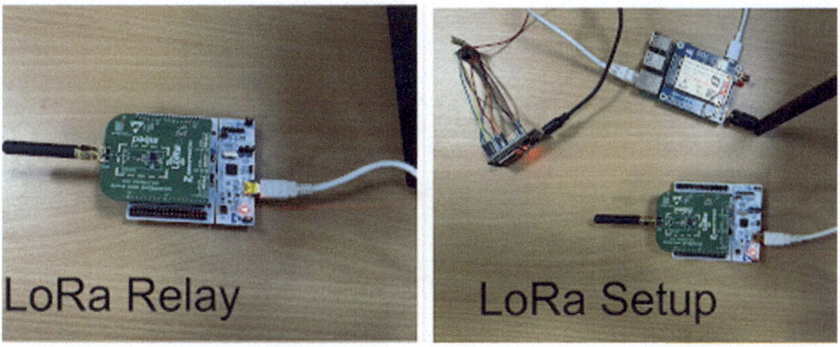

Fig. 6 LoRa communication setup

models the physical transmission behavior and is designed to simulate realistic propagation and channel effects across space, air, and ground links.

Routing functionality is encapsulated in the `SaginRouting` class, derived from the `ns3::Object` base. It includes mechanisms for path computation and dynamic re-routing to adapt to topology changes introduced by mobile or orbital nodes. This is particularly useful in studying delay-tolerant networking (DTN) extensions or hybrid routing protocols suitable for SAGIN scenarios.

The `NodeAddress` and `NodeList` utilities provide logical addressing and centralized management of nodes deployed across the three tiers. `NodeAddress` allows tagging and identification of nodes based on their domain and role, while `NodeList` maintains global references and helps in efficiently locating or querying nodes during simulation runtime.

Simulation setup and node configuration are streamlined using the `SaginHelper` class, defined in the helper directory. This class allows researchers to instantiate ground, aerial, and space nodes with appropriate parameters, configure inter-node communication links, and set mobility patterns. The module supports easy integration with other NS-3 components and routing stacks (e.g., AODV with DTN extensions), facilitating cross-layer experimentation.

Example scenarios demonstrate typical use cases such as inter-orbital relaying, UAV-aided backhaul formation, and dynamic topology adaptation in mobile edge-cloud environments. These examples serve as templates for designing more complex SAGIN experiments involving latency-aware routing, traffic prioritization, or network slicing.

Overall, the SAGIN NS-3 module provides a flexible, extensible, and high-fidelity simulation framework for researchers aiming to explore and evaluate communication paradigms in integrated space-air-ground architectures. Its modular design and abstraction hierarchy make it suitable for studying next-generation connectivity challenges such as dynamic topology management, joint trajectory-resource optimization, and AI/ML-based orchestration across heterogeneous network layers. Different sub-module of the SAGIN module and the different node types of `ns3::SaginNode` with their properties are shown in Figs. 7 and 8, respectively.

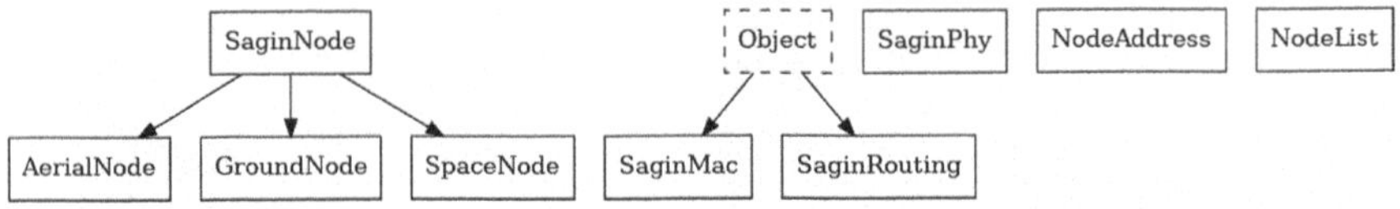

Fig. 7 Different sub-module of the SAGIN module

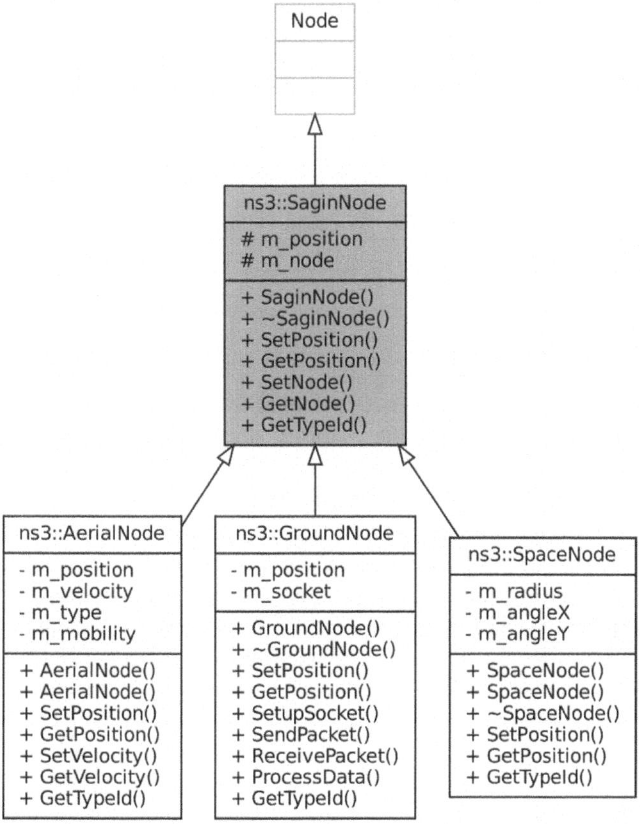

Fig. 8 Different node types in `ns3::SaginNode`

4 Proposed Architecture

The LoRaWAN-to-Satellite communication system is designed to overcome the limitations of terrestrial networks by integrating LoRaWAN technology with satellite communication. This architecture (shown in Fig. 9) provides seamless global connectivity, enabling IoT applications in remote and underserved areas such as oceans, forests, mountains, and polar regions. The system consists of three primary layers: IoT end devices, satellite-enabled gateways, and ground stations with cloud processing, each playing a crucial role in ensuring efficient data transmission, low power consumption, and reliable connectivity.

At the IoT end devices layer, low-power sensors and IoT devices are deployed in remote locations to collect and transmit data using LoRa modulation. These devices operate on minimal power, often using duty cycling and adaptive spreading factors to optimize energy efficiency and prolong battery life. Unlike traditional LoRaWAN networks, where IoT devices communicate with terrestrial gateways, this architecture

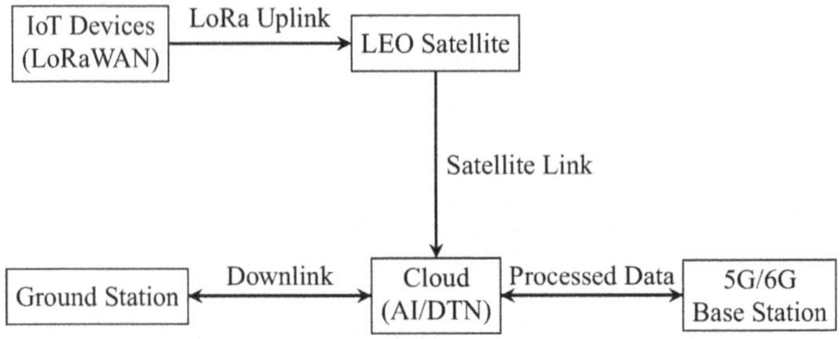

Fig. 9 Integration of LoRaWAN, LEO satellite, and terrestrial networks in 6G

allows devices to transmit data directly to satellites equipped with LoRa receivers. However, due to intermittent satellite visibility, store-and-forward mechanisms may be necessary to ensure reliable data delivery. The satellite-enabled gateway layer acts as an intermediary between IoT devices and ground stations. Satellites equipped with LoRaWAN-compatible receivers collect data from end devices and relay it to Earth for further processing. Low Earth Orbit (LEO) satellites, positioned between 500–1,500 km, offer low latency (50–100 ms) and frequent data transmission, making them ideal for real-time or near-real-time IoT applications. Meanwhile, Medium Earth Orbit (MEO) satellites provide a balance between coverage and latency, while Geostationary Earth Orbit (GEO) satellites, positioned at 35,786 km, offer continuous coverage but suffer from high latency (250–600 ms), making them less suitable for real-time applications. To improve reliability, inter-satellite communication can be utilized for optimized data routing before relaying the information to Earth. Additionally, adaptive modulation and coding techniques are used to optimize spectral efficiency and reduce packet loss under varying link conditions.

At the ground station and cloud processing layer, data is received from satellites via high-speed radio frequency (RF) or optical links. These ground stations process the data and forward it to cloud-based platforms, where real-time monitoring, AI-driven analytics, and decision-making occur. Network servers manage LoRaWAN network traffic, handling packet deduplication, device authentication, and security protocols. Additionally, cloud computing infrastructure ensures efficient storage and processing of IoT data, allowing users to access valuable insights through dashboards, APIs, or mobile applications. The integration of AI-driven data prioritization helps optimize bandwidth usage by reducing redundant transmissions while ensuring critical data is delivered in a timely manner. Furthermore, this architecture can interconnect with 5G networks, edge computing, and terrestrial LoRaWAN systems, providing a hybrid communication framework for seamless connectivity.

The end-to-end data flow in this system begins with IoT devices collecting sensor data and transmitting it using LoRa modulation. LEO/MEO/GEO satellites receive these signals and forward them to ground stations using high-speed RF or optical links. The ground stations then process and filter the data before forwarding it to cloud platforms for real-time analytics and application services. Users can access and visualize IoT data through intuitive dashboards, enabling informed decision-making in applications such as disaster management, environmental monitoring, smart agriculture, and military surveillance.

Despite its advantages, LoRaWAN-to-Satellite communication faces several challenges, including high latency, intermittent connectivity, spectrum efficiency, and power constraints of IoT devices. GEO satellites introduce significant latency, making them unsuitable for real-time applications, while IoT devices must optimize power consumption to ensure long-term operation. Additionally, LoRaWAN operates in unlicensed frequency bands, making it vulnerable to interference, necessitating effective spectrum management techniques. Security is another crucial concern, requiring lightweight cryptographic solutions to protect data integrity and confidentiality. To overcome these challenges, advanced techniques such as Delay-Tolerant Networking (DTN), AI-driven network optimization, adaptive modulation, and multipath routing across LEO, MEO, and GEO satellites can be employed to enhance network resilience and efficiency.

5 Challenges in IoT-to-Satellite Communication

While IoT-to-Satellite communication offers significant advantages in extending connectivity to remote and underserved areas, several challenges must be addressed to ensure efficient, reliable, and sustainable operations. These challenges stem from the fundamental differences between terrestrial IoT networks and satellite communication, including factors such as high latency, intermittent connectivity, spectral efficiency, interference management, and energy constraints of IoT devices. One of the primary challenges in IoT-to-Satellite communication is high latency, particularly when using Geostationary Earth Orbit (GEO) satellites, which are positioned at 35,786 km above the Earth. The round-trip signal delay for GEO satellites can exceed 500 ms, making them unsuitable for real-time applications such as industrial automation and emergency response. While Low Earth Orbit (LEO) satellites offer lower latency (typically 50–100 ms), their high-speed movement across the sky introduces additional challenges in maintaining continuous connectivity, requiring frequent handovers between satellites. The intermittent visibility of LEO satellites can result in packet loss, necessitating store-and-forward mechanisms and Delay-Tolerant Networking (DTN) to ensure reliable data transmission.

Another major issue is *spectrum efficiency and interference management.* LoRaWAN operates in unlicensed frequency bands, which are prone to interference from other wireless technologies, terrestrial networks, and even adjacent satellite networks. Unlike traditional cellular networks, LoRaWAN has limited bandwidth, and optimizing spectral efficiency is critical to avoiding congestion in satellite-based LoRaWAN systems. Adaptive modulation and coding techniques are needed to dynamically adjust data rates and transmission power based on changing channel conditions. Additionally, as satellite networks expand, inter-satellite interference could become a significant issue, requiring advanced frequency planning and interference mitigation strategies to ensure reliable communication.

Energy constraints of IoT devices present another critical challenge. Most IoT sensors deployed in remote locations are battery-powered, and replacing or recharging these batteries is often impractical. Unlike terrestrial LoRaWAN networks that rely on nearby gateways, satellite-based IoT communication requires longer transmission distances, leading to increased power consumption. To address this, energy-efficient transmission strategies such as duty cycling, adaptive spreading factors, and low-power wake-up schemes must be implemented. Additionally, AI-driven power optimization can help dynamically allocate resources based on network conditions, further extending the operational lifetime of IoT devices.

Intermittent connectivity and network disruptions are also significant hurdles. Unlike terrestrial LoRaWAN, where gateways are permanently available, satellite-based networks experience frequent connectivity blackouts due to orbital movement, weather conditions, and link congestion. The store-and-forward mechanism is essential to buffer data during disruptions and ensure eventual delivery. However, network congestion and limited satellite bandwidth can further delay data transmission, especially when dealing with high-density IoT deployments. Multipath routing across LEO, Medium Earth Orbit (MEO), and GEO satellites can help mitigate this issue by enabling dynamic path selection to minimize packet loss and improve Quality of Service (QoS).

Security and privacy are additional concerns in IoT-to-Satellite communication. The open nature of LoRaWAN's unlicensed spectrum makes it vulnerable to eavesdropping, jamming, and replay attacks. Implementing lightweight encryption mechanisms is essential, but these solutions must be designed to minimize computational overhead to avoid draining the battery life of IoT devices. Furthermore, authentication and access control mechanisms need to be adapted for satellite-based IoT networks, ensuring secure data transmission without introducing excessive complexity or delays.

Lastly, *scalability and network management* present operational challenges as satellite constellations grow. With the increasing number of LEO satellites in orbit, effective network orchestration is required to balance traffic loads, avoid congestion, and optimize data routing. AI-driven network optimization can play a key role in predicting congestion patterns and dynamically allocating bandwidth and transmission priorities to ensure efficient resource utilization. However, integrating AI with satellite-based LoRaWAN networks requires advanced edge computing capabilities to process data locally before forwarding it to cloud-based platforms. These challenges are listed in Table 1.

5.1 Security Challenges in IoT-to-Satellite Communication

The integration of IoT networks with satellite systems presents multidimensional security complications due to the inherent weaknesses of resource-constrained IoT

Table 1 Challenges in IoT-to-satellite communication

Challenges	Description
High latency (GEO/LEO)	GEO satellites introduce >500 ms round-trip delays, making real-time applications impractical. LEO satellites reduce latency (50–100 ms) but require frequent handovers due to high orbital speeds
Intermittent connectivity	LEO satellites experience visibility gaps, causing packet loss and requiring store-and-forward mechanisms. Weather, orbital movement, and congestion further disrupt continuous data transmission
Spectrum efficiency	Interference and Limited bandwidth in unlicensed LoRaWAN bands leads to congestion. Interference from terrestrial networks, adjacent satellites, and poor spectral efficiency necessitates adaptive modulation and coding techniques
Energy constraints	Battery-powered IoT devices face high power demands for satellite uplinks. Energy-efficient strategies (duty cycling, adaptive spreading factors) and AI-driven power optimization are critical for longevity
Security and privacy	Vulnerabilities include eavesdropping, jamming, replay attacks, and weak encryption. Resource-constrained IoT devices struggle with advanced cryptography, while distributed architectures complicate authentication
Scalability and network management	Growing LEO constellations require AI-driven orchestration to balance traffic, avoid congestion, and optimize routing. Edge computing is needed to preprocess data before cloud transmission
Lack of standardized security frameworks	Absence of unified protocols for space-terrestrial systems hinders threat detection/mitigation. Solutions like lightweight cryptography, blockchain authentication, and AI-based intrusion detection are needed

devices, vulnerable wireless satellite links, and the integrated terrestrial-space data pathway. First, IoT devices usually have limited computational power to support advanced cryptographic algorithms. These cryptographic solutions are needed for spoofing, eavesdropping, and physical tampering. Second, satellite communication links are low-orbit communication networks. They are vulnerable to interception, signal jamming, and replay attacks because of long propagation delays and broad coverage. Third, IoT-satellite networks consist of spanning edge gateways, satellites, and ground stations. Such a diverse nature introduces vulnerability to unauthorized access to mission-critical data during aggregation or relay. Moreover, the distributed model introduces difficulty in key managing procedures and authentication across intermittent connections. It raises risks of man-in-the-middle (MITM) attacks or anomalous nodes. Scalability further escalates these challenges because traditional security solutions are difficult to apply to massive IoT deployments with varying latency and bandwidth limitations. Finally, the lacks of standardized cross-domain security frameworks for space-terrestrial systems restrict threat detection and mitigation. It raises a need for novel solutions on lightweight cryptography, blockchain-based authentication, and AI-driven intrusion detection.

6 Conclusion and Future Work

This chapter explores the integration of LoRaWAN with satellite communication to enable global IoT connectivity beyond terrestrial constraints. By leveraging LEO satellites, LoRaWAN-based IoT-to-satellite systems support applications in environmental monitoring, disaster management, and defense. A three-layer architecture ensures efficient data transmission, but challenges like latency, intermittent connectivity, and power constraints persist. AI-driven optimizations, DTN, and adaptive modulation can enhance efficiency. With 6G and ITNTN, future research should focus on security, resource allocation, and inter-satellite communication, ensuring scalable, resilient, and energy-efficient IoT networks for remote and critical applications.

References

1. Castro-Carrera, A.: A systematic review of leo satellite services for iot. Multidisciplinary Reviews **8**(3), 2025083–2025083 (2025)
2. Centenaro, M., Costa, C.E., Granelli, F., Sacchi, C., Vangelista, L.: A survey on technologies, standards and open challenges in satellite iot. IEEE Communications Surveys & Tutorials **23**(3), 1693–1720 (2021)
3. Choquenaira-Florez, A.Y., Ohs, R., Fraire, J.A., Rivano, H.: Florasat 2: Simulating cross-linked direct-to-satellite iot leo constellations. In: 2025 12th Advanced Satellite Multimedia Systems Conference and the 18th Signal Processing for Space Communications Workshop (ASMS/SPSC). pp. 1–8. IEEE (2025)
4. Dave, J., Choudhury, N.: Security enhancement of otaa based joining procedure in lorawan for satellite communication. In: 2024 IEEE 99th Vehicular Technology Conference (VTC2024-Spring). pp. 1–5 (2024). https://doi.org/10.1109/VTC2024-Spring62846.2024.10683277
5. Deng, J., Benkhelifa, F., Alouini, M.S.: Orthogonality analysis in lora uplink satellite communications affected by doppler effect. arXiv preprint arXiv:2502.16179 (2025)
6. Fraire, J.A., Céspedes, S., Accettura, N.: Direct-to-satellite iot - a survey of the state of the art and future research perspectives. In: Palattella, M.R., Scanzio, S., Coleri Ergen, S. (eds.) Ad-Hoc, Mobile, and Wireless Networks. pp. 241–258. Springer International Publishing, Cham (2019)
7. Gorrela, A., Choudhury, N.: A clustering-based adaptive data rate technique for industrial lorawan-iot networks. IEEE Internet of Things Journal **12**(6), 6506–6518 (2025)
8. Gorrela, A., Choudhury, N., Hazarika, A., Lloret, J.: Contention congestion collision adaptive data rate for lorawan-based challenging industrial iot. In: 2023 IEEE Globecom Workshops (GC Wkshps). pp. 1021–1026 (2023)
9. Janssen, T., Koppert, A., Berkvens, R., Weyn, M.: A survey on iot positioning leveraging lpwan, gnss, and leo-pnt. IEEE Internet of Things Journal **10**(13), 11135–11159 (2023)

10. Jouhari, M., Saeed, N., Alouini, M.S., Amhoud, E.M.: A survey on scalable lorawan for massive iot: Recent advances, potentials, and challenges. IEEE Communications Surveys & Tutorials **25**(3), 1841–1876 (2023). https://doi.org/10.1109/COMST.2023.3274934
11. Kamra, S., Walia, A., Jajodia, H.V., Ojha, T., Maiti, R.R.: Space-aerial-ground integrated network (SAGIN) NS-3 module. https://github.com/Kal-El-pt2/SAGIN-ns3-module/ (2025), accessed: 2025-05-22
12. Le, T.T.T., Hassan, N.U., Chen, X., Alouini, M.S., Han, Z., Yuen, C.: A survey on random access protocols in direct-access leo satellite-based iot communication. IEEE Communications Surveys & Tutorials **27**(1), 426–462 (2025). https://doi.org/10.1109/COMST.2024.3385347
13. Ledesma, O., Lamo, P., Fraire, J.A.: Trends in lpwan technologies for leo satellite constellations in the newspace context. Electronics **13**(3), 579 (2024)
14. Lee, C., Kim, T., Jung, C., Yoon, Z.: Iot-ntn with vleo and leo satellite constellations and lpwan: A comparative study of lora, nb-iot, and mioty. Electronics **14**(9), 1798 (2025)
15. Lin, K., Ullah, M.A., Lei, L., Alves, H., Mikhaylov, K., Hao, T.: Performance analysis of lorawan underground-to-satellite connectivity: An urban underground pipelines monitoring case study. Ad Hoc Networks **169**, 103747 (2025)
16. LoRa Alliance: Lorawan relay specification v1.0.0 (2022), https://resources.lora-alliance.org/technical-specifications/ts011-1-0-0-relay, accessed: Jan. 20, 2025
17. Maurya, P., Hazra, A., Kumari, P., Sørensen, T.B., Das, S.K.: A comprehensive survey of data-driven solutions for lorawan: Challenges and future directions. ACM Transactions on Internet of Things **6**(1), 1–36 (2025)
18. Qu, Z., Cao, H., Cheng, Y., Wu, S., Zhang, G.: A lorawan-based network architecture for leo satellite internet of things. In: 2019 IEEE International Conference on Consumer Electronics-Taiwan (ICCE-TW). pp. 1–2. IEEE (2019)
19. Qu, Z., Zhang, G., Cao, H., Xie, J.: Leo satellite constellation for internet of things. IEEE access **5**, 18391–18401 (2017)
20. Sahu, S., Solanki, S., Solanki, S.N., Gaur, K., Choudhury, N.: Lorawan ns-3 module. https://github.com/SayanSahu99/lorawan (2025), accessed: 2025-05-22
21. Salah, M.M., Saad, R.S., Zaki, R.M., Rabie, K., ElHalawany, B.M.: Multi-armed bandits for resource allocation in uav-assisted lora networks. IEEE Internet of Things Magazine **8**(2), 40–45 (2025)
22. Susilo, H.E., Suryana, J.: Research on lpwan direct to satellite iot: A survey technology and performance on leo satellite. In: 2023 29th International Conference on Telecommunications (ICT). pp. 1–7. IEEE (2023)
23. Temim, M.A.B.: Low-Earth-Orbit satellite communications using LoRa-like signals. Ph.D. thesis, Université de Bordeaux (2022)
24. Ullah, M.A., Souza, R.D., Pasolini, G., de Souza Sant'Ana, J.M., Höyhtyä, M., Mikhaylov, K., Alves, H., Paolini, E., Al-Houran, A.: Extending the lora direct-to-satellite limits: Doppler shift pre-compensation. IEEE Open Journal of the Communications Society (2025)
25. Varma, A.M., Choudhury, N., Dave, J., Hazarika, A., Nasralla, M.M.: Lorawan scheduling mechanism for 6g-based leo satellite communications. In: 2024 IEEE 99th Vehicular Technology Conference (VTC2024-Spring). pp. 1–5 (2024). https://doi.org/10.1109/VTC2024-Spring62846.2024.10683512
26. Zhou, Z., Afhamisis, M., Palattella, M.R., Accettura, N., Berthou, P.: Pervasive lpwan connectivity through leo satellites: trading off reliability, throughput, latency, and energy efficiency. In: Low-Power Wide-Area Networks: Opportunities, Challenges, Risks and Threats, pp. 85–110. Springer (2023)

Machine Learning Approach to Determine and Predict the Scattering Coefficients of Myocardium Tissue in the NIR Band for In-Vivo Communications—6G Networks

Raja Manjula, Adi Vishnu Avula, Abdul Jawad Khan, Chiranjeevi Thota, Venkata Kavyanjali Munipallle, and Sabita Langkam

1 Introduction

The scattering coefficient μ_s of optical signals monitoring the myocardium is useful for assessing tissue properties and dynamics [1, 2]. It provides valuable information about the microstructural properties of the myocardium, including cell density, arrangement, and the presence of extracellular matrix components. Changes in these properties can occur due to various pathological conditions, such as ischemia, fibrosis, or inflammation, affecting light scattering patterns. With light scattering analysis within the myocardium tissue, researchers can gain insights into tissue structure, blood perfusion, and oxygenation levels. This information is vital for detecting abnormalities in cardiac function, diagnosing conditions like ischemia or infarction, and guiding interventions for heart health management. Overall, the scattering coefficient of optical signals serve as a valuable biomarker for monitoring myocardial health and guiding clinical decision-making in cardiology.

R. Manjula (✉) · A. V. Avula · A. J. Khan · C. Thota · V. K. Munipallle
Department of Computer Science and Engineering, SRM University AP, Andhra Pradesh, India
e-mail: rajamanjula12@gmail.com

A. V. Avula
e-mail: adivishnu_avula@srmap.edu.in

A. J. Khan
e-mail: jawad_khan@srmap.edu.in

C. Thota
e-mail: chiranjeevi_thota@srmap.edu.in

V. K. Munipallle
e-mail: venkatakavyanjali_m@srmap.edu.in

S. Langkam
Nayang DSP Research Centre (NDRC), Raipur, India

T. Ojha et al. (eds.), *Edge-Enabled 6G Networking*,
https://doi.org/10.1007/978-3-032-19042-0_14

Optical techniques, such as diffuse reflectance spectroscopy, optical coherence tomography (OCT), and diffuse optical imaging, utilize the scattering coefficient to minimally-invasively probe tissue characteristics [3]. By measuring the scattering properties of myocardial tissue over time, clinicians and researchers can track disease progression, assess treatment efficacy, and predict outcomes. However, each of these has certain limitations. OTC, for instance, has (i) Limited Penetration Depth (typically 1–2 mm in tissue), which restricts its ability to visualize deeper structures within the tissue and (ii) Movement of the tissue, such as the beating of the heart, can introduce artifacts and degrade image quality, making it challenging to obtain clear images of moving organs. These limitations require immediate attention to mitigate them. One such upcoming technology we suggest is the usage of in-vivo wireless nanosensor networks (i-WNSNs).

In-vivo wireless nanosensor nodes potentially address some of these limitations through several innovative approaches [4–6]:

- Enhanced Penetration Depth: Nanosensors can employ advanced light sources such as supercontinuum lasers or other light sources that provide a broad spectrum of wavelengths [7]. These sources can improve the penetration depth by allowing the use of longer wavelengths, say 800–1100 nm, that can penetrate deeper into the tissue.
- Mitigating Motion Artifacts: Wireless nanosensor nodes can be designed to acquire data in real time, reducing the impact of motion artifacts. The ability to capture data quickly can help synchronize with the cardiac cycle, minimizing distortions due to heartbeats. Embedding motion sensors within the nanosensor nodes can help detect and compensate for tissue movement. This data can be used to correct for motion artifacts in the OCT images.
- Expanding Field of View: Multiple nanosensor nodes can be distributed over a larger area to simultaneously capture data from different regions. This networked approach can effectively expand the field of view without the need for multiple scans.
- Miniaturization and Mobility: Nanosensors injected into the bloodstream are designed to gather and transmit data from various parts of the body, enabling the detection and pinpointing of abnormalities [8]. Nanosensors can be miniaturized and made mobile, allowing them to navigate through tissue and cover larger areas. This mobility can provide comprehensive imaging over extended regions of interest.
- Wireless communication capabilities can simplify the setup and use of nanosensor nodes. Eliminating the need for complex wiring and external equipment can make the technology more user-friendly and easier to deploy in clinical settings.
- Additional Advantages: Nanosensor nodes can be designed to target specific tissues or cells, providing high-resolution imaging of particular areas of interest. This targeted approach can enhance the diagnostic capabilities of OCT.

- Multimodal Sensing: Nanosensor nodes can integrate multiple sensing modalities, combining OCT with other optical techniques like fluorescence or Raman spectroscopy. This multimodal approach can provide complementary information, enhancing overall tissue characterization.

The enlisted qualities of in-vivo wireless nanosensor nodes make them a prospective candidate for medical imaging and data collection applications.

Given the background information on the importance of the scattering coefficients in optical bands and the advantages of using iWNSNs for medical diagnostics purpose, we now discuss the potential benefits of using Machine Learning techniques for computing and predicting the scattering coefficient values of biological tissues in medical applications.

Machine learning (ML) is a subfield of artificial intelligence (AI) focused on the development of algorithms and statistical models that enable computers to perform specific tasks without using explicit instructions, relying instead on patterns and inference. Data mining, computer vision, voice recognition, self-driving vehicles, and many more industries have recently adopted machine-learning-based techniques. These assignments fall within the categories of unsupervised and supervised learning. The aim of supervised learning using labeled data is to develop a generic and precise function between inputs and outputs, which makes it appropriate for handling regression and classification issues. Conversely, algorithms for unsupervised learning must characterize the hidden structure from unlabeled data. Scattering coefficient prediction is a supervised regression issue that may be handled using supervised machine learning methods like Linear Regression (LR), Polynomial Regression (PR), Gradient Boost (GB), and Artificial Neural Network (ANN). There have been reports that machine learning-based models outperform deterministic ones in terms of computing efficiency and accuracy compared to empirical models. Current literature uses machine learning for predicting optical properties of tissues [9], turbid medium [10] and skin [11]. However, to the best of our knowledge, there is no work in the literature that has demonstrated the application of machine learning for predicting the scattering coefficient of myocardial tissue in the NIR (333–425 THz) band for in-vivo applications. In addition, to understand the power of machine learning tools, we have also studied the data expansion aspect of machine learning. We aim to predict the scattering coefficient values for 425–500 THz frequency band and compare them with the existing data for validation. This strategic approach enables us to unravel the complexities of scattering loss in the myocardium layer and understand its behavior across different frequencies that are critical for heart health monitoring.

1.1 Problem Statement

To improve the understanding and prediction of scattering loss in myocardial tissues for applications in wireless health monitoring.

- Existing literature lacks analysis of scattering loss in the human heart.
- This is surprising as heart tissues cause spreading loss, absorption loss, and scattering loss.
- This research aims to fill this critical research gap by exploring heart tissue scattering

1.2 Contribution of This Work

The following are the contributions of this work:

- Estimate the scattering coefficient of the optical signal (NIR band) for the myocardium layer of the human heart using existing analytical models.
- Predict the scattering coefficient for the myocardium layer using ML models and data generated using the analytical model.
- Validate the results using a cross-validation technique.

The rest of the report is organized as follows: Sect. 2 provides the related literature works; Sect. 4 discusses the analytical model employed in the work and the various ML techniques studied. In Sect. 5 we provide results and discussion on the work and finally conclude the work in Sect. 6.

2 Literature Review

The authors in [12] present a method to determine the complex permittivity of lossy materials, such as tissue-mimicking phantoms, from observed reflection coefficients using an open-ended coaxial probe (OECP) and a deep learning model (DLM). The DLM is trained with a synthetic dataset generated using the admittance model and the Cole-Cole relaxation model. This approach accurately predicts complex permittivity from 0.5 to 20 GHz with a 50-MHz resolution, eliminating the need for actual measurements. Real reflection coefficient data from the skin, muscle, blood, and fat phantoms showed percent relative errors ranging from 2.08 ± 0.4 to 10.84 ± 2.43. This research offers a reliable and effective method for determining complex permittivity in biological tissues using deep learning and synthetic datasets, overcoming the limitations of traditional measurement techniques and providing a practical solution for real-world applications.

The work in [13] reviews recent advancements in using artificial intelligence (AI), specifically machine learning (ML) and deep learning (DL), to solve complex electromagnetic (EM) problems, including EM imaging and inverse scattering (IS). AI methods offer unprecedented computational efficiency and improved accuracy. The paper provides a detailed analysis of these applications, highlighting the strengths and limitations of AI in solving EM vision problems. The paper reviews the use of

AI for real-time inverse scattering and electromagnetic imaging, showcasing AI's potential to offer efficient and accurate solutions. It calls for further research to overcome current challenges and explore new AI applications in electromagnetics.

Khalid et al. [14] review examines the integration of artificial intelligence (AI) with microwave imaging (MWI) in biomedical applications. It highlights how AI enhances the accuracy and performance of MWI, discusses historical evolution, current advancements, and potential future applications, and addresses clinical challenges. The work has examined the latest MWI methods in healthcare; reviewed AI-supported MWI approaches and applications; identified research challenges in AI-supported MWI and finally evaluated recent AI and MWI advancements and their impact on medical diagnosis. The work investigates the application of multivariate and machine-learning techniques to assess the composition and biomechanical features of articular cartilage.

This study by Kafin et al. [15] demonstrates the possibility of real-time, quantitative tissue characterization through the use of optical spectroscopic techniques in conjunction with machine learning. This could result in improved diagnosis and treatment outcomes for degenerative joint illnesses such as osteoarthritis. Measured using techniques such as near-infrared spectroscopy or optical coherence tomography, the scattering (μ_s) and reduced scattering ($\mu_s^{'}$) coefficients can provide insights into the biochemical composition and structural integrity of cartilage, enabling early detection of degenerative changes. By combining these characteristics with machine learning algorithms, it is possible to enhance current diagnostic techniques while also increasing the precision and dependability of cartilage diagnoses.

Rodrigues work in [16] delves into the minimally-invasive in vivo monitoring of breast tumor progression by the utilisation of machine learning in conjunction with photoacoustic spectroscopy (PAS). Using an aseptic chamber that has been carefully built and connected with a photoacoustic (PA) probe, the research shows how PAS can be used to detect biochemical changes in tumors. In order to create breast tumors in the study, MCF-7 cells were implanted into naked mice, and PA spectra were taken at different intervals. The PA data was classified using machine learning models, particularly support vector machines (SVM), which demonstrated excellent sensitivity and specificity. The outcomes show that PAS is useful for diagnosing breast cancer early on and that it has the potential to be translated into clinical settings. This study demonstrates the great promise of PAS as a minimally-invasive, sensitive, and targeted approach for early disease identification in the diagnosis of breast cancer. Incorporating machine learning improves analytical capacities and opens the door to better patient outcomes and diagnostic accuracy in the treatment of breast cancer.

In order to improve diffuse optical tomography (DOT) reconstruction, the work in [17] study provides a machine learning model with physical constraints (ML-PC). DOT is confronted with a number of practical challenges, including noise and difficult boundary conditions, in addition to its ill-posed character. The novel method enhances reconstruction accuracy by combining physical restrictions, a neural network-based auto-encoder, and ultrasound-guided DOT. Reconstruction mistakes are greatly decreased in both phantom and clinical studies by the model, which performs better than conventional techniques. The ML-PC model, which offers better accuracy and clinical viability, is a noteworthy development in DOT reconstruction. This method solves the problems with DOT and opens the door to more accurate breast cancer monitoring and detection by combining machine learning with physical limitations.

3 Background

This section describes the necessary background information on the biological model of the heart, particularly the myocardium tissue, the subject of the work under the influence of optical signals; and description of the scattering model employed for complex structures such as myocardium that has nonuniform refractive indices throughout and finally explain the various machine learning models used in this work for estimation and prediction of scattering coefficients of NIR signal traveling through myocardium tissue.

3.1 Model of the Myocardium Tissue

The mammalian heart comprises of 3 walls and they are described as follows: (i) Epicardium: The outer layer of the heart wall, also known as the visceral layer of the serous pericardium, (ii) Myocardium: The middle, thickest layer, composed primarily of cardiac muscle cells, and (iii) Endocardium: The inner layer, lining the heart chambers and covering the heart valves as shown in Fig. 1. While all three

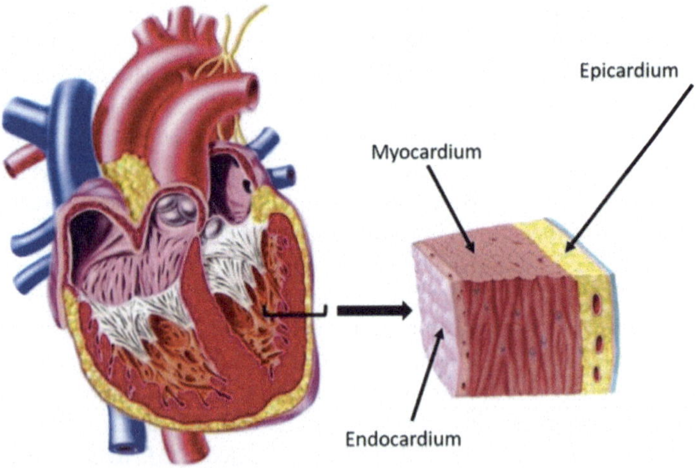

Fig. 1 Layers of the heart wall [18]

Table 1 Refractive index of myocardium tissue [19]

Description	Notation/Values
Wavelength (nm)	600–900 nm
Refractive index of sarcoplasm	1.35
Refractive index of myofibril	1.53
Volume fraction of sarcoplasm	$f_{sarco} = 0.875$
Volume fraction of myofibrils (cylinders)	$f_{cyl} = 1 - f_{sarco} = 0.126$
Radius of the particle (r)	1 μm
The average refractive index	n_0
Refractive index of the scatterers	n_s
Relative refractive index	$m = n_s/n_0$
Wavelength of the signal in vacuum	$\lambda_0 = c/f$

layers of the heart wall are important, the myocardium is the most critical due to its role in generating the contractile force required for pumping blood. This function is essential for maintaining circulation and supporting life, making the myocardium indispensable in the overall function of the heart. Therefore, in this preliminary investigation, we primarily focus on understanding the behavior (scattering analysis) of the myocardium tissue (particularly the myocardiocytes) when NIR signals are transmitted through it.

The heart's myocardium is a unique type of striated muscular tissue. Sarcolemma, the cytoplasm of the cardiomyocyte, is the kind of intracellular fluid of the carciac cell and myofibrills are cell components (scatterers) among others. Sarcoplasm includes myoglobin, which is responsible for binding oxygen molecules that are transferred from interstitial fluid into muscle fibers. The primary absorber in the muscles is myoglobin. The diameter of myofibrils ranges from 0.5 to 2 μm [19], which is equivalent to visible and near-infrared wavelengths. Actin and myosin are the two protein chains that makeup myofibrils. Large quantities of glycosomes, which are granules of stored glycogen, are also present in sarcoplasm. The myocardium scatters light strongly due to its intricate fiber structure. The refractive index values measured for human myocardium tissue are summarized in Table 1. We take the average values of the refractive index of myocardium tissue as 1.376 and sarcoplasm as 1.350. The effective refractive index of protein (fibrils) in muscle tissue is 1.530. The volume fraction of sarcoplasm denoted by f_{sc} is taken as 0875 [19].

3.2 *Scattering Model for Biological Tissues*

The model considered in this work is described as follows: we consider a single cardiac cell, known as a cardiomyocyte, consisting of a number of myofibrils suspended in sarcoplasm as shown in Fig. 2.

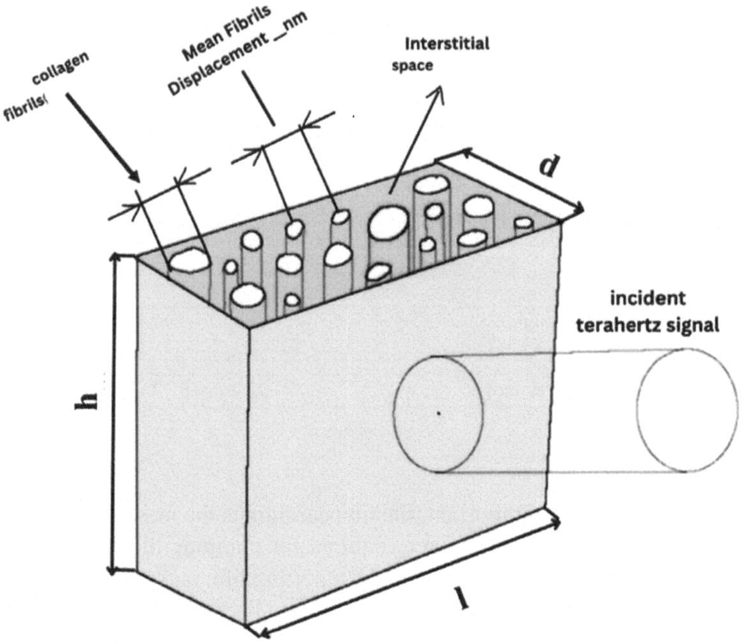

Fig. 2 Schematic representation of human myocardium tissue (see Ref. [19])

A considerable mismatch in refractive indices between myofibrils and ground substance, sarcoplasm, makes the system turbid, i.e., causes multiple scattering and poor transmittance of propagating light.

The optical properties of tissue are related to its microstructure and refractive index distribution. In the current literature the works have considered skin or fat tissue as discrete cells having homogeneous refractive indices [20–23]. However, there are tissues like the myocardium that comprise of myocardiocytes (cardiac cells) having heterogeneous refractive indices. Heart muscle cells, or cardiomyocytes, are the building blocks of the heart. The myocardium tissue, in the simplest form, is composed of a closely packed group of cells i.e., cardiomyocytes entrapped in a network of fibers through which fluid percolates. On a tiny scale, the tissue components have no clear borders. Their refractive indices seem to blend into a continuous structure with spatial fluctuations.

Based on the size (r_s) of the particle, we can either use the Rayleigh scattering model if the diameter of the particle is less than one-tenth the wavelength of the signal or the Mie scattering model, otherwise [24, 25]. Since the diameter ($2 * r$) of the scatterers i.e., the myofibrils (2 μm) which is larger than the wavelength of the NIR signals (600–900 nm), we consider Mie scattering model in our research [26].

The scattering coefficient μ_s [cm^{-1}] of the cardiomyocyte is determined by the following expression:

$$\mu_s = \rho_s * \sigma_s \tag{1}$$

where ρ_s is the volume density of the scatterers (i.e., myofibrils) and is given by

$$\rho_s = \frac{V f_{\text{myofibrils}}}{\frac{4}{3}\pi r^3} \tag{2}$$

and $\sigma_s = Q_s * A_s$ is the effective cross-section [cm^2] of the scattering geometry, Q_s is the scattering efficiency, and A is the geometric cross-section of the scatterer.

3.3 *Machine Learning Models*

Machine learning, a subset of artificial intelligence, enables systems to learn and make predictions without explicit programming. The underlying principle of the scattering coefficient prediction based on machine learning is shown in Fig. 3. Since we know both the output (i.e., scattering coefficient) and the input features such as the radius of the scatterers, refractive indices of the media, volume fraction, and the wavelength of operation, we can use supervised machine learning techniques to find a good estimation for the scattering coefficients.

In our research, machine learning proves instrumental by analyzing patterns in data to estimate scattering coefficients for myocardial tissue. Advanced algorithms and statistical models explore the relationships between frequency, tissue type, and scattering loss. Through iterative learning, the ML models can estimate coefficients for frequencies not present in the training data. By taking an adaptive approach, machine learning enhances the precision and versatility of our cardiac health monitoring research.

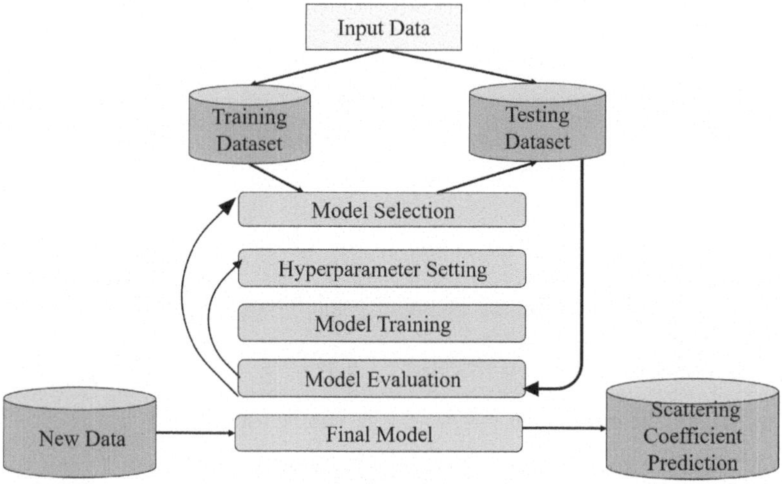

Fig. 3 Machine learning based scattering coefficient estimation

3.3.1 Linear Regression

Linear regression is a type of supervised machine learning algorithm that computes the linear relationship between a dependent variable and one or more independent features by fitting a linear equation to observed data. Simple Linear Regression occurs when there is only one independent feature, whereas Multiple Linear Regression occurs when there are multiple features. Similarly, when there is only one dependent variable, it is referred to as Univariate Linear Regression, whereas Multivariate Regression is used when there are multiple dependent variables.

The equation for Simple Linear Regression can be given as follows:

$$y = \beta_0 + \beta_1 x + \delta \tag{3}$$

The coefficients β_0 and β_1 are calculated as:

$$\beta_1 = \frac{\sum_{i=1}^{n}(x_i - \bar{x})(y_i - \bar{y})}{\sum_{i=1}^{n}(x_i - \bar{x})^2} \tag{4}$$

$$\beta_0 = \bar{y} - \beta_1 \bar{x} \tag{5}$$

where:

$$\bar{x} = \frac{1}{n}\sum_{i=1}^{n} x_i$$

$$\bar{y} = \frac{1}{n}\sum_{i=1}^{n} y_i$$

The equation for Multiple Linear Regression can be given as follows:

$$y = \beta_0 + \beta_1 x_1 + \beta_2 x_2 + \cdots + \beta_n x_n + \delta \tag{6}$$

The coefficients $\beta_0, \beta_1, \ldots, \beta_n$ are calculated by solving the normal equations:

$$\mathbf{X}^\top \mathbf{X} \beta = \mathbf{X}^\top \mathbf{y} \tag{7}$$

where:

- $\mathbf{X}$ is the matrix of input features, including a column of ones for the intercept term.
- $\mathbf{y}$ is the vector of output values.
- β is the vector of coefficients $[\beta_0, \beta_1, \ldots, \beta_n]^\top$.

Specifically, the coefficients $\beta_0, \beta_1, \ldots, \beta_n$ can be found using:

$$\beta = (\mathbf{X}^\top \mathbf{X})^{-1} \mathbf{X}^\top \mathbf{y} \tag{8}$$

where:

$$\mathbf{X} = \begin{bmatrix} 1 & x_{11} & x_{12} & \cdots & x_{1n} \\ 1 & x_{21} & x_{22} & \cdots & x_{2n} \\ \vdots & \vdots & \vdots & \ddots & \vdots \\ 1 & x_{m1} & x_{m2} & \cdots & x_{mn} \end{bmatrix} \quad \text{(design matrix with a column of ones for the intercept term)}$$

$$\mathbf{y} = \begin{bmatrix} y_1 \\ y_2 \\ \vdots \\ y_m \end{bmatrix} \quad \text{(vector of output values)}$$

$$\beta = \begin{bmatrix} \beta_0 \\ \beta_1 \\ \vdots \\ \beta_n \end{bmatrix} \quad \text{(vector of coefficients)}$$

The interpretability of linear regression is a significant advantage. The model's equation includes clear coefficients that show how each independent variable affects the dependent variable, allowing for a better understanding of the underlying dynamics. Linear regression is transparent, simple to implement, and serves as a foundation for more complex algorithms.

3.3.2 Polynomial Regression

Polynomial regression is a form of regression in which the dependent variable that is denoted by y and the independent variable denoted by x is in the form of nth degree polynomial. Hence, it is the expansion of the linear regression and is applied when the data show a non-linear pattern or trend.

The equation for Polynomial Regression can be given as follows:

$$y = \beta_0 + \beta_1 x + \beta_2 x^2 + \cdots + \beta_d x^d + \delta \tag{9}$$

The coefficients $\beta_0, \beta_1, \ldots, \beta_d$ are calculated by solving the normal equations for the transformed feature matrix:

$$\mathbf{X}^\top \mathbf{X}\beta = \mathbf{X}^\top \mathbf{y} \tag{10}$$

where:

- $\mathbf{X}$ is the matrix of input features, including polynomial terms up to degree d.
- $\mathbf{y}$ is the vector of output values.
- β is the vector of coefficients $[\beta_0, \beta_1, \ldots, \beta_d]^\top$.

Specifically, the coefficients $\beta_0, \beta_1, \ldots, \beta_d$ can be found using:

$$\beta = (\mathbf{X}^\top \mathbf{X})^{-1}\mathbf{X}^\top \mathbf{y} \tag{11}$$

where:

$$\mathbf{X} = \begin{bmatrix} 1 & x_1 & x_1^2 & \cdots & x_1^d \\ 1 & x_2 & x_2^2 & \cdots & x_2^d \\ \vdots & \vdots & \vdots & \ddots & \vdots \\ 1 & x_n & x_n^2 & \cdots & x_n^d \end{bmatrix} \quad \text{(design matrix with polynomial terms)}$$

$$\mathbf{y} = \begin{bmatrix} y_1 \\ y_2 \\ \vdots \\ y_n \end{bmatrix} \quad \text{(vector of output values)}$$

$$\beta = \begin{bmatrix} \beta_0 \\ \beta_1 \\ \vdots \\ \beta_d \end{bmatrix} \quad \text{(vector of coefficients)}$$

The best part of Polynomial Regression is that the points in the data set need not be in a straight linear arrangement. When data is in a non-linear fashion, then building a linear model would not be suitable huge errors will follow and accuracy suffer. With polynomial terms added against linear regression equations, it can create more intricate and nonlinear functions, and the sets of data easily.

3.3.3 Gradient Boost

Ensemble approaches in machine learning integrate numerous models to produce a single, more accurate predictive model. Ensemble approaches improve performance, reduce volatility, and increase generalization by combining the predictions of multiple base models. Bagging and boosting are two often used ensemble procedures. Bagging, also known as Bootstrap Aggregation, involves training many models on various subsets of data and then averaging their predictions to reduce overfitting and variation. Boosting generates models consecutively, with each model correcting the faults of the preceding one, lowering bias and improving overall performance.

Gradient boosting successively combines the predictions of several weak learners, usually decision trees. By refining the model's weights based on the mistakes of earlier iterations, seeks to enhance overall predictive performance by progressively lowering prediction errors and raising the model's accuracy. Gradient Boosting improves our project's prediction skills by successively developing an ensemble of models, each of which corrects the flaws of the previous one. In this project, the Gra-

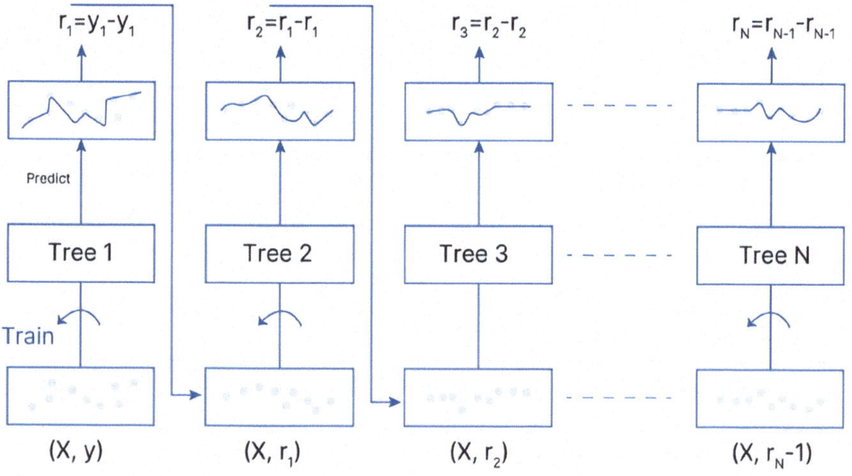

Fig. 4 Working of gradient boost model [27]

dient Boosting Regressor is employed to forecast scattering coefficients accurately. Gradient Boosting lowers bias and captures intricate patterns in data by iteratively fitting decision trees to the prior model's residual errors. This approach produces a resilient and precise model that accurately predicts scattering coefficients for specific wavelengths (Fig. 4).

3.3.4 Artificial Neural Networks

Artificial Neural Networks (ANNs) are inspired by the structure and functioning of the human brain. There are roughly 86 billion neurons in the human brain, each connected by synapses. Electrical impulses are the means by which neurons exchange information. Each neuron takes in inputs, processes them, and then produces an output. The brain is able to carry out complex functions like learning, pattern recognition, and decision-making because of its intricate network of neurons (Fig. 5).

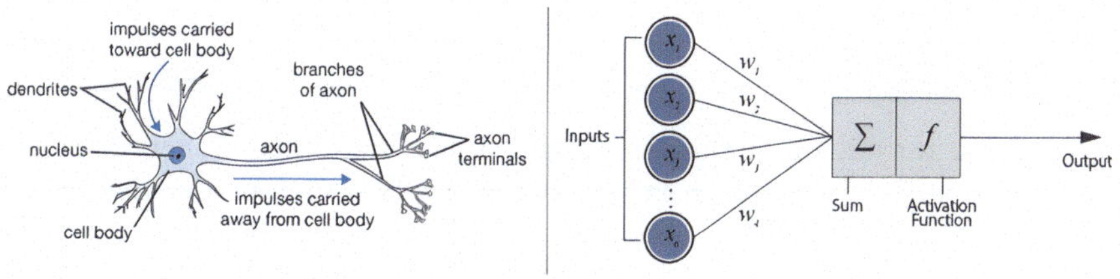

Fig. 5 Biological neuron versus artificial neuron [28]

$$z(sum) = \sum_{i=1}^{n} w_i x_i + b \tag{12}$$

The activation function, commonly denoted as (a = f(z)), can be expressed using different functions. Below is an example using the sigmoid activation

$$a = \sigma(z) = \frac{1}{1 + e^{-z}} \tag{13}$$

ANNs seek to simplify and mimic this structure of biological brain networks. They are correlated as follows:

- **Nodes and Neurons:** Artificial neurons, or nodes, in ANNs simulate the functions of real neurons. Every node takes in inputs, processes them, and outputs something.
- **Weights and Synapses:** In an ANN, weights are comparable to synapses in the brain. The input signals' relevance and strength are determined by their weights. These weights are changed during training in order to reduce mistake.
- **Layers:** ANNs are made up of several layers of neurons:
  Input Layer: Reacts to stimuli received by sense organs from outside the body.
  Hidden Layers: Showcase the brain's internal functioning. From the input data, they compute and extract features.
  Output Layer: produces the end result, similar to how the brain makes judgments or responds.

4 Methodology

This section provides in-depth details about the data created for training and testing using machine learning models; and discusses various parameters and hyperparameters used in this research for the machine learning part. Initially, we begin with data preparation followed by machine learning tools. Then finally we discuss the various metrics used in this work for measuring the effectiveness of the machine learning approach and validation.

4.1 Data Preparation

In our work, we initially performed analytical analysis on the scattering coefficient based on the details given in [19, 29]. Particularly, the information related to sarcoplasm's and myofibril's refractive indices and volume fraction were taken from [29]. These values were then plugged into Eq. 1 to obtain the scattering coefficient values for frequencies between 600 and 1000 nm. This data is then used for training the machine learning models.

4.2 Machine Learning Tools and Performance Metrics

This portion explains various tools used in each model of machine learning.

- **Linear Regression:** In this study, the link between the myocardial tissue's scattering coefficients and the NIR band wavelength was examined using Linear Regression as the fundamental model. From our datasets, the scattering coefficient was selected as the target variable (y) and wavelength as the feature (X) for data preparation. There were no hyperparameters specifically stated when the Linear Regression model was first started; it was initialized using default settings. The relationship between the input wavelength and the matching scattering coefficients was learned by the model by training on the training set of data. The model was used to predict scattering coefficients for the wavelengths in the bigset dataset once it had been trained. We assess model performance with metrics like MAE, MSE, RMSE and R2 score. Visualizing the analytical and predicted data provides insights into how well the linear regression model captures scattering coefficient trends across the specified frequencies.
- **Polynomial Regression:** Compared to linear models, polynomial regression provides a more flexible method that enables us to capture intricate correlations between the myocardial tissue's wavelength and scattering coefficients. We extracted the wavelength as the feature (X) and the scattering coefficient as the target variable (y) from our datasets. The input features were transformed into polynomial features of degree 2. This allowed us to capture the quadratic relationships between the wavelength and scattering coefficients. We evaluate performance using MAE, MSE, RMSE, and R2 scores. This polynomial regression approach enhances understanding of how well such models adapt to complex scattering loss trends in cardiac monitoring.
- **Gradient Boosting:** Gradient Boosting Regression is a great option for modeling the non-linear relationship between wavelength and scattering coefficients because it can capture complex patterns and interactions in the data. Gradient Boosting improves predictive accuracy by creating numerous decision trees consecutively, which allows for a thorough examination of tissue scattering behavior. From our datasets, we extracted the scattering coefficient as the goal variable (y) and the wavelength as the feature (X). In order to prevent any dominance of particular characteristics during model training, the input features were standardized to guarantee that all features were on a same scale. The following hyperparameters were used to initialize a Gradient Boosting Regression model:
  - n_estimators: The quantity of stages used for boosting. We employed a total of 1000 boosting stages in our implementation.
  - learning_rate: Each estimator's shrinkage factor. The learning rate is set at 0.01.
  - max_depth: The maximum depth of each regression estimator is
  - max_depth. We have 5 as the maximum depth.

- random_state: A reproducible seed for the creation of random numbers. A random state of 42 was used. The target variable and standardized features were used to train the model.

The prediction curve and comparison to analytical data in Sect. 5.1 demonstrate the model's effectiveness in modeling the complex scattering behavior across the frequency range of interest. Performance metrics such as MAE, MSE, RMSE, R2 score are calculated to evaluate the model's accuracy and effectiveness.

- **ANN:** ANNs are excellent at capturing non-linear patterns and interactions because they make use of numerous layers of interconnected neurons. Hence, they are a good fit for our research's scattering coefficient prediction. From our datasets, we extracted the scattering coefficient as the target variable (y) and the wavelength as the feature (X). An 80–20 split ratio was used to divide the dataset into training and testing sets. To guarantee that every feature was on the same scale, input features were standardized, which aided in model convergence and increased training effectiveness. The architecture for ANN Model used is as follows:

  - Input layer: Single neuron corresponding to the wavelength feature.
  - Hidden layers: Two dense layers with 64 and 32 neurons, respectively, and ReLU activation functions.
  - Output layer: Single neuron representing the predicted scattering coefficient.

  The Adam optimizer was used to create the model, with a mean squared error loss function and a learning rate of 0.001. With a batch size of 32, the ANN model was trained for 100 epochs using the standardized training set. The model was used to forecast scattering coefficients for the wavelengths in the testing set after it had been trained.
  In the evaluation phase, the model is tested on the initial dataset, and the performance metrics are calculated, including MAE, MSE, RMSE, R2 score. The visual representation of the original and extended datasets, along with the ANN's prediction curve, provides insights into how well the model generalizes scattering coefficient trends.

The following metrics are used to evaluate the performance of the ML models.

4.2.1 Mean Absolute Error (MAE)

It quantifies the average absolute difference between predicted and actual values, offering a straightforward measure of model accuracy

$$\text{MAE} = \frac{1}{N}\sum_{i=1}^{N} |y_i - \hat{y}| \tag{14}$$

where, $\hat{y}$: predicted value of y

4.2.2 Mean Squared Error (MSE)

It assesses the average squared difference between predicted and actual values, penalizing larger errors more significantly.

$$\mathrm{MSE} = \frac{1}{N}\sum_{i=1}^{N}(y_i - \hat{y})^2 \tag{15}$$

where, $\hat{y}$: predicted value of y

4.2.3 Root Mean Squared Error (RMSE)

It represents the square root of MSE, providing a measure in the original units.

$$\mathrm{RMSE} = \sqrt{\mathrm{MSE}} = \sqrt{\frac{1}{N}\sum_{i=1}^{N}(y_i - \hat{y})^2} \tag{16}$$

where, $\hat{y}$: predicted value of y

4.2.4 R-Squared (R^2)

It indicates the proportion of the variance in the dependent variable that is predictable from the independent variable(s). It ranges from 0 to 1, with higher values signifying better model fit

$$R^2 = 1 - \frac{\sum(y_i - \hat{y})^2}{\sum(y_i - \bar{y})^2} \tag{17}$$

where, $\hat{y}$: predicted value of y
$\bar{y}$: mean value of y

4.3 Data Augmentation for Prediction

The technique of artificially creating new data from pre-existing data is known as data augmentation. It is one of the benefits of machine learning which helps us in getting data for unexperimented scenarios. For instance, in our case, the literature provides experimental data on the optical properties of sarcoplasm (background media) and myofibrils (scatterers) only for the wavelength range of 600–900 nm. If we have to determine the scatter coefficients or path loss using these values, then one has to repeat the experiments to obtain these optical values. However, this entails costly affairs as these experimental setups are either too costly or not in reach of many people. One way to get the newer data is to employ extrapolation methods, however, this approach might not be accurate for critical applications such as medical domains. Therefore, in this work, we explore the potential of machine learning to predict the scattering coefficients in the unexplored wavelength bands and help researchers and other medical related personnel to use this data for their applications.

To improve the prediction power of our machine learning models, we used data augmentation approaches in our study. By creating more artificial data points based on the available datasets, the augmentation method increased the model's capacity to generalize to new data. The steps for implementing data augmentation for prediction are as follows:

- The datasets contained the frequency and tissue parameters required to predict the NIR band scattering coefficients of cardiac tissue.
- To increase the resilience of our models and the diversity of the dataset, we used a variety of augmentation strategies. Among these methods were:
  - Data Transformation: Adding new synthetic data (wavelength and scattering coefficient) to the existing data points (frequency) by applying transformations like translation and scaling.
  - Bootstrapping: Creating new data points with comparable properties by sampling and replacing existing data points from the original dataset.
- We combined the real data with the synthetic data points using the augmented methods previously discussed to create a larger augmented dataset.

5 Results and Discussion

This section presents and evaluates the effectiveness of several machine learning models in predicting the scattering coefficients of myocardium tissue. We analyze the accuracy and efficacy of the models based on multiple performance measures and provide visualizations to demonstrate their prediction power.

5.1 Analytical and Machine Learning Results

Using the details of the cardiac cell (i.e., the cardiomyocyte) as given in Table 1, computed the scattering coefficient values of the myocardium i.e., the cardiac cell in the frequency band 600–900 nm using Eq. 1. The scattering coefficient values thus obtained analytically are plotted in Fig. 6. This figure shows the variation of the scattering coefficient for different frequencies. It is observed that the scattering coefficient is significantly large, beginning with 2200 [cm] for 600 [cm] nm and

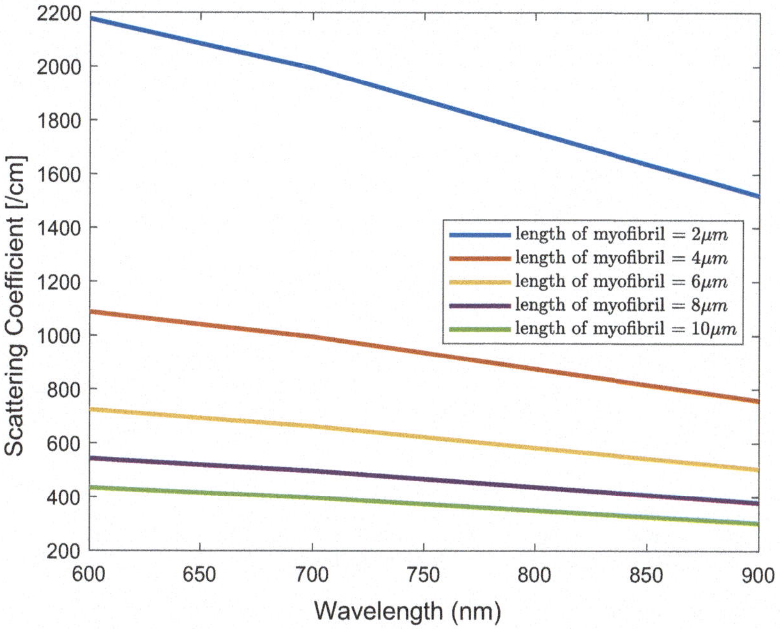

Fig. 6 Scattering coefficient of myocardium tissue for different sizes (length of the Myofibrils)

gradually reducing to 1580 [cm] at 900 nm for the length of the myofibril of 2 μm. As the length of the myofibril increases the magnitude of the scattering coefficient drastically reduces. For the myofibril length of 10 μm, the scattering coefficient has a value of 420 [cm] at 600 nm and it decreases to 380 [cm] at 900 nm. This finding indicates that scattering is significantly high in the NIR band as a result has reduced penetration depth and decreased image contrast. Accordingly, for a given length of the myofibril, it is recommended NIR signals in 900 nm wavelength are suitable as they have lesser scattering losses compared to other wavelength bands.

5.2 *Results Obtained from Linear Regression*

The graphs below illustrate the results of using a Linear Regression Model to forecast scattering coefficients based on frequencies. In Fig. 7, the grey line represents the analytical data from 600 to 900 nm.[1] The red line shows the data predictions done by

[1] Note: The original data and analytical data are the data generated using Eq. 1. Here, we are using two different terms to indicate that grey color data was used for training ML models for prediction purposes while the blue colored portion is used to compare ML predicted (unknown) values with the analytical data. To make this differentiation, we have renamed the blue-colored portion as analytical data. This is true for all the four figures i.e., Figs. 7, 8, 9 and 10.

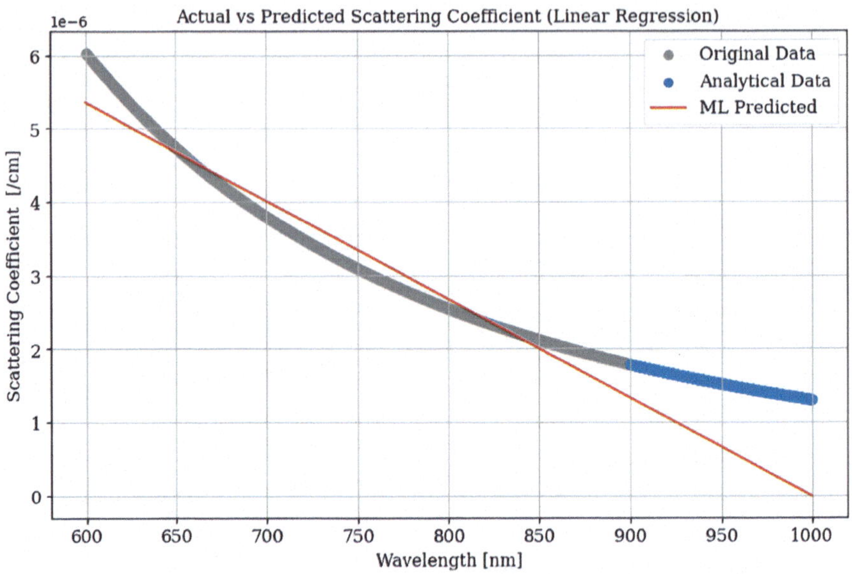

Fig. 7 Linear regression

training the Linear Regression model from 900 to 1000 nm, beginning from 600 nm data sets and extending up to 900 nm. Furthermore, the blue color line extending after the grey color line is the data-generated analytical model. We use this line in all four models to indicate the trend of how the original data varies with wavelength when compared with the ML-predicted data. The plot's appearance is due to the model assuming a straight-line relationship between frequency and scattering coefficient, with the line's slope indicating how much the coefficient changes for each frequency unit.

The performance metrics of the Linear Regression model are presented in Table 2. These metrics include the Mean Absolute Error (MAE), Mean Squared Error (MSE), Root Mean Squared Error (RMSE), and the R-squared (R^2) score, which indicate the accuracy and reliability of the model's predictions.

Table 2 Performance metrics and value

Metric	Value
MAE	0.00073252
MSE	0.00000113
RMSE	0.00106435
R^2 Score	0.98238456

5.3 Results Obtained from Polynomial Regression

In Fig. 8, the grey line represents the analytical data from 600 to 900 nm, and the blue line indicates the analytical data used for comparisons with the ML predicted output for the case of future samples. The red line shows the data predictions made by training the Polynomial Regression model from 600 to 900 nm and extending it to 1000 nm. The Polynomial Regression model captures the nonlinear relationship between Frequency and Scattering Coefficient through a quadratic equation, a polynomial with degree 2. Despite being a linear regression method due to its linearity in coefficients, Polynomial Regression can model nonlinear data, giving the plot its distinctive curved shape. The coefficients provide key insights, showing the change in the dependent variable (scattering coefficient) for unit changes in both the independent variable (frequency) and its square.

The performance metrics of the Polynomial Regression model are presented in Table 3. These metrics include the Mean Absolute Error (MAE), Mean Squared

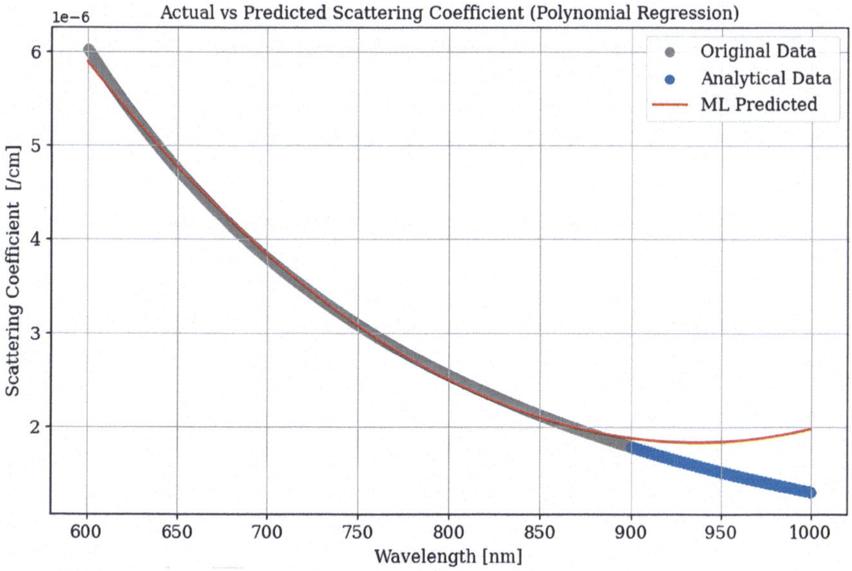

Fig. 8 Polynomial regression

Table 3 Performance metrics and Values

Metrics	Values
MAE	0.00009972
MSE	0.00000004
RMSE	0.00019544
R^2 Score	0.99940604

Error (MSE), Root Mean Squared Error (RMSE), and the R-squared (R^2) score, which indicates the accuracy and reliability of the model's predictions.

5.4 *Results Obtained from Gradient Boost*

The graphs below show how Gradient Boosting Regression helps us stretch our data beyond its original limits by combining weak learners to make stronger predictions. It's like teamwork to improve accuracy.

In Fig. 9, the grey line represents the analytical data from 600 to 900 nm wavelength. The red line shows the data predictions made by training the Gradient boost model from 600 to 900 nm and extending it to 100 nm. The blue line indicates the analytically generated data. The red line, ML predicted data, from 900 to 1000 nm is deviating largely from the analytical data values because Gradient Boosting, despite its precision in fitting existing data, may not be ideal for extrapolation because it tends to closely follow observed patterns, potentially leading to overfitting and inaccurate predictions when extended beyond the known data range. Other modeling approaches that emphasize generalization may be more suitable for scenarios requiring reliable predictions outside the observed range.

The performance metrics of the Gradient Boost model are presented in Table 4. These metrics include the Mean Absolute Error (MAE), Mean Squared Error (MSE),

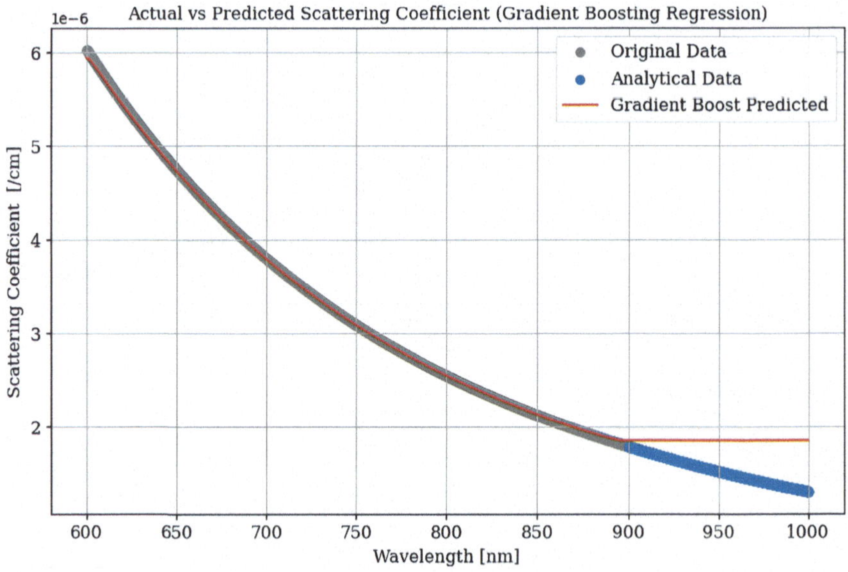

Fig. 9 Terahertz range—gradient boost

Table 4 Performance metrics and values

Metrics	Value
MAE	0.00043321
MSE	0.00000150
RMSE	0.00122496
R^2 Score	0.97666722

Root Mean Squared Error (RMSE), and the R-squared (R^2) score, which indicates the accuracy and reliability of the model's predictions.

5.5 *Results Obtained from ANN*

This graph illustrates the profound impact of Artificial Neural Network (ANN) modeling on broadening the insights within our dataset. By harnessing the collaborative strength of interconnected nodes, akin to a synchronized team effort, the ANN enhances predictive accuracy.

In Fig. 10, the grey line represents the original data from 600 to 900 nm and the blue line indicates the analytical data from 900 to 100 nm. The red line shows the data predictions made by training the ANN model from 600 to 900 nm and extending

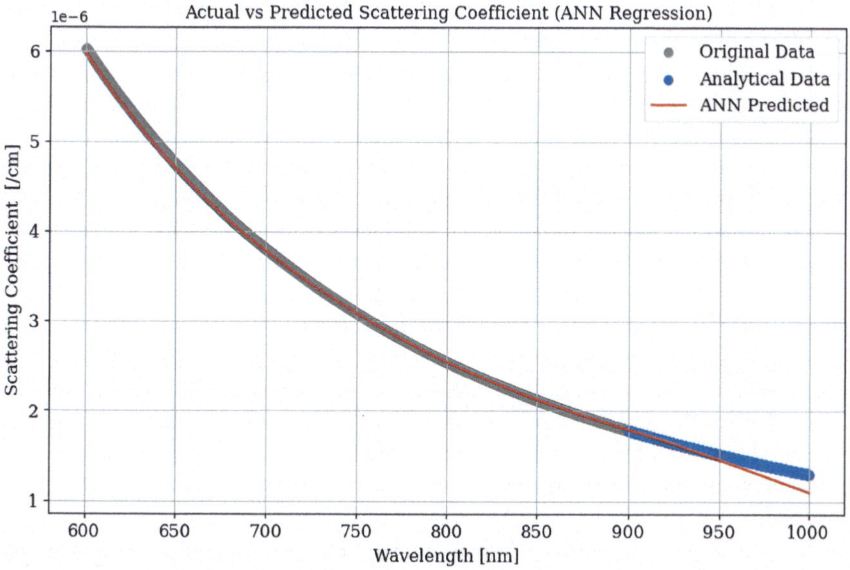

Fig. 10 ANN

Table 5 Performance metrics and values

Metrics	Values
MAE	0.00011652
MSE	0.00000004
RMSE	0.00020988
R^2 Score	0.99931505

it to 1000 nm. In contrast to other methods, ANNs excel at modeling nonlinear relationships, making them especially well-suited for extrapolation tasks. Their adaptive nature enables them to analyze complex datasets, detect subtle patterns, and generate highly accurate predictions. In situations requiring precision beyond observed data, ANNs are a compelling choice, offering unrivaled predictive accuracy.

The performance metrics of the ANN model are presented in Table 5. These metrics include the Mean Absolute Error (MAE), Mean Squared Error (MSE), Root Mean Squared Error (RMSE), and the R-squared (R^2) score, which indicates the accuracy and reliability of the model's predictions.

5.6 *Inferences on Data Augmentation*

At times it is either difficult or expensive to get data of scattering information of biological tissues for wide band of frequency spectrum. In this situation we expect to have tool and techniques that help us to predict the scattering values for un-experimented data. For instance, in our case, the research has reported the dielectric properties of cardiac cell in the wavelength band of 600–900 nm and thus we determined the scattering values i this band. However, we are interested to have the information of the scattering values in the wavelength band beyond 900 nm to see if the scattering of the cardiac cell is either increasing or decreasing. To answer this question we tried to explore the capability of machine learning to predict un-known data i.e., scattering coefficient. We experimented (through simulations) using all the four models namely, linear regression, polynomial regression, gradient boosting and ANN, to understand how each of these models perform in predicting new scattering values. This prediction is seen in Figs. 7, 8, 9 and 10. In these figures, the red colored portion between 900 and 1000 nm is the predicted values of the scattering coefficient obtained using the four machine learning models. It is seen that linear regression and ANN are performing better compared to polynomial regression and gradient boosting. Tables 2, 3, 4 and 5 gives the respective performance metrics indicating machine learning can serve as a better tool for exploring un-known data in case of non-availability.

The comparison of performance metrics, such as Mean Absolute Error (MAE), Mean Squared Error (MSE), Root Mean Squared Error (RMSE), and R^2, offers valuable insights into the influence of hyperparameter tuning on model performance. By analyzing these metrics across different models and configurations, we can identify patterns that highlight the strengths and limitations of each approach. For instance, the consistently lower MAE and RMSE values achieved through Gradient Boosting and Artificial Neural Network (ANN) models suggest that tuning hyperparameters, such as learning rate, depth of decision trees, and the number of neurons in hidden layers, significantly enhances predictive accuracy.

Moreover, observing R^2 scores across frequency bands helps gauge the models' ability to generalize beyond the training data. Such comparisons are instrumental in refining hyperparameter settings to strike a balance between overfitting and underfitting, ultimately leading to robust models capable of capturing complex scattering loss trends in myocardial tissues. This process ensures that the predictive models are both accurate and adaptable, providing deeper insights into the scattering behavior over terahertz and optical frequency bands.

6 Conclusion

In conclusion, our research endeavors to enhance the understanding and prediction of scattering loss in myocardial tissues for applications in wireless health monitoring. Machine learning (ML) emerged as a powerful tool in our methodology, with a particular focus on linear regression, polynomial regression, gradient boosting, and artificial neural networks (ANN). These models were carefully selected and systematically applied to capture and predict scattering coefficients across varying frequency ranges. The exploration of ML tools and techniques showcased their utility and relevance in our research, providing valuable insights into the complex relationships inherent in scattering loss phenomena. Furthermore, the incorporation of metrics such as Mean Absolute Error (MAE), Mean Squared Error (MSE), Root Mean Squared Error (RMSE), and R-squared (R2) facilitated a robust evaluation of model performance.

Our future work includes developing a phantom model of the cardiac cell, with two components named sarcoplasm and myofibrils, in COMSOL Multiphysics and validating the scattering coefficient values for different volume fractions of myofibrils.

Acknowledgements This work is supported by the Commissioned Research through SRM University-AP Seed Fund, India under Grant No. SRMAP/URG/SEED/2023-24/012 and is carried out in the Nano Communication and Networking Lab at SRM University-AP.

References

1. M. L. Oelze and J. Mamou, "Review of quantitative ultrasound: Envelope statistics and backscatter coefficient imaging and contributions to diagnostic ultrasound," *IEEE transactions on ultrasonics, ferroelectrics, and frequency control*, vol. 63, no. 2, pp. 336–351, 2016.
2. J. Yan, B. Huang, J. Tonko, M. Toulemonde, J. Hansen-Shearer, Q. Tan, K. Riemer, K. Ntagiantas, R. A. Chowdhury, P. D. Lambiase *et al.*, "Transthoracic ultrasound localization microscopy of myocardial vasculature in patients," *Nature Biomedical Engineering*, pp. 1–12, 2024.
3. L. Waszczuk, J. Ogien, F. Pain, and A. Dubois, "Determination of scattering coefficient and scattering anisotropy factor of tissue-mimicking phantoms using line-field confocal optical coherence tomography (lc-oct)," *Journal of the European Optical Society-Rapid Publications*, vol. 19, no. 2, p. 39, 2023.
4. K. M. K and M. G, "Nanosensors success in cardiovascular diseases," *Research and Reviews: Journal of Pharmaceutics and Nanotechnology*, no. 2, p. pp. 7, 2016.
5. A. Savchenko, D. Kireev, R. T. Yin, I. R. Efimov, and E. Molokanova, "Graphene-based cardiac sensors and actuators," *Frontiers in Bioengineering and Biotechnology*, vol. 11, p. 1168667, 2023.
6. Q. H. Abbasi, K. Yang, N. Chopra, J. M. Jornet, N. A. Abuali, K. A. Qaraqe, and A. Alomainy, "Nano-communication for biomedical applications: A review on the state-of-the-art from physical layers to novel networking concepts," *IEEE Access*, vol. 4, pp. 3920–3935, 2016.
7. https://fyla.com/the-use-of-supercontinuum-laser-sources-in-biomedical-diffuse-optics-unlocking-the-power-of-multispectral-imaging/, [Online; accessed 17-April-2024].
8. J. T. Gómez, A. Kuestner, J. Simonjan, B. D. Unluturk, and F. Dressler, "Nanosensor location estimation in the human circulatory system using machine learning," *IEEE Transactions on Nanotechnology*, vol. 21, pp. 663–673, 2022.
9. B. H. Hokr and J. N. Bixler, "Machine learning estimation of tissue optical properties," *Scientific Reports*, vol. 11, no. 1, p. 6561, 2021.
10. I. Hassaninia, R. Bostanabad, W. Chen, and H. Mohseni, "Characterization of the optical properties of turbid media by supervised learning of scattering patterns," *Scientific reports*, vol. 7, no. 1, p. 15259, 2017.
11. D. Cunha, "Determination of optical properties of skin tissues using spatial domain frequency imaging and random forests," in *IX Latin American Congress on Biomedical Engineering and XXVIII Brazilian Congress on Biomedical Engineering: Proceedings of CLAIB and CBEB 2022, October 24–28, 2022, Florianópolis, Brazil—Volume 2: Biomedical Signal Processing and Micro-and Nanotechnologies*, vol. 99. Springer Nature, 2024, p. 250.
12. S. Joof, C. Aydinalp, I. Dilman, M. N. Akinci, T. Yilmaz, M. Çayören, and I. Akduman, "A guideline for complex permittivity retrieval of tissue-mimicking phantoms from open-ended coaxial probe response with deep learning," *IEEE Transactions on Microwave Theory and Techniques*, vol. 70, no. 11, pp. 5105–5115, 2022.
13. M. Salucci, M. Arrebola, T. Shan, and M. Li, "Artificial intelligence: New frontiers in real-time inverse scattering and electromagnetic imaging," *IEEE Transactions on Antennas and Propagation*, vol. 70, no. 8, pp. 6349–6364, 2022.
14. N. Khalid, M. Zubair, M. Q. Mehmood, and Y. Massoud, "Emerging paradigms in microwave imaging technology for biomedical applications: unleashing the power of artificial intelligence," *npj Imaging*, vol. 2, no. 1, p. 13, 2024.
15. I. Kafian-Attari, E. Nippolainen, D. Semenov, M. Hauta-Kasari, J. Töyräs, and I. O. Afara, "Tissue optical properties combined with machine learning enables estimation of articular cartilage composition and functional integrity," *Biomedical Optics Express*, vol. 11, no. 11, pp. 6480–6494, 2020.
16. J. Rodrigues, A. Amin, S. Chandra, N. J. Mulla, G. S. Nayak, S. Rai, S. Ray, and K. K. Mahato, "Machine learning enabled photoacoustic spectroscopy for noninvasive assessment of breast tumor progression in vivo: A preclinical study," *ACS sensors*, 2024.

17. Y. Zou, Y. Zeng, S. Li, and Q. Zhu, "Machine learning model with physical constraints for diffuse optical tomography," *Biomedical optics express*, vol. 12, no. 9, pp. 5720–5735, 2021.
18. A. Krishnan, H. Sharma, D. Yuan, A. F. Trollope, and L. Chilton, "The role of epicardial adipose tissue in the development of atrial fibrillation, coronary artery disease and chronic heart failure in the context of obesity and type 2 diabetes mellitus: a narrative review," *Journal of Cardiovascular Development and Disease*, vol. 9, no. 7, p. 217, 2022.
19. V. V. Tuchin *et al.*, "Tissue optics." Society of Photo-Optical Instrumentation Engineers (SPIE) Bellingham, WA, USA, 2015.
20. H. Elayan, R. M. Shubair, and J. M. Jornet, "Bio-electromagnetic thz propagation modeling for in-vivo wireless nanosensor networks," in *2017 11th European Conference on Antennas and Propagation (EuCAP)*. IEEE, 2017, pp. 426–430.
21. H. Elayan, R. M. Shubair, and J. M. Jornet, "Characterising thz propagation and intrabody thermal absorption in iwnsns," *IET Microwaves, Antennas & Propagation*, vol. 12, no. 4, pp. 525–532, 2018.
22. P. Johari and J. M. Jornet, "Nanoscale optical channel modeling for in vivo wireless nanosensor networks: A geometrical approach," in *2017 IEEE International Conference on Communications (ICC)*. IEEE, 2017, pp. 1–6.
23. Z. Ameri and F. Jahangiri, "Comparison on the scattering path loss of terahertz waves in fat layer under air-enclosed and tissue-enclosed conditions," *International Journal of Optics and Photonics*, vol. 16, no. 2, pp. 139–144, 2022.
24. D. Jing and D. Song, "Optical properties of nanofluids considering particle size distribution: experimental and theoretical investigations," *Renewable and Sustainable Energy Reviews*, vol. 78, pp. 452–465, 2017.
25. H. Elayan, R. M. Shubair, J. M. Jornet, and P. Johari, "Terahertz channel model and link budget analysis for intrabody nanoscale communication," *IEEE transactions on nanobioscience*, vol. 16, no. 6, pp. 491–503, 2017.
26. S. Jacques and S. Prahl, "Optical properties," ": https://omlc.org/classroom/ece532/class3/index.html", 1998, [Online; accessed 13-Feb-2024].
27. A. Saini, "BWorld Robot Control Software," ": https://www.analyticsvidhya.com/blog/2021/09/gradient-boosting-algorithm-a-complete-guide-for-beginners/ ", 2008, [Online; accessed 12-March-2024].
28. "Keras Tutorial: Deep Learning in Python," ": https://www.datacamp.com/tutorial/deep-learning-python ", 2019, [Online; accessed 19-May-2024].
29. D. K. Tuchina, A. N. Bashkatov, E. A. Genina, and V. V. Tuchin, "Quantification of glucose and glycerol diffusion in myocardium," *Journal of Innovative Optical Health Sciences*, vol. 8, no. 03, p. 1541006, 2015.

Dielectric Characterization of Ovine Heart Tissues at Terahertz Frequencies via Machine Learning: A Use Case for In-Vivo Wireless Nano-Communication

Raja Manjula, Nalluri Sai Kusum Sarayu, Nelluri Sai Sruthi, Damavarapu Samaya, Kudeti Tarun Teja, and Langkam Sabita

1 Introduction

Dielectric properties, such as permittivity and conductivity, are critical to understanding the electrical behavior of heart tissues [1]. Permittivity reflects the tissue's ability to store electrical energy, while conductivity measures its ability to conduct electric current. These properties are vital for several reasons. They directly influence the propagation of electrical signals within the heart, essential for synchronized cardiac contractions [2]. Accurate knowledge of these properties is crucial for developing precise models that can predict how the heart responds to electrical stimuli, thereby aiding in the design of medical devices such as pacemakers and defibrillators.

More importantly, the dielectric properties of the heart are essential for understanding the tissue's response to various medical treatments and interventions. Particularly, the endocardium, the innermost layer of the heart, plays a critical role in the overall electrical activity and health of the heart. Here are some more key reasons:

R. Manjula (✉) · N. Sai Kusum Sarayu · N. Sai Sruthi · D. Samaya · K. Tarun Teja
Department of Computer Science and Engineering, SRM University AP, Andhra Pradesh, India
e-mail: rajamanjula12@gmail.com

N. Sai Kusum Sarayu
e-mail: saikusumsarayu_n@srmap.edu.in

N. Sai Sruthi
e-mail: saisruthi_nelluri@srmap.edu.in

D. Samaya
e-mail: samaya_damavarapu@srmap.edu.in

K. Tarun Teja
e-mail: tarunteja_kudeti@srmap.edu.in

L. Sabita
Nanyang DSP Research Centre (NDRC), Raipur, India

T. Ojha et al. (eds.), *Edge-Enabled 6G Networking*,
https://doi.org/10.1007/978-3-032-19042-0_15

- *Electro-physiological Studies*: Dielectric properties influence the propagation of electrical signals within the heart. Accurate knowledge of these properties can improve the interpretation of electro-physiological studies, such as electrocardiograms (ECGs), by providing better models of how electrical signals travel through the cardiac tissue.
- *Radio-frequency Ablation*: Radio-frequency (RF) ablation is a common treatment for arrhythmias, where precise delivery of RF energy is used to destroy abnormal electrical pathways [3]. The effectiveness and safety of this procedure depend on the dielectric properties of the tissue, as they affect how RF energy is absorbed and dissipated. Understanding these properties helps in optimizing the energy delivery and minimizing damage to surrounding healthy tissues.
- *Imaging and Diagnostic Tools*: Techniques like electrical impedance tomography (EIT) and magnetic resonance imaging (MRI) rely on the dielectric properties of tissues to generate images. Accurate knowledge of the dielectric properties of the endocardium can improve the resolution and accuracy of these imaging methods, aiding in better diagnosis and treatment planning.
- *Tissue Characterization and Pathology*: Dielectric properties can change with different pathological conditions, such as fibrosis, ischemia, or infarction. By studying these properties, clinicians and researchers can develop non-invasive diagnostic tools to detect and characterize various cardiac conditions based on dielectric measurements.
- *Development of Medical Devices*: Pacemakers, defibrillators, and other implantable cardiac devices interact with the heart tissue. Knowledge of the dielectric properties helps in designing electrodes and other components that can interface more effectively and safely with the heart tissue, ensuring reliable performance and longevity of the devices.
- *Biophysical Research*: For researchers studying the fundamental properties of cardiac tissues, understanding dielectric properties provides insights into the biophysical processes governing cellular and tissue behavior. This knowledge can lead to the development of new therapeutic approaches and a better understanding of heart function and dysfunction.

The need for dielectric properties in the terahertz band (0.1–10 THz) is driven by the development of new-generation sensing, processing, and communicating devices made possible by nanotechnology as shown in [4–6]. In-vivo wireless nanosensor nodes (iWNSNs) offer revolutionary potential for medical imaging and data collection [7, 8]. Such tiny devices, operating at the THz band, promise to transform healthcare applications by enabling efficient communication between nanonodes floating in the circulatory system and gateway devices fixed in the skin. Understanding in-vivo channel characteristics at this frequency range is essential to achieve efficient and reliable in-vivo communication [9], which can significantly improve non-invasive (or minimally invasive) sensing and real-time health monitoring cardiac during surgery in a networked healthcare environment.

Having given the information on the importance of the need for the dielectric properties of heart tissues and the benefits of in-vivo nanosensor communication technology, we now focus on the machine learning aspect. Machine learning (ML) is a branch of artificial intelligence (AI) that focuses on developing algorithms that enable computers to learn from and make decisions based on the data [10]. This involves training models on large datasets to identify patterns and relationships, allowing the system to improve its performance over time without explicit programming for each task. ML is significant because it enables automation and enhances decision-making across various industries by providing insights and predictive analytics that were previously unattainable. Machine Learning Algorithms (MLAs) are used in numerous fields, including healthcare (predicting patient outcomes, diagnosing diseases, personalizing treatment plans), and technology (enhancing search engines, improving voice recognition systems, developing virtual assistants and classification of liver tissue as shown in [11]). The algorithms are typically categorized into supervised learning, which involves training a model on labelled data for tasks like regression and classification, and unsupervised learning, which involves training a model on unlabelled data to uncover patterns and structures for tasks like clustering and dimensionality reduction. Overall, machine learning is a transformative technology that drives innovation and efficiency across various sectors, making it an essential tool in the modern technological landscape. Our research focuses on predicting the dielectric properties (permittivity and conductivity) of biological tissue, the endocardium, using different MLAs. Machine learning can enhance accuracy in predicting tissue properties across a wide frequency range, vital for precise diagnostics and treatment planning [12]. This approach enables real-time monitoring and deeper insights into tissue dynamics, advancing personalized healthcare and medical diagnostics significantly.

1.1 Problem Statement

Predicting the permittivity and conductivity of the material is critical for the fabrication of nano-scale sensors in the THz range (0.1–10 THz). Traditional methods and literature give information about the permittivity and conductivity only up to 20 GHz which is not sufficient for in-vivo applications. Therefore, to fill this research gap, we aim to examine how MLAs can be employed to predict the dielectric properties (permittivity and conductivity) at frequencies ranging from 20 GHz MHz to 10 THz, unavailable data in the literature, based on the available experimental data i.e., between 500 MHz and 20 GHz in the existing literature. The goals are to use ML to calculate dielectric properties within 500 MHz–20 GHz and also explore extrapolation to determine new dielectric values in the 20 GHz–10 THz range.

To this end, our research investigates the electrical properties intrinsic to the ovine heart tissues to enhance precision in parameter extraction and advance research methodologies. Leveraging Origin Software and the 3-Debye model [1], the study integrates machine learning techniques to comprehend heart tissue dynamics comprehensively. By evaluating machine learning models' effectiveness and comparing them with analytical models, the research elucidates their predictive capabilities. Utilizing Origin Software, the study fits mathematical models to assess data correlation, facilitating visual assessment of model quality. This research anticipates significant contributions to research methodologies and healthcare applications.

1.2 Contribution of This Work

The following are the contributions of this work:

- Assessing machine learning models Linear Regression, Polynomial Regression, Gradient Boosting, K-Nearest Neighbors (KNN) for predicting cardiac tissue dielectric properties in the terahertz band using data from the 3-pole Debye Model.
- Validating predictions against analytical models and using Origin software for additional verification.
- Exploring machine learning's potential in predicting unknown dielectric properties, advancing non-invasive sensing technologies for 6G healthcare applications.

The rest of the paper is organized as follows: in Sect. 3, a concise background on the 3-Debye model and ML models and metrics are provided. Section 4, the methodology section, outlines the approach, covering data collection, preparation, Python library integration, and extrapolation. This is followed by the presentation of Machine Learning, Origin results, and extrapolation results in the next section. Finally, in the conclusion section, we summarize the key findings and implications of the research.

2 Literature Review

There have been reports that machine learning-based models outperform deterministic ones in terms of computing efficiency and accuracy compared to empirical models. Current literature uses machine learning to predict the optical properties of tissues, turbid mediums, and skin. For instance, Neural Networks, Gaussian Processes, and Random Forests have been used in these applications. However, to the best of our knowledge, there is no work in the literature that has demonstrated the application of machine learning for predicting the dielectric properties of endocardial tissue in the lower frequency bands for in-vivo applications.

Authors in [1] say that knowledge of the dielectric effects of biological tissues stands important for medical diagnostics, monitoring, and therapeutic technologies. Previous studies have treated the heart as a homogeneous organ, but their study aims to provide a more comprehensive understanding by considering the heart as a hybrid organ. The authors measured the dielectric effects at different locations within and outside of the heart in the frequency range of 500 MHz–20 GHz. They identified various parts of an ovine heart based on structure and function and reported the dielectric properties of each part. The results showed significant differences in dielectric properties between various parts of the heart, with differences in some cases. The authors also developed Debye models and provided single-frequency dielectric properties for each part of the heart. These findings can be used to develop more accurate models for electro-magnetic simulations and improve the efficacy of microwave ablation treatment for atrial fibrillation.

Authors in [13] examine the dielectric properties of rat muscle tissue and how they change with varying levels of dehydration. Measurements were taken both in vivo and ex vivo, spanning a frequency range from 500 MHz to 50 GHz. The study used four rats, each undergoing multiple measurements at different stages of dehydration, resulting in a detailed dataset of 25,149 data points. The research process included data loading and cleaning, visualizing the measurements, and structuring the data for training regression models. Various machine learning regression models were tested using nested cross-validation to predict dielectric properties based on tissue hydration levels. The findings reveal that dehydration has a significant impact on permittivity, with greater variability observed at higher dehydration levels. This study sheds light on the crucial relationship between tissue hydration and dielectric properties, which is essential for biomedical applications such as non-invasive diagnostics and therapeutic monitoring.

The study by authors in [14] presents a novel approach for diagnosing liver cancer by leveraging differences in dielectric properties between malignant and healthy tissues. Utilizing an open-ended coaxial probe for in vivo measurements across 500 MHz–6 GHz, the study applies a Support Vector Machine (SVM) algorithm to classify tissue types with a remarkable 99.2% accuracy. This method not only enhances diagnostic precision but also potentially reduces the need for multiple measurements, offering a significant advancement in non-invasive cancer diagnostics and improving surgical outcomes by ensuring clearer surgical margins and minimizing healthy tissue loss.

The study in [15] presents a comprehensive examination of in vivo rat breast tissue dielectric properties (DPs) from 0.5 to 6 GHz, aiming to enhance microwave medical device development and demonstrate their diagnostic potential. Using the open-ended coaxial probe (OECP) technique, 1180 measurements from normal and diseased tissues of 18 Sprague-Dawley female rats were collected and analyzed with Cole-Cole parameters. The study addresses the scarcity of in vivo DP data, especially for diseased tissues, and validates that rat DPs closely resemble those of human tissues, with less than ±11% discrepancy. The OECP method, which enables broadband measurements without sample preparation, shows promise despite historically high error rates, which are mitigated through machine learning (ML) algorithms. Among the seven ML algorithms tested, support vector machines (SVMs) achieved the highest classification accuracy for malignant, benign, and normal tissues, with a median accuracy of 94.4%, alongside strong recall, precision, and F1 scores. These findings suggest significant potential for OECP-based microwave diagnostic systems to improve breast cancer detection, emphasizing the importance of integrating advanced ML techniques to enhance diagnostic accuracy and reliability.

The authors in [16] focus on the early detection of human breast cancer by analyzing the dielectric properties of normal and malignant tissues at low frequencies (α dispersion). Malignant tissues exhibit higher electric permittivity and conductivity due to their higher water and electrolyte content and lower fat content. By measuring these properties in the range 50–100 Hz for 15 malignant and corresponding normal tissues, the researchers identified a threshold separating the two tissue types. This threshold was verified using mathematical calculations and support vector machine (SVM) analysis. The dielectric data were then used as input for deep learning neural networks, achieving an accuracy of 91.7%, sensitivity of 85.7%, and specificity of 100% in distinguishing between normal and malignant tissues. This method shows potential for both cancer diagnosis and prognostic follow-up.

A deep-learning-enabled microwave-induced thermoacoustic tomography (DL-MITAT) approach is shown in [17] for reconstructing the dielectric properties of biological samples with high permittivity and conductivity. Utilizing a novel network structure called DBResU-Net, which features a coarse model and a fine-tuning model, the method accurately reconstructs permittivity and conductivity from preliminary thermoacoustic images. Simulations and experimental tests, including those with breast-mimicking samples, demonstrate the technique's high quality and reliability, achieving an experimental reconstruction error of only 5%. The network exhibits excellent generalization capabilities, handling inhomogeneous samples with various compositions and moderately mismatched shapes. This work provides a promising alternative for quantitative reconstruction in biomedical imaging, detection, and non-destructive testing applications, paving the way for practical implementations.

3 Background

In this segment, we'll begin with exploring the fundamentals of the three-pole Debye model formula.

3.1 Three-Pole Debye Model

The 3-Debye model is a mathematical representation used for dielectric characterization as depicted in [18], particularly in the context of complex biological tissues. This model extends the simpler Debye model, which describes the dielectric behavior of materials based on a single relaxation time. The 3-Debye model accounts for multiple relaxation processes, making it more suitable for characterizing complex tissues that exhibit a range of relaxation times.

The general formula for the 3-Debye model taken from [1] can be expressed as:

$$\epsilon = \epsilon_\infty + \frac{\Delta\epsilon_1}{1 + j\omega\tau_1} + \frac{\Delta\epsilon_2}{1 + j\omega\tau_2} + \frac{\Delta\epsilon_3}{1 + j\omega\tau_3} + \frac{\sigma_s}{j\omega\epsilon_0} \quad (1)$$

where,

$$\begin{aligned}
\epsilon &: \text{Complex Permittivity (F/m)}\\
\Delta\epsilon_1 &: \text{Difference between } \epsilon_1 \text{ and } \epsilon_2\\
\Delta\epsilon_2 &: \text{Difference between } \epsilon_2 \text{ and } \epsilon_3\\
\Delta\epsilon_3 &: \text{Difference between } \epsilon_3 \text{ and } \epsilon_\infty\\
\sigma_s &: \text{Static Ionic Conductivity (S/m)}\\
\epsilon_0 &: \text{Permittivity of free Space (F/m)}\\
\epsilon_\infty &: \text{Permittivity at high Frequency (F/m)}\\
\omega &: \text{Angular Frequency (rad/sec)}\\
\tau &: \text{Relaxation Time (ns)}
\end{aligned}$$

The equation for angular frequency, ω, is given by:

$$\omega = 2\pi f \tag{2}$$

where f is the frequency value in Hertz (Hz).

3.2 Machine Learning Models

Machine learning is a facet of AI that empowers computers to learn from data without explicit programming. It involves crafting algorithms for computers to discern patterns and make predictions. Machine learning algorithms are crucial for automating intricate tasks and addressing data-centric challenges. Applications span various domains, including image recognition, recommendation systems, predictive analytics, industrial automation, natural language processing, healthcare diagnostics, fraud detection, and autonomous vehicles and in accounting research [19].

The following are the ML algorithms used in our research:

1. **Linear Regression:** Linear regression is a simple and widely used statistical method to model the relationship between a dependent variable y and one or more independent variables X. The model assumes a linear relationship between the input variables and the output.
   For a single predictor variable:

$$y = \beta_0 + \beta_1 x + \tilde{\epsilon} \tag{3}$$

   For multiple predictor variables:

$$y = \beta_0 + \beta_1 x_1 + \beta_2 x_2 + \cdots + \beta_n x_n + \tilde{\epsilon} \tag{4}$$

where:

- y is the dependent variable.
- x or x_i are the independent variables.
- β_0 is the intercept.
- $\beta_1, \beta_2, \ldots, \beta_n$ are the coefficients of the independent variables.
- $\tilde{\epsilon}$ is the error term.

2. **Polynomial Regression:** Polynomial regression is an extension of linear regression where the relationship between the independent variable and the dependent variable is modeled as an n-degree polynomial.

$$y = \beta_0 + \beta_1 x + \beta_2 x^2 + \cdots + \beta_n x^n + \tilde{\epsilon} \tag{5}$$

where:

- y is the dependent variable.
- x is the independent variable.
- β_0 is the intercept.
- $\beta_1, \beta_2, \ldots, \beta_n$ are the coefficients.
- $\tilde{\epsilon}$ is the error term.

3. **Gradient Boosting:** Gradient boosting is a machine-learning technique for regression and classification problems. It builds the model in a stage-wise fashion from weak learners (typically decision trees) and optimizes for a loss function using gradient descent.
For regression, the model can be represented as:

$$F(x) = \sum_{m=1}^{M} \alpha_m h_m(x) \tag{6}$$

where:

- $F(x)$ is the final model.
- M is the number of trees.
- α_m is the weight applied to the mth tree.
- $h_m(x)$ is the mth weak learner (decision tree).

The model is trained to minimize a loss function $L(y, F(x))$ using gradient descent.
4. **K-Nearest Neighbors:** K-Nearest Neighbors is a non-parametric method used for classification and regression. The model makes predictions based on the k closest training examples in the feature space.
For regression:

$$\hat{y} = \frac{1}{k} \sum_{i=1}^{k} y_i \tag{7}$$

For classification:

$$\hat{y} = \text{mode}\{y_1, y_2, \ldots, y_k\} \tag{8}$$

where:

- $\hat{y}$ is the predicted value.
- k is the number of nearest neighbors.
- y_i are the values (labels) of the k nearest neighbors.

In regression, the prediction is the average of the values of the nearest neighbors while in classification, it is the mode of the nearest neighbors' labels.

3.3 *Performance Metrics*

Performance metrics provide a computable measure of how efficiently a model is performing on a given task as illustrated in [20].

1. Mean Squared Error (MSE): It calculates the average squared difference between the predicted values and the actual values. The formula for MSE is as follows:

$$MSE = \frac{1}{n}\sum_{i=1}^{n}(y_i - \hat{y}_i)^2 \tag{9}$$

where, $\hat{y}$: predicted value of y

2. Root Mean Square Error (RMSE) is calculated as the square root of the average of the squared differences between actual and predicted values, providing a comprehensive measure of model accuracy.

$$RMSE = \sqrt{\frac{\sum_{i=1}^{n}(y_i - \hat{y}_i)^2}{n}} \tag{10}$$

where, $\hat{y}$: predicted value of y

3. Mean Absolute Error (MAE) is a metric used to measure the average absolute differences between actual and predicted values in regression analysis.

$$MAE = \frac{\sum_{i=1}^{n}|y_i - \hat{y}_i|}{n} \tag{11}$$

where, $\hat{y}$: predicted value of y

4. R-squared as a vital measure in regression analysis, gauging how well independent variables explain variance in the dependent variable.

$$R^2 = 1 - \frac{\sum(y_i - \bar{y})^2}{\sum(y_i - \hat{y}_i)^2} \tag{12}$$

where, $\hat{y}$: predicted value of y
$\bar{y}$: mean value of y

4 Methodology

Our approach comprises the following steps and we explain each step in detail in the subsequent sections:

- Integration of 3-Debye model in origin software.
- Data extraction using the 3-Debye model for training the machine learning models.
- Discuss various Python libraries used in this work.
- Finally, we also discuss the need for extrapolation in the realm of the medical domain.

4.1 Integration of 3-Debye Model in Origin Software

Curve fitting is a widely-used analytical technique for identifying the best-fitting relationship between predictors (independent variables) and a response variable (dependent variable). In this work, Origin software serves as the primary tool for curve fitting. A user-defined function representing the 3-Debye model was integrated into the Origin tool. Using 101 experimental data points (as described in [1] and partially illustrated in Table 1), curve fitting was performed. Three models were evaluated: linear regression and polynomial regression (both pre-built in Origin) and the custom 3-Debye model. These models were applied to experimental data comprising frequency, permittivity, and conductivity of endocardial tissue. Fitted curves were compared against the experimental data (see Figs. 3, 4 and 5). Black curves represent the experimental dataset, while yellow and green curves depict predictions from linear regression, polynomial regression, and the 3-Debye model for permittivity and conductivity, respectively.

Table 1 Data set (partial set) of dielectric properties for endocardium. Tissue [1]

Frequency	ϵ' real part of permittivity	ϵ'' imaginary part of Permittivity
2E+08	67.8314	77.2174
2.12E+08	66.9644	73.28
2.23E+08	66.1777	69.4738
2.35E+08	65.5925	66.1826
2.47E+08	65.0772	63.2122
2.58E+08	64.5911	60.5305
2.7E+08	64.1475	57.9756
2.82E+08	63.6713	55.8456
2.94E+08	63.3343	53.6916
3.05E+08	63.0895	51.7846

4.2 Data Extraction Using 3-Debye Model

In this phase, we extract 5000 examples of the parameters from the 3-Debye model as the data for training the machine learning models. This data is generated using the values as shown in Table 2. The 5000 data examples are generated by putting these values in the 3-Debye model given in Eq. 1. This dataset is used for training the machine learning models. The dataset is now prepared to meet the specific requirements of our analysis, ensuring a robust foundation for subsequent modeling.

4.3 Python Libraries and Hardware Specification

- NumPy: NumPy is a library designed for numerical computing in Python.
- Matplotlib: Matplotlib is a 2D mapping library for Python for effective data representation.
- `from sklearn.preprocessing import PolynomialFeatures`: To generate polynomial features from input data.
- `from sklearn.linear_model import LinearRegression`: The `LinearRegression` class in scikit learn implements this algorithm, facilitating the training and utilization of linear regression models.

Table 2 Parameters obtained after fitting 3-Debye model [1]

ϵ_∞	σ (S/m)	$\Delta\epsilon_1$	τ_1 (ns)	$\Delta\epsilon_2$	τ_2 (ns)	$\Delta\epsilon_3$	τ_3 (ns)
7.53	0.124	311.85	3.41	4.70	$6.24*10^{-2}$	48.61	$8.41*10^{-3}$

- `from sklearn.pipeline import make_pipeline`: The `make_pipeline` function in scikit learn streamlines the creation of processing pipelines.
- `from sklearn.metrics import mean_squared_error`: The `mean_squared_error` function in scikit learn evaluates model performance, guiding our analysis.
- The machine used to train the models had 16GB RAM, 1TB hard disk, Windows 11 with 64-bit OS, and a Core i7 processor with a speed of 2.8 GHz.

4.4 Application of Machine Learning Models

Our study evaluates machine learning models to predict dielectric properties using three algorithms: Linear Regression, Gradient Boosting, and Polynomial Regression.

We first prepare and load the dataset, including frequency-dependent permittivity values. Polynomial Regression is applied with a degree of two (quadratic), and the results are visualized by comparing actual and predicted permittivity values for both real and imaginary components.

Linear Regression models are created separately for the real and imaginary parts of epsilon (permittivity). After loading and preparing the frequency and permittivity values, predictions are generated and visualized through comparative plots.

Gradient Boosting, with hyperparameters like 100 estimators, a learning rate of 0.1, a maximum depth of 3, and a fixed random state, models the real and imaginary parts of epsilon. Results are compared to experimental data for accuracy and reliability.

Using initial data from the three-pole Debye model, we trained the machine learning models to fill gaps in experimental data across the target frequency range. This comprehensive approach facilitates efficient in-vivo communication system development by providing accurate predictions of dielectric properties.

4.5 Relevance for Cardiac Health Monitoring

The paper explores the dielectric characterization of ovine heart tissues at terahertz frequencies, with implications for cardiac health monitoring. Key findings and their biological relevance include:

- **Dielectric Properties as Health Indicators:** The study focuses on permittivity and conductivity, which influence electrical signal propagation in cardiac tissue. Changes in these properties can signal pathological conditions like fibrosis or ischemia, aiding in early diagnosis and treatment.

- **Enhancements to Medical Imaging and Diagnostics:** The dielectric data can improve the accuracy of imaging modalities such as electrical impedance tomography (EIT) and MRI. This enables better visualization and assessment of cardiac tissue health.
- **Implications for Minimally Invasive Monitoring:** The research emphasizes the role of machine learning (ML) in predicting tissue properties beyond current measurement limits, facilitating the development of non-invasive nanosensors for real-time cardiac monitoring. This is particularly relevant in the terahertz band, which is critical for advanced in-vivo communication systems.
- **Advancements in Medical Device Design:** Insights from this study can optimize the design of implantable devices like pacemakers or defibrillators by tailoring their interaction with specific cardiac tissue types.
- **Potential for Personalized Healthcare:** The combination of ML and terahertz-frequency analysis allows for personalized monitoring and treatment, improving outcomes by providing data-driven, patient-specific insights.

The findings bridge a critical gap in knowledge of cardiac tissue dynamics and pave the way for innovative diagnostic tools and monitoring systems, contributing significantly to precision medicine and networked healthcare environments.

5 Results and Evaluations

5.1 Validation Using Origin Software

The results for 500 MHz–20 GHz (experimental data of endocardium of the heart tissue) obtained after fitting each of these three models are as shown in Figs. 2, 3 and 4. In these figures, black curves indicate the original experimental data permittivity and conductivity of dielectric values of the endocardium tissue. The yellow curves indicate the fitted data for permittivity and the green curves indicate the fitted data for conductivity (Figs. 6, 7 and 8).

5.2 Machine Learning Results

5.2.1 Performance Metrics

Four machine learning models, Linear Regression, Polynomial Regression, Gradient Boosting, and K-nearest neighbors (KNN), are applied and their performance comparison is done. The performance metrics used are Mean Squared Error (MSE), Root Mean Squared Error (RMSE), Mean Absolute Error (MAE), and R-Square (Coefficient of Determination).

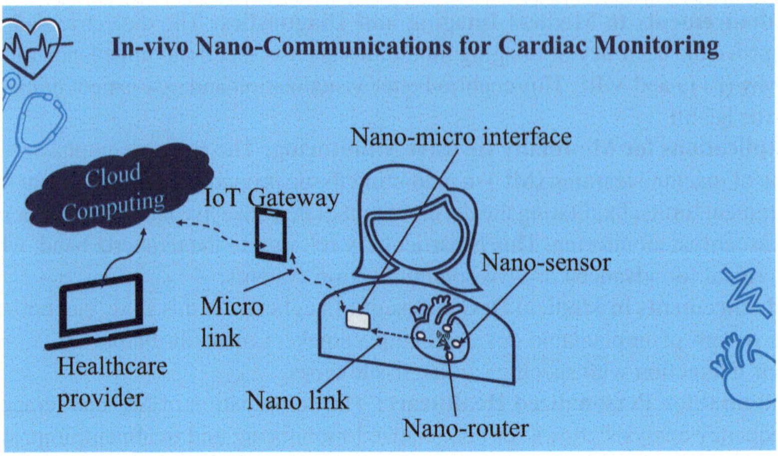

Fig. 1 In-vivo nanosensor network for cardiac monitoring

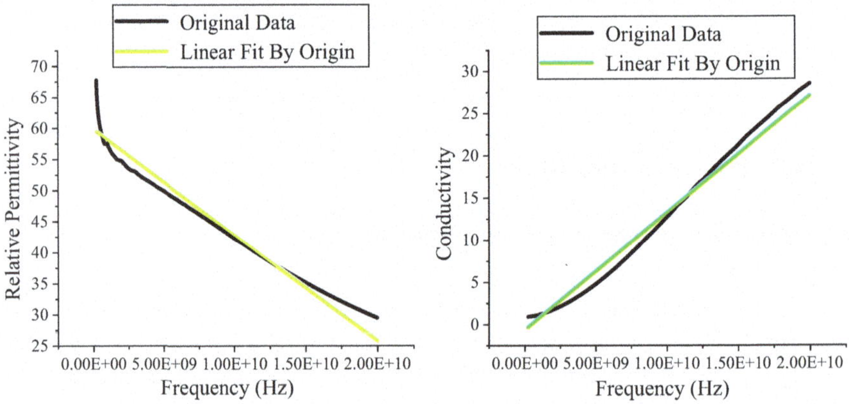

(a) Permittivity vs Frequency

(b) Conductivity vs Frequency

Fig. 2 Linear fit in origin

Among these, Gradient Boosting achieved the best performance with near-perfect R^2 values of 0.9999 for both permittivity and conductivity, and the lowest MSE, RMSE, and MAE metrics. Its ensemble approach effectively captured the complex patterns in the data, demonstrating robustness and high predictive accuracy. KNN, while competitive, exhibited slightly higher errors, particularly in RMSE and MAE, due to its sensitivity to the choice of $k = 5$ and the use of the Minkowski distance metric ($p = 2$). Linear Regression struggled significantly, reflecting the model's inability to handle the non-linearity inherent in the data. Polynomial Regression (degree $d = 2$) improved over Linear Regression but fell short of capturing more nuanced rela-

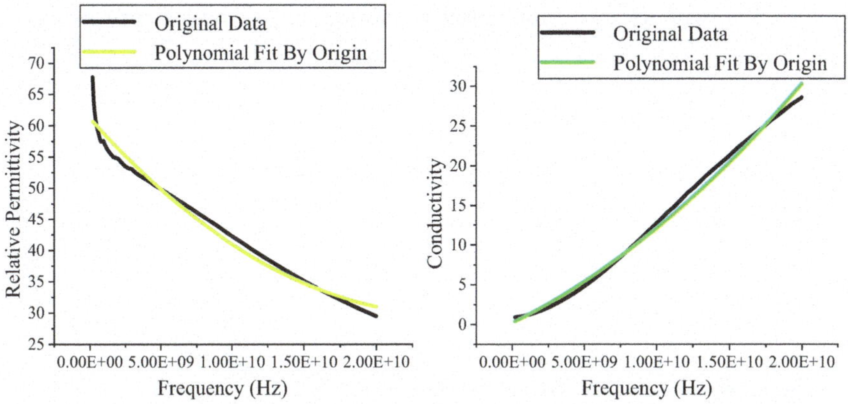

(a) Permittivity vs Frequency (b) Conductivity vs Frequency

Fig. 3 Polynomial fit in origin

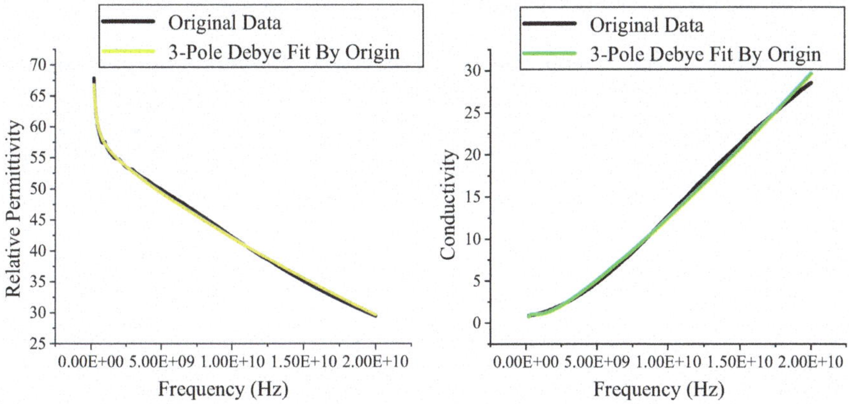

(a) Permittivity vs Frequency (b) Conductivity vs Frequency

Fig. 4 3-Debye fit in origin

tionships, indicating the importance of fine-tuning the polynomial degree to balance underfitting and overfitting.

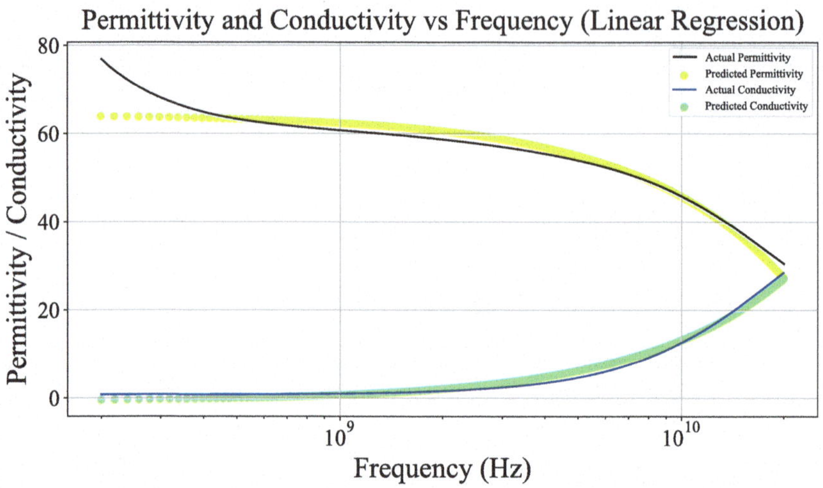

Fig. 5 Linear regression (Permittivity and conductivity vs. frequency; endocardium tissue)

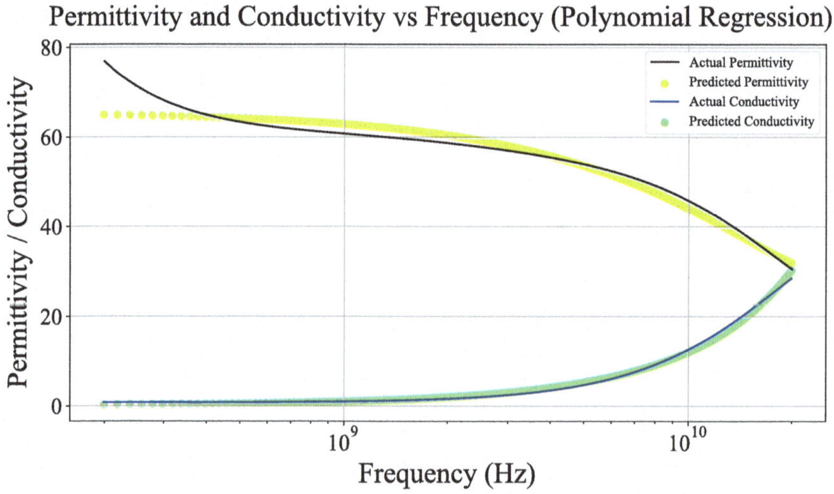

Fig. 6 Polynomial regression (Permittivity and conductivity vs. frequency; endocardium tissue)

These results highlight the critical role of hyperparameter optimization in model performance. For Gradient Boosting, further tuning of parameters such as learning rate, number of estimators, and tree depth could enhance performance even further. Similarly, adjusting the number of neighbors and distance metrics in KNN could potentially reduce errors. The comprehensive performance metrics of the models are summarized in Tables 3 and 4, emphasizing Gradient Boosting as the most suitable model for this dataset.

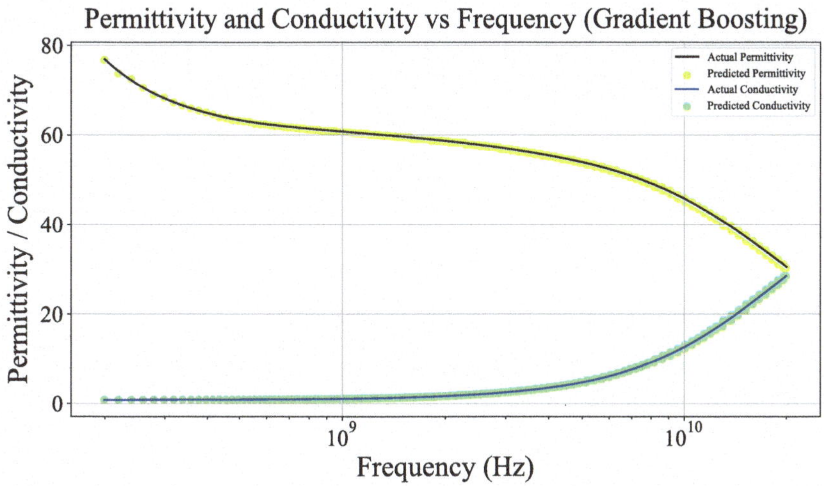

Fig. 7 Gradient boosting (Permittivity and conductivity vs. frequency; endocardium tissue)

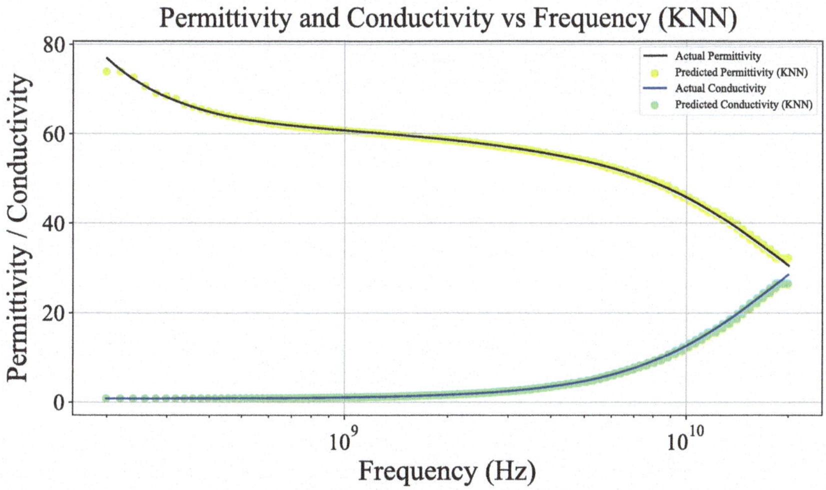

Fig. 8 KNN (Permittivity and conductivity vs. frequency; endocardium tissue)

Table 3 ML predicted permittivity metrics

ML Model	MSE	RMSE	MAE	R-Square
Gradient Boosting	0.0014	0.03818	0.0230	0.9999
KNN	0.2043	0.4520	0.1940	0.9979
Linear Regression	8.7329	2.9551	2.0220	0.9126
Polynomial Regression	7.2096	2.6850	1.8956	0.9278

Table 4 ML predicted conductivity metrics

ML Model	MSE	RMSE	MAE	R-Square
Gradient Boosting	0.0806	0.0092	0.0051	0.9999
KNN	0.0981	0.3132	0.1035	0.9981
Linear Regression	0.9764	0.9881	0.8763	0.9814
Polynomial Regression	0.2616	0.5115	0.4233	0.9950

5.3 Extrapolation Results and Inferences

Here, we begin with addressing the question *'why extrapolation'?*. We know that in-vivo wireless nanosensor networks [9] the nanosensor nodes operate in the terahertz band owing to their physical dimensions. Even though terahertz signals are known to have high absorption in this band (0.1–10 THz), the works in [5, 9] have shown the feasibility of employing nanosensor nodes for monitoring internal health parameters and deliver this information to the outside world (for in-vivo nano network, see Fig. 1). However, to study the behavior of such networks, it is essential to have a thorough knowledge of the channel condition so that this knowledge might be used for developing efficient media access control (MAC) and routing protocols. Since the literature gives the dielectric properties of the endocardium tissues for up to 20 GHz, we aimed to exploit the potential benefits of machine learning in predicting these values beyond 20 GHz (experimentally determined data in the literature). To this end, this study explores the extrapolation capability of machine learning and its effectiveness in predicting new and unknown values (permittivity and conductivity values). Machine learning algorithms learn patterns from data and make predictions about future data which indicates that MLAs can be used to extrapolate. We have considered data that falls beyond the range of training data and hence it would be interesting to see how ML extrapolation works for us.

The predicted permittivity and conductivity values, using ML extrapolation, of cardiac tissue (endocardium) across a frequency range from 500 MHz to 10 THz using the gradient Boosting, kNN machine learning models, and 3-Debye models are shown in Figs. 9, 10 and 11.

The permittivity and conductivity values generated between 20 GHz and 10 THz using the 3-Debye (analytical) model will help us understand the correctness of the prediction of the two ML models. Looking at these three figures Figs. 9, 10 and 11, it is clear that machine learning models can predict the new and unseen values of permittivity and conductivity. However, we stress that these extrapolated values need to be validated by comparing them with the experimental data obtained in the 20 GHz–10 THz band so that these models can be used in medical applications.

Both the ML models and the 3-Debye model show that permittivity decreases with increasing frequency. The sharp decline and eventual leveling off in the Gradient Boosting prediction align well with the 3-Debye model's behavior. This suggests that the ML models are able to capture the overall trend of decreasing permittivity with increasing frequency.

Both methods predict a rise in conductivity as frequency increases, followed by a plateau at higher frequencies. The shape of the conductivity curve in the ML model plots matches closely with the 3-Debye model, indicating that the machine learning model effectively approximates the conductivity behavior across the frequency range.

Tables 5 and 6 show various scores for extrapolation of the two machine learning models.

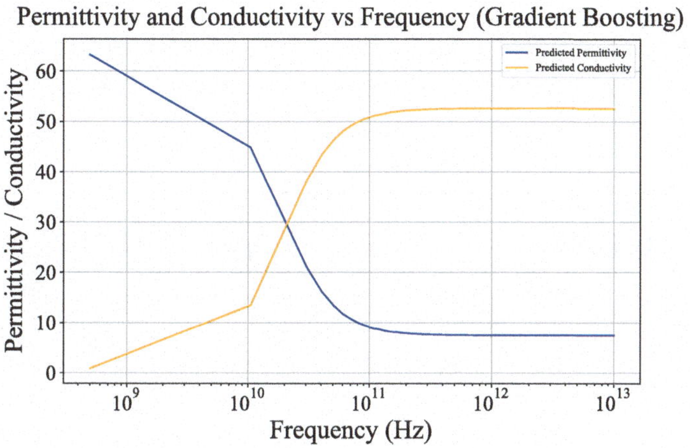

Fig. 9 Gradient boosting (Permittivity and conductivity vs. frequency)

Table 5 Extrapolated permittivity metrics

ML Model	MSE	RMSE	MAE	R-Square
Gradient Boosting	1.7472	0.0041	0.0007	0.9999
KNN	0.0337	0.1836	0.0087	0.9912

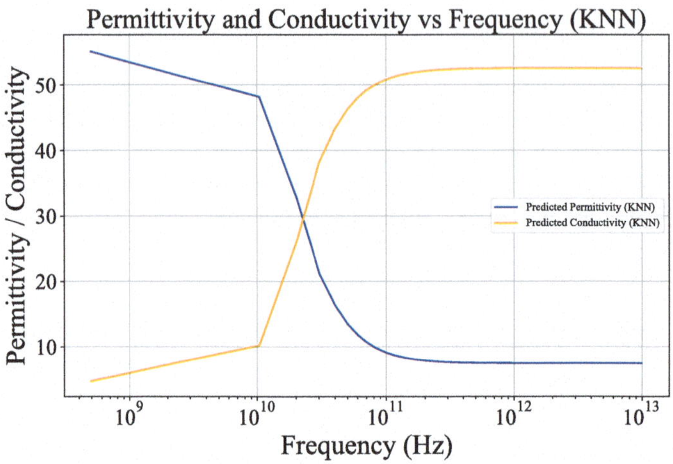

Fig. 10 KNN (Permittivity and conductivity vs. frequency)

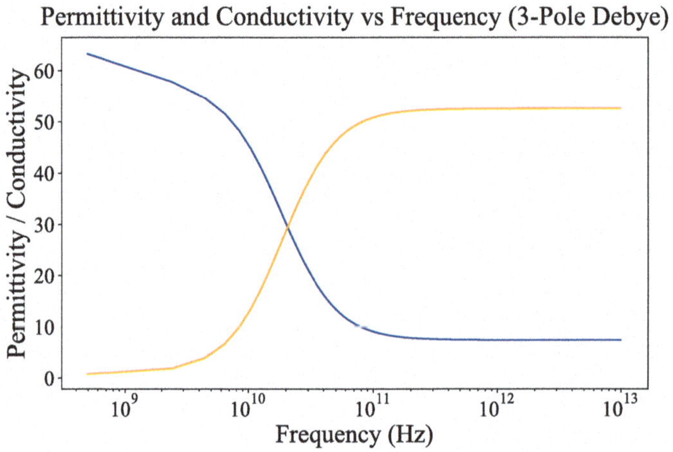

Fig. 11 3-Pole Debye (Permittivity and conductivity vs. frequency)

Table 6 Extrapolated conductivity metrics

ML Model	MSE	RMSE	MAE	R-Square
Gradient Boosting	1.7408	0.0041	0.0007	0.9999
KNN	0.0223	0.1494	0.0077	0.9944

6 Conclusion

In our research, we delved into a detailed comparative analysis of ML algorithms applied to the assessment of ovine heart tissues' complex permittivity within two distinct frequency cases (Case-1: 500 MHz–20 GHz, Case-2: 500 MHz–8.5 GHz). This investigation aimed to understand the electrical characteristics of the tissues, with a focus on the real part representing relative permittivity and the imaginary part signifying conductivity. Throughout our rigorous examination, three prominent algorithms–Linear Regression, Gradient Boosting, and Polynomial Regression, and KNN–were thoroughly investigated for their efficacy in predicting complex permittivity. Our analyses involved comprehensive visualizations and a meticulous breakdown into real and imaginary components. We have successfully portrayed the relationships through insightful graphs. Upon careful evaluation, it was evident that the gradient-boosting algorithm demonstrated exceptional performance. The predictions aligned remarkably well with the actual scatter loss values, achieving higher accuracy. The plots illustrating the actual versus predicted curves showcased the model's outstanding precision, with data points closely aligning along the reference line. This underscores the remarkable predictive capabilities of the Gradient Boosting algorithm in capturing the nuanced electrical behavior of ovine heart tissues across the specified frequency range. The Gradient Boosting model accurately reflects the key trends observed in the 3-Debye model for both permittivity and conductivity. Permittivity decreases and then stabilizes with increasing frequency. Conductivity increases sharply and then plateaus at higher frequencies. This consistency validates the use of Gradient Boosting for predicting the dielectric properties of cardiac tissues and suggests it can be effectively used for extrapolation in biomedical applications, particularly when experimental data is sparse or incomplete. In essence, our research not only provides valuable insights into the dielectric characterization of ovine heart tissues but also highlights the superior performance of the Gradient Boosting algorithm in this specific context. This outcome has significant implications for advancing the understanding of tissue properties and underscores the potential of machine-learning approaches in biomedical research and healthcare technology.

Future work will focus on using COMSOL Multiphysics simulations to investigate the interactions of terahertz (0.1–10 THz) and microwave (200 MHz–20 GHz) frequency bands with six ovine heart tissues. This includes analyzing the transmittance, reflectance, and absorptance properties within these bands. Understanding these optical properties will enhance our knowledge of signal propagation and interaction with tissues, leading to optimized in-vivo nano-communication networks. These insights will contribute to the development of more precise and minimally invasive diagnostic tools and medical devices, improving healthcare applications and protocols.

Acknowledgements This work is supported by the Commissioned Research through SRM University-AP Seed Fund, India, under Grant No. SRMAP/URG/SEED/2023-24/012 and is carried out in the Nano Communication and Networking Lab at SRM University-AP.

References

1. N. Ištuk, E. Porter, D. O'loughlin, B. McDermott, A. Santorelli, S. Abedi, N. Joachimowicz, H. Roussel, and M. O'halloran, "Dielectric properties of ovine heart at microwave frequencies," *Diagnostics*, vol. 11, no. 3, p. 531, 2021.
2. I. F. Akyildiz, J. M. Jornet, and M. Pierobon, "Nanonetworks: A new frontier in communications," *Communications of the ACM*, vol. 54, no. 11, pp. 84–89, 2011.
3. J. K. Wray, B. Dixon, and R. Przkora, "Radiofrequency ablation," in *StatPearls [Internet]*. StatPearls Publishing, 2023.
4. K. Yang, A. Pellegrini, A. Brizzi, A. Alomainy, and Y. Hao, "Numerical analysis of the communication channel path loss at the thz band inside the fat tissue," in *2013 IEEE MTT-S International Microwave Workshop Series on RF and Wireless Technologies for Biomedical and Healthcare Applications (IMWS-BIO)*. IEEE, 2013, pp. 1–3.
5. K. Yang, A. Alomainy, and Y. Hao, "In-vivo characterisation and numerical analysis of the thz radio channel for nanoscale body-centric wireless networks," in *2013 USNC-URSI Radio Science Meeting (Joint with AP-S Symposium)*. IEEE, 2013, pp. 218–219.
6. O. Smolyanskaya, N. Chernomyrdin, A. Konovko, K. Zaytsev, I. Ozheredov, O. Cherkasova, M. Nazarov, J.-P. Guillet, S. Kozlov, Y. V. Kistenev *et al.*, "Terahertz biophotonics as a tool for studies of dielectric and spectral properties of biological tissues and liquids," *Progress in Quantum Electronics*, vol. 62, pp. 1–77, 2018.
7. I. F. Akyildiz, M. Pierobon, S. Balasubramaniam, and Y. Koucheryavy, "The internet of bio-nano things," *IEEE Communications Magazine*, vol. 53, no. 3, pp. 32–40, 2015.
8. I. F. Akyildiz and J. M. Jornet, "The internet of nano-things," *IEEE Wireless Communications*, vol. 17, no. 6, pp. 58–63, 2010.
9. H. Elayan, R. M. Shubair, A. Alomainy, and K. Yang, "In-vivo terahertz em channel characterization for nano-communications in wbans," in *2016 IEEE International Symposium on Antennas and Propagation (APSURSI)*. IEEE, 2016, pp. 979–980.
10. S. Badillo, B. Banfai, F. Birzele, I. I. Davydov, L. Hutchinson, T. Kam-Thong, J. Siebourg-Polster, B. Steiert, and J. D. Zhang, "An introduction to machine learning," *Clinical pharmacology & therapeutics*, vol. 107, no. 4, pp. 871–885, 2020.
11. P. Samaddar, A. K. Mishra, S. Gaddam, M. Singh, V. K. Modi, K. Gopalakrishnan, R. L. Bayer, I. C. Igreja Sa, S. Khanal, P. Hirsova *et al.*, "Machine learning-based classification of abnormal liver tissues using relative permittivity," *Sensors*, vol. 22, no. 24, p. 9919, 2022.
12. B. H. Hokr and J. N. Bixler, "Machine learning estimation of tissue optical properties," *Scientific Reports*, vol. 11, no. 1, p. 6561, 2021.
13. B. Gerazov, D. A. Caligari Conti, L. Farina, L. Farrugia, C. V. Sammut, P. Schembri Wismayer, and R. C. Conceiç ao, "Application of machine learning to predict dielectric properties of in vivo biological tissue," *Sensors*, vol. 21, no. 20, p. 6935, 2021.
14. T. Yilmaz, M. A. Kılıç, M. Erdoğan, M. Çay"oren, D. Tunaoğlu, I. Kurtoğlu, Y. Yaslan, H. Çay"oren, A. E. Arıkan, S. Teks"oz *et al.*, "Machine learning aided diagnosis of hepatic malignancies through in vivo dielectric measurements with microwaves," *Physics in medicine and biology*, vol. 61, no. 13, p. 5089, 2016.
15. N. P. Ozsobaci, E. Onemli, C. Aydinalp, and T. Yilmaz, "Measurement and analysis of in vivo microwave dielectric properties collected from normal, benign, and malignant rat breast tissues: Classification using supervised machine learning algorithms," *IEEE Transactions on Instrumentation and Measurement*, 2024.
16. M. M. Shawki, M. M. Azmy, M. Salama, and S. Shawki, "Mathematical and deep learning analysis based on tissue dielectric properties at low frequencies predict outcome in human breast cancer," *Technology and Health Care*, vol. 30, no. 3, pp. 633–645, 2022.
17. Z. Luo, C. Li, D. Liu, B. Wang, L. Zhang, Y. Ma, K. Xu, and X. Wang, "Quantitative reconstruction of dielectric properties based on deep-learning-enabled microwave-induced thermoacoustic tomography," *IEEE Transactions on Microwave Theory and Techniques*, 2023.
18. P. Mantas, "Dielectric response of materials: extension to the debye model," *Journal of the European Ceramic Society*, vol. 19, no. 12, pp. 2079–2086, 1999.

19. J. Krupa and M. Minutti-Meza, "Regression and machine learning methods to predict discrete outcomes in accounting research," *Journal of Financial Reporting*, vol. 7, no. 2, pp. 131–178, 2022.
20. A. Botchkarev, "A new typology design of performance metrics to measure errors in machine learning regression algorithms," *Interdisciplinary Journal of Information, Knowledge, and Management*, vol. 14, p. 045–076, 2019. [Online]. Available: http://dx.doi.org/10.28945/4184

Chapter 16
Evolution of Intelligent Transportation Systems for the Next Generation: IRS Enabled 6G

Shaik Rajak, Vineela Chandra Dodda, Lakshmi, Koduru Hajarathaiah, Mohd Hamza Naim Shaikh Hamza, Inbarasan Muniraj, and Sunil Chinnadurai

16.1 Introduction

16.1.1 Evolution of Transportation System

Transportation is essential in modern life, with significant economic and social consequences. Ground-based, air, sea, and space are the most popular means of transportation today, with each providing distinct mobility and capability. The growing demand for mobility has overloaded large cities with automobiles, resulting in increased gridlock in traffic and unanticipated incidents and accidents. These challenges reveal considerable bottlenecks in travel, emphasizing the need to build solutions that encourage safer, more effective movement. One strategy to tackle these

S. Rajak (✉) · V. C. Dodda
Amrita Vishwa Vidyapeetham, Amaravthi, India
e-mail: r_shaik@av.amrita.edu

V. C. Dodda
e-mail: c_vineela@av.amrita.edu

Lakshmi
Department of Electronics and Communication Engineering, Koneru Lakshmaiah Educational Foundation (KLEF), Vaddeswaram 522302, Andhra Pradesh, India

K. Hajarathaiah
School of Computer Science and Engineering, VIT-AP University, Amaravthi, India

M. H. N. Shaikh Hamza
Department of Electronic and Electrical Engineering, University College London, London, UK

I. Muniraj
Department of Electronic Engineering, Maynooth University, Maynooth, Ireland

S. Chinnadurai
Electronics and Communication Engineering, SRM University AP, Andhra Pradesh, India

T. Ojha et al. (eds.), *Edge-Enabled 6G Networking*,
https://doi.org/10.1007/978-3-032-19042-0_16

difficulties is to use recent communication research results to handle transportation. This may be accomplished by utilizing intellectual networking concepts and establishing systems for managing transportation with learning features that enable the forecasting of prospective hazards and the subsequent modification of vehicle behavior.

Intelligent Transportation Systems (ITS) involve incorporating advanced technologies into transportation infrastructure and vehicles to enhance safety, efficiency, and overall mobility. ITS includes a diverse array of applications and technologies aimed at solving traffic issues, providing better traveler information, and aiding in transportation planning and management. By leveraging technology, ITS creates smarter, safer, and more efficient transportation networks, leading to improved quality of life and economic growth. ITS have emerged in response to the increasing transportation demands in recent years [1]. ITS utilizes a modern wireless data network, integrating intelligence, connectivity, technology, and other innovations to facilitate seamless interaction among humans, roadways, and automobiles [2, 3]. Numerous studies have combined vehicle-to-vehicle (V2V) and vehicle-to-infrastructure (V2I) communications within vehicular networks to enhance ITS performance [4]. The future success and efficiency of ITS will rely on the integration of V2V and V2I networking and the optimal use of resource allocation and frequency sharing. However, the rapid development of automated vehicles presents a growing challenge in meeting ITS demands [5]. A significant volume of data needs to be transferred quickly within ITS, necessitating the use of sixth-generation (6G) communications, which require higher transmission power and bandwidth.

16.1.2 Introduction to IRS and Its Potential in 6G

Despite the fifth-generation (5G), wireless communication system is still in use, experts are currently trying to define the next-generation, or 6G communications radio network. The goal is to meet far superior performance criteria, such as exceptional throughput, super-high trustworthiness, ultra-low latency, and extremely low energy utilization [6]. However, depending simply on current developments, such as massive multi-input multi-output (MIMO) and millimeter wave (mmWave), may not be sufficient to meet these requirements. In contrast, these developments can improve performance, but they additionally raise power and hardware expenses. Furthermore, wireless network performance is essentially constrained by channel imperfections such as route loss, shadowing, and small-scale fading, which standard wireless communication approaches can only slightly address.

ITS requires highly accurate and near-zero latency communication for faster and safer operations. Additionally, signal blockages caused by tall buildings and other obstacles can impede ITS functionality. To address these challenges, the Intelligent Reflecting Surfaces (IRS) is utilized in ITS. IRS helps overcome signal blockages, increase received signal strength, and reduce power consumption by reflecting inci-

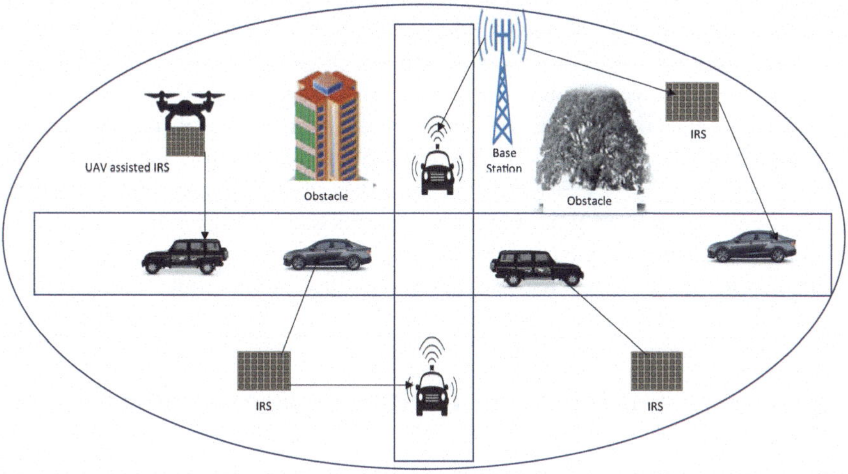

Fig. 16.1 ITS network by using IRS in 6G communications. IRS is deployed between the users when there is a signal blockage or obstacle

dent signals through numerous passive elements as shown in Fig. 16.1, where IRS is placed to direct the reflected signal towards the user. Future communication systems are poised to handle the substantial data traffic and increased network capacity anticipated in 6G wireless networks. However, THz communications face significant challenges in practical implementation, including propagation loss, signal blockage, and high hardware costs. It explores the emerging paradigm of IRS-assisted communication systems, which addresses these challenges by combining active and passive beamforming to enhance communication quality and reduce overhead. It provides the current methods for achieving THz active/passive beam steering at the transmitter and IRS, focusing on practical implementation. Recognized as one of the most revolutionary technologies, IRS can significantly enhance the capabilities of future wireless networks [7]. The phase shifts of the reflecting elements in IRS are adjusted to reconfigure the transmission signal between the source and destination, thereby improving system performance [8].

16.1.3 Role of 6G in Shaping the Future ITS

Modern communication mechanisms are becoming more essential as transportation networks grow in size and complexity. Numerous research studies looked into improving transport systems with 5G and previous generations of wireless networks. 6G intends to surpass 5G in terms of data throughput, connectivity, and efficiency. It also aims to give more support for maximum mobility by allowing gadgets on high-speed vehicles and even airplanes to communicate via terrestrial wireless networks.

However, there remain transportation circumstances in which connectivity is rare or throughput is severely constrained. In the coming years, the 6G network is expected to enable ubiquitous connection for users and objects across all modes of travel, covering even the most distant and unpopulated corners of the earth. Furthermore, 6G's superior communication capabilities enable effective traffic control and optimization via continuous V2I connectivity, which reduces jams and improves travel times. In addition, 6G's low latency and high speed of data allow wireless vehicle control, which improves the protection of autonomous cars and provides remote support in difficult circumstances. For customers, 6G enables improved entertainment services, including effective multimedia and virtual reality applications while in traveling.

16.2 Overview of Intelligent Transportation Systems (ITS)

Intelligent Transportation systems encompass a wide array of technologies aimed at enhancing the safety, efficiency, reliability, and environmental sustainability of transportation systems without requiring extensive infrastructure modifications. These technologies include sensors, control systems, communications networks, and computer informatics, drawing on expertise from disciplines such as transportation, engineering, telecommunications, computer science, finance, electronic commerce, and automotive manufacturing. As a growing global trend, ITS benefits both public and private sectors by facilitating the implementation of government regulations and processes more cost-effectively, while also increasing corporate productivity through time savings, reduced operating costs, energy efficiency, and improved reliability. The major goals of ITS are enhancing mobility, sustainability, and efficiency. Mobility focuses on increasing the efficiency and performance of transportation networks. Sustainable mobility prioritizes traffic safety and ecologically responsible improvements to infrastructure. Finally, convenience aims to provide conveniently accessible services to travelers.

16.2.1 History and Development of ITS

The electronic route guiding system (ERGS) was the first application in America [9]. After that, the American government established the Vehicle Infrastructure Integration (VII) project [10, 11], which offers communication between automobiles and transportation systems to increase safety. Later on, another project aimed at improving safety and mobility, Cooperative Vehicle-Highway Automation Systems (CVHAS) [12], commenced. Recently, America's study emphasis has shifted to linked vehicles and associated automation technology.

Europe pioneered the introduction of ITS in the first decade of the 1970s, resulting in substantial advances in Road Transport Informatics (RTI) [13]. Subsequently, other projects have been initiated to accelerate the advancement of ITS. The most notable program Dedicated Road Infrastructure for Vehicle Safety in Europe (DRIVE) [14], began in 1989 as the European Union's first telematics advancement program, with 72 distinct projects. In 1991, the European Union founded the European Road Transport Telematics Implementation Coordination Organisation (ERTICO) to use technology for communication and information to improve active hazard and driver autonomy [15]. The eSafety project began in 2003 to incorporate safety technologies in automobiles to improve road safety.

16.2.2 Key Features and Technologies in Current ITS

Intelligent Transport Systems include significant aspects that transform the way we navigate in urban areas. One of the most notable features of ITS is real-time traffic surveillance and management, which uses data from sensors and cameras to optimize traffic flow and reduce congestion. Furthermore, modern information systems give commuters real-time traffic alerts, alternate route ideas, and public transit timetables, which improves overall mobility accuracy. Another essential element is adaptive traffic signal control, which adjusts traffic lights in real-time on the rate of traffic and congestion levels, therefore optimizing traffic flow and lowering travel time. By incorporating these and other elements, ITS contributes significantly to the development of safer, smarter, and more efficient modes of transportation for future generations as shown in Fig. 16.2. A few of ITS features are listed as follows,

Traffic management: Traffic management is critical in intelligent transportation systems optimizing traffic flow and improving total road network efficiency. Trans-

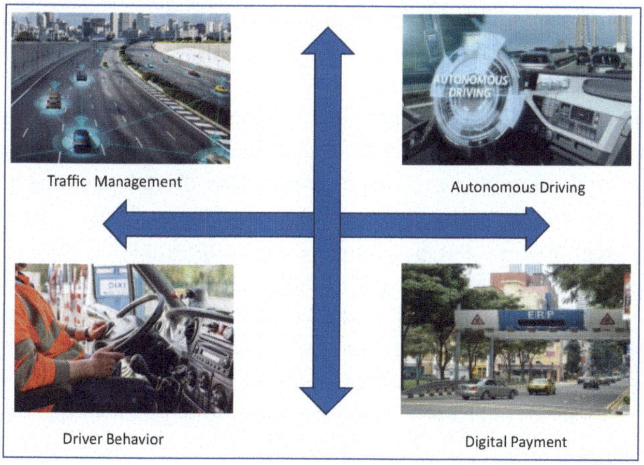

Fig. 16.2 Application of IRS in ITS to improve the performance and collect the vehicle and driving conditions

portation authorities may use sophisticated technology like real-time traffic monitoring, analytical modeling, and adaptive signal control to proactively detect congested areas, dynamically modify traffic signals, and deliver actionable information for better decision-making. These solutions allow experts to respond quickly to traffic problems, cut delays, lower emissions, and, ultimately, enhance the commuting experience for vehicles and pedestrians. Adopting intelligent transportation technologies enables transportation experts to develop more secure, feasible, and efficient city environments.

Autonomous Driving: Autonomous driving has transformed ITS, leading to a new era of efficiency and safety on our roadways. Autonomous cars can negotiate complicated traffic circumstances with incredible precision because of new technology such as artificial intelligence, sensors, and real-time data processing. This unique strategy not only decreases the possibility of human mistakes but also improves traffic flow and reduces congestion. Furthermore, automated driving technologies have the potential to drastically reduce accident rates, making our roads safer for all drivers. As we go forward in this industry, it is critical to prioritize rigorous testing, rules, and infrastructure development to enable the seamless integration of self-driving vehicles into our transportation systems.

Driver information and behavior: In the context of ITS, driver information and behavior are critical in influencing the future of road safety and traffic efficiency. Real-time insights about driver behavior may be gathered by leveraging modern technology like GPS, sensors, and data analytics, resulting in better decision-making. This information may be used to optimize traffic flow and prevent accidents while strengthening overall transportation facilities. Furthermore, by promoting desirable driving behaviors such as adhering to speed limits and keeping safe following distances, the potential advantages of these intelligent devices are enhanced. Finally, by realizing the importance of driver information and behavior in ITS, the objective of establishing a safer and more efficient transportation system may be achieved.

Digital Payments: Intelligent transport systems that use digital payments are changing the way we commute and pay for transport services. Passengers may enjoy a more pleasant and efficient travel experience when digital payment methods are smoothly integrated into intelligent transportation systems. These solutions not only speed the payment process, but also improve the entire transportation infrastructure by decreasing congestion, increasing traffic flow, and giving real-time data insights to help decision-makers. The use of modern technology such as RFID cards, mobile payment applications, and contactless payment systems represents an important step towards a more connected and smart transportation ecosystem. Implementing electronic payment methods in ITS is critical for encouraging green and accessible mobility and providing travelers with a smoother and more user-friendly travel experience.

16.3 Role of IRS and 6G in ITS

As we approach the 6G communications, wireless connections are expected to improve data throughput, connectivity, and accuracy while reducing latency and power usage. To meet the different demands of vertical businesses, 6G will prioritize three new cases: integrated sensing and communication (ISAC), artificial intelligence (AI), and ubiquitous connection. These applications and capacities will revolutionize communication and benefit specific sectors like transportation. Urban locations see more impact from IRS on energy efficiency (EE) and spectral efficiency (SE) than semi-urban and rural areas. Relays are highly successful in both semi-urban and rural locations. Increasing the number of IRS leads to considerable training costs for ITS and complicated channel estimates due to their inherent instability and reconfigurability [16]. Developing a preliminary model with a large number of training sets allows Deep Learning (DL) to compute the IRS channel with minimal training time and difficulty [17]. DL is effective in extracting features and understanding input data for IRS-assisted communication networks [18]. Furthermore, DL outperforms model-based techniques, which rely primarily on mathematical models. IRS-aided wireless systems leverage deep learning to provide sophisticated 6G technologies with high data speeds, like ITS. The work in [19] presents a unique DL-based ITS architecture that optimizes computing complexity, efficiency, and reliability.

16.3.1 IRS Functions and Applications in 6G Network

IRS is estimated to enhance transmission efficiency in 6G wireless networks due to its ease of installation and reconfiguration, affordable costs for implementation, and low power demand. A large number of channel simulations have been presented for various conditions and frequencies. These models are unable to be updated or rebuilt and need complex transmitting and receiving techniques to adapt. In 6G wireless networks, focusing just on end-points may not fulfill KPI criteria for ultra-high throughput, low latency, and high dependability. IRS is a game-changing technology that allows wireless environments to be optimized and regulated, rather than merely adapted to. The IRS-assisted intelligent connection can be beneficial in several 6G network applications.

In urban areas, glass is commonly used for exterior walls of tall structures. Smart glasses with IRSs [20, 21] can efficiently regulate radio wave propagation. IRS can provide high-speed connection in busy environments like huge buildings, university campuses, offices, and classrooms, eliminating the need for many access points. Intelligent clothing can monitor people's health in real-time by inserting IRSs and smart sensors into wearable body area networks. These IRS-assisted applications lay the groundwork for the implementation of an intelligent data society. IRS-assisted

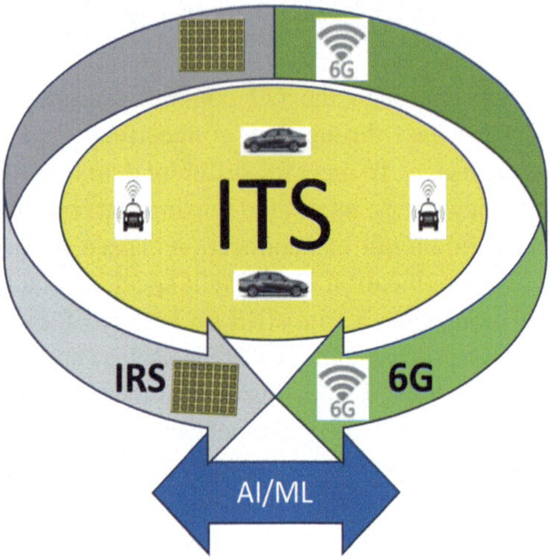

Fig. 16.3 AI/ML techniques to improve efficiency and reduce the computational complexity in ITS by 6G enabled IRS

connectivity can greatly improve 6G network access in many circumstances because of low power consumption and ease of installation. In metropolitan areas, buildings' outside walls can be covered with IRS. This presents chances to improve the coverage and power consumption of 6G networks in cities. IRS may be put on the roofs of high buildings to provide a simulated LoS link between the access point and the IRS. This is particularly insightful when the straight path is heavily obscured [22]. The IRS's widespread implementation can significantly lower electromagnetic radiation (EM) from city network facilities. IRS coating on interior walls can improve local access to wireless gadgets like mobile phones and iPads. IRS, in particular, may be installed in ceilings and subterranean walls to give coverage to a large number of subscribers at the same time. IRS coatings on vehicles, high-speed trains, and airplanes can act as moving, nearly passive relays to improve 6G network access in both air and land situations as shown in Fig. 16.3.

16.3.2 Advantages of IRS in ITS

IRS and ITS are becoming more prevalent in the transportation business, aiming to improve efficiency and management for both terrestrial and aerial vehicles. Both conventional automobile makers and Digital auto businesses, including BMW and Tesla, are interested in automated driving and creating driver-aid systems [23]. Latest studies on infrastructure and material demonstrate the ability to continuously regulate reflection, allowing for real-time beamforming and serving numerous users. IRS's tunable passive beamforming enhances physical layer security in both terrestrial and aerial vehicle connectivity. Research indicates that a vehicular network with IRS has reduced outage rates and greater resilience compared to a system without IRS. The impact of topographical geography on vehicle communication can't be ignored. Dhruvakumar et al. [24] used IRS to improve signal propagation in wireless channels across two terrains. The simulation results show that theÃƒÆ'Ã¢â‚¬Å¡ÃƒâŁšÃ‚Â IRS improves transmission consistency and communication range. Enabling swift communication in terrestrial vehicle networks necessitates highly precise location.

IRS-aided methods provide additional channel details so they can track and identify vehicles depending on incoming wave patterns. In [25], IRSs were used to place mobile phone users, resulting in greater reliability and accessibility compared to non-IRS systems. IRS can improve finding quality and boost connectivity by predicting locations after establishing a reliable connection. Scientific study indicates that considering the period when the antenna's signal arrives at the car and when it is reflected by a regular wall might improve vehicle location accuracy [26]. IRS can intelligently alter the direction and polarization of redirected waves, unlike regular walls. IRS can allow passengers to converse with others outside the car. A hybrid-equivalent surface-edge present model is suggested to analyze radiation from vehicle transmitters. This research could create a theoretical foundation for installing IRS on vehicle panels. Huang et al. [27] investigated the use of IRS in high-speed transport vehicles to improve passenger communication with roadside BSs. IRS-enabled passive beamforming effectively reduces rapid channel fading induced by the Doppler effect of high-speed vehicles.

16.3.3 Integration of IRS with 6G in ITS

Modern mobility requires more sophisticated infrastructure, including crosswalks, d-junctions, tunnels, and pedestrian overpasses Transportation units have varying effects on wireless connectivity. In 6G vehicular communications, radio waves in the mmWave or THz frequency spectrum have short wavelengths and poor penetration [28]. Wireless signal transmission can be limited by dynamic as well as static impediments, such as buildings, fences, trees, and passing cars and pedestrians. Previous research has mostly focused on the deployment of Road Side Units (RSUs) [29, 30], which can be challenging and costly to relocate once placed. In 6G metropolitan contexts, a large number of RSUs are needed, yet certain locations may not be feasible owing to topography, leading to increased building costs. To achieve LoS and reliable channels in 6G vehicle communications, a more adaptable and efficient approach is required.

Enabling high-speed connectivity in ground-based vehicle networks necessitates highly precise location. To initiate communication, you'll need to find the user. The exact location can also be utilized for tracking. IRS-aided techniques provide additional channel status and can monitor and locate cars depending on incident wave propagation. In [31], IRSs were used to place mobile phone users, resulting in improved accuracy and coverage compared to non-IRS systems. IRS can improve finding accuracy and boost communication by predicting locations after establishing a robust connection. IRS allows passengers to converse with others outside the car.

In [32], a hybrid-equivalent surface-edge present prototype was suggested to analyze radiation from vehicle antennas. This research might establish a theoretical foundation for installing IRS on vehicle panels. Later works investigated the use of IRS in high-speed autonomous vehicles to improve passenger communication with roadside BSs. IRS-enabled passive beamforming effectively reduces fast channel fading produced by the Doppler effect of high-speed vehicles [33], the authors analyze and examine the challenge of allocating information and communication facilities for IRS-aided MEC-served vehicle networks.

The simulation findings show that the system has a greater computational efficiency using IRS. IRS has the potential to positively impact computing resource allocation. While there is limited study on IRS in edge computing for ITS, it is expected to become more relevant as autonomous vehicle algorithms need more processing power.

16.4 Enhanced Connectivity and Efficiency

IRS enhances network coverage and transmission dependability. The IRS may maintain the link between an aerial vehicle and a fixed target over the line of sight (LoS) by reflection, enabling 3D reflect beamforming [34]. In [35], the authors use IRS to improve air-ground interaction efficiency. They show that IRS-assisted UAV interaction systems can achieve ten times larger ergodic capacity than traditional UAV networks. THz technology will be used in 6G, making THz for ITS a critical study area. The small bandwidth of ultra-high frequency transmissions causes significant attenuation and limited penetration. Terahertz transmissions are unstable when transmitted via physical impediments like buildings and landscapes. IRS's capacity to operate outside LoS has significant advantages for THz communications. IRS enables signal reconfiguration and transmission beyond LoS, boosting system connection and preventing penetration loss [36, 37]. The capability of the IRS to provide beyond-LoS and energy-efficient transmission has enormous potential in 6G vehicle networks. IRSs in 6G transport networks have the potential to improve multipath propagation and communication connectivity for V2V, V2I, and V2P networks.

The IRS is deployed in the ITS to analyze the EE. Here two scenarios are considered to estimate the EE. In case one IRS, relay, and hybrid IRS-relay aided ITS are assumed to analyze the EE. Where EE is more when the vehicle is nearer to the IRS block, it gradually decreases with an increase in distance as shown in Fig. 16.4. We assume there is no physical connection between the BS and the vehicle. The path loss exponent has been fixed at 2.2, and the Nakagami-m fading channel variables range from 0.5 to 3. In the multi-IRS arrangement, all IRS elements' reflection coefficients are fixed to be close to 0.8. The speed is 50 km/h, with the ITS moving towards the IRS. To maximize EE our computational model sets the power dissipation for each IRS element $P_e i$ as 3 mW, and the overall power consumption of the $BS = ITS = R = 50\,\text{mW}$ for real-time implementation. Furthermore, the multiple IRS blocks concept is implemented to verify the EE and compared with IRS-relay-aided ITS [38, 39]. Results showed that 3-IRS block-assisted ITS outperformed the hybrid IRS-relay network. From the above, it is observed that an increase in IRS blocks or elements can help the ITS performance in terms of area coverage and EE.

16.4.1 Examples of IRS Enabled ITS

The work in [40] explored using IRS-assisted vehicular wireless systems with earth-based vehicles to improve quality of service (QoS). The model aimed to optimize average throughput for V2I while maintaining SINR for V2V across different channel connections. To simplify the aforementioned optimization, use the dual-phase alternating approach. The first phase addressed the combined power distribution and IRS propagation patterns, whereas phase two focused on spectrum utilization for both V2I and V2V. Simulations show that the IRS may enhance channel impairments and V2I sum capabilities in-vehicle networks.

Accurately detecting and anticipating driving trends is crucial for autonomous transportation security. In [41], deep learning-based techniques like LSTM and PJTSM were used to predict driving behaviors and vehicle movement across different energy levels. AI-enabled wireless networks have a significant influence on reliability and speed improvement. In [42], wireless sensors and IoT networks for ITS were explored to improve energy efficiency. This paper proposes a fresh method to ITS challenges utilizing distributed AI (DAI) and neural networks, in addition to earlier efforts. DAI invented the self-organizing map (MOP) methodology, which improves scheduling efficiency in contrast to traditional techniques.

In a recent study [43], ITS was analyzed in the SWIPT approach and various parameters to address the fusion problem. The issue has become non-convex due to the EE maximization limitations. The non-convex issue is addressed using a high

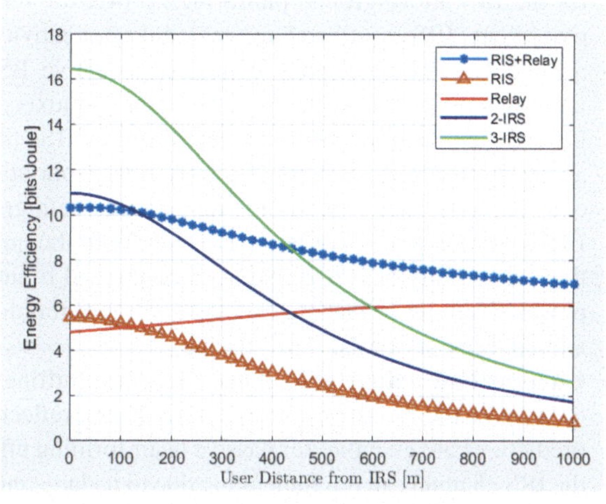

Fig. 16.4 EE analysis for ITS by using multiple IRS blocks and hybrid IRS-relay aided network

SNR approximation approach. The Lambert W function and Lagrange technique were used to determine several components, including minimum transmitting power, number of antennas, and reception placement. Simulation findings indicate that the suggested model can assist ITS with implementing SWIPT technology. The research published in [44] presented reflecting surfaces for ITS design (REITS). The first focus was on identifying defects in the RF-based projection model for self-driving automobiles. REITS is utilized to create reflective surfaces using both constructive and detrimental beamforming approaches. Numerical findings show that the suggested REITS with Van Atta type array reflector can identify signals in each direction.

16.5 Challenges and Future Trends

IRS can significantly increase the functionality of ITS, however, there still exist construction and execution issues. The following part focuses on significant issues that require immediate attention.

- **Reconfiguration of IRS elements**: The present IRS technology allows for the multi-channel, multi-user distribution, and accurate beamforming, nevertheless, it is not yet commonly employed in in-vehicle communications. The present IRS can provide multi-user beamforming in mobile networks with weak user position changes. Due to the increased mobility of automobiles, the IRS must keep a close eye on the situation at all times. In the ITS, the IRS and base station have established connections due to their stable position. The IRS simply must change to communicate with the user. In vehicular communications, each vehicle is in a moving particle, therefore IRS must modify the phase shift to manage the link to the sender and the network to the target individually. IRSs require more processing power and accurate phase-shifting controlling techniques.
- **Optimal Position of IRS**: IRS's flat shape allows for simple deployment. Except for the IRS above-ground platform, the IRS site remains reasonably stable after placement. IRS is utilized for regional connectivity and coverage, resulting in a limited operational range compared to active BSs. The deployment place is important to contemplate. In fixed user contexts, IRS-aided systems perform better when installed with adjacent users or BSs [45]. When installing IRSs in above-groundÃƒÆ’Ã¢â‚¬Å¡Ãƒâ€šÃ‚Â transportation systems, it's important to consider landscape and altitude interactions with grounded devices. To optimize IRS locations, it's important to consider both the quantity and size of IRSs. IRSs that are too tiny or ineffective in size may end in unsatisfactory reflecting signal power, while those that are excessively big or too many can contribute to unused and unnecessary costs.
- **Channel Estimation**: IRS adjusts the phase shifting of metamaterial components to regulate the transmission of signals during reflection. Precise forecast channel predictions are essential for passive beamforming efficiency. However, estimating the IRS channel can be challenging due to its large number of passive components.

Current IRS-aided ITS research mostly uses the perfect Channel State Information (CSI) model. Most research on channel estimates in IRS-assisted wireless networks use static conditions and do not account for cellular users' movement [46, 47]. Without proper planning, combining ITS and IRS might negatively impact system efficiency and resource utilization. Enhancing reliability in forecasting channels requires significant investments in learning and power usage, resulting in higher system expenses. Ensuring reliable CSI estimates and energy utilization remains a significant challenge in IRS-aided ITS.

- **Beamforming at IRS**: Future 6G wireless networks will use millimeter-wave frequencies. Deploying IRS in between transmitter and receiver improves signal quality in ITS. IRS phase shift optimization is required at the sender for better beamforming conditions. Further investigation is needed to determine the ideal combined active and passive beamforming strategies.
- **Mobility and Doppler Shifts**: In IRS-assisted vehicle communication, mobility difficulties such as Doppler shifts and phase variations demand rapid, adaptive IRS element modification and exact channel state information estimation. Optimized interference control, beamforming, and resource allocation are critical to maintaining communication quality for multiple vehicles. Doppler shifts generated by vehicle movement result in fast channel variations, which can be minimized by algorithms that dynamically track and adjust for these effects. To handle phase variations, IRS systems can use adaptive phase-shifting to modify the signal's phase in real-time, reducing disturbances. Furthermore, wide-angle beamforming may cover a larger area, ensuring consistent communication with fast-moving vehicles even while changing lanes or accelerating.

16.6 Conclusion

This chapter studies the use of IRS as an essential technology to improve the efficiency and effectiveness of 6G-enabled ITS systems. It also provides a thorough discussion of the basic concepts behind IRS technology, with an emphasis on its potential applications and benefits in the 6G environment. Intelligent IRS formulation and execution are significant areas of priority for dealing with challenges including beamforming, phase-shift optimization, channel conditions, deployment strategies, and interference. To better understand the problems of adopting IRS in 6G ITS, it is essential to gain knowledge of the most recent studies on this emerging communication model. The investigation offers an overview of the IRS for 6G ITS and reviews key resources on the topic. Most importantly, the application of AI/ML to optimize the IRS configuration in real-time was examined, leading the way for ITS. The combined efforts of IRS and 6G are expected to alter the ITS landscape, bringing in a new age of reliability, safety, security, low latency, and high-throughput connectivity. We discussed and summarized the existing work on IRS-aided 6G ITS, and later highlighted limitations as well as other promising research possibilities.

References

1. George Dimitrakopoulos and Panagiotis Demestichas. Intelligent transportation systems. *IEEE Vehicular Technology Magazine*, 5(1):77–84, 2010.
2. Junping Zhang, Fei-Yue Wang, Kunfeng Wang, Wei-Hua Lin, Xin Xu, and Cheng Chen. Data-driven intelligent transportation systems: A survey. *IEEE Transactions on Intelligent Transportation Systems*, 12(4):1624–1639, 2011.
3. Wei Song, Shaik Rajak, Shuping Dang, Ruijun Liu, Jun Li, and Sunil Chinnadurai. Deep learning enabled irs for 6g intelligent transportation systems: A comprehensive study. *IEEE Transactions on Intelligent Transportation Systems*, 2022.
4. Kakan Chandra Dey, Anjan Rayamajhi, Mashrur Chowdhury, Parth Bhavsar, and James Martin. Vehicle-to-vehicle (v2v) and vehicle-to-infrastructure (v2i) communication in a heterogeneous wireless network–performance evaluation. *Transportation Research Part C: Emerging Technologies*, 68:168–184, 2016.
5. Brian L Smith and Ramkumar Venkatanarayana. Realizing the promise of intelligent transportation systems (its) data archives. *Journal of Intelligent Transportation Systems*, 9(4):175–185, 2005.
6. Shaik Rajak, Poongundran Selvaprabhu, Sunil Chinnadurai, ASM Sanwar Hosen, Aldosary Saad, and Amr Tolba. Energy efficient mimo–noma aided iot network in b5g communications. *Computer Networks*, 216:109250, 2022.
7. Qingqing Wu and Rui Zhang. Towards smart and reconfigurable environment: Intelligent reflecting surface aided wireless network. *IEEE communications magazine*, 58(1):106–112, 2019.
8. Jia Ye, Shuaishuai Guo, Shuping Dang, Basem Shihada, and Mohamed-Slim Alouini. On the capacity of reconfigurable intelligent surface assisted mimo symbiotic communications. *IEEE Transactions on Wireless Communications*, 21(3):1943–1959, 2021.
9. Dan A Rosen, Frank J Mammano, and Rinaldo Favout. An electronic route-guidance system for highway vehicles. *IEEE Transactions on vehicular technology*, 19(1):143–152, 1970.
10. Ram Kandarpa, Mujib Chenzaie, Justin Anderson, Jim Marousek, Tim Weil, Frank Perry, Ian Schworer, Joe Beal, and Chris Anderson. Vehicle infrastructure integration proof-of-concept results and findings–infrastructure. Technical report, 2009.
11. Yangxin Lin, Ping Wang, and Meng Ma. Intelligent transportation system (its): Concept, challenge and opportunity. In *2017 ieee 3rd international conference on big data security on cloud (bigdatasecurity), ieee international conference on high performance and smart computing (hpsc), and ieee international conference on intelligent data and security (ids)*, pages 167–172. IEEE, 2017.
12. Yafeng Yin, Mark A Miller, and Steven E Shladover. Assessment of the applicability of cooperative vehicle-highway automation systems to freight movement in chicago. In *Transportation Research Board 2004 Annual Meeting.(http://database. path. berkeley. edu/reports/index. cgi.* Citeseer, 2004.
13. Ian Catling and Bob McQueen. Road transport informatics in europe-major programs and demonstrations. *IEEE Transactions on Vehicular Technology*, 40(1):132–140, 1991.
14. R LIBBRECHT. Dedicated road infrastructure for vehicle safety in europe (drive). In *Conference on Metros at the 1992 European Horizon (1989: Brussels Belgium). Metros at the 1993 European horizon*, 1989.
15. Xinping Yan, Hui Zhang, and Chaozhong Wu. Research and development of intelligent transportation systems. In *2012 11th International Symposium on Distributed Computing and Applications to Business, Engineering & Science*, pages 321–327. IEEE, 2012.
16. Ertugrul Basar, Marco Di Renzo, Julien De Rosny, Merouane Debbah, Mohamed-Slim Alouini, and Rui Zhang. Wireless communications through reconfigurable intelligent surfaces. *IEEE access*, 7:116753–116773, 2019.
17. Shun Zhang, Muye Li, Mengnan Jian, Yajun Zhao, and Feifei Gao. Airis: Artificial intelligence enhanced signal processing in reconfigurable intelligent surface communications. *China Communications*, 18(7):158–171, 2021.

18. Tao Jiang, Hei Victor Cheng, and Wei Yu. Learning to reflect and to beamform for intelligent reflecting surface with implicit channel estimation. *IEEE Journal on Selected Areas in Communications*, 39(7):1931–1945, 2021.
19. Aidin Ferdowsi, Ursula Challita, and Walid Saad. Deep learning for reliable mobile edge analytics in intelligent transportation systems: An overview. *ieee vehicular technology magazine*, 14(1):62–70, 2019.
20. Marco Di Renzo, Alessio Zappone, Merouane Debbah, Mohamed-Slim Alouini, Chau Yuen, Julien De Rosny, and Sergei Tretyakov. Smart radio environments empowered by reconfigurable intelligent surfaces: How it works, state of research, and the road ahead. *IEEE journal on selected areas in communications*, 38(11):2450–2525, 2020.
21. Wenxuan Long, Rui Chen, Marco Moretti, Wei Zhang, and Jiandong Li. A promising technology for 6g wireless networks: Intelligent reflecting surface. *Journal of Communications and Information Networks*, 6(1):1–16, 2021.
22. Qingqing Wu, Shuowen Zhang, Beixiong Zheng, Changsheng You, and Rui Zhang. Intelligent reflecting surface-aided wireless communications: A tutorial. *IEEE transactions on communications*, 69(5):3313–3351, 2021.
23. Yishi Zhu, Bomin Mao, and Nei Kato. Intelligent reflecting surface in 6g vehicular communications: A survey. *IEEE Open Journal of Vehicular Technology*, 3:266–277, 2022.
24. T Dhruvakumar and Ashvini Chaturvedi. Intelligent reflecting surface assisted millimeter wave communication for achievable rate and coverage enhancement. *Vehicular Communications*, 33:100431, 2022.
25. Ertugrul Basar, Ibrahim Yildirim, and Fatih Kilinc. Indoor and outdoor physical channel modeling and efficient positioning for reconfigurable intelligent surfaces in mmwave bands. *IEEE Transactions on Communications*, 69(12):8600–8611, 2021.
26. Emil Björnson, Luca Sanguinetti, Henk Wymeersch, Jakob Hoydis, and Thomas L Marzetta. Massive mimo is a reality—what is next?: Five promising research directions for antenna arrays. *Digital Signal Processing*, 94:3–20, 2019.
27. Zixuan Huang, Beixiong Zheng, and Rui Zhang. Transforming fading channel from fast to slow: Irs-assisted high-mobility communication. In *ICC 2021-IEEE International Conference on Communications*, pages 1–6. IEEE, 2021.
28. Shanzhi Chen, Ying-Chang Liang, Shaohui Sun, Shaoli Kang, Wenchi Cheng, and Mugen Peng. Vision, requirements, and technology trend of 6g: How to tackle the challenges of system coverage, capacity, user data-rate and movement speed. *IEEE Wireless Communications*, 27(2):218–228, 2020.
29. Wern-Yarng Shieh, Wei-Hsun Lee, Shen-Lung Tung, Bor-Shenn Jeng, and Cheng-Hsin Liu. Analysis of the optimum configuration of roadside units and onboard units in dedicated short-range communication systems. *IEEE Transactions on Intelligent Transportation Systems*, 7(4):565–571, 2006.
30. Christian Lochert, Björn Scheuermann, Christian Wewetzer, Andreas Luebke, and Martin Mauve. Data aggregation and roadside unit placement for a vanet traffic information system. In *Proceedings of the fifth ACM international workshop on VehiculAr Inter-NETworking*, pages 58–65, 2008.
31. Sha Hu, Fredrik Rusek, and Ove Edfors. Beyond massive mimo: The potential of positioning with large intelligent surfaces. *IEEE Transactions on Signal Processing*, 66(7):1761–1774, 2018.
32. Huapeng Zhao, Xinhui Zhang, Jun Hu, Zhizhang David Chen, and Ying-Chang Liang. A hybrid-equivalent surface-edge current model for simulation of v2x communication antennas with arbitrarily shaped contour. *IEEE Internet of Things Journal*, 8(10):8064–8077, 2020.
33. Yishi Zhu, Bomin Mao, and Nei Kato. A dynamic task scheduling strategy for multi-access edge computing in irs-aided vehicular networks. *IEEE Transactions on Emerging Topics in Computing*, 10(4):1761–1771, 2022.
34. Hongyao Li, Yanhong Zhang, Jianxiang Xi, and Wenxin Guo. 3d beam tracking method based on reconfigurable intelligent surface assistant for blocking channel. In *2021 36th Youth Academic Annual Conference of Chinese Association of Automation (YAC)*, pages 684–689. IEEE, 2021.

35. Abdulla Mahmoud, Sami Muhaidat, Paschalis C Sofotasios, Ibrahim Abualhaol, Octavia A Dobre, and Halim Yanikomeroglu. Intelligent reflecting surfaces assisted uav communications for iot networks: Performance analysis. *IEEE Transactions on Green Communications and Networking*, 5(3):1029–1040, 2021.
36. Yijin Pan, Kezhi Wang, Cunhua Pan, Huiling Zhu, and Jiangzhou Wang. Sum-rate maximization for intelligent reflecting surface assisted terahertz communications. *IEEE Transactions on Vehicular Technology*, 71(3):3320–3325, 2022.
37. Xinying Ma, Zhi Chen, Wenjie Chen, Zhuoxun Li, Yaojia Chi, Chong Han, and Shaoqian Li. Joint channel estimation and data rate maximization for intelligent reflecting surface assisted terahertz mimo communication systems. *IEEE Access*, 8:99565–99581, 2020.
38. Shaik Rajak, Inbarasan Muniraj, Karthikeyan Elumalai, ASM Sanwar Hosen, In-Ho Ra, and Sunil Chinnadurai. Energy efficient hybrid relay-irs-aided wireless iot network for 6g communications. *Electronics*, 11(12):1900, 2022.
39. Shaik Rajak, Inbarasan Muniraj, Poongundran Selvaprabhu, Vinoth Babu Kumaravelu, Md Abdul Latif Sarker, Sunil Chinnadurai, and Dong Seog Han. A novel energy efficient irs-relay network for its with nakagami-m fading channels. *ICT Express*, 2023.
40. Yuanbin Chen, Ying Wang, Jiayi Zhang, and Marco Di Renzo. Qos-driven spectrum sharing for reconfigurable intelligent surfaces (riss) aided vehicular networks. *IEEE Transactions on Wireless Communications*, 20(9):5969–5985, 2021.
41. Yang Xing, Chen Lv, Xiaoyu Mo, Zhongxu Hu, Chao Huang, and Peng Hang. Toward safe and smart mobility: Energy-aware deep learning for driving behavior analysis and prediction of connected vehicles. *IEEE Transactions on Intelligent Transportation Systems*, 22(7):4267–4280, 2021.
42. Pratik Goswami, Amrit Mukherjee, Ranjay Hazra, Lixia Yang, Uttam Ghosh, Yinan Qi, and Hongjin Wang. Ai based energy efficient routing protocol for intelligent transportation system. *IEEE Transactions on Intelligent Transportation Systems*, 23(2):1670–1679, 2021.
43. Baofeng Ji, Zhenzhen Chen, Shahid Mumtaz, Jianghui Liu, Yong Zhang, Jia Zhu, and Chunguo Li. Swipt enabled intelligent transportation systems with advanced sensing fusion. *IEEE Sensors Journal*, 21(14):15643–15650, 2020.
44. Zhiqiang Wei, Yuanxin Cai, Zhuo Sun, Derrick Wing Kwan Ng, Jinhong Yuan, Mingyu Zhou, and Lixin Sun. Sum-rate maximization for irs-assisted uav ofdma communication systems. *IEEE Transactions on Wireless Communications*, 20(4):2530–2550, 2020.
45. Ertugrul Basar. Reconfigurable intelligent surface-based index modulation: A new beyond mimo paradigm for 6g. *IEEE Transactions on Communications*, 68(5):3187–3196, 2020.
46. Keming Feng, Xiao Li, Yu Han, Shi Jin, and Yijian Chen. Physical layer security enhancement exploiting intelligent reflecting surface. *IEEE Communications Letters*, 25(3):734–738, 2020.
47. Zhihan Lv, Yang Han, Amit Kumar Singh, Gunasekaran Manogaran, and Haibin Lv. Trustworthiness in industrial iot systems based on artificial intelligence. *IEEE Transactions on Industrial Informatics*, 17(2):1496–1504, 2020.

The manufacturer's authorised representative in the EU is Springer Nature Customer Service Centre GmbH, Europaplatz 3, 69115 Heidelberg, Germany. If you have any concerns regarding our products, please contact ProductSafety@springernature.com

Printed and bound by CPI Group (UK) Ltd, Croydon, CR0 4YY
07/10/2026
02229349-0015